Manufacturing and the Circular Economy

Scrivener Publishing
100 Cummings Center, Suite 541J
Beverly, MA 01915-6106

Publishers at Scrivener
Martin Scrivener (martin@scrivenerpublishing.com)
Phillip Carmical (pcarmical@scrivenerpublishing.com)

Manufacturing and the Circular Economy

Edited by

Jeyaprakash Natarajan

Milon Selvam Dennison

M. Bhuvanesh Kumar

and

Ganapathy Thirukkotti

Scrivener Publishing

WILEY

This edition first published 2027 by John Wiley & Sons, Inc., 111 River Street, Hoboken, NJ 07030, USA and Scrivener Publishing LLC, 100 Cummings Center, Suite 541J, Beverly, MA 01915, USA

For more information about Scrivener publications please visit www.scrivenerpublishing.com.

Wiley Global Headquarters
111 River Street, Hoboken, NJ 07030, USA

For details of our global editorial offices, customer services, and more information about Wiley products visit us at www.wiley.com.

The manufacturer's authorized representative according to the EU General Product Safety Regulation is Wiley-VCH GmbH, Boschstr. 12, 69469 Weinheim, Germany, e-mail: Product_Safety@wiley.com.

Library of Congress Cataloging-in-Publication Data

ISBN 978-1-394-40340-0

Cover image: Generated with AI using Adobe Firefly
Cover design by Russell Richardson

Set in size of 11pt and Minion Pro by Manila Typesetting Company, Makati, Philippines

Printed in the USA

10 9 8 7 6 5 4 3 2 1

Contents

Preface

It gives us immense satisfaction to present this volume on manufacturing and the circular economy to readers from academia, industry, government, and civil society. Manufacturing has long been a backbone of economic growth and national development, yet it has also been closely associated with intensive resource use, growing waste streams, and environmental stress. Around the world, industries are now confronted with a simple but demanding question: How can we continue to grow and innovate without exhausting the very ecological and social foundations on which our progress depends?

The idea of the circular economy offers a thoughtful and practical response to this question. Instead of the familiar pattern of take, make, and dispose, circular thinking urges us to keep materials, components, and products in productive use for as long as possible, to design out waste from the very beginning, and to align economic value creation with environmental regeneration. The chapters in this book demonstrate that this is not only a philosophical shift but also a deeply technical, managerial, and policy-oriented transformation for the manufacturing sector.

The opening chapter introduces the circular economy as a pivotal transformation in manufacturing. It moves beyond a purely linear mindset and explains how resource efficiency, waste minimization, and supply chain resilience can be systematically advanced by keeping products and materials at their highest value for extended periods. The chapter also draws attention to the importance of digital technologies and policy frameworks, while honestly recognizing the real-world challenges of investment needs, infrastructure gaps, and organizational change. This sets the tone for the rest of the book, which does not treat circularity as an abstract slogan but as a practical agenda embedded in concrete production decisions.

Building on this foundation, the second chapter turns to circular design and the product lifecycle. It shows that the way we design a product largely decides how long it will last, how easily it can be repaired, disassembled, or upgraded, and how efficiently its materials can be recovered. Through concepts such as durability, modularity, and recyclability, along with life-cycle assessment and ecodesign approaches, the chapter traces how design teams can embed circularity from the earliest stages of product conception. The experiences of firms such as Patagonia, IKEA, Interface, and Fairphone illustrate that responsible design is compatible with strong commercial performance when supported by suitable business models, user engagement, and policy support.

The third chapter addresses material flow optimization and resource efficiency, reinforcing the idea that efficient movement and use of materials are central to any serious circular manufacturing strategy. Lean practices, design for disassembly, industrial symbiosis, and circular business models are discussed as ways to minimize material usage and extend product life. The chapter also highlights the role of responsibly sourced raw materials backed by international standards, as well as the growing contribution of connected devices, virtual replicas, and traceable records in providing real-time visibility of material flows. Case studies from automotive, electronics, textile, and construction sectors show that substantial gains in material efficiency and competitiveness can be achieved when technology, policy, and skills are aligned.

From here, the discussion moves outward to the wider value chain. The fourth chapter examines closed-loop supply chains and reverse logistics as central pillars of modern sustainable business practices. It traces the evolution from linear to circular to fully closed-loop systems and explains how regulations, extended producer responsibility, and economic incentives have accelerated this shift. Conceptual frameworks for reverse logistics and closed-loop supply chains are presented, and their practical relevance is demonstrated through examples from Apple, H&M, Caterpillar, and HP. The chapter is balanced in its treatment of both benefits and barriers, and it provides a set of strategic recommendations to address challenges such as capital intensity, organizational resistance, fragmented regulations, and the need for customer participation.

Chapters 5 and 6 delve into the heart of value recovery through remanufacturing, refurbishment, waste reduction, and recycling. The chapter on remanufacturing and product refurbishment explains how used products can be restored to like-new condition through systematic disassembly, cleaning, repair, and replacement of parts. It shows that these activities can significantly reduce material and energy consumption and open new revenue streams, while also identifying obstacles such as technological limitations, regulatory inconsistencies, and consumer perceptions. The chapter on waste reduction and recycling highlights the serious environmental and health hazards posed by poorly managed waste streams, especially in developing regions that receive large volumes of obsolete equipment. It discusses waste data reliability, realistic recycling strategies, and standard procedures for safe management and offers lessons for experts and policy-makers working to build robust circular manufacturing ecosystems.

Recognizing that no firm can become circular in isolation, the seventh chapter focuses on collaborative partnerships and ecosystem building. It argues that circular economy outcomes depend on shared responsibility and systems thinking that cut across organizational boundaries. The chapter explores how producers, suppliers, customers, financial institutions, and policy actors can cocreate value through industrial symbiosis, blended finance, and collaborative governance. It also highlights the role of digital tools such as connected networks, distributed ledgers, and virtual replicas in monitoring and optimizing material and energy flows across entire ecosystems. At the same time, it does not shy away from discussing barriers such as fragmented governance structures and a lack of trust, offering both conceptual and practical insights on how to build resilient circular ecosystems across sectors ranging from renewable energy and agriculture to automotive and urban systems.

Measurement and accountability are addressed in the eighth chapter, which deals with metrics and performance assessment for the circular economy. Transitioning from linear systems to circular practices requires indicators that can capture not only economic output but also material efficiency, environmental performance, social value, and regenerative capacity. This chapter presents widely used tools and standards, such as the Material Circularity Indicator, Circular Transition Indicators, BS 8001, and ISO 14040 and 44, and explains their complementary roles. It also underscores the importance of life-cycle assessment and material flow analysis for quantifying impacts and trade-offs and highlights the growing integration of circular metrics with environmental, social, and governance frameworks. The message is clear: What gets measured can be managed, and robust indicators are essential to move the circular economy from aspiration to verifiable practice.

The ninth and tenth chapters look at enabling conditions inside and outside the factory gates. Regulatory compliance and policy considerations are explored through global, regional, and national examples, with a particular focus on how different instruments, from market-based incentives to command and control approaches, are being used to operationalize circular principles in manufacturing. Issues such as policy fragmentation, compliance costs, and regulatory gaps for emerging technologies are examined through comparative case studies from the European Union, Asia, and developing countries. Material handling inside production shops is discussed in the following chapter, which shows how movement, storage, control, and protection of materials directly influence productivity, safety, and quality. By combining lean concepts, layout design, and advanced technologies, such as connected tracking systems, robotics, and autonomous vehicles, the chapter presents material handling as a strategic lever for intelligent and sustainable manufacturing.

The later chapters of the book turn toward emerging trends, sector-specific applications, and key enablers of circular manufacturing. Chapter 11 surveys future trends and opportunities, examining the interplay between current and emerging industrial paradigms. It explores how digital twins, connected devices, robotics, additive manufacturing, modular design, and big data-driven analysis are accelerating circular practices across construction, polymers, and textiles. Chapter 12 extends the discussion into the biomedical field, where the choice of materials and manufacturing methods for implants and medical devices has direct implications for performance, biocompatibility, and long-term integration with human tissues. An overview of metals, polymers, ceramics, and composite biomaterials is provided, highlighting how advances in this field can support more responsible, regenerative approaches in circular manufacturing.

Sustainable supply chain management and procurement strategies are examined in Chapter 13. Here, procurement is presented not as a narrow, cost-driven function but as a strategic lever for advancing circularity through green sourcing, supplier collaboration, life-cycle costing, and closed-loop resource use. The chapter also gives due space to ethical dimensions that influence procurement choices, including labor rights, fair trade, and transparency in multitier global supply chains. It proposes pathways for embedding sustainability into supplier evaluation, contract design, and performance monitoring, while acknowledging the challenges of balancing cost, risk, and sustainability goals.

Digital technologies and energy systems receive focused attention in Chapters 14 and 15. The chapter on digital integration explains how principles of the circular economy can be combined with connected devices, virtual replicas, distributed ledgers, and cyberphysical systems to enable real-time monitoring, predictive analytics, smart inventory management, and transparent closed-loop supply chains. It also notes the barriers related to uneven digital infrastructure, cybersecurity, and skills gaps and points to the need for unified sustainability metrics and more transparent decision support. The chapter on energy efficiency and renewable energy utilization situates circular manufacturing within the global transition to low-carbon energy. It reviews the status of renewable energy systems, modeling techniques, site analysis methods, energy management strategies, storage technologies, reliability tools, and maintenance approaches, with particular attention to challenges faced by remote communities and developing countries.

No transition is complete without investment in people and finance. Chapter 16 examines human capital, workforce training, and skills development as decisive factors in the adoption of the circular economy. Using data from numerous international initiatives, it shows how structured reskilling programs, modular learning pathways, and well-designed competency frameworks can significantly improve resource recovery, reduce waste, and enhance remanufacturing productivity. It also analyzes regional experiences in which skill indicator dashboards are linked to eco-innovation outcomes and proposes a multitier architecture that connects firm-level training, institutional mechanisms, and ecosystem-level governance.

The final chapter turns to investment, business models, and financial strategies for circular manufacturing. It explains how circular production is supported by government incentives; environmental, social, and governance requirements; and investor demand for sustainable practices. Global trends in venture capital, green bonds, and blended finance are discussed along with the critical role of development banks and public–private partnerships. The chapter explores business models such as product-as-a-service, remanufacturing systems, and take-back schemes, illustrated through examples including Philips Lighting Services, Xerox, and Caterpillar remanufacturing initiatives and circular strategies of brands such as H&M and Renault. It also introduces the Circular Investment Readiness Model and newer indicators, such as lifecycle cost savings, the Material Circularity Indicator, and return on circular investment, to guide investors and managers through this evolving landscape.

Taken together, the 17 chapters in this book offer a rich and carefully structured journey from foundational concepts to practical tools, sectoral applications, human and financial enablers, and future directions. They bring together perspectives from engineering, management, policy studies, and social sciences, and they speak to the realities of both advanced and developing economies. The book will be of value to students seeking an entry point into circular manufacturing, to researchers seeking conceptual and empirical insights, to practitioners seeking tested strategies and case examples, and to policymakers and financial actors who must create the enabling conditions for circular practices to flourish.

As editors and contributors, we hope this volume will encourage readers to view manufacturing not as an unavoidable burden on the environment but as a powerful instrument for regeneration and shared prosperity. If it helps even a few organizations redesign their products, reimagine their supply chains, invest in people and technology with a circular lens, and engage more deeply with policy and society, the purpose of this book will be well served. We invite you to engage with these chapters with an open, reflective mind, to question, adapt, and extend the ideas presented here and to actively participate in the ongoing global journey toward a truly circular manufacturing economy.

1

Introduction to Circular Economy in the Manufacturing Sector

Uma Sankar Behera[1] and Sourav Poddar[2*]

[1]*Department of Chemical and Biomolecular Engineering, Chonnam National University, Yeosu, Jeonnam, South Korea*
[2]*Department of Chemical Engineering, Haldia Institute of Technology, Haldia, West Bengal, India*

Abstract
Circular economy (CE) signifies a pivotal transformation in manufacturing, transitioning from the conventional linear "take–make–dispose" model to a regenerative system that prioritizes resource efficiency and waste minimization. CE fundamentally aims to reduce waste and optimize resource use by maintaining products, components, and materials at their maximum usability and worth for extended periods. The advantages of adopting CE principles in the manufacturing industry are numerous. Therefore, these encompass improved resource efficiency, diminished environmental impact, and increased supply chain resilience. Digital technologies (DTs), including Internet of Things, artificial intelligence, and big data analytics, are essential for facilitating CE practices through enhanced resource management and supply chain transparency. The shift to a CE has several obstacles. Substantial investment expenditures, inadequate infrastructure, and the necessity for considerable alterations in industrial processes may hinder implementation. Addressing these difficulties necessitates inventive strategies and conducive policy structures. Numerous international case studies underscore the promise of CE. Policy and regulatory frameworks are crucial catalysts for CE. In the future, technological innovation will be pivotal in promoting CE. DT, sophisticated materials, and innovative business models present substantial prospects for the establishment of more circular and sustainable production systems. The integration of Industry 4.0 technologies with CE concepts is expected to drive further innovation and efficiency improvements.

**Corresponding author*: souravpoddarsxc@gmail.com; souravpoddar@hithaldia.ac.in; spoddar@nitt.edu

Jeyaprakash Natarajan, Milon Selvam Dennison, M. Bhuvanesh Kumar and Ganapathy Thirukkotti (eds.) Manufacturing and the Circular Economy, (1–34) © 2027 Scrivener Publishing LLC

Keywords: Circular economy, sustainable manufacturing, PLS, industry 4.0, resource efficiency, remanufacturing

1.1 Introduction

Circular economy (CE) in manufacturing aims to minimize waste and optimize resource use by implementing the principles of reduction, reuse, and recycling throughout product life cycles [1, 2]. Digital technologies (DTs), such as the Internet of Things (IoT), artificial intelligence (AI), and big data analytics, are crucial for enhancing the implementation of CE practices in manufacturing processes [1, 3]. Therefore, these technologies facilitate resource efficiency (RE), improve supply chain transparency, enable predictive maintenance, and promote the development of circular business models. The shift from a linear "take–make–dispose" model to a CE represents a significant transformation in resource management, prioritizing sustainability and waste minimization as fundamental principles.

The growing utilization of AI in facilitating CE models enhances RE, product design, waste management, and recycling [4, 5]. The implementation of AI in circular systems, despite its potential environmental and economic benefits, presents ethical dilemmas that may impact the practical adoption of CE principles. The incorporation of AI into CE systems can augment sustainability by optimizing resource use, minimizing waste, and enhancing supply chain operations. AI-driven advancements, such as predictive maintenance, waste sorting, and big data analytics, facilitate the successful application of CE principles [6].

The implementation of CE methods in the manufacturing sector can lead to more sustainable company models. AI capabilities transform labor activities, data flows, and organizational processes, impacting CE practices in the manufacturing sector [7]. Digital transformation, driven by AI, provides a disruptive avenue for attaining sustainable innovation through process optimization, improved decision-making, and systemic enhancement. Therefore, this transition demands innovative approaches that transcend traditional linear methods [8].

The influence of AI driven by big data analytics has increased in recent years, improving supply chain efficiency. Institutional theory and the resource-based view theory elucidate the rationale behind enterprises' involvement in manufacturing operations and their use of AI driven by big data analytics [9]. AI algorithms can expedite design processes or modifications by scrutinizing extensive datasets. AI designers generate more accurate designs and evaluate their applicability across various domains, thereby augmenting the longevity and value of materials and goods in a CE [10].

Nonetheless, obstacles to the adoption of CE persist, including substantial investment costs and insufficient infrastructure [1]. Balancing quality and cost while accommodating diverse client requirements is essential as remanufacturing evolves into a burgeoning sector. Pursuing excellence could augment the drive and incentive of remanufacturers. The literature suggests that organizations' strategies for leveraging CE opportunities to enhance their positioning are inadequately defined [11].

The synergistic potential of AI and product-based learning methodologies is crucial for students to acquire skills and competencies in the emerging circular bioeconomy. The conventional approach to materials engineering education, characterized by passive information absorption, is insufficient in the present context. AI may provide content for research papers, educational resources, and product descriptions about biobased materials, facilitate information discovery, generate innovative concepts for product development, and enhance standard operating procedures. AI can facilitate the effective planning of experiments and produce scientific visuals to aid in visualizing intricate structures and processes in biobased materials [12]. Companies are undertaking strategic measures to adopt CE solutions, such as establishing leadership in CE practices, enhancing responsible and transparent sourcing within the supply chain, commercializing sustainability through proprietary brand products, developing data-driven services for customers and society utilizing customer data and AI ethically, broadening communal responsibility initiatives, and minimizing energy consumption while augmenting renewable energy production [13]. Detailed schematic steps are shown in Figure 1.1.

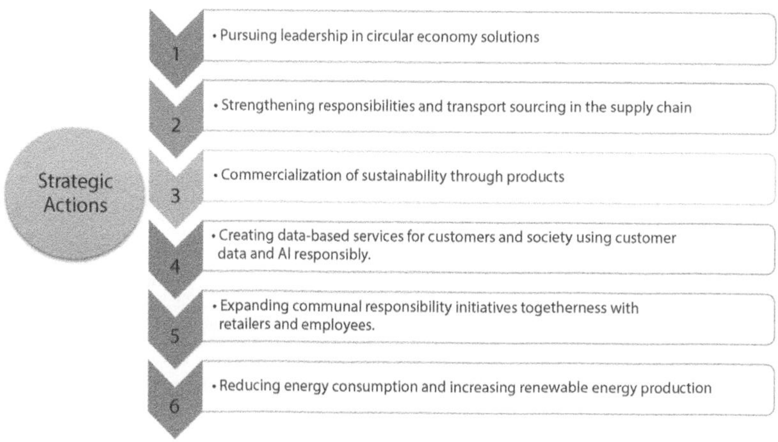

Figure 1.1 Strategic actions are generally considered for a retail company [13].

The integration of digital twins with AI can optimize material flows and address the inefficiencies inherent in linear economic models. Therefore, this new concept of circular-AI twin integration (CAT-I) provides a systematic approach for implementing, advancing, and verifying CE principles. The importance of AI in energy-efficient industrial systems is substantial, as AI approaches are specifically designed to address the challenges inherent in these systems [14].

AI and virtual reality can enhance logistics and intelligent manufacturing through preventive diagnostics, product development and optimization, knowledge transfer regarding behavior, human–robot interaction, equipment training, hand-tracking and control, digital twin development for shop floors, and quality control and management. Figure 1.2 represents the variation of logistics and intelligent manufacturing.

AI is utilized throughout the production life cycle in several stages, including design, scheduling, commissioning, operation, maintenance, and recycling. It is observed that as these manufacturing life-cycle steps progress, the number of stakeholders involved increases. The combination of cognitive AI and additive manufacturing techniques enables the establishment of mass customization enterprises, streamlining the oversight of complex production processes [16].

AI significantly enhances CE processes by delivering data-driven insights for improved resource management and waste reduction (WR) initiatives. It facilitates agricultural endeavors, promoting more efficient

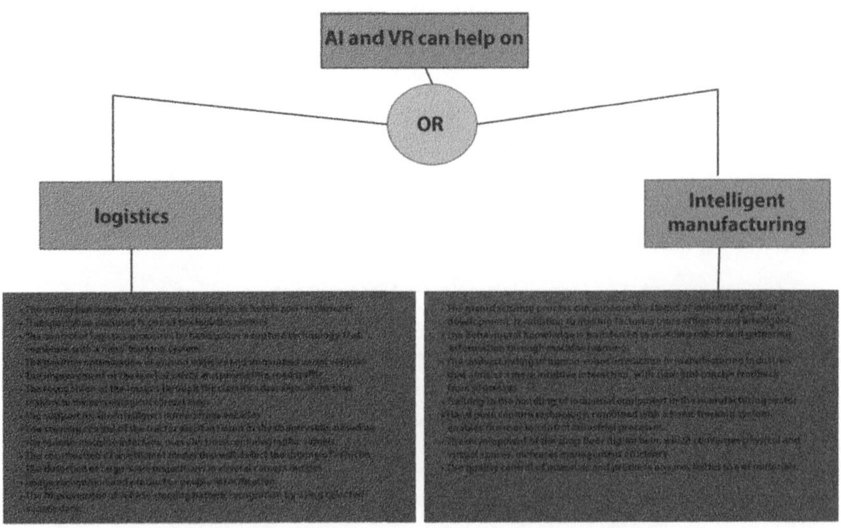

Figure 1.2 The variation of logistics and intelligent manufacturing [15].

resource utilization, enhanced environmental stewardship, and superior decision-making in farming operations [17]. Nonetheless, the growing dependence on AI within CE also presents cybersecurity vulnerabilities. Addressing these cybersecurity concerns is crucial for the effective and secure implementation of AI-driven CE processes [18]. Figure 1.3 illustrates the integration of sustainable agriculture, AI, and CE.

The integration of AI within CE poses ethical dilemmas. The ability of AI to automate labor-intensive processes, such as literature reviews and data analysis, has created opportunities for unethical practices, as scholars may incorporate AI-generated content into their articles, potentially compromising academic integrity. Addressing these ethical challenges is crucial for the responsible and sustainable use of AI in CE [19].

Figure 1.4 illustrates the framework for the impact of AI on the job market. AI innovation exerts a dual influence on the labor market, fostering job creation in upstream areas while precipitating job destruction in downstream sectors that implement AI technologies [20]. AI-driven interventions can have a significant impact on the labor market, influencing employment, income, job attributes, productivity, and the broader labor market framework [21]. Therefore, this chapter focuses on the role of CE in the manufacturing sector, including its economic benefits, challenges in implementing CE, global case studies, policies, and regulatory frameworks, and, finally, the future outlook and opportunities associated with it. Furthermore, this chapter will deal with the role of CE, followed by the benefits and challenges of CE. The chapter will also emphasize global case studies, policies, and the regulatory framework, as well as future outlook and opportunities.

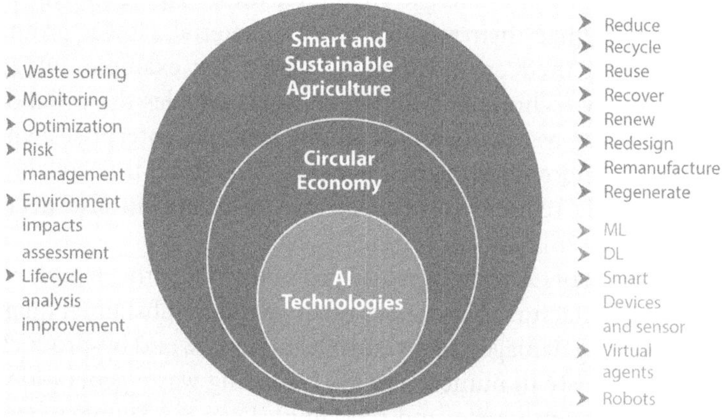

Figure 1.3 Sustainable agriculture, artificial intelligence, and CE are integrated [17].

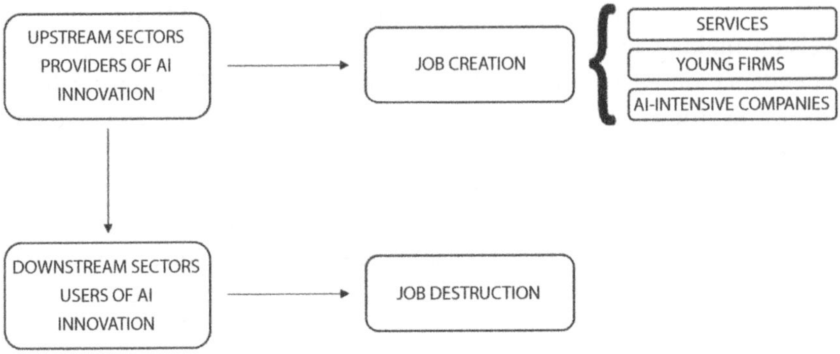

Figure 1.4 Conceptual framework on AI impact on the job market [20].

1.2 Role of CE in the Manufacturing Sector

CE is increasingly recognized as a vital framework for transforming the manufacturing sector, followed by sustainable promotion and, finally, enhanced RE. Therefore, this approach aims to decouple economic growth from resource consumption by minimizing waste and ultimately maximizing the lifespan and utility of both the finished product and raw materials. The manufacturing sector, which comprises resources and generators of waste, stands to gain significantly from adopting CE principles [22–24].

CE in manufacturing primarily aims to enhance RE. Previously, linear supply chains followed a take–make–dispose model, which is now contributing to resource depletion and environmental degradation [25]. In contrast, CE prioritizes initiatives such as reducing, reusing, recycling, and recovering materials and energy. Therefore, these strategies help manufacturers to minimize their reliance on raw materials, lower production costs, and reduce their environmental impact. For example, integrating industrial ecology techniques with CE concepts enables the collaborative utilization of waste as raw materials among multiple enterprises, yielding both economic and environmental benefits. Therefore, this collaborative approach not only reduced the cost of raw materials but also decreased waste generation [26].

The application of CE principles also promotes WR in the manufacturing sector [24]. Manufacturing processes often generate substantial quantities of waste, including damaged items, surplus materials, and by-products. CE aims to reduce waste in numerous ways (reducing waste generation from the source, reusing products, and recycling). Lean Six Sigma approaches can be combined with CE principles to enhance industrial operations, minimize waste, and increase RE. Green Lean Six Sigma methodologies specifically emphasize the eradication of waste and pollution, the enhancement of resource circulation, and the preservation of environmental resources [23, 27]. Furthermore, digital transformation technologies, such as the IoT, AI, and big data, are crucial for WR by enabling enhanced monitoring, optimization, and management of resources [28].

CE promotes innovation in product design and production methodologies. Creating products that prioritize durability, disassembly, and recyclability is a fundamental tenet of CE [29]. Therefore, this methodology, termed ecodesign, ensures that items are readily repairable, reusable, or remanufacturable, thereby prolonging their lifespan and reducing the need for new resources.

A vital function of CE is to bolster the robustness of supply chains. Conventional supply chains frequently exhibit susceptibility to disturbances, including resource scarcity, price fluctuations, and geopolitical instability. By diversifying resource origins, advocating for local procurement, and establishing closed-loop processes, CE can enhance the resilience and adaptability of supply chains. Reconfigurable manufacturing systems, capable of swiftly adapting to evolving requirements, are crucial for improving supply chain resilience within a CE [31]. Moreover, the incorporation of DT, such as blockchain, enhances transparency and traceability within supply chains, facilitating improved oversight of product and material movement [32].

CE enhances environmental sustainability within the manufacturing sector. By reducing resource consumption, minimizing waste, and promoting cleaner production processes, CE helps mitigate ecological impacts, including climate change, pollution, and biodiversity loss [28]. The adoption of CE principles in the automotive manufacturing sector has led to increased recycling rates and the widespread application of sustainability criteria for assessing environmental performance.

However, the implementation of CE principles in the manufacturing sector faces several challenges, including insufficient awareness and comprehension of CE principles, a lack of supportive policies and regulations, and a need for enhanced collaboration among stakeholders. Overcoming these obstacles necessitates a comprehensive strategy that encompasses education and training, regulatory reforms, and the development of new business models and technologies [33]. Therefore, these strategies are discussed in the following sections. Furthermore, it is essential to evaluate the social and economic dimensions of CE, guaranteeing equitable labor practices, secure working environments, and community welfare [30].

The amalgamation of Industry 4.0 technologies with CE concepts presents novel prospects for enhancing sustainable production. Cyberphysical systems, the IoT, AI, big data analytics, and digital twins facilitate the advancement of intelligent and sustainable manufacturing methodologies. Therefore, these technologies enable real-time surveillance of resource flows, enhance manufacturing processes, and improve waste and emissions management [34]. Furthermore, Industry 5.0, which advances the developments of Industry 4.0 by emphasizing a more human-centric paradigm, can further augment the sustainability and resilience of the manufacturing industry [35].

1.3 Benefits of CE in the Manufacturing Sector

CE offers a viable alternative to the conventional linear methods, providing significant advantages to the industrial sector by reducing waste, enhancing RE, and promoting economic growth [36]. By implementing circular methods, manufacturers can enhance the sustainability of their processes, reduce environmental impact, and gain a competitive advantage in the global market [37].

A key benefit of CE is its emphasis on RE. Conventional linear supply chains lead to resource depletion and environmental harm, prompting a shift to more resilient and resource-efficient approaches. The incorporation of CE principles into sustainable supply chain management offers opportunities for improving WR and resource recovery. By optimizing raw material and energy utilization, manufacturers can substantially decrease operational expenses and enhance profitability. Manufacturers can considerably lower operational costs and improve profitability by optimizing the utilization of raw materials and energy [38]. CE is aiming to create closed-loop systems that eliminate the detrimental environmental effects of waste [39]. Therefore, this can be accomplished through diverse ways, including remanufacturing, refurbishing, and recycling. Reconfigurability in manufacturing enables systems to swiftly adjust to changing requirements, which is essential for markets to sustain operations amid unforeseen setbacks. Simultaneously, the concept of a CE is gaining increasing prevalence in industry, aiming to reduce waste and enhance RE [31].

Furthermore, CE stimulates innovation and generates new business opportunities within the manufacturing sector. DTs, including the IoT, AI, blockchain, and big data, are integrated with CE concepts to enhance sustainable manufacturing methods. Therefore, these technologies are essential for improving resource management and minimizing waste. AI and digital twin technologies can facilitate a CE by reducing emissions and waste, safeguarding biodiversity, and ensuring the purity of air, land,

and water. The use of CE concepts can generate new employment opportunities in sectors such as sustainable manufacturing, recycling, and DT development [17].

Implementing CE techniques can enhance a company's brand equity and strengthen its competitive edge. Consumers are increasingly seeking sustainable products and activities, and they are more likely to trust and remain loyal to brands perceived as ecologically and socially responsible. By implementing CE principles and promoting them effectively, organizations can enhance their brand image and attract new customers [40].

A principal obstacle is the lack of thorough assessment frameworks for implementing CE. Therefore, this complicates the ability of organizations to assess their progress and pinpoint areas that necessitate improvement [41]. Furthermore, organizations may exhibit resistance to change, coupled with a lack of awareness and comprehension of CE concepts. To address these difficulties, collaboration among governments, industry associations, and research institutes is vital to offer guidance and support to producers [42].

To facilitate the transition to a CE, enterprises must develop innovative business models that align with the principles of circularity. Therefore, this may entail transitioning from a product-centric strategy to a service-oriented approach, when clients compensate for the utilization of a product instead of possessing it outright. Furthermore, this incentivizes producers to create goods that are durable and long-lasting, as they maintain ownership and bear responsibility for maintenance and repair [43]. Moreover, enterprises may investigate avenues for collaboration and alliances with other entities to establish closed-loop systems and exchange resources [30].

The incorporation of DT is essential for facilitating CE within the manufacturing sector. Digital platforms can enable the exchange of materials and goods among enterprises, establishing a marketplace for secondary resources. Therefore, these platforms facilitate transparency and traceability in supply chains, allowing organizations to monitor the movement of commodities and verify their sustainable management [44].

CE presents a substantial opportunity for the industrial sector to enhance sustainability, mitigate environmental damage, and foster economic growth. By utilizing circular processes, manufacturers can optimize RE, minimize waste, foster innovation, enhance brand equity, and secure a competitive edge. The transition to a CE presents challenges; nevertheless, these can be overcome through collaboration, innovation, and the integration of DT. As the world progresses toward a more sustainable future, CE is expected to emerge as a progressively significant paradigm for the manufacturing sector [45].

1.4 Challenges in Implementing CE

The transition of the manufacturing sector to a CE offers substantial prospects for sustainability and RE; yet, its execution encounters various obstacles. Therefore, these problems encompass technical, economic, regulatory, and organizational areas, obstructing the smooth transition from linear approaches to closed-loop systems. Surmounting these challenges is essential for actualizing the complete potential of CE in manufacturing [28, 46].

A primary obstacle lies in the technical aspects of CE deployment. Conventional manufacturing methods are typically optimized for linear production, complicating the integration of circularity without substantial alterations. Therefore, this requires the implementation of sophisticated technology for recycling, remanufacturing, and waste minimization. Implementing efficient reverse logistics for the collection and processing of end-of-life products presents a significant challenge [36]. The absence of standardized procedures for evaluating the quality and composition of recycled materials hampers their incorporation into manufacturing processes. Overcoming the aforementioned technical hurdles necessitates significant investments in research and development to devise novel solutions customized for the industrial sector's specific requirements [47].

Economic uncertainties hinder the extensive implementation of CE in manufacturing. The preliminary expenses associated with transitioning to circular business models, including investments in new machinery, infrastructure, and workforce training, can be substantial. The economic feasibility of CE efforts relies on several key elements, including market demand for recycled goods, variations in material pricing, and the presence of financial incentives. Numerous manufacturers exhibit reluctance to participate in CE owing to perceived financial concerns and the absence of a definitive return on investment. Addressing the aforementioned economic obstacles necessitates favorable government policies, inventive financing strategies, and the establishment of resilient markets for secondary materials [32, 48].

Regulatory obstacles pose a substantial challenge to the adoption of CE in the manufacturing sector. Inconsistent environmental regulations, waste management strategies, and product standards across various areas complicate operations for firms in global marketplaces. The lack of standardized criteria for defining and measuring circularity impedes the advancement of successful CE plans. Furthermore, several existing restrictions may unintentionally dissuade CE efforts by privileging the utilization of virgin materials over recycled alternatives. To tackle these regulatory obstacles, enhanced coordination among governments, industry stakeholders, and international organizations is essential for formulating clear, consistent, and supportive policy frameworks for CE [49].

Organizational obstacles within manufacturing firms can hinder the effective execution of CE. Insufficient awareness, comprehension, and commitment to CE concepts among employees and management may impede the implementation of circular practices. Resistance to change, entrenched linear thinking, and an emphasis on short-term profitability at the expense of long-term sustainability can engender inertia inside organizations. Surmounting the aforementioned organizational obstacles requires robust leadership, efficient communication, and the incorporation of CE principles into the company's culture and decision-making frameworks.

Furthermore, the intricacies of supply chains present a considerable obstacle to the implementation of CE practices. Establishing closed-loop supply chains that enable the collection, sorting, and recycling of end-of-life products requires meticulous collaboration and coordination among multiple stakeholders, including suppliers, manufacturers, distributors, and customers. The absence of transparency and traceability in supply networks can impede the tracking and management of goods. Resolving these supply chain difficulties requires the development of breakthrough technologies, collaborative platforms, and innovative business models that promote circularity throughout the entire value chain.

The shift to a CE in manufacturing requires a comprehensive strategy that addresses technical, economic, regulatory, and organizational challenges. Manufacturers can overcome these obstacles and realize the full potential of CE by investing in research and development, fostering collaboration, developing supportive policies, and cultivating a culture of sustainability. Adopting the aforementioned new strategies will be essential for facilitating the extensive implementation of CE principles in the manufacturing industry and realizing a genuine CE [50].

1.5 Global Case Studies

Global case studies exemplify CE in manufacturing through sustainable techniques such as waste recovery and material recycling. Industries implement eco-innovative designs to prolong product life cycles and minimize resource consumption. The automotive industry exemplifies the importance of recycling and sustainability, whereas the electronics and textile sectors are adopting circularity for both sustainability and profitability. CE is gaining prominence in the manufacturing sector, providing a means to reconcile economic growth with environmental sustainability. It entails transitioning from a linear approach paradigm to a regenerative system that maximizes the utilization of resources for an extended duration. Therefore, this change necessitates innovative strategies, cooperation, and a thorough reevaluation of production and consumption habits.

1.5.1 Global Case Studies in Circular Manufacturing

Several case studies demonstrate the application of CE principles across various manufacturing sectors and geographic locations.

Automotive industry: The automotive industry is increasingly adopting CE practices, with a focus on recycling and sustainability [51]. The investigation indicates that approximately 68% of automotive companies have initiated CE practices, achieving a recycling rate of 45% [51]. Therefore, the practices mentioned above include designing vehicles for easier disassembly, using recycled materials, and implementing remanufacturing processes to extend product life cycles. Findings also reveal that a significant shift toward the adoption of CE practices has occurred, with 68% of surveyed automotive companies implementing these practices. Therefore, these initiatives are demonstrated by an admirable recycling rate of 45% and the extensive adoption of sustainability criteria (72%) for evaluating environmental performance [51].

Construction sector: The construction sector, a major consumer of resources and generator of waste, is exploring CE models to minimize environmental impact [52, 53]. One approach involves plastic recycling, where waste plastics are repurposed for construction materials [52]. Additionally, green building rating systems, such as LEED (Leadership in Energy and Environmental Design), promote the minimization of construction waste, although performance varies across countries [54]. A comparison of LEED-certified projects in the United States and China reveals differences in construction waste minimization performance, highlighting the need for tailored strategies [54].

Electronics industry: The electronics industry faces significant challenges related to e-waste. CE strategies focus on extending product lifespans, improving recyclability, and

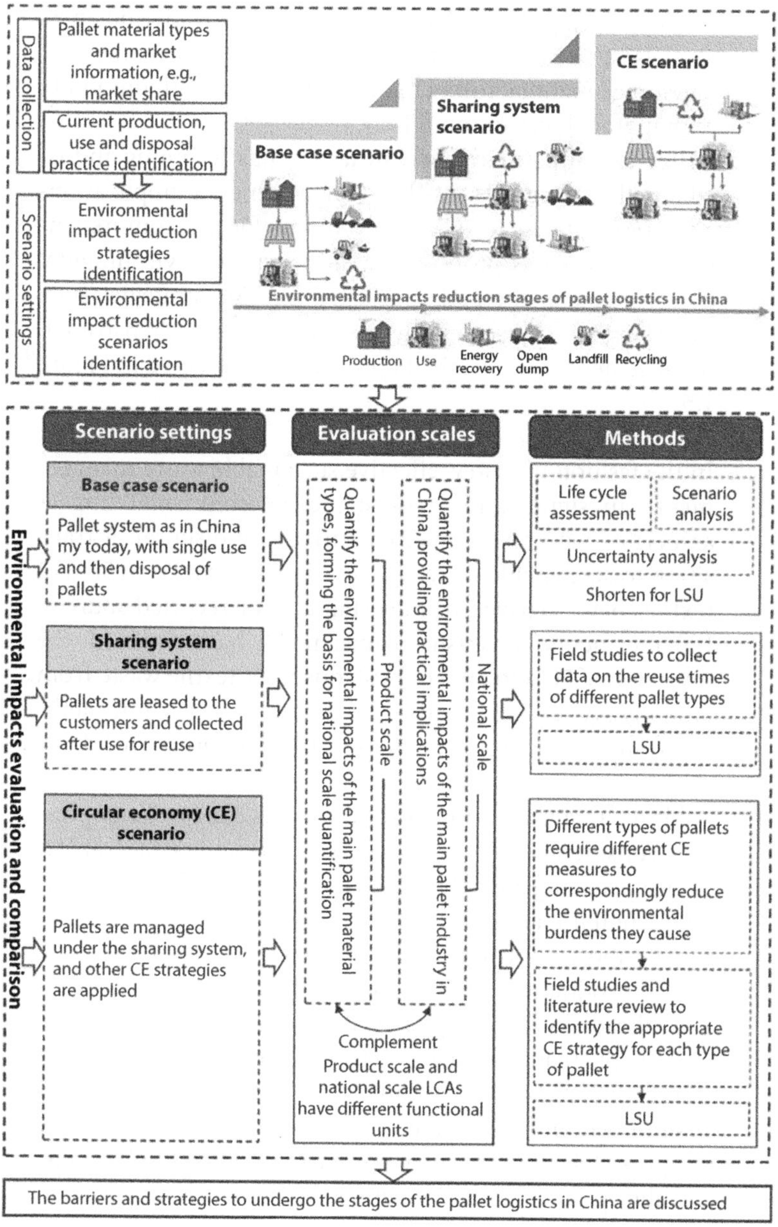

Figure 1.5 Approaches to CE that can help China's developing industrial pallet industry [56].

implementing take-back programs [55]. Innovative business models, such as product leasing and service-based offerings, encourage manufacturers to design products with durability and upgradability in mind [55].

Pallet manufacturing in China: China's booming industrial pallet usage presents both environmental implications and opportunities for CE interventions [56]. A comprehensive framework is proposed to enhance the environmental performance of the pallet industry through strategies such as leasing and reuse systems, as well as comprehensive CE management [56]. Detailed procedure is presented in Figure 1.5.

(1) In the fashion industry, effective sustainable waste management can significantly reduce the environmental impact associated with textile manufacturing and disposal. A transition to sustainable materials could result in 40% to 50% of textiles being derived from sustainable or recycled sources. Enhancements in waste management have enabled the diversion of 70% to 80% of postconsumer textile waste from landfills *via* recycling and reuse. Water conservation methods result in a decrease of 50 to 100 L of water for each kilogram of textile manufactured [59].

(2) Additive manufacturing, also known as 3D printing, presents considerable opportunities for enhancing heat transfer in heat exchangers, with a focus on sustainability and environmental impact [60].

(3) Furthermore, incorporating bioeconomy concepts into bionic production may enhance sustainability and ecological efficacy by utilizing renewable biological resources and sustainable manufacturing methods [30].

(4) Manufacturing in India: Small- and medium-sized enterprises (SMEs) in India are crucial to the nation's GDP, and adopting CE practices can significantly enhance their sustainability and competitiveness [57]. However, various social, technological, and economic barriers hinder the adoption of CE in the Indian manufacturing sector [57, 58]. Overcoming these barriers requires tailored strategies and policy interventions.

1.5.2 CE Assessment Metrics

Assessing the effectiveness of CE strategies requires appropriate metrics that capture the multidimensional aspects of circularity [61–63]. These metrics should consider technical, economic, and environmental dimensions at both the planning and life-cycle levels [61]. The types of assessment metrics are based on the type of metrics, the framework of assessments, and, finally, the integration of DT.

Types of metrics: The types of metrics that CE generally follows are material flow analysis (MFA), life-cycle analysis (LCA), and circularity indicators (CIs). MFA tracks the flow of materials through the economy to identify opportunities for reducing waste and improving RE. LCA evaluates the environmental impacts associated with a product or service throughout its entire life cycle [62, 63]. CI quantifies the circularity of products, processes, or systems, considering factors such as recycled content, recyclability, and product lifespan [63, 64].
Frameworks for assessment: The types of assessment frameworks followed by CE are multilevel assessment (MLA1), microlevel assessment (MLA2), and, finally, Urban Circularity Assessment Framework (UCAF). MLA1 suggests that manufacturing systems often use multiple CE strategies simultaneously, necessitating assessment frameworks that capture the combined impact of these strategies [61]. MLA2 focuses on indicators and metrics specific to individual companies, enabling them to track and improve their CE performance [65]. UCAF is designed for planning, monitoring, and evaluating CE transitions in cities, considering governance, CE strategies, and urban stocks and flows [64].
Integration with DT: The types of DT followed by CE are IoT and AI. IoT devices can be utilized to monitor and manage resource utilization, waste generation, and product life cycles [51]. Assessment tools evaluate the socioenvironmental effectiveness of IoT in manufacturing supply chains, taking into account sustainability and circularity principles [51]. AI can optimize resource allocation, predict waste generation, and facilitate the development of circular business models [1, 66]. The details of the assessment metrics for CE are shown in Table 1.1, along with descriptions and their applications. Case studies of DT are described below.

Table 1.1 Assessment metrics for CE: some examples.

Metrics	Description	Application
Recycled content	Percentage of recycled material in a product	Measuring the use of recycled materials in manufacturing
Recyclability rate	Percentage of a product that can be recycled	Assessing the end-of-life potential for recycling
Product lifespan	Average duration a product is used before disposal	Evaluating the durability and longevity of products
Waste generation rate	Amount of waste generated per unit of production	Tracking WR efforts
Energy consumption	Energy used in production, transportation, and disposal	Assessing energy efficiency and carbon footprint
Water consumption	Water used in production and processing	Evaluating water resource management
Material circularity indicators	Measures how well material loops are closed	Evaluating the circularity performance of products and processes

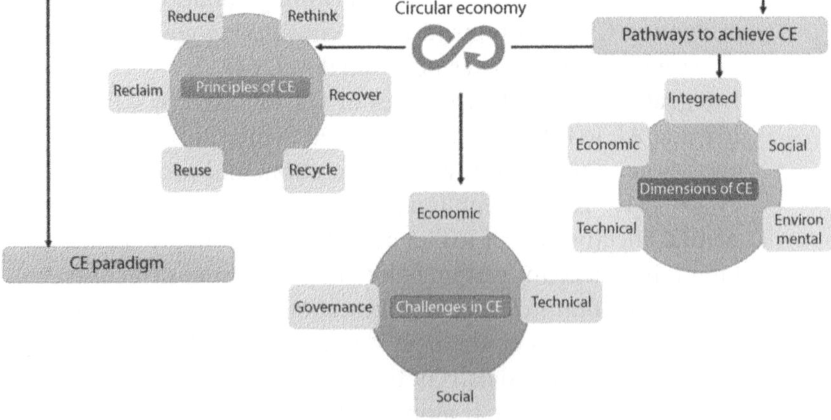

Figure 1.6 Principles behind CE methods for use in the water industry [67].

- **Agriculture in China**: AI and digital twin: DT, such as AI and digital twins, are being integrated with CE practices in Chinese agriculture to minimize consumption and waste [17]. These involve using AI for waste sorting, risk management, and LCA. Detailed graphical representation is shown in Figure 1.3.
- **Water and wastewater sector**: Innovative approaches: The water sector is exploring CE approaches to address urbanization and resource depletion [67]. These include reducing water use, reusing treated water, and reclaiming resources from wastewater. Detailed graphical representation is shown in Figure 1.6.
- **3D positioning framework**: Selecting the best CE assessment approach requires considering the type of information needed (socioeconomic indicators), the system level (macro, meso, micro, or nano), the sector and subsector, and the cycle (technical, biological, or mixed) [68]. Detailed graphical representation is shown in Figure 1.7.

1.5.3 Company-Level Classification Framework

This framework clarifies assessment targets and methods, linking CE indicators to organizational functions [69]. Therefore, Company-Level Classification Framework comprises the UCAF and Recycling Technology Selection Framework.

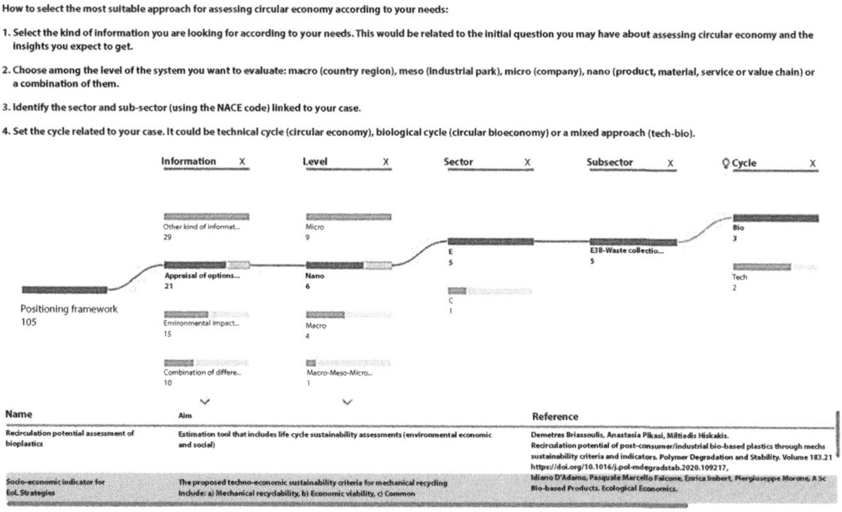

Figure 1.7 Evaluate CE using the selected method [68].

1.5.4 Urban Circularity Assessment Framework

The UCAF is designed for planning, monitoring, evaluating, and learning from CE transitions in cities [64]. The framework incorporates aspects such as governance, CE strategies, urban resource stocks and flows, and the triple bottom line, focusing on social, environmental, and economic outcomes. Detailed graphical representation is shown in Figure 1.8.

1.5.5 Recycling Technology Selection Framework

This framework assesses the effectiveness of plastic recycling technologies in advancing CE. Circularity metrics, assessment tools, and measurement indices are used to evaluate comprehensively circularity [70]. Detailed graphical representation is shown in Figure 1.9.

1.5.6 Role of AI

AI is increasingly significant in enabling and assessing CE practices [1, 17, 66]. AI algorithms can optimize resource use, predict waste generation, and facilitate the development of circular business models in the manufacturing sector [1]. For instance, AI can analyze large datasets to identify patterns and opportunities for reducing waste, reusing materials, and promoting recycling. AI and digital twin technologies promote

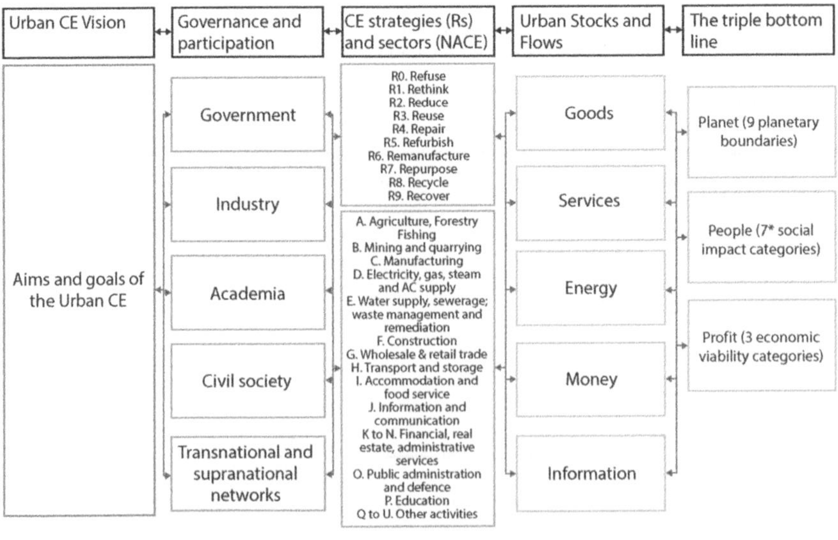

Figure 1.8 Framework for an Urban CE [64].

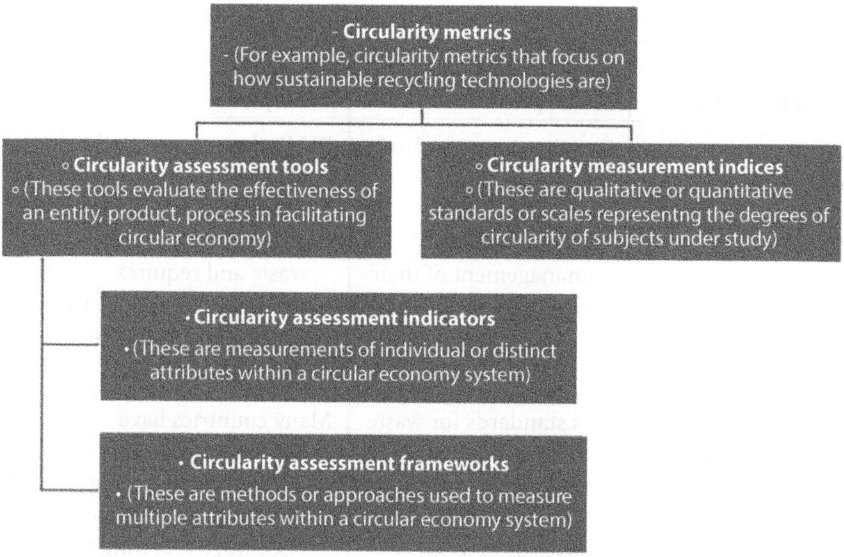

Figure 1.9 Circularity metrics features [70].

sustainable practices in agriculture by optimizing RE and reducing waste [17].

Moreover, AI can enhance the assessment of CE strategies by automating data collection, analysis, and reporting. AI-powered tools can monitor material flows, track product life cycles, and assess the environmental impacts of manufacturing processes [71].

1.6 Policies and Regulatory Frameworks

Transitioning toward a CE in the manufacturing sector necessitates a supportive policy and regulatory framework [55, 72]. Traditional linear models have led to environmental degradation, resource depletion, and economic inefficiencies. A well-designed policy landscape can incentivize circular practices, overcome systemic barriers, and drive sustainable business models [55, 73]. Therefore, this section examines the key components of such a framework, exploring its role in promoting the adoption of CE within the manufacturing sector. The details of the policy tools to encourage a CE in the manufacturing sector are shown in Table 1.2 with descriptions and examples.

1.6.1 The Role of Policy in Driving Circularity

Policies play a crucial role in setting the direction and pace of CE implementation. They can create a level playing field, stimulate innovation, and

Table 1.2 Policy tools to encourage a CE in the manufacturing sector.

Policy instrument	Description	Example
Extended producer responsibility	Requires manufacturers to assume accountability for the defective management of their products	EU Packaging and Packaging Waste Directive, which sets targets for recycling and recovery of packaging waste and requires producers to finance the collection and treatment of packaging [79]
Waste management regulations	Sets standards for waste collection, treatment, and disposal and may include landfill taxes or bans on certain materials	Many countries have implemented landfill taxes to discourage the disposal of waste in landfills and encourage recycling and other forms of waste recovery [17]
Standards and certifications	Provides benchmarks for circular products and processes, helping consumers and businesses make informed choices	Cradle-to-Cradle Certified (CCC), a multiattribute ecolabel that assesses products based on material health, material reutilization, renewable energy, water stewardship, and social fairness [72]
Incentives and subsidies	Offers financial support to manufacturers who invest in circular technologies or adopt circular business models	Tax credits for companies that use recycled materials in their products or subsidies for research and development of circular technologies [75]
Public procurement	Prioritizes circular products and services in government purchasing decisions	The EU's Green Public Procurement criteria, which guide the incorporation of environmental considerations into public procurement contracts [76]

ensure that the environmental and social costs of manufacturing are appropriately accounted for [74]. Key policy interventions include the following:

Extended producer responsibility schemes: Extended producer responsibility programs assign manufacturers the responsibility for handling their goods when their useful lives end [73]. Therefore, this incentivizes them to design for durability, repairability, and recyclability, thereby reducing waste and promoting resource recovery [55].

Waste management regulations: Stricter waste management regulations, including landfill taxes and bans on certain types of waste, can encourage manufacturers to minimize waste generation and explore alternative disposal routes such as recycling and remanufacturing [55].

Standards and certifications: Standards and certifications can provide clear benchmarks for circular products and processes, enabling consumers and businesses to make informed choices [70]. These standards can cover aspects such as material content, recyclability, and energy efficiency.

Incentives and subsidies: Financial incentives, such as tax breaks or subsidies for CE investments, can encourage manufacturers to adopt circular practices [75]. These can help offset the initial costs of transitioning to new business models and technologies.

Public procurement: Governments can increase demand for circular goods and services using their purchasing power [76]. By prioritizing circularity in public acquisition contracts, they can create a market for innovative solutions and support CE businesses [77].

1.6.2 Designing an Effective Regulatory Framework

A robust regulatory framework is essential for translating policy goals into concrete action [78]. Key elements of such a framework include the following:

Clear definitions and targets: Clear explanations of CE concepts, along with measurable targets for RE, WR, and recycling rates, can provide a common understanding and guide policy implementation [79].

Streamlined permitting processes: Complex and time-consuming permitting processes can discourage manufacturers from investing in CE technologies and infrastructure. Streamlining these processes can reduce administrative burden and accelerate the transition [80].

Enforcement mechanisms: Effective enforcement mechanisms, such as inspections, fines, and penalties for noncompliance, are crucial for ensuring that manufacturers adhere to CE regulations [81].

Data collection and monitoring: Robust data collection and monitoring systems are essential for tracking progress toward CE goals and identifying areas where further policy interventions are needed [75].

Collaboration and stakeholder engagement: Effective regulatory frameworks are developed in collaboration with industry, academia, and civil society organizations [82]. Therefore, this ensures that regulations are practical, feasible, and aligned with the needs of all stakeholders.

1.6.3 Overcoming Barriers to Policy Implementation

Despite the potential benefits of CE policies, several barriers can hinder their effective implementation:

a. **Lack of awareness and understanding**: Many manufacturers are not fully aware of the benefits of CE or how to implement circular practices in their operations [82].
b. **High upfront costs**: Transitioning to circular business models often requires significant upfront expenditures for infrastructure, new technologies, and training [75].
c. **Lack of access to finance**: Manufacturers, particularly SMEs, may struggle to access the financing needed to invest in CE initiatives [83].
d. **Regulatory uncertainty**: Unclear or inconsistent regulations can create uncertainty and discourage manufacturers from making long-term investments in circularity [80].
e. **Lack of collaboration**: A lack of cooperation between stakeholders, including manufacturers, suppliers, customers, and policymakers, can hinder the development and implementation of effective CE policies [84].

1.6.4 The Imperfect Regulatory Framework in Ukraine

Ukraine's inadequate regulatory system poses challenges to the incorporation of environmental standards across various industries. Addressing this problem necessitates a holistic strategy and strengthened legislative efforts [80]. Additionally, war-related issues can impact the implementation of CE approaches.

1.7 Future Outlook and Opportunities Involved

The industrial sector is presently experiencing a substantial shift driven by AI and other technological innovations, offering both opportunities and problems for the future [85, 86].

AI is set to transform multiple facets of manufacturing, encompassing design, production, supply chain management, and quality assurance. AI-driven solutions can facilitate the creation of creative designs, enhance production processes, and forecast equipment problems, resulting in heightened output and diminished expenses. The integration of AI in manufacturing also enables greater flexibility and agility, allowing companies to respond quickly to changing market demands and customer needs. Gamification, as an emerging trend, can increase manufacturing operations by augmenting worker engagement and motivation [87, 88].

A key opportunity in the manufacturing sector lies in advancing and implementing intelligent manufacturing systems. Therefore, these systems utilize AI, the IoT, and big data analytics to establish highly efficient, adaptable, and networked manufacturing processes. AI algorithms can scrutinize extensive data from diverse sources, including sensors, machinery, and supply chains, to discern trends, forecast results, and enhance operations in real-time. Therefore, this may result in optimized resource utilization, diminished waste, and augmented sustainability in manufacturing [89, 90].

The growing implementation of AI in manufacturing prompts ethical and legal concerns regarding intellectual property and copyright violations. As AI systems increasingly generate creative output, including designs, models, and written documentation, it is essential to confront the matters of authorship and ownership. Current copyright legislation may be insufficient to safeguard works produced by AI, resulting in ambiguity and possible conflicts around intellectual property rights [86, 91].

The emergence of generative AI poses difficulties regarding plagiarism and academic integrity. AI-driven technologies can produce language that is challenging to differentiate from human-authored content, facilitating plagiarism or the misrepresentation of AI-generated work as original. Therefore, this requires a reassessment of plagiarism policies and the creation of novel techniques for identifying and mitigating AI-facilitated academic misconduct [91].

To mitigate the risks of plagiarism and copyright infringement in the industrial sector, it is crucial to implement robust intellectual property protection measures and promote ethical guidelines for AI utilization. Organizations must have explicit policies about the ownership and utilization of AI-generated content and offer training to staff on intellectual property rights and moral implications. Moreover, it is essential to cultivate AI literacy and proficiency among those used in the industry. Therefore, this encompasses comprehending the powers and constraints of AI, along with the ethical and legal ramifications of its application [92].

The incorporation of AI in manufacturing has ramifications for the workforce and the employment market. Although AI can automate specific processes and enhance efficiency, it may also result in job displacement in particular sectors. Consequently, it is imperative to invest in educational and training initiatives to furnish workers with the requisite skills to adjust to the evolving requirements of the manufacturing industry. AI can also create new job opportunities in areas such as AI development, data analysis, and intelligent manufacturing system management [20].

The growing collaboration between humans and AI will undoubtedly influence the future of the industrial sector. AI can enhance human talents by delivering insights, automating monotonous jobs, and facilitating more informed decision-making. It is essential to uphold human monitoring and control over AI systems to guarantee their ethical and responsible utilization. Therefore, this necessitates an emphasis on creating AI systems that are transparent, explicable, and congruent with human ideals [89, 93].

1.8 Conclusion

CE in manufacturing signifies a transition from the conventional linear take–make–dispose model to a regenerative system that optimizes resource utilization and minimizes waste. Therefore, this transformation is motivated by escalating apprehensions regarding resource depletion, environmental deterioration, and the necessity for sustainable development.

CE is based on the principles of reduction, reuse, recycling, and recovery of materials and energy across the product lifespan. Its objective is to dissociate economic growth from resource use by establishing closed-loop systems that minimize waste and prolong the utilization of resources.

The benefits of implementing CE practices in the manufacturing sector are wide-ranging. It mitigates resource depletion, diminishes waste production, and reduces greenhouse gas emissions. Economically, it can result in cost savings *via* optimal resource utilization, generate new business prospects in recycling and remanufacturing, and improve competitiveness. It can generate employment, enhance public health, and encourage sustainable consumption practices.

Notwithstanding the myriad advantages, the adoption of CE principles in the manufacturing sector encounters various obstacles. Therefore, these encompass financial risks, technological challenges in implementing efficient reverse logistics, and organizational barriers such as insufficient awareness and internal resistance to change. The absence of standardized criteria and certifications, substantial initial investment expenditures, and regulatory obstacles can impede the adoption of circular practices.

Numerous international case studies illustrate the practical application of CE principles within the industrial sector. The automobile sector has achieved notable advancements in material recycling and reuse, with several businesses attaining elevated recycling rates. In the electronics sector, initiatives such as product take-back programs and design for disassembly are gaining prominence. Similarly, other industries, such as pharmaceuticals, chemicals, oil and gas, textiles, food manufacturing, and processing industries, are now considering product development-related programs to convert to Industry 4.0. Therefore, these examples underscore the potential for the adoption of CE practices across diverse manufacturing sectors.

Robust policy and regulatory frameworks are essential for facilitating the transition to a CE in the manufacturing sector. Governments can significantly influence WR and recycling by setting targets, offering incentives for circular business models, and implementing policies that promote sustainable product design and expanded producer responsibility. Cooperation among government, business, and research organizations is crucial for formulating and executing efficient CE policies.

The prospects for CE within the manufacturing sector are optimistic. Emerging trends, including DT such as IoT, AI, and big data analytics, present opportunities to augment RE, boost supply chain transparency, and facilitate novel circular business models. Moreover, the rising customer demand for sustainable products and heightened knowledge of environmental concerns are prompting corporations to use circular processes.

Future research opportunities encompass examining the possibilities of novel materials and technologies for circular manufacturing, establishing standardized metrics for assessing circularity, and analyzing the social and economic ramifications of CE projects. Furthermore, additional study is required to address the obstacles to the implementation of a CE, especially within SMEs.

In conclusion, CE provides a route to a more sustainable and resilient manufacturing industry. By adopting circular concepts, manufacturers can mitigate their environmental impact, improve their competitiveness, and foster a more sustainable future. Realizing the full potential of CE necessitates overcoming hurdles, promoting teamwork, and enacting appropriate policies and regulations. Digitalization, innovation, and a transformation in mentality are essential for realizing the potential of CE within the manufacturing sector.

AI disclosure statement: The author acknowledges the use of AI-based tools for minor language editing or grammatical correction. However, all intellectual contributions, analyses, and conclusions presented in this chapter are entirely the author's own.

References

1. Ronaghi, M.H., The influence of artificial intelligence adoption on circular economy practices in manufacturing industries. *Environ. Dev. Sustain.*, 2023, https://doi.org/10.1007/s10668-022-02670-3.
2. Revathi, P., *et al.*, AI Assistance in Circular Business Models for Sustainable Development in India, in: *2024 International Conference on Science Technology Engineering and Management (ICSTEM)*, 2024, https://doi.org/10.1109/ICSTEM61137.2024.10560744.
3. Cui, L., *et al.*, Selecting a remanufacturing quality strategy based on consumer preferences. *J. Cleaner Prod.*, 2017, https://doi.org/10.1016/j.jclepro.2017.03.056.
4. Aroul, G.G., Enabling Circular Economy through Integrated Digital Twins: A Framework for AI-Driven Business Transformation. *Int. J. Sci. Res. Eng. Manag.*, 2024, https://doi.org/10.55041/ijsrem28351.
5. Baduge, S.K., *et al.*, Artificial intelligence and smart vision for building and construction 4.0: Machine and deep learning methods and applications. *Autom. Constr.*, 2022, https://doi.org/10.1016/j.autcon.2022.104440.
6. Bishnoi, M.M., *et al.*, Impact of AI and COVID-19 on manufacturing systems: An Asia Pacific Perspective on the two Competing exigencies. *Prod. Manuf. Res.*, 2023, https://doi.org/10.1080/21693277.2023.2236684.
7. Wongsa, A., *et al.*, Mechanical and thermal properties of lightweight geopolymer mortar incorporating crumb rubber. *J. Cleaner Prod.*, 2018, https://doi.org/10.1016/j.jclepro.2018.06.003.

8. Chen, D., *et al.*, Photocatalytic degradation of organic pollutants using TiO2-based photocatalysts: A review. *J. Cleaner Prod.*, 2020, https://doi.org/10.1016/j.jclepro.2020.121725.
9. Bag, S., *et al.*, Role of institutional pressures and resources in the adoption of big data analytics powered artificial intelligence, sustainable manufacturing practices and circular economy capabilities. *Technol. Forecasting Social Change*, 2021, https://doi.org/10.1016/j.techfore.2020.120420.
10. Bhatt, J. and Singh, S., Sustainable innovation through digital transformation: Leveraging Ai for circular economy models. *Int. J. Adv. Res. Sci. Commun. Technol.*, 2025, https://doi.org/10.48175/IJARSCT-24869.
11. Solomon, N.O., *et al.*, Circular Economy Principles and Their Integration into Global Supply Chain Strategies. *Finance Account. Res. J.*, 2024, https://doi.org/10.51594/farj.v6i5.1133.
12. Liu, M., *et al.*, Investigating students' cognitive processes in generative AI-assisted digital multimodal composing and traditional writing. *Comput. Educ.*, 2024, https://doi.org/10.1016/j.compedu.2023.104977.
13. Mäkelä, M. and Onkila, T., Domination of Managerial and Technical Frames—How the Circular Economy Is Reported in Finnish Business. *Circ. Econ. Sustainability*, 2024, https://doi.org/10.1007/s43615-023-00335-5.
14. Abadi, M.M.K.F., *et al.*, Leveraging AI for energy-efficient manufacturing systems: Review and future prospectives. *J. Manuf. Syst.*, 2025, https://doi.org/10.1016/j.jmsy.2024.11.017.
15. De Oliveira, T.R., *et al.*, Virtual Reality Solutions Employing Artificial Intelligence Methods: A Systematic Literature Review. *ACM Comput. Surv.*, 2023, https://doi.org/10.1145/3565020.
16. Becue, A., *et al.*, AI's effect on innovation capacity in the context of industry 5.0: a scoping review. *Aritif. Intell. Rev.*, 2024, https://doi.org/10.1007/s10462-024-10864-6.
17. Anwar, A.Z., *et al.*, Circular Economy Advances with Artificial Intelligence and Digital Twin: Multiple-Case Study of Chinese Industries in Agriculture. *J. Knowl. Econ.*, 2025, https://doi.org/10.1007/s13132-024-02101-w.
18. Bashynska, I. and Prokopenko, O., Mitigating Cyber Risks in AI-Driven Circular Economy Implementations. *ASEJ Sci. J.*, 2024, https://doi.org/10.19192/wsfip.sj4.2024.10.
19. Miao, J., *et al.*, Ethical Dilemmas in Using AI for Academic Writing and an Example Framework for Peer Review in Nephrology Academia: A Narrative Review. *Clin. Pract.*, 2024, https://doi.org/10.3390/clinpract14010008.
20. Damioli, G., *et al.*, Drivers of employment dynamics of AI innovators. *Technol. Forecasting Social Change*, 2024, https://doi.org/10.1016/j.techfore.2024.123249.
21. Ghosh, D., *et al.*, AI-exposure and labour market: a systematic literature review on estimations, validations, and perceptions. *Manag. Rev. Q.*, 2025, https://doi.org/10.1007/s11301-023-00393-x.

22. Kharayat, T.S. and Gupta, H., A Novel Grey Causal Modelling (GCM) Approach to Enhance Resource Efficiency and Minimizing Waste in the Manufacturing Supply Chain Through Circular Economy. *Bus. Strategy Environ.*, 2025, https://doi.org/10.1002/bse.70087.
23. Orlov, A.K., *et al.*, Circular Economy in Manufacturing: Optimization using Lean Six Sigma. *E3S Web Conf.*, 2024.
24. Dennison, M.S., *et al.*, Realization of circular economy principles in manufacturing: obstacles, advancements, and routes to achieve a sustainable industry transformation. *Discover Sustainability*, 2024, https://doi.org/10.1007/s43621-024-00689-2.
25. Siratan, E.D., *et al.*, Optimizing Sustainable Supply Chain Management with a Circular Economy Approach in the Manufacturing Industry. *Int. J. Sci. Rev.*, 2025, https://doi.org/10.71364/ijfsr.v2i4.22.
26. Petrova, V., Industrial symbiosis in raw material sector as an overarching solution in circular economy. *Sustain. Extr. Process. Raw Mater.*, 2022, https://doi.org/10.58903/c16182120.
27. Farrukh, A., *et al.*, Green-lean-six sigma practices and supporting factors for transitioning towards circular economy: A natural resource and intellectual capital-based view. *Resour. Policy*, 2023, https://doi.org/10.1016/j.resourpol.2023.103789.
28. Oladapo, B.I., *et al.*, AI-Driven Circular Economy of Enhancing *Sustainability* and Efficiency in Industrial Operations. *Sustainability*, 2024, https://doi.org/10.3390/su162310358.
29. Ijassi, W., *et al.*, Development of a circularity design methodology for urban factories based on systemic thinking and stakeholders engagement. *Sustainable Prod. Consumption*, 2024, https://doi.org/10.1016/j.spc.2024.02.031.
30. Tišma, S. and Škrtić, M.M., Integrating Bioeconomy Principles in Bionic Production: Enhancing Sustainability and Environmental Performance. *J. Risk Financ. Manag.*, 2023, https://doi.org/10.3390/jrfm16100437.
31. Hassan, H., *et al.*, Resilient Circularity in Manufacturing: Synergies Between Circular Economy and Reconfigurable Manufacturing. *J. Manuf. Sci. Eng.*, 2024, https://doi.org/10.1115/1.4065744.
32. Manudu, U.U., *et al.*, Circular economy in the manufacturing sector: Digital transformation and sustainable practices. *Int. J. Sci. Res. Arch.*, 2025, https://doi.org/10.30574/ijsra.2024.12.2.1217.
33. Chhimwal, M., *et al.*, Challenges in the implementation of circular economy in manufacturing industry. *J. Model. Manag.*, 2022, https://doi.org/10.1108/JM2-07-2020-0194.
34. Nikam, H. and Somatkar, A., Developing Frameworks for Reducing Waste and Improving Resource Efficiency in Manufacturing using Industry 4.0. *Int. J. Sci. Res. Eng. Manag.*, 2025, https://doi.org/10.55041/ijsrem49973.

35. Rejeb, A., *et al.*, When Industry 5.0 Meets the Circular Economy: A Systematic Literature Review. *Circ. Econ. Sustainability*, 2025, https://doi.org/10.1007/s43615-025-00570-y.
36. Constance Obiuto, N., *et al.*, Implementing Circular Economy Principles to Enhance Safety and Environmental Sustainability in Manufacturing. *Int. J. Adv. Multidiscip. Res. Stud.*, 2024, https://doi.org/10.62225/2583049x.2024.4.2.2432.
37. Aparecido, R., *et al.*, Synergizing lean management and circular economy: Pathways to sustainable manufacturing. *Corp. Soc. Responsib. Environ. Manag.*, 2024, https://doi.org/10.1002/csr.2962.
38. Sulista, *et al.*, Turning waste into profit: Circular economic optimization of quartz sand from tin mining and processing. *Sustainable Prod. Consumption*, 39, 2023, https://doi.org/10.1016/j.spc.2023.05.002.
39. Brinsi, W., Evaluating sustainability through resource efficiency: A case study of circular economy proacticses in three companies. *Oradea J. Bus. Econom.*, 2024, http://doi.org/10.47535/1991ojbe200.
40. Mostaghel, R., *et al.*, The transformative impact of the circular economy on marketing theory. *Technol. Forecasting Social Change*, 2023, https://doi.org/10.1016/j.techfore.2023.122780.
41. Yosep, Y., *et al.*, Unleashing the Sustainable Transition of Circular Economy: A Case Study of SMEs Tapioca Industry in Lampung, Indonesia. *Circ. Econ. Sustainability*, 2024, https://doi.org/10.1007/s43615-024-00358-6.
42. Shahin, V. and Alimohammadlou, M., Current status and emerging trends on urban circular economy: a bibliometric analysis. *Environ. Dev. Sustainability*, 2024, https://doi.org/10.1007/s10668-024-05169-1.
43. Habibollahi Najaf Abadi, H., *et al.*, Measuring and Indexing the Durability of Electrical and Electronic Equipment. *Sustainability (Switzerland)*, 2023, https://doi.org/10.3390/su151914386.
44. Bhawna, *et al.*, Bridging the gap: a systematic analysis of circular economy, supply chain management, and digitization for sustainability and resilience. *Oper. Manage. Res.*, 2024, https://doi.org/10.1007/s12063-024-00490-4.
45. Oliveira, A.M.C.P. de, *et al.*, Building Rehabilitation: A Sustainable Strategy for the Preservation of the Built Environment. *Sustainability (Switzerland)*, 2024, https://doi.org/10.3390/su16020553.
46. Hettiarachchi, B.D., *et al.*, Challenges and Opportunities for Implementing Additive Manufacturing Supply Chains in Circular Economy. *IFAC-PapersOnLine*, 2022, https://doi.org/10.1016/j.ifacol.2022.09.545.
47. Kotyal, K., Sustainable Waste Management in the Circular Economy: Challenges and Opportunities. *Environ. Rep.*, 2024, https://doi.org/10.51470/ER.2023.5.2.01.
48. Nademi, Y. and Khochiani, R., The Pursuit of Happiness in a Circular Economy. *J. Knowl. Econ.*, 2024, https://doi.org/10.1007/s13132-024-01739-w.

49. Bayram, B., *et al.*, Product Quality in the Circular Economy: A Systematic Review of its Definition and Contexts in Scientific Literature. *Circ. Econ. Sustainability*, 2024, https://doi.org/10.1007/s43615-024-00396-0.
50. Cavalieri, A., *et al.*, Socioenvironmental assessment and application process for IOT: A comprehensive approach. *J. Cleaner Prod.*, 2024, https://doi.org/10.1016/j.jclepro.2023.140348.
51. Madrid, J.A., Circular Economy in Automotive Manufacturing: Recycling and Sustainability. *Int. J. Adv. Res. Sci. Commun. Technol.*, 2023. https://doi.org/10.48175/ijarsct-11964.
52. Soroka, A., *et al.*, Circular Economy Models in the Construction Sector: A Plastics Recycling Use Case. *Smart Innov. Syst. Technol.*, 2023, https://doi.org/10.1007/978-981-19-9205-6_14.
53. Bilal, M., *et al.*, Current state and barriers to the circular economy in the building sector: Towards a mitigation framework. *J. Cleaner Prod.*, 2020, https://doi.org/10.1016/j.jclepro.2020.123250.
54. Chi, B., *et al.*, Construction waste minimization in green building: A comparative analysis of LEED-NC 2009 certified projects in the US and China. *J. Cleaner Prod.*, 2020, https://doi.org/10.1016/j.jclepro.2020.120749.
55. Hassan, S.M., Circular Economy and ESG: Building Sustainable Business Models in the Manufacturing Sector. *J. Bus. Econom. Stud.*, 2025.
56. Zhang, T., *et al.*, Circular economy strategies for the booming industrial pallet use in China. *Sustainable Prod. Consumption*, 2024, https://doi.org/10.1016/j.spc.2024.02.028.
57. Sharma, M., *et al.*, Analysis of circular economy barriers in manufacturing context for indian industries: a BWM ranking process. *Environ. Dev. Sustainability*, 2023, https://doi.org/10.1007/s10668-023-03868-9.
58. Badhotiya, G.K., *et al.*, Analyzing barriers for the adoption of circular economy in the manufacturing sector. *Int. J. Product. Perform. Manag.*, 2022, https://doi.org/10.1108/IJPPM-01-2021-0021.
59. Rehman, M., *et al.*, Sustainable fashion: Mapping waste streams and life cycle management. *J. Cleaner Prod.*, 2024, https://doi.org/10.1016/j.jclepro.2024.141279.
60. Anwajler, B., Potential of 3D Printing for Heat Exchanger Heat Transfer Optimization—Sustainability Perspective. *Inventions*, 2024, https://doi.org/10.3390/inventions9030060.
61. Castiglione, C., *et al.*, Multidimensional and multi-level assessment of circular economy strategies in manufacturing systems. *Procedia CIRP*, 2024, https://doi.org/10.1016/j.procir.2024.01.004.
62. Wang, Q., *et al.*, Life cycle assessment and the willingness to pay of waste polyester recycling. *J. Cleaner Prod.*, 2019, https://doi.org/10.1016/j.jclepro.2019.06.123.
63. Brändström, J. and Saidani, M., Comparison between circularity metrics and LCA: A case study on circular economy strategies. *J. Cleaner Prod.*, 2022, https://doi.org/10.1016/j.jclepro.2022.133537.

64. Vanhuyse, F., The Urban Circularity Assessment Framework (UCAF): a Framework for Planning, Monitoring, Evaluation, and Learning from CE Transitions in Cities. *Circ. Econ. Sustainability*, 2024, https://doi.org/10.1007/s43615-023-00314-w.
65. Baratsas, S.G., *et al.*, A quantitative and holistic circular economy assessment framework at the micro level. *Comput. Chem. Eng.*, 2022, https://doi.org/10.1016/j.compchemeng.2022.107697.
66. Mamudu, U.U., *et al.*, Circular economy in the manufacturing sector: Digital transformation and sustainable practices. *Int. J. Sci. Res. Arch.*, 2024, https://doi.org/10.30574/ijsra.2024.12.2.1217.
67. Vinayagam, V., *et al.*, Envisioning the innovative approaches to achieve circular economy in the water and wastewater sector. *Environ. Res.*, 2024, https://doi.org/10.1016/j.envres.2023.117663.
68. Macias Aragonés, M. and Arroyo Torralvo, F., How to select the best approach for circular economy assessment? 3D positioning framework, decision support tool and critical analysis for bio-based systems. *Environ. Impact Assess. Rev.*, 2024, https://doi.org/10.1016/j.eiar.2024.107493.
69. Vinante, C., *et al.*, Circular economy metrics: Literature review and company-level classification framework. *J. Cleaner Prod.*, 2021, https://doi.org/10.1016/j.jclepro.2020.125090.
70. Kunlere, I.O. and Shah, K.U., A recycling technology selection framework for evaluating the effectiveness of plastic recycling technologies for circular economy advancement. *Circ. Econ.*, 2023, https://doi.org/10.1016/j.cec.2023.100066.
71. Pham, H.T., *et al.*, Artificial intelligence (AI) development in the Vietnam's energy and economic systems: A critical review. *J. Cleaner Prod.*, 2024, https://doi.org/10.1016/j.jclepro.2024.140692.
72. Gupta, H., *et al.*, Industry 4.0, cleaner production and circular economy: An integrative framework for evaluating ethical and sustainable business performance of manufacturing organizations. *J. Cleaner Prod.*, 2021, https://doi.org/10.1016/j.jclepro.2021.126253.
73. Neramballi, A., *et al.*, Toward a policy landscape to support the product-as-a-service design process for a circular economy. *J. Ind. Policy*, 2024, https://doi.org/10.1111/jiec.13535.
74. Milios, L., Advancing to a Circular Economy: three essential ingredients for a comprehensive policy mix. *Sustainability Sci.*, 2018, https://doi.org/10.1007/s11625-017-0502-9.
75. Gue, I.H.V., *et al.*, Environmentally-extended input-output analysis of circular economy scenarios in the Philippines. *J. Cleaner Prod.*, 2022, https://doi.org/10.1016/j.jclepro.2022.134360.
76. Valli Buttow, C. and Weerts, S., Public sector information in the European Union policy: The misbalance between economy and individuals. *Big Data Soc.*, 2022, https://doi.org/10.1177/20539517221124587.

77. Strupeit, L., *et al.*, Towards a Circular Solar Power Sector: Experience with a Support Framework for Business Model Innovation. *Circ. Econ. Sustainability*, 2024, https://doi.org/10.1007/s43615-024-00377-3.
78. Sharma, S. and Sud, M., Impact of regulatory framework on bidding behavior of firms: Policy implications for the oil & gas sector. *Energy Policy*, 2019, https://doi.org/10.1016/j.enpol.2019.01.075.
79. Preisner, M., *et al.*, Indicators for resource recovery monitoring within the circular economy model implementation in the wastewater sector. *J. Environ. Manage.*, 2022, https://doi.org/10.1016/j.jenvman.2021.114261.
80. Salashenka, T.I. and Samoilenko, V.S., Regulatory Support for the Development of the Circular Approach in Ukraine. *Bus. Inform.*, 2024, https://doi.org/10.32983/2222-4459-2024-10-159-174.
81. Karovic Maricic, V., *et al.*, Serbian oil sector: A new energy policy regulatory framework and development strategies. *Energy Policy*, 2012, https://doi.org/10.1016/j.enpol.2012.08.021.
82. Torgautov, B., *et al.*, Circular economy: Challenges and opportunities in the construction sector of Kazakhstan. *Buildings*, 2021, https://doi.org/10.3390/buildings11110501.
83. Munir, R. and Fausiah, R., The Role of Circular Economy in Green Entrepreneurship: Sustainable Business Models. *J. Indones. Sch. Soc. Res.*, 2025, https://doi.org/10.59065/jissr.v5i1.173.
84. Shebanin, V., *et al.*, Circular economy of the agricultural sector: Strategies and challenges in the context of globalisation. *Sci. Horiz.*, 2024, https://doi.org/10.48077/scihor9.2024.148.
85. Espina-Romero, L., *et al.*, Challenges and Opportunities in the Implementation of AI in Manufacturing: A Bibliometric Analysis. *Sci.*, 2024, https://doi.org/10.3390/sci6040060.
86. Cebi, E., *et al.*, The Influence of Artificial Intelligence on Copyright Law. *Interdiscip. Stud. Soc. Law Polit.*, 2023, https://doi.org/10.61838/kman.isslp.2.2.5.
87. Akhtar, Z.B., Artificial intelligence (AI) within manufacturing: An investigative exploration for opportunities, challenges, future directions. *Metaverse*, 2024, https://doi.org/10.54517/m.v5i2.2731.
88. Keepers, M., *et al.*, Current state of research & outlook of gamification for manufacturing. *J. Manuf. Syst.*, 2022, https://doi.org/10.1016/j.jmsy.2022.07.001.
89. Bending, D. and Braunche, A., The role of artificial intelligence algorithms in information systems research: a conceptual overview and avenues for research. *Manag. Rev. Q.*, 2024, https://doi.org/10.1007/s11301-024-00451-y.
90. Shankar, R. and Gupta, L., An integrated AI framework for managing organizational risk and climate change concerns in B2B market. *Ind. Mark. Manag.*, 2024, https://doi.org/10.1016/j.indmarman.2023.12.019.
91. Dwivedi, Y.K., *et al.*, Opinion Paper: "So what if ChatGPT wrote it?" Multidisciplinary perspectives on opportunities, challenges and implications

of generative conversational AI for research, practice and policy. *Int. J. Inf. Manage.*, 2023, https://doi.org/10.1016/j.ijinfomgt.2023.102642.
92. Chiu, T.K.F., *et al.*, What are artificial intelligence literacy and competency? A comprehensive framework to support them. *Comput. Educ. Open*, 2024, https://doi.org/10.1016/j.caeo.2024.100171.
93. Androutsopoulou, M., *et al.*, Leveraging AI for Enhanced eGovernment: Optimizing the Use of Open Governmental Data. *J. Knowl. Econ.*, 2, 2024, https://link.springer.com/article/10.1007/s13132-024-02317-w.

2

Understanding Circular Design and Product Lifecycle

Milad Heidari*, Jeyaprakash Natarajan, Khalid Anwar and Amirhossein Ali Memari

Global College of Engineering and Technology (GCET), Muscat, Sultanate of Oman

Abstract

A shift away from conventional linear models towards a model of a circular economy has drastically changed Product Design, Development, and Lifecycle Management. However, an exploration into Circular Design Concepts and Strategies as critical tools for helping to create Sustainable Manufacturing continues and forms the basis of this Chapter. Through the exploration of how product design choices can allow for increased product durability, modularity, and recyclability, it will be established that these design methods can help conserve finite resources, reduce waste, and extend the lifespan of products. It will also be discussed how Systemic Thinking (e.g., 3D Modeling) and Data-Driven Approaches (e.g., Life Cycle Assessment (LCA) and Eco-Design) can assist in facilitating environmentally responsible decisions for all stages of product development. Apart from discussing the difficulties and compromises involved in the implementation of circular design, the chapter also focuses on the environmental, social, and economic justifications for the shift to circular design, as observed in an increasing number of companies. The chapter discusses some of the most prominent cases of companies like Patagonia, IKEA, Interface, and Fairphone to prove that incorporating circular design is beneficial for the achievement of sustainable development. The cases discussed in the chapter indicate that to achieve sustainable development, it is necessary to transform business models, engage people, strengthen regulatory environments, and create innovative materials and processes. The concluding part of the chapter offers a framework for the implementation of circular design in product development, and it is discussed as a means to build a regenerative economy. From the chapter, it is evident that circular design is an effective means to enhance resource efficiency, build sustainable production, and move toward a circular economy.

**Corresponding author*: milad@gcet.edu.om

Jeyaprakash Natarajan, Milon Selvam Dennison, M. Bhuvanesh Kumar and Ganapathy Thirukkotti (eds.) Manufacturing and the Circular Economy, (35–64) © 2027 Scrivener Publishing LLC

Keywords: Circular design, product lifecycle, sustainable manufacturing, life cycle assessment, eco-design

2.1 Introduction

The economic model referred to by many people as the "take–make–use–dispose" model has always influenced the way industries work, the way products are made, and the way the economy is growing globally. This model has seen the use of natural resources extracted from the environment, made useful and bought by people, worn out or consumed by them, and finally discarded as waste. Though the model has seen the economy grow enormously and some developments in the way industries have worked, it is increasingly being viewed as having negative consequences for the environment and being a waste of precious resources. The main assumption of the model, which has influenced the way the economy has worked over the years, has proven not to work. This is because there is now ample evidence of the glaring disconnect between the amount of use and the environment's ability to sustain the same. The use of natural resources has tripled globally since 1970, exceeding 100 billion tons annually, while only 7.2% is recovered and recycled [1]. Figure 2.1 illustrates the disconnect between the traditional model and the new regeneration model.

2.1.1 Importance of Circular Design in Sustainable Manufacturing

Climate change, depletion of natural resources, and loss of biodiversity are examples of crucial environmental challenges that help to justify the need

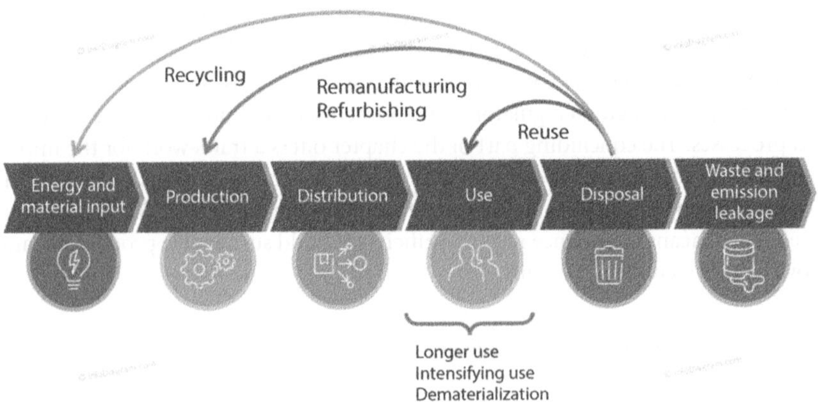

Figure 2.1 Circular economy vs. linear approach diagram [2].

to utilize circular design principles in production systems. Traditional linear industrial systems or "take-make-dispose" models are major contributors to environmental destruction. For example, according to the European Environment Agency [3], the average European produces 190 kg of packaging waste per year, a portion of which is not recycled. In that sense, circular design principles can be applied to reduce waste and pollution; to keep products and resources in circulation for as long as they hold utility and value; and to create a framework for restoring and creating natural systems. By applying circular design principles, manufacturers can help reduce the negative impacts of production on the environment, thereby leading to a substantial decrease in the ecological footprint of industrial systems [3].

The economic benefits of circular design principles are multiple: improved efficiency in manufacturing processes; reduced costs of producing goods; and opportunities to generate new revenue streams through diversification. Manufacturers can improve their bottom lines by creating longer-lasting products with greater ease of repair and recyclability, thereby helping them to minimize their use of materials and their vulnerability to variations in the price of raw materials. Furthermore, through new ways of doing business that focus on remanufacturing, taking back old products, and providing the product as a service (e.g., "lighting as a service" by Philips, where the customer pays only for the light produced, not for ownership of the fixture), manufacturers may find opportunities to enter new markets and develop new value propositions for customers [4].

Modern society is witnessing a rise in both consumer demand for sustainable products and increased transparency throughout the product lifecycle (Figure 2.2). Due to greater public awareness of how product consumption affects both the environment and society, consumers are increasingly choosing to support companies that demonstrate a commitment to sustainability. The pressure on companies to comply with new regulatory requirements is also rising. In many countries throughout the world, governments have established new regulations designed to encourage product lifecycle thinking, such as eco-design and Extended Producer Responsibility (EPR) policies. The implementation of circular design will not only help organizations meet the regulatory requirements but will also enable them to respond to consumer demands, thus establishing themselves as competitive players within their respective markets.

Not only is circular design a group of technical solutions (as shown in Figure 2.3), but it is also a holistic strategic approach to how organizations will design, engineer, and manage their products over the entire life cycle. This includes designing the product to have attributes such as recyclability,

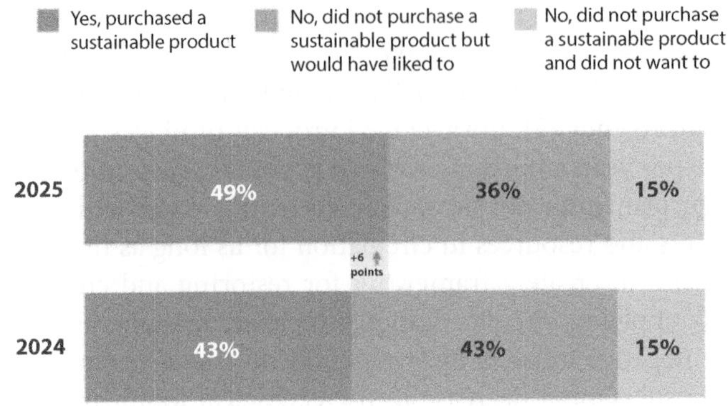

Figure 2.2 A significant percentage of consumers in the US have purchased environmentally sustainable products, indicating this growing demand for sustainable alternatives [5].

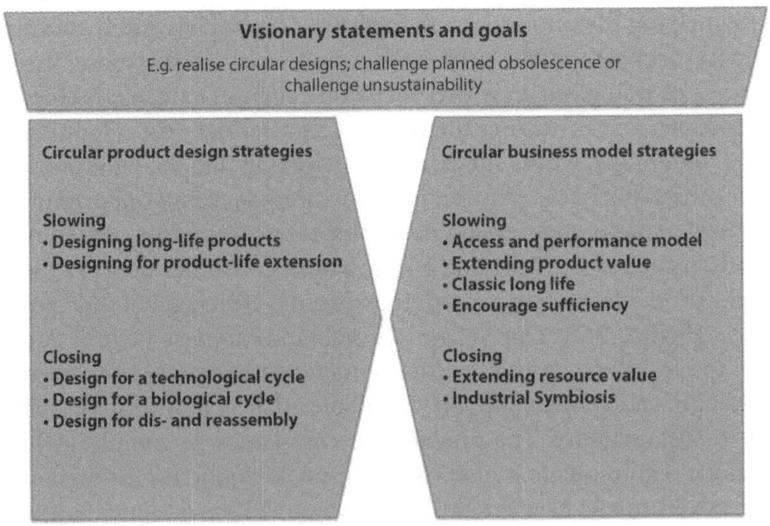

Figure 2.3 The circular economy product and business model strategy framework identifies a distinct path for the incorporation of circular economy concepts into product development processes and business strategies. This framework also highlights the simultaneous incorporation of circular product development strategies, such as product durability, modularity, and material recovery, with business model innovations, such as product-as-a-service concepts and product take-back systems, into business strategies [6]

reusability, and recoverability, while developing product-related business models. All parties associated with the life cycle of the product need to work together to promote this transformation. As a result, by integrating the concept of circular design throughout the entire industrial process, organizations can facilitate the creation of an innovative and sustainable economy.

This chapter aims to provide a comprehensive overview of circular design and its significant contribution to the development of sustainable manufacturing practices. This chapter begins with the development of a theoretical background based on the precise differentiation between linear and circular economy concepts. Following the development of the theoretical background, the chapter aims to provide a critical analysis of the contribution of circular design concepts to the development of sustainable practices, such as environmental, economic, and social sustainability, with the assistance of examples. In addition, the chapter also aims to provide a critical discussion on the circular design concepts, including durability, modularity, and recyclability, with the assistance of examples. In addition, the chapter also aims to provide a critical discussion on the application of eco-design methodologies and the use of life cycle analysis (LCA) as tools for the evaluation of environmental sustainability. In addition, the chapter also aims to provide a critical discussion on the application of the circular economy concept with the assistance of the latest technological innovations, such as digital twins, the Internet of Things (IoT), and artificial intelligence (AI), for the development of sustainable product development practices. In addition, the chapter also aims to provide a critical discussion on the application of circular economy concepts with the assistance of case studies from leading organizations, such as Patagonia, Fairphone, Philips, and IKEA, with the assistance of examples.

2.2 Importance of Circular Design in Sustainable Manufacturing

2.2.1 Environmental Drivers

One of the biggest issues facing the world today is climate change, and industrial activities have been identified as one of the major contributors to greenhouse gas emissions. The conventional linear economy model, with its "take-make-dispose" philosophy, only adds to this issue by creating waste and contributing to the depletion of resources. On the other hand, the concept of a circular economy provides a solution to this issue through the reuse, recycling, and remanufacturing of materials, which in turn helps to minimize the emission of greenhouse gases. This helps to meet some of the major issues facing the world today, like the Paris Agreement's goal of limiting global warming to well below 2°C. For example, the implementation of circular design in industries like electronics and textiles has been found to have huge potential for emission reductions, thus demonstrating the importance of circular design in the fight against climate change [7].

Rising global population levels and industrial activities are causing increasing demand for the use of natural resources. Resource scarcity is now a major global issue. The UN projects that world consumption of natural resources will be approximately 60% higher in 2060 than it was in 2020. As these projections highlight, the urgency to shift towards sustainability and resource efficiency cannot be overstated. Through the use of renewable resources and through extending product life, circular design provides opportunities for the relief of scarce resources while also providing access to future generations who may rely on these same resources [8–10].

The link between limited resources and climate change highlights the ecological need for implementing circular design principles in manufacturing systems. By implementing circular economy operations, companies can help to limit climate change's impact on greenhouse gases and can also

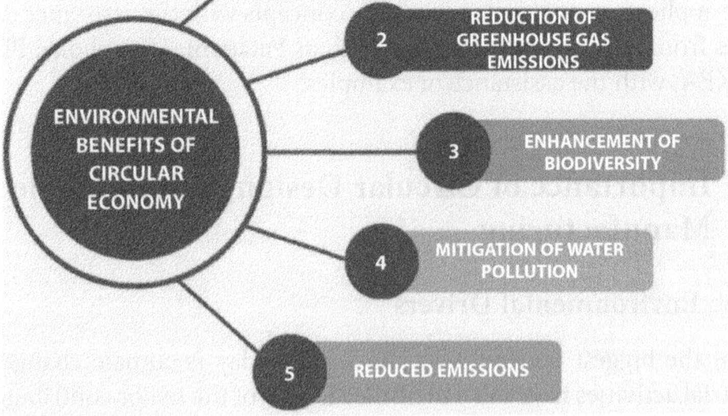

Figure 2.4 Greenhouse gas emissions, limited extraction of natural resources, and limited pollution in the environment are all possible results of the implementation of circular economy models. In addition, the strategy of utilizing design-for-disassembly and sustainable materials provides positive effects on the environment compared to traditional linear manufacturing methods of production [11].

significantly limit the need for harvesting limited materials from the natural world. Circular design can help limit environmental impacts in several ways, including selecting sustainable materials for use and incorporating design-for-disassembly strategies, which can limit harm to the environment through natural resource extraction (Figure 2.4). The implementation of circular manufacturing design in the production of consumer goods (i.e., manufactured items) has also been positively correlated with limiting waste (both material and energy) in the environment, thus resulting in improved air and water quality. By demonstrating that circular design has strategic value as an environmentally viable option for sustaining and creating a successful manufacturing operation, companies are able to ultimately contribute toward creating environmental sustainability and resiliency [9].

2.2.2 Social Drivers

Consumer awareness of sustainability has increased considerably. This means that consumer behavior is showing a greater preference for products that feature a circular design. The 2024 Report indicated that 54% of consumers were willing to pay more for products and services featuring circular design elements compared to prior years. Additionally, nearly 50% of consumers in the USA said they purchased an environmentally-friendly product in the last month (indicating that while there may be a high demand for environmentally-friendly products, they are being purchased by more than just a small percentage of the consumer market). The different consumer groups involved have significantly influenced the movement (especially the younger generation). For example, 60% of millennials exhibited a preference to pay more for products that featured circular design elements, while 59% of Generation Z displayed the same tendency. Therefore, as consumer behavior continues to change, manufacturers are adopting the principles of circular design more heavily in order to respond to the market and establish a brand identity that will create long-term customer loyalty as well as shorter-term [12–14].

In addition to the shift in consumer behavior, changes in regulations and legislation from governments worldwide will also encourage manufacturers to adopt circular design principles. Many governments have been creating regulations with the intention of addressing environmental concerns, as well as promoting sustainable development. For example, many governments now have a circular economy action plan that outlines goals related to improving the recycling rate, limiting the introduction of microplastics, and revising legislation pertaining to waste management. In addition, many government agencies, such as the SEC, have created regulations regarding how companies must report on their sustainability efforts. Through these requirements, companies are being encouraged to consider sustainability in their overall processes and business models.

Environmental, Social, and Governance (ESG) factors increasingly influence the strategies employed by manufacturers who recognize the strategic importance of conducting business in a manner that is environmentally sustainable and socially responsible. By embedding ESG factors into the fabric of the manufacturing processes employed by a firm, not only does the firm enhance its reputation, but it also fosters a level of trust among its investors and consumers. By embedding ESG factors into the day-to-day operations of a firm, the latter is able to create a level of value that is sustainable over the long term. In a business environment where regulatory authorities exert a higher level of scrutiny and where consumers increasingly demand ESG performance from manufacturers, the latter is more likely to weather the dynamics of the market and sustain a level of competitiveness.

Table 2.1 offers a meaningful and relevant comparative analysis of the differences in environmental impact between the linear and circular economy manufacturing models. As shown in the table, the conventional linear approach is associated with a level of environmental degradation through excessive extraction of natural resources, excessive use of energy, significant levels of greenhouse gas emissions, and excessive levels of waste. Such an

Table 2.1 An evaluation highlighting the differences between the impacts of linear and circular economic models concerning resource extraction, energy consumption, waste generation, greenhouse gas emissions, and ecosystem stress; demonstrating the benefits of circular models through reductions in the above.

Impact category	Linear economy model	Circular economy model
Resource Extraction	The extreme reliance on virgin raw materials causes rapid depletion of non-renewable resources, which in turn creates an extreme dependence on raw materials with corresponding endings through extractive industries (mining, logging, etc.).	Decreased reliance upon raw materials, preference for reuse and recycling, and usage of renewable resources; lengthen the lifespan of resources by utilizing closed-loop systems.

(*Continued*)

Table 2.1 An evaluation highlighting the differences between the impacts of linear and circular economic models concerning resource extraction, energy consumption, waste generation, greenhouse gas emissions, and ecosystem stress; demonstrating the benefits of circular models through reductions in the above. (*Continued*)

Impact category	Linear economy model	Circular economy model
Energy Consumption	Each step in an extraction cycle (extraction, production of raw materials, transportation of raw materials, and disposal of product) has a very high energy requirement.	Decreased total energy consumption through remanufacturing, recycling, and optimizing the product's life-cycle, as well as creating lower-impact manufacturing processes.
Greenhouse Gas Emissions (GHG)	The production, transportation, and disposal of numerous products with short (or single) product life cycles produce a large number of emissions.	Significant reductions in overall greenhouse gas emissions are achieved when utilizing closed-loop systems to design products with a long lifespan and using services rather than goods.
Waste Generation	A significant portion of waste produced will go to landfills or incineration, with little recovery of material and less efficient recovery of metals, plastics, or paper through recycling.	Waste generation is minimized; raw materials are treated as resources that are valuable to the company; products are designed to be disassembled and/or repaired, thereby facilitating their reuse and the generation of high-value returns.
Water Use & Pollution	Large amounts of water will be used and contaminated at each step of this cycle.	Reduced water usage in the process of using resources more efficiently, implementing more sustainable methods of producing goods, and using closed-loop water systems.

(*Continued*)

Table 2.1 An evaluation highlighting the differences between the impacts of linear and circular economic models concerning resource extraction, energy consumption, waste generation, greenhouse gas emissions, and ecosystem stress; demonstrating the benefits of circular models through reductions in the above. (*Continued*)

Impact category	Linear economy model	Circular economy model
Biodiversity & Ecosystem Impact	The environmentally destructive process of extracting virgin raw materials affects soils, waters, and atmospheres through habitat destruction created by the extraction process itself.	Reduction in pressure on the environment from regenerating the materials used to produce goods, reducing the amount of land that is disturbed, and producing a minimum amount of pollution.
Circularity & Material Flow	There is an inherently linear process ("Take → Make → Dispose") with limited opportunities to close loops/ reintegrate materials back into the system.	The "circular flow" is a process that consists of "design → use → reuse/recycle/ regenerate." The goal of the "circular flow" is to maintain the functional value of the materials being used to make the products for as long as possible.

approach also leads to habitat destruction, loss of biodiversity, and water pollution. On the other hand, the circular economy approach focuses on the regeneration of natural resources, the extension of product lifespan, the reuse and recycling of products, and the ease with which products may be disassembled. By keeping the material at the highest level of usability for a longer period, the environmental impact is minimized through the reduction of greenhouse gas emissions, the improvement of energy efficiency, and the elimination of waste. As such, the circular economy is a fundamental mechanism for the creation of a sustainable manufacturing approach through the reconfiguration of the manner in which products are designed.

2.3 Design Principles: Durability, Modularity, and Recyclability

A fundamental principle of circular design is durability, or the design of products that will last for a long time (or, in other words, continue to serve their function, provide quality performance, and maintain an aesthetic appearance) without having to be replaced. By designing for durability, a manufacturer reduces how often a product needs to be replaced, which in turn decreases the number of materials used to produce the product as well as the energy used to manufacture the product and all other environmental impacts of replacing the product (e.g., waste generated). Ensuring that a product has a long service life helps to keep the materials that are embedded in the product in productive use as long as possible, thus reducing the amount of waste generated by the product and also increasing overall resource efficiency. Durability can be achieved through good engineering practices, utilizing high-quality materials, and designing a product so that it can be metabolized (i.e., maintained, repaired, or have its components replaced). A good example of how this is accomplished in the electronics industry is with many laptops and smartphones, which are designed with removable batteries and other durable components. As a result, some laptops and smartphones are capable of functioning longer than the anticipated lifecycle for those devices. Companies such as Patagonia also demonstrate that they can achieve high durability through carefully selected and developed materials and supply chain practices intended to promote the length of time garments remain usable (i.e., durable) [15, 16].

Modular design is a method of developing products that are developed together as an intact system of modules that work together as one full product. The use of modules supports achieving a circular economy because modules can be reused in multiple ways or customized, upgraded over time, and when one module fails, you do not necessarily need to throw away the entire product. The concept of modularity is important because it provides a way to save resources and minimize waste by not having to throw away a functional item, as long as you can simply replace the broken module. An excellent example of modular design is the Fairphone, and its modular design allows users to replace each piece of hardware (such as display, battery, or camera) independently of each other to extend the life of their phone. Industries like furniture and industrial cannot be left out when it comes to modularity in their respective industries, as they can often develop modular styles of furniture or equipment that can be easily reconfigured, refurbished, or repurposed for use in other ways. Although modular designs provide a great deal of flexibility and can also increase the effectiveness of managing products throughout their entire lifecycles, the implementation of this philosophy to product design does require a significant amount of engineering to achieve compatibility, structural integrity, and cost-effectiveness.

The recyclable design principle is focused on enabling efficient material recovery at the end of a product's useful life, through the reintegration of those materials back into new production cycles so that material loops can be closed, less reliance on virgin resources, and minimization of environmental impacts such as landfill waste, pollution, or excessive energy use. Recyclable design includes the selection of materials that are easily separable, avoiding the use of complex composites, which make recovery difficult, and creating product architectures that are consistent with current recycling infrastructures. A few examples of recyclable design would include the increased use of paper-based packaging and recyclable PET containers in the packaging industry, as well as the way in which automotive products are designed to allow for the recovery of metals, plastics, and electronic components at the end of a vehicle's lifecycle. Recycling is an important component of the circular design process; however, there are still challenges to the practicability of recycling, such as material contamination, inadequacies in current infrastructure, and possible trade-offs with durability and performance, which require a balanced and systems approach to the development of new products [17, 18].

2.3.1 Challenges, Compromises, and Implementation Barriers

Table 2.2 provides a list of key obstacles to manufacturers' introduction of durability as an essential criterion for circular design. Among these several obstacles, high upfront investment in superior-quality raw material and superior engineering solutions is one of the greatest obstacles to designing products that last for an extended period; this is particularly challenging in highly competitive (i.e., price-sensitive) marketplaces. Designing for long-lasting products also brings with it a concern about product obsolescence (i.e., the product remains physically intact but loses functionality)—this is particularly important in high-tech industries (i.e., consumer electronics) where technology advances so quickly. Another significant limitation to introducing durable products is the complexity of repair and maintenance. Products that are designed for long-term use typically require a greater degree of technical expertise to service, as well as more costly maintenance service infrastructure, and access to spare parts; this results in higher operational costs and a greater burden of logistical requirements to provide ongoing support for the product during its expected life cycle. Furthermore, creating more durable products often results in design compromises with respect to a product's weight, flexibility, appearance, and compatibility with other circular strategies (e.g., modularity and recyclability), due to the use of thicker materials and enhanced structural integrity,

Table 2.2 Challenges associated with the implementation of durability with circular design.

Challenge	Description	Impact on implementation	Examples across sectors
High Upfront Material and Production Costs	Generally speaking, durable products often require superior materials, advanced manufacturing techniques, and enhanced engineering design.	Upgraded durability increases capital and production costs and potentially reduces competitiveness in price-sensitive markets.	Electronics: Smartphones with reinforced hardware and extended battery life; Automotive: Usage of high-grade materials in hybrid/electric automobiles; Textiles: Usage of premium materials in Patagonia clothing items.
Technological Obsolescence	Products designed for long-lasting physical performance are likely to become functionally obsolete as a result of rapid technological advancements.	There is a risk of reduced market relevance because of structural durability, which could reduce consumer adoption potential.	Consumer Electronics: Smartphones with aging software platforms and reinforced hardware; Automotive: Hybrid vehicle battery systems that require certified maintenance; Industrial Equipment: Long-lasting equipment that requires specialized technical expertise.

(*Continued*)

Table 2.2 Challenges associated with the implementation of durability with circular design. (*Continued*)

Challenge	Description	Impact on implementation	Examples across sectors
Maintenance and Repair Complexity	Durable products often require servicing, specialized maintenance, or replacement parts.	Upgraded durability increases operations and logistics requirements, including supporting infrastructure and human resources.	Electronics: Reinforced enclosures that add to the overall weight of the device; Textiles: Increased weight that can reduce overall comfort.
Design Trade-offs	Upgraded durability could also affect other performance or design attributes such as weight, flexibility, and appearance.	Upgraded durability could also affect consumer experience, appeal, and modularity and recyclability strategies.	Automotive: Limited availability of minerals used in hybrid vehicle battery systems; Textiles: Limited availability of certified durable organic fibers.
Supply Chain Constraints	There is also a potential constraint on access to superior materials with high-performance and durability attributes.	This type of durability also increases sourcing risk, production lead times, and supply chain complexity.	Automotive: Long-life battery materials are scarce; Textiles: Durable organic fibers may have limited suppliers.

as well as the difficulty of obtaining high-quality, durable components from the supply chain (e.g., costs associated with sourcing high-performance, long-lasting components, unavailability of high-performance, long-lasting components, and the potential for market volatility). Taken together, these challenges demonstrate the need for strategic lifecycle planning, collaboration across industries, and innovative business models to successfully incorporate durability in circular design while keeping the economics of the product affordable for consumers and economically viable for the manufacturer [19–21].

2.3.1.1 *Compromises Associated with Modularity*

Modularity, as a design concept, can be seen as having several benefits, especially in terms of maintainability, upgradability, and reusability. However, there are several trade-offs associated with modularity, especially in terms of the production process, the integration of the components, and the overall optimization of the design. When modularity is used as a design concept, there are several drawbacks, especially in terms of the ability of the designer to ensure the integration of the components and the overall optimization of the design. For example, Fairphone, which offers modular smartphones, can be seen as having several benefits, especially in terms of circularity. However, there are several challenges, especially in terms of ensuring compactness and lightness, as seen in non-modular smartphones. Similarly, modular furniture, such as that offered by IKEA, can be seen as having several benefits, especially in terms of circularity. However, there are several challenges, especially in terms of ensuring the availability of replacement modules.

2.3.1.2 *Barriers to Recyclability*

The recyclability of materials is subject to several technical and systemic barriers, including the presence of impurities in materials, the use of composite materials, and the lack of recycling facilities. In the packaging industry, while the use of multi-layer polymer materials improves performance in terms of functional properties, there is a major negative impact on recyclability. Similarly, while electronic devices are subject to design optimization in terms of durability and upgradeability, there are challenges in terms of recyclability due to the use of toxic materials, rare earth materials, and the miniaturization of components. Table 2.3 presents a summary of the major technical and systemic constraints to recyclability in circular design approaches as reported in the literature [20–23].

2.4 Product Lifecycle Assessment (LCA) and Eco-Design Strategies

LCA is a scientific approach that is standardized and is used as a tool for determining and measuring the environmental impacts of a product,

Table 2.3 Barriers to recyclability within circular design.

Barrier	Description/cause	Impact on circularity	Examples across sectors
Material Contamination	Presence of organic residues, dirt, or chemical pollutants in recyclable materials.	Recycling efficiency and quality are reduced; potential consequences of reduced recycling efficiency and quality are downcycling or disposal of materials.	Packaging: Contaminated polyethylene terephthalate bottles, packaging papers; Electronics: Presence of substances on the circuit boards that affect material recycling.
Composite or Mixed Materials	Presence of products made of bonded materials such as plastics, metals, adhesives, and multiple materials that are difficult to separate.	Presence of difficulties in separating materials; need for advanced and costly recycling techniques.	Packaging: Multilayer films; Electronics: Printed circuit boards, composite casings.
Lack of Recycling Infrastructure	Limited availability of collection and processing facilities for specific waste materials.	Recyclable materials are sent to landfills and incinerators, limiting the potential of circular design systems.	Electronics: Informal electronics recycling in developing countries; Automotive: Lack of recycling infrastructure for lithium-ion batteries.

(*Continued*)

Table 2.3 Barriers to recyclability within circular design. (*Continued*)

Barrier	Description/cause	Impact on circularity	Examples across sectors
Presence of Hazardous Materials	Presence of toxic materials and critical materials requiring careful handling.	The presence of increased costs and technical complexity of recycling processes restricts safe recovery of materials.	Electronics: Heavy metals contained in the batteries; Consumer products: Rare earth metals contained in the micro-components.
Design for Longevity / Modularity Conflicts	Presence of long-lasting and modular products that utilize adhesives and assemblies.	Presence of increased difficulties in disassembling products requires specialized tools and protocols for disassembly.	Electronics: Modular assemblies of the smartphone; Industrial equipment: Durable equipment with interlocked parts.

service, or process throughout its entire life cycle. This means that it considers all of the stages of a product or service, from raw material acquisition through end of life, including the use phase. The primary goal of LCA is to ensure that it is comprehensive and does not shift burdens between life cycle stages or categories. LCA is different from approaches that address specific issues such as global warming, water use, natural resource depletion, and human toxicity because it is comprehensive and offers a broad view of sustainability. The key benefit of LCA is its holistic approach and its relevance to organizations seeking to apply circular economy principles in their operations [24, 25]. Following the ISO 14040 protocol, the LCA framework has four interconnected phases, namely, Goal and Scope Definition, Life Cycle Inventory (LCI) Analysis, Life Cycle Impact Assessment (LCIA), and Interpretation. This framework provides a scientific approach to the identification, quantification, and assessment of the environmental impacts associated with a product, process, or service throughout its complete life cycle, which includes all the phases from the extraction of raw materials to the disposal or recycling phase (Figure 2.5).

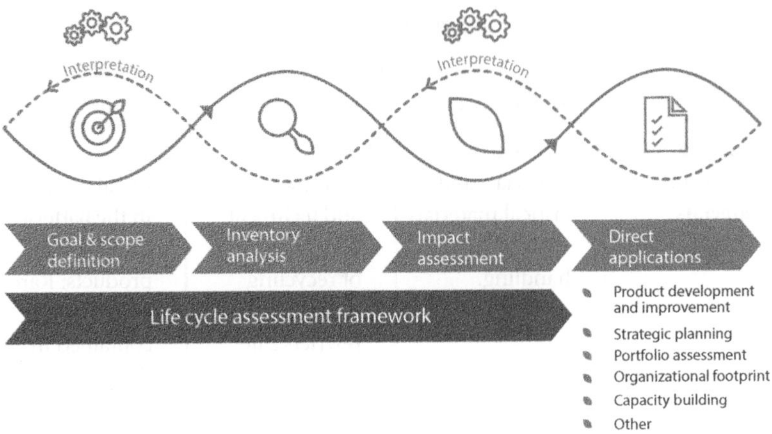

Figure 2.5 LCA methodology [26].

The LCA methodology has been formally defined by the ISO 14040 and ISO 14044 standards. The ISO standards have defined the overall methodological structure, requirements, and principles for conducting life cycle assessments. According to the ISO standards, the overall LCA methodology includes four interconnected phases for conducting the life cycle assessment. The first phase of the LCA methodology is the goal and scope definition, where the overall objective of the study is defined. The second phase of the overall methodology is the life cycle inventory, where the overall material and energy flows within the system are quantified. The third phase of the overall methodology is the life cycle impact assessment, where the overall inventory data collected from the system is categorized into impact categories. The final phase of the overall methodology is the interpretation, where the overall results of the study are used for decision-making. The overall methodology for conducting life cycle assessments has been found to be robust and has been used for various industrial and research applications [27, 28].

From an industrial and research point of view, it is evident that life cycle assessment is becoming one of the integral components of sustainable product design and development. Based on LCA, there is a scope for developing strategies for sustainable product design and development, where there is a need for carrying out modularization, lightweight design, and substitution of materials. In the European Union, life cycle assessment is one of the integral components of Product Environmental Footprint (PEF), where there is a need for carrying out harmonized impact assessments of products. In addition, there is a greater scope for carrying out life cycle assessments with the advent of digital technologies, where there is greater accuracy and scope for carrying out predictive analysis based on big data analytics, artificial intelligence, and digital twin concepts. In addition, with the advent of sustainable practices and sustainable products, life cycle assessment is becoming one of the integral components of market competitiveness and is becoming one of the key drivers for sustainable product design and development. [29].

2.4.1 Stages of the Product Lifecycle and Hotspots

The lifecycle of a product is typically described in terms of five major phases, namely, raw material extraction, manufacturing and processing, distribution, usage by the end user, and end-of-life management. All these phases make significant but unique contributions to the overall environmental profile of the product, and taken together, they present a comprehensive picture of the sustainability of the product. For example, raw material extraction and processing have been found to result in high energy demands and emission of greenhouse gases. The usage phase has been found to dominate the lifecycle phases in terms of hotspots, which are defined as those lifecycle phases in which any change is most likely to result in the largest sustainability benefits [30, 31].

Hotspot analysis represents one of the most important applications of LCA, which helps to identify the areas where the impact of changes will have the largest sustainability benefits. For the automobile industry, for example, the fuel consumption during the use phase has been reported to be the dominant impact area, while the raw material extraction and processing phases have also been reported to have a major impact due to the use of steel and aluminum. For the packaging industry, the end-of-life management phase has been reported to be the dominant impact area, especially for plastics, where the landfill and incineration rates are still high, and the recycling efficiency is also poor. For the electronics industry, the raw material extraction phase, especially with respect to the extraction of raw materials such as rare earth elements and critical metals, and the end-of-life management phase due to the presence of hazardous components, have been reported to be the dominant impact areas [32].

This identification assists organizations in maximizing the general impact of their interventions by identifying the lifecycle hotspots that need to be addressed. This ensures that organizations can strike the perfect balance between the environment and the associated economic and social gains. For instance, the improvement of energy efficiency in household appliances not only reduces emissions but also provides the end-user with cost savings, thus providing a win-win situation. Similarly, the improvement of material efficiency in the extraction and production phases not only reduces the scarcity of scarce resources but also reduces the risks associated with the supply chain. However, the improvement of hotspots is not without its challenges. For example, the improvement of the lightweighting material in the automotive sector may reduce emissions in the end-user phase, but may create challenges in the recyclability phase, thus creating a problem with composite materials. This, in essence, creates the need to utilize LCA to create a move towards sustainability, thus avoiding burden shifting and piecemeal gains.

2.4.2 How LCA Informs Eco-Design

LCA offers an analytically sound basis, which allows us to integrate the environmental dimension into each step of the design process. By thoroughly and systematically analyzing the environmental effects of the entire lifecycle of the product, from cradle to grave, LCA underlines the critical design intervention points where the most significant positive effects on the environment can be achieved. Thus, for example, if the results of the LCA indicate that the use phase accounts for the largest proportion of the overall energy consumption of the product, then the design team is encouraged to focus on improving the efficiency of the product in terms of energy consumption, or on developing design solutions that allow the best possible interaction with the user. Conversely, in cases where the results of the analysis indicate that the material extraction phase is the most critical, then the design team might focus on the use of recycled, recyclable, and/or sustainable materials. The main strength of the LCA method is based on scientific principles. This allows design teams to make eco-design decisions based on scientific data rather than relying on intuition and only using data based on single attributes. This way, the data-driven approach of the LCA method fits perfectly with the principles of the circular economy, which are based on assessing all the effects on the environment. By integrating the lifecycle concept into the early stages of design, organizations can avoid unintended consequences and ensure that sustainability benefits are reaped throughout the system, rather than just at the component level. Figure 2.6 below shows the eco-design methodology, focusing on the role of the LCA method.

LCA can enable a comprehensive evaluation of trade-offs and synergies among a range of different eco-design strategies, such that improvements in any one life cycle phase are not offset by negative impacts in another. For example, reducing the weight of a product in order to minimize energy consumption in the use phase may make subsequent material recyclability

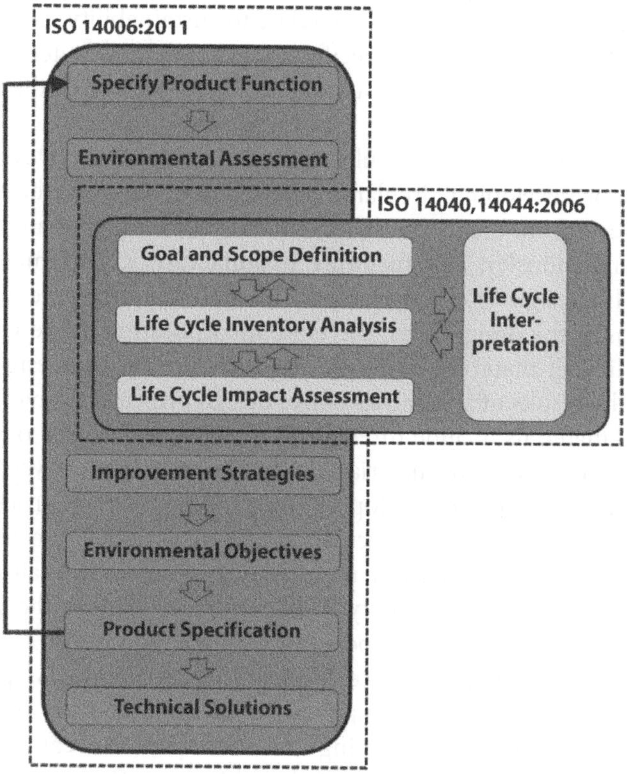

Figure 2.6 Eco-design methodology flowchart [33].

more difficult in the end-of-life phase. LCA can provide a quantitative basis for such scenarios to be simulated, and designers can thus optimize their designs in terms of their overall impacts. The combination of LCA and advanced digital technologies, such as simulation, digital twin, and AI-based predictive technologies, can also help to increase the potential for decision support. These technologies can assist designers in efficiently evaluating different possible designs and in identifying those designs that can balance different criteria, such as environmental, technical, and economic performance. The integration of LCA into the product design process can help organizations to systematically align their innovation activities with their sustainability, regulatory, and consumer-facing strategies.

2.5 Case Studies of Circular Design in Practice

The application of circular design and life cycle-based strategies to real-world applications in multiple industries demonstrates the feasibility of circular economy principles as they relate to sustainability and economic viability. Details on industry-specific applications and outcomes of the circular economy in real-world settings will be described in the following section.

Industry Utilization of Circular Composite Materials: Design methodologies for developing circular composite materials have been studied through several different industries, such as automotive manufacturing, the building industry, and furniture manufacturing. This methodology includes the design of circular composite material with potential recovery options at the design level, therefore incorporating the re-use, repair, and recycling of materials and products directly into the design process [34–36]. The results of an analysis of five design projects involving circular composite materials include three projects that were focused on optimizing the composition of the materials used to increase their recyclability and two projects that involved developing circular materials and products. One of the practical examples of a circular composite material is an automotive dashboard manufactured from recyclable thermoplastic materials with better recyclability and durability. This example illustrates the successful implementation of circular composites in other applications.

Levi's Jeans and Surgical Face Masks: The company has applied the concept of circular design to improve the use and recovery of materials in products such as jeans, ensuring that these products can be recycled or reused more easily at the end of their lifecycle. The extension of the lifecycle of materials used in products like jeans has reduced the chances of waste being generated in the long term. The same concept has been applied in circular design for products such as face masks in the medical sector, addressing all phases of the lifecycle from production to the end of the lifecycle. The environmental impact can be reduced, and products like face masks can be made easy to recycle by using biodegradable materials in their production. The author has used examples like face masks and jeans to show that circular design can be applied in different settings or industries, such as medical textiles and denim wear, for instance, Levi Strauss & Co. This study applies LCA to reduce the environmental impact of products such as jeans throughout their entire lifecycle, from raw material acquisition to the end-of-life stage.

A multi-hierarchical framework for circular design was proposed to improve the understanding and application of concepts like recycling, reusing, and maintaining products within circular design. It was evaluated using various case studies. To apply these concepts in a practical environment, four companies—Patagonia, Bugaboo, Loop by Terracycle, and Fairphone—were chosen as examples. Each of these companies was chosen because of its unique way of applying circular design strategies in its business models. For instance, Patagonia emphasizes sustainable business practices and designing products for longevity, while Loop by Terracycle focuses on reusing products through packaging that can endure up to 100 use cycles. This shows that circular design is not a single solution applicable to all businesses but can vary in its implementation depending on specific contexts.

While these case studies prove successful implementation, there are still hindrances to a complete transformation into a circular economy. Circular design methodologies may not function as well as expected due to factors such as government circumstances, logistics, and business circumstances. To address these challenges and support a circular economy on a large scale, a comprehensive strategy must be employed [34]. Table 2.4 presents a comparison of the Circular Design Case Study.

Patagonia, IKEA, and Interface offer different stories of transformation towards the common goal of circular design, impacting both product architecture and business model innovation. Patagonia's focus on reparability and consumer involvement proves that the extension of product life can be a powerful driver for the development of a strong brand identity that can influence consumer behavior. IKEA's story points to the challenges in bridging the gap between consumer intentions and actual behavior. Despite having a strong base of design principles and a buy-back policy, the reality is that the consumer is still driven by convenience rather than the recyclability of products. Interface represents the new state of the art in industry practice that incorporates the principles of circular design into the business model. All three stories show that the strategy of circular design has the greatest impact when it is integrated throughout the entire life cycle of the product, including material selection, design, reuse, recycling, and recovery. The application of circular design also has some challenges, such as the costs of operation, the significant role of consumer involvement, and the need for data systems to facilitate circular design. However, the stories of the three companies show that the strategy of circular design is not limited to engineering and technological innovation; it also requires the coordination of different players in the value chain, including the consumer, which points to a new understanding of the role of products in the eyes of both the consumer and the companies.

Best Practices for Circular Design (Four Key Principles)

Circular design is a new paradigm in the field of strategic design that questions the conventional approaches to product development by focusing on the life cycle of products and the potential to reduce waste while generating

Table 2.4 Comparative analysis of circular design case studies.

Company/focus area	Circular design strategies	Outcomes	Critical assessment	Design implications
Patagonia — Repair, Resale & Circular Business Model [37, 38]	- Focus on durability and reparability in design - Execute the Worn Wear program that includes repair, resale, and recycling - Execute consumer engagement strategies that encourage sustainable consumption	- Extend the life of products through repair and secondary markets - Align business strategy with sustainability goals	- Scalability is constrained by logistical complexity and consumer participation - There is limited quantitative lifecycle evidence regarding the environmental benefits of repair and reuse.	- Integrating product and service design for LCS extension - Development of repair infrastructure and education of consumers
IKEA — Circular Consumption and Home Textiles [39, 40]	- Focus on disassemblability and recyclability in design - Use renewable and recycled materials in products - Create buy-back programs to promote resale - Create circular economy-based initiatives for consumers	- Consumers exhibit positive attitudes toward repair and resale but tend to show low engagement in these activities. - Early internal design guidelines institutionalize lifecycle thinking.	- There remains an apparent gap between consumers' stated intentions and their actual behaviors in repairing or reselling products, thereby implying an "intention-action gap." - Lack of empirical data on LCS extension and material recovery rates	- Combining product development with service design and behavioral engagement - Using digital tools for LCS monitoring and circular performance metrics
Interface — Circular Materials and Take-Back in Flooring [41, 42]	- Use carpet tile design that can be replaced and recycled - Execute the Re-Entry program that provides take-back and material recovery services - Use recycled and biobased materials in products - Use Life Cycle Sustainability Assessment (LCSA) to measure sustainability	- Achieve significant reductions in the use of virgin materials and waste generation - Demonstrate environmental benefits through closed-loop recycling - Improve resource efficiency through material innovation	- High costs are involved in establishing collection and recycling infrastructure - Methodological difficulties in comparing LCSAs - Lack of transparency related to material processing after recovery	- Integrating modularity and mono-materialism into design - Integrating product design with reverse logistics and recovery - Using lifecycle assessment for trade-off analysis

value in the life cycle of products. The following section outlines the best practices of circular design by synthesizing different theories and studies on circular design strategies by different authors in the field of design.

1. Design for Longevity and Reuse: Create products that maintain their functionality throughout extended usage periods because they support maintenance needs and show the ability to provide upgrades and recycling options. This approach will work to stop waste production while protecting existing resources from depletion.
2. Employ Sustainable and Recoverable Materials: The company must establish a product development process that uses materials which renewable resources, recycled content, and biodegradable components. The product needs material components that either consist of single materials or materials that can be recycled through standard processes.
3. Enable Disassembly and Circular Recovery Systems: Your product design needs to support easy disassembly because this helps achieve sustainable practices through material recovery. The product design must include circular recovery systems as an essential requirement.
4. Integrate Systems Thinking and Collaboration: Life cycle assessment tools help product designers apply circular economy principles to their designs, which evaluate environmental impacts. The success of the circular economy depends on creating partnerships that provide opportunities for shared progress.

2.6 Conclusion and Future Outlook

A shift toward circular economic systems has caused companies to take an entirely different approach when designing, manufacturing, using, and recycling products than they did before when utilizing a linear approach. As evidenced in this chapter, the concept of circular design goes beyond simply offering a set of different techniques and includes a complete framework that incorporates sustainability, resource efficiency, and regenerative approaches across all phases of the product lifecycle. Moreover, by utilizing circular design methodologies, manufacturers are able to minimize their environmental impacts and optimize their use of resources, and preserve the value of their products throughout the entire industrial lifecycle. There is a link between LCA and eco-design; collectively, they offer a means of providing a variety of data-driven means of meeting the need to balance sustainability, functionality, and economic performance. In today's world of growing environmental awareness and increasing environmental regulation, circular design represents a way to create both environmental resilience and business advantage by creating compliance with environmental, social, and economic imperatives. The following organizations are doing this through circular design: Patagonia, IKEA, Interface, and Fairphone. Through a systems approach, collaboration, and innovation in new business models, these organizations realize that circular design acts as an essential mechanism to decouple the environmental impact of their activities from the value created. There are many difficulties that must be addressed: behavioral, technological, and financial; thus, creating the need to support new policy creation, continual innovation, and working with our interest groups. The primary vehicle for growing regenerative industrial systems and sustainable manufacturing methodologies will be Circular Design. This will allow for a lower amount of waste, resulting in the design being used as the primary vehicle for supporting the environmental and society's well-being. Therefore, it will support a worldwide shift towards a new economic model that is built on renewing and regenerating the systems within it to avoid ecological destruction.

AI disclosure statement: The author acknowledges the use of AI-based tools for minor language editing or grammatical correction. However, all intellectual contributions, analyses, and conclusions presented in this chapter are entirely the author's own.

References

1. https://circularity-gap.world/2023.
2. https://www.infodiagram.com/slides/circular-economy-vs-linear-approach-diagram/.
3. European Environment Agency, Circular economy in Europe — Developing the knowledge base, EEA Report, 2016. doi:10.2800/51444.
4. Ellen MacArthur Foundation, Circular Desig, 2021. https://www.ellenmacarthurfoundation.org/topics/circular-design/overview.
5. https://trellis.net/article/survey-nearly-half-of-u-s-consumers-say-they-buy-sustainable-products/.
6. Bocken, N., de Pauw, I., Bakker, C.A., van der Grinten, B., Circular economy product and business model strategy framework. *J. Ind. Ecol.*, 20, 3, 476–490, 2016.

7. Ellen Macarthur Foundation, Completing the picture, Material Economics, 2021.
8. https://www.weforum.org/stories/2024/03/sustainable-resource-consumption-urgent-un/.
9. Synergies and trade-offs in the transition to a resource-efficient and circular economy, OECD Environment Policy Paper, 2022.
10. Yang, M., Chen, L., Wang, J., Msigwa, G., Osman, A.I., Fawzy, S., Rooney, D.W., Yap, P.-S., Circular economy strategies for combating climate change and other environmental issues. *Environ. Chem. Lett.*, 21, 55–80, 2023, https://doi.org/10.1007/s10311-022-01499-6.
11. Karki, J.R., Rafiq, I., Ilić, P., Riaz, S., Environmental Benefits of Circular Economy. In *Circular Economy and Sustainable Consumption*, 2024.
12. Consumer Perception towards Eco-Friendly Products: A Quantitative Study. *J. Informatics Educ. Res.*, 2023, https://doi.org/10.52783/jier.v3i2.79.
13. Iannuzzi, A., Green Marketing. In: *Greener Products: The Making and Marketing of Sustainable Brands,* 3rd ed., CRC Press, Boca Raton, FL, pp. 201–221, 2024. https://doi.org/10.1201/9781003441939-10.
14. Aisyah, D.D., Cahyasita, D., Nugroho, A.D., Willingness to Pay and Barriers in Gen Z's Pro-Environmental Product Consumption. *BIO Web Conf.*, 69, 04024, 2023. https://doi.org/10.1051/bioconf/20236904024.
15. Rahee, S.P. and Sarker, Md.R., Circular product design strategies in the apparel industry: toward the circular economy. *Discov. Sustain.*, 5, 1, 2024, https://doi.org/10.1007/s43621-024-00654-z.
16. Jetti, R. and Dhar, D., Product Durability: A Systematic Literature Review. *Arch. Des. Res.*, 37, 5, 93–128, 2024, https://doi.org/10.15187/adr.2024.11.37.5.93.
17. Quinn, E.C., Knauer, K.M., Beckham, G.T., Chen, E.Y.-X., Mono-material product design with bio-based, circular, and biodegradable polymers. *One Earth*, 6, 6, 582–586, 2023, https://doi.org/10.1016/j.oneear.2023.05.019.
18. The role of product design in closing material loops. *International Symposium on Environmentally Conscious Design and Inverse Manufacturing*, 605–610, 2003. https://doi.org/10.1109/ECODIM.2003.1322742.
19. Bocken, N.M.P., de Pauw, I., Bakker, C., van der Grinten, B., Product design and business model strategies for a circular economy. *J. Ind. Prod. Eng.*, 33, 5, 308–320, 2016, https://doi.org/10.1080/21681015.2016.1172124.
20. Geissdoerfer, A., Savaget, P., Bocken, N.M.P., Hultink, E.J., The Circular Economy – A new sustainability paradigm?. *J. Clean. Prod.*, 143, 757–768, 2017, https://doi.org/10.1016/j.jclepro.2016.12.048.
21. Kirchherr, J., Reike, D., Hekkert, M., Conceptualizing the circular economy: An analysis of 114 definitions. *Resour. Conserv. Recycl.*, 127, 221–232, 2018.
22. Karatum, O., Bhuiya, M.M.H., Carroll, M.K., Anderson, A.M., Plata, D.L., Life Cycle Assessment of Aerogel Manufacture on Small and Large Scales: Weighing the Use of Advanced Materials in Oil Spill Remediation. *J. Ind. Ecol.*, 22, 6, 1365–1377, 2018. https://doi.org/10.1111/jiec.12720.

23. Kumar, A., Holuszko, M., Espinosa, D.C.R., E-waste: An overview on generation, collection, legislation and recycling practices. *Resour. Conserv. Recycl.*, 122, 32–42, 2017. https://doi.org/10.1016/j.resconrec.2017.01.018.
24. Curran, M.A., Overview of Goal and Scope Definition in Life Cycle Assessment. In: Curran, M. (eds) *Goal and Scope Definition in Life Cycle Assessment. LCA Compendium – The Complete World of Life Cycle Assessment.* Springer, Dordrecht, 2017. https://doi.org/10.1007/978-94-024-0855-3_1.
25. Hellweg, S. and Mila i Canals, L., Emerging approaches, challenges and opportunities in life cycle assessment. *Science*, 344, 6188, 1109–1113, 2014, https://doi.org/10.1126/science.1248361.
26. https://pre-sustainability.com/articles/life-cycle-assessment-lca-basics/.
27. ISO, *ISO 14040: Environmental management—Life cycle assessment—Principles and framework.* International Organization for Standardization, 2006.
28. Hauschild, M.Z., Rosenbaum, R.K., Olsen, S.I. (Eds.), *Life Cycle Assessment: Theory and Practice*. Springer, Cham, Switzerland, 2018. https://doi.org/10.1007/978-3-319-56475-3.
29. Finnveden, G., Hauschild, M.Z., Ekvall, T., Guinée, J., Heijungs, R., Hellweg, S., Koehler, A., Pennington, D., Suh, S., Recent developments in Life Cycle Assessment. *J. Environ. Manage.*, 91, 1, 1–21, 2009 Oct, Epub 2009 Aug 29. PMID: 19716647. doi: 10.1016/j.jenvman.2009.06.018.
30. Baumann, H. and Tillman, A.-M., The Hitch Hiker's Guide to LCA: An orientation in life cycle assessment methodology and application. *Int. J. Life Cycle Assess.*, 11, 2, 142–142, 2006. https://doi.org/10.1065/lca2006.02.008.
31. Hertwich, E.G., Lifset, R., Pauliuk, S., Resource efficiency and climate change: Material efficiency strategies for a low-carbon future. International Resource Panel, UNEP, 2020.
32. Gonçalves, M., Monteiro, H., Iten, M., Life Cycle Assessment studies on lightweight materials for automotive applications - An overview. *Energy Rep.*, 8, 338–345, 2022, https://doi.org/10.1016/j.egyr.2022.01.067.
33. Navajas, A., Uriarte, L., Gandía, L.M., Application of Eco-Design and Life Cycle Assessment Standards for Environmental Impact Reduction of an Industrial Product. *Sustainability*, 9, 10, 1724, 2017, https://doi.org/10.3390/su9101724.
34. Joustra, J., Bakker, C., Bessai, R., Balkenende, R., Circular Composites by Design: Testing a design method in industry. *Sustainability*, 14, 13, 7993, 2022.
35. Patil, R.A., van Langen, S.K., Ramakrishna, S., Circularity at Nano Level: A Product/Service Perspective. In *Circularity Assessment: Macro to Nano: Accountability Towards Sustainability* (pp. 87–98). Singapore: Springer Nature Singapore, 2023.
36. Franconi, A., Ceschin, F., Peck, D., Structuring circular objectives and design strategies for the circular economy: a multi-hierarchical theoretical framework. *Sustainability*, 14, 15, 9298, 2022.

37. Rattalino, F., Circular advantage anyone? Sustainability-driven innovation and circularity at Patagonia, Inc. *Thunderbird Int. Bus. Rev.*, 60, 5, 747–755, 2018.
38. Fürst, T. and Akdağ, H.C., Integrating Circular Economy Principles in the Fashion Industry: A Case Study of Patagonia. In *The International Symposium for Production Research* (pp. 325–338). Cham: Springer Nature Switzerland, 2024, October.
39. Lehner, M., Mont, O., Mariani, G., Mundaca, L., Circular economy in home textiles: Motivations of IKEA consumers in Sweden. *Sustainability*, 12, 12, 5030, 2020.
40. Seidel, A., Closing the Loop: Exploring IKEA's Transition to the Circular Economy, 2018.
41. Lama, V., Righi, S., Quandt, B.M., Hischier, R., Desing, H., Resource pressure of carpets: guiding their circular design. *Sustainability*, 14, 5, 2530, 2022.
42. Luthin, A., Crawford, R.H., Traverso, M., Assessing the circularity and sustainability of circular carpets—a demonstration of circular life cycle sustainability assessment. *Int. J. Life Cycle Assess.*, 29, 10, 1945–1964, 2024.

3

Material Flow Optimization and Resource Efficiency

N. Prakash*, P. Karthikeyan, M. Dharshne, K. Nakul, T. Soundaryalaksmi and M. Tishitaa

Department of Management Studies, Kongu Engineering College, Perundurai, Erode, Tamil Nadu, India

Abstract

Maximizing material flow and promoting resource efficiency are key elements in realizing sustainable production in the context of a circular economy. It emphasizes relevant practices such as lean production, material efficiency, disassembly design, industrial symbiosis, and circular business models that focus on minimizing material usage and extending product life. In addition, the chapter highlights the promise of responsibly sourced raw materials, ensuring quality, traceability, and accountability throughout the supply chain, based on internationally recognized standards and certifications. Industry 4.0 technologies, such as digital twins, Internet of Things, artificial intelligence, and blockchain, provide real-time visibility of material flows, predictive control, and closed-loop synchronization. Furthermore, sophisticated production methods and recovery procedures for materials enable the reuse and recycling of secondary materials, facilitating source reduction. Examples based on actual applications in the automotive, electronics, textile, and construction industries describe real-world cases that have led to significant improvements in material efficiency and circularity. This chapter critically addresses the challenges posed by economic barriers, organizational inertia, technological limitations, and gaps in regulatory approaches. It proposes a set of strategic recommendations for policy approaches, sustainable technologies, cross-industry engagement, workforce skills development, and other relevant areas. This chapter ultimately positions material flow optimization as a fundamental enterprise operating system for achieving scalable circular manufacturing, reducing embodied environmental impacts, and enhancing long-term industrial competitiveness.

**Corresponding author*: np.mba@kongu.edu

Jeyaprakash Natarajan, Milon Selvam Dennison, M. Bhuvanesh Kumar and Ganapathy Thirukkotti (eds.) Manufacturing and the Circular Economy, (65–106) © 2027 Scrivener Publishing LLC

***Keywords*:** Material flow optimization, resource efficiency, circular economy, sustainable manufacturing, industrial symbiosis, sustainable sourcing, Industry 4.0, digital twins

3.1 Introduction

Following the abstract's high-level map, this introduction defines material flow as an integrated system and explains why its optimization is pivotal to circular outcomes.

3.1.1 Background and Importance of Material Flow Optimization

Reduce waste and variability and maximize value delivery through material flow optimization, which is the methodical design and management of how materials are specified, sourced, converted, moved, stored, assembled, and recovered throughout the manufacturing value stream. Cost reduction through reduced scrap and rework, lead time compression through coordinated logistics, quality improvement through stable processes, and resilience through decreased reliance on erratic input streams are the primary forces behind material flow optimization [1].

Material flow is more comprehensible as an interconnected system rather than a series of disconnected activities because it is an interrelated process that encompasses intralogistics, production scheduling, warehouse management, packaging, and supplier management. The role of material flow and its effect on performance are exacerbated by varying product complexity, short product life cycles, and increased customization seen in modern manufacturing environments. In some ways, this is a product of the variability we all experience within the material flow system [2]. Rigid structures for material flow are established by technically designing the process, visual control, standardized work, and inventory replenishment as to suit the process of the product and the required flow rate of materials (such as by pull system or by demand-driven material requirement planning) with respect to the pace of production (i.e., takt time rate), while accounting for the variation that the system will invariably introduce. Improvement occurs when our decisions regarding material flow are aligned with a product's architecture, equipment capabilities, and the conventional reliability of suppliers.

Hence, the optimization of material flow is paramount and serves as the foundational cornerstone of the circular economy. Material flow is further classified by the location, quality, and timing of the flow, which directly influence the value retained through processes such as remanufacturing, refurbishing, reuse, and recycling [3]. These processes rely on predictable and traceable moves of materials. The optimization of material flow is a precursor to enabling repeatable circularity, through aligning throughput with the definition of information and quality grades of materials, such that the materials can retain their value while recovering value [4].

3.1.2 Link between Material Efficiency and Circular Economy

Having shown how stable, system-wide flow underpins quality, cost, and resilience, the next subsection connects material efficiency directly to circular economy principles that prioritize value retention and inner loops. Material efficiency involves achieving functional performance while minimizing mass and environmental impact. This practice aligns closely with the core principle of the circular economy, which aims to sustain the utility and value of materials at their highest feasible level for extended periods. Material efficiency decreases primary extraction, alleviates environmental externalities, and reduces cumulative energy demand throughout the life cycle, thus diminishing the overall environmental impact of products and systems. The circular economy enhances material efficiency through design strategies that facilitate disassembly, allow for component interchangeability, and maintain material purity for reuse and recycling. It also encourages business models that advance processes for extending product life and determining the optimal end-of-use asset return rates. Material efficiency systematically enables inner loops that prioritizes repair, refurbishment, and remanufacturing over recycling; thus, products are designed for maintainability, upgradability, and compatibility with harvesting. Further enhancements are made in material efficiency by utilizing materials in primary manufacturing processes to minimize the amount of residual waste that requires recovery. At the same time, high levels of material identification and traceability further ensure the quality of the recirculation process. This relationship is reciprocal insofar as circular business models, such as product-as-a-service, themselves incentivize material efficiency by transferring value away from throughput and toward performance.

3.1.3 Global Challenges: Resource Scarcity, Industrial Waste, and Climate Change

Although material efficiency and circularity are mutually reinforcing, global pressures, resource scarcity, rising waste, and climate constraints clarify why accelerating these practices is now imperative. Resource scarcity, rising waste output, and climate change all pose simultaneous challenges to the global industrial system, making material flow optimization and resource efficiency improvements imperative. Rare earth elements, cobalt, nickel, and premium graphite are examples of critical raw resources that are subject to supply chain hazards, price volatility, and geopolitical concentration. These factors increase input uncertainty and capital exposure in new product development and capacity planning.

1. Industrial waste streams are significant in both established and developing manufacturing areas, with considerable portions of production scrap, packaging waste, and post-consumer returns not being utilized in high-value recovery pathways. This is attributed to inadequate product design, fragmented collection systems, and variable quality of secondary materials.
2. The carbon budget created by climate change is incompatible with linear models that permit higher energy and material throughput. This puts pressure on manufacturers to reduce their embodied emissions by using lighter materials, incorporating more recycled content, utilizing renewable energy, and implementing more efficient processes.

3.1.4 Chapter Objectives and Structure

To support the circular economy, this chapter aims to achieve four goals that collectively enhance the practice of material flow optimization. The first goal is to create business models that prolong useful life, design strategies that reduce mass and increase recoverability, and codify methods that reduce material consumption at the source through lean operations. The second goal is to codify frameworks and principles for sustainable sourcing and effective use of raw materials, including the function of procurement standards and certification as governance tools that communicate accountability and quality. The third goal is to focus on advanced manufacturing, digitalization, material recovery, and simulation-based decision support. The fourth goal is to put ideas into practice by using industry-specific case studies and best practices.

Figure 3.1 illustrates the system-level view of material flows in a circular manufacturing enterprise, showing primary conversion stages, intralogistics nodes, information feedback from quality and sensors, and closed-loop return channels for repair, refurbishment, remanufacturing, and recycling.

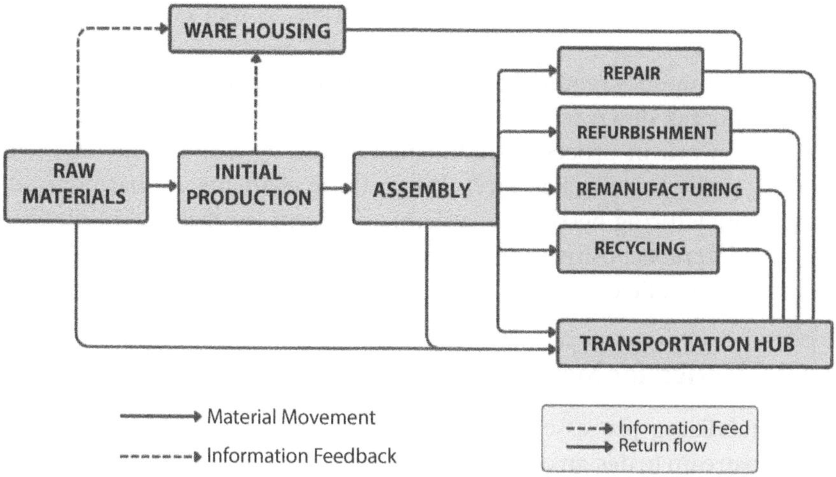

Figure 3.1 Systemic nature of material flow and how they enable closed-loop manufacturing.

3.2 Strategies for Minimizing Material Consumption

Translating intent into action, this section presents four complementary strategies that reduce material intensity at the source and across interconnected value networks.

3.2.1 Lean Manufacturing and Waste Elimination

By emphasizing the elimination of non–value-added processes that manifest as overproduction, waiting, transportation, overprocessing, inventory accumulation, motion, and defects, lean manufacturing provides a methodical approach to reducing material consumption. Defects and overproduction are particularly significant in the context of material efficiency because they result in wasted materials that have already incurred conversion costs and embodied environmental impacts. Small lot sizes, demand-level production sequence design, and flow stabilization at takt time all increase responsiveness while lowering the risk of overproduction. Standardized work and visual management combine best practices to prevent variability from resurfacing, resulting in reduced material losses [5].

When lean is applied with material efficiency as a clear goal, decisions about line balancing, cell design, and layout are assessed not only for labor and equipment use but also for the shortest material paths, the fewest handling steps, and the least amount of packaging required. This reduces handling and logistics-related indirect materials, as well as direct material usage [6].

The transparency required to prioritize interventions is generated by loss trees that break down scrap and rework by cause, inventory turns for raw materials, work-in-process, and finished goods, as well as material yield metrics at the process step level. When these elements are harmonized, lean manufacturing becomes a systemic platform for material minimization that interacts positively with design decisions, maintenance practices, and sourcing policies [7].

3.2.2 Design for Material Efficiency and Disassembly

After stabilizing processes and eliminating operational waste, attention shifts upstream to design decisions that lightweight, simplify geometry, and enable disassembly to lock in efficiency before production begins Because the choice of materials, geometries, and assembly techniques affects downstream process complexity, yield, and end-of-life recoverability, design is the oldest and most significant lever for lowering material consumption. Lightweighting, structural optimization, and functional integration are all combined in material efficient design to meet performance goals while using less mass. Techniques such as generative design and topology optimization create geometries that eliminate non–load-bearing material while preserving strength and stiffness. When paired with additive manufacturing or near-net shape processes, the decreased machining allowances further reduce scrap.

To ensure that improvements in use-phase energy efficiency do not compromise end-of-life recyclability or disassembly complexity, material substitution with high-specific-strength alloys, engineered polymers, or hybrid composites must be assessed using full-life-cycle models. Clear access routes to valuable components, modular subassemblies that can be replaced separately to increase service life, and joints and fasteners that can be disassembled and reassembled without causing damage are all prioritized in disassembly design. The purity of recovered streams is maintained, and secondary processing is simplified using compatible materials and the prevention of contamination through coatings or nonseparable layers. Digital passports, clear material identification, and the incorporation of disassembly instructions into product documentation or data carriers increase the speed and dependability of value recovery procedures [8]. Upgrades that add new functionality without completely replacing products are made possible by modularity, thereby delaying the need for new material inputs as long as performance standards can be met.

Wear-resistant surfaces, redundancy when failure is unacceptable, and corrosion or heat protection increase durability by extending service hours and mitigating embodied impacts. Because features that streamline production lower defect rates and shorten cycle times, which in turn improve material yield, design for manufacturability and assembly continue to be crucial. The likelihood that material value will be preserved at high-quality grades is increased when design for material efficiency and disassembly is combined to create coherence between first-pass production efficiency and the viability of inner-loop recovery strategies.

3.2.3 Industrial Symbiosis and Byproduct Utilization

Complementing product-level design levers, the discussion now broadens to industrial symbiosis, where byproducts and secondary streams are matched to functional uses across firms. Industrial symbiosis is a cooperative approach in which waste heat, energy streams, and byproducts from one process are utilized as inputs for another. The objective is to reduce the extraction of primary resources by utilizing byproducts that satisfy functional requirements. Reclassifying waste as secondary resources reduces the need for disposal and waste management. Knowledge of material specifications, variability ranges, and pretreatment requirements is necessary for success. Despite secondary inputs, receiving processes must maintain quality [9].

3.2.4 Circular Business Models and Life Cycle Extension

To reinforce technical pathways, the next subsection recasts incentives *via* circular business models that monetize longevity, upgrades, and take-back to sustain material value over time. Instead of using volume-based throughput, circular business models reshape incentives and operational procedures to optimize value from materials and products over time. Manufacturers are financially motivated to design long-lasting, maintainable products and to retain control over assets at the end of their useful life through product-as-a-service contracts, leasing, deposit return programs, and buyback guarantees. Business units dedicated to remanufacturing and refurbishing turn into profit centers that recover components from returns, bring them back to performance standards, and then reintroduce them to the market with warranties that reassure customers. The demand for entirely new products and related material inputs is reduced when spare parts and upgrade strategies are coordinated to increase functionality and make maintenance more efficient. To ensure that return flows have sufficient capacity, tracking, and condition assessment capabilities, take-back and reverse logistics networks are designed in tandem with outbound distribution networks. Although providing information about component lifetimes and failure modes that can be incorporated into design and process planning, digital monitoring of in-use products *via* embedded sensors and connectivity supports predictive services that lower catastrophic failures and material intensive replacements [10].

Strategies from various time scales are integrated through life-cycle extension. Whereas medium-term strategies rely on remanufacturing and module upgrades, short-term actions concentrate on repair and refurbishment. Effective disassembly and high-quality material recycling at product retirement are guaranteed by long-term planning. Cost structures, asset intensity, and residual values all affect financial results, necessitating accurate modeling. Effective circular models maintain revenue while using less material, but they also require new skills and organizational alignment.

Figure 3.2 explains the framework of strategies to reduce material consumption, showing four reinforcing pillars. Lean operations control process variability and stabilize material flow. Design for material efficiency and disassembly reduces mass and preserves recoverability. Industrial symbiosis transforms by-products into secondary inputs across firms. Circular business models extend product life cycles and maintain asset control for value recovery.

Through precise torque, sequenced parts delivery, point-of-use supplier logistics, and stable assembly lines, lean waste elimination aims to increase yield, decrease defects, and minimize inventory. Whereas optimizing

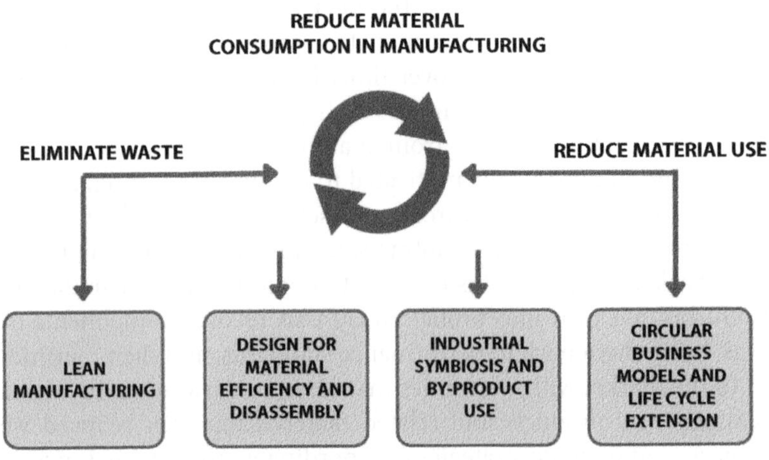

Figure 3.2 Framework of strategies to reduce material consumption.

the cutting room, marker efficiency, and quality at source reduces fabric waste, high-mix, low-volume operations require strict line clearance and error-proofing to prevent material misplacement. Reduced storage damage, less over-ordering, and consistent product quality are ensured by just-in-time site logistics, batch control of aggregates, and avoidance of dye lot mixing. Circular business models, such as remanufacturing, refurbishment, take-back programs, and service-based models, extend product life cycles, reduce the demand for raw materials, and capture residual value. Industrial symbiosis further reinforces circularity by reusing scrap metals, solvents, fibers, and construction by-products.

Table 3.1 compares the application of material consumption reduction strategies across the automotive, electronics, textile, and construction industries. Designing for material efficiency and disassembly enables lightweighting with durable materials, modular assemblies, and quick-release fasteners that improve recovery and fuel efficiency. Modular boards, standardized connectors, and upgradable firmware promote reuse, whereas clothing modularity, nanomaterials, and replaceable trims facilitate recycling.

Table 3.1 Comparison of strategies across industries.

Strategy and focus area	Automotive sector	Electronics and IT industry	Textile and fashion industry	Construction and infrastructure
Lean waste elimination	High	High	High	High
Design for material efficiency and disassembly	Moderate	High	Low	Moderate
Industrial symbiosis and by product use	High	Moderate	Moderate	High
Circular business models and life-cycle extension	High	High	Moderate	Moderate

3.3 Efficient Use of Raw Materials and Sustainable Sourcing

Material efficiency also depends on what is purchased and how it is governed, so this section codifies principles for sustainable sourcing and raw material stewardship.

3.3.1 Principles of Sustainable Sourcing and Procurement

The strategic process of acquiring goods and services in a way that protects the environment, promotes social welfare, and ensures long-term economic viability is known as sustainable sourcing. These core principles include supply chain transparency, human rights and labor due diligence, biodiversity and water conservation, climate-aligned procurement that considers embodied emissions, and circularity standards that prioritize end-of-life recoverability and the use of recycled materials. Procurement departments incorporate these ideas into supplier qualification, category strategies, and contract conditions that set performance benchmarks and reporting requirements. Material specifications incorporate sustainability characteristics such as minimum percentages of recycled content, limitations on hazardous materials, and traceability to confirmed production zones for commodities with conflict or deforestation hazards [11].

Supplier development programs promote the growth of capabilities in energy management, waste reduction, and process control, all of which contribute to improved cost performance and sustainability. Life-cycle costs, including potential regulatory exposures and waste disposal responsibilities, are factored into total cost of ownership approaches. These factors influence decisions about suppliers and materials that are effective under current and future policy regimes. Cross-functional governance encompasses design, quality, operations, and compliance, ensuring that sourcing decisions align with product specifications and process capabilities and that trade-offs are managed systematically rather than on an *ad hoc* basis.

Sustainable procurement also requires data infrastructure and verification methods. Digital traceability systems track provenance and custody changes, allowing claims such as verified origin, recycled material, or compliance with specific social and environmental criteria to be validated. Risk assessment tools identify geographies and supply category hotspots that need targeted actions or diversification. Long-term contracts with suppliers help to stabilize demand and pave the way for cooperative investments in regenerative agriculture, renewable energy, and recycling capacity.

These guidelines transform sustainability goals into legally binding and auditable procedures that consistently raise the effectiveness and accountability of raw material usage [12].

3.3.2 Sustainable Raw Material Management Including Renewable and Nonrenewable Inputs

From governance principles, the focus turns to managing renewable and nonrenewable materials differently to maximize lifetime utility and recovery potential. Sustainable raw material management recognizes the distinctions between renewable and nonrenewable resources, aligning material portfolios with long-term availability, environmental sustainability, and optimal functionality. Natural fibers, biobased polymers, and sustainably managed timber are examples of renewable materials that can promote circularity when they originate from systems that preserve or enhance ecosystem function and when products are designed to last for several use cycles before eventually biodegrading under the right conditions. To slow depletion and reduce embodied impacts, nonrenewable materials such as metals, minerals, and polymers derived from fossil fuels must be stewarded with an emphasis on recycled content, effective first-use, and high-quality recovery at the end of life.

To reduce downgrading, strategies that design components for easy separation and clear alloy labeling are supported by the thermodynamic advantage of closed loop recycling at high purity for metals. Although chemical recycling can address otherwise unrecyclable combinations, it must be implemented with energy-efficient processes and strong emissions controls. For polymers, compatibility and additive management are crucial to enabling mechanical recycling without property loss. Because ceramics and composites are frequently heterogeneous and bonded in ways that make separation difficult, they pose special challenges that necessitate design decisions that allow for disassembly or the creation of secondary applications that absorb these materials without endangering the environment.

Recyclability and material criticality should be reflected in inventory management policies. Plans for substitution and the qualification of secondary sources, such as recycled feedstock, can be used to supplement safety stocks for essential materials. When standards permit the use of recycled content, suppliers can utilize secondary materials and make investments in quality enhancement without compromising performance. Process planning that minimizes offcuts and produces near-net forms reduces the amount of raw material required per completed unit. The integration of renewable and nonrenewable materials must optimize their individual lifetime benefits while avoiding combinations that lower recovery potential.

3.3.3 Global Standards and Certifications Including FSC, ISO 20400, and EU Green Public Procurement

Because stewardship requires credible proof, the discussion now details global standards and certifications that verify provenance, recycled content, and environmental performance. International standards and certifications establish a unified framework for sustainable sourcing, ensuring the quality, traceability, and accountability of materials across supply chains. Certifications such as FSC safeguard forests and indigenous rights, whereas ISO 20400 guides sustainable procurement and ISO 14001 improves environmental management. The Global Organic Textile Standard ensures compliance in textile production, and plastics certifications validate recycled

Table 3.2 Certifications and benefits.

Certification	Industry application	Key benefits
Forest Stewardship Council	Wood, paper, textiles	Protects biodiversity, ensures ethical labor, enables traceability
ISO 20400	All sectors	Provides guidance on sustainable procurement processes
ISO 14001	Plastics, chemicals	Reduces emissions and waste, improves environmental management
Global Organic Textile Standard	Textile, apparel	Promotes organic materials, responsible water use, and supply chain transparency
Recycled content and mass balance certifications	Plastics, chemicals, and complex value chains	Validates recycled content, drives investment in recycling technologies
European Union Green Public Procurement	Public sector purchasing	Scales demand for products with recycled content and low environmental impact

content using traceable methods or mass balance. Frameworks such as the EU Green Public Procurement further fuel the market's demand for products that are low-emission, recyclable, and highly durable.

Table 3.2 summarizes major sustainability certifications and standards, their industry applications, and key benefits. The implementation of these certifications and standards enhances data comparability and quality, reduces the workload associated with bilateral audits, and clarifies supplier expectations. Companies should include requirements in contracts, outline proof of conformance, and set up procedures for ongoing development and remediation. With internal performance goals that surpass minimum requirements when feasible and that complement climate science-based pathways and circularity aspirations, certification should be viewed as a floor rather than a ceiling. Standards and internal metrics should be harmonized to avoid duplication of effort and enhance auditing and reporting efficiency.

3.3.4 Circular Supply Chain

Equipped with standards, the narrative advances to circular supply chain practices that embed take-back, alloy management, and verified secondary inputs at scale. When incorporated into business plans and operations, sustainable sourcing dramatically increases material efficiency and reduces risks. Advanced sorting and alloy management preserve material quality and prevent downcycling. At the same time, closed-loop aluminum supply chains in the metals sector collect production scrap and postconsumer returns for remelting, lowering embodied carbon and dependency on primary aluminum. Reputational and regulatory risks in the electronics sector are mitigated through procurement policies that require certified, conflict-free, and responsible sourcing of minerals such as tantalum, tin, tungsten, and gold. Design decisions also increase the use of recycled aluminum and plastics without compromising performance. With the help of take-back programs that increase recycling rates, textile companies that source certified organic cotton and incorporate mechanically or chemically recycled fibers reduce their reliance on virgin materials and water-intensive cultivation.

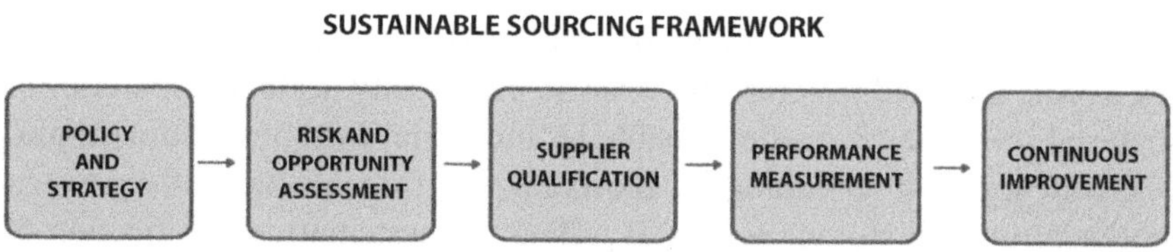

Figure 3.3 Flowchart of sustainable sourcing framework.

These examples show generalizable patterns. Explicit contracts and specifications establish the foundation for supplier compliance. Long-term partnerships and volume commitments support capital deployment in the recycling and renewable energy sectors. To ensure that materials chosen for their sustainability attributes can be processed consistently without yield losses, internal cross-functional teams connect design, procurement, and operations. Data systems document performance and provenance, facilitating ongoing development and reliable external communication. In addition to improving environmental outcomes, sustainable sourcing stabilizes the supply of materials, reduces exposure to price volatility, and lowers compliance costs when these factors are present.

Figure 3.3 illustrates the flowchart of the sustainable sourcing framework, which outlines the steps involved in policy and strategy definition, risk and opportunity assessment, supplier qualification and development, contract and specification integration, performance measurement and traceability, and continuous improvement cycles.

3.4 Technologies for Improving Material Efficiency

Real-time data, advanced fabrication, recovery methods, and virtualized decision-making together raise material yields and secure traceable loops. The next section examines technologies that operationalize high-yield, traceable flows.

3.4.1 Role of Industry 4.0 and Digitalization

As required by circular economy strategies, digitalization incorporates sensing, connectivity, analytics, and automation into the operational fabric of manufacturing systems to enable high temporal fidelity observation, prediction, and control of material flows across procurement, intralogistics, conversion, and reverse loops. Scheduling and dispatch decisions can be continuously updated as conditions change, thanks to real-time visibility provided by connected sensors and production intelligence [13]. This minimizes waiting and excess inventory while averting starvation and blockage events that lead to scrap and rework. The facility-scale transparency of material movements, made possible by industrial Internet platforms and real-time location technologies, allows for the traceable handoffs between workstations and storage nodes, as well as the systematic identification of bottlenecks and misroutes [14].

To implement interventions before defects and shortages spread throughout the value stream, predictive signals for material replenishment, equipment condition, and quality drift can be generated by fusing data from enterprise systems and shop floor sensors. In addition to providing adaptive policies that balance throughput, cycle time, and material exposure, artificial intelligence supports operational decision-making by orchestrating fine-grained responses, such as autonomous intralogistics tasking and dynamic sequencing, to maintain a steady flow in the face of variability. Blockchain-based ledgers are increasingly being utilized for tamper-resistant provenance records that link material efficiency to a verifiable chain of custody by certifying recycled content, confirming responsible sourcing, and maintaining material identity for high-quality recovery [15].

Digital twins reduce the risk and expense of change while speeding up cycles of continuous improvement for yield and waste reduction by combining virtual models with real-time plant data to simulate and test flow adjustments before physical implementation. In smart factories, layout-aware analytics reduce handling distances and dwell times by combining positional data and work-in-process attributes. This reduces indirect materials and damage mechanisms that arise from excessive touches and transfers. When digital technologies work together, the material flow becomes self-aware and self-correcting, enabling the consistent achievement of desired yields and the dependable capture of returns for inner-loop operations, such as remanufacturing, refurbishment, and repair. The resulting data infrastructure improves alignment between operational excellence and circular economy outcomes by quantifying waste avoidance and recovery rates with auditable evidence, supporting sustainability reporting and supplier engagement [16].

3.4.2 Advanced Manufacturing

Having established sensing, analytics, and orchestration for flow stability, the discussion now moves to fabrication capabilities that cut mass and defects at the source. By matching physical transformation procedures with part functionality, advanced manufacturing increases material efficiency by reducing excess mass and the amount of corrective work needed to meet specifications. At the same time, it enhances precision and repeatability, thereby preventing waste caused by defects. When proper design guidelines and quality controls are followed, additive manufacturing can minimize machining allowances and scrap associated with subtractive processes while enabling near-net shape fabrication and topology-optimized geometries that use less material to deliver equivalent structural performance.

In addition to reducing overcuts, rework, and part rejection, precision machining with in-process metrology and adaptive control maintains tight tolerances, which in turn minimize material damage from forced fits and misalignments, as well as downstream assembly problems. To minimize part damage, consumable use, and contamination—all of which would otherwise impair material yields and recovery potential—robotics facilitates consistent handling, assembly, and joining at regulated speeds and forces. Reconfigurable robot cells and programmable fixtures enable flexible automation, allowing for frequent changeovers and small-batch production without the need for oversized safety stocks that could become obsolete or buffer inventories. In addition to simplifying packaging requirements for internal moves, process integration and multitasking machines reduce exposure to loss and environmental degradation by reducing routing times and eliminating the need for intermediate transport and storage.

When high-value materials and intricate multimaterial assemblies are involved, advanced inspection that uses machine vision and sensor fusion to identify deviations early on ensures that the material is corrected at the least embodied stage or diverted to the proper recovery pathways. To support both first-pass yield and end-of-life material purity, digital work instructions that are synchronized with configuration data minimize misguides and cross-part contamination, which make disassembly and recycling more difficult. Advanced manufacturing achieves higher capability indices with lower scrap rates when these capabilities are combined with robust maintenance and disciplined process development. This allows for more accurate material accounting and predictable circular flows [17].

3.4.3 Material Recovery and Recycling Technologies

Even with better first-pass yield, recirculation is essential, so the next subsection examines mechanical, chemical, and biological recovery routes and their quality constraints. To reduce reliance on primary extraction and minimize embodied environmental impacts, material recovery technologies transform production residues, returns, and post-use products into secondary feedstock with predictable quality and stable supply. This makes circular manufacturing feasible [18]. To recover materials such as metals and single-polymer streams, mechanical recycling involves sorting, size reduction, and reprocessing of these materials to extract their value. Its efficacy is dependent on contamination control, material identification, and the maintenance of physical characteristics throughout processing cycles [19]. By depolymerizing or solvolyzing mixed or contaminated plastic streams into monomers or intermediates, chemical recycling advances the technical envelope. This can result in higher-quality output, but it usually necessitates close attention to energy intensity and emissions to achieve system-level net benefits [20].

Although throughput and selectivity are still context-dependent and necessitate strict process integration with upstream segregation and pre-treatment, biological recovery pathways transform organic residues into biogas, compost, or platform molecules. New biocatalytic processes also target polymer backbones [21]. Secondary smelting and refining are well-established processes for metals; however, alloy management and control of tramp elements remain essential for preventing down-cycling. This encourages the design of products and processes that avoid incompatible combinations and enable effective separation during disassembly.

When physical segregation is impractical, mass balance certification and digital traceability are being used more to validate recycled content. This helps to maintain credible claims in complex chemical and polymer value chains and encourages investment in recovery capacity. Recovery technology integration with manufacturing planning enhances feedstock stability and collection rates for recycling assets by reducing backhaul empties and

Table 3.3 Comparative performance of recycling technologies.

Technology	Suitable input streams	Typical energy and process intensity	Output quality and use cases
Mechanical recycling	Metals, single polymer or well sorted plastic streams	Moderate energy demand for sorting, size reduction, and melt processing	Property retention depends on contamination; supports closed loop uses
Chemical recycling	Mixed or contaminated plastics, complex polymer combinations	Higher energy and solvent use; requires strict emissions control	Monomer or feedstock outputs compatible with virgin quality production
Biological recovery	Organic residues, specific polymer backbones	Variable intensity; depends on substrate and bioprocess design	Outputs biogas, compost, or platform molecules with variable quality
Certified mass balance	Complex chemical/ polymer value chains without physical segregation	Process intensity as per conversion; adds audit and governance overhead	Allocates recycled content credibly, enabling recycling investment

utilizing reverse logistics for consolidated return streams. The selection and configuration of materials with recirculation performance as an explicit criterion enhance overall material productivity due to feedback from recovery processes to design and sourcing functions, which gradually closes quality loops. Digital identifiability, certification frameworks, and technological maturation all work together to make recovery a co-equal pillar of material efficiency with source reduction and process yield improvement [22]. Table 3.3 presents a comparative assessment of material recovery and recycling technologies, highlighting their suitable input streams, process intensity, and output quality characteristics.

3.4.4 Simulation and Digital Twins for Process Optimization

Because changes are costly on live systems, simulation and digital twins now provide a safe, data-linked test bed to optimize buffers, routing, and control for yield and circularity. The cost and risk of achieving material efficiency goals are significantly reduced by utilizing simulation and digital twins to create a computational representation of production systems, enabling the design, testing, and validation of material flow scenarios without disrupting ongoing operations. To quantify buffer sizing, line balancing, and sequencing strategies that reduce waiting, overproduction, and inventory-induced damage, discrete-event simulation models are used to capture routing logic, resource contention, and variability in processing and transportation times. Digital twins are created by continuously connecting virtual models with real-time plant data. These digital twins can detect deviations from expected behavior, update state estimates in real-time, and suggest or carry out corrective actions to maintain flow, yield, and quality.

Digital twins can resolve the spatial and temporal dynamics of materials in motion when combined with real-time location and condition monitoring. This enables the localization of loss mechanisms that degrade material value, such as mishandling, environmental exposure, and misplacement. With traceable assumptions and sensitivity analyses that increase organizational confidence in selected designs, scenario analysis carried out in the twin environment enables planners to assess several layouts, material handling devices, and control policies for their effects on throughput, cycle time, and scrap. Additionally, digital twins facilitate closed-loop optimization, in which planning and scheduling are informed by parameter updates gleaned from operations. This establishes a positive feedback loop that continuously lowers waste and enhances resource use.

When twin representations are extended to reverse flows in circular systems, it is possible to synchronize forward production with take-back,

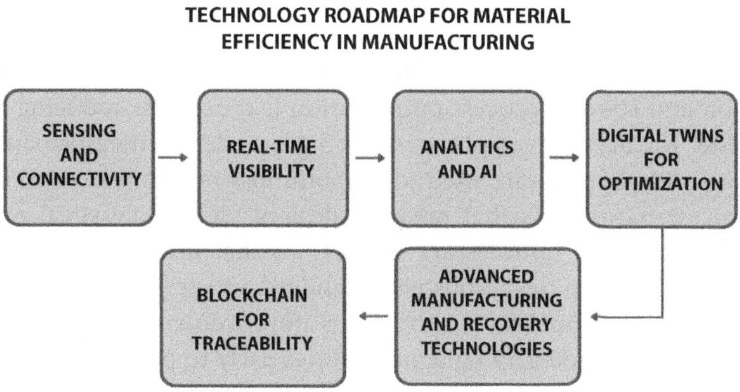

Figure 3.4 Technology roadmap for material efficiency.

inspection, and reprocessing. This ensures that recovered materials with known properties arrive when needed, preventing degradation and storage losses. Because design, operations, and logistics can all examine the same model and come to an agreement on modifications that optimize material efficiency without sacrificing service or cost, the institutionalization of simulation and twin-driven decision-making speeds up cross-functional alignment. As capabilities grow, the twin serves as a governance tool that records the attainment and upkeep of material efficiency goals, assisting with both regulatory compliance and ongoing improvement initiatives.

Figure 3.4 illustrates the technology roadmap for material efficiency. The figure shows a layered progression from sensing and connectivity to real-time visibility and traceability, followed by analytics and artificial intelligence for predictive and prescriptive control. Digital twins for closed-loop optimization and, finally, advanced fabrication and recovery technologies orchestrated by interoperable data standards to deliver sustained yield improvement, enhanced resource efficiency, and circular material flows across manufacturing systems. Grayscale, 300 dots per inch, with callouts referencing applications such as dynamic scheduling, autonomous intralogistics, near-net shape fabrication, and certified recycled content allocation reduces material intensity per unit of functional output.

3.5 Best Practices for Reducing Material Waste in Manufacturing

The following practices translate technology and strategy into disciplined routines that consistently lower scrap, rework, and incidental losses.

3.5.1 Process Optimization

By establishing stable, predictable production processes with minimal variation and rework, process optimization is crucial for reducing material waste. The data-driven phases of Six Sigma—define, measure, analyze, improve, and control—are used to pinpoint loss mechanisms and establish process parameters that preserve desired yields. Statistical process control helps avoid unnecessary corrections that increase scrap by differentiating between deviations with standard and special causes. Kaizen encourages operational-level continuous improvement by standardizing best practices and identifying abnormalities early to prevent faults. Total quality management minimizes material loss downstream by extending quality assurance throughout the value chain and preventing defects at their source. Digital process instrumentation's real-time data enable the quick identification and containment of out-of-control situations, reducing the quantity of scrap generated. Material flow analysis and automated tracking reveal hidden losses, such as damage or misroutes, which are missed by aggregate reports. Model-based layout and route optimization reduce handling and dwell times, which in turn minimize indirect material use and damage. When process capability data are combined with real-time scheduling, waiting and starvation are decreased. Batch sizes and sequences are carefully tailored to minimize material waste resulting from overprocessing and rework. Short interval controls and tiered accountability continuously assess competence, despite production pressures, ensuring the prompt correction of aberrations and sustainable waste savings. By institutionalizing these improvements through digital feedback systems and governance, waste reduction is integrated into the business culture. This continuous process optimization supports consistent material efficiency, which is necessary for stable circular material flows. By utilizing analytics and maintaining discipline across operations, manufacturers can achieve sustainable waste reductions and enhance overall resource sustainability [23].

3.5.2 Closed-Loop Manufacturing

Beyond stabilizing primary processes, the narrative now integrates reverse flows—remanufacturing, refurbishment, and component harvesting—into day-to-day operations. Closed-loop manufacturing extends beyond source reduction by reintegrating components, end-of-life products, residuals, and byproducts into production cycles to enhance material productivity and reduce the reliance on primary inputs. Remanufacturing restores used products to like-new conditions while maintaining the original energy and material through disassembly, examination, and reconditioning. Faster returns are made possible by refurbishment, which restores functionality without requiring a complete teardown and is suitable for items with limited wear. High-value parts that meet safety regulations are recovered selectively for reuse or new construction through a process known as component harvesting. To minimize idle inventory and match recovered materials with production schedules, reverse logistics arranges for the collection and quality grading of these materials. Traceability is made possible by digital product passports, which also increase customer trust and minimize qualification efforts.

Product-as-a-service and take-back agreements are examples of circular contracts that enhance return rates and product condition, boosting recovery yields and reducing expenses. By combining recovery and manufacturing, damage in reverse flows is minimized, and transportation and packaging costs are decreased. By recapturing scrap, tooling remnants, and packaging for reuse or recycling, supplier collaboration improves feedstock quality and expands the closed loop to tiered suppliers. Transparent reporting and ongoing improvement are made possible by measurement and governance, which monitor recovery metrics and avoid material use. Closed-loop manufacturing, when properly integrated, supports the objectives of the circular economy, mitigates supply chain risks, and structurally reduces waste.

3.5.3 Waste Hierarchy

To prioritize actions, the next subsection frames decisions with the waste hierarchy, emphasizing reduction and reuse ahead of quality-preserving recycling. The waste hierarchy prioritizes reduction first, followed by reuse, and then recycling, ranking actions according to their material and environmental efficiency. This methodical approach prevents waste from being diverted to high-volume, less valuable recovery techniques. By redesigning products with fewer parts and lower mass, optimizing processes, and balancing demand to minimize overproduction, reduction aims to prevent waste. By maintaining functionality through repair, refurbishment, and redistribution, reuse maximizes the utility gained per material input and prolongs product life [24].

Because it maintains complex structures and embodied energy, performs comparably to new products, and often yields better environmental results even when additional stages such as transportation are considered, remanufacturing is special. Recycling should only be done as a last resort, even though it is crucial. High-quality outputs that maintain material integrity should be sought after to prevent cycling.

To make the hierarchy workable, organizations need to integrate its principles into their sourcing policies, design processes, and service models. This will ensure that reduction and reuse are prioritized above recycling. Governance should focus on measures such as reduced material inputs, more extended utilization periods, and improved recycled material quality, rather than just recycling volumes, which could promote shaky compliance.

Through education and training, teams are empowered to select high-impact strategies that sustain material output. Policy assistance strengthens the hierarchy and encourages the growth of the market for circular goods and services by promoting repair and remanufacturing through standards and procurement processes. Ultimately, the waste hierarchy serves as a comprehensive guide that helps businesses achieve actual material efficiency and circularity by moving beyond short-term waste diversion programs.

Figure 3.5 describes the hierarchy of waste reduction practices represented as a tiered framework where reduction is the highest priority followed by reuse through repair, refurbishment, and remanufacturing and recycling as a last resort with quality preservation as a central design and operations constraint, presented in grayscale at 300 dots per inch with clear labels and process linkages suitable for manufacturing system training and governance deployment.

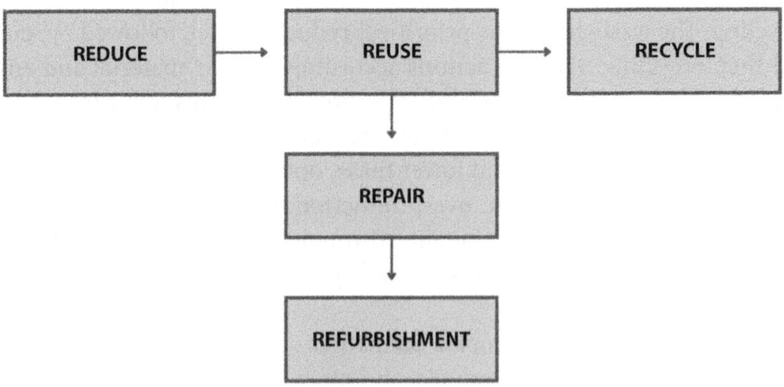

Figure 3.5 Hierarchy of waste reduction.

3.6 Challenges and Barriers

These practices face real-world headwinds, so the next section surfaces economic, organizational, technological, and policy barriers to adoption.

3.6.1 Economic Challenges: Cost of Sustainable Materials and Investment Needs

The cost structures and capital requirements involved in switching from linear throughput to circular and resource-efficient operations present economic challenges. Due to limited supply, certification costs, quality assurance requirements, and the emergence of secondary markets, sustainable materials often have higher prices than their incumbent counterparts. These premiums are introduced into product bills of materials and must be supported by life-cycle performance and risk reduction, rather than short-term unit costs. The payback profile of material efficiency programs and capital budgeting horizons is not aligned because the investment requirements for enabling infrastructure, such as advanced sorting, high-quality recycling, remanufacturing cells, and digital traceability platforms, can be significant and upfront. At the same time, the benefits accrue over several planning cycles. Due to limited access to low-cost capital, internal cash flows that are susceptible to market cycles, and the uncertainty surrounding the collateral value of new equipment or intangible data systems, small- and medium-sized businesses are particularly challenged with financing, which may cause adoption to be delayed or scaled back. Investment cases that depend on stable spreads or policy-derived incentives are undermined by price volatility in commodity markets, which makes returns from recycled content and secondary feedstock strategies less predictable because cost advantages over virgin materials can reverse in the short term [25].

Because throughput determines unit costs, economies of scale are crucial in recovery operations and reverse logistics networks. Until return flows reach a specific density and consistency, operations may be subscale and uncompetitive, particularly in cases where geography disperses customers and products, increasing handling steps and backhaul distances. In procurement and capital planning, total cost of ownership models that account for avoided compliance costs, decreased exposure to supply disruptions, and reputational value are not consistently applied, which biases decisions towards options with lower upfront costs, even when circular pathways offer greater long-term material productivity and risk management benefits. Because residual values and salvage credits are not fully recognized, accounting procedures may unintentionally penalize reuse and remanufacturing. At the same time, warranty provisioning and liability considerations for recovered components increase perceived financial risks. Furthermore, taxation and tariff regimes may not be neutral regarding secondary materials and cross-border return movements, which would raise transaction costs and lead to jurisdictional arbitrage, making the design of a consolidated network more difficult. Unless governance mechanisms, policy instruments, and internal decision rules are explicitly aligned with life-cycle value creation and risk mitigation, the combined effect of these economic factors is to increase the hurdle rate for material efficiency investments, especially those that require coordinated action across multiple actors.

3.6.2 Organizational and Cultural Barriers

Because capital profiles and commodity volatility affect incentives, the discussion now turns to internal alignment—goals, metrics, and collaboration needed to execute circular strategies. Strategies, structures, metrics, and mindsets that have been optimized for linear production and sales growth, rather than for circular value retention and material productivity, give rise to organizational and cultural barriers. Because operational targets are still centered on throughput, short-cycle delivery, and unit cost minimization, whereas sustainability is framed as a corporate narrative, strategic intent is frequently fragmented. This dissonance leads to trade-offs being made in favor of immediate output over long-term material efficiency. For closed-loop models that require coordinated specifications, supplier engagement, reverse logistics, and condition-based remanufacturing or refurbishment operations, functional silos hinder collaboration between design, procurement, operations, service, and finance. Operations may prioritize throughput without yield quality weighting that includes recovery potential; procurement may optimize for price and on-time delivery without valuing recycled content or verified sourcing; design teams may be rewarded for cost and speed to market without accountability for end-of-life recoverability; and service teams may be evaluated on turnaround time without accounting for component harvesting and failure mode learning loops. Performance metrics and incentives are generally out of sync. When concerns about perceived product quality, brand positioning, or the cannibalization of new product sales are prevalent, cultural inertia makes it challenging to adopt new practices such as product-as-a-service, take-back programs, or the introduction of recovered components into production.

Because material efficiency necessitates cross-disciplinary competence in life-cycle design, data analytics, materials science, quality engineering for recovered parts, and contract design for circular models, skill gaps exacerbate these problems. In the absence of targeted capability building, teams often revert to tried-and-true linear solutions. Similarly, customer relationships may not be structured to support high return rates, predictable reverse flows, or the acceptance of certified remanufactured components. Supplier relationships can also be transactional and adversarial, which hinders the trust and data sharing necessary for provenance tracking, collaborative investment in secondary materials, and the cooperative development of recovery standards. Because change control boards, design gates, and capital committees may not have criteria that specifically value material efficiency, promising options are frequently filtered out early for failing to meet legacy templates. This is an example of how governance processes are often not modified for circular decisions. Finally, organizational narratives and success stories frequently highlight the introduction of new products and expansion milestones rather than ongoing advancements in material productivity. This lowers the prominence and prestige of the circular transformation effort, which in turn restricts funding and sponsorship.

3.6.3 Technological Limitations in Recycling and Recovery

Structural alignment alone is insufficient without fit-for-purpose recycling and recovery technologies that meet quality and cost thresholds. High-quality recirculation is technically complex and economically sensitive due to persistent technological limitations across the spectrum of recovery and recycling processes, which are caused by contamination, material complexity, and thermodynamic constraints. Even when disassembled, cross-contamination can deteriorate properties and force outputs into lower-grade applications, resulting in down-cycling that reduces material value with each loop. Composite and multimaterial assemblies that combine metals, polymers, ceramics, adhesives, and coatings in inseparable layers or complex geometries are resistant to cost-effective separation. Although chemical recycling technologies offer paths for mixed streams, they also come with high energy requirements, problems managing solvents, and expanded risks associated with emissions controls, reactor fouling, and product purification. Polymer incompatibility, additive packages, flame retardants, and colorants limit the recycling of plastics by reducing mechanical property retention and creating variability that makes specification-compliant reuse more difficult. Although metal recovery is a well-established concept, it is complicated by alloying constituents and tramp elements that accumulate and alter the composition beyond acceptable bounds. Especially for complicated alloys used in high-performance applications, this calls for costly and energy-intensive sorting, sensor-based identification, and refining procedures.

As manufacturers seek to reintroduce recovered materials into high-energy-density cells, yield and purity targets for cathode and anode materials are becoming increasingly stringent. Lithium-ion battery recycling is on the rise, but it remains heterogeneous due to the variety of chemistries, form factors, and pack designs that complicate disassembly automation, thermal runaway risk safety management, and process selection among pyrometallurgical, hydrometallurgical, and direct recycling approaches [26]. Miniaturization, adhesive bonding, and encapsulation hinder the accessibility of valuable components in electronics recovery, and regulatory requirements for handling hazardous substances and data destruction complicate processing, reducing throughput. Digital product passports and other traceability technologies are crucial for quality control; however, they also require scalable systems integration with enterprise resource planning and manufacturing execution systems, robust tagging that endures use and disassembly, cybersecurity to protect intellectual property, and interoperable data standards. Although generalized robotic solutions face challenges in perception, dexterity, and adaptability in unstructured environments where product variance is high and conditions are uncertain, automation in disassembly and sorting can lower costs and increase safety. Lastly, differences between mass balance and physical segregation approaches can lead to uncertainty in market claims and acceptance, slowing adoption by risk-averse industries that require clear assurance of material performance. Measurement and verification of recycled content and circular flows rely on certification schemes and audit trails that are still developing.

3.6.4 Regulatory and Policy Gaps

Finally, even proven solutions require coherent rules, interoperable data, and frictionless cross-border flows to scale reliably. Fragmentation, inconsistency, and misaligned incentives are examples of regulatory and policy gaps that impede the spread of material efficiency and circular practices across sectors and jurisdictions. Multinational manufacturers must adapt their operations to local regulations rather than maximizing a unified reverse logistics network, which can result in uneven return rates, disparate collection infrastructures, and increased compliance complexity. Extended producer responsibility (EPR) frameworks vary significantly in their scope, targets, and enforcement. Even when movements occur between certified facilities for high-quality recovery, waste classification, and transboundary movement, regulations can limit adequate cross-border flows of returns and secondary materials by imposing permitting burdens and delays that raise costs and deteriorate the condition of materials. This issue is particularly severe for specialized streams, such as batteries and electronics, where processing capacity is geographically concentrated. To suppress demand signals that would otherwise drive market growth for circular products and services and justify private investment in recovery capacity and material-efficient design, public procurement criteria often place more emphasis on the lowest upfront price than on life-cycle value, recycled content, repairability, or take-back provisions.

When value-added tax is applied more heavily to repair services than to sales of new products, or when landfill and incineration fees are low in comparison to the capital and operating costs of high-quality recycling and remanufacturing, these fiscal and tax policies can be neutral or even detrimental to circularity, which distorts economic comparisons at the margin. A lack of standard data models and interoperability across digital traceability systems further undermines effective compliance and market transparency. Although standards and certification systems for recycled content, product durability, repairability, and remanufacturing quality are improving, they are still insufficient or nonharmonized, which breeds uncertainty among producers and buyers and raises the transaction costs of verification. Intellectual property and liability frameworks can deter third-party repair, refurbishment, and component reuse by limiting access to repair information, diagnostic software, and spare parts and shifting blame to parties that had no control over the original design decisions. This can stifle emergent circular ecosystems and concentrate capabilities in a small number of vertically integrated actors. Environmental permitting for recovery facilities can be time-consuming and resource-intensive, adding a delay that is out of pace with the speed of product innovation and return flows. Periodic capacity shortages may result, slowing recovery rates and disrupting the secondary feedstock supply [27].

Lastly, there is frequently insufficient policy coordination across the domains of climate, waste, labor, and trade, which leads to conflicting signals. For example, aggressive decarbonization targets that rely on recycled materials without parallel support for infrastructure for collection, sorting, and processing, or labor standards that increase recovery operations costs without corresponding productivity and technology support, limit the competitiveness of domestic circular industries [28].

3.7 Case Studies and Industrial Applications

The following cases translate the playbook into concrete applications across automotive, electronics, textiles, and construction.

3.7.1 Automotive Sector

Case: DELMIA

The application of DELMIA, a digital platform created to maximize material flow in automotive manufacturing. To provide manufacturers with real-time visibility and control over materials, inventory, resources, and quality status throughout the production process, DELMIA serves as an integrated solution that connects warehouse management and production scheduling. By coordinating the direct delivery of parts and subassemblies to production lines at specific times, this platform supports just-in-time and just-in-sequence manufacturing strategies. By reducing or eliminating inventory buffers, which DELMIA enables, waste and storage requirements are reduced, resulting in more efficient operations and lower costs [29].

Due to DELMIA's versatility and support for multiple manufacturing models, including make-to-stock, make-to-order, and configure-to-order, automakers are better equipped to respond to shifting market demands. By monitoring material movements and status, the platform's real-time data capabilities enhance traceability, ensuring that quality and compliance standards are consistently met. By improving operational visibility and coordination, this integrated approach enables manufacturers to quickly identify and address disruptions or quality issues before they escalate.

DELMIA promotes lean manufacturing concepts by streamlining production and warehouse processes, reducing lead times, minimizing waste, and enhancing overall productivity. By providing teams with actionable insights that help them simplify procedures and reduce material consumption, the system also encourages continuous improvement. All things considered, DELMIA is a comprehensive tool that allows automakers to achieve a highly effective, responsive, and sustainable material flow—all of which are essential in a highly complex, high-volume production setting [30].

3.7.2 Electronics and IT Industry

Case: Dell Technologies

From real-time flow control on assembly lines, the narrative moves to closed-loop plastics and precious metals that validate high-quality secondary inputs in electronics. The goal of Dell Technologies' closed-loop recycling program is to recover plastics from returned electronic devices, process them, and then use the recycled material to create new products. By separating plastics from take-back streams, melting them, and then molding them into new parts, this method preserves the quality of the polymers. From collection to the reuse of the plastic in new Dell products, including laptops, desktops, and monitors, the process usually takes less than 6 months. To ensure that the recycled plastics meet stringent engineering specifications, including strength, flame retardance, and aesthetic standards, Dell collaborates closely with supply chain partners, such as recyclers and material manufacturers. Dell maintains consistent material performance throughout manufacturing cycles by combining recycled content with virgin plastic [31].

Compared to products made entirely of virgin plastics, this closed-loop approach reduces carbon emissions by approximately 11% by reducing reliance on virgin raw materials.

The initiative helps stabilize material costs, reducing exposure to volatile oil prices, while also impacting the price of virgin plastic and conserving resources by decreasing plastic waste. In addition, Dell applies the closed-loop concept to precious metals, recovering recycled gold from e-waste, which considerably reduces environmental harm compared to conventional mining. By encouraging circularity, reducing e-waste, and cultivating a supply chain that facilitates material reuse without compromising product quality or performance, Dell is advancing sustainability in the electronics sector [32].

3.7.3 Textile and Fashion Industry

Case: Shakti Textiles (India)

Next, logistics optimization in textiles shows how route and process redesign reduce transport distance, cost, and material exposure. India-based Shakti Textiles utilized LINGO software, a powerful tool for resolving complex optimization issues, to optimize its transportation routes and supply chain. Before optimization, Shakti Textiles' transportation route required multiple locations for the procurement of raw materials, dyeing, printing, and final processing, resulting in inefficient longer travel distances and increased expenses.

Shakti Textiles found an optimal route that decreased the gross travel distance from 1810 km to 1600 km by modeling and analyzing the supply chain logistics using LINGO. This modification significantly reduced transportation expenses and optimized the material flow from raw material acquisition to dyeing, printing, and manufacturing processes.

The improved delivery lead times resulting from the revised route enabled faster order fulfillment and reduced operational stress [33].

To further reduce costs and complexity, optimization recommended rearranging order processing to eliminate unnecessary supply chain processes. This example illustrates how supply chain and material flow optimization, utilizing state-of-the-art software such as LINGO, can increase output, reduce expenses, and enhance overall manufacturing performance in the textile industry.

3.7.4 Construction and Infrastructure

Case: Kerala, India Construction Study

Finally, site logistics in construction highlight on-time delivery, waste reduction, and stock movement control in a complex, dynamic environment. The Kerala construction site case study focuses on measuring and optimizing material flow and stock movement to boost efficiency and reduce resource consumption. Efficient material flow is the process of delivering the right amounts of resources at the correct times without interruption. This can be challenging due to issues such as material shortages, delivery delays, subpar transportation, waste, and inadequate storage space.

By distributing a questionnaire survey to 65 industry participants, the study identified the primary determinants of material flow, including labor availability, equipment availability, material availability, time constraints, and costs. Using these factors, researchers developed material flow paths that were optimal for the construction activities at the site. These routes contribute to the effective management of logistics and material transportation on site by reducing delays and material waste [34].

The study highlights the crucial role of efficient logistics and material management in infrastructure projects, promoting resource efficiency and the principles of the circular economy. Projects can improve timely delivery, reduce waste, and minimize cost overruns by streamlining the flow of materials. Underpinning sustainable and effective construction methods in Kerala and comparable contexts, this all-encompassing approach guarantees that materials are better coordinated throughout the supply chain and onsite processes.

Figure 3.6 demonstrates the case study process diagram illustrating the generic pathway from strategic intent and design for circularity through material flow optimization in production and construction, to reverse logistics, triage, remanufacturing and refurbishment, material recycling, and reintegration into forward supply, with data and governance layers ensuring traceability, quality assurance, and performance monitoring across the whole loop.

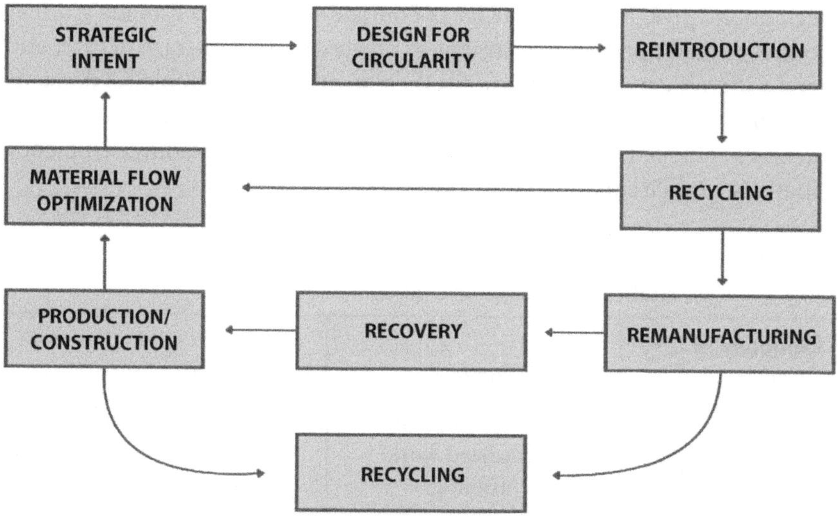

Figure 3.6 Key stages in circular manufacturing.

3.8 Strategic Recommendations

Scaling circular performance requires aligned rules, interoperable data, shared platforms, and upgraded skills.

3.8.1 Policy and Regulatory Interventions

Because they establish market conditions that incentivize the retention of high-quality materials and penalize their wasteful disposal, policy and regulatory interventions are essential in facilitating the shift to a circular economy. To maintain uniform collection goals, enforce design for circularity specifications, and encourage performance-driven strategies for reuse, remanufacturing, and high-quality recycling, regulators should standardize EPR laws across geographical boundaries. In addition to stabilizing reverse material flows, this alignment promotes private investment in material traceability and recovery infrastructure [35]. Secondary feedstock markets can grow more quickly if mandatory recycled content targets specific to each product type are implemented, along with open conformance evaluations and enforcement. Demand for long-lasting and upgradable products can be increased by requiring repairability and durability disclosures at the point of sale. By defining requirements such as verified recycled content, material passports, take-back clauses, and maintenance-friendly designs, green public procurement policies encourage suppliers to provide circular products, attract private investment to create enabling infrastructure, and thereby increase market demand for these products [36]. Table 3.4 presents case studies from different industrial sectors and highlights measurable outcomes achieved through material flow optimization, resource efficiency initiatives, and circular economy practices.

Table 3.4 Case studies and measurable outcomes.

Company or sector	Practice focus	Representative outcomes
Automotive manufacturing	Lean production with standardized work, error proofing, and supplier synchronization	Documented reductions in scrap and rework rates in assembly and body operations and improved alloy segregation increasing quality of recycled offcuts
Electronics and IT	Trade-in and take-back integrated with component harvesting and certified recovery processes	Increased return rates for used devices and higher recovery of precious and base metals reducing primary extraction needs
Textile and fashion	Collection, resale, incorporation of recycled fibers, and monomaterial design for recyclability	Extended garment lifetimes in secondary markets and improved yield and quality of recovered fibers for reintegration
Construction and infrastructure	Specification of supplementary cementations materials and design for disassembly with certified timber	Reduced primary material demand and increased component reuse lowering demolition waste
Cross sector digitalization	Real-time material visibility and predictive control of handling, storage, and changeovers	Reduced incidental losses from misroutes and exposure, higher first-pass yield through timely interventions

By reducing taxes on labor-intensive repair and remanufacturing services and raising fees on disposal techniques that destroy material value, fiscal policies can change incentives. For advanced sorting, reprocessing, and digital traceability technologies that enable quality-assured material recirculation, accelerated depreciation and investment tax credits should be implemented. To remove obstacles to the cross-border movement of returns and secondary materials among certified facilities while upholding social and environmental protections, trade and customs laws need to be updated. Cost-effective circular operations require effective regional networks, particularly in industries with specialized recovery technologies. The most effective control technologies should be integrated into modern environmental permitting procedures to expedite approvals while maintaining stringent protection standards. For facilities handling batteries, electronics, and complex polymers—where return flows are constrained by limited capacity—this is crucial [37].

Lastly, to share provenance, composition, and processing histories among authorized parties, regulatory frameworks should require data interoperability standards, such as open material identities and secure digital product passports. This lowers transaction costs, improves quality assurance for secondary inputs, and enables the evaluation of compliance using circular material productivity and retained utility, rather than just focusing on wasted diversion volumes. When combined, these regulations offer a thorough framework for accelerating the widespread adoption of the circular economy [38].

3.8.2 Digital Transformation Synopsis

Standardized EPR, recycled-content targets, and green procurement create demand certainty that justifies digital traceability and predictive control investments. An architecture-driven roadmap that combines short-term yield and scrap reduction with medium-term closed-loop synchronization and long-term autonomous flow control across forward and reverse value streams is the best way to pursue the adoption of Industry 4.0 and digital technologies [39]. To make losses from misroutes, handling damage, and environmental exposure visible and enable prompt containment through short interval control and digital Andon, organizations should start with a strict material flow baseline that equips critical processes with sensors and real-time location capabilities.

Digital twins connected to live data offer a low-risk setting for testing layout modifications, buffer sizing, and control policies before physical implementation. In contrast, production intelligence based on interoperable data platforms must integrate enterprise data with shop floor signals to enable predictive replenishment, dynamic sequencing, and constraint-based dispatching that reduce overproduction and waiting-induced defects. Tamper-evident provenance records and material identity management systems that maintain property data and processing history across loops should be used to address chain of custody requirements for secondary materials and recovered components [40]. Specification-bound applications must accept remanufactured parts and recycled content. Artificial intelligence can assist planners and supervisors by proposing actions that together optimize throughput, cycle time, and material exposure under variability. It can also learn from results to enhance control policies over time without destabilizing operations. Integration between product life-cycle management, manufacturing execution, and quality systems must be improved to prevent cross-part contamination and misguided decisions that lower material yield and recyclability, as well as to ensure that engineering changes are consistently reflected in work instructions, inspection plans, and recovery pathways. As more actors and interfaces share sensitive product and material data through circular processes, access control and cybersecurity become crucial. Strong governance enables verification and compliance, ensuring that traceability does not compromise intellectual property.

To increase the impact, companies should implement open standards for data models and interfaces to prevent vendor lock-in, enable participation in shared recovery platforms and industrial symbiosis, and institutionalize value measurement that connects digital investments to material productivity metrics such as recovery yield, verified recycled content reintroduction rates, scrap intensity per unit of output, and first-pass yield. For change management to be effective, production leaders and engineers must be trained to use decision support tools. Confidence must be bolstered through pilots with clear counterfactuals, and deployments must be sequenced from high-return bottlenecks to system-wide rollout, with governance that maintains gains under demand changes and new product introductions.

3.8.3 Cross-Industry Collaborations and Knowledge Sharing

Because no firm can build circular networks alone, the focus shifts to symbiosis hubs, shared specifications, and pooled reverse logistics. Distributed, small-scale projects are transformed into coordinated systems that deliver dependable circular performance at lower costs and with higher quality through knowledge exchange and cross-industry collaborations. Industrial symbiosis networks should be explicitly formed through regional hubs and Internet marketplaces by mapping product streams and balancing supply and demand to optimize resource utilization. These platforms use standardized material specifications, quality testing, and liability frameworks to convert disposal liabilities into lucrative feedstock assets [41]. Establishing standards for digital product passports, remanufacturing quality, and verified recycled content helps reduce negotiation costs and boost buyer confidence—two criteria that are critical in regulated industries. Through shared grading and reverse logistics pooling between manufacturers and logistics providers, not only are unit costs lowered and return density increased, but recovery predictability is also enhanced, leading to better secondary material planning [42].

Precompetitive research collaborations among public entities, academia, and industry address technological obstacles such as battery recycling and multimaterial separation, freely exchanging knowledge to spur advancement. By using outcome-based contracts and blended models, shared financing lowers investment risks and raises funds for infrastructure that individual actors cannot support on their own [43].

Knowledge platforms compile benchmarks and case studies to facilitate the adoption of circular practices more quickly. Beyond written documentation, peer exchanges and secondments develop the organizational and human skills required. Lean governance structures with explicit guidelines for IP, data sharing, and dispute resolution are necessary to preserve engagement, prevent collaboration fatigue, and uphold trust. By showcasing value creation and risk reduction, transparency through established key performance indicators promotes involvement. When combined, these tactics boost the adoption of the circular economy by establishing cooperative, efficient, and scalable industrial ecosystems [44].

3.8.4 Workforce Training, Education, and Skill Development

Common standards and platforms only deliver when people have the cross-disciplinary skills to design, run, and improve circular. Because material flow optimization and circularity require cross-disciplinary competencies that are uncommon in traditional manufacturing roles, workforce education, training, and skill development are the cornerstones of long-lasting transformation. Life-cycle design, materials science (with an emphasis on recycled and bio-based inputs), quality engineering for recovered components, process capability and statistical control, reverse logistics planning and triage, disassembly and remanufacturing engineering, environmental health and safety for handling residuals and returned goods, procurement for circular and responsible sourcing, and data analytics for real-time decision support and digital twin operation are all skills that should be mapped out in a competency framework. Learning architecture should combine foundational academies with role-specific pathways and hands-on labs, where operators, technicians, and engineers practice disassembly, diagnosis, reconditioning, and reassembly on real assemblies, and simulate flow optimization in digital environments that mirror production systems. Assessment should be based on demonstrated capability rather than seat time. Whereas formal certification in remanufacturing, recycling, and sustainable procurement can professionalize circular economy roles and create clear career ladders that attract and retain personnel, microcredentials allow for continuous learning that keeps pace with evolving regulations and technologies [45].

To integrate material efficiency and circular outcomes with safety, delivery, quality, and cost, supervisors and middle managers must be trained in change leadership for improvement procedures, tiered responsibility, and problem-solving approaches. This will help coordinate day-to-day operations with strategic objectives. Teams that demonstrate improvements in product valuation, modular upgrades, and repair capability should be highlighted in recognition programs. In addition to throughput, incentive schemes should lead to enhancements, improved recovery rates, and the successful reintroduction of secondary materials. Partnerships with academic institutions and technical schools can support applied research projects that tackle real plant problems while improving student competencies, provide apprenticeship programs for technicians in recycling and remanufacturing, and align curricula with industry priorities [46].

Finally, a robust safety culture tailored to circular operations is essential due to the variable product conditions, embedded energy, and hazardous materials introduced by reverse flows, which necessitate specialized handling and risk assessment. To ensure that circularity strengthens rather than compromises the integrity of industrial operations, training must equip teams to manage these risks while preserving productivity, quality, and environmental performance.

3.9 Conclusion

Material flow optimization and resource efficiency are key aspects of sustainable manufacturing. They are also crucial for transitioning to a circular economy. As global industries face increasing resource constraints, stricter environmental regulations, and shifting market demands, optimizing material flows has evolved from a technical task to a strategic necessity.

Taking a comprehensive approach to material flow helps ensure that resources are used wisely, waste is reduced methodically, and all outputs, including by-products, are treated as valuable materials for further use within or outside the organization. Using tools such as material flow analysis, businesses can identify inefficiencies, redesign systems for better circularity, and encourage cooperation across supply chains to close material loops. This not only leads to cost savings and operational improvements but also reduces reliance on new materials and lessens vulnerability to unstable resource markets.

These practices are the foundation of the circular economy. They focus on eliminating waste, extending the life of products and materials, and restoring natural systems. By incorporating resource efficiency and process improvement into their manufacturing strategy, organizations build resilience, spark innovation in product and process design, and capitalize on new market opportunities tied to sustainability goals. Material flow improvement is more than just a technical need; it is a key driver of the circular economy. It changes manufacturing from a resource-heavy, linear model into a flexible engine for sustainable success in the 21st century. As the circular approach becomes a global norm, manufacturers that excel at managing efficient, circular material flows will not only meet future regulations but also lead the way, surpass competitors, and create new paths to success for future generations [47].

Combining design, sourcing, production, service, and recovery through shared data, standards, and continuous improvement practices, material flow optimization is not a discrete project but rather an enterprise operating system for circularity that maximizes material productivity and minimizes embodied environmental burdens at scale.

AI disclosure statement: The author acknowledges the use of AI-based tools for minor language editing or grammatical correction. However, all intellectual contributions, analyses, and conclusions presented in this chapter are entirely the author's own.

References

1. Chaudhari, U.S., Sedaghatnia, K., Reck, B.K., Maguire, K., Johnson, A.T., Watkins, D.W., ... Shonnard, D.R., PET and polyolefin plastics supply chains in Michigan: present and future systems analysis of environmental and socio-economic impacts. *Front. Sustainability*, 5, 1405427, 2024.

2. Zocco, F., Sopasakis, P., Smyth, B., Haddad, W.M., Thermodynamical material networks for modelling, planning, and control of circular material flows. *Int. J. Sustainable Eng.*, 16, 1, 1–14, 2023.
3. Shaikh, A.M. and Ghatge, D.A., CFD Simulation for fluid flow through a circular chamber by using ANSYS, in: *Recent Advances in Material, Manufacturing, and Machine Learning*, pp. 1025–1034, CRC Press, Boca Raton, FL, USA, 2023.
4. Huang, Q., Zhao, T., Lin, M., Li, W., Zhou, Q., Chen, C., Insights and practices for industrial solid waste management under "zero-waste city" construction in China. *Circ. Econ.*, 100155, 2025.
5. Amir, S., Asif, F.M., Roci, M., Towards circular economy: enhanced decision-making in circular manufacturing systems, in: *Sustainable Consumption and Production, Volume II: Circular Economy and Beyond*, pp. 257–279, Springer International Publishing, Cham, 2020.
6. Lieder, M., Asif, F.M., Rashid, A., Mihelič, A., Kotnik, S., Towards circular economy implementation in manufacturing systems using a multi-method simulation approach to link design and business strategy. *Int. J. Adv. Manuf. Technol.*, 93, 5, 1953–1970, 2017.
7. Blomsma, F., Pieroni, M., Kravchenko, M., Pigosso, D.C., Hildenbrand, J., Kristinsdottir, A.R., ... McAloone, T.C., Developing a circular strategies framework for manufacturing companies to support circular economy-oriented innovation. *J. Cleaner Prod.*, 241, 118271, 2019.
8. Chauhan, P.R., Kumar, R., Bharj, R.S., Optimisation of the circular microchannel heat sink under viscous heating effect using entropy generation minimisation method. *Therm. Sci. Eng. Prog.*, 13, 100365, 2019.
9. Hofstetter, J.S., De Marchi, V., Sarkis, J., Govindan, K., Klassen, R., Ometto, A.R., ... Vazquez-Brust, D., From sustainable global value chains to circular economy—different silos, different perspectives, but many opportunities to build bridges. *Circ. Econ. Sustainability*, 1, 1, 21–47, 2021.
10. Geissdoerfer, M., Pieroni, M.P., Pigosso, D.C., Soufani, K., Circular business models: A review. *J. Cleaner Prod.*, 277, 123741, 2020.
11. Xu, S., Han, Z., Yuan, K., Qin, P., Zhao, W., Lin, T., ... Huang, F., Upcycling chlorinated waste plastics. *Nat. Rev. Methods Primers*, 3, 1, 44, 2023.
12. Singh, G., Singh, S., Daultani, Y., Chouhan, M., Measuring the influence of digital twins on the sustainability of manufacturing supply chain: A mediating role of supply chain resilience and performance. *Comput. Ind. Eng.*, 186, 109711, 2023.
13. Sabale, D.B., Kaswan, M.S., Rathi, R., Development of a circular economy model using Industry 4.0's machine learning techniques to improve performance metrics of MSMEs. *Int. J. Interact. Des. Manuf.*, 1–19, 2024.
14. Bhojwani, A. and Gupta, A., Investigating the Integration of Industry 4.0 and Circular Economy Practices for Sustainable Manufacturing, in: *Digital Technologies to Implement the UN Sustainable Development Goals*, pp. 375–398, Springer Nature Switzerland, Cham, 2024.

15. Lu, H., Zhao, G., Liu, S., Integrating circular economy and Industry 4.0 for sustainable supply chain management: a dynamic capability view. *Prod. Plan. Control*, 35, 2, 170–186, 2024.
16. Hossain, M.S., Sikdar, M.S.H., Chowdhury, A., Bhuiyan, S.M.Y., Mobin, S.M., AI-driven aggregate planning for sustainable supply chains: A systematic literature review of models, applications, and industry impacts. *Am. J. Adv. Technol. Eng. Solutions*, 1, 01, 382–437, 2025.
17. Lasi, H., Fettke, P., Kemper, H.G., Feld, T., Hoffmann, M., Industry 4.0. *Bus. Inf. Syst. Eng.*, 6, 4, 239–242, 2014.
18. Okogwu, C., Agho, M.O., Adeyinka, M.A., Odulaja, B.A., Eyo-Udo, N.L., Daraojimba, C., Banso, A.A., Exploring the integration of sustainable materials in supply chain management for environmental impact. *Eng. Sci. Technol. J.*, 4, 3, 49–65, 2023.
19. Chatterjee, A., Mathur, N., Figola, D., Triebe, M.J., Hapuwatte, B., Hartwell, A., Morris, K.C., Quantifying High-Density Polyethene Flows in the United States Using Material Flow Analysis, in: *International Manufacturing Science and Engineering Conference*, 2024, June, vol. 88100, American Society of Mechanical Engineers, p. V001T04A010.
20. Radhakrishnan, H., Chemical upcycling of waste plastics *via* non-thermal plasma and advanced pyrolysis. Doctoral dissertation, Iowa State University, 2024.
21. Mangla, S.K., Luthra, S., Jakhar, S.K., Kumar, A., Rana, N.P. (Eds.), *Sustainable procurement in supply chain operations*, CRC Press, Boca Raton, FL, USA, 2019.
22. Rene, E.R., Sethurajan, M., Ponnusamy, V.K., Kumar, G., Dung, T.N.B., Brindhadevi, K., Pugazhendhi, A., Electronic waste generation, recycling and resource recovery: Technological perspectives and trends. *J. Hazard. Mater.*, 416, 125664, 2021.
23. Castillo, E.D., *Process optimisation: a statistical approach*, Springer US, Boston, MA, 2007.
24. Thielmann, L.S., Smart Circularity: Exploring the Impact of Artificial Intelligence on the Circular Economy: Building Block C: Cross-Sector Collaboration. Master's thesis, Universidade NOVA de Lisboa (Portugal), 2023.
25. Gaur, T.S., Yadav, V., Mittal, S., Sharma, M.K., A systematic review on sustainable E-waste management: challenges, circular economy practices, and a conceptual framework. *Manag. Environ. Qual.: Int. J.*, 35, 4, 858–884, 2024.
26. Uekert, T., Singh, A., DesVeaux, J.S., Ghosh, T., Bhatt, A., Yadav, G., ... & Carpenter, A.C., Technical, economic, and environmental comparison of closed-loop recycling technologies for common plastics. *ACS Sustainable Chem. Eng.*, 11, 3, 965–978, 2023.
27. Martínez-Falcó, J., Sánchez-García, E., Marco-Lajara, B., Andreu, R., Green supply chain management and sustainable performance: exploring the role

of circular economy capability and green ambidexterity innovation. *Br. Food J.*, 126, 11, 3985–4011, 2024.

28. Buzbee, W.W., Recognising the regulatory commons: A theory of regulatory gaps. *Iowa L. Rev.*, 89, 1, 2003.
29. Curran, R., Gomis, G., Castagne, S., Butterfield, J., Edgar, T., Higgins, C., McKeever, C., Integrated digital design for manufacturing for reduced life cycle cost. *Int. J. Prod. Econ.*, 109, 1–2, 27–40, 2007.
30. Bzymek, Z.M., Nunez, M., Li, M., Powers, S., Simulation of a machining sequence using Delmia/Quest software. *Comput. Aided Des. Appl.*, 5, 1–4, 401–411, 2008.
31. Dubey, S., Shashikanth, T., Nayak, D.M., Optimising the supply chain system in the textile industry. *Int. J. Eng. Res. Technol. (IJERT)*, 10, 2, Article IJERTV10IS020096, 2021.
32. Prados, T.M., Barroso, T.L.C.T., Forster-Carneiro, T., Lovón-Canchumani, G.A., Colpini, L.M.S., Life cycle assessment and circular economy in the production of rare earth magnets: an updated and comprehensive review. *Clean Technol. Environ. Policy*, 27, 2, 471–494, 2025.
33. Chen, G., Geng, D., Zhu, Q., Implementation Barriers to the Circular Supply Chain Mode for Pre-Consumer Textile Waste Reprocessing in China. *Resour. Conserv. Recycl.*, 206, 107621, 2024.
34. Babu, S.S. and Eldhose, S., Material flow in construction sites – a case study. *Sustain. Agri Food Environ. Res.*, 10, 1, 329–342, 2022.
35. Chen, P. and Steuer, B., A first assessment of Hong Kong's circular economy for wastepaper: Material flows, value chains and the role of the semi-formal informal recycling sector. *J. Cleaner Prod.*, 450, 141939, 2024.
36. Gahlaut, T. and Dwivedi, G., Policy recommendations to enhance the circular economy of LIBs in an emerging economy. *Environ. Syst. Dec.*, 44, 2, 398–411, 2024.
37. Ada, N., Kazancoglu, Y., Sezer, M.D., Ede-Senturk, C., Ozer, I., Ram, M., Analysing barriers of circular food supply chains and proposing Industry 4.0 solutions. *Sustainability*, 13, 12, 6812, 2021.
38. Lahane, S. and Kant, R., Evaluating the circular supply chain implementation barriers using the Pythagorean fuzzy AHP-DEMATEL approach. *Cleaner Logist. Supply Chain*, 2, 100014, 2021.
39. Ejaz, M.R., The Relationship between Industry 4.0 & Circular Economy in the context of Sustainability, in: *Shape the Future Together! IV. BBS International Sustainability Student Conference Proceedings*, pp. 223–230, Budapest Business School, Budapest, Hungary, 2021.
40. Teigland, R., Wiberg, M., Borgen, J.E., de Freitas, M., Landberg, J., Rouhi, M., ... Wiest, W., Circular material flows, the twin transition of manufacturing, and the future of labour: Insights from a case study of the Peniche Ocean Watch initiative, in: *The Future of Labour*, pp. 234–251, Routledge, London, UK, 2025.

41. Choueiri, Y. and Perrotti, D., Informality in Urban Metabolism, in: *Interdisciplinary and Transdisciplinary research for Sustainable Development*, 2022.
42. Shao, J., Huang, S., Lemus-Aguilar, I., Ünal, E., Circular Business Model Generation for the Automobile Remanufacturing Industry in China: Barriers and Opportunities. *J. Manuf. Technol. Manag.*, 31, 3, 542–571, 2020.
43. Yadav, K., Shweta, Tanwar, S., Mathur, H., Yadav, C.S., Barriers in the Implementation of Blockchain Technology in Indian Food Supply Chains: A Study Through ISM and MICMAC Analysis, in: *Flexibility and Emerging Perspectives in Digital Supply Chain Management*, pp. 165–186, Springer Nature Singapore, Singapore, 2025.
44. Salvador, R., Barros, M.V., Da Luz, L.M., Piekarski, C.M., de Francisco, A.C., Circular business models: Current aspects that influence implementation and unaddressed subjects. *J. Cleaner Prod.*, 250, 119555, 2020.
45. Singh, G., Misra, S.C., Daultani, Y., Singh, S., Electric vehicle adoption and sustainability: Insights from the bibliometric analysis, cluster analysis, and morphology analysis. *Oper. Manage. Res.*, 17, 2, 635–659, 2024.
46. de Padua Pieroni, M., McAloone, T., Pigosso, D., Business model innovation for circular economy: Integrating literature and practice into a conceptual process model. *Proc. Des. Soc.: Int. Conf. Eng. Des.*, 1, 1, 2517–2526, 2019, July, Cambridge University Press.
47. Leipold, S., Petit-Boix, A., Luo, A., Helander, H., Simoens, M., Ashton, W.S., ... Xue, B., Lessons, narratives, and research directions for a sustainable circular economy. *J. Ind. Ecol.*, 27, 1, 6–18, 2023.

4

Impact on Closed-Loop Supply Chains and Reverse Logistics in Modern Sustainable Business Practices

N. Prakash*, P. Karthikeyan, M. Dharshne, S. Nithish and S. Sangavi

Department of Management Studies, Kongu Engineering College, Perundurai, Erode, Tamil Nadu, India

Abstract

As industries around the world shift toward circularity and sustainability, closed-loop supply chains (CLSCs) and reverse logistics have become key pillars of modern business strategy. The take–make–dispose paradigm-based linear supply chains are being increasingly substituted by longevity, resource recovery, and eco-friendliness–based models. The present chapter gives a comprehensive analysis of CLSC and reverse logistics as two central drivers of the circular economy in manufacturing industries, bringing together conceptual roots and empirical evidence. The theoretical development of supply chains from linear to circular and ultimately to closed-loop structures is described at the beginning of the chapter. It outlines why green regulation such as the European Union's WEEE (Waste Electrical and Electronic Equipment) directive and extended producer responsibility legislation, joined by economic motivations and technology innovation, has accelerated this transition. Theoretical models such as the reverse logistics maturity model and the CLSC framework are referenced to provide structural and strategic guidance for execution. Impact on CLSCs and reverse logistics in modern sustainable business practices key elements of effective CLSC systems are addressed, including product recovery design, reverse logistics operations (collection, sorting, remanufacturing, recycling), instantaneous information flow, digital technology (Internet of Things, artificial intelligence, blockchain), and multistakeholder cooperation. Integration of these pillars constructs the foundation for sustainable performance, enabling businesses to recover value from end-of-life products, reduce virgin material dependence, and minimize waste. The impact of implementing CLSC practices

**Corresponding author*: np.mba@kongu.edu

Jeyaprakash Natarajan, Milon Selvam Dennison, M. Bhuvanesh Kumar and Ganapathy Thirukkotti (eds.) Manufacturing and the Circular Economy, (107–140) © 2027 Scrivener Publishing LLC

on business is then evaluated in this chapter. Economic benefits include increased asset utilization, access to secondary markets for recovered products, and cost savings from material recovery. Customers are paying more for transparent, ethically sourced, and circular products, which increases brand value. Large corporations such as Apple, H&M, Caterpillar, and HP provide empirical support. Apple's application of robotics to break down smartphones, H&M's in-store collection program for clothing, Caterpillar's remanufacturing of industrial components, and HPs closed-loop cartridge recycling program are highlighted to demonstrate scalable and profitable CLSC models. These cases demonstrate how strategic alignment, customer engagement, and technology investment can translate circular theory into tangible outcomes. Although it has its advantages, implementation of CLSC is not free of challenges. Some of these challenges include high capital expenditure, organizational resistance to change, integration challenges of technology, regulatory fragmentation, and poor consumer participation. The chapter presents strategic recommendations on how to address these challenges such as phased implementation, building capability, public–private collaborations, and leveraging digital supply chain platforms. In short, the chapter positions CLSC and reverse logistics as leaders in achieving environmental sustainability, economic competitiveness, and long-term resilience. With the further unfolding of global value chains, the companies that dynamically integrate CLSC principles will better be equipped to deal with pressures from regulation, expectations from stakeholders, and volatility in the marketplace. This research contributes to academic literature and applied guidance for firms making the circular transition.

***Keywords*:** Circular economy, closed-loop supply chains, reverse logistics, sustainable manufacturing, remanufacturing, resource efficiency, digital supply chain, environmental sustainability

4.1 Introduction

Over the past decades, the growing imperative of climate change, scarcity of resources, and environmental degradation has sparked a revolution in the way that global supply chains are imagined and executed. Conventional linear supply chains—characterized by an outbound flow of materials from raw extraction to product use and ultimate disposal—have been the foundation of industrial production regimes for centuries. But this "take–make–dispose" system is increasingly considered to be unsustainable, especially in light of the finite availability of a great many natural resources and the environmental impact of waste and emissions. Consequently, the evolution toward circular and finally closed-loop supply chains (CLSCs) is one of the most important trends in sustainable business practice today.

CLSC model transcends the typical boundaries of forward logistics. It encompasses reverse logistics, where products, components, and materials are sent back to the supply chain after initial customer utilization. Unlike traditional supply and demand recycling or waste management, CLSCs are based on proactive design and systems integration of restoration procedures. It encompasses reuse, remanufacturing, refurbishment, and recycling—each aiming to achieve residual value, minimize the use of virgin materials, and decrease environmental external effects [1].

Global efforts aim to shift to a circular economy (CE), focused on eliminating waste and where materials are utilized for an extended duration, have heightened the importance of CLSCs. Externally, this is driven by policymaking all over the world, for example, the European Union's (EU's) WEEE (Waste Electrical and Electronic Equipment) directive and the EPR (Extended Producer Responsibility) systems wherein companies have to take back their products throughout their life cycle, even when the product ends up at the end-users' site. In addition to these regulatory drivers, evolved consumer perspectives, and in particular those of environmentally conscious shoppers, have driven the need for companies to display their sustainability credentials *via* transparent, defensible regulations in their supply chain.

The role of technology has been crucial in enabling the operational feasibility of CLSCs as Table 4.1 elaborates. With the advent of Industry 4.0 technologies such as the Internet of Things (IoT), blockchain, artificial intelligence (AI), and big data analytics, it has become possible for companies to create more agile, transparent, and responsive supply networks. For instance, products embedded with smart sensors may be able to monitor usage life and condition, thereby enabling reverse logistics to notify when and how and to collect the products for remanufacturing or recycling. Material flows can be transparently documented, with the help of blockchain technology, which improves accountability and compliance with sustainability standards.

Economic resilience is another important factor driving this change. The global impact of COVID-19 has highlighted vulnerabilities of traditional supply chains, particularly those that relied heavily on single-source vendors and international trade logistics. In contrast, CLSCs represent a more robust model, thanks to the localized loops of recovery and production, which are less vulnerable to volatile global markets and can allow firms to recover valuable resources at much shorter lead times and costs.

The value proposition of CLSCs has not simply remained a theoretical concept; it is being increasingly supported by evidence. Companies not only in electronics and fashion, but also in auto and industrial equipment,

Table 4.1 Technologies and role in CLSC and reverse logistics.

Technology	Role in CLSC and reverse logistics	Example applications	Benefits
Internet of Things	Real-time tracking of products and materials	Siemens MindSphere for asset tracking	Improved visibility, reduced losses
Artificial intelligence (AI)	Predictive analytics for returns, sorting, and routing optimization	Walmart's AI-driven returns forecasting	Cost reduction, optimized logistics
Blockchain	Transparent, immutable tracking of product provenance	De Beers' Tracr platform for diamond traceability	Enhanced trust, fraud reduction
Digital twins	Virtual simulation of product life cycle and recovery processes	GE's wind turbine digital twins	Process optimization, predictive maintenance
Robotics and automation	Automated disassembly and sorting of returned products	Apple's Daisy robot for iPhone disassembly	Increased recovery rates, labor cost savings

are now starting to implement these closed-loop systems not as part of a CSR effort, but as a fundamental strategic driver. These systems reduce operations costs and lead to new revenue.

Despite the promise, transitioning to CLSC is fraught with challenges. The consolidation of forward and reverse logistics mandates fundamental re-engineering of business strategy, product design, and supplier interactions, as well as customer behavior [2]. Implementation is hard; costly issues such as high upfront capital costs, technology integration, retraining staff, and patchy regulatory inconsistencies are moderating implementation.

This chapter seeks to offer a comprehensive analysis of CLSCs and reverse logistics in the context of sustainable business operations. The chapter starts with a conceptual development of CLSCs, discussing their importance, organization, and strategic concerns. The subsequent sections examine the elements and functioning of reverse logistics, followed by implementation strategies. With in-depth case analyses of industry giants such as Apple, H&M, Caterpillar, and HP, the chapter demonstrates the breadth of strategies and innovations in this area. The final sections address the most significant obstacles and suggest strategic recommendations for organizations wishing to navigate and prosper within this changing landscape.

Although global supply chains remain affected by environmental, economic, and technological disruption, closing the loop on material flow is no longer a choice but a requirement. Companies that adopt CLSC not only join the cause of world sustainability but also prepare themselves for long-term competitiveness and resilience in the CE age.

4.2 Concept of Closed-Loop Supply Chains and Their Significance

The CE and CLSCs, keeping it technical, are not just some trendy buzzwords. CLSCs are real, structural shift in the way industries operate. Forget the old-school linear model where stuff goes from raw material to product to landfill. In a CLSC, building a perpetual motion machine for materials, items are designed, used, then scooped back up, broken down, and circulated into new products. In other words, the end is just the beginning. This is not just about "feeling green"—it is a strategic overhaul of both operational and design paradigms.

Figure 4.1 illustrates the circular flow of materials and products in a CLSC. The cycle includes stages such as forestry, paper manufacturing, corrugated packaging manufacturing, manufacturer/packer/filler, consumer product use, distribution center, retail, used packaging collection, and reprocessing, emphasizing sustainability and resource reuse. From a systems engineering perspective, the transition to CLSCs introduces a complex layer of reverse logistics and integrated product life-cycle management. The technical core is about optimizing the flow of goods both forwards (manufacturing, distribution, sales) and backward (collection, disassembly, reprocessing) [3]. It is not as simple as tossing old stuff in a bin and hoping for the best. Companies need to build robust infrastructure: collection points, sorting facilities, traceability systems, and advanced disassembly lines. Automation and digitalization—IoT sensors and blockchain tracking—are increasingly essential. Real-time data on where assets are, what condition they are in, and how much value can be extracted from each return are required for processing.

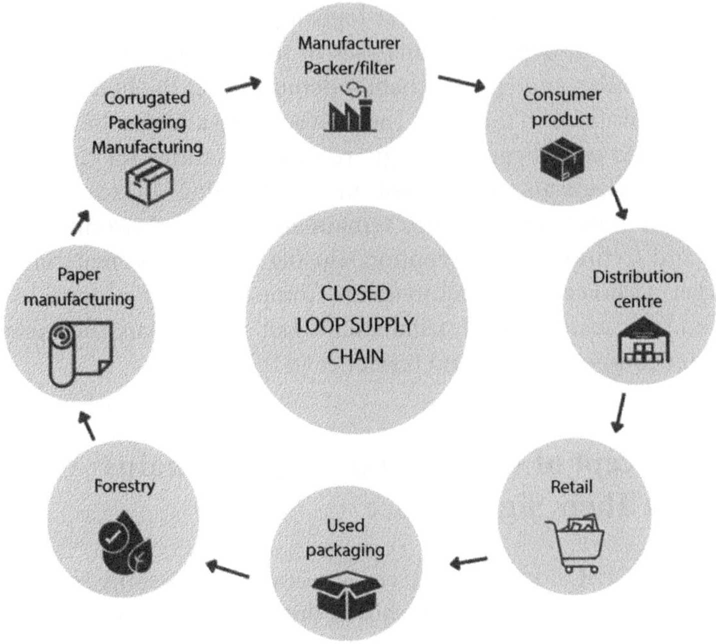

Figure 4.1 Concept of CLSC.

4.2.1 Design for Disassembly and Modularity

A crucial technical distinction in CLSCs is design for disassembly and modularity. Engineers are embedding features that facilitate efficient teardown—standardized fasteners, nondestructive joining techniques, and clear labeling of materials. These design decisions save work and energy during recovery of a system and perform a direct impact on the overall efficiency of that system. In electronics, that means being able to replace circuit boards and battery packs in minutes. Full engine assemblies are rebuilt using used parts that fit OEM standards, in automotive. The technical problem is to make such modular products strong and cost-effective compared to classic monolithic designs.

On the regulatory and compliance front, CLSCs are increasingly governed by EPR regulations and international standards. Organizations are not only motivated to do so; it is quite frequently mandated from a legal perspective to monitor and manage product end-of-life [4]. This includes investment in compliance software, reporting tools and environmental impact assessments in the supply chain workflow. The failure to do this is not just bad optics—it exposes participants to penalties and market exclusion.

4.2.2 Economic and Strategic Benefits

CLSCs' resource efficiency is revolutionary from an economic standpoint.

Volatility of the supply chain: Consider how businesses can recover and repurpose essential materials to significantly reduce rare earth shortages, geopolitical trade disruptions, and volatile commodity prices. The technical solution often involves advanced sorting and separation technologies: AI-driven robotics, chemical recycling, and precision remanufacturing. These allow for recovery of high-value components with minimal degradation. For example, battery recycling in the EV sector is leveraging hydrometallurgical processes to recover lithium and cobalt at purity levels that rival virgin material.

There is also a resilience angle. Localizing loops—setting up regional recovery and remanufacturing centers—reduces overreliance on global shipping and creates buffer capacity when disruptions hit. Technically, this requires agile supply chain modeling and simulation to optimize asset flows and minimize bottlenecks. Companies can use digital twins and predictive analytics to forecast returns, schedule refurbishments, and balance inventory in real time.

4.2.3 Industry Applications and Case Examples

Industries from automotive to electronics, fashion, and FMCG are already deploying these strategies. The likes of BMW and Renault have embedded remanufacturing as a core function, using data analytics to determine which parts are most viable for recovery. Consumer tech companies are using modular architectures and service-based business models to keep products in use longer [5]. Even CPG giants are piloting refillable packaging, which requires technical integration with logistics and retail systems for tracking and cleaning.

Ultimately, the critical technical insight is that CLSCs are not just about "being sustainable" on paper. It demands a holistic integration of product design, digital infrastructure, regulatory compliance, and advanced recovery technologies. Success hinges on shifting both the engineering mindset and the operational model: seeing used products not as waste, but as assets to be strategically recaptured and redeployed. The result? Reduced costs, enhanced supply chain agility, and a measurable reduction in environmental impact—delivered by robust, technically sophisticated systems.

4.3 Reverse Logistics for Product Returns, Remanufacturing, and Recycling

Reverse logistics has undergone a major transformation in supply chain strategy. In the past, it was basically the annoying afterthought, the line item that made the CFO sigh. But now, as CLSCs and CE principles get real traction, reverse logistics is a linchpin. It is not just about shuffling returns—it has become core to resource recovery, regulatory compliance, and sustainability metrics that matter to both boards and customers.

4.3.1 Strategic Evolution of Reverse Logistics in CLSC

Reverse logistics has evolved from a cost burden into a strategic enabler. At its heart, reverse logistics refers to the systematic management of products and materials as it moves backward through the supply chain, postconsumer. This is not just about a customer sending back a defective toaster.

Suite of activities: product take-back initiatives, trade-in programs, warranty returns, and even the retrieval of products reaching end-of-life [6]. Companies leverage a range of channels to collect these items—think brick-and-mortar drop-off points, mail-back kits, and specialized third-party logistics (3PL) services. The operational challenge is huge, honestly. Geographic dispersion of customers means collection networks require sophisticated routing algorithms and, increasingly, the support of digital tracking systems to optimize costs and minimize environmental impact.

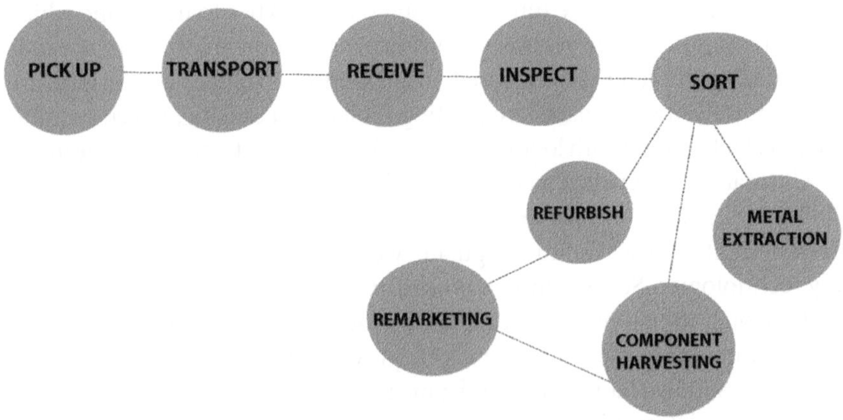

Figure 4.2 Reverse logistics.

If data analytics and IoT sensors are not used for route planning and tracking, then probably money is been wasted.

Figure 4.2 outlines the key stages in a reverse logistics system, starting from product pickup, transport, receiving, and inspection. Items are then sorted and directed toward appropriate end-of-life strategies: repair/refurbishment and remarketing, component harvesting, or metal extraction through recycling—supporting sustainability and value recovery in the supply chain.

4.3.2 Technical Processes: From Inspection to Remanufacturing and Recycling

Once products re-enter the logistics stream, the next critical phase is triage—sorting and inspection. This is where human expertise plus AI-driven automation can make a difference. Each item gets assessed for functionality, cosmetic condition, and potential value recovery. Here, companies face a classic "repair or recycle" dilemma. Remanufacturing is the gold standard for value retention. It involves comprehensive disassembly, replacement of worn components, reassembly, and end-to-end testing to restore original performance specs. This is not just a wipe-down and a sticker—think full teardown, with quality assurance that rivals new production. Refurbishment is a bit lighter—restoring basic function and appearance, but not necessarily meeting "like new" standards [7]. Both these processes extend product life cycles and drastically cut demand for virgin materials.

Products or components that fail the repair/refurbishment test are routed to material recovery—recycling. This involves mechanical or chemical processes to extract metals, plastics, and sometimes rare earth elements. The tech here is evolving fast: advanced robotics for disassembly, AI vision systems for material sorting, closed-loop processes that feed reclaimed materials directly back into manufacturing lines. For companies in electronics, automotive, or heavy industry, the ability to recover high-value materials such as copper, aluminum, or cobalt is a serious hedge against volatile commodity markets [8]. And, being real, it is not just about cost—regulations around waste management and material recovery are getting tighter, especially in the EU and Asia. Failing to comply can mean fines, loss of market access, or reputational damage that sticks.

Table 4.2 illustrates that once items have been remanufactured, refurbished, or recycled, the output needs to re-enter the value chain. Secondary markets, outlet stores, and online resale platforms are booming, driven by consumer demand for lower-cost, sustainable options. Companies now build dedicated sales channels just for these goods. Recovered materials

Table 4.2 Reverse logistics.

Industry	Avg. return rate (%)	Remanufacturing rate (%)	Recycling rate (%)	Avg. cost savings per unit (USD)	CO_2 emissions reduced (tons/year)	Notable example/ company
Electronics	32	18	62	$13	120,000	Apple (iPhone)
Automotive	40	35	55	$50	150,000	Caterpillar, Renault
Fashion/ apparel	28	12	45	$3	76,000	H&M
Consumer goods	22	10	38	$2	40,000	HP (cartridges)
Heavy equipment	55	48	80	$180	200,000	Caterpillar

Sources: Ellen MacArthur Foundation [26], Company Sustainability Reports [27–30], Capgemini Research Institute [31].

are fed back into production, either in-house or *via* supply agreements with external partners. Reusing existing materials offers clear economic advantages by reducing procurement expenses and increasing resilience to supply chain disruptions. It also supports sustainability reporting, as each ton of recovered material contributes valuable data for investors and regulatory compliance. Waste that cannot be economically or technically recovered gets processed for compliant, environmentally sound disposal. Again, regulations dictate the playbook here—think certified e-waste recycling centers, hazardous materials handling, and so on.

Strategically, effective reverse logistics delivers a triple win: cost reduction, environmental stewardship, and regulatory compliance. In sectors with high material intensity—electronics, automotive, industrial equipment—the savings and risk management benefits are enormous. Companies that invest in advanced reverse logistics systems (think: real-time tracking, AI-powered decision engines, blockchain for chain-of-custody) are not just ticking boxes—AI is building real supply chain resilience and competitive advantage. Reverse logistics is not just "nice to have" anymore. It is table stakes for any company that wants to stay relevant, profitable, and compliant in a world that is only getting more circular.

Reverse logistics is not only a backdoor for cost reduction—it has become a strategic lever for both revenue generation and market expansion, especially in industries where margins are tight, and sustainability is now a competitive edge. When a company refurbishes or remanufactures a product, it is not simply reducing waste, it is also breaking into the secondary and developing markets with a product that is cheaper to manufacture but still holds significant value. For example, to bring back into use certified preowned electronics or remanufactured auto parts is not just about selling off inventory—it is about extending the customer base, getting into price-sensitive segments, obsolescence recovery, and utilization cycles.

From a brand management angle, a strong reverse logistics system indicates a company's focus on being eco-friendly and sustainable. As ESG (environmental, social, governance) performance has become a primary decision-making criterion for institutional investors, companies that are leaders in this area typically see an enhancement in their corporate reputation and capital access. An efficient reverse logistics operation directly contributes to better ESG scores, which can boost investor confidence and gain access to sustainability-minded investment funds.

There is already a layer of rapidly growing complexity involved in regulatory compliance. The number of EPR programs worldwide is increasing, and producers need to reconcile the postconsumer collection, recycling, or disposal of products. Failure to comply can result in significant fines for businesses; however, more importantly, it leaves organizations vulnerable to reputational harm that is often far harder to regain. Proactively embracing reverse logistics is more than simply risk avoidance; it is an approach toward future-proofing operations as regulations tighten.

From a technology perspective, the inclusion of tracking and data analytics tools has revolutionized the way reverse logistics functions. Barcode scanning and RFID mean the entirety of product flows can be traced with high precision to prevent loss. From the perspective of companies, IoT sensors—when installed in devices—provide real-time data about their condition and use, so that they can better plan returns in terms of both timing and logistics. Together, AI and machine learning are being used to predict return volumes, optimize sorting and routing procedures, and even determine which parts are most likely to break—leading to more efficient operations and economies of scale. The use of blockchain technology and IoT, in contrast, allows for a level of trust and transparency that guarantees returns chain of custody and authenticated sustainability claims—a vital element as supply chains increasingly come under the microscope [9].

Established companies are defining what quick and easy mean. Apple's "Daisy" robot is one example of a high-throughput method for disassembly, allowing rare earth metals to be recovered that would otherwise be lost—demonstrating closed-loop material recovery. HP's cartridge recycling program showcases scale and circularity in action—dramatically reducing the use of virgin plastics and significantly reducing landfill. Caterpillar's remanufacturing of heavy machinery, for example, demonstrates how industrial companies can mitigate life-cycle emissions and resource intensity by designing for recovery from the start. Even in consumer goods, initiatives such as H&M's garment take-back programs show how reverse logistics can support both recycling and upcycling process, minimizing landfill impact by feeding new product streams.

But the operational challenges should not be dismissed. Volume, condition, and geography of returns are variable and add a high level of complexity to planning and asset management. Contrary to order fulfillment that is essentially demand driven and predictable, reverse logistics necessitates more flexible resource allocation, such as capacity of the system and the flexibility of the inspection and triage process. The fact that the level of consumer participation is considered part of system demand adds an extra level of ambiguity; if participants are not adequately motivated to participate, or if return itself is not maximally frictionless, participation levels can undercut the strength of implementation.

Another substantial impediment is the high capital expenditure—investment in collection points, reverse logistics hubs, dedicated inspection, and refurbishment infrastructure is not inconsiderable, and return on investment (ROI) timescales can be long. In SMEs or in commoditized industries, it can be an uphill challenge to make these investments pay off, even if there is acknowledgement that longer-term strategic gains will be evident. The more important question, though, regards product quality and brand risk: Secondary offerings need to hold up, because even one failure can damage brand reputation and erode customer trust.

The answer lies in ecosystem engagement as reverse logistics being inherently multistakeholder needs to involve logistics service providers, retailers, recyclers, tech vendors, consumers, and even governments. Operational efficiency and scalability depend on clear contractual frameworks, integrated data, and performance-based partnership. Specialized third-party logistics (3PL) providers focused on returns management use modular solutions that enable companies to scale their reverse supply chains without investing heavily in dedicated infrastructure.

In the end, reverse logistics has shifted from a cost center to a strategic asset—one that, when done in a technically sophisticated way, will provide economic, environmental, and reputational value to the enterprise. The companies that invest in reverse logistics capabilities now are not just mitigating risk—they are building the logistics systems of tomorrow. Partnering up with NGOs and public agencies is not just a box-ticking exercise; it is the best way for companies to amplify their impact. These collaborations can turbocharge awareness campaigns, set up robust collection networks, and bring in new expertise for capacity-building.

4.3.3 Metrics, Collaboration, and the Future of Reverse Logistics

On the technical side, performance measurement in reverse logistics is pretty complicated. Companies are no longer satisfied with just counting the number of returns—they are digging into metrics such as return rate (basically, what percentage of sold products boomerang back), recovery yield (how much value a company can wring out of those returns), and time-to-recover (how fast the company can flip those returns into resale or reuse). Cost per return is another big one, because nobody wants a reverse logistics operation that bleeds money. Seriously, if it is not tracked, then it is like flying blind.

But wait, there is more: customer satisfaction and environmental impact are now front and center. It is not enough for companies to just move stuff efficiently—stakeholders want to see hard numbers on landfill diversion, carbon savings, and how happy customers are with the returns process.

These are not just feel-good stats. It is becoming central to compliance, branding, and even investor relations, thanks to tightening sustainability regulations and growing demand for ESG transparency.

The operational backbone or lifeblood of any CLSC is not exaggeratedly, reverse logistics. It is the place where an abstract notion of circularity gets translated into hard-nosed business value. Recycling and reverse logistics—such as the recycling technology offered by Australia's Compac Group based in Auckland—eliminates waste and closed the loop, while common dilemma of refusing to cede environmental impact from the landfill to raw material extraction is given a new answer. A company that nails reverse logistics can pivot faster when supply chains turn into a mess, thus becoming more resilient.

As a result, the worldwide supply chain players are under pressure to take back their products due to the strengthening of climate policies and consumers' right to know forcing consumers to demand transparency, and for this reason, the reverse logistics is no longer a matter of option. It is a technical skill that falls at the convergence of operational efficiency, compliance, and sustainability thought leadership. Companies that take it seriously stand to future-proof their operations and unlock new revenue streams and competitive edge in an increasingly circular economy.

4.4 Implementation Strategies for Creating Circular Supply Chains

4.4.1 Product Design for Circularity

Creating a circular supply chain in actual production is not just a matter of flipping a switch or slapping a "recyclable" label on a bottle. The technical difficulty is colossal here. Examining a multifaceted transformation that touches every part of a company's operations, including product design and data architecture, logistics, and cross-industry partnerships.

Design is at the heart of circularity, far more than any other enabling technology that we might pursue. The engineering problem, he said, is to make products that can identify and reconfigure themselves, rather than simply being thrown into a basic recycling stream. These features are modular architectures and universal connectors and are free from a point when broken down from harmful waste materials. Technical specifications need to include things such as single-material casings, snap-fit assemblies, and digital identification (RFID, barcodes) embedded in every product component. That way, when the product comes back, automated systems can sort, diagnose, and route each part for reuse, refurbishment, or recycling—no guesswork involved.

Take Philips Lighting and their "Lighting as a Service" model. Here, the engineering extends beyond the fixture itself. It is about designing fixtures that can be upgraded with new LEDs or drivers without scrapping the whole unit. This means specifying universal sockets, modular PCBs, and firmware that can be remotely updated. The circularity here is not only a sustainability buzzword; it is a set of technical standards baked into every stage of the development life cycle. The impact? Products stay in circulation longer, and residual value is extracted at every step [10].

4.4.2 Building the Digital Backbone

Design is only half the technical battle. The digital backbone is where things get both challenging and fascinating. It requires an enterprise-level ERP systems that do not just track outgoing products, but also orchestrate the entire reverse logistics process—returns, inspections, inventory of used components, refurbishment schedules, and compliance tracking. IoT comes into play with embedded sensors monitoring product health and usage in real time. These data feed predictive maintenance algorithms, so they can retrieve products before it fails completely, increasing the recovery chances and reducing downtime.

The workflow is also more optimized with AI. Machine learning models also can predict return volumes based on usage, forecast that components have the greatest residual value, and propose the most efficient remanufacturing routes. For example, Michelin uses sensor in the tires to gather wear data and plan tire retrievals with pinpoint surgical accuracy. As a result, the advantages in terms of retreading are reduced retreading work, less waste, and lower cost per kilometer.

4.4.3 Leveraging Blockchain for Traceability and Compliance

Blockchain technology is another technical pillar, particularly for industries where product provenance and regulatory compliance are nonnegotiable. Immutable ledgers track every handoff, material origin, and compliance checkpoint. This builds trust across the ecosystem and supports automated auditing, reducing friction in multiparty collaborations.

Now, none of these systems operate in a vacuum. The closed-loop model demands a robust network of ecosystem partners. Technically, this means integrating disparate information technology (IT) systems—suppliers, logistics providers, recyclers, even regulators—into a unified data exchange.

Standardized APIs, data sharing protocols, and secure digital identities become critical. 3PL providers need access to product status and return schedules, whereas recyclers require granular material data to optimize recovery processes. Public–private partnerships help fill infrastructure gaps, especially in urban environments with complex waste streams [11]. Human factor should not be overlooked in technical architecture. Consumer engagement platforms must be designed for frictionless returns—QR codes, mobile apps, automated deposit-refund transactions—so participation is effortless. Gamification and customized incentives, powered by customer analytics, increase return rates and drive behavioral change.

4.4.4 Innovation Hubs and Knowledge-Sharing Networks

The Ellen MacArthur Foundation's CE100 initiative operates as a sophisticated, cross-disciplinary collaboration engine, uniting corporates, municipalities, and research institutions to design, pilot, and scale CE frameworks. It is not just a networking club; it is a structured environment for prototyping and knowledge transfer, leveraging collective intelligence to de-risk circular innovation. Participants contribute data, case studies, and technical expertise, building a repository of best practices and operational models that others can adapt. This ecosystem approach actively accelerates adoption by bridging gaps between sectors and fostering precompetitive collaboration—critical, given the systemic complexity of supply chains and the need for shared standards.

Transitioning from linear to circular business models is a massive operational and strategic lift. It is not just tweaking the supply chain; it is fundamentally re-architecting how value is generated and retained. Service-based propositions—think product-as-a-service (PaaS) or equipment-as-a-service—align incentives around product durability, reparability, and modularity. For instance, in a PaaS scenario, manufacturers remain asset owners, which creates a business case for designing products that are robust, easily upgradeable, and simple to disassemble at end-of-life. This design-for-circularity mandate cascades down to material selection, supply chain contracting, and aftersales logistics [12]. Companies such as Xerox have operationalized this for decades: their leasing model enables them to manage asset life cycles tightly, recover high-value components, and optimize remanufacturing throughput. Meanwhile, secondary markets, trade-in programs, and certified refurbishment streams are becoming embedded features in sectors such as consumer electronics and mobility, opening up new layers of revenue and capturing residual product value that would otherwise be lost.

4.4.5 Scaling through Circular Pilots and Agile Iteration

Scalability is another beast altogether. Circular supply chain transformation is not a "big bang" deployment—it is a calibrated, iterative process. Companies tend to initiate with pilots: controlled, low-risk implementations targeted at a particular SKU, market niche, or geography. These pilots serve as live testbeds for validating business logic, technical feasibility, and customer acceptance. Data gathering is nonnegotiable—return rates, recovery yields, life-cycle emissions, refurbishment costs, and customer satisfaction metrics are tracked relentlessly. Process mapping is used to engineer integration points between forward and reverse flows, uncover bottlenecks, and enable closed-loop logistics. Agile feedback loops—drawing on input from frontline staff, supply partners, and end-users—feed into continuous improvement cycles. IKEA's phased deployment of its take-back and refurbishment program provides a textbook example: start small, iterate based on empirical data, and then ramp up once operational risks are contained and the value proposition is proven [13].

Regulatory frameworks are moving from carrot to stick. Global governments are rolling out policy instruments that mandate, incentivize, or penalize specific behaviors. EPR schemes shift postconsumer waste management costs onto manufacturers, compelling them to invest in product recovery, recycling infrastructure, and eco-design. "Right to repair" laws are dismantling artificial barriers to maintenance, forcing OEMs to provide repair manuals, diagnostic software, and spare parts. Fiscal levers such as landfill bans and eco-taxes raise the cost and reduce the attractiveness of disposal, tipping the economics in favor of recovery and reuse. Public procurement policies have been gravitating toward the requirement that circular criteria be met—in effect, conditioning success in the pursuit of contracts on sustainable design and the ability to prove it—increasingly so in the EU, where the Circular Economy Action Plan lays out technical standards, reporting requirements and even a roadmap of sectoral evolution.

4.4.6 Circularity as a Competitive Advantage

Embedding circularity is a systematic transformation that touches every function of R&D, procurement, manufacturing, logistics, IT, customer service, and compliance. Success hinges on cross-functional coordination, robust data infrastructure, and a willingness to iterate. The long-term upside? Reduced resource dependency, enhanced supply chain resilience, regulatory risk mitigation, and the unlocking of new revenue stream from previously untapped value pools. Firms that build circularity into their operational DNA are positioning themselves at the vanguard of sustainable business, not only meeting ESG expectations but also reinforcing their competitive edge in a resource-constrained world [14].

In summary, implementing circular supply chains demands a convergence of technical innovation, organizational agility, and strategic foresight. The companies that "get it right" will not only drive environmental outcomes, but also future-proof their business models against shifting market and regulatory dynamics. Circularity, in this context, is not a buzzword—an operational imperative.

4.5 Case Studies on Companies Implementing Closed-Loop Supply Chains

CLSC principles are not only abstract theories—transforming how some of the world's biggest companies operate, and honestly, the technical sophistication here is impressive. Breaking down what is actually happening with the major players: Apple, H&M, Caterpillar, and HP, each of these organizations has embedded circularity into their business models, but what stands out is the way they leverage technology, process engineering, and stakeholder engagement to scale these efforts.

4.5.1 Apple: AI-Driven Disassembly and Materials Recovery

Apple, for example, is not just collecting old iPhones for show. Behind the scenes, there is a carefully engineered reverse logistics system. Devices flow from end-users back to regional hubs, where advanced sorting algorithms (think: AI-driven diagnostics) determine whether a phone is destined for refurbishment or for disassembly. The Daisy robot—Apple's proprietary, modular disassembly line—does more than just pull phones apart. It is calibrated to extract high-value materials such as rare earth magnets, tungsten, and precision aluminum with minimal contamination, preserving purity and yield [15]. That is not trivial; rare earth extraction is one of the nastiest, most resource-intensive processes on the planet, so Apple's ability to close the loop on these materials is a legit technical achievement. And then, integrating that recycled material back into flagship products? Not only does it reduce upstream supply risk (less reliance on volatile mining operations), but it also embeds sustainability directly into the product life cycle. That is vertical integration, CE style.

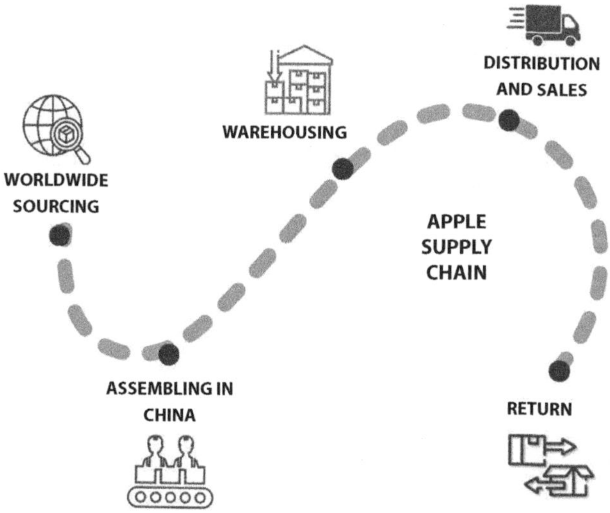

Figure 4.3 Closed loop supply chain of apple.

Figure 4.3 represents the streamlined supply chain of Apple Inc., starting with global sourcing of components, followed by product assembly in China. The process continues through warehousing, distribution and sales, and concludes with the return phase, illustrating the company's integration of forward and reverse logistics.

4.5.2 H&M: Decentralized Textile Recycling and Process Engineering

H&M's approach is a master class in process engineering and material science adaptation at scale. The logistics of collecting, sorting, and processing tens of thousands of tons of textiles annually is a nontrivial systems challenge. Garment collection bins feed a distributed network of sorting facilities, where items are triaged using both manual inspection and, increasingly, machine vision to identify what can be reworn, what gets downcycled (think: industrial cleaning cloths), and what is a candidate for fiber-to-fiber recycling. The Loop machine in Stockholm is basically a microfactory: It mechanically shreds, cleans, and re-spins old fabric into new yarn, in a closed system that eliminates water and chemical usage. This is not just a sustainability win; it is a proof of concept for decentralized, urban textile recycling. If it is scaled that up, then it could fundamentally change how fashion supply chains operate, reducing waste and localizing production [16].

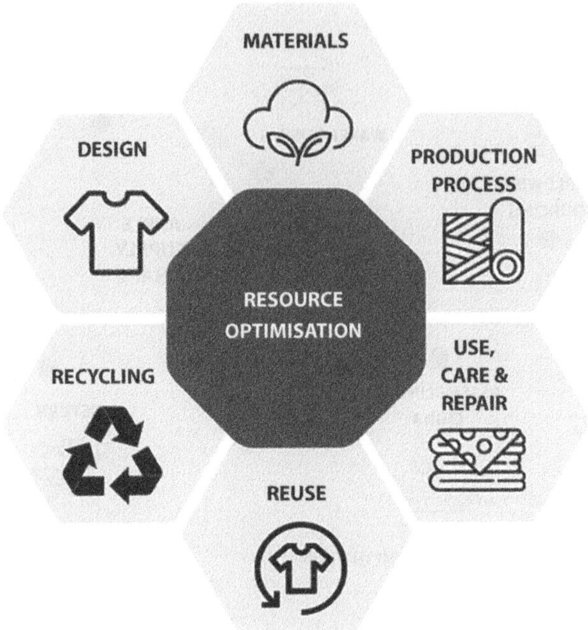

Figure 4.4 Resource optimization of H&M.

Figure 4.4 illustrates a circular approach to fashion, emphasizing sustainable resource use across six key stages: design, materials, production processes, use/care/repair, reuse, and recycling. At the center, resource optimization acts as the core goal, promoting longevity, waste reduction, and circularity in the textile life cycle.

4.5.3 Caterpillar: Advanced Remanufacturing and Digital Integration

Caterpillar's remanufacturing division, Cat Reman, is another technical powerhouse. They have designed engines, transmissions, and hydraulic systems with modularity and durability in mind, which is rare in heavy equipment. When a component comes back, it is not just patched up—the part is reverse-engineered, subjected to nondestructive testing (ultrasound, X-ray), and rebuilt to meet or exceed original specs. The process reduces raw material input by as much as 85%, and energy consumption drops dramatically compared to conventional manufacturing. But here is the kicker: Remanufactured parts are integrated into Caterpillar's digital

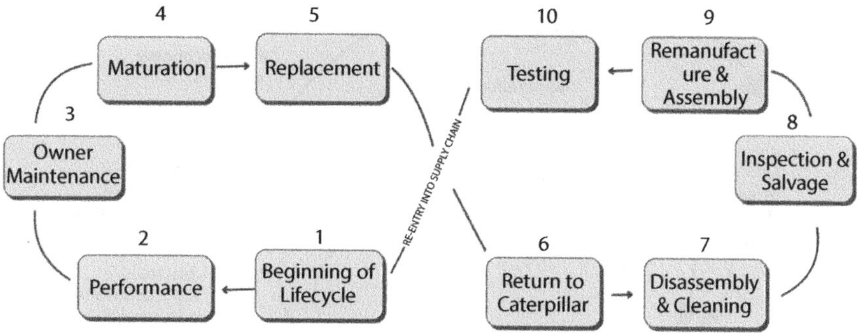

Figure 4.5 Supply chain of caterpillar.

asset management platforms, so customers get real-time data on performance and life-cycle cost savings. This closes the feedback loop, allowing for predictive maintenance and further optimization of remanufacturing processes. It is not just green—it is smart [17].

Figure 4.5 illustrates the continuous cycle of a product's life, from its beginning, performance, and maintenance through maturation and eventual replacement. It then transitions into the remanufacturing process, including return, disassembly, inspection, reassembly, and testing, before re-entering the supply chain. The model emphasizes sustainable reuse and life-cycle extension.

4.5.4 HP: Plastic Circularity and Reverse Logistics at Scale

HP, meanwhile, has taken a data-driven approach to closing the loop on plastics. Their Planet Partners Program operates in more than 60 countries, handling the reverse logistics of collecting and processing used ink and toner cartridges at scale. HP's supply chain team has mapped out the entire process, from customer drop-off points to regional sorting centers, all the way to polymer reprocessing plants. The integration of ocean-bound plastic, particularly through partnerships in Haiti, is technically complex. HP must ensure that the recovered material meets strict quality standards for use in precision components such as ink cartridges. This involves advanced washing, sorting, and compounding processes. HP's supply chain is not just about recycling—it is about reengineering the flow of materials to maximize both environmental and economic outcomes [18].

Figure 4.6 illustrates HP's circular approach centered on the user, emphasizing sustainable strategies such as maintenance/upgrade models,

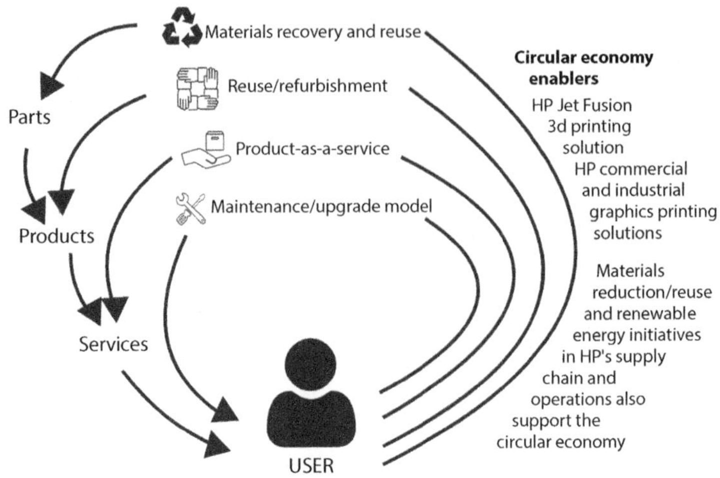

Figure 4.6 CLSC of HP.

PaaS offerings, reuse or refurbishment programs, and materials recovery and reuse. It highlights the flow of services, products, and parts, supported by CE enablers such as 3D printing and energy-efficient supply chain operations.

Table 4.3 states that what emerges from these cases is a set of technical best practices that other organizations can adopt. First, user participation is key, but it requires robust incentive structures and seamless collection mechanisms integrated into existing supply chains. Second, advanced automation and digital technologies—robotics, AI, IoT—are essential to identify, sort, and process returned goods efficiently. Third, cross-sector partnerships matter, not only for PR, but also for access to new materials streams, logistics capabilities, and technical know-how. Finally, rigorous measurement and transparent reporting are nonnegotiable; it underpins continuous improvement and build trust with stakeholders.

Table 4.4 sums up that CLSC is not just about being "less bad" for the environment. When executed with technical rigor, it is a strategic lever for supply chain resilience, resource efficiency, and competitive differentiation. These companies are demonstrating that circularity, when backed by engineering and data, is not just feasible—it is a smart bet for the future.

Table 4.3 CLSC strategy and technologies used.

Company	Industry	CLSC strategy	Technologies used	Outcomes/benefits	Lessons learned
Apple	Electronics	Robotics-driven iPhone disassembly	Robotics ("Daisy"), IoT, AI	95% material reuse, 40% reduction in virgin mining	Technology investment critical; consumer engagement essential
H&M	Fashion	In-store garment collection	Reverse logistics networks	76,000 tons textiles recycled, 120,000 tons CO_2 reduced	Consumer incentives increase returns
Caterpillar	Heavy equipment	Engine remanufacturing	Advanced remanufacturing tech	85% energy savings, extended product life cycles	Strong engineering and quality control
HP	Printing	Cartridge recycling	Reverse logistics, recycling tech	Hundreds of millions of cartridges diverted from landfills	Transparency and accountability build trust
Philips	Lighting	Lighting as a service	IoT, product-as-a-service model	Reduced waste, long-term customer relationships	Business model innovation drives circularity

Table 4.4 Sustainability reports.

Company	Sector	Annual CO_2 reduction (tons)	Cost savings (million US $)	Return rate (%)	Notable outcome
Apple	Electronics	120,000	$40	30	95% material recovery in iPhones
H&M	Fashion	76,000	$25	22	76,000 tons textiles recycled
Caterpillar	Heavy equipment	150,000	$50	60	85% energy savings in remanufacturing
HP	Printing	80,000	$18	25	400M cartridges recycled

Source: Company Sustainability Reports, 2023–2024.

4.6 Challenges in CLSC and Reverse Logistics

Implementing CLSCs and reverse logistics may sound like the holy grail of sustainable operations, but peel back that shiny exterior and that will find some seriously gnarly challenges—especially for SMEs—breaking down the real-world technical barriers and why so many companies end up stuck at the starting line.

4.6.1 High Capital Investment and Infrastructure Complexity

The capital requirements are brutal. It is not just talking about a few new bins in the warehouse. Setting up CLSC means investing in an entire ecosystem: collection points, inspection tech, advanced sorting systems, and dedicated facilities for disassembly and remanufacturing. On top of that, the digital backbone—IoT sensors for tracking, ERP systems for process integration, and blockchain for traceability—demands both serious upfront cash and specialized expertise to implement and maintain. For many firms, especially those without deep pockets, these investments can feel like a leap of faith. The business case for CLSC often hinges on uncertain long-term returns, and that lack of short-term financial payoff is a major deterrent [19].

Now, dig into product design. Circularity is not just about taking stuff back; it is about engineering products from the ground up for easy disassembly, component reuse, and material recovery. This approach drives up R&D costs and forces companies to rethink their supply chain relationships (try convincing the suppliers to switch to modular, recyclable parts—good luck). The upfront engineering work and material selection often clash with existing cost-optimization models, and the ROI is tricky to quantify, especially before economies of scale kick in.

4.6.2 Organizational Resistance and Change Management Gaps

Organizational resistance is another massive roadblock where many companies are still entrenched in linear supply chain thinking, laser-focused on throughput and cost minimization. Implementing a closed-loop model requires a fundamental rewire of workflows and KPIs. Cross-functional collaboration becomes nonnegotiable—procurement, design, ops, logistics, marketing, and sustainability teams have to align, which is easier said than done. Cultural inertia and risk aversion frequently kick in, especially when leadership does not provide a clear mandate or adequate resources for change management. In practice, this means promising pilot programs often fizzle out before scaling.

On the technology front, most organizations are saddled with legacy IT infrastructure that cannot support the data integration and real-time analytics needed for closed-loop operations. Seamlessly connecting forward and reverse logistics, ensuring data integrity, and maintaining visibility over complex multitier networks require robust digital platforms—which, again, come with a hefty price tag and steep learning curve [20]. Interoperability issues and lack of industry-wide standards make integration a technical headache, particularly for midsized players.

4.6.3 Fragmented Regulatory Environment

Regulatory complexity only makes the situation worse. Environmental regulations such as EPR, right to repair regulations, and waste reduction regulations are fragmented across multiple areas. Definitions of compliance, the rigor of enforcement, and reporting requirements vary widely, resulting in global companies configuring their reverse logistics systems on a per-market basis. This piecemeal regulatory framework complicates operations, raises compliance costs, and frequently results in inefficient *ad hoc* fixes that compromise the efficient operation of CLSC systems.

The inconsistency of what condition a returned product is in makes it even worse. In contrast to forward logistics of well-behaved new goods, reverse logistics must accommodate to the mess of the predictability across the spectrum of use conditions, undocumented failures, missing parts and even so on. Attempting to sort, grade, and recondition such returns, however, not only slows processing, but also detracts from cost-efficiency, particularly when residual value is not high, or when use information is lacking. Automated inspection and sorting systems are improving, although widespread adoption remains challenged by expensive costs and immaturity of technology.

Table 4.5 states that consumer behavior is another wild card. Effective CLSC depends on high participation rates—consumers need to return used products in a usable condition. Yet, low awareness of return programs, misperceptions about the quality of refurbished goods, and the sheer inconvenience of return logistics all conspire to keep participation rates low. Technical solutions such as digital product passports, take-back kiosks, and incentive platforms are emerging, but adoption is slow, and consumer trust remains a significant barrier.

Table 4.6 illustrates that addressing these challenges demands a holistic strategy: substantial investment in digital infrastructure, integrated product and process redesign, robust change management, and dedicated stakeholder engagement. On top of that, the development of harmonized standards and policy frameworks is essential to lower technical and regulatory barriers, foster cross-industry collaboration, and unlock the full potential of circular supply chains. Until these issues are tackled head-on, the road from linear to circular will remain bumpy—no matter how compelling the sustainability business case might look on paper.

Brand protection and intellectual property (IP) concerns loom large as well. Companies fear that once products re-enter the market through secondary channels, counterfeit or poorly refurbished items could erode brand equity and customer trust. Enforcing quality assurance and IP protection in decentralized, open-loop systems is technically and logistically challenging—especially as secondary markets grow and the risk of unauthorized refurbishing rises [21].

Finally, the lack of standardized metrics, benchmarking frameworks, and best practices for CLSC implementation stifles industry progress. Without universal standards for material classification, process validation, and sustainability reporting, organizations struggle to measure performance, share knowledge, or benchmark against peers. This gap slows the adoption of circular models and makes it difficult for stakeholders to demonstrate tangible business value to investors and regulators.

Table 4.5 CLSC of accenture.

Barrier	Frequency (%)	Example/comment
High initial investment	68	Cost of robotics, IT, and reverse logistics infrastructure
Lack of consumer participation	55	Low product return rates
Regulatory complexity	51	Varying EPR laws across regions
Technology integration challenges	47	Legacy ERP/IT systems
Supply chain partner collaboration	44	Data sharing and trust issues
Lack of skilled workforce	39	Need for training in new processes

Source: Accenture Circular Supply Chain Survey, 2023.

Table 4.6 Challenges and strategies recommended.

Challenge	Description	Strategic recommendation
High capital expenditure	Significant upfront investment in technology and infrastructure	Phased implementation; pilot projects to manage costs
Organizational resistance	Employee and management reluctance to change	Capability building; training and change management
Technological integration	Difficulty integrating legacy systems with new digital tools	Use of modular, scalable IT solutions; cross-functional teams
Regulatory fragmentation	Inconsistent regulations across regions	Advocacy for harmonized global standards; public–private partnerships
Consumer participation	Low rates of product returns and recycling	Incentives, education campaigns, convenient return options

4.7 Strategic Recommendations

A serious approach to building an effective CLSC and high-performing reverse logistics system requires more than surface-level tactics. Stripping away the corporate gloss reveals a complex system that demands technical depth and structured problem-solving. By dissecting key challenges and applying sound engineering principles, it becomes possible to design a resilient, enduring solution.

4.7.1 Governance and Accountability Structures

Effective governance requires a clearly defined accountability structure and hope things fall into place. Explicit accountability is required for mapping out for every CLSC activity. Think of it like an engineering control system—every function (procurement, R&D, ops, marketing, sustainability) gets its own parameters and feedback loops. Because manufacturers face more depletion of natural resources and due to growing environmental concerns, the CE presents a regenerative model that prioritizes resource efficiency, waste reduction, and closed-loop systems [22], integrating circular objectives right into the corporate KPIs, so that it is as nonnegotiable as revenue or productivity metrics. Regulatory compliance must be treated as a strategic priority, not an optional consideration. The EU's Circular Economy Action Plan is not only a suggestion, and India's E-Waste rules have real teeth, integrating regulatory monitoring into the regular risk assessment cycles, building alerts and dashboards to track compliance, and spotting opportunities for tax incentives or grants. These are not only nice-to-haves; they are core to competitive advantage.

4.7.2 Digital Infrastructure and Intelligent Technology Adoption

Digital transformation is not only a buzzword; it is the backbone of any scalable circular supply chain. For instance, embedding IoT sensors into products gives granular, real-time data on usage patterns, end-of-life triggers, and logistics bottlenecks. This is not only about tracking, it is about predictive maintenance and optimizing reverse flows. Blockchain? Think secure, tamper-proof records for provenance and chain-of-custody—it is critical when dealing with warranty returns or regulatory audits. AI and big data analytics are optimization engines, helping the model recovery pathways, forecast returns, and dynamically allocate resources. The technical infrastructure should include robust APIs to connect these tools, plus digital dashboards that deliver actionable metrics such as return rates, recovery yield, and emissions reductions [23]. These are not vanity stats; it is operational levers.

Now, operations. Here is where process engineering meets supply chain execution. Standardization is everything: Define return logistics protocols, inspection checklists, and refurbishment workflows in detail. Use value stream mapping to identify waste—whether that is excess handling, rework, or transport miles. Modular product design is not only an R&D novelty; it is an operational strategy that slashes recovery times and boosts refurbishment rates. Distributed recovery hubs? It is about network optimization—reducing last-mile costs and localizing emissions impacts. And do not forget to codify best practices in SOPs, so knowledge transfers across shifts and sites.

4.7.3 Ecosystem Collaboration and Stakeholder Integration

Collaboration is more than just a buzzword; it is systems integration across the value chain. Incentivize consumers at the interface—trade-ins, loyalty perks, and carbon offset reports work best when these are data-driven and personalized. Form consortia with industry peers to harmonize standards and share technology investments—think pooled reverse logistics fleets or shared recycling infrastructure. Rethink supplier engagement as a closed-loop partnership: Specify recycled-content requirements, audit upstream processes, and integrate circularity metrics into supplier scorecards. Public–private partnerships can be powerful: Use them to coinvest in collection depots, recycling plants, or even digital traceability platforms.

Culture change is the glue that holds all this together. Technical training on CE principles and life-cycle analysis should be mandatory for every relevant role, not only the sustainability team. Build in innovation laboratories—literal or virtual—where teams can prototype new business models, test reverse logistics pilots, and fail fast. Recognize and promote internal champions who drive CLSC progress and make sure circular performance shows up in bonus schemes and annual reviews [24]. If performance is not measured and rewarded, it does not happen—it is that simple.

And about frameworks: the "5-P" model is actually a solid architecture. Purpose (clear, measurable circular goals), processes (engineered workflows for recovery and reuse), people (multiskilled teams trained in circular thinking), partnerships (integrated, cross-sector collaborations), and platforms (digital and physical infrastructure for end-to-end visibility). Each pillar should have its own technical roadmap, KPIs, and feedback cycles [25].

To sum up, the technical path to an effective CLSC and reverse logistics system involves systems thinking, rigorous process design, digital integration, and a relentless focus on measurement and improvement. Automation alone cannot overcome cultural inertia, and operations cannot succeed without deliberate planning. Success lies with companies that approach circularity not as a marketing strategy, but as a core systems engineering challenge—addressed through the right combination of technology, process, and people. This is the approach that future-proofs the supply chain and ensures competitiveness as regulatory and market pressures intensify.

4.8 Conclusion

The landscape of supply chain management is not just shifting—it is undergoing a seismic overhaul, and anyone still clinging to the good old-fashioned linear model is already behind the curve. The rise of CLSCs and reverse logistics is testimony to a systemic shift, one that is literally transforming every touchpoint in the way companies source, make, recover, and reintegrate materials. This is not merely a matter of operational tweak age. It is also a necessity as regulation continues to bear down, resources diminish, and, honestly, the inevitable global drive toward sustainability becomes a nonnegotiable requirement to meet.

At the technical core, CLSC is about engineering a feedback loop into supply chains. Traditional model? It is one-and-done: raw material in, product out, waste to the landfill. CLSC flips that on its head, designing systems in which products and components and materials cycle back into the production process. What was once the neglected budgetary black hole of reverse logistics turns out to be a linchpin. Rather than considering end-of-life items as liabilities, successful companies recover value by remanufacturing, recycling, or even placing them in secondary markets. This is not only theory; it is already changing P&Ls in categories where the processes have been dialed in.

Drilling into the operational frameworks, success in CLSC hinges on granular tracking and control across the product life cycle. This is where digitalization becomes more than a buzzword. IoT sensors, RFID tags, and machine learning algorithms are enabling real-time monitoring of product flows, quality, and usage patterns. Blockchain, with its immutable ledgers, is rapidly gaining traction for authenticating provenance and tracking compliance—no small feat when managing global, multitiered supply networks. This convergence of digital tech with physical logistics is turbocharging transparency and driving process optimization that was impossible even a decade ago.

Look at the heavy hitters—Apple, H&M, Caterpillar, and HP. Each has architected bespoke CLSC models to fit their industry's profile. Apple's material recovery robots and closed-loop aluminum initiatives, H&M's garment collection and fiber-to-fiber recycling, Caterpillar's remanufacturing of engine components, and HP's printer cartridge return systems—they are all leveraging advanced logistics, predictive analytics, and innovative product design to close the loop. What unites these efforts is a technical commitment to circularity at the design stage, seamless reverse logistics integration, and a data-driven approach to continuous improvement.

But complexity is formidable. The deployment of CLSC brings in technical challenges such as how to handle products quality after multiple cycles, how to optimize reverse logistics flows, and how to integrate heterogeneous information systems. Regulatory patchwork over jurisdictions is an additional headache, particularly for dynamic standards of material recovery and reporting. The capital cost is a biggie—there are plants to retrofit new tech to put into the field and people to be trained, and none of that happens without some serious capital planning. And then there is the age-old consumer participation hurdle: Create systems and incentives that really cause people to return and reuse.

Strategically, the blueprint for overcoming these challenges is multifaceted. Leadership must commit to circularity not as a peripheral CSR exercise, but as a core strategic pillar. Governance structures need to embed accountability for circular metrics. Investment in enabling technologies—digital twins, advanced robotics, predictive analytics—should be prioritized based on value chain analysis. Operationally, lean principles and agile methodologies can help organizations iterate and adapt as it scales up CLSC initiatives. Strategic partnerships—both up and downstream—are crucial for sharing risk, resources, and technical know-how.

Looking forward, several technical trends warrant close attention. PaaS models are shifting ownership dynamics and enabling manufacturers to retain control over product life-cycle recovery. Regulatory harmonization, especially in the EU and Asia-Pacific, is likely to set new baselines for minimum recycled content, recovery rates, and transparency. The proliferation of digital CE platforms—essentially cloud-based marketplaces and traceability networks—will further enable real-time data sharing, collaborative logistics, and secondary market liquidity. Meanwhile, consumer demand for sustainability and transparency is driving the adoption of digital product passports, which embed life cycle and recycling data directly into products.

In sum, CLSC and reverse logistics represent a technical and strategic transformation—one that moves far beyond incremental process improvement. For businesses, the opportunity is clear: Those that master the integration of digital technology, operational excellence, and circular design will not only capture new revenue streams but also build resilient, future-proof supply chains. Waste is no longer just a byproduct—it is a resource stream waiting to be unlocked. The organizations that recognize and capitalize on this will define the next era of industrial competitiveness and sustainability. In this context, the question is not whether to adopt CLSC, but how quickly organizations can retool their supply chains to meet the technical and strategic demands of a truly circular economy.

AI disclosure statement: The author acknowledges the use of AI-based tools for minor language editing or grammatical correction. However, all intellectual contributions, analyses, and conclusions presented in this chapter are entirely the author's own.

References

1. Mishra, A., Dutta, P., Jayasankar, S., Jain, P., Mathiyazhagan, K., A review of reverse logistics and closed-loop supply chains in the perspective of circular economy. *Benchmarking: An Int. J.*, 30, 3, 975–1020, 2023.
2. Daramola, O.M. and Apeh, C.E., Optimizing reverse logistics for circular economy: Strategies for efficient material recovery and resource circularity. *Int. J. Soc. Sci. Except. Res.*, 2, 1, 16–31, 2023.
3. Chizaryfard, A., Lapko, Y., Trucco, P., Strategic closed-loop supply chain configuration in the transition towards the circular economy of EV batteries: an evolutionary analytical framework. *Int. J. Logist. Manag.*, 34, 1, 1–23, 2023.
4. Tran, T.Y.A., Herat, S., Kaparaju, P., Current status and compliance management of EPR regulations for packaging waste in Vietnam. *Circ. Econ. Sustainability*, 3, 7, 1–18, 2025.
5. McKinsey, Powering the remanufacturing renaissance with AI, McKinsey & Company Insights, March 21, 2025, pp. 1–10, 2025.
6. Butta, A.S., Alib, I., Govindan, K., The role of reverse logistics in a circular economy for achieving sustainable development goals: a multiple case study of retail firms. *Prod. Plan. Control*, 35, 12, 1490–1502, 2023.
7. Ayres, R.U., Pelton, S., van der Voet, E., Value-retained vs. impacts avoided: The differentiated contributions of remanufacturing, refurbishment, repair, and reuse within a circular economy. *J. Remanuf.*, 12, 1, 19–35, 2022.
8. Howley, J., The rise of critical material recovery in automotive recycling. *Adv. Mater. World*, 2024, 9, 1–8, 2024.
9. Sangaiah, A.K. and Sakthivel, N., Recent advances in blockchain-enabled supply chains: Transparency, traceability, and trust. *J. Intell. Manuf.*, 36, 4, 789–804, 2025.

10. Forti, V., Baldé, C.P., Kuehr, R., Bel, G., *The Global E-waste Monitor 2020: Quantities, flows and the circular economy potential.* United Nations University (UNU)/United Nations Institute for Training and Research (UNITAR)–co-hosted SCYCLE Programme, International Telecommunication Union (ITU), & International Solid Waste Association (ISWA), Bonn/Geneva/Rotterdam, 2020.
11. Kumar, R. and Nair, A., Role of digital technologies and partnerships in circular supply chain collaboration. *Int. J. Oper. Supply Chain Manag.*, 14, 1, 33–47, 2025.
12. Hidalgo-Crespo, J., *et al.*, Facilitating circularity: challenges and design guidelines of Product-as-a-Service (PaaS) business model offers for electrical and electronic equipment. *Procedia CIRP*, 128, 1, 567–572, 2024.
13. Nilsson, P. and Johansson, M., Optimizing reverse logistics in circular supply chains: The role of process mapping and feedback loops. *J. Sustain. Logist.*, 18, 2, 134–147, 2023.
14. Amir, A., Towards circular economy: A guiding framework for circular supply chain implementation. *Bus. Strategy Environ.*, 32, 4, 456–472, 2023.
15. Apple Inc., Environmental progress report, Apple Inc., 2023.
16. H&M Group, Sustainability report, H&M Group, 2023.
17. Caterpillar Inc., Remanufacturing solutions, Caterpillar Inc., 2023.
18. HP Inc., Sustainable impact report, HP Inc., 2023.
19. Hu, Y., Perspectives in closed-loop supply chains network design considering risk and uncertainty factors. *arXiv Preprint*, 2023, 6, 1–15, 2023.
20. Austin-Gabriel, S., Ezeife, C., Oliván, M., Real-time analytics in fragmented supply chains: Integration hurdles and investment implications. *J. Ind. Data*, 12, 1, 45–59, 2021.
21. Ganin, C., Park, M., Stanton, G.H., How fashion brands can protect their IP in the recommerce market. *Bloomberg Law US Law Week*, 2022, 10, 1–8, 2022.
22. Dennison, M.S., Kumar, M.B., Jebabalan, S.K., Realization of circular economy principles in manufacturing: Obstacles, advancements, and routes to achieve a sustainable industry transformation. *Discover Sustainability*, 5, Article No. 438, 2024.
23. Mdpi *Sustainability*, Big Data Analytics in Sustainable Supply Chain Management: A Focus on Manufacturing Supply Chains. *Sustainability*, 13, 13, 7101–7120, 2021.
24. Subramanian, N., Roscoe, S., Jabbour, C.J.C., Green human resource management and the enablers of green organisational culture: Enhancing a firm's environmental performance for sustainable development. *Bus. Strategy Environ.*, 28, 5, 771–784, 2019.
25. Song, H., *et al.*, Enabling Industry 5.0-Driven Circular Economy Transformation: A Strategic Roadmap. *Sustainability*, 16, 22, 1–20, 2023.
26. Ellen MacArthur Foundation, *Completing the Picture: How the Circular Economy Tackles Climate Change*, Ellen MacArthur Foundation, Cowes, UK, 2019.
27. Apple Inc., Environmental Progress Report 2024, 2024.

28. HP Inc., Sustainable Impact Report 2024. Palo Alto, CA: HP Inc., 2024.
29. H&M Group., Sustainability Disclosure Report 2024. Stockholm, Sweden, 2024.
30. Caterpillar Inc., Sustainability Report 2024. Deerfield, IL: Caterpillar Inc., 2024
31. Capgemini Research Institute. *Sustainable Supply Chains: Balancing Sustainability and Resilience*. Capgemini Research Institute, Paris, France, 2024.

5

Remanufacturing and Product Refurbishment

Awafung Emmanuel Adie[1]*, George Uwadiegwu Alaneme[2], Sharon Kiprotich[3]*, Peter O. Ohiero[4] and Val Hyginus Udoka Eze[5]

[1]Department of Biomedical Engineering, School of Engineering, Kampala International University, Western Campus, Iahaka, Uganda
[2]Department of Civil Engineering, School of Engineering, Kampala International University, Western Campus, Iahaka, Uganda
[3]Department of Physical and Biological Sciences, Murang'a University of Technology, Nairobi, Kenya
[4]Department of Electrical and Electronic Engineering, University of Cross River State, Calabar, Nigeria
[5]Department of Electrical, Telecommunications and Computer Engineering, Kampala International University, Western Campus, Ishaka, Uganda

Abstract

Reliability product refurbishment and remanufacturing are key to improving the sustainability, resource, and waste management of contemporary manufacturing. These approaches are attracting growing recognition as a way of extending the life cycle of products and achieving the so-called circular economy in the face of global worries about climate change and resource scarcity. The chapter explains the procedures, advantages, difficulties, and future of remanufacturing and refurbishment and explains their contribution to environmentally friendly manufacturing. Remanufacturing turns used products back to a like-new condition by following a series of steps, including disassembly, cleaning, repair, and replacement of parts, which considerably saves on materials, energy, and emissions. Refurbishment is less extensive, but increases product usability and longevity. These practices have been successfully implemented in industries such as the automotive industry, electronic industry, and machinery industry with cost savings, increased competitiveness,

**Corresponding author*: awafungadie@kiu.ac.ug; ORCID: https://orcid.org/0009-0007-3574-7234
Val Hyginus Udoka Eze: ORCID: https://orcid.org/0000-0002-6764-1721

Jeyaprakash Natarajan, Milon Selvam Dennison, M. Bhuvanesh Kumar and Ganapathy Thirukkotti (eds.) Manufacturing and the Circular Economy, (141–178) © 2027 Scrivener Publishing LLC

and new sources of revenue. Nevertheless, such obstacles as technological constraints, consumer distrust, and regulatory discontinuities should be dealt with. Digital technologies such as artificial intelligence, Internet of Things, and blockchain are changing the process of remanufacturing, making it more efficient and traceable. Wider adoption is dependent on consumer awareness and enabling policies. It is concluded in this chapter that remanufacturing and refurbishment are key to a sustainable manufacturing paradigm, waste reduction, resource conservation, and increased circularity.

Keywords: Remanufacturing, product refurbishment, circular economy, artificial intelligence (AI), sustainable manufacturing, resource efficiency

5.1 Introduction

The global concern of environmental sustainability and the conservation of resources have changed the industrial practice considerably across the globe. Renewal and product refurbishment among them have become essential alternatives to extending the life of a product, while simultaneously complying with the ideas of a circular economy. Remanufacturing and refurbishing can be used to enhance sustainability in the production process as organizations become more and more pressured to eliminate wastage and carbon emissions [42]. Remodeling used objects to a like-new condition through dismantling, cleaning, repairing, and replacing worn-out parts is referred to as remanufacturing. The approach will be able to minimize the ecological footprint related to the creation of new products in terms of decreasing the reliance on raw materials and the consumption of energy. Product refurbishment, on the other hand, involves repairing and upgrading the old products to increase their lifespan without necessarily restoring them to their original specifications. Although refurbishment might not be as effective in restoring a product as remanufacturing, it plays a vital role in product life cycle extension as well as waste minimization [2]. Recent reports and statistics within the industry have seen a high level of economic and environmental benefits of remanufacturing and refurbishment. Remanufacturing can save the production cost by 40% to 60% and can provide businesses with the opportunity to sell the products at 45% to 65% of the original price at which they were sold at the retail point [44]. Remanufacturing methods have also been reported to be linked to a lighter raw material and energy use of around 6883% and lower CO_2 emissions of up to 87% [10]. Refurbishment, often not as intensive as remanufacturing, nevertheless, makes a significant contribution to sustainable development through extending life cycle and minimizing e-waste, particularly in electronics and medical devices. The cost of production can also be lowered up to 40% to 60% by manufacturing methods so that companies can sell items at 45% to 65% of the original retail cost [30].

The international market on remanufactured and refurbished products is growing at a high rate. According to a report by the International Data Corporation [21], this will significantly increase because companies will be involved in corporate responsibility, and more customers will be demanding sustainable options. These processes have been successfully used by industries such as automotive, electronics, and machinery demonstrating their cost-effectiveness and possible cost reduction. Remanufactured and refurbished product market has been growing globally at a very high rate. According to the report by the IDC, the market in remanufactured goods is set to grow significantly in the future due to corporate responsibility and a growing consumer need of sustainable solutions. The automotive, electronics, and machinery industries are good examples of industries that have successfully used the remanufacturing and refurbishment process, demonstrating that they are economically viable and can reduce costs [21]. Implementation of the Internet of Things (IoT) technologies will make it possible to monitor the performance of the products in real time so that the refurbishment strategy can be arranged proactively to increase the lifespan of the products. Selling of remanufactured and reconditioned products should be promoted with a high level of customer interactions and awareness. Companies who communicate well on the environmental and economic advantages of their sustainable products are also able to increase market share and brand recognition as consumers are increasingly concerned about eco-conscious decisions. The promotion of demand in this expanding industry requires education of consumers on the benefits of remanufactured products, including saving money and impact on the environment [48].

More and more, the role of refurbishment and remanufacturing as regulatory frameworks is beginning to be appreciated as a critical component of sustainable manufacturing practices. To promote the principles of the circular economy, governments are pursuing policies to motivate enterprises to consider refurbishing and remanufacturing processes to reduce waste and increase efficiency of their resources, which will be able to help the shift toward a more sustainable manufacturing ecosystem. Sustainable manufacturing requires remanufacturing, product refurbishment as key aspects of the circular economy. Increasing product life cycles and decreasing waste, these approaches align with the global efforts to curb environmental impact and resource conservation. However, there are still obstacles that need to be addressed to ensure that they are widely implemented. Through innovation, customer engagement, and enabling legislative environments, industries will be able to use the remanufacturing and refurbishing potential to create more sustainable goods [38]. Besides environmental and economic gains, remanufacturing and refurbishment increase the integrity of supply chains and create jobs on a regional level. They minimized the use of new materials, thus making the supply networks less vulnerable to the geopolitical shocks or raw materials deficiencies. At the same time, these processes contribute to the formation of local jobs in the field of reverse logistics, quality control, disassembly, and testing. The principles of the circular economy and its focus on resource and waste reduction, as well as overall sustainability, are deeply embedded in the methods of remanufacturing and refurbishment. A digital change is essential, which makes it easier to track products and predictive maintenance and optimize processes using data. By applying concepts of the circular economy in the manufacturing sector, the industry will encourage the development of innovation and allow companies to meet the emerging regulatory and consumer pressure of sustainability [8].

5.2 Objectives

1. To prolong product lifespan by enabling the reuse and continued functionality of existing components through remanufacturing and refurbishment processes.
2. To mitigate environmental effects by reducing waste generation, minimizing resource extraction, and lowering emissions associated with traditional manufacturing.
3. To reduce production expenses through cost-effective recovery and reuse of materials, thereby decreasing the need for new raw materials and lowering overall manufacturing costs.
4. To improve resource efficiency by maximizing the use of existing materials and components, aligning with the principles of a circular economy and minimizing material losses.

5.3 Definition of Remanufacturing and Refurbishment

Remanufacturing and refurbishment, although frequently conflated, are different processes characterized by differing objectives, operational scopes, technological complexities, and quality results as summarized in Table 5.1. Both solutions are essential for attaining circular economy objectives by prolonging product lifespans and reducing waste. Nonetheless, comprehending their functional, technological, and commercial distinctions is essential for manufacturers, legislators, and consumers in establishing efficient recovery and reuse systems. Remanufacturing is a systematic, standardized industrial procedure designed to restore used or degraded

Table 5.1 A comparative summary highlighting the key distinctions between remanufacturing and refurbishment.

Aspect	**Remanufacturing**	**Refurbishment**
Objective	Restore product to 'like-new' performance	Improve condition and usability
Process depth	Complete disassembly, inspection, and rebuild	Partial repair, cleaning, and reconfiguration
Part replacement	Critical and worn parts are replaced with new or equivalent	Only visibly or functionally defective parts may be replaced
Standards and certification	Meets or exceeds OEM specifications; often certified	No uniform technical standards; variable quality
Testing	Comprehensive functional and performance testing	Basic operational or visual checks
Warranty	Often carries same warranty as new product	Limited or no warranty depending on the provider
Output quality	Functionally equivalent to new	Better than used, but not "as new"
Automation and standardization	Highly standardized, suitable for automation	Often manual, nonstandardized
Examples	Remanufactured engines, jet turbines, industrial gearboxes	Refurbished laptops, mobile phones, medical monitors
Common industries	Aerospace, automotive, heavy equipment, healthcare	Electronics, furniture, appliances, IT equipment
Environmental impact	High resource and energy savings; long life cycle	Moderate environmental benefits; short- to medium-term use

products to a condition comparable to new or even enhanced, frequently accompanied by a complete warranty. It entails total disassembly, examination, substitution of essential components, reassembly, and thorough testing. Refurbishment denotes a partial or cosmetic restoration process aimed at enhancing a product's functionality, aesthetics, or resale value, generally without complete disassembly or total component replacement. It is less stringent than remanufacturing and may not satisfy the same technical or warranty criteria [38].

5.4 Core Processes in Remanufacturing

The goal of remanufacturing and refurbishment is to make used or broken materials workable or new-like manner. This is done through a series of planned, interconnected steps. The goal of these processes is to get the most value out of existing goods while causing the least amount of damage to the environment and waste. The success of remanufacturing and repair depends on the smooth running of these main steps, from collecting used items to sending them out again after being put back together and checked for quality. Companies can make backward logistics easier in a number of ways, such as:

1. **Incentivized returns**: Customers are more likely to return used items if they are offered benefits such as discounts or trade-in credits.
2. **Collection points**: Giving customers a place to drop off their things makes it easier for them to return them.
3. **Partnerships**: Working together with stores or other groups can make it easier to collect items and reach more people through return programs.

5.4.1 Collection and Reverse Logistics

The remanufacturing cycle begins with a systematically collection of end-of-life or used products, which are commonly referred to as cores. Extended producer responsibility schemes mandated by government policy may require consumers to return these cores through trade-in programs or collection. The primary collection procedure is facilitated by reverse logistics, a specialized supply chain system that operates in the opposite direction of conventional product flows [5]. Unlike traditional logistics, which transports finished goods from manufacturers to consumers, reverse logistics focuses on returning discarded goods from consumers to processing

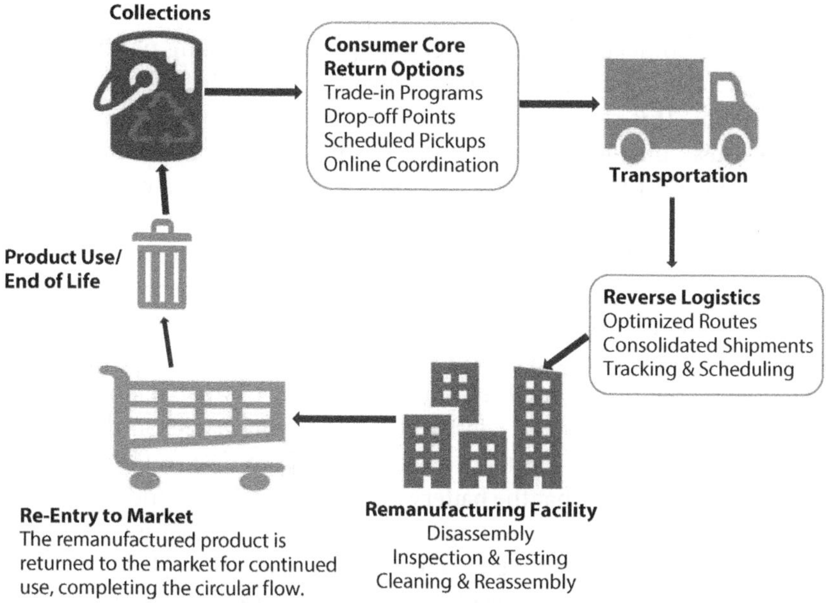

Figure 5.1 Schematic representation of the collection and reverse logistics process in remanufacturing systems, showing product return pathways, reverse logistics operations, remanufacturing stages, and re-entry into the market within a circular economy framework.

facilities. This reverse flow is critical for ensuring a regular supply of cores, which are the major raw materials for remanufacturing. As a result, developing effective and sustainable reverse logistics systems is critical to the success of any remanufacturing company. These systems often incorporate drop-off stations, scheduled collections, and online coordination platforms to help with return handling. Furthermore, to reduce transportation emissions and costs, reverse logistics solutions are carefully designed with sustainability in mind, including route optimization and consolidated shipping methods. The effectiveness of this first step, which sets the tone for the entire remanufacturing process, has an impact on timelines, costs, and resource usage [32]. An overview of the collection and reverse logistics process is illustrated in Figure 5.1.

5.4.2 Inspection and Sorting

This step is instrumental because it identifies whether every item gathered could be reused in the form of materials, remanufactured, reconditioned, or disposed of. The inspection process typically begins by the visual examination of the external state of the product. Every unit is examined by trained technicians or automated equipment regarding physical signs of wear, including cracks, warping, rust, abrasion, distortion, and lost components. This step is essential because it will help to instantly filter out obviously unsuitable goods and put units that may need additional investigation on the radar. They can also be visually inspected to identify any form of manipulation, as well as past repair, and severe wear-and-tear, which may affect the viability of the product to be remanufactured. Surface-level damage can be spotted visually, but often internal or subsurface issues are not revealed. Consequently, nondestructive testing (NDT) methods are used to gain a clearer knowledge on structural and functional integrity without destroying the component. Some of these methods are as follows: Functional tests can consist of the following based on the type of product performed on: Electrical testing is done to ensure that electrical devices are connected, that the battery has enough lifespan, and the devices are functioning. Mechanical testing is undertaken to test the functionality of parts under stress and load, e.g., in engines or in machinery [17].

The functional performance of a product is analyzed by the use of diagnostic tools after it has been physically and structurally tested. Diagnostic software can be connected to electronic control units to confirm data processing, signal output, and error codes. Likewise hydraulic systems can be pressure tested, and motors can be loaded to check power output, vibration, and thermal characteristics. Functional testing is used to verify that a component or product is able to perform the intended functionality within the operating parameters that have been established. In other situations, the benchmarks of the original manufacturer are used to test whether the reconditioned equipment meets the required specifications. Passing units may then move on to cleaning, repair, and reassembly. The ones that fail can be dismantled to retrieve useful components or can be recycled [6]. After the inspection and testing process, the products are categorized based on their condition and their remanufacturing possibility. These groups frequently contain the following: can be fully remanufactured, can be slightly refurbished or repaired, harvesting of components (useable only components), recycling of materials (e.g., metals, plastics), and non-recoverable (ethical disposal required). All inspection and testing records are also stored in a central database to be traceable, quality controlled, and compliant. This recordkeeping proves crucial in controlled industries such as aerospace, automobiles, and healthcare. It can also be used to make data-driven decisions, warranties, and life-cycle management. This is to see that only viable objects go to the next stage. The sorting process helps to minimize waste, avoid unnecessary labor, and make the most out of available assets.

To achieve these objectives effectively, a number of best practices in inspection and collection have been put in place, such as the following:

1. **Standardized procedures**: It is important to specify collecting and inspection rules so as to increase efficiency and consistency. All the members of staff involved in such activities should be provided with information concerning the design and use of standard operating procedures (SOPs).
2. **Training programs**: Training programs should be undertaken regularly to ensure that the employees involved in collection and inspection have the skills and knowledge needed to carry out their work effectively.
3. **Data management systems**: With the installation of reliable data management systems, it is possible to trace the number of returned goods and inspection outcomes. This knowledge can be applied in the process of strategic decision-making, as well as in the process of ongoing development.
4. **Customer engagement**: The customer involvement in the collection programs can be increased by informing the customers about the advantages of returning used products. Good communication approaches can present a feeling of responsibility and sustainability of the customers.

5.4.3 Disassembly

Having been checked and sorted, the products that can be remanufactured are dismantled. Taking a product to pieces is known as disassembly, which is the meticulous deconstruction of a product into its separate parts to allow a product to be fully cleaned, repaired, or replaced. This may be a labor-intensive and careful process, particularly in cases where the components are delicate or tightly connected together or were not designed to be reused in the first place. When the reusable parts are prone to the destruction by the human judgment and care, manual disassembly is generally used. Specialized hand tools may also be used by technicians, and they should follow elaborate disassembly procedures. The automated disassembly machines using robotic arms, conveyor, and machine vision are becoming increasingly popular in performing high-volume operations with standardized products. In most of the facilities, there are hybrid systems that involve the use of manual finesse and speed of automation to improve efficiency and safety. The concepts of design for disassembly are becoming more significant in the contemporary product development.

Future disassembly products facilitate quicker, safer, and less expensive recovery of parts during the reprocessing of the product [16]. The importance of disassembly involves the following:

1. **Resource recovery**: With disassembly, it is possible to recover valuable parts (circuit boards and batteries) to reuse or recycle, and so save materials and minimize waste.
2. **Quality assurance**: It allows the adequate inspection and analysis of single items, which ensures that only feasible parts proceed to the next phase of remanufacturing and therefore does not compromise product quality.
3. **Cost efficiency**: Disassembly will reduce the necessity to purchase new components, by recycling recovered components, reduce the cost of production and disposal, and increase economic sustainability.

5.4.4 Cleaning

Once dismantled, all the components that are to be reused are washed. It should be cleaned not only on a cosmetic basis, but also to avoid the interference of impurities including oil, dust, rust, or biological residues with the performance, dependability, or safety of the product. Cleaning operations can differ depending on the character of the contamination, as well as the kind of component. Manual cleaning involves the procedure of rubbing or wiping parts using solvents or cleaning chemicals. The ultrasonic cleaning applies to the parts with complex geometry or delicate structures, and in this technique, high-frequency sound waves in a liquid bath are used to remove particles trapped in small crevices [12]. High-pressure chemical or steam cleaning can be used to clean industrial items to eliminate tenacious filth or scale. After cleaning, components are reinspected again to assure cleanliness. In certain industries, e.g. healthcare or food production, sterilization might be mandatory to comply with regulatory requirements. Clean parts are then prepared in the next stage, which is repair or replacement.

Cleaning may be done using the following:

1. **Manual cleaning**: Manual cleaning is the process of removing pollutants with hand tools and cleaning solutions. This method is commonly used for complex items that require delicate handling. Manual cleaning provides for more focused attention to specific areas, making it ideal for fragile components. However, this procedure can be laborious and time-consuming.

2. **Automated cleaning**: Automated cleaning systems use technology to do cleaning tasks such as ultrasonic cleaning, spray washing, and vapor degreasing. These solutions enhance cleaning efficiency and consistency by removing human error and increasing throughput [24]. Automated cleaning is particularly beneficial in high-volume industrial environments where speed and efficiency are important.
3. **Chemical cleaning**: Chemical cleaning is the use of solvents, detergents, or other cleaning agents to dissolve and eliminate pollutants. This method is important in breaking down tough residues such as grease and oils. However, cleaning solutions are carefully selected to avoid harming components or leaving dangerous residues.

5.4.5 Repair and Replacement

At this phase, the condition of each component determines whether it can be repaired or replaced. Repair is the process of restoring functionality to defective or broken components. The repair and replacement process are a critical phase in the remanufacturing and maintenance cycle, focused on restoring the functionality and reliability of a defective component. It begins with a comprehensive assessment of the component's condition to determine the extent of damage or wear. This step typically involves visual inspections, NDT methods, and operational checks to identify whether the component can be salvaged. Following the assessment, a diagnostic analysis is conducted to pinpoint specific defects, such as structural cracks, electrical failures, or surface degradation. Accurate diagnostics are essential for making an informed decision on the next course of action. Based on the results, a decision is made whether to repair or replace the part. This choice is influenced by cost–benefit analysis, safety implications, component availability, and the criticality of the part within the larger system. In sectors such as aerospace or automotive safety systems, replacement is often prioritized due to high reliability standards. If the component is deemed repairable, technicians perform targeted repair operations, such as soldering electronic circuits, remachining worn surfaces, recalibrating mechanisms, or reinforcing weak areas. Conversely, if the component is irreparable or unreliable, it is replaced with a new or certified remanufactured part sourced from original equipment manufacturers (OEMs) or trusted suppliers. In some cases, upgraded components may be used to enhance performance or extend the product's service life. Once repaired or replaced, the component undergoes rigorous quality control and functional testing to ensure it meets required standards for performance, safety, and durability. This includes load testing, system integration, and inspection under operational conditions. Finally, the entire process is documented, capturing details such as the nature of the fault, method of correction, technician involved, and serial numbers of replaced parts. This documentation ensures traceability, supports future maintenance, and aligns with industry regulations and warranty requirements.

Figure 5.2 illustrates the repair and replacement workflow in remanufacturing. The process begins with component condition assessment, followed by diagnostic analysis to identify faults. Based on technical feasibility, safety requirements, and cost considerations, a decision is made to either repair or replace the component. The selected action is implemented, after which the component undergoes quality control and functional testing. Finally, all actions are documented to ensure traceability and compliance with industry standards.

The following are some repair and replacement techniques commonly used:

1. **Manual repair**: Manual repair entails experienced technicians diagnosing and repairing product defects. This method is frequently used for complicated items, such as electronics

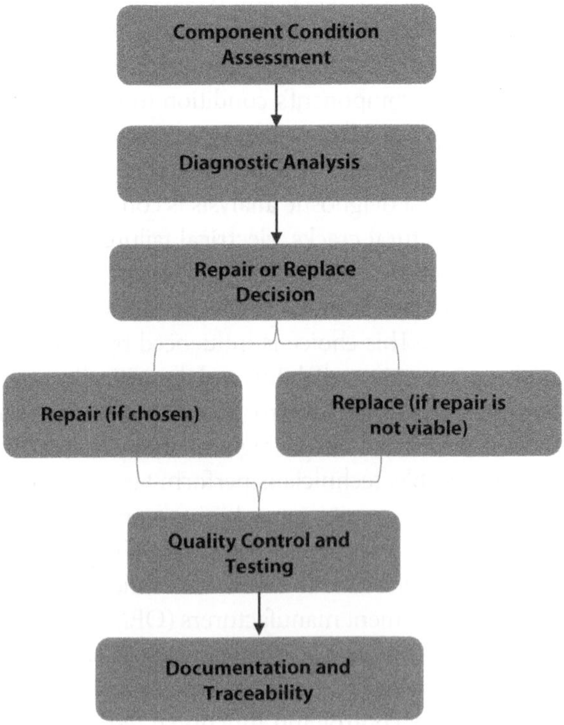

Figure 5.2 Repair and replacement flowchart.

and equipment, which required deep knowledge and specialized abilities. Manual repairs provide extensive inspections and customized solutions, but they can be time-consuming and labor-intensive.

2. **Automated repair systems**: As technology advances, automatic repair systems become more prevalent. These systems combine robotics and artificial intelligence (AI) to perform repairs, resulting in greater efficiency and uniformity. Automated solutions can minimize human mistake and speed up repair times, making them suitable for high-volume environments.
3. **Replacement parts**: When repair is neither possible or cost-effective, replacement parts are utilized to restore function. Manufacturers frequently offer standardized replacement parts designed to fit certain products, ensuring compatibility and functionality. This is especially common in industries such as automotive, where components might wear out over time and need to be replaced.

5.4.6 Reassembly

Once the components are clean and functional, technicians start reassembling the product. Usually, reassembly is done carefully to guarantee that every part is precisely aligned, firmly secured, and compatible. Errors at this stage could cause product faults and jeopardize the entire remanufacturing process. Depending on how complex the product is, reassembly can be done automatically or by hand. When it comes to complex or customized gadgets that require specialized work, manual reassembly is commonly used. Automated reassembly is used in large-scale processes where precision and speed are essential. To help employees along the way, assembly lines may make use of augmented reality systems, torque-control devices, and programmable logic controllers. Every reassembled product is put through validation procedures before final testing [35]. To ensure traceability and compliance with quality assurance procedures, accurate documentation is kept up to date. Reassembly techniques include the following:

1. **Manual reassembly**: Manual reassembly requires skilled personnel to manually put the parts together. This method works especially well for intricate items that need accuracy and close attention to detail, such electronic devices and machinery. By checking the state of each component during reassembly, technicians can make sure that only high-quality

parts are utilized. However, reassembly by hand can be labor-intensive and time-consuming.

2. **Automated reassembly**: In contrast, automated reassembly uses robotics and machines to complete assembly duties. Automated methods can improve efficiency by enhancing the speed and consistency of reassembly. These technologies are especially effective in high-volume manufacturing scenarios where standardization and quick turnaround are required. However, the initial investment in automation technologies may be large [14].

Table 5.2 Reassembly process comparison table.

Process	Description	Importance	Challenges	Best practices
Manual reassembly	Requires skilled personnel to manually assemble components, ideal for intricate items requiring precision, such as electronics and machinery	Allows detailed inspection during assembly, ensuring high-quality parts and precision fitting	Labor-intensive and time-consuming; relies heavily on skilled labor availability	Uses skilled technicians, standardizes reassembly procedures, ensures regular training
Automated reassembly	Uses robotics and machines for assembly; enhances speed and consistency; suited for high-volume, standardized manufacturing environments	Improves efficiency and consistency in repetitive tasks, reduces human error in large-scale operations	High initial investment; may lack flexibility for complex, nonstandard tasks	Invest in adaptable automation systems, perform regular maintenance, and frequent calibration
Hybrid methods	Combines manual and automated methods; simple tasks are automated, whereas complex tasks are handled by skilled personnel	Optimizes labor and technology use, increasing productivity while maintaining flexibility and quality control	Requires careful coordination; potential for integration issues between manual and automated systems	Defines clear task division, uses interface tools for coordination, and continuously evaluates workflow efficiency

3. **Hybrid methods**: Many businesses use hybrid systems that mix manual and automated reassembly techniques. Automated systems, for example, can handle simple, repetitive activities, whereas expert personnel can focus on intricate assembly issues. This strategy takes advantage of the characteristics of both methods, increasing overall efficiency and ensuring high-quality outcomes [18]. A comparison of reassembly methods is provided in Table 5.2.

5.4.7 Testing and Quality Control

Before a product is reintroduced into the market, a remanufactured or refurbished product has been heavily tested and controlled in terms of quality. This phase makes sure that the product will perform the same or more than the performance specification of the original product. Testing can be done in terms of operational testing in normal conditions, stress testing in extreme ones, and accuracy and precision calibration. NDT is reexamined where structural integrity is required but not by disassembly. Firmware updates and software compatibility are also tested in the case of electronic equipment. Any test results are noted down, and only those products, which meet the internal and regulatory standards, are accepted to be distributed. This can be done by use of ISO 9001 or Six Sigma processes to guarantee process consistency and continuous improvement [3]. Important are the testing and quality assurance as it entails,

1. **Assuring product reliability**: Testing will be essential in ensuring the reliability of the reconditioned products and remanufactured products. Through large-scale testing, manufacturers are able to identify defects and also ensure that their products will perform well in varying circumstances. Trustful goods do not only make clients happier, but also ensure brand loyalty and trust [40].
2. **Quality assurance methods**: Quality assurance methods are used to guarantee that products meet the industry regulations and standards. The nature of most industries such as aerospace, healthcare, or automotive industry demands compliance with safety and quality requirements. Quality assurance and testing help companies achieve these requirements, minimize the risk of legal issues and enhance the brand [1].
3. **Cost efficiency**: A good testing and quality assurance system may help save money by minimizing product failure and

recall. When the flaws are detected at the initial stage of the remanufacturing process, companies will avoid incurring expensive repairs and damage of the brand. Such a strategic approach encourages the culture of constant development.

The testing process plays a significant role in the remanufacturing/refurbishing process because it proves the operation, reliability, and safety of items recovered and released into the market again [40]. Different testing method as summarized in Figure 5.3 are applied according to the type of product, industry standards, and the intended use. Such processes can be as simple as following visual transfers to more complex NDT and performance appraisals. This is to ensure that every part or full unit is up to or exceeding performance requirements and within regulatory limits. These are the general testing processes that are typically used during remanufacturing.

1. **Functional testing**: This is the simplest and most vital in that the product or component is tested to ensure that it is functioning its intended purpose within the normal operating range. Considering the example of turning on an electronic device or the working of a motor with an average load [46].
2. **Performance testing**: The product is subjected to simulated or real working conditions to test the efficiency of products, output, durability and responsiveness. This involves load tests, endurance tests, and speed/throughput tests.

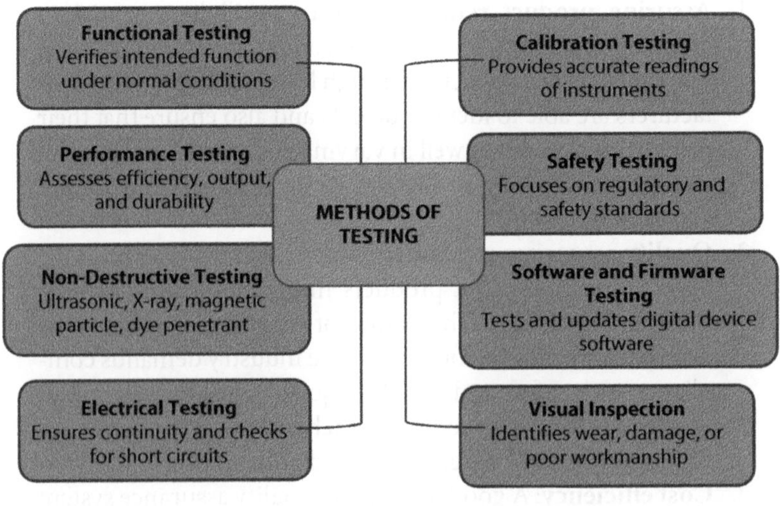

Figure 5.3 Testing and quality control processes in remanufacturing and refurbishing.

3. **NDT**: The NDT technologies enable nondestructive inspection of the component. Widely used methods of NDT are as follows: Ultrasonic testing is a method that utilizes sound waves of high frequency to locate internal defects. X-ray or radiographic testing is a visualization technique of internal structures and defects. Surface and near subsurface discontinuities in ferromagnetic materials are detected by magnetic particle testing. Dye penetrant testing reveals cracks and porosity on the surface [22].
4. **Electrical testing**: This is used on electrical circuit components to test continuity, insulation resistance, and the lack of short circuits, typically of electronics and electrical appliance remanufacturing.
5. **Calibration testing**: Tests the instruments and measuring tools to ensure that they give accurate measurements. This is essential in the process of remanufacturing medical equipment, pressure gauges, or industrial control tools.
6. **Safety testing**: It is concerned with the compliance of the refurbished product to regulatory and safety standards. Examples are as follows: electric insulation and grounding tests of appliances, fluid-handling system pressure and leak tests, and consumer product sharp edge and fire test.
7. **Software and firmware testing**: In the case of remanufactured digital equipment, testing should include software/firmware reinstallation/reupdating, and verification of user interface responsiveness, system stability, and compatibility with peripheral equipment.
8. **Visual inspection**: Visual testing is a mandatory procedure, nonetheless rudimentary. Researchers inspect those indicators of wear, corrosion, damage, or bad workmanship that may compromise reliability or looks.

5.4.8 Finishing and Packaging

The last process in product preparation is finishing, which is done after the product is ready to be released into the market. It can be used as a functional and aesthetic item. Such surface treatments as polishing, powder coating, painting, and anodizing are designed to enhance durability and esthetic appeal. Branding strategies such as logos, labels, and compliance certifications are reused to suit the initial standard. Packaging has no other purpose but to ensure the safety of delivered goods in transit and storage but also serve as a manifestation of the quality of the product brand and its sustainability [5]. Environmentally friendly packaging materials, e.g., recyclable and biodegradable, are becoming more and more widespread and used to reduce the impact on the environment. To be a full-fledged professional customer experience, the device is supplied with instructions manuals, warranty information, and product registration documentation. The way in which goods are packaged varies depending on the product and the market the product is aimed at. Common types of packaging would be:

1. **Protective packaging**: Foam, bubble wrap, and molded pulp are regarded as protective materials that cushion the goods and minimize their damages during transportation.
2. **Shrink wrapping**: This technique is used to package goods in a plastic film, which is shrunk to a tight-fitting layering, which ensures a tamper-evident seal and protection against dust and moist air.
3. **Retail packaging**: Retail packaging is used to make the products visible in the shelves and to provide vital information to the customers.

It is good to set up and follow SOPs to have consistency in the process of testing and quality assurance. SOPs give strict guidelines to each stage of the review process and ensure that all are trained and subjected to the same standards [45]. The testing results and quality assurance procedures should be documented accurately and accounted for and traced. Detailed documentation assists in the recognition of trends in the performance of the products and supports the work toward the continuous enhancement. Additionally, paperwork in most instances is vital in matters of regulation. It is important to create a culture of continuous improvement so that it can improve the process of testing and quality assurance. Companies should also continuously review their operations, obtain feedback, and undergo employee training to keep up with the changing technologies and industry standards. The importance of getting things done contains the following:

1. **Quality improvement**: Finishing, such as painting, polishing, and coating the surface, improves the aesthetic appeal of the surface and surface quality of the remanufactured products. These additions renew or uplift the product aesthetics, making it more attractive and competitive in the market.

2. **Damage protection finishing**: Finishing provides a protective coating to prevent the corrosion, wear, and environmental degradation. This increases the longevity of the components and, in particular, metallic parts through avoiding rust and surface corrosion.
3. **Brand perception**: The professionalism and perceived value of the product are strengthened through a high-quality finish, which has a positive impact on customer confidence and brand image. In such industries as automotive and electronics, excellent finishing is a direct contribution to customer satisfaction and their buying.

5.4.9 Distribution

The last activity in remanufacturing process is distribution. This involves delivery of the completed product to the clients either directly or indirectly. Direct distribution involves retail storefronts and e-commerce platforms owned by the company and gives the producer control over the sales process, as well as it enables the producer to deal directly with the customer. An example of an indirect channel of distribution includes wholesalers, third-party sellers, and Internet market places. Warehousing, order fulfillment, and transportation are also included in logistics of distribution. Modernized logistics systems enhance the delivery path, decrease the time of shipping goods, and decrease emissions [23]. Also, strategies such as reverse logistics are embedded in distribution strategies to address product returns, warranties and remanufacturing cycles thereof. The effective and sustainable distribution system is associated with timely delivery as well as enhances customer satisfaction and reflects to the circular economy by maintaining the value loop of the product. Distribution is important and involves the following:

1. **Availability of the market**: Proper distribution chains are necessary to make remanufactured products reach many consumers. Organizations facilitate sustainability objectives through access and encouragement of the utilization of used goods instead of new ones [4].
2. **Cost efficiency**: A lean distribution process will reduce the cost of logistics by optimizing routes, consolidating shipments, and using the most economical transportation options. Such savings may be transferred to customers,, and

remanufactured products may be even more competitive in terms of prices [28].

3. **Customer satisfaction**: The satisfaction of customer is largely dependent on the distribution process. Timely delivery and good conditions guarantee that products are received in a good state, hence enhancing satisfaction, loyalty, and good reviews [31].

Table 5.3 describes the key steps of the remanufacturing process and highlights their fundamental functions, strategic significance, frequent challenges, and potential recommendations to follow. This methodological survey presents a viable model when it comes to defining the role of every process toward the general effectiveness, sustainability, and quality of remanufactured products.

Table 5.3 Summary of core remanufacturing processes: functions, challenges, and best practices.

Process	Description	Importance	Challenges	Best practices
Collection and reverse logistics	Gathering used products (cores)	Ensures reusable parts availability	High logistics cost, coordination	Retailer partnerships, return incentives
Disassembly	Dismantling into components	Identifies reusable elements	Complex/nonmodular designs	Design for disassembly
Inspection and sorting	Evaluate component quality	Decide repair feasibility	Subjective evaluations	Automated diagnostics
Cleaning and reprocessing	Remove contaminants	Prepare for reuse	Chemical waste	Eco-friendly cleaning agents
Component replacement and reassembly	Replace parts and rebuild	Restore function	Compatibility issues	OEM part use
Testing and quality control	Verify performance	Ensure trust and standards	Cost of equipment	Automated testing and logging

5.5 Applications of Remanufacturing in Key Industries

Remanufacturing has gained traction across various sectors due to its ability to reduce costs, conserve resources, and meet sustainability targets. Below are key industries actively implementing remanufacturing practices.

5.5.1 Automotive Industry

The automobile industry is a key focus for remanufacturing, with worldwide companies such as Caterpillar, Cummins, and Volvo spearheading efforts to restore engines, brake systems, and drivetrains. These companies have adopted remanufacturing not merely as a cost-cutting approach, but also as a commitment to sustainability. Core components are recovered, inspected for wear and structural integrity, and then restored to OEM specs using advanced machining and testing technology. This has been extremely useful in extending vehicle life cycles and reducing environmental impact, particularly in fleet maintenance and heavy-duty vehicles [41].

5.5.2 Aerospace and Defense

In the aerospace and defense industries, remanufacturing high-value components is important for reducing cost and operational reliability. Boeing and GE Aviation specialize in refurbishing turbine blades, landing gear, and avionics equipment. Given the industry's demanding safety and performance standards, remanufactured parts are subjected to comprehensive NDT, precision engineering, and tight regulatory compliance [36].

5.5.3 Consumer Electronics

Apple and Dell have authorized refurbishment programs for smartphones, tablets, and computers. Devices returned for warranty or trade-in purposes are dismantled, tested, repaired, and packed for resale. These programs drastically reduce e-waste while also providing more inexpensive options for customers, especially in price-sensitive markets [33].

5.5.4 Industrial Machinery

Industrial firms such as Siemens and ABB remanufacture electric motors, gear systems, and control units used in manufacturing and automation. These components are critical for plant uptime and performance. By refurbishing such parts, companies can reduce procurement lead times, control costs, and decrease the environmental impact of new production [34].

5.5.5 Healthcare

In the healthcare sector, companies such as Philips and Siemens Healthineers refurbish diagnostic imaging systems, including magnetic resonance imaging (MRI) and computed tomography (CT) scanners. The refurbishment of medical equipment is done under strict hygiene, quality control, and regulatory oversight to ensure patient safety. These remanufactured devices provide lower-cost access to cutting-edge technology in underresourced healthcare settings [43].

5.5.6 Energy Sector

The goal of remanufacturing in the energy sector is to increase the lifespan of solar panels, wind turbine parts, and energy storage devices such as batteries. The functionality of these technologies can be restored or even improved through remanufacturing, as they frequently deteriorate with time. By increasing clean energy systems' sustainability and cost-effectiveness, this strategy aids in the switch to renewable energy [9]. Table 5.4 summarizes these industry applications, including examples, key products, benefits, and challenges.

5.6 Economic and Environmental Impacts of Remanufacturing

Remanufacturing provides considerable economic and environmental advantages; thus, it is a part of the circular economy strategies.

5.6.1 Cost Efficiency

Remanufacturing is also very cost-effective, typically saving the company 40% to 60% of the cost of production compared to using raw materials to produce products. The reuse of the available components and the decrease in the necessity of the new resources are the key factors contributing to it. Moreover, research has revealed that as many as 85% of the materials used during the manufacture of the original product can be recycled so as to help in saving on resources. This will save resources and energy because remanufactured products consume 60% to 90% less energy than new manufactured products. All these factors interact to decrease carbon emissions and promote environmental goals in the world [30].

5.6.2 Material Conservation

Remanufacturing gives an opportunity to reuse as much as 85% of the original product materials. Instead of discarding used items, precious resources such as metals, polymers, and electronic parts are stored and recycled. This greatly decreases the need to require new resources and minimizes the environmental harm that mining and extraction operations would create [11].

Table 5.4 Industry applications of remanufacturing.

Industry	Examples	Key remanufactured products	Benefits	Challenges
Automotive	Caterpillar, Cummins, Volvo	Engines, brake systems, transmissions	Cost savings, reduced emissions, extended vehicle life	Component wear variability, consumer trust, logistics complexity
Aerospace and defense	Boeing, GE Aviation	Avionics systems, turbine components	Lower maintenance costs, operational reliability, compliance with safety standards	Stringent safety regulations, precision requirements, certification
Consumer electronics	Apple, Dell	Smartphones, laptops, tablets	Reduced e-waste, affordable devices, increased accessibility	Data wiping, software updates, consumer skepticism
Industrial machinery	Siemens, ABB	Electric motors, control systems	Decreased downtime, improved resource efficiency	Custom part handling, system integration issues
Healthcare	Philips, Siemens Healthineers	Imaging devices (MRI, CT scanners)	Cost-effective diagnostics, increased access to advanced healthcare equipment	Regulatory compliance, sanitization, high-tech component reliability
Energy sector	Wind turbines, batteries, solar panels	Energy storage systems, turbine blades	Extended lifespan of renewable infrastructure, improved sustainability	Component degradation, technical requalification, storage challenges

5.6.3 Energy Savings

Remanufacturing maintains the fundamental form of goods; processes such as smelting and molding are not involved, leading to a 60% to 90% use of energy compared to the normal manufacturing. This assists in attaining carbon neutrality targets particularly in energy-intensive sectors [26].

5.6.4 Carbon Emissions Reduction

Recycling and conservation of energy would save a lot of carbon. It has been shown that remanufactured products have the potential to reduce CO_2 emissions by up to 87%. Besides assisting the industries in complying with environmental rules, the reduction has an advantage in global climate objectives [29].

5.6.5 Waste Minimization

Remanufacturing saves much garbage that would be found in the landfills, and it does not need hazardous waste disposal. Instead of going to waste management facilities, components would be reused elsewhere, decreasing the strain on waste management systems [25].

5.7 Problems and Issues of Remanufacturing

Although it has the advantages, remanufacturing is associated with a number of operational and market-related challenges:

1. **Irregular product quality and availability**: Product quality and availability of cores returned may be inconsistent, and this may influence production schedules and the end result.
2. **Technological gaps**: Some remanufacturers do not have access to the latest technologies such as automation, AI-based sorting, and robotics, which reduces efficiency.
3. **Consumer skepticism**: There are customers who feel that products that have been remanufactured are inferior, although they have been shown to be equally effective or even more so.
4. **Regulatory fragmentation**: The legal definitions, standards, and labeling requirements differ across the nations, and this makes global remanufacturing activities more complicated.

These issues need concerted efforts in standardization of policies, education of the masses, and investment in technology to deal with them.

5.8 Best Practices of an Efficient Remanufacturing

An effective distribution system during remanufacturing aligns with the environmental sustainability objectives by the following:

1. Lessening the emissions of long-haul shipping by cutting down carbon footprints by local transport paths.
2. Waste can be minimized using solutions such as product returns and end-of-life item take-back programs as part of the solutions called reverse logistics.
3. Offering inexpensive environmentally sound technologies and equipment to push the consumers to sustainable decisions.

5.9 Effective Distribution in Remanufacturing: Examples and Sustainability Integration

Distribution system in remanufacturing does not only enhance efficiency in operations but also correlates with the objective of environmental sustainability by the following:

1. Regionalized and centralized transport paths may decrease carbon footprints and lower long-distance shipping carbon emissions.
2. Minimizing waste by use of reverse logistics such as product returns and end-of-life take-back programs.
3. Greater availability of inexpensive and eco-friendly technology and equipment may motivate consumers to be more sustainability-focused.

5.10 Linkage with Sustainability Goals

A good distribution system in remanufacturing enhances efficiency in operation besides complying with the environment sustainability strategic objectives by the following:

1. The use of localized routes of transport and consolidated routes can help curb carbon footprints and reduce shipping long distances emissions.
2. Eliminating waste by implementing reverse logistics strategies such as product returns, end-of-life take-back programs.

3. Consumers can be motivated to make sustainable decisions by increasing their availability of cheap and eco-friendly technologies and equipment.

5.11 Remanufacturing and Digitalization and Artificial Intelligence

Modern technologies and the digital transformation are transforming remanufacturing using digital tools, such as AI, the IoT, digital twins, robotics, and blockchain. These tools improve operational efficiency as well as increase traceability, sustainability, and accuracy at all stages in the remanufacturing process. The following subsections provide a detailed analysis of the role and advantages that are associated with each technology. The integration of these digital technologies, along with their benefits and challenges, is summarized in Table 5.5.

5.11.1 Fault Detection and Predictive Maintenance with AI

Predictive maintenance takes advantage of the past and present data to address equipment issues and to optimize maintenance plans. When applied to remanufacturing, AI algorithms process the data sent back by the returned components (e.g., the number of hours of use, vibration patterns, fluid viscosity) to determine the extent of wear and predict failure. Volvo and Cummins are companies in the automobile remanufacturing industry that are using AI-powered predictive analytics to manage engine telemetry. Such systems are found to identify faults such as overheating, oil wear, or pressure changes before mechanical failure. Hence, only elements proving to be dangerous functionally are selected to be disassembled, whereas useful parts are left unprocessed, and the resource of time and materials is saved. The factors and processes that cause the wear and tear of parts can be correlated with the complexities of usage behavior by machine learning models that have been trained on failure datasets. It will use a neural network to identify individual sensor signatures that predict alternator failures when subjected to high thermal loads. As a result, returned alternators can be sorted in advance at remanufacturing plants with the help of AI-based diagnostics and therefore enhanced efficiency and reliability are achieved [39].

5.11.2 IoT-Enabled Condition Monitoring

IoT enables real-time data acquisition from embedded sensors within industrial equipment, consumer electronics, or automotive components. These

Table 5.5 Integration of digital technologies in remanufacturing: processes, benefits, challenges, and best practices.

Process	Description	Importance	Challenges	Best practices
Predictive maintenance and AI-driven fault detection	Uses AI and machine learning to predict component failures by analyzing operational data such as vibration, temperature, and usage history	Enables early detection of defects, reduces downtime, improves sorting efficiency, and avoids unnecessary rework	Requires large datasets and training models; initial setup cost is high	Develop robust datasets; uses cloud-based diagnostics; combined with expert systems for model accuracy
IoT-enabled condition monitoring	IoT sensors capture real-time operational data (e.g., vibration, torque, heat) from in-service equipment and components	Enables condition-based refurbishment, reduces premature disassembly, and supports preemptive logistics planning	Data overload; hardware and integration costs; cybersecurity risks	Uses edge computing for processing; uses data filtering algorithms; integrates with return forecasting systems
Digital twin technology	Creates virtual replicas of physical systems for simulation, performance testing, and degradation prediction under different conditions	Reduces trial-and-error, improves part salvage accuracy, and supports safety-critical compliance in regulated industries	Requires high-fidelity models; needs real-time data updates; high computational demand	Integrates CAD/CAM systems with IoT data; prioritizes use for high-cost or mission-critical components
Smart disassembly and robotics	Use AI-driven robots and vision systems to disassemble products, recognize components, and automate removal processes	Reduce disassembly time, increase part recovery rates, and prevent damage to delicate components	High setup cost; complex programming for variant handling; product design incompatibility	Adopt design-for-disassembly standards; use hybrid (manual + robotic) lines; apply barcode/ image recognition systems

(Continued)

Table 5.5 Integration of digital technologies in remanufacturing: processes, benefits, challenges, and best practices. (*Continued*)

Process	Description	Importance	Challenges	Best practices
Blockchain for traceability	Records tamper-proof digital histories of components (e.g., service logs, refurbishment stages) accessible by OEMs, customers, and regulators	Ensures product authenticity, prevents counterfeit parts, enhances regulatory compliance, and builds consumer trust	Requires cross-platform standardization; data privacy issues; high latency in some blockchain models	Combines with RFID and IoT tags; uses permissioned blockchain networks; standardizes record formats across stakeholders

sensors measure operational metrics such as vibration, torque, temperature, pressure, and usage cycles. ABB uses IoT-based monitoring in electric motor systems to assess component fatigue, overheating, and energy efficiency. These data help remanufacturing centers prioritize motors for refurbishment, minimizing unnecessary dismantling and enabling condition-based remanufacturing rather than reactive processes [49]. In remanufacturing, condition monitoring through IoT supports two key activities:

1. **Preemptive core collection**: IoT-enabled devices can alert OEMs when a product approaches its end-of-life, streamlining reverse logistics and core acquisition.
2. **Component viability assessment**: Continuous data logging allows remanufacturers to evaluate whether a component has operated within acceptable thresholds. If it has, it may qualify for minor refurbishment rather than full remanufacturing.

5.11.3 Digital Twin Technology

A digital twin is a virtual version of a physical product or system that is constantly updated with real-time operational information. It enables engineers to model behavior, stress situations, and degradation patterns prior to making refurbishment decisions. In aircraft remanufacturing, businesses such as GE Aviation and Rolls-Royce use digital twins of turbine blades and landing gear to mimic heat fatigue, stress fractures, and airflow dynamics. Before physical disassembly begins, AI-enhanced simulations determine whether components are salvageable, need repair, and should be discarded. Digital twins are dynamic digital duplicates of physical components or systems that are constantly updated with sensor and user input. These models support real-time simulation and performance prediction. In the wind energy industry, digital twins of turbine blades may track structural integrity over time, allowing organizations to determine if a blade should be reconditioned, retired, or updated [37].

5.11.4 Smart Disassembly and Robotics

Disassembly is frequently labor-intensive and represents one of the major steps in the remanufacturing cycle. Smart robotic disassembly systems use AI, machine language, and automation to improve dismantle speed and precision. In consumer electronics, for example, corporations such as Apple use robotic arms such as "Liam" and "Daisy" to automate iPhone disassembly. These robots can detect various screw kinds, determine battery positions, and remove fragile components without causing harm, resulting in high component recovery rates. Advanced AI systems can also modify disassembly tactics based on product variants recognized using barcodes or image recognition, allowing them to handle many models in a single workflow. Benefits include reducing disassembly time by over 50%, preventing damage to delicate components, and enabling high-volume, uniform refurbishing production [19].

5.11.5 Blockchain for Traceability

Blockchain technology provides tamper-proof records of component history, which is important in businesses that require stringent traceability and regulatory compliance. In medical device or aerospace remanufacturing, knowing a product's whole lifespan history (e.g., number of refurbishments, sterilization dates, maintenance records) is important. Blockchain provides a secure log for all of these occurrences, which may be shared with parties such as OEMs, regulators, and customers. By combining blockchain with RFID and IoT tags, remanufacturers can ensure component authenticity.

Detection of counterfeit parts and accurate warranty tracking. For example, Philips Healthcare is looking into using blockchain to track CT scanner components during maintenance. Each part has a distinct digital identity that documents disassembly, sterilization, reassembly, and the final testing stages [47].

5.12 Circular Economy Integration in Remanufacturing

Remanufacturing is a critical element of the circular economy, which enables the transformation between the traditional linear paradigm of take–make–dispose to a restorative, regenerative industrial system. It also adopts the main ideas of the circular economy, which is to lengthen the lifespan of products, components, and resources. This part discussed the way certain remanufacturing strategies reinforce and supplement the concepts of the circular economy.

5.12.1 Loop Closed and Reverse Logistics

The collection of abandoned products (cores) to refurbish or remanufacture them is essential to the solution of the loop, which is one of the foundations of circularity. Reverse logistics prevents the dumping of valuable materials because postconsumer products are gathered to be processed into the manufacturing cycle once more, and this is where the business can recover the value of inherent worth. Reverse logistics systems in automotive corporations, such as Renault and Caterpillar, allow central collection of end-of-life engines and components and reuse them as fully warranted items in the market. This will greatly decrease the need of virgin materials and lower emissions that are related to new production [7].

5.12.2 Material Transformation

Raw materials once extracted are then converted through transformation processes to ready inputs in terms of manufacturing. This involves melting, refining, and treatment in form of chemicals. Circular strategies at this level focus on the incorporation of secondary raw materials with those recycled out of end-of-life products, thus lessening energy density and pollution linked with processing of primary materials.

5.12.3 Take Apart and Design Circularly

During the disassembly process, things are broken down to form reusable and recyclable components. It is purposefully consistent with the concepts introduced as the design for disassembly and the design for circularity, which can promote the creation of objects that can be easily assembled and restructured to be used many times. Within the electronic remanufacturing industry, modular design businesses, such as Dell, can be disassembled and have easy access to individual parts (e.g., motherboards, RAM, cooling fans) that can be repaired and updated separately, significantly extending the lifespan of the device and reducing e-waste [27].

5.12.4 Recovery of Components and Looping of Materials

Remanufacturing by methods such as part harvesting makes sure that useful parts of the product are reclaimed and reused again in the process. This encourages looping of materials whereby materials continuously recycle in the economy, instead of turning out to be waste. Components of the imaging devices (e.g., X-ray tubes and control panels) are also frequently requalified and reused when preparing medical equipment. This keeps in place high-value materials such as rare-earth metals and reduces the ecological footprint of making new devices [13].

5.12.5 Cleaning, Reprocessing, and Extension of Life

Remanufacturing is among the best solutions to circular economy as it helps lengthen the life of the product by getting rid of impurities and repairing or replacing the product to create a new one. The less the duration of the product or component, the less its environmental impact is over a life cycle. The cleaning, rewinding, and readjustment of industrial motors can increase operating life by 10 to 15 years, which is two times as much efficient in terms of material and has a lower environmental impact than buying a new case [20].

5.12.6 Circular Flow Packaging and Distribution

Finishing and packaging are also influenced by the ideas of a circular economy, which promotes the application of reusable, recyclable, and biodegradable materials. One form of distribution strategy is the reversed distribution systems where the discarded products are remade. Firms are utilizing more and more closed-loop logistics; i.e., the same supply chain to deliver refurbished devices is utilized to collect cores, reducing transportation-related emissions and increasing the cycle with which products are recycled [15].

5.12.7 Users

The user step takes the center stage when it comes to deciding duration and prospective circular recovery of a product. Circular strategies are even more effective when they are applied responsibly, regularly serviced, and

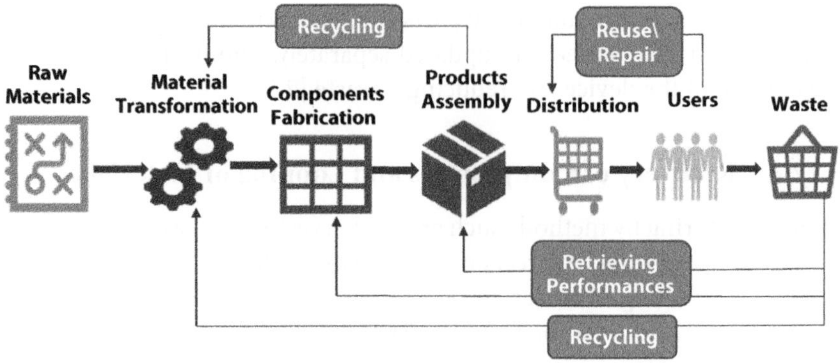

Figure 5.4 Manufacturing and circular economy flowchart.

enrolled in take-back or leasing programs. The data that users create can also be used to make improvements with the design in the future and optimize products.

5.12.8 Waste and Recovery Loops

Instead of considering waste as the dead end, the circular economy considers it as a store of resources. The products returned are sorted into three broad recovery streams:

1. **Reuse and repair**: in which small scale defects are corrected and products are returned to the market.
2. **Retrieving performances**: in which products are functionally reconstructed by means of technical reconditioning.
3. **Recycling**: which involves converting the material and reusing it in previous production.

These loops decrease reliance on landfills and encourage resources efficiency, which is where a regenerative industrial system begins. The overall integration of remanufacturing within the circular economy framework is presented in Figure 5.4.

Conclusion

Remanufacturing and product refurbishment are indispensable for achieving manufacturing sustainability and advancing the circular economy. This chapter has elucidated the critical distinctions and core processes involved in both practices, demonstrating their significant role in prolonging product life cycles, reducing waste, and conserving resources. The economic and environmental benefits are clear, with substantial cost savings, material conservation, and emissions reduction. However, widespread adoption is hindered by challenges such as inconsistent core quality, technological gaps, consumer skepticism, and fragmented regulatory landscapes.

The integration of digital technologies such as AI, IoT, and blockchain presents a transformative opportunity to enhance the efficiency, traceability, and reliability of remanufacturing operations. Future success will depend on strategic investments in these technologies, the development of supportive policy frameworks, and initiatives to boost consumer awareness and trust. Future research should focus on standardizing remanufacturing protocols, optimizing reverse logistics networks, exploring business models that incentivize circularity, and further investigating the socioeconomic impacts of a large-scale shift toward remanufacturing. By addressing these areas, industries can fully leverage the potential of remanufacturing and refurbishment to build a more sustainable and resilient future.

AI disclosure statement: The author acknowledges the use of AI-based tools for minor language editing or grammatical correction. However, all intellectual contributions, analyses, and conclusions presented in this chapter are entirely the author's own.

References

1. Aguilar, F.J., *Managing corporate ethics: Learning from America's ethical companies how to supercharge business*, Oxford University Press, New York, NY, 1994.
2. Alkouh, A., Keddar, K.A., Alatefi, S., Remanufacturing of industrial electronics: A case study from the GCC region. *Electronics*, 12, 9, 1960, 2023, https://doi.org/10.3390/electronics12091960.
3. Alyahya, M., Agag, G., Aliedan, M., Abdelmoety, Z.H., Understanding the factors affecting consumers' behaviour when purchasing refurbished products: A chaordic perspective. *J. Retail. Consum. Serv.*, 75, 103492, 2023, https://doi.org/10.1016/j.jretconser.2023.103492.
4. Barkhi, F., Ahmadi, S., Shokouhyar, S., Filieri, R., Ramezaninia, M., Key drivers and priorities of consumer decisions for refurbished electronics: A mix-method approach. *Heliyon*, 10, 24, e40977, 2024, https://doi.org/10.1016/j.heliyon.2024.e40977.

5. Berssaneti, F.T., Berger, S., Saut, A.M., Vanalle, R.M., Santana, J.C.C., Value generation of remanufactured products: Multi-case study of third-party companies. *Sustainability*, 11, 3, 584, 2019, https://doi.org/10.3390/su11030584.
6. Betancur, J.A., Castillo, A., Ramos, E., Vargas, H., Ochoa, J., Sanchez, C., Diagnostic methodology for vehicles equipped with antilock braking system and electronic stability control. *Discov. Appl. Sci.*, 6, 9, 1–22, 2024, https://doi.org/10.1007/s42452-024-06069-.
7. Butt, A.S., Ali, I., Govindan, K., The role of reverse logistics in a circular economy for achieving sustainable development goals: A multiple case study of retail firms. *Prod. Plann. Control*, 35, 12, 1490–1502, 2024, https://doi.org/10.1080/09537287.2023.2197851.
8. Celestin, M., Impact of global supply chain disruptions on business resilience: Strategies for adapting to pandemics and geopolitical conflicts. Zenodo, 2015, https://doi.org/10.5281/zenodo.13887198.
9. Charles, R.G., Davies, M.L., Douglas, P., Hallin, I.L., Mabbett, I., Sustainable energy storage for solar home systems in rural Sub-Saharan Africa – A comparative examination of lifecycle aspects of battery technologies for circular economy, with emphasis on the South African context. *Energy*, 166, 1207–1215, 2019, https://doi.org/10.1016/j.energy.2018.10.053.
10. Chaudhari, S., Research on remanufacturing process and its impact on the environment. *Int. J. Res. Appl. Sci. Eng. Technol.*, 11, 11, 1621–1630, 2023, https://doi.org/10.22214/ijraset.2023.56567.
11. Chen, L., Yang, M., Chen, Z., Xie, Z., Huang, L., Osman, A.I., Farghali, M., Sandanayake, M., Liu, E., Ahn, Y.H., Al-Muhtaseb, A.H., Rooney, D.W., Yap, P.S., Conversion of waste into sustainable construction materials: A review of recent developments and prospects. *Mater. Today Sustainability*, 27, 100930, 2024, https://doi.org/10.1016/j.mtsust.2024.100930.
12. Chrysalidis, A. and Kyzas, G.Z., Applied cleaning methods of oil residues from industrial tanks. *Processes*, 8, 5, 569, 2020, https://doi.org/10.3390/pr8050569.
13. Ciulli, F., Kolk, A., Boe-Lillegraven, S., Circularity brokers: Digital platform organizations and waste recovery in food supply chains. *J. Bus. Ethics*, 167, 2, 299–331, 2020, https://doi.org/10.1007/s10551-019-04160-5.
14. Davila Delgado, J.M., Oyedele, L., Ajayi, A., Akanbi, L., Akinade, O., Bilal, M., Owolabi, H., Robotics and automated systems in construction: Understanding industry-specific challenges for adoption. *J. Build. Eng.*, 26, 100868, 2019, https://doi.org/10.1016/j.jobe.2019.10086.
15. De Abreu, V.H.S., Da Costa, M.G., Da Costa, V.X., De Assis, T.F., Santos, A.S., D'Agosto, M.deA., The role of the circular economy in road transport to mitigate climate change and reduce resource depletion. *Sustainability*, 14, 14, 8951, 2022, https://doi.org/10.3390/su14148951.
16. Fegade, V., Shrivatsava, R.L., Kale, A.V., Design for remanufacturing: Methods and their approaches. *Mater. Today: Proc.*, 2, 4–5, 1849–1858, 2015, https://doi.org/10.1016/j.matpr.2015.07.130.

17. Gao, C.M., Wong, K.Y., Key factors influencing building components' remanufacturing strategy: A comprehensive literature review. *Buildings*, 15, 6, 934, 2025, https://doi.org/10.3390/buildings15060934.
18. Gao, R.X., Krüger, J., Merklein, M., Möhring, H.C., Váncza, J., Artificial Intelligence in manufacturing: State of the art, perspectives, and future directions. *CIRP Ann.*, 73, 2, 723–749, 2024, https://doi.org/10.1016/j.cirp.2024.04.101.
19. Goli, F., Wang, Y., Saadat, M., Perspective of self-learning robotics for disassembly automation, in: *2022 27th International Conference on Automation and Computing (ICAC)*, IEEE, 2022, https://doi.org/10.1109/ICAC55051.2022.9911085.
20. Haupt, M. and Hellweg, S., Measuring the environmental sustainability of a circular economy. *Environ. Sustainability Indic.*, 1–2, 100005, 2019, https://doi.org/10.1016/j.indic.2019.100005.
21. International Data Corporation (IDC), Deliverable D2.4 First report on facts and figures, 2023.
22. Inês Silva, M., Malitckii, E., Santos, T.G., Vilaça, P., Review of conventional and advanced non-destructive testing techniques for detection and characterization of small-scale defects. *Prog. Mater. Sci.*, 138, 101155, 2023, https://doi.org/10.1016/j.pmatsci.2023.101155.
23. Islam, M.T. and Iyer-Raniga, U., Circular business model value dimension canvas: Tool redesign for innovation and validation through an Australian case study. *Sustainability*, 15, 15, 11553, 2023, https://doi.org/10.3390/su151511553.
24. Kang, M., Kim, J., Kim, H., Ultrasonic cleaning system for removal of oil and grease from metal parts. *J. Mech. Sci.Technol.*, 30, 5, 2321–2327, 2016.
25. Kumar, R., Gupta, G., Hussain, A., Rani, A., Thapliyal, A., Gunsola, D., Chattaraj, S., Ganguly, A., Panneerselvam, P., Guerra-Sierra, B.E., Mitra, D., Pioneering zero-waste technologies utilization and its framework on sustainable management: International, national and state level. *Discov. Appl. Sci.*, 7, 3, 1–30, 2025, https://doi.org/10.1007/s42452-025-06693-z.
26. Liu, T., Chen, L., Yang, M., Sandanayake, M., Miao, P., Shi, Y., Yap, P.S., Sustainability considerations of green buildings: A detailed overview on current advancements and future considerations. *Sustainability*, 14, 21, 14393, 2022, https://doi.org/10.3390/su142114393.
27. Mesa, J.A., Design for circularity and durability: an integrated approach from DFX guidelines. *Res. Eng. Des.*, 34, 4, 443–460, 2023, https://doi.org/10.1007/s00163-023-00419-1.
28. Milioti, C., Kepaptsoglou, K., Deloukas, A., Apostolopoulou, E., Valuation of man-made incident risk perception in public transport: The case of the Athens metro. *Int. J. Transp. Sci. Technol.*, 11, 3, 578–588, 2022, https://doi.org/10.1016/j.ijtst.2021.07.003.
29. Min, J., Yan, G., Abed, A.M., Elattar, S., Amine Khadimallah, M., Jan, A., Elhosiny Ali, H., The effect of carbon dioxide emissions on the building energy efficiency. *Fuel*, 326, 124842, 2022, https://doi.org/10.1016/j.fuel.2022.124842.

30. Modak, N.M., Sinha, S., Ghosh, D.K., A review on remanufacturing, reuse, and recycling in supply chain—Exploring the evolution of information technology over two decades. *Int. J. Inf. Manage. Data Insights*, 3, 1, 100160, 2023, https://doi.org/10.1016/j.jjimei.2023.100160.
31. Namakula, S., Transportation management systems and freight cost reduction in Uganda. *Int. J. Supply Chain Logist.*, 9, 2, 41–52, 2025, htps://doi.org/10.47941/ijscl.2531.
32. Nunes, L.J.R., Reverse logistics as a catalyst for decarbonizing forest products supply chains. *Logistics*, 9, 1, 17, 2025, https://doi.org/10.3390/logistics9010017.
33. Petrisor, I. and Cozmiuc, D., Global supply chain management organization at siemens in the advent of industry 4.0, in: *Global intermediation and logistics service providers*, pp. 123–142, IGI Global, Hershey, PA, 2017, https://doi.org/10.4018/978-1-5225-2133-4.ch007.
34. Petrisor, I. and Cozmiuc, D., Global supply chain management organization at Siemens in the advent of industry 4.0, in: *Supply chain and logistics management: Concepts, methodologies, tools, and applications*, pp. 1095–1114, IGI Global, Hershey, PA, 2019, https://doi.org/10.4018/978-1-7998-0945-6.ch051.
35. Petropoulos, F., Laporte, G., Aktas, E., Alumur, S.A., Archetti, C., Ayhan, H., Battarra, M., Bennell, J.A., Bourjolly, J.M., Boylan, J.E., Breton, M., Canca, D., Charlin, L., Chen, B., Cicek, C.T., Cox, L.A., Currie, C.S.M., Demeulemeester, E., Ding, L., ... & Zhao, X., Operational Research: methods and applications. *J. Oper. Res. Soc.*, 75, 3, 423–617, 2024, https://doi.org/10.1080/01605682.2023.2253852.
36. Pop, G.I., Titu, A.M., Pop, A.B., Enhancing aerospace industry efficiency and sustainability: Process integration and quality management in the context of industry 4.0. *Sustainability*, 15, 23, 16206, 2023, https://doi.org/10.3390/su152316206.
37. Pregnolato, M., Gunner, S., Voyagaki, E., De Risi, R., Carhart, N., Gavriel, G., Tully, P., Tryfonas, T., Macdonald, J., Taylor, C., Towards Civil Engineering 4.0: Concept, workflow and application of Digital Twins for existing infrastructure. *Autom. Constr.*, 141, 104421, 2022, https://doi.org/10.1016/j.autcon.2022.104421.
38. Psarommatis, F., May, G., Azamfirei, V., Product reuse and repurpose in circular manufacturing: A critical review of key challenges, shortcomings and future directions. *J. Remanuf.*, 2025, Advance online publication. https://doi.org/10.1007/s13243-025-00153-y.
39. Rana, S., AI-driven fault detection and predictive maintenance in electrical power systems: A systematic review of data-driven approaches, digital twins, and self-healing grids. *Am. J. Adv. Technol. Eng. Solutions*, 1, 01, 258–289, 2025, https://doi.org/10.63125/4p25x993.
40. Realyvásquez-Vargas, A., Robles-Heredia, R., García-Alcaraz, J.L., Díaz-Reza, J.R., Reliability tests as a strategy for the sustainability of products and

production processes—A case study. *Mathematics*, 11, 1, 208, 2023, https://doi.org/10.3390/math11010208.

41. Rönkkö, P., Ayati, S.M., Majava, J., Remanufacturing in the heavy vehicle industry—Case study of a Finnish machine manufacturer. *Sustainability*, 13, 19, 11120, 2021, https://doi.org/10.3390/su131911120.
42. Sakao, T., Bocken, N., Nasr, N., Umeda, Y., Implementing circular economy activities in manufacturing for environmental sustainability. *CIRP Ann.*, 73, 2, 457–481, 2024, https://doi.org/10.1016/j.cirp.2024.06.002.
43. Shukla, S., Kalaiselvan, V., Raghuvanshi, R.S., How to improve regulatory practices for refurbished medical devices. *Bull. World Health Organ.*, 101, 6, 412–414, 2023, https://doi.org/10.2471/BLT.22.289416.
44. Sierra-Fontalvo, L., Polo-Cardozo, J., Maury-Ramírez, H., Mesa, J.A., Diagnosing remanufacture potential at product-component level: A disassemblability and integrity approach. *Resour. Conserv. Recycl.*, 205, 107529, 2024, https://doi.org/10.1016/j.resconrec.2024.107529.
45. Simandjuntak, S. and Shibli, A., Practical use of defect assessment procedures for industrial component integrity assessment. *Mater. High Temp.*, 28, 3, 245–253, 2011, https://doi.org/10.3184/096034011X13124750650 71.
46. Sposito, G., Ward, C., Cawley, P., Nagy, P.B., Scruby, C., A review of non-destructive techniques for the detection of creep damage in power plant steels. *NDT & E Int.*, 43, 7, 555–567, 2010, https://doi.org/10.1016/j.ndteint.2010.05.012.
47. Xiao, L., Sun, W., Chang, S., Lu, C., Jiang, R., Research on the construction of a blockchain-based industrial product full life cycle information traceability system. *Appl. Sci.*, 14, 11, 4569, 2024, https://doi.org/10.3390/app14114569.
48. Zhang, Y., Liu, S., Liu, Y., Yang, H., Li, M., Huisingh, D., Wang, L., The 'Internet of Things' enabled real-time scheduling for remanufacturing of automobile engines. *J. Cleaner Prod.*, 185, 562–575, 2018, https://doi.org/10.1016/j.jclepro.2018.02.061.
49. Zhong, R.Y., Wang, L., Xu, X., An IoT-enabled real-time machine status monitoring approach for cloud manufacturing. *Procedia CIRP*, 63, 709–714, 2017, https://doi.org/10.1016/j.procir.2017.03.349.

6

Waste Reduction and Recycling Strategies

Ismaila Mahmud[1], Sulaiman Haruna Sulaiman[1], Abubakar Abdulkarim[1,2*], Mutiu Shola Bakare[2] and Ibrahim Sani Madugu[3]

[1]Department of Electrical Engineering, Ahmadu Bello University, Zaria, Kaduna, Nigeria
[2]Department of Electrical Engineering, Kampala International University, Kampala, Uganda
[3]Department of Electrical Engineering, Aliko Dangote University, Kano, Nigeria

Abstract

Due to continuous rapid technological advancements, devices become obsolete in a matter of months. However, most of these obsolete and out-of-use devices, systems, and equipment end up being exported to the developing countries. These journeys could happen during end-of-life, useful-age, and wear-out periods of these devices and eventually find their ways into landfills. Unfortunately, they pose many health and environmental hazards to human and the ecology. This chapter reviews issues relating to waste initiative, reduction, benefits of circular economy, waste data reliability, and recycle strategies, as well as management in a circular economy. In addition, the chapter identifies the sources of waste in circular economy, including their component and associated dangers. Realistic strategies of managing waste as well as recycling in circular economy are proposed. Furthermore, to make the environment safe, standard procedures on how to manage waste as well as appropriate recycling models are proposed. Eventually, lessons learned have also been explained in the chapter in detail. It is expected that the chapter could be used by the experts, academics, and policymakers to develop a robust circular manufacturing environment.

***Keywords*:** Waste management, circular economy

**Corresponding author*: aabdulkarim@kiu.ac.ug

Jeyaprakash Natarajan, Milon Selvam Dennison, M. Bhuvanesh Kumar and Ganapathy Thirukkotti (eds.) Manufacturing and the Circular Economy, (179–212) © 2027 Scrivener Publishing LLC

6.1 General Introduction

The European Union (EU) has defined waste as "any substance or object that the holder discards or intends or is required to discard." The definition was also accompanied by a list of several examples of objects and items that could be regarded as waste in the European Waste Catalogue [1]. The generation of waste differs in most of the countries across the world, which depends on locations and affluence. As seen in Figure 6.1, projections for 2050 indicate that waste creation is predicted to increase in every part of the world. Waste management (WM), on the other hand, was defined based on the Basel Convention as a way of collecting, transporting, processing, and disposal of both hazardous and nonhazardous forms of waste. It also includes the aftercare of the waste disposal sites [2].

Electronic waste (e-waste), as a prevalent type of waste in both the developed and the developing economies, can be regarded as one of the persisting types of wastes. It is one of the rapidly growing wastes that can adversely affect human lives and significantly aid environmental pollution due to various degrees of toxic materials that constitute them. In this regard, many countries have intensified efforts in the introduction of various protocols that focus on the management of e-waste and also reutilizing them

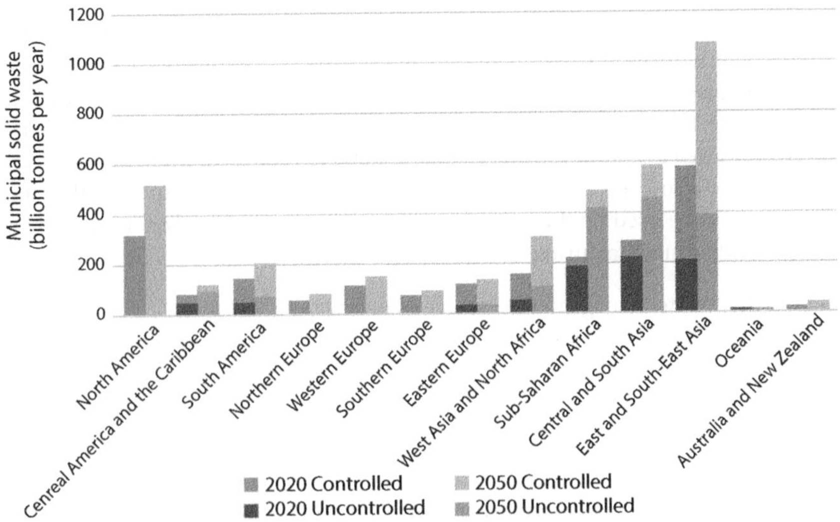

Source: UNEP (2024a).

Figure 6.1 Continental projection of waste generation.

as raw materials in the production of other items by way of up-cycling and down-cycling [3].

Therefore, the Basel Convention requires that for effective management of e-waste and other types of wastes, it is essential to develop devices that are eco-friendly as well as putting in place proper mechanisms and technologies for e-wastes collection and disposal, as well as ensuring safe recovery and recycling of materials. The two most important things to take into account so as to achieve effective e-waste management are wider awareness on their impacts and prohibiting the exportation of secondhand e-gadgets to the developing nations. Contrary to the provision of the Basel Convention and similar protocols, several African and Asian countries have seen an influx of hazardous e-wastes [4, 5].

Along with the many millions of personal computers that are thought to reach their "useful life" annually, the Environmental Protection Agency estimates that e-waste makes up around 5% of the total waste volume produced worldwide. Thus, a large quantity of hazardous materials from these wastes will further contaminate the environment. Despite this, however, with proper WM strategy, many companies worldwide are using appropriate technologies to recover a wide range of invaluable components and minerals from e-waste, including ferrous metals, aluminum, copper, plastics, acrylonitrile butadiene styrene (ABS), high-impact polystyrene, polycarbonates (PC), and ABS-PC [6].

Several reasons have been identified to contribute the production of wastes. These include, but are not limited to:

(i) Short lifespan of the product. This mainly affects items such as garments, foods, electronic appliances and devices;
(ii) Overproduction of goods; excess production of foods can always translate to food wastage, which, in 2011, was identified to account for over one billion tons per year [7];
(iii) Lack of sufficient awareness on WM. WM practices as well as reuse, recycling, and materials recovery have generally seen little awareness in media outlets. This is, in part, due to the lack of interest in such programs from the viewers;
(iv) Disposing unwanted material such as leftovers from contractions resulting from economic processes;
(v) Urbanization and improved standard of living. As the world sees continues rise in urbanization, the population as well as the purchasing powers of individuals also increases. This, in turn, causes surge in the amount of waste generated across the globe [8, 9];

(vi) Industrialization and climate change. Urbanization correlates to industrialization and economic development. These, generally, pose a great rise in the volume of the generated solid waste;
(vii) Lack of motivation and market size;
(viii) Political maneuvers and interference. Relationships with political parties and political elections; and
(ix) The impact of advertising and brainwashing to purchase superfluous goods.

6.2 Waste Management Initiatives

Many EU member states such as the Netherlands, Germany, and Sweden had, since the late 19th century, developed respective national policies aimed at curtailing the increasing problems of waste productions as detailed in Table 6.1. However, There is still need for the harmonization of these policies and also extending them to other EU member states so that a workable single market that will cover all the EU states could be achieved [10]. Hence, the EU responded through the introduction of the Landfill Directive and legislation on Extended Producer Responsibility (EPR) as its two major policies.

The Landfill Directive tasked both the EU and the UK Government to regulate both the issuance of permits and licenses for the establishment of new landfill sites based on proper assessment of fulfilling all the necessary operating standards and to also ensure that, by 2020, landfill municipal wastes were reduced to one-third of its value 5 years earlier as the countries were running out of spaces for efficient waste disposal. Landfill tax was then imposed that charged defaulters a significant amount per ton of waste [11, 12]. In this regard, the Waste Strategy 2000 for England and Wales [13], belonging to the UK Government was made to have four levels, in order of importance, as indicated in Figure 6.2. Thus, based on the strategy, establishing landfills will always be considered as a last resort to the management of solid waste, whereas Table 6.1 summarizes WM initiatives across diverse geographies and sectors.

The EPR principle, on the other hand, mandates that importers and manufacturers of goods take a large amount of accountability for the environmental effects of their goods. This includes the choice of raw materials, the process of manufacturing, the usage of the final goods, and proper disposal of the waste. EPR is therefore the "polluter pays" principle's logical progression. This is based on the claim that producers may significantly

Table 6.1 Summary of waste management initiatives across diverse geographies and sectors.

References	Geographic scope	Initiative type	Key findings/results	Challenges identified	Recommendations
[14]	India (National)	Waste-to-energy (WtE)	Successful WtE plants; policy support *via* Swachh Bharat Mission	Technological, financial, regulatory barriers	Integrated systems; stronger regulations; PPPs
[15]	Noveleta, Cavite (Philippines)	Community waste management	Recycling and segregation practices developed	Lack of infrastructure	Build waste facilities; promote sustainability
[16]	Tanzania	Financing models	Hybrid models proposed	Limited financing options	Hybrid public–private financing
[17]	Philippines (Barangay Pili)	Strategic management framework	High satisfaction in pollution control	Waste collection gaps	Boost community involvement; awareness campaigns
[18]	India (rural)	Rural waste management	Successful total sanitary campaign	Limited scalability	Involve local stakeholders
[19]	Malaysia (Pahang)	Construction waste	Contractors comply with policies	Weak policy enforcement	Strengthen policies and compliance

(Continued)

Table 6.1 Summary of waste management initiatives across diverse geographies and sectors. (*Continued*)

References	Geographic scope	Initiative type	Key findings/results	Challenges identified	Recommendations
[20]	India (national)	Urban waste management	Formal sector importance	Urban system gaps	Strengthen formal sector role
[21]	Malaysia	3Rs (university-led)	Community-based 3Rs model	Lack of environmental literacy	Promote environmental education
[22]	Tanzania (Keko Machungwa)	Informal settlements SWM	Only ~29% waste collected	Low public participation; financial constraints	Community alliances; awareness campaigns
[23]	Indonesia (Bunaken Island)	Marine waste management	Community-based "Rubbish Bank" model	Marine ecosystem degradation	Community empowerment; replication of Rubbish Bank
[24]	Philippines (Tanauan, Leyte)	Legal framework evaluation	Poor ESWMA law implementation	Lack of institutional support	Proactive ESWMA enforcement

(*Continued*)

Table 6.1 Summary of waste management initiatives across diverse geographies and sectors. (*Continued*)

References	Geographic scope	Initiative type	Key findings/results	Challenges identified	Recommendations
[25]	EU (Multi-country)	Healthcare waste (operating rooms)	New model for OR waste lifecycle	High OR waste and energy use	Develop reusable tools; healthcare worker training
[26]	Vietnam and Indonesia	Tourism and university–community partnerships	Student/community involvement	Funding; cultural resistance	Enhance university-community partnerships
[27]	Indonesia (Kajartengguli Village)	Household composting	Successful composting program	Initial low awareness	Community training and organic waste composting
[28]	Tanzania (Dar es Salaam slums)	Public health focus	Direct link between waste and disease	Inadequate collection and education	Increase collection frequency; community-led initiatives
[29]	EU (UK, Germany)	Plastic waste EPR and DRS	EPR/DRS effective but with limitations	Industry resistance; recycling challenges	Standardization; better infrastructure and partnerships

(*Continued*)

Table 6.1 Summary of waste management initiatives across diverse geographies and sectors. (*Continued*)

References	Geographic scope	Initiative type	Key findings/results	Challenges identified	Recommendations
[30]	Global	E-waste management	EPR, PRO, and biotech solutions	Toxicity; limited tech adoption	Promote advanced recycling technologies
[31]	Pakistan (Karachi slums)	Community collection initiatives	Community-based primary collection	Geographical and legal marginalization	Strengthen community-based models
[32]	Global South (Argentina, Brazil, Canada, Kenya, etc.)	Grassroots waste picker cooperatives	Waste pickers generate livelihoods and recycling	Limited resources; policy challenges	Support waste picker networks; participatory governance
[33]	Indonesia (vocational polytechnic)	Green campus evaluation	Low sustainability compliance score	Inefficient segregation and recycling	Improve recycling; engage campus community
[34]	India (plastic waste)	Start-up–led plastic management	Start-ups and waste pickers inclusion	Informal sector fragmentation	Support ecosystem approach; formalization of informal sector
[35]	Costa Rica	Waste Innovation Index	Low recycling rate (9.6%); urban–rural disparity	Infrastructure, public awareness	AI, blockchain, public education, infrastructure upgrades

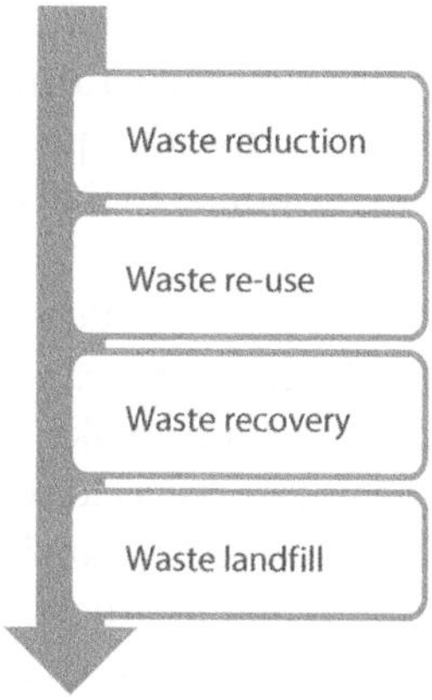

Figure 6.2 Waste strategy 2000 for England and Wales.

contribute to environmental sustainability through the selection of materials and processing techniques [36]. The EPR is explicitly applied most in the waste electrical and electronic equipment (WEEE).

Electrical and electronic equipment (EEE) wastes generally contain materials that can have adverse effects on the environment whether they are when disposed of in landfills or through incineration processes. They are also accountable to over threefold of the total volume of general waste [37]. All appliances powered by electricity with a voltage of no more than 1 kV for AC and 1.5 kV for DC are considered electrical and electronic trash. Because of their high value, products that operate at higher voltages are not included in the waste. The main goals of the WEEE Directive include the following:

1. Reduction of EEE waste.
2. Improvement on waste recycling, recovery and re-use of EEE waste, and
3. Environmental impacts due to the treatment of EEE waste should be minimized.

It has been established in the United Kingdom that the effects of EEE could be reduced by 0.1% due to high level of recycling activities [38]. However, this statistics ignored the EEE waste generated due to the production of the electrical engineering products; unfortunately, every ton of the electrical engineering products produced 5 and 20 tons of manufacturing waste and waste due to extraction, respectively [39]. Thus, if the WEEE

Directive were to lead to an increase in product repair and remanufacture, which would decrease waste from manufacturing, consumers, and resource extraction. Furthermore, the directive's unquestionable consequence is to shift the burden of WM from the public to the individual OEMs, regardless of the measured difference in waste.

Information technology (IT) devices such as PCs, printers, and photocopiers produce 39% of all WEEE, whereas large home appliances such as refrigerators and laundry machines make up 43%. Additionally, only roughly 40% of IT equipment gets recycled, compared to 88% of bigger household appliances [40]. These discrepancies are generally attributed to two primary causes. Among them is the ease with which large appliances could be separated from the waste stream. Same could, however, not be said with smaller components such as the ferrous metal from computer hardware.

It could be argued that the 1957 Treaty of Rome was "guilty" because it addressed only environmental protection in the following way: "the harmonization of environmental legislation and uniformity in the fight against certain forms of aid, so that technical barriers to the free circulation of goods would not arise due to different national links." This is because the global economy is developing according to a linear model, which means that we take something, develop it, use it, and then dispose of it. It was stated during the 1972 Stockholm Agreement amendment (UN, 1972) that member states should take into account the current environmental protection technology and know-how. In November 1973, the first Environmental Action Plan (EAP) was decided upon, based on the 1972 promises made by the European Council to create a Community environmental policy. To protect the environment against waste accrual, prevention plans were mentioned as a top priority in the first EAP in 1973 of the EU, which ran from 1973 to 1977. "Sustainable development is the development that meets the needs of the present without compromising the ability of future generations to meet their own needs," according to the Norwegian prime minister in 1987 [41].

Between 1992 and 1999, treaties (such as the Maastricht Treaty on the Council of the European Communities, 1992) and conferences (UN Conference on Environment, 1992) have focused on enhancing the economic dimension of Europe as well as achieving agreements on penalties to be imposed. The directives on the landfill on waste were then issued by the EU in 1999. The directive requires the establishment of a strategy by the EU member states that will ensure significant reduction of the biodegradable substances for more than 2 years in landfills. Recycling goals, composting, biogas production, and materials and energy recovery are a few aspects of the initiative. Generally speaking, the 1999/31/EC directive mandated that current member states should make effort to dispose 10% of the biodegradable waste generated starting in 2015, whereas new members were required do same on all biodegradable wastes generated in 2019. It also required that, in the whole of Europe, all existing landfills seize to operate in the near future.

Other treaties such as the Treaties of Amsterdam developed in 1997 and implemented in 1999 and Treaties of Nice in 2001 that got into effect in 2003 focused on other key issues of democratic legitimacy throughout the EU as well as environmental protection (contained in the Lisbon Treaty of 2007 that got into effect in 2009) without proper planning on the management of waste. It was later agreed in subsequent treaties, as contained in the Directive 2008/98, that a knowledge-based economy set to be achieved in the states must be able to provide a sustainable strategy for the management of solid waste.

The regulation explains the distinction between waste and by-products as well as how waste turns into a secondary raw material from garbage (end-of-waste criteria). Additionally, the WFW mandated that the member states create a number of initiatives with a focus on energy recovery, prevention, reuse, reduction, and recycling. Accordingly, the WFD establishes several fundamental WM guidelines, one of which is the evaluation of WM's impact on human health. Furthermore, WFD established the Producer Responsibility and the Polluter Pays Principle (PPP) [42].

To improve practices, it is essential to have a significant understanding of WM in the context of circular economy (CE). However, WM in a CE remains limited [43–45]. Due to the increased complexity of WM and the practice problems in a CE, several challenges and opportunities arise in the WM for a CE.

Some of the fundamentals that cement any regions position in a CE for the role it plays in enhancing the quality of municipal planning and regulation frameworks include adequate proximity of resources for market supply and demand of products [44]. This can be demonstrated in the EU's policy implementation and endorsement of new procedures that will help in enhancing the acceptability of CE through the European Commission 2018 that is widely regarded as a state-of-the-art waste legislation. The idea includes recyclable materials such as paper, glass, and plastics, as well as reusable items. It also includes the use of organic waste to produce goods [44]. Thus, effective functioning of a CE to be able to recycle and up-cycle waste is characterized by judicious selection and usage of materials as well as labor and financial strength and the level of innovation and technological advancement of the area [46]. A CE emphasizes recycling, reuse, and trash reduction over disposal throughout North America, especially the United States [47]. In Asia, China and Japan were the two countries to officially present a CE.

According to Diaz, Latin America, the Caribbean, and Africa are considered backward in terms of adopting CE mainly due to little or no laws and policies and laws governing proper management of waste, inexperienced personnel, lack of trainings, awareness, and knowledge, as well as a lack of political will. These factors gave rise to unofficial markets for recycling, recovery, and reuse as well as a number of queries about the CE idea [48]. Therefore, by providing an excellent alternative model that replaces conventional linear processes, investigating WM is anticipated to enhance the economy, preserve the environment, and safeguard social justice [43, 49].

Table 6.2 Environmental, social, and economic benefits derived from CE.

Benefits	CE	References
Environmental	CE promotes recycling, waste reduction, GHG emission control, and environmental protection by modifying end-of-life items. Because some of the raw materials used in production might be locally sourced from the materials in transition, it also guarantees a large reduction in resource importation.	AUDA-UNEP Dung [52] Schröder *et al.* [94] Guarnieri *et al.* [95] Marino and Pariso [96]
Social	The youth are able to make a life because CE generates employment chances. As a result, it reduces poverty, transforms society, and lessens the effects of climate change and other social issues.	Debrah *et al.* [97] AUDA-UNEP
Economic	CE stimulates competition among local and worldwide organizations, which advances technological and corporate change, innovation, and economic progress.	Smol *et al.* [98] Awan *et al.* [99] Bressanelli *et al.* [100]

Practical measures such as building WM infrastructure are essential requirements that are needed to overcome the challenges hampering the transformation of WM from a linear economy to a CE [50]. Governments, private WM firms, researchers, nongovernmental organizations, and entrepreneurs are important players in this. They must fund the CE projects. Although WM is witnessing a lot of investment efforts in its full-scale transformation into a CE, such as the assistance in gradually cutting off the utilization of plastic bags to promote environmentally friendly ways of life in some countries through partnerships with development banks, a lot will be needed to accomplish intended outcomes.

According to Barbaritano *et al.* [51] and Dung [52], social transformation and economic innovation are just two of the many advantages of CE projects in developing nations. Table 6.2 summarizes the sustainability benefits, which include environmental, social, and economic ones.

6.3 Issues on Reliable Data on Waste

Effective waste administration management requires accurate data on waste generation, but there are considerable problems as shown in Table 6.3, especially for nations with developing economies. Among the typical problems is inconsistency of information regarding waste generation, as illustrated by the variation between city and national data in India, where the use of narrow datasets results in biased estimation [53]. In Ghana, participatory engagement models have been suggested as a way to improve data credibility and reliability through emphasizing stakeholder collaboration towards addressing endemic data gaps [54]. Additionally, research in Asian newly industrialized nations has established that a high proportion of available datasets do not conform to current statistical standards and therefore possess limited informational content, for which deeper analyses become requisite [55]. Serbia has lacked adequate, reliable data in terms of waste composition, and therefore, significant inconsistencies in decision-making have been experienced, with variations in indicators surpassing 300% [56].

Ideally, SWOT and/or PESTEL are applied to evaluate the area in which any WM strategy is to be applied using real data as depicted in Figure 6.3. The advantages are beneficial, whereas shortcomings are adverse effects related to the inner features of the system under assessment. Prospects are outside variables having beneficial relationship with the system, whereas the adverse consequences of the system environment are present [57, 58]. This technique is a simple qualitative and quantitative tool that can assist stakeholders in making policies [58]. PESTEL, on the other hand, means

Table 6.3 Issues and solutions for reliable waste data collection and analysis.

References	Geographic scope	Key issues identified	Proposed solution/ approach	Additional remarks
[53]	India	Inconsistent national, state, and city-level waste generation data; reliance on limited CPCB and NEERI data	Involve academic institutions in data handling; technical and policy reforms	Large variability due to population estimation errors
[54]	Ghana	Lack of reliable data; absence of participatory data gathering; no climate burden monitoring	Stakeholder engagement, participatory waste audits, climate action plans	Collaborative evidence-based framework to close chronic data gaps
[55]	Asia (especially India)	Inconsistent MSW data across city sizes; improper data collection methodologies	Adopt international solid waste sampling standards; detailed MSW composition analysis	Lower data quality in smaller urban areas
[56]	Serbia (Bor municipality)	Discrepancies in waste quantity data across sources	Standardized data reporting across agencies; harmonization of cost indicators	Variability up to 300% can mislead decision-making
[63]	Poland (mining waste)	Inconsistent reporting between mining companies and national statistics	Mandatory reporting by waste codes; integrate company data into centralized platform (e.g., Eurostat)	Key for monitoring industrial symbiosis and CE progress
[64]	Serbia (Timok County)	Lack of municipal waste composition data for LCA modeling	Implement reliable local and national data systems for informed LCA-based waste management	Essential for EU approximation process

(Continued)

Table 6.3 Issues and solutions for reliable waste data collection and analysis. (*Continued*)

References	Geographic scope	Key issues identified	Proposed solution/ approach	Additional remarks
[65]	USA	Incomplete data for landfill modeling; missing long-term parameter measurements	Develop full-scale landfill models requiring fewer parameters	Longitudinal monitoring of large landfills remains costly
[66]	Europe	Inaccuracies in automated volume measurement (ultrasonic sensors) due to irregular waste shapes and sensor failures	Improve sensor systems; integrate ML models for predictive accuracy	Environmental variability affects automated waste data
[67]	USA	Lack of standardized national technical waste data system	Pilot national waste data network to support engineers, planners, decision-makers	Early vision for national solid waste data system
[68]	Global (construction waste focus)	Lack of big data in construction waste management (CWM); reliance on small, sample-based data	Develop big data acquisition, storage, and analytics for more comprehensive CWM	Transferable insights for general waste management community
[69]	Developing countries	Lack of organized reporting systems; use of indirect data methods	Use of indicator-based indirect data; recommends government-supported sampling surveys	Indirect data useful but lacks error measurement precision
[70]	Pakistan (Mahmood Booti dumping site)	Lack of environmental impact data for dumping sites	Apply risk assessment models such as EASEWASTE for environmental impact estimation	Heavy metal leaching significant contributor to human and ecotoxicity

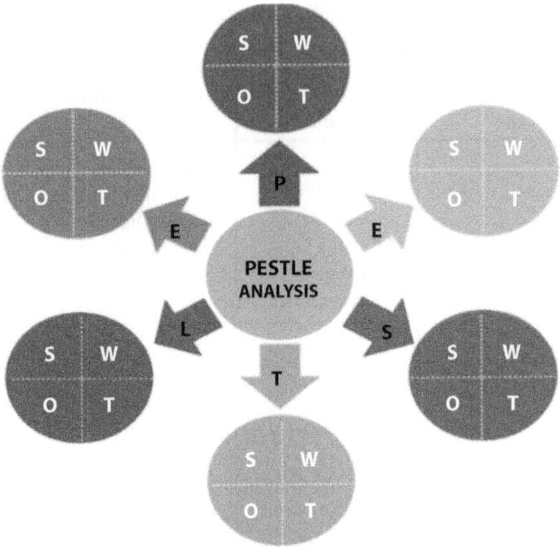

Figure 6.3 SWOT in conjunction with PESTEL analysis.

political, economic, social, technical, environmental, and legal analysis. It is an analysis technique that is used to observe potential benefits as well as challenges that may result from the implementation of renewable energy policies [59]. These tools have been applied by researchers to analyze the feasibility of a certain event at various countries. Fons *et al.* [60] applied the SWOT technique to evaluate Aragón, Spain's Sustainable Tourism Development, whereas Srdjevic *et al.* [101] incorporated the PESTEL technique into SWOT to identify the internal and external obstacles influencing Servia's water supply. Symeonides *et al.* assessed the Cyprus End of Life Tire using SWOT analysis [58]. Additionally, Tsangas *et al.* assessed the hydrocarbons industry in insular communities using a SWOT analysis in each PESTEL pillar [61].

Demographics; population size; waste protection; eating habits; daily routines; ethics; incomes; current laws; economic, environmental, and social criteria analysis; clean and accumulation waste index; economic activities; and the names of the primary polluters should all be included in the data used to assess any chosen area to develop WM strategies. Equation (6.1) is used to determine the Clean Index (CI) [62].

$$\mathrm{CI} = \left(\frac{I_{\mathrm{col}}}{S}\right)K \tag{6.1}$$

where S is the fixed section's surface area measured in m^2, K is a constant, and I_{col} is the number of substances gathered on a defined portion of an area.

Although the accumulation index accounts for the waste litter accumulation rates (ARs), the AR estimates the level of waste accumulation in a certain item per unit area per unit time.

The AR accumulation index is computed using Equations (6.2) and (6.3), respectively.

$$\mathrm{AR} = I_{col}/S/T \tag{6.2}$$

$$\mathrm{AI} = \log_{10}(\mathrm{AR} \times 10^6) \tag{6.3}$$

where AI is accumulation index.

Another indicator is the waste generation rate (WGR), which is calculated using Equation (6.4). It is a product of the total daily waste produced in any area and the number of people for the study area on the same day.

$$\mathrm{WGR} = \text{Waste production in kg} \times \text{citizens in 1 day} \tag{6.4}$$

Hence, WGR can be computed for any given area using Equations (6.5) and (6.6).

$$\mathrm{WGR} = \Sigma\ (Bzi - BAi)/T \tag{6.5}$$

$$\mathrm{WGR} = \Sigma\ (Ci \times Ei)/T \tag{6.6}$$

where T is the monitoring and measuring time period (in days), Bzi represents the weight of each garbage truck in kilograms, and BAi represents the tare also in kilograms. The capacity of the truck, Ci, and the bulking density, Ei, are measured in m^3 and kg/m^3, respectively.

6.4 Waste Management Technologies

Several technologies have emerged over the years to ensure effective management of both the municipal and the industrial wastes. The emergence of these technologies is mainly inspired by the need to reduce the negative impacts of waste on the environment as well as increasing the effectiveness with which waste could be managed with relative ease. Several conventional techniques, such as the composting and landfilling, as well as emerging technologies, such as the Internet of Things (IoT), have been covered in the literature. Some of the recent WM technologies (WMTs) are discussed below, with a detailed breakdown in Table 6.4.

6.4.1 Greening Waste Management through Taxation

This is one of the initiatives aimed at enhancing effective WM. The multidimensional view of environmental taxation has been demonstrated in recent researches reported in the literature through incineration and other sustainability initiatives. These results shed light on sustainable WM and provide stakeholders and policymakers with guidance. Carbon pricing incentives were shown to reduce incineration facility emissions [71]. As economic incentives align with ecological aims, reduction in the emissions caused by greenhouse gases (GHGs) encourages the adoption of greener technology.

Incineration practices have been suggested by the US Department of Energy as a means of reducing CO_2 emissions arising from heavy industry production and hence emphasized the importance and strictness of hazardous emissions. However, Briguglio (2021) warned against outrageous emission levies as they are capable of encouraging illegal garbage disposal and also make incineration, a legal waste-to-energy option, difficult to practice. Danish and Erdogan (2022) examined how nuclear energy affected CO_2 emissions from both production and consumption in nations that are members of the Organization for Economic Co-operation and Development (OECD). The experimental results demonstrate that nuclear energy helps reduce CO_2 emissions resulting from production. Furthermore, emissions arising from either the production or the demand side tend to decline as a result of globalization. The long-term factors influencing carbon emissions in 19 EU nations were examined by Khan *et al.* in 2023. The results show that technology, clean energy, and tax all help to reduce emissions [72].

Abbasi *et al.* observed how environmental tax policies that are efficiently drafted can aid eco-friendly waste-to-energy conversion strategies and good incineration as a WM alternative [73]. Gupt (2023) examined how producer responsibility expansion is connected to taxes on the environment. The analysis demonstrated that, by promoting product design that reduces waste carbon emissions and simplifies incineration, growing producer responsibility programs can supplement carbon levies. The combination promotes incineration as a sustainable approach to trash management.

According to European sustainability goals, the Commission, in 2013, explored the impacts of environmental tax measures and recommended well-implemented tax adjustments to encourage incineration operations to adopt cleaner technologies. Wurzel [102] illustrated the substantial rise in incineration and other waste-to-energy technologies in EU member states. Lastly, waste-to-energy technology, CE principles, and environmental taxation were examined by Achinas *et al.* [103]. According to the analysis, taxes can promote circular practices, which would allow incineration to play a vital role in EU sustainable WM programs. Evaluations of recent studies demonstrate the intricate relationship between incineration, production-based CO_2 emissions, and EU environmental taxes. These studies highlight the necessity of well-written rules that minimize hazards and unforeseen consequences while promoting incineration as a sustainable waste-to-energy alternative. For stakeholders and politicians negotiating WM and environmental sustainability, this research offers crucial insights and a comprehensive perspective.

6.4.2 Smart Waste Bin

A significant amount of the waste produced is municipal rubbish. Generally speaking, about 5 metric tons of garbage were produced per EU resident in the year 2020, compared to 530 kg per capita in 2021 (Eurostat, 2023). This accounts for over 10% of the trash generation contribution. An estimated 3.4 billion tons of municipal waste will be generated annually by 2050, requiring management costs of about $635.5 billion. To help manage garbage more effectively, a smart waste that is outfitted with a variety of sensors and technology offers a simple way to handle all other waste bins [74]. These sensors in a smart waste bin (SWB) can identify a number of characteristics, such as the waste weight, gas emissions, fill level, etc. [75]. Software provision is an essential part of bins that help them to work properly. Additionally, for additional analysis, the database shall contain the whole data gathered from all the sensors. Storage is crucial for additional analysis. SWBs can be added to existing bins or used as autonomous devices. Additionally, they can be powered by several technologies, such as batteries, solar photovoltaic, or even the kinetic energy produced due to movement of people in the course of waste disposal. WM firms can more efficiently schedule pick-ups by keeping an eye on the bin's fill level, which lowers the number of trucks on the road and the emissions that go along with it. In trash management, other technologies such as GPS tracking and RFID tags with low-power sensors are also becoming more and more common [76, 77]. Garbage trucks and rubbish containers with RFID tags attached can send information about their position and condition. Several IoT technologies exist, including the following: WM firms can schedule waste pick-ups from the bins through careful monitoring of the level of garbage contained. This practice will significantly reduce truck traffics as well as potential emission they can cause. In trash management, other technologies such as GPS tracking and RFID tags with low-power sensors are also becoming more and more common [76, 77]. Garbage trucks and rubbish containers with RFID tags attached can send information about their location and operational conditions. Several IoT technologies exist, including the following:

- **Message Queuing Telemetry Transport**
SWBs are connected to a network using them, a low-power IoT application that uses a lightweight Message Queuing Telemetry Transport (MQTT) protocol. It makes use of the publish/subscribe model, in which subscribers receive data after devices publish it to a broker [78]. The protocol is highly dependable and transmits data *via* TCP/IP. The gateway, which connects to the cloud using a MQTT bridge made for low-power IoT applications, may use each waste bin as a client.
- **Low-Power Wide Area Network**
This IoT protocol for wireless communication was created for long-range, low-power applications [79].
- **Bluetooth**
It is a gadget for communicating across small distances. Its inability to be used for long-distance communication is a drawback. In the event of a system failure, staff can perform maintenance *via* Bluetooth [80].
- **Global System for Mobile Communications (GSM)**
Smart bins frequently communicate with one another using this cellular network technology. It offers quick data transfer speeds and a large bandwidth. It is typically inexpensive and simple to use [81].

The selection of communication technology for SWBs is contingent upon a number of criteria, including coverage, energy consumption, technological cost, and application requirements. For SWBs, GSM is a popular technology, although alternative choices such as MQTT or Low-Power Wide Area Network (LoRaWAN) might also work well.

6.4.3 Artificial Intelligence and Robots

Due to its great precision and accuracy in tasks such as speech and image recognition, decision-making, image classification, and forecasting, artificial intelligence (AI) has become a fascinating tool that finds application in many areas of life [82]. The main aim of the AI technology is to create machines and systems that can mimic the human brain capability in terms of learning, adaptation, and decision-making so that they can be deployed to solve complex problems. AI technology through computer vision can be deployed in WM so that AI-based robotic machines can detect and correctly classify waste based on their shape and color [83]. It may also be useful in sorting waste onto trucks and conveyors, where individual pieces are automatically transported to the right container for proper disposal and possible recycling. AI-powered software could be used to locate illegal waste dumping sites that can prevent further environmental pollution [84]. Effective sorting, which can be time-consuming, laborious, and a precise procedure, is essential to efficient waste recycling. Many automated systems that can accomplish that more quickly and efficiently have been developed in response to this. AI systems using computer vision are able to differentiate between different forms of garbage [37, 38] and separate them using robotic arms, air pressure, or magnets. With products such as the Heavy Picker and Fast Picker, the Finnish company ZenRobotics invented automated waste-sorting technology utilizing robotics and AI. The Heavy Picker has a 3D laser sensing system, a high-resolution RGB camera, an image metal detector, NIR sensors, and other sensors, whereas the Light Picker has only a visible light sensor [39]. Computer vision–equipped robots can separate recyclables from nonrecyclable garbage. Different forms of plastic can be distinguished by AI algorithms, allowing for separation. Manually doing it is difficult for human workers [40]. Additionally, waste collection and routing can be optimized with AI algorithms, which can cut down on the labor and assets needed for gathering waste.

6.4.4 Automated Vacuum Collection System

Garbage collectors, using garbage trucks, are in most cases responsible for house-to-house by garbage collection. They have to optimize their routes with consideration of all factors. The trucks usually have to travel long distances and are required to be efficient in terms of their capacity, volume ratio, speed, and overall health, in addition to the waste density [85]. This renders their use quite demanding. Automated vacuum collection (AVAC) has therefore been suggested as alternative to the conventional garbage collection method. The AVAC principle requires that once waste is thrown into the inlet, pipes are used to convey it to the collection point. Although the AVAC has for long been in use to manage waste, it is still not very common. In 2015, the system was deployed to provide a simple underground means of collecting household waste. Today, a form of AVAC, MetroTaifun, is in operation in over 40 countries. The literature has examined the ecological and economic effects of managing waste with AVAC systems. Three New York cities' pneumatic trash pipes were examined by Miller *et al.* [49]. Maintaining a conventional waste collection operation comes at a high financial and environmental cost [49]. The High Line pneumatic facility, the Second Avenue Subway pneumatic facility, and potential upgrades to the current Roosevelt Island pneumatic system were the three particular situations taken into consideration in this study. It was discovered that because of design features, the expenses and effects of AVAC installations vary from those of traditional collecting.

6.4.5 Software in Waste Management

Automation of processes such as WM can be achieved through the use of AI, the IoT, and other software packages [86]. The end-user does not directly access it; instead, it uses sensors and electromechanical components that interact with the actual world to automate manual tasks that they would otherwise perform. Epifancev *et al.* in 2020 compared the effectiveness of popular waste disposal software packages in Russia and Europe using performance metrics such as logistics, landfill selection, disposal cost calculation, and user-friendly interface. These days, the Internet is being used to help with trash management through desktop, mobile, and Internet applications, as well as to influence ecological consciousness. According to the Global Connectivity Report 2022, 63% of people used the Internet in 2021, and 95% of people were connected to a broadband network (3G, 4G, or 5G). Applications designed for casual users include buying small food packages and identifying unlawful garbage in the neighborhood, which has an impact on the ecology and dozens of individuals.

6.4.6 Incineration

Because of its many advantages, incineration is essential in contemporary WM efforts. It helps in significantly reducing air and environmental pollution as well as landfill requirements through efficient transformation of nonbiodegradable and nonrecyclable waste into useful energy [104]. It helps in the diversification of energy sources and significantly reduces overdependence on fossil fuels for electricity and heat generation. Hence, according to the European Commission (2020) incineration helps in improving energy security. Therefore, as a way to combat air pollution challenges, the utilization of it throughout sustainable WM and energy management programs needs to be controlled.

Additionally, incineration contributes to sustainable development in the EU and its member nations. It supports the CE goals of the EU by extending landfill lifespans and improving WM efficiency. By producing dependable, sustainable energy, it also improves energy security and lowers GHG emissions, especially landfill methane. By increasing resource efficiency, incineration also helps the EU achieve its WM and recycling goals. Additionally, it lessens the negative environmental effects of rubbish disposal, enhancing the quality of the air and water in densely populated EU cities.

Conversely, environmental taxes support environmental initiatives and promote ecologically conscious behavior. Incineration is impacted by these EU levies. Greener energy production and emissions reduction in incineration operations are encouraged by carbon taxes and emissions trading schemes. The choice of energy source may be influenced by energy taxes, which have an impact on the incinerator facilities' economic feasibility. Taxes and fees on garbage disposal influence WM choices, favoring incineration over landfill disposal. To maximize the economic and environmental benefits of incineration, taxes and environmental technologies must be harmoniously integrated to lessen the environmental impact, encourage responsible WM, and create a circular, low-carbon economy in the EU.

Furthermore, WM regulations in the EU depend heavily on the interaction of environmental technologies, tariffs, carbon emissions, and incineration. The environmental effects of incineration facilities throughout the EU have been lessened, thanks in large part to developments in environmental technology, such as enhanced filtration systems and waste-to-energy technologies. To encourage the adoption of cleaner incineration processes and reduce carbon emissions, the EU has also put in place a number of taxation policies and carbon pricing mechanisms. By encouraging incinerators to invest in pollution control technologies and investigate alternate waste disposal techniques, these regulations seek to internalize the external costs related to pollution and carbon emissions.

Building on the previous conversation, the intricate relationship between carbon emissions for incineration that are based on production and consumption emphasizes how difficult it is to assess the environmental effects of waste-to-energy. Incineration is a production-based solution with lower GHG emissions, thanks to advanced emissions control systems. But because incineration produces emissions, indirect emissions from waste treatment, facility building, maintenance, and waste transportation must be included in the carbon footprint.

Table 6.4 Overview of emerging waste management Technologies (WMTs).

Technology	Core function	Key components/ features	Benefits	Challenges	Real-world applications/ studies
1. Greening waste management through taxation	Economic incentive alignment	• Carbon pricing • Environmental levies • Producer responsibility schemes	• Reduces GHG emissions (e.g., 22% drop in EU incinerator emissions) • Funds green tech R&D	• Illegal dumping incentives • Implementation complexity • Regional compliance gaps	EU incineration facilities [73]; OECD nuclear energy integration [87]
2. Smart waste bins (SWB)	Real-time waste monitoring	• Fill-level/gas sensors • IoT networks (MQTT/ LoRaWAN/GSM) • Solar/kinetic power	• 30% fewer collection trips • Dynamic routing optimization • 15% fuel savings	• High upfront costs (\$200+/bin) • Network vulnerability • Power dependency	EU municipal systems [88]; RFID-GPS integration [76]
3. AI and robotics	Automated sorting/ optimization	• Computer vision (waste identification) • Robotic arms (ZenRobotics) • Illegal dumping detection AI	• 95% sorting accuracy • Four times faster than manual • Route optimization (20% efficiency gain)	• High CAPEX (\$500K+/system) • Maintenance complexity • Limited material recognition	ZenRobotics Heavy Picker (Finland) [89]; conveyor sorting systems [83]

(Continued)

Table 6.4 Overview of emerging waste management Technologies (WMTs). (*Continued*)

Technology	Core function	Key components/ features	Benefits	Challenges	Real-world applications/ studies
4. Automated vacuum collection (AVAC)	Centralized waste transport	• Underground pneumatic pipes • Collection terminals • Vacuum propulsion	• 80% fewer collection vehicles • Odor/pest control • Space optimization	• $2M+/km installation cost • Inflexible infrastructure • High energy demand	MetroTaifun systems (40+ countries); NYC pneumatic trials [90]
5. Waste management software	Digital workflow optimization	• IoT integration platforms • Disposal cost calculators • Public reporting apps	• 25% operational cost reduction • Real-time analytics • Citizen engagement boost	• Data security risks • Digital literacy barriers • System interoperability	EU-Russia logistics software [90]; illegal waste reporting apps [91]
6. Advanced incineration	Waste-to-energy conversion	• Emission scrubbers • Heat recovery systems • Ash processing units	• 90% landfill diversion • Energy security (500kW/ton) • Methane reduction	• Air pollution concerns • $100M+ facility costs • Public perception issues	EU WtE plants [92]; circular economy integration [93]

6.5 Conclusion

WM remains a significant challenge in many developing countries. Some countries have made partial investments in related infrastructure, logistics, and equipment, for instance, by acquiring waste collection trucks, but limited progress has been made toward adopting a CE model. Transitioning from the traditional "take–make–dispose" approach to a repair, reuse, and recycling framework turning garbage into fresh goods could produce significant societal benefits, yet this transformation is far from complete. In addition, the key recommendations and findings from this paper are as follows:

- The application of emerging technological approaches to properly manage waste holds great prospect in reducing its general effects on the environment. Such innovations can improve the productivity of processing operations while influencing sociocultural attitudes toward waste, thereby reducing nonrecyclable materials and minimizing waste generation.
- Advanced software, alternative ways of transporting waste, contemporary communication protocols, and sensor-based WM are just a few innovations that can aid in reducing waste and delivering financial and environmental gains. However, many of these solutions remain expensive, which restricts their application, and they have some technical requirements that may not be realistic in all settings. Furthermore, each technology has its own pros and cons that should be carefully evaluated prior to implementation. Additional research is needed to identify the most effective technologies for each context.
- Lastly, entrepreneurs in the developing countries should consider investing in modern WM technologies to enable their countries' transition toward a CE. Strict policy implementation and regulations connected to the CE should be enforced by the governments to aid this process and contribute to additional sustainable practices on effective management of wastes.

AI disclosure statement: The author acknowledges the use of AI-based tools for minor language editing or grammatical correction. However, all intellectual contributions, analyses, and conclusions presented in this chapter are entirely the author's own.

References

1. Christensen, T., *Solid waste technology and management*, John Wiley & Sons, 2011
2. Ahmed, I., The Basel convention on the control of transboundary movements of hazardous wastes and their disposal: a legal misfit in global ship recycling jurisprudence. *Wash. Int'l L.J.*, 29, 411, 2019.
3. WHO, Electronic waste (e-waste), World health organization, 2024.
4. Kiddee, P., Naidu, R., Wong, M.H., Electronic waste management approaches: An overview. *Waste Manage.*, 33, 5, 1237–1250, 2013.
5. Rasul, G. and Manandhar, P., *Prospects and problems in promoting tourism in South Asia: A regional perspective. South Asia Econ. J.*, 10, 1, 187–207, 2009.
6. Group, C., CP Group appoints Jarshire to represent in UK and European Market, 2012.
7. Loizia, P., Neofytou, N., Zorpas, A.A., The concept of circular economy strategy in food waste management for the optimization of energy production through anaerobic digestion. *Environ. Sci. Pollut. Res.*, 26, 15, 14766–14773, 2019.
8. Zorpas, A.A., Voukkali, I., Loizia, P., Socio economy impact in relation to waste prevention, in: *Sustainable economic development: green economy and green growth*, pp. 31–48, Springer, 2016.
9. Zorpas, A.A., Voukkali, I., Loizia, P., *Effectiveness of waste prevention program in primary students' schools. Environ. Sci. Pollut. Res.*, 24, 16, 14304–14311, 2017.
10. Cooper, T., WEEE, WEEE, WEEE, WEEE, all the way home? An evaluation of proposed electrical and electronic waste legislation. *Eur. Environ.*, 10, 3, 121–130, 2000.
11. EU, Council Directive 1999/31/EC of 26 April 1999 on the landfill of waste, 1990.
12. Treasury, H.M., Tax and the environment: using economic instruments, HM Treasury, 2002.
13. Detr, *Waste strategy 2000 for England and Wales*, DETR, London, 2000.
14. Sati, K. and Vats, A., Turning Trash into Treasure: The Current Landscape and Future of Waste-to-Energy Initiatives in India. *Int. J. Environ. Agric. Biotechnol.*, 9, 6, 2024.
15. Rane, A.K., *et al.*, Community-driven Waste Management Initiatives: Exploring Barangay Strategies for Cleaner and Greener Noveleta. *Int. J. Adv. Multidiscip. Res. Stud.*, 4, 3, 527–534, 2024.
16. Ilomo, M. and Charles, G., Financing grassroots initiatives in solid waste management: benchmarking the Tanzanian experience against international practices. *Environ. Res. Commun.*, 7, 1, 015012, 2025.
17. Udanga, G.E. and Cuevas, A., Assessing Government Service Delivery in Barangay Pili, Mogpog, Marinduque: A Resident Satisfaction Survey. *Cogniz. J. Multidiscip. Stud.*, 7, 3, 341–359, 2023.

18. Kumar, R., Waste Management Initiatives in Rural India, in: *Promoting Socio-Economic Development through Business Integration*, pp. 338–354, IGI Global Scientific Publishing, 2015.
19. Aishah, T.S.D.S.N., *et al.*, Identifying the initiatives of construction waste management in Malaysia towards achieving sustainable construction. *Construction*, 3, 1, 130–134, 2023.
20. Agarwal, R., Chaudhary, M., Singh, J., Waste management initiatives in India for human well being. *Eur. Sci. J.*, 2015.
21. Hashim, K.S.H.-Y., Mohamed, A.H., Redza, H.Z.M.S., Developing a waste minimization awareness model through community based movement: A case study of the IIUM Green Team. *Geografia*, 8, 5, 2012.
22. Kasala, S.E., Critical analysis of the challenges of solid waste management initiatives in Keko Machungwa informal settlement, Dar Es Salaam. *J. Environ. Prot.*, 5, 12, 1064, 2014.
23. Tallei, T.E., Local community-based initiatives of waste management activities on Bunaken Island in North Sulawesi. *Res. J. Environ. Earth Sci.*, 5, 12, 737–743, 2013.
24. Ibañez, E.P. and Torrentira Jr, M.C., Problems and recommendations to improve the solid waste management initiatives of the local government unit of Tanauan, Leyte, Philippines. *Eur. J. Dev. Stud.*, 2, 4, 1–3, 2022.
25. Lorenzon, L., *et al.*, CARING NATURE (ClimAte neutRal INitiatives for GrowiNg heAlTh and care Unmet REquirements)-Waste Management in Health Care. *Impact Surg.*, 1, 2, 64–64, 2024.
26. Singer, J., Kieu, K.T., Pravitasari, A.E., Solid waste management in tourist destinations in developing nations: case studies in Hoi An, Vietnam, and Puncak, Indonesia, in: *Environmental Sustainability and Education for Waste Management: Implications for Policy and Practice*, pp. 189–206, 2019.
27. Marodiyah, I., Cahyana, A.S., Nurmalasari, I.R., Empowering Communities Through Household Organic Waste Management: A Case Study in Kajartengguli Village, Indonesia. *Indones. J. Cult. Community Dev.*, 14, 2, 2023.
28. Kitole, F.A., *et al.*, The Impact of Poor Waste Management on Public Health Initiatives in Shanty Towns in Tanzania. *Sustainability*, 16, 24, 10873, 2024.
29. Ramasubramanian, B., *et al.*, Recent advances in extended producer responsibility initiatives for plastic waste management in Germany and UK. *Mater. Circ. Econ.*, 5, 1, 6, 2023.
30. Garlapati, V.K., E-waste in India and developed countries: Management, recycling, business and biotechnological initiatives. *Renewable Sustainable Energy Rev.*, 54, 874–881, 2016.
31. Mansoor, A., Community Initiatives in Solid Waste, in: *21st WEDC Conference*, 1995.
32. Adalberto, M., *et al.*, Inclusive Waste Governance and Grassroots Innovations for Social, Environmental And Economic Change. Report on first research

outcomes of the project Recycling Networks & Waste Governance Recycling Networks. Recuperado el, 13, 7, p. 2022, 2018.
33. Bismoko, A.H., *et al.*, Green Campus Initiative Assessing Waste Management at a Technical Polytechnic. *Academia Open*, 9, 2, 2024, 10.21070/acopen. 9.2024. 8591–10.21070/acopen. 9.2024. 8591
34. Sahni, H., Chopra, N., Gadhavi, P., The social rendition of plastic waste management initiatives in India, in: *Socially Responsible Plastic: Is This Possible?* pp. 31–58, Emerald Publishing Limited, 2023.
35. Jiménez, A.N., Overcoming Waste Management Challenges in Costa Rica: Evaluating Practices, Government Initiatives, and Future Strategies, 2024.
36. Ofori, D. and Opoku Mensah, A., Sustainable electronic waste management among households: a circular economy perspective from a developing economy. *Manag. Environ. Qual.: An Int. J.*, 33, 1, 64–85, 2022.
37. King, A.M., *et al.*, *Reducing waste: repair, recondition, remanufacture or recycle? Sustainable Dev.*, 14, 4, 257–267, 2006.
38. Ji, G. and Huang, W., Effective implementation of WEEE take-back directive. *J. Manag. Sci. China*, 15, 1–9, 2012.
39. Meadows, D., Meadows, D., Randers, J., *Beyond the limits: Global collapse or a sustainable future Earthscan*, London, 1992.
40. Rajalakshmi, S., Amzad Basha, K., Asif Jamal, G., *A manual on waste management audit*, 163p, Laser Park Publish House, Coimbatore, Tamil Nadu, India, 2023.
41. McManus, P., *Defining sustainable development for our common future: a history of the World Commission on Environment and Development (Brundtland Commission)*, Taylor & Francis, 2014.
42. Hansen, W., Christopher, M., Verbuecheln, M., EU waste policy and challenges for regional and local authorities, Ecological Institute for International and European Environmental Policy, Berlin, Germany, 2002.
43. Korhonen, J., *et al.*, Circular economy as an essentially contested concept. *J. Cleaner Prod.*, 175, 544–552, 2018.
44. Zeller, V., *et al.*, Urban waste flows and their potential for a circular economy model at city-region level. *Waste Manage. (Oxford)*, 83, 83–94, 2019.
45. Pires, A. and Martinho, G., Waste hierarchy index for circular economy in waste management. *Waste Manage. (Oxford)*, 95, 298–305, 2019.
46. Omoloso, O., *et al.*, Corporate sustainability disclosure: a leather industry perspective. *Emerg. Sci. J.*, 4, 1, 1–11, 2020.
47. Van Ewijk, S. and Stegemann, J., Limitations of the waste hierarchy for achieving absolute reductions in material throughput. *J. Cleaner Prod.*, 132, 122–128, 2016.
48. Diaz, L.F., *Waste management in developing countries and the circular economy*, pp. 1–2, SAGE Publications, Sage UK: London, England, 2017.
49. Miller, B., Spertus, J., Kamga, C., Costs and benefits of pneumatic collection in three specific New York City cases. *Waste Manage. (Oxford)*, 34, 11, 1957–1966, 2014.

50. Hull, C.E., Millette, S., Williams, E., Challenges and opportunities in building circular-economy incubators: Stakeholder perspectives in Trinidad and Tobago. *J. Cleaner Prod.*, 296, 126412, 2021.
51. Barbaritano, M., Bravi, L., Savelli, E., Sustainability and quality management in the Italian luxury furniture sector: A circular economy perspective. *Sustainability*, 11, 11, 3089, 2019.
52. Dung, T., Circular Economy—Key to Reduct Pollution, Promote Sustainable Development.
53. Hujare, R. and Telsang, K., Solid Waste Generation Data Variability in India—An Unnoticed Hurdle, in: *Recent Developments in Waste Management: Select Proceedings of Recycle 2018*, Springer, 2020.
54. Oduro-Appiah, K. and Afful, A., Sustainable Pathway for Closing Solid Waste Data Gaps: Implications for Modernization, in: *Strategies of Sustainable Solid Waste Management*, p. 25, 2021.
55. Speier, C.J., Mondal, M.M., Weichgrebe, D., Data reliability of solid waste analysis in Asia's newly industrialised countries. *Int. J. Environ. Waste Manage.*, 22, 1–4, 124–146, 2018.
56. Stevanović, Č.H.D., *et al.*, The importance of reliability of data on waste generation in decision-making processes determining the optimal waste management options in the Municipality of Bor. Recycling and Sustainable Development, 6, 1, 1–7, 2013.
57. Fertel, C., *et al.*, Canadian energy and climate policies: A SWOT analysis in search of federal/provincial coherence. *Energy Policy*, 63, 1139–1150, 2013.
58. Symeonides, D., Loizia, P., Zorpas, A.A., Tire waste management system in Cyprus in the framework of circular economy strategy. *Environ. Sci. Pollut. Res.*, 26, 35, 35445–35460, 2019.
59. Kolios, A. and Read, G., A political, economic, social, technology, legal and environmental (PESTLE) approach for risk identification of the tidal industry in the United Kingdom. *Energies*, 6, 10, 5023–5045, 2013.
60. Fons, M.V.S., Fierro, J.A.M., y Patiño, M.G., Rural tourism: A sustainable alternative. *Appl. Energy*, 88, 2, 551–557, 2011.
61. Tsangas, M., *et al.*, The application of analytical hierarchy process in combination with PESTEL-SWOT analysis to assess the hydrocarbons sector in Cyprus. *Energies*, 12, 5, 791, 2019.
62. Zorpas, A.A., Strategy development in the framework of waste management. *Sci. Total Environ.*, 716, 137088, 2020.
63. Kulczycka, J., Dziobek, E., Szmiłyk, A., Challenges in the management of data on extractive waste—The Polish case. *Miner. Econ.*, 33, 341–347, 2020.
64. Carapina, H.S., *et al.*, Importance of municipal waste data reliability in decision making process using LCA model-case study conducted in Timok County (Serbia). *Int. J. Waste Resour.*, 4, 4, 1–7, 2014.
65. Lamborn, J., Issues in using medium to large scale landfill data for modelling, model calibration and prediction, 2011.

66. Maus, T., *et al.*, Volume Determination Challenges in Waste Sorting Facilities: Observations and Strategies. *Sensors*, 24, 7, 2114, 2024.
67. Clark, R.M., Sweeten, J.M., Greathouse, D.G., Basic data for solid waste pilot study. *J. Sanit. Eng. Div.*, 98, 6, 897–907, 1972.
68. Lu, W., *et al.*, Big data in construction waste management: Prospects and challenges. *Detritus*, 2018.
69. Sheshinski, R.H., Indirect data collection for waste statistics and waste indicators. *Stat. J. U.N. Econ. Comm. Eur.*, 19, 1–2, 53–63, 2002.
70. Alam, A., *et al.*, Application of EASEWASTE model for assessing environmental impacts from solid waste landfi lling. *Arch. Environ. Prot.*, 47, 4, 2021.
71. Abbasi, S. and Erdebilli, B., Green closed-loop supply chain networks' response to various carbon policies during COVID-19. *Sustainability*, 15, 4, 3677, 2023.
72. Khan, M.T. and Imran, M., Unveiling the carbon footprint of Europe and Central Asia: insights into the impact of key factors on CO2 emissions, 2023.
73. Abbasi, G., Khoshalhan, F., Hosseininezhad, S.J., Municipal solid waste management and energy production: A multi-objective optimization approach to incineration and biogas waste-to-energy supply chain. *Sustainable Energy Technol. Assess.*, 54, 102809, 2022.
74. Shyam, G.K., Manvi, S.S., Bharti, P., Smart waste management using Internet-of-Things (IoT), in: *2017 2nd international conference on computing and communications technologies (ICCCT)*, IEEE, 2017.
75. Noiki, A., *et al.* Smart waste bin system: a review. *IOP Conf. Ser.: Earth Environ. Sci.*, 2021, IOP Publishing.
76. Chowdhury, B. and Chowdhury, M.U., RFID-based real-time smart waste management system, in: *2007 Australasian telecommunication networks and applications conference*, IEEE, 2007.
77. Joshi, S., Singh, U.K., Yadav, S., Smart dustbin using GPS tracking. *Int. Res. J. Eng. Technol.*, 6, 156–170, 2019.
78. Fawwaz, D.Z., *et al.*, Optimal distributed MQTT broker and services placement for SDN-edge based smart city architecture. *Sensors*, 22, 9, 3431, 2022.
79. Baldo, D., *et al.*, A multi-layer lorawan infrastructure for smart waste management. *Sensors*, 21, 8, 2600, 2021.
80. Ogunwolu, L., *et al.*, Design and Implementation of an IoT Based Smart Waste Bin for Fill Level and Biodegradability Monitoring. 2020.
81. Wijaya, A.S., Zainuddin, Z., Niswar, M., Design a smart waste bin for smart waste management, in: *2017 5th International Conference on Instrumentation, Control, and Automation (ICA)*, IEEE, 2017.
82. Harkut, D.G. and Kasat, K., Introductory chapter: artificial intelligence-challenges and applications, in: *Artificial Intelligence-Scope and Limitations*, 2019.
83. Wang, Z., Li, H., Zhang, X., Construction waste recycling robot for nails and screws: Computer vision technology and neural network approach. *Autom. Constr.*, 97, 220–228, 2019.

84. Fayomi, G., *et al.*, Smart waste management for smart city: impact on industrialization. *IOP Conf. Ser.: Earth Environ. Sci.*, 2021, IOP Publishing.
85. Vu, H.L., *et al.*, Interactions of residential waste composition and collection truck compartment design on GIS route optimization. *Waste Manage.*, 102, 613–623, 2020.
86. Sheng, T.J., *et al.*, An internet of things based smart waste management system using LoRa and tensorflow deep learning model. *IEEE Access*, 8, 148793–148811, 2020.
87. NEA, Nuclear nenergy data, Nuclear Technology Development and EconomicsNuclear Technology Development and Economics, 2021.
88. Eurostat, Municipal waste down by second consecutive year, News articles, 2025.
89. ZenRobotics, Safe Sorting - Superior Waste Recycling Robots, 2007.
90. Czekała, W., Drozdowski, J., Łabiak, P., Modern technologies for waste management: a review. *Appl. Sci.*, 13, 15, 8847, 2023.
91. winpol, An app to fight illegal dumping, 2022.
92. CEWEP, Waste-to-Energy Plants in Europe in 2020, 20220.
93. Tuboalabo, A., *et al.*, Circular economy integration in traditional business models: Strategies and outcomes. *Finance Account. Res. J.*, 6, 6, 1105–1123, 2024.
94. Schröder, P., Lemille, A., Desmond, P., Making the circular economy work for human development. *Resour., Conserv. Recycl.*, 156, 104686, 2020.
95. Guarnieri, P., Silva, L.C., Trojan, F., Lizot, M., Transition to the Circular Economy in Brazil: A Multicriteria Decision Model from the Perspective of New Institutional Theory. *Revista de Administração de Empresas*, 65, e2024–0216, 2025.
96. Marino, A. and Pariso, P., The transition towards to the circular economy: European SMEs' trajectories. *Entrep. Sustain. Issues*, 8, 4, 431, 2021.
97. Debrah, J.K., Teye, G.K., Dinis, M.A.P., Barriers and challenges to waste management hindering the circular economy in Sub-Saharan Africa. *Urban Sci.*, 6, 3, 57, 2022.
98. Smol, M., Kulczycka, J., Avdiushchenko, A., Circular economy indicators in relation to eco-innovation in European regions. *Clean Technol. Environ. Policy*, 19, 3, 669–678, 2017.
99. Awan, U. and Sroufe, R., Sustainability in the circular economy: insights and dynamics of designing circular business models. *Appl. Sci.*, 12, 3, 1521, 2022.
100. Bressanelli, G., Pigosso, D.C., Saccani, N., Perona, M., Enablers, levers and benefits of Circular Economy in the Electrical and Electronic Equipment supply chain: a literature review. *J. Clean. Prod.*, 298, 126819, 2021.
101. Srdjevic, Z., Lakicevic, M., Srdjevic, B., Approach of decision making based on the analytic hierarchy process for urban landscape management. *Environ. Manag.*, 51, 3, 777–785, 2013.

102. Wurzel, R.K., Policy in the EU: Actors, Institutions and Processes on 6th May 2021, available online: https://www. routledge. com/ Environmental-Policy-in-the-EU-Actors-Institutions-and-Processes/Jordan-Gravey/p/book/9781138392168.
103. Achinas, S., Longinos, S., Achinas, V., Euverink, G.J.W., Scale-up operations for biogas production: Analysis on critical factors governing large-scale operations, in: *Biogas Production: From Anaerobic Digestion to a Sustainable Bioenergy Industry*, pp. 263–283, Springer International Publishing, Cham, 2021.
104. Trinh, V.L. and Chung, C.K., Advances in triboelectric nanogenerators for sustainable and renewable energy: Working mechanism, tribo-surface structure, energy storage-collection system, and applications. *Processes*, 11, 9, 2796, 2023.

7

Collaborative Partnerships and Ecosystem Building

A.U. Lawan[1]*, Abubakar Abdulkarim[2,3], Ibrahim Sani Madugu[2,4] and Mutiu Shola Bakare[2]

[1]Department of Electrical Engineering/Center for Renewable Energy and Sustainable Transition, Bayero University Kano, Kano, Nigeria
[2]Department of Electrical Engineering, Kampala International University, Kampala, Uganda
[3]Department of Electrical Engineering, Faculty of Engineering, Ahmadu Bello University, Zaria, Nigeria
[4]Department of Electrical Engineering, Aliko Dangote University, Wudil, Kano, Nigeria

Abstract

The movement toward a circular economy is inevitable globally; for this to be realistic, there is a need for innovative approaches in the form of value creation. This development is a move beyond conventional approaches driven by conventional efficiency driven approaches. However, the circular economy needs a collaborative approach that tales share responsibility, system thinking, and realistic governance. This chapter has shown that within energy industries and manufacturing chains, the development of an ecosystem that can connect suppliers, producers, consume and policy makers is the best pathway for closing. In addition, it has explained the roles of ecosystem building and collaboration in the advancements of the circular economy across all sectors of society. Other contributions of this chapter are the analysis of the contributions of artificial intelligence (AI), blockchain, Internet of Things (IoT), and digital twins towards the implementation of the circular economy. Furthermore, discussions on case studies from different countries on various circular economic integrated models have been provided, and eventually, lessons learned from them have been highlighted. Finally, various policy directions have been discussed that can enable all the stakeholders to be committed in order to provide many possible options for realistic implementations and development

**Corresponding author*: aulawan.ele@buk.edu.ng

Jeyaprakash Natarajan, Milon Selvam Dennison, M. Bhuvanesh Kumar and Ganapathy Thirukkotti (eds.) Manufacturing and the Circular Economy, (213–252) © 2027 Scrivener Publishing LLC

of the circular economy. It is expected that the chapter can assist policymakers, researchers, and all stakeholders in better understanding and possible options for the development of circular economic models across the globe. This can assist the developing nations to be more proactive in the circular economy, so that they will not be left behind in the scheme of things.

Keywords: Circular economy, collaborative partnerships, renewable energy, industrial ecosystems, digitalization, policy, sustainability, industrial symbiosis

7.1 Introduction

To address the global sustainability crisis recently, the circular economy (CE) has been widely considered as one of the most influential paradigm shifts that emphasizes keeping materials and products in use for as long as possible, maximizing value retention, and ensuring regeneration of natural systems [1–3]. This is unlike the traditional linear model defined by the "take, make, dispose" approach; this transformation represents not only an environmental strategy but also a restructuring of industrial systems, business models, and socio-economic relations [2].

Progressively, the increasing use of the circular economy is recognized as a driver of innovation, competitiveness, and resilience, most importantly in areas where resource scarcity and environmental degradation are of serious concern. The manufacturing sector is a global giant in the area of carbon emission and energy use; therefore, they are at the center of the circular economy. In addition, industries are faced with the issue of climate change policies and fuel price volatility. These issues have changed the customer's perspective about them. Therefore, the circular economy has been the leader in maintaining stability and ensuring profits are maintained. One of the examples of this transition is the EU circular economy action plan 2020, which was designed to stimulate large-scale innovations that are eco-friendly and assist in waste reduction [3]. There are some efforts on the African continent; some of the prominent countries that have developed circular economic models are Kenya, Nigeria, and South Africa. These countries have been integrating national policies for renewable energy, industrial development, and waste management, and these are some of the top priorities for the advancement of the circular economy. To develop these models, collaboration is a central factor, such that without collaboration, no single actor can achieve the purpose. Therefore, when these actors work together, a more complex circular economy model can be developed to solve societal problems. The manufacturing sector is a typical example that can provide a practical illustration of how to collaborate and adopt a circular economy. This can be demonstrated in high-energy industries. In this case, renewable energy resources such as wind, solar, and biomass can be used together with the help of power electronic devices to reduce greenhouse gas emissions and decentralized power supply [4, 5].

Another area of development when looking into the circular economy is value creation when considering it from the business angle. Traditionally, a business model is maximizing profits on short term; however, the circular economy gives more consideration to long-term resilience and value creation [6]. This comprised new models' example product-as-a-service in which the firm retained the ownership and at the same time satisfied the customers by providing access, sharing economies, and logistics. This also depends on transparency, governance trust, and the number of possible collaborative partnerships. From this analysis, one can see that one of the enablers of the circular economy is digitization. This is possible with the help of the internet and other technologies. That can assist in areas of maintenance predictions, recycling, real-time monitoring, and management [7]. A typical example is the recycling of solar panels in Kano, Nigeria, which is an AI-driven model entrusted with the responsibility of tracking solar panels to allow manufacturers, recyclers, and the government to trace them after use. Other initiatives are agricultural circular models developed in the same state. This is designed to assist farmers in solar energy irrigation systems [8]. Also, it can show how developing nations can enhance agriculture for more industrial revolutions in various sectors of society with the help of circular economic models.

This introduction has established how collaborative partnerships can assist in ecosystem building, which is critical for operating a circular economy. They provide technological, innovative, instructional, and societal scaffolding needed to connect all the stakeholders for successful economic model building.

7.2 The Strategic Importance of Collaboration in Circular Economy Implementation

Presently, collaboration is critical to the actualization of the circular economy rather than optional. This is because the system is to be designed in such a way that resources can be extracted, processed, consumed, and reintegrated into the economy in a circular manner; therefore, for this to be possible, collaboration must be at all levels, such as technical, social, institutional, and financial levels.

7.2.1 Why Collaboration Matters in CE

In the circular economy, value chains are multidimensional and interdependent, unlike the case of linear value chains; the system is straightforward and, in most cases, vertically integrated. One of these is the life cycle extension of a product. For this to be achieved, all stakeholders require a coordinated approach between designers, manufacturers, logistic providers, and recyclers, to name just a few. This type of interconnection is better handled by more than one actor, and therefore, an ecosystem-level coordination is desired. In this regard, it is clear that collaboration can provide several benefits, such as system-level innovation, risk sharing, cost reduction, policy alignment, trust, and legitimacy.

7.2.2 Multidimensional Nature of Collaboration

Multi-dimensional approaches of collaborations ensure that the circular economy is across various layers, such as technical, institutional, and behavioral, and in many dimensions of each, as explained; that is,

a) Technical collaboration: Joint R&D between industry, academia, and startups, on eco-design, renewable integration, digital twins, and material science.
b) Economic and financial collaboration: blended finance models, risk-sharing partnerships, and Co-investment platforms.
c) Regulatory collaboration and policy: multi-level governance (local, national, and international) to harmonize regulations and standards.
d) Social collaboration: Engagement of civil society, consumer groups, and communities to promote awareness and adoption of CE behaviors.

7.2.3 Collaboration in Energy-Intensive Manufacturing

In energy-intensive sectors such as steel, cement, chemicals, and electronics, collaboration is critical to overcoming entrenched barriers. High energy demand is faced by these industries, carbon intensity, and complex supply chains. Collaborative CE approaches can include [9–11]:

a) Shared renewable energy platforms: Industrial parks in China and Europe increasingly rely on shared solar or wind energy installations to reduce costs and emissions.

b) Joint material recovery systems: Electronics manufacturers collaborate with recyclers to recover rare earth metals.
c) Digital monitoring ecosystems: IoT and AI platforms are developed jointly by tech firms and manufacturers to enable real-time tracking of energy and material flows.

For example, the Kalundborg Symbiosis project in Denmark is one of the most cited cases of industrial symbiosis that emerged through collaboration between power plants, pharmaceutical companies, and municipal authorities. The waste heat from a power station is used to warm homes, while by-products such as gypsum are supplied to construction industries [12]. Without trust-based, multi-stakeholder collaboration, such inter-sectoral exchanges would not be feasible.

7.2.4 Collaboration for Policy and Governance

Governments play a pivotal role in orchestrating CE ecosystems. As such, their efforts are most effective when co-designed with industry and academia. For example, the European Battery Alliance (EBA) was established to secure sustainable battery value chains through collaboration between EU institutions, research centers, and more than 400 industrial actors. This initiative not only boosts Europe's competitiveness but also embeds CE principles such as recycling and second-life applications of batteries [13].

In African contexts, collaborative governance platforms are emerging under the African Circular Economy Alliance (ACEA), which brings together governments, businesses, and think tanks to co-develop strategies for circular value chains in textiles, plastics, and renewable energy [14]. Similarly, in Nigeria, collaborative policy making between the Ministry of Power, Universities, and renewable energy start-ups is enabling localized CE approaches in energy access projects.

7.2.5 Digitalization and Collaborative CE

Due to the present global shift in information technology, digital technology has become one of the hearts to enabling collaboration in the circular economy ecosystem. In this regard, exchange of resources is done digitally, and recording in immutable ledgers is done using IoT-enabled means. Furthermore, IoT networks enable data sharing in real time, and sharing can be achieved in real time with the support of IoT for the circular economy to be realistic and get the expected attention [15, 16]. Other digital tools support maintenance and lifecycle optimization, and these also constitute pillars of modern circular economic models. There are some efforts by researchers to develop models, such as recycling coins by [17]. This model is developed to incentivize stakeholders through a blockchain-enabled solar panel recycling model. Additionally, effort is presented in [18], where AI-driven maintenance allowed equipment operators and recyclers to share information on the degradation of components. This allowed for prompt refurbishment and recycling. This model required both hardware and software manufacturers to collaborate and ensure the system is reliable, economical, and available. These are also attributes of circular economic models.

7.2.6 Collaboration as a Driver of Social Acceptance

Reports have shown that people are more likely to adopt new models, such as product-as-a-service or take-back schemes, when there is visible collaboration between companies, governments, and civil society [19]. This is beyond technical and policy domains, as collaboration is crucial for consumer acceptance of CE. In urban CE projects in Melbourne and Amsterdam, municipalities have worked closely with NGOs, local communities, and groups of start-ups to build trust and ensure that CE systems are aligned with citizen needs [20].

In the context of Africa, consumer acceptance has often been tied to affordability, cultural appropriateness, and awareness. On the other hand, collaborative efforts such as partnerships between microfinance institutions, solar providers, and women's cooperatives have improved the adoption of solar lanterns and pay-as-you-go systems, linking inclusive finance with circular design for CE [21].

7.3 Forms of Collaboration and Thematic Synthesis of Collaboration Trends

In the circular economy, collaboration can manifest in diverse forms depending on the sectoral context, the actors involved, and the stage of the value chain. These diverse forms range from formal partnerships such as public–private partnerships (PPPs) to less formal arrangements such as community-driven networks or cross-sector innovation platforms. Regardless of the structure, each form can play a selective role in enabling the transition from linear to circular models through the exchange of fostering knowledge, co-innovation, and resource sharing.

7.3.1 Public Private Partnerships (PPPs)

Public-private partnerships (PPPs) are some of the most visible forms of the circular economy. Governments, through their corridors such as ministries and local authorities, often have a low level of technical expertise and financial resources as gaps to implement CE solutions independently on their own. Thus, partnering with private companies can help to bridge these gaps for ensuring scalability and efficiency [22, 23]. For instance, the Stadler GmbH project in Germany, in partnership with universities and government agencies, has made closed-loop PET recycling systems much more feasible; waste plastics have been collected, reprocessed, and reintegrated into manufacturing [24] through co-investment and shared governance.

In Africa, through an implementing agency, Rural Electrification Agencies (REA), PPPs in renewable energy through Nigeria's solar mini-grid initiatives funded jointly by international donors, state governments, and private developers have demonstrated how some CE principles, such as collaboration, can be embedded in energy access programs. Similarly, PPPs are particularly critical in infrastructure-heavy CE projects such as waste-to-energy plants, eco-industrial parks, and urban circular systems. These project initiatives need long-term trust, financing, and stable governance, all of which are enhanced through collaborative PPP frameworks [25].

7.3.2 Academic Industry Research Collaborations

Universities and other research institutions have been key contributors to CE through research, development, and innovation (RDI) in materials, renewable technologies, and digital solutions, when these are partnered with industry, innovations can be up-scaled and commercialized effectively. For instance, academic industry consortia in the European automotive sector, where universities co-design and develop modular vehicle components with manufacturers. These project initiatives enable remanufacturing, recycling, and resource-efficient production.

7.3.3 Supplier Manufacturer Agreements

Manufacturers drive design and production, while suppliers are at the front line of material sourcing. Thus, collaboration between these two players is critical for circular product development. Agreements may involve:

a) Material substitution (e.g., replacing virgin plastics with bio-based polymers),
b) Modular component design (to allow disassembly and reuse),
c) Reverse logistics for returning end-of-life products to manufacturers.

Suppliers have partnered with Apple to source recycled aluminum for MacBook production, which is a typical example. One of the circular models in Africa is seen in the cement manufacturer's collaboration with farmers for the supply of used crop residue as alternative fuel, thereby reducing the dependency on fossil fuel for the energy requirements of their plants.

7.3.4 Cross-Sector Platforms and Networks

The majority of the transformative circular economic models are possible when there are collaborations across different sectors. In this case, different institutions and industries co-designed and proposed solutions. These enable cross-sector initiatives and result in providing space for discussions, innovative proposals, and pilot project development. In this regard, the Ellen MacArthur Foundation's circular economic platforms bring academia, government, and business together in order to develop many innovative strategies for global best practices of circular economic model development and implementations. Another effort in Africa is done by the Renewable Energy Association of Nigeria (REAN) and the African Circular Economy Alliance (ACEA). These developed mechanisms for circular approaches in energy material management, renewable energy, plastics, and textiles within Africa and some African countries such as Nigeria, Rwanda, Kenya, and South Africa [26–28].

7.3.5 Community-Based and Civil Society Collaborations

Community-level collaborations and civil society can play a vital role in ensuring local adoption of CE practices, while NGOs, cooperatives, and grassroots organizations often act as intermediaries between technical experts and end-users [16]. For instance, women's cooperatives in Kenya collaborated with solar companies and microfinance institutions to distribute pay-as-you-go solar home systems through energy initiatives bodies such as Eco was Center for Energy Efficiency (ECREE). This model not only enhances energy access but also integrates circular features through modular design and product take-back schemes [17]. Also, community-based waste collection and recycling networks in Lagos, Nigeria, have shown how local participation enhances circular material flows while also creating more jobs [28].

7.3.6 Thematic Synthesis of Collaboration Trends

A report of a review of 59 high-impact CE studies has revealed recurring themes that shape collaboration outcomes [20–30]. These themes highlight both opportunities and challenges for ecosystem building:

(a) Supply Chain Collaboration
Recently, the supply chain collaboration has become one of the most frequently documented themes. This is because the circular practices such as eco-design, remanufacturing, and reverse logistics have been integrated across the value chain [29]. For instance, cross-firm agreements in the electronics sector allow recovery of the critical minerals from discarded devices to reduce dependency on virgin mining [30].

(b) Digital Tools (Industry 4.0)
IoT, blockchain, AI, and digital twins, which are Industry 4.0 technologies, have increasingly been used to coordinate collaboration [31]. This is to provide predictive insights, traceability, and real-time monitoring that make CE models feasible at both prototype and scale [32].

(c) Governance and Regulation
Regulatory incentives and governance frameworks remain essential to aligning stakeholders toward common goals in CE [23]. Public sectors that co-create policies with industry and institutions, such as in the EU's eco-design directive, have become more successful, especially at scaling CE, than those relying solely on top-down mandates.

(d) Cross-Sector Partnerships
To foster innovation, the use of cross-sector platforms by connecting stakeholders from diverse industries, particularly valuable in emerging markets where institutional support is weak, has been achieved. This has really helped CE development across different sectors [33].

(e) Institutional Support and Consumer Engagement
Universities, NGOs, and think tanks provide legitimacy, training, and research inputs. Without institutional support, CE initiatives often fail to achieve long-term adoption [33]. Although less frequently reported,

Table 7.1 Key themes in circular economy collaboration literature.

Theme	Frequency	Focus
Supply Chain Collaboration	High	Electronics recycling, modular automotive parts
Digital Tools (Industry 4.0)	Moderate	Blockchain-enabled recycling, IoT monitoring
Governance & Regulation	High	EU Eco-design, African CE Alliance
Cross-Sector Partnerships	Moderate	Ellen MacArthur CE100, REAN Nigeria
Institutional Support	Moderate	Academic–industry R&D projects
Consumer Engagement	Low	Pay-as-you-go solar, take-back schemes

consumer engagement is vital. Without end-user participation, CE systems such as take-back schemes or product-as-a-service cannot function effectively [34]. Table 7.1 presents the themes and their corresponding number of occurrences in terms of their impact, given as frequencies with their respective supporting study areas.

7.4 Actor Roles in Circular Ecosystems

To sustain circular ecosystems, diverse stakeholders whose roles differ but are interdependent are usually considered. Each player contributes specific capacities, technical, financial, social, or institutional roles that allow closing, narrowing, and slowing of resource loops in CE. Understanding these roles is important for achieving incentives, collaborative platforms, and governance mechanisms to align with circular principles.

7.4.1 Suppliers: Gatekeepers of Circular Inputs

To determine the type, quality, and circular potential of inputs entering production processes, suppliers play a foundational role in CE by influencing material sustainability through:

a) Eco-design components: by providing modular, repairable, and standardized components to enable simple disassembly and reuse of materials.
b) Material Replacement: Substituting new materials with renewable, bio-based inputs or recycled materials.
c) Reverse logistics: Playing as nodes for the collection of used materials and means of channeling them back into complete value chains.

A typical example of the above processes is in the electronics sector; suppliers have increasingly been required to supply parts with higher recyclability and compliance with extended producer responsibility (EPR) laws. In Africa, agricultural suppliers and cement manufacturers in Kenya and Nigeria, through collaboration, allow the substitution of fossil fuels with crop residues, reducing emissions while valorizing agricultural waste [35].

7.4.2 Manufacturers: Architects of Circular Design

Manufacturers are the center of the circular economy because they determine how products are designed, assembled, and coupled to markets. Their main responsibility is designed for disassembly, development of modular components, facilitation of repair, recycling, and manufacturing. Efficient resource production, for example, the use of renewable energy for energy-efficient power electronics to reduce waste due to operation, digital integrations, system performance prediction, etc., at global levels, companies like Renault and BMW collaborate with both suppliers and recyclers for plastics and metal into vehicles, while considering other designs for second life applications of systems such as batteries. In Nigeria, small-scale solar PV assemblers partner with local researchers to develop modular charge controllers and inverters that can be refurbished and reused, extending product lifetimes [36].

7.4.3 Consumers: Enablers of Circular Behaviors

Consumers are the main actors in CE; their purchase decisions and how they use and dispose of circular products. Their major roles may include some of the following:

a. New Business Models Adoption: This involves engagement in products and services, leasing, and sharing schemes.

b. Take Back Opportunities: End-of-life products can be returned to the manufacturers for recycling or reprocessing.
c. The Demand for Eco-friendly Goods: Producing market enticements for corporations to plan circular products.

The successes of rental apparel and gadgets companies in Europe have attracted strong consumer participation. However, the African cultures prioritized affordability and accessibility. For instance, the pay-as-you-solar enterprise in Nigeria and Kenya demonstrated that consumers can maintain circularity by upgrading or replacing modular components rather than replacing the entire system [36].

7.4.4 Academia and Research Establishments: Drivers of Knowledge and Innovation

Research centers, such as universities, promote research, innovation, and capacity-building within CE ecosystems through collaborations with other organizations, such as the Ellen MacArthur Foundation. For years, this foundation has collaborated with some African scholarly and research institutions like Stellenbosch University and Bayero University Kano in South Africa and Nigeria, respectively. Together, they achieved milestones in CE, promoting renewable energy, circular agriculture, and many industrial symbioses [37]. To buttress these achievements, these collaborations may consider some of the following roles:

a. Carrying out a pragmatic study on eco-materials, waste valorization, and renewable energy.
b. Training of engineers, policymakers, and entrepreneurs in the CE values.
c. Acting as unbiased knowledge brokers, connecting industry, government, and the communities.

7.4.5 Government and Policymakers: Enablers of Institutional Frameworks

Governments continue to extend their influence on the CE ecosystem. They formulate policies and regulations governing the implementation of the frameworks and provide incentives.

There are various successes recorded *via* these interventions by governments. Some of these interventions include: implementation of the eco-design policies for Extended Producer Responsibility (EPR); provision of fiscal encouragement such as tax holiday, subsidies, and blended financing; synchronizing cross-sectional collaboration with the national and regional stratagems [36].

Some key instances of these government interventions include the following:

a. Europe's Circular Economy Action Plan has demonstrated how legal frameworks drive CE innovation [37].
b. Rwanda's ban on the single-use of plastic, but instead promoted reuse.
c. The Nigeria's Energy Transition Plan, 2022, that incorporates circularity, especially in renewable energy and waste-to-value systems [38].

7.4.6 Financial Institutions: Catalysts for Scaled Investment

The risks involved in circular projects and longer payback times posed a serious challenge to financiers. However, despite those challenges, banks, development finance institutions, and venture capitalists continue to support circular projects *via* some schemes that involve:

a. Provision of green bonds and sustainability-related loans.
b. Supporting a blended financing systems that reduce risks to private investors.
c. Provision of funds to start-ups, incorporating the CE prototypes into renewable energy, recycling waste, and product servicing innovations [39].

The Circular Economy Facility by the African Development Bank (AfDB) emerges as a good method in mobilizing resources for CE-related infrastructure and SMEs.

7.4.7 NGOs and Civil Society: Social Mobilization Agents

Non-governmental organizations (NGOs) and civil society act as advocates, educators, and brokers within the CE ecosystems. They support sensitization, community mobilization, and track how industries perform in environmental protection. Some examples are the Lagos Recycle Points, an NGO that works with households and businesses to collect plastics. They award points to participants, leading to an increase in consumer engagement and behavioral change. In Kenya, an NGO working with microfinance institutions provides rural dwellers with circular, affordable solar systems to female entrepreneurs.

7.4.8 Technology Providers: Digital and Technical Enablers

Technology industries provide hardware and software that enhance some of the following CE practices:

a. Development of an IoT-enabled sensor for tracking energy and material flows.
b. Create a blockchain platform for translucent material relations.
c. Supply an AI predictive model for maintenance and optimization.

Authors in [40] demonstrated that a blockchain can improve accountability in solar panel recycling by paying actors with digital tokens. It was clear that AI-driven prognostics can extend the lifecycle of renewable energy assets and enable resource-efficient maintenance.

7.4.9 Case Synthesis of Actor Roles

In Table 7.2, a summary of the key contributions of ecosystem actors is given with illustrations.

Table 7.2 Contributions of ecosystems actors.

Actor	Contribution to CE	Case example
Suppliers	Material substitution, modular components, reverse logistics	Cement industry using crop residues (Kenya, Nigeria)
Manufactures	Eco-design, resource-efficient production, digital integration.	BMW: recycled materials in EVs; Nigerian PV assemblers
Consumers	Product-as-a-service, take-back schemes, and eco-friendly demand	Pay-as-you-go solar adoption in Kenya and Nigeria

(*Continued*)

Table 7.2 Contributions of ecosystems actors. (*Continued*)

Actor	Contribution to CE	Case Example
Academia	Research and Development, training, knowledge brokering	CREST (Nigeria), Stellenbosch (South Africa)
Government	Regulation, incentives, governance platforms	EU CE Action Plan, Rwanda plastic ban
Financial institutions	Green bonds, blended finance, venture capital	AfDB Circular Economy Facility
NGOs/Civil Society	Advocacy, education, grassroots mobilization	Recycle Points in Lagos, Kenya, and solar cooperatives
Technology Providers	IoT, blockchain, AI tools	Blockchain solar recycling (Chowdhury), AI prognostics (Afridi)

7.4.10 Comparative Perspectives: Africa and Beyond

Circular-economy transitions vary by region due to differences in institutional maturity, structure, and cultural norms that influence collaboration [41]. In developed countries, CE arose through regulatory change and technical advancement. The European Union's action plans, China's Circular Economy Promotion Law, and Japan's 3R (Reduce-Reuse-Recycle) strategy have all incorporated circular principles into policy and industrial design [42]. In Africa and South America, CE had advanced through informal recycling, repair economies, and renewable-energy cooperatives to address governance deficiencies [43].

7.4.10.1 Governance and Institutional Pathways

Governments in Europe and East Asia use top-down institutional frameworks to mandate eco-design standards and extended producer responsibility (EPR) systems. The policies made by these governments created robust markets for secondary materials and financing digital traceability. However, the African pathways prefer to develop from the grassroots through Small and Medium Enterprises (SMEs), non-governmental organizations (NGOs), and receive donations from donor-supporting institutions. Kenya's Sustainable Waste Management Act (2022) formulated the recycling networks with the established city-level partnership [44].

While government maturity differs, both ways emphasized the same standard: partnership moves procedure from rhetoric to preparation. Cross-regional cooperation, such as EU-Africa investigation programs on sustainable materials, indicates reciprocal institutional learning. Africa brings real expertise in inclusive business strategies, whereas Europe provides lessons on regulatory harmonization [45].

7.4.10.2 Financial and Market Mechanisms

Europe has institutionalized the CE financing by providing green bonds and circular innovation funds. In the African systems, the blended-finance schemes that combine concessions and integrate private investments remain the most popular scheme. In Nigeria, for example, the Nigeria Sovereign Investment Authority (NSIA) impact on the co-financing strategy with partners to provide funding for waste-to-energy and renewable power projects. Indeed, it can be deduced that collaborative systems for ecosystem finance reduce risk, promote responsibilities, and increase technological partnership [46].

Furthermore, there is a frequent discouragement in a long-term investment in CE because of volatility in the Forex market and policy somersaults [47]. But it is important to improve on transparent financing, credit guarantees, and carbon pricing mechanisms [48]. The main lessons learnt from the European models can be studied and integrated into the African strategies [49]

7.4.10.3 Technological and Digital Readiness

Digitalization regulates the rate of CE maturity. Europe's digital product permits enable material traceability from design to recycling [50]. In Africa, digital invention arises in mobile platforms for waste collection, pay-as-you-go solar systems, and AI-enabled logistics, which are examples of leapfrogging technologies. These solutions prioritized community adoption over outdated infrastructure. According to an analysis of digital-readiness indicators, countries with more than 60% broadband penetration experience faster CE digitization. Africa's future competitiveness in CE will depend on investments in open-data platforms and regional interoperability standards [51].

7.4.10.4 Socio-Cultural Dimensions and Cross Learning

Traditions influence how societies estimate waste. While Northern Europe, for instance, encourages participation of consumers in sorting and take-back processes, most African cultures promote social enterprise through youth and women's associations in transforming waste to wealth [50]. The hurdle is ensuring these models do not erode their authenticity in such communities. In comparison, evidence suggests that culturally influenced methods embodied stronger collaboration and responsibility as against externally imposed policies [52].

Cross-learning for North-South and South-South Cooperation can facilitate cross-comparison, with North-South policymakers adapting EU traceability standards and Europe adopting low-cost community innovations. The South-South countries, such as Nigeria, Kenya, and Ghana, can share CE knowledge through ACEA and ECOWAS Renewable-Energy Programs. This bidirectional interchange enhances global circular governance and promotes a diverse perspective of CE evolution.

7.5 Industrial Symbiosis and Shared Platforms

Industrial symbiosis (IS) remains among the most practical examples of the circular economy CE in action. The practice of using waste streams, by-products, energy, and water from one industry as resources in another creates mutually advantageous exchanges. The IS connects enterprises, towns, and infrastructure systems, transforming industrial zones into closed-loop ecosystems of materials and energy. Shared platforms are generally powered by digital technology and serve as the coordinating mechanism that makes such transactions visible and efficient. IS and shared platforms play a crucial role in implementing CE in industrial and energy-intensive sectors.

7.5.1 Principles and Mechanisms of Industrial Symbiosis

At its foundation, the industrial symbiosis relies on 3 main principles, as follows:

a. Inputs Substitution: Here, one firm's by-product is used by another company as a raw material.
b. Utility Sharing: This means sharing common infrastructure such as renewable energy plants, heat recovery systems, water recycling, and so on.

c. Exchange of Knowledge: This principle epitomizes firms' information sharing on innovations, flow of material, and optimized practices.

There are two major common models in the IS networks, which include:

a. Hub-and-Spoke: This is where one firm, called a central anchor firm (example: a refinery, cement manufacturer, or power plant), serves as the primary source of raw materials for smaller companies clustered around it. They may use its by-products like waste heat, water, and so on.
b. Network Model: This is where numerous firms cooperate on equal equilibrium, designing shared exchanges of materials, energy, and logistics for optimum delivery.

7.5.2 Global Examples of Industrial Symbiosis

The Kalundborg Symbiosis in Denmark has been in operation for almost 40 years, making it a well-known example of industrial symbiosis. A power plant, pharmaceutical firm, oil refinery, and local municipality exchange steam, water, and by-products like gypsum, resulting in a cost-effective industrial network.

China's eco-industrial parks have expanded industrial symbiosis to national levels. Tianjin Eco-City firms work together to share treated wastewater, exchange industrial by-products, and invest in renewable energy infrastructure.

In Europe, urban-industrial symbiosis programs have evolved where construction companies employ demolition trash for new housing projects, and municipalities offer material matching platforms.

7.5.3 African Context: Emerging Industrial Symbiosis

Though recently, the industrial symbiosis is gaining ground in African countries through:

a. Linkages between cement and agriculture: In Nigeria and Kenya, cement factories use agricultural leftovers (maize stalks, rice husks) from farmers instead of fossil fuels.
b. Valorizations of urban waste: Recycling cooperatives in Lagos provide plastics and metals to local industry, promoting circular flows in building and packaging [9].

c. South African industrial zones are experimenting with pooled solar PV plants and microgrid systems, allowing multiple enterprises to invest and share renewable electricity [10].

In the above instances, industrial symbiosis from Africa's perspective can be seen to be closely tied to energy security and utilization of agricultural products, thereby reflecting its priorities.

7.5.4 Role of Shared Digital Platforms

A major hindrance to IS adoption is the disposal of properties; firms may lack data on possible partners or access to by-products. Shared platforms, both physical and digital, close this gap.

a. Material conversation stages: Online portals enable trades to list accessible by-products and pursue required inputs.
b. Internet of Things (IoT) Monitoring: Real-time sensors track energy and waste flows, allowing companies to find conceivable swaps.
c. Blockchain-based Traceability: Distributed ledgers deliver transparent archives of materials exchanges, promoting responsibility and trust among parties.

In the Netherlands, AI-powered waste-matching platforms are used to identify data that matches industrial waste producers with users, while blockchain pilots in solar panel recycling ensure that waste that is recycled is verified and traced [53]. In Nigeria, a digital small-scale platform is used to connect waste collectors with recyclers. Some of these apps were used in mapping the available plastic waste for collection and resale [54, 55].

7.5.5 Enablers of Industrial Symbiosis

There are abundant determinants to positive IS systems:

a. Physical juxtaposition amongst enterprises saves transportation expenses and permits businesses [56].
b. Transparency in data: Open reportage of material streams and environmental consequences builds confidence.
c. Contracts and governance: Long-term contracts validate exchanges while dropping risks.

d. Infrastructure investment: Shared services, including water treatment or microgrid systems, offer physical size for exchanges [17].

These enablers are regularly supported by government policies, such as eco-industrial park certification or tax enticements for resource exchanges.

7.5.6 Barriers to Industrial Symbiosis

Despite its potential, IS faces significant challenges:

a) Reluctance to share data: Firms often view material flows as proprietary information.
b) High upfront investment: Infrastructure for pipelines, microgrids, or treatment plants requires capital.
c) Trust deficits: Without strong governance, firms may fear dependence on partners.
d) Policy fragmentation: In developing regions, the lack of clear regulations discourages collaboration.
e) For instance, attempts to create symbiotic industrial clusters in West Africa have been slowed by weak governance and limited investment in digital platforms. Table 7.3 presents the enablers of the circular economy and their corresponding level of impacts.

Table 7.3 Enablers of industrial symbiosis.

Enabler	Impact	Illustrative example
Geographic Proximity	High	Kalundborg Symbiosis (Denmark)
Data Transparency	High	Dutch AI waste-matching platforms
Trust & Contracts	High	Long-term PPP waste-to-energy projects
Infrastructure	Medium	Shared microgrids in South African industrial zones

7.5.7 Industrial Symbiosis and Renewable Energy

The age of centralized power systems is gradually reducing by the day; as such, there are several initiatives globally. These initiatives allow the sharing of solar, wind, and biomass plant development in modular forms. This development reduced the dependence on fossil fuels for the energy needs of many communities globally. Some of the industrial parks can be found in India and Ethiopia; these projects have shown how renewable energy symbiosis can align CE goals with climate mitigation [20]. In another development, agro-industrial clusters have been developed in Nigeria to use biogas from agricultural waste, which created both security and waste management benefits [19–21].

7.6 Case Studies of Circular Partnerships

Case studies provide concrete illustrations of how collaborative partnerships drive circular economy outcomes in practice. They highlight the mechanisms, actors, and enabling conditions that transform circular principles into real-world impacts. The following examples cover global best practices and African emerging experiences, focusing on renewable energy, manufacturing, agriculture, and urban systems.

7.6.1 European Experiences: Mature Circular Partnerships

(a) Stadler GmbH – Closed-loop PET Recycling
In Europe, Germany has developed a good example of a circular project. The project has partners from the universities and government agencies for implementation. Eventually, the partnership has achieved a closed loop recycling, in which the post-consumer PET bottles are collected, processed, and returned into used for food grade packaging. The project has shown that with the developed model, partnerships with universities and government agencies make it possible to create a profitable, environmentally friendly circular economic model in the country.

(b) The Melbourne Circular Economy City Project
In Melbourne, Australia, the city government, business, and NGO developed a city-wide circular economy model that combined waste recycling, renewable energy, and urban faming. In this project, solar cooperatives generate electricity in a decentralized manner for local industries, and community groups collect food waste for composting. The project

successfully demonstrated circularity by suing realistic local partnership in the community.

(c) European Battery Alliance (EBA)

This project could be regarded as one of the most successful of its kind globally, this is due to the diversity in the number of companies, about 400. EU institutions and universities are involved. Furthermore, it is called one of the most ambitious multi-stakeholder collaborations in Europe. The project aims to create thousands of green jobs in the EU. The focal point is on securing the battery supply chain, whereby recycling, reuse, and second-life applications are integrated.

7.6.2 African Case Studies: Emerging Collaborative Ecosystems

(a) Nigerian Mini-Grids and Solar Value Chains

In Africa, there are many efforts to see that microgrids assist the circular economy in many ways; one of these efforts is in Nigeria. In Nigeria, there are many partners such as the World Bank, states, and local government programs that assist in ensuring that microgrids in modular forms have gained national acceptance. It has been cleared that the majority of these projects centered on circular economic model. For these initiatives to assist the circular economy, they are normally designed in modular forms such that refurbishments and take-back systems are carefully considered for the end-of-life recycling of such systems. These considerations are linked to the circular economy, sustainability, and social equity.

(b) Rwanda's Plastic Ban and Circular Enterprises

Rwanda was not left behind in the scheme of things on how to collaborate with relevant agencies of government to enforce the national ban on single-use plastics in the country. However, this was achieved by a policy developed by the government to ensure that a partnership is achieved between all the stakeholders, ranging from the construction materials, government agencies, and consumers. This has shown how realistic leadership can assist in achieving a comprehensive circular economy in society. Therefore, other countries in Africa and beyond can actually learn from the Rwandan government initiatives on the circular economy [55].

(c) Kenya's Pay-As-You-Go Solar Ecosystem

In Kenya, the country has developed a pay-as-you-go (PAYG) solar system. This model has been built and strongly supported by solar companies, community cooperatives, and microfinance banks, to name just a few. In these models, the solar systems are designed in modular forms, and consumers can pay over a period of time, and the system is transferred to them after payments. During the period of the payments, companies are responsible for maintenance and repairs in case of any systematic damage.

7.6.3 Renewable Energy Case Studies

(a) Blockchain-Enabled Solar Panel Recycling

A model has been proposed by [56] in order to give incentives to manufacturers, users, recyclers, and government agencies on how to manage the end of life of solar panels. The system introduced is called "recycling coin", and has actually shown a framework that ensures accountability, fairness, and adequate distribution. Eventually, it has clearly shown how digital technology could strengthen collaborations based on trust.

(b) IoT-Based Dependable Control in Microgrids

Several efforts are presented in the literature, especially on how the circular economy can align the architecture of solar-enabled microgrids, especially using IoT-based controllers. These types of controllers ensure that real monitoring is activated, maintenance predictions are possible, and fault location in some systems is always available for complete reliability, availability, and efficient microgrid networks. These attributes are useful in the system, thereby having the ability to increase the lifespan of solar panels, batteries, and power electronics devices in the microgrid. Also, it enables the system to generate streams of data that can be shared across power systems, manufacturers, recyclers, embedding collaboration into the entire energy lifecycle [57].

Furthermore, in order to achieve the objectives of enabling systems that assist the circular economy in power systems, some systems energy management controllers have been developed to manage the energy of solar microgrid as shown in Figure 7.1. The proposed system consists of a solar panel dual axis mechanism that can adjust the panel's azimuth and tilt angles. In this system, communication is handled through a gateway that translates Modbus Serial signals into Modbus TCP. Furthermore, battery storage stores the excess energy for later use and ensures the load is satisfied at all times. This type of network ensures the availability of electricity, and thereby one of the objectives of having a circular economy can be handle satisfactory.

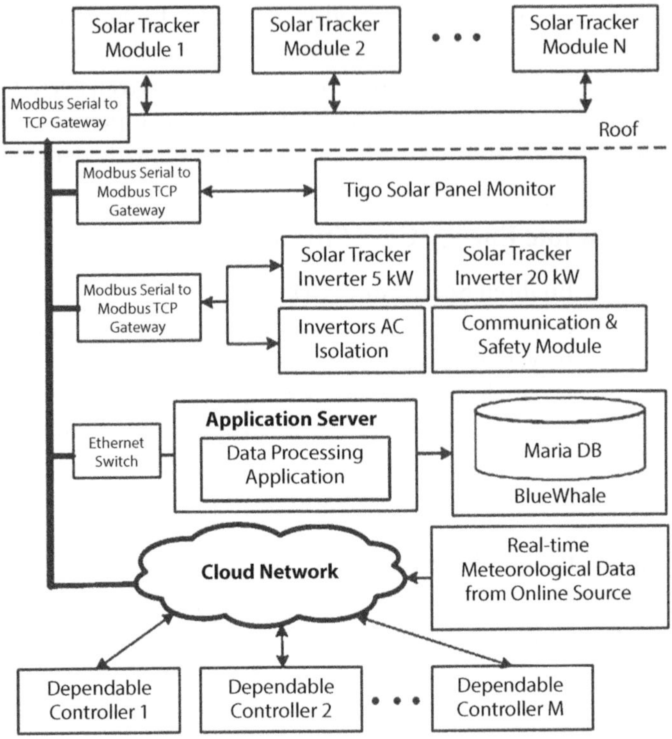

Figure 7.1 Overview of the solar energy management in microgrids [58].

(c) AI-Based Prognostic Maintenance

The circular economic model needs the AI-based prognostic maintenance strategy development to reduce downtime and cost associated with the system. The AI-based maintenance is a strategy that uses real-time data and AI to predict an estimated remaining useful life (RUL). The key aspect of this approach includes. Core objective, methodology, prognostic technique, and the corresponding benefits. The system key considerations are uncertainty, data quality, and the process involved in executing the strategies developed. When all these are combined, there is high possibility of improving circular economy in the future.

7.6.4 Industrial Symbiosis in Practice

(a) Kalundborg Symbiosis, Denmark

The Kalundborg industrial is used as one of the global examples of a cluster benchmark for CE. It consists of power plants, oil refineries, pharmaceutical firms, steam, municipal water exchangers, and other byproducts, to name just a few. In this cluster, gypsum from the plants supplies construction companies, while households receive waste heat frameworks. This demonstrated how trust and geographical proximity make it possible for long-term symbiotic relationships.

(b) South African Industrial Parks

Another example of an eco-friendly industrial park is the South African industrial park. The park integrated symbiosis with renewable energy. The park has a solar power plant that supplies electricity to many firms, while waste is converted into biogas. This park has shown that in Africa, industries can use the concept of CE to supply energy and resource sharing, which are some of the enablers of the CE.

7.6.5 Urban and Agricultural Partnerships

(a) Lagos Waste-to-Wealth Model

In Logos, Nigeria, recycling companies, NGO, and state authorities were able to develop a waste-to-wealth ecosystem. This is possible because waste is collected on an incentive-based scheme, processed by recyclers, and reintroduced into packaging and construction. The initiative is also possible because civil societies are at the forefront in mobilizing local households; on the other hand, companies take the responsibility of providing logistics and processing.

(b) Circular Agriculture in Ethiopia

Circular agricultural project in South Africa is another success story for CE. The project consists of government agencies, universities, and cooperatives. From the plant, animal manure, and crop residues are converted into biogas and organic fertilizers for farm utilization. The system has shown less reliance on synthetic fertilizers and the possibility of using renewable energy.

However, several challenges persist, including financing gaps, reluctance to share data, and capacity limitations in developing regions. Table 7.4 presents case studies of successful CE collaborations from across the world.

Table 7.4 Successful case studies in CE collaboration.

Case study	Partners	Outcomes
Stadler GmbH, Germany	Universities, government, and private firms	Closed-loop PET recycling
Melbourne CE City Project	NGOs, city gov, businesses	Urban circular ecosystems
European Battery Alliance	EU, academia, 400+ companies	Sustainable battery supply chains
Nigerian Solar Mini-Grids	Start-ups, donors, state gov	Energy access + modular circularity
Rwanda Plastic Ban	Government, SMEs, civil society	Elimination of single-use plastics
Kenya PAYG Solar	Solar firms, microfinance, cooperatives	Affordable, modular solar access
Blockchain Solar Recycling	Manufacturers, recyclers, gov, consumers	Traceability + incentives
IoT in Microgrids	Utilities, manufacturers, software developers	Predictive maintenance, efficiency
AI Prognostics in Renewables	Researchers, operators, recyclers	Lifecycle extension, optimized reuse
Kalundborg Symbiosis	Power plants, pharma, oil, municipality	Resource + energy sharing
South African Eco-Industrial Parks	Firms, municipalities, and renewable developers	Shared solar, biogas symbiosis
Lagos Waste-to-Wealth	NGOs, recyclers, government	Plastic recycling ecosystem
Ethiopian Circular Agriculture	Farmers, cooperatives, universities, gov	Biogas + organic fertilizers

7.7 Barriers and Enablers to Effective Collaboration and Sectoral Insights into CE Adoption

There are still many barriers hindering the transition to the circular economy; unfortunately, the transition is possible only if there is a strong collaborative ecosystem. However, the ecosystems are faced with many challenges while benefiting from some of these enablers. However, there is a need for understanding of both sections in order to design strategies that can be centered toward context and sector sensitive. Furthermore, some of the barriers are more critical in some regions, institutional environments, and industries, to mention just a few. This section explores some of them, that is

7.7.1 Barriers to Effective CE Collaboration

(a) Policy Fragmentation
Policy cross-sectoral collaboration is critical towards achievements of CE in many countries, example in West Africa, renewable energy and waste management are still in active and operate in silos, making it impossible to actualized some of the developed initiatives on waste-energy for more understanding and implementations of the CE models in the region, and many parts of the world are experiencing the same or similar problems especially in the developing nations.

(b) Limited Digital Infrastructure
Presently, digital tools such as AI, IoT, and blockchain are becoming more central to the achievement of CE collaborations globally. Unfortunately, many developing nations lack a strong, reliable internet network, which could be a reason for the limited adoption and implementation of CE in many parts of the world. Hence, without reliable data systems, the symbiosis opportunities, or track material flows, would be difficult for the concerned firm to explore.

(c) Data-Sharing Reluctance
Lack of trust is one of the critical reasons for difficulty in sharing/exchange of materials and energy in many industrial symbioses globally. This is making it worse since sensitive data cannot be shared, even though their availability of digital systems and networks across the globe, making it difficult to achieve some of the objectives of the CE.

(d) Financing Gaps
Circular initiatives often involve high upfront costs for infrastructure, renewable systems, or recycling facilities. Access to credit and blended finance remains a major barrier in Africa, where small enterprises struggle to secure loans for CE investments.

(e) Capacity and Skills Shortages
In order to fully actualize the concept of CE, development across the African continent, Universities, and higher institutions of learning need to integrate that in the curricula. This can assist in human development for the scaling of a collaborative ecosystem when implemented. Thus, suggesting a shortage of skilled workers trained in the design of CE, renewable energy technologies, and digital integration, leading to slow adoption of the model.

(f) Cultural and Institutional Resistance
The advancements of enhanced linear model business models have discouraged the use of experimental models, especially the collaborative or circular economic models. Industries are now hesitant to enter into partnerships due to some factors, such as loss of proprietary advantage.

7.7.2 Enablers of Effective CE Collaboration

Despite these barriers, several enablers have been shown to accelerate CE adoption:

(a) National and Sub-National Policy Integrated
It has been seen that in countries where the CE is integrated into national, regional, or local polices usually provides clear directions to stakeholders in order to achieve the goal of its development. This can be seen in EU countries, in which there is an action plan on how alignment is created to allow research institutes, industry, and civil societies to work together. A similar strategy has been seen in Rwanda and South Africa. Therefore, other countries should adopt a similar package in order to implement the circular economy in a comprehensive manner.

(b) Digital Infrastructure Development
In order to realistically implement the circular economy, there is a need for massive infrastructure development globally. Some of the possible areas to develop include IoT, blockchain, and other AI platforms. Some countries to use as models here are Dutch and Nigeria. The model in Dutch is AI-based, in which material matching platforms have been developed for the

reduction of waste by connecting industries with possible users. In the case of Nigeria, a mobile-based recycling app has been developed to connect waste buyers. All these innovations can assist other nations, even if the resources are not adequate.

(c) Blended Finance and Green Investment
Innovative finance mechanisms such as green bonds, sustainability-linked loans, and blended public–private funding help overcome financing gaps. The African Development Bank's CE Facility is an emerging enabler supporting SMEs in waste recycling and renewable energy. It is interesting to note that the African Development Bank has proposed a CE on waste recycling and renewable energy in the form of small and medium enterprises. The approach could be a mechanism in which public–private funding helps overcome financing gaps can be overcome, and assist in achieving the expected outcome in the implementation of the model.

(d) Knowledge-Sharing and Leadership Platforms
Cross-sector platforms such as the Ellen MacArthur Foundation's CE100 and the African Circular Economy Alliance (ACEA) provide spaces for dialogue, training, and co-innovation. These forums act as trust-building mechanisms and knowledge-dissemination hubs.

There are other innovations, such as cross-sector sharing platforms, such as the MacArthur Foundation's and African circular economy alliance (ACEA), that provide an enabling environment for training, innovations, and dialogue in this direction. The main function of this organization is to allow knowledge sharing and dissemination hubs across the continent.

7.7.3 Sectoral Insights into CE Adoption

CE adoption varies widely across sectors. While some industries demonstrate maturity, others remain in early stages.

(a) Manufacturing
The manufacturing sector leads in CE adoption due to strong supply chain pressures and regulatory requirements. Eco-design, remanufacturing, and modular production are widely implemented. For instance, the automotive sector integrates recycled plastics and metals into production, while electronics firms collaborate with recyclers to recover rare earths. More details of this insight towards adoptions of the circular economy could be seen in Table 7.5. In similar manner, circular economy sectoral maturity details are presented in Table 7.6. the table has shown adoption levels and

Table 7.5 Table of barriers and enablers.

Factor	Type	Effect size	Illustrative example
Policy Fragmentation	Barrier	High	West Africa waste-to-energy disconnect
Digital Infrastructure	Barrier/ Enabler	High	Dutch AI waste matching; Nigerian apps
Trust & Data Sharing	Barrier	Moderate	Firms' reluctance in industrial symbiosis
Financing Gaps	Barrier	High	African SMEs lack access to green loans
Knowledge Platforms	Enabler	High	ACEA, CE100 initiatives
Demonstration Projects	Enabler	High	Kalundborg, Nigeria solar pilots

Table 7.6 Sectoral CE maturity.

Sector	Adoption level	Key features
Manufacturing	High	Modular design, remanufacturing, eco-design
Agriculture	Moderate	Biogas, organic fertilizers, waste reuse
Urban Planning	Moderate	Local loops, waste-to-wealth, renewable integration
Automotive	High	Battery recycling, modular vehicles, eco-innovation
Waste Management	Moderate	Policy-led recycling, tech-assisted platforms

key enablers for each of the key items, ranging from manufacturing, agriculture, planning, automotive and waste management.

(b) Waste Management

For realistic collaborations in the circular economy. There are many initiatives in some parts of the world. One of these is the waste management in the circular economy in Lagos, Nigeria. This one is developed for the recycling and management of waste from households. The circular economic model in Rwanda is for the waste management of plastic into construction materials, and each of these has been successfully implemented in the country in which the model is designed.

7.8 Digital Tools and Platforms for Ecosystem Integration and Collaboration

Without digital platforms, resource loops often remain invisible, and trust between actors is weak. By contrast, digitalization ensures that materials, energy, and product lifecycles are monitored transparently, enabling collaboration at scale. The two figures presented in Figures 7.2 and 7.3 are clear indications that digital technologies are now indispensable tools critical to the implementation of the circular economy. The model enables all stakeholders to work together towards a common goal. The tool can avoid visibility, predictability, traceability, and alignment needs between the stakeholders. Without these platforms, resources remained invisible, and weak links were created between the stakeholders. Furthermore, digitization ensures energy, product lifecycle can be monitored for easy collaboration at larger scales. Figure 7.3 presents the tools needed for the realistic implementation and development of the circular economy.

Another application in the area of energy, with a clear example from Kano State, Nigeria. The project is piloted to enable and support energy

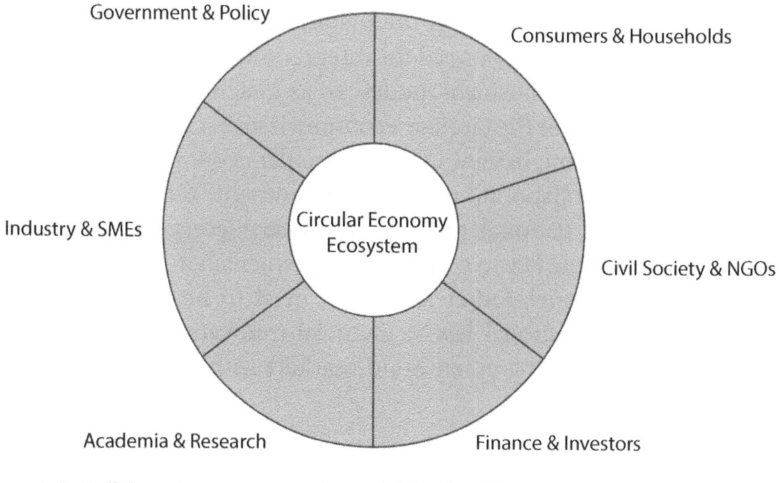

Figure 7.2 Collaborative ecosystem pie model for the CE.

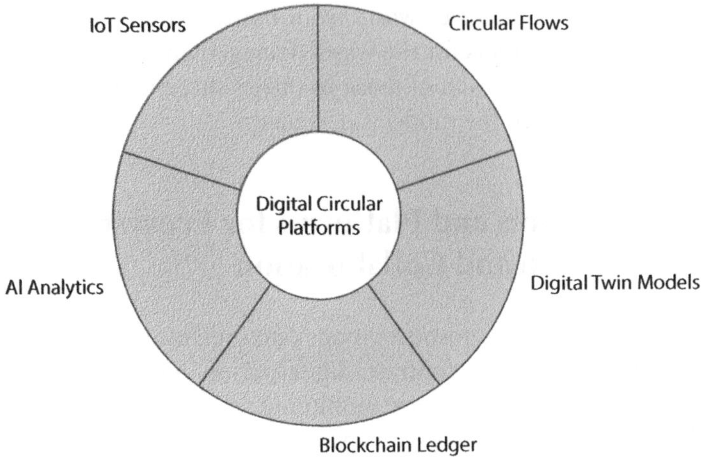

Figure 7.3 Digital tool integration pie model.

sharing. In addition, blockchain secure date and enables smart contracts for resource exchange. The flowchart is presented in Figure 7.4, that enable collaborative implementation of AI+IoT in the renewable sector. This model could help in achieving circularity in power electronics, energy lifecycle, and recovery.

7.9 Conclusion and Policy Recommendations

This chapter has shown that collaborative partnership is one of the backbones of the circular economy in the manufacturing process. For this to assist in this regard, there is a need for integrations between technical systems, stakeholders, and business models so as to achieve sustainability. In addition, the strength of the circular economy is also a function of innovations and value creation. In view of this, a circular economy can be possible if all stakeholders collaborate between government, academia, industry, and communities, at national, regional, and global levels. However, intelligent collaboration is the key to sustainable implementation and development of the circular economy. Other areas that need to be stretched include transparency at institutional levels; financial innovation remains central to this process. Expanding green-bond markets with a clear taxonomy of

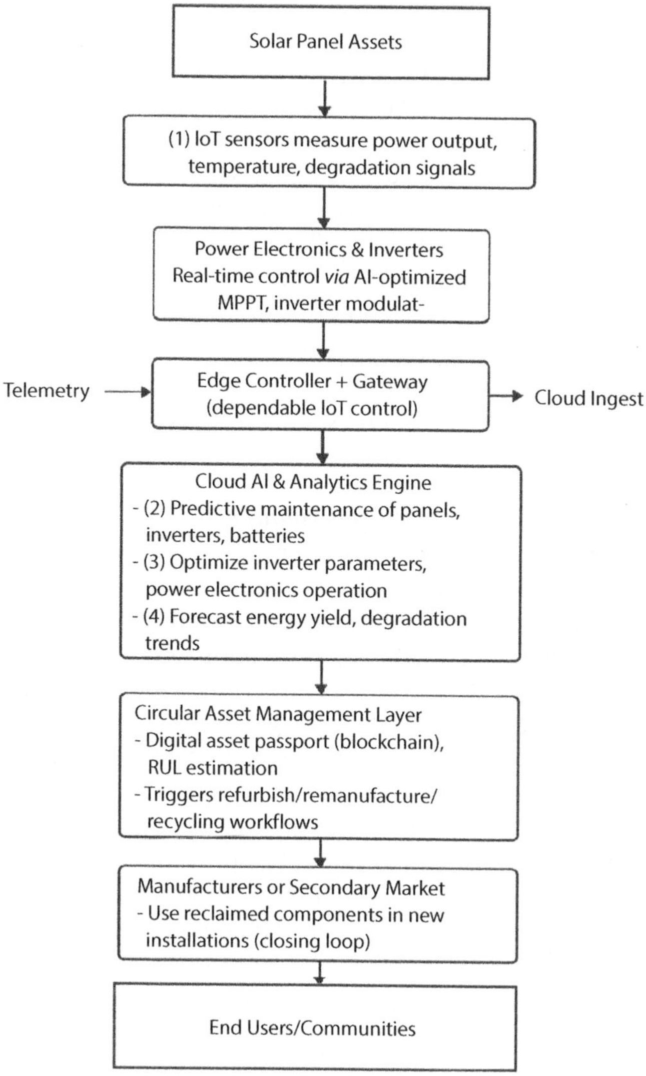

Figure 7.4 Flow chart diagram on how a collaborative implementation of an AI + IoT in renewable energy circular economy drives circularity.

eligible activities can unlock private investment and drive project bankability. Technology and innovation are among the sensitive pillars of scaling the circular economy; monitoring and evaluation should be robust. Finally, regular publication of the updates is also needed for accountability in all directions.

7.9.1 Future Research Directions

Although collaborative partnerships have gained significant global attention, research gaps persist in understanding and scaling CE ecosystems. These gaps span technological, institutional, financial, and socio-behavioral domains and must be addressed to design next-generation CE models that are adaptive, inclusive, and digitally robust. This chapter has shown that, though there are many efforts in a collaborative direction in order to gain more global attention towards the circular economy, research gaps exist in order to scale up the entire concept and implementation of the circular economy. These gaps range from technical, institutional, financial, and socio-behavioral domains. Therefore, in order to resolve them, especially for the future generation of circular economy models, the following points are noted here.

Digital intraoperative and data governance:
Future research direction should explore open-architecture frameworks to ensure secure information without compromising information privacy. Thereafter, more can be done on the areas of AI ethics, Digital trust, cybersecurity, and digital collaborations across continents.

Industrial symbiosis and network scaling:
Scaling some of the developed circular economic models globally presents a real challenge of scaling up for further investigations. Projects such as Ulsan (South Korea), Kalundborg (Denmark), and Kano industrial corridors provided many lessons. However, they present many challenges, and little is known about how infrastructural upgrades are needed to enable these project upgrades on a large scale. Quantitative modeling or system dynamic modeling could enable cross-country research on maturity and cultural norms to enable understanding of governments and network resilience.

Circular finance and investment analytics:
There is a need to develop a framework suitable for measuring environmental and social returns on circular investment. Using machine learning models, it is possible to predict circular economic risks by simply analyzing the macroeconomics and environmental databases. This necessitated the development of unified circular-finance models for cross-border investments and cooperation.

Socio-cultural and behavioral:
Future studies need to explore how local values, gender, religion, and community identities in order to shape global perceptions of waste, repair, and consumption. Understanding these dynamics can enhance the design of communication, education, and government frameworks to aid public engagement and adoption of modern circular economic model. The modern circular economy can include innovation ecosystems that are technologically and socially grounded.

Policy coherence and regional integration:
Presently, there are a few comparative studies of ACEA, ECOWAS, and the European Union that could enable the transfer of government mechanisms. Further research is needed across regional and national levels to allow integration and understand how these circular economic strategies can align with international frameworks. Developing regional CE monitoring indicators, especially those reflecting digital performance and industrial symbiosis, would strengthen data-driven policymaking. Finally, the education and skills dimension requires urgent attention. Universities and technical institutes should design interdisciplinary curricula that bridge engineering, economics, and behavioral sciences.

AI disclosure statement: The author acknowledges the use of AI-based tools for minor language editing or grammatical correction. However, all intellectual contributions, analyses, and conclusions presented in this chapter are entirely the author's own.

References

1. Aarikka-Stenroos, L., Chiaroni, D., Kaipainen, J., Urbinati, A., Companies' circular business models enabled by supply chain collaborations: An empirical-based framework, synthesis, and research agenda. *Ind. Mark. Manag.*, 105, 322–339, 2022.
2. Adner, R. and Kapoor, R., Value creation in innovation ecosystems: How the structure of technological interdependence affects firm performance in new technology generations. *Strateg. Manag. J.*, 31, 3, 306–333, 2010.
3. Adediran, Y.A. and Abdulkarim, A., Challenges of electronic waste management in Nigeria. *Int. J. Adv. Eng. Technol.*, 4, 1, 640, 2012.
4. Grose, S.O., Abdulkarim, A., Eze, V.H.U., A comprehensive review of power generation from solid waste using gasification and integrated gasification combined cycle systems. *Discov. Electron.*, 3, 11, 2026, https://doi.org/10.1007/s44291-026-00166-2.

5. Lawan, A.U., Babani, S., Abdulkarim, A., Shehu, G.S., Jibril M, Y., Madugu, I.S., Power compensation for vector-based current control of a modular multilevel converter (MMC) based STATCOM. *Int. J. Power Electron. Drive Syst.*; Yogyakarta, 10, 4, 1781–1796, 2019.
6. Andersen, J., A relational natural-resource-based view on product innovation: The influence of green product innovation and green suppliers on differentiation advantage in small manufacturing firms. *Technovation*, 104, 102254, 2021.
7. Madugu, I.S., Abdulkarim, A., Bakare, M.S., A novel forecasting-based sizing technique for cost-optimal autonomous solar PV-battery microgrids: a case study of Kano, Nigeria. *Discov. Electron.*, Springer, 3, 19, 1–26, 2026, https://link.springer.com/article/10.1007/s44291-026-00176-0.
8. Sarker, S.A., Zhu, N., Almutlaq, F., Adnan, K.M.M., Huq, M.E., Financial impact and adoption of solar irrigation in Rangpur, Bangladesh. *Energy Strategy Rev.*, 59, 2025.
9. Butt, A.S., Ali, I., Govindan, K., The role of reverse logistics in a circular economy for achieving sustainable development goals: A multiple case study of retail firms. *Prod. Plann. Control*, 1–13, 2023.
10. Camilleri, M.A., Troise, C., Strazzullo, S., Bresciani, S., Creating shared value through open innovation approaches: Opportunities and challenges for corporate sustainability. *Bus. Strateg. Environ.*, 32, 7, 4485–4502, 2023.
11. Cavicchi, C. and Vagnoni, E., The role of performance measurement in assessing the contribution of circular economy to the sustainability of a wine value chain. *Br. Food J.*, 124, 5, 1551–1568, 2022.
12. Valentine, S.V., Kalundborg Symbiosis: fostering progressive innovation in environmental networks. *J. Clean. Prod.*, 118, 65–77, 2016.
13. Tang, D., Cao, J., Yu, J., Remaining useful life prediction for engineering systems under dynamic operational conditions: A semi-Markov decision process-based approach. *Chin. J. Aeronaut.*, 32, 3, 627–638, 2019.
14. Abdulkarim, A., Faruk, N., Alozie, E., Olagunju, H., Aliyu, R.Y., Imoize, A.L., Adewole, K.S., Imam-Fulani, Y.O., Garba, S., Baba, B.A., Hussain, M., Oloyede, A.A., Abdullahi, A., Usman, D.J., Advances on Design of Renewable Energy Power Supply for Rural Health Clinics, Case Studies, and Future Directions" published by Clean Technol. 2024.
15. Cillo, V., Petruzzelli, A.M., Ardito, L., Del Giudice, M., Understanding sustainable innovation: A systematic literature review. *Corp. Soc. Responsib. Environ. Manag.*, 26, 5, 1012–1025, 2019.
16. Ciulli, F., Kolk, A., Boe-Lillegraven, S., Circularity brokers: Digital platform organizations and waste recovery in food supply chains. *J. Bus. Ethics*, 167, 299–331, 2020.
17. De Angelis, R., Howard, M., Miemczyk, J., Supply chain management and the circular economy: Towards the circular supply chain. *Prod. Plann. Control*, 29, 6, 425–437, 2018.

18. De Marchi, V. and Grandinetti, R., Knowledge strategies for environmental innovations: The case of Italian manufacturing firms. *J. Knowl. Manag.*, 17, 4, 569–582, 2013.
19. Farooque, M., Zhang, A., Liu, Y., Hartley, J.L., Circular supply chain management: Performance outcomes and the role of eco-industrial parks in China. *Transp. Res. Part E: Logist. Transp. Rev.*, 157, 102596, 2022.
20. Farooque, M., Zhang, A., Thürer, M., Qu, T., Huisingh, D., Circular supply chain management: A definition and structured literature review. *J. Clean. Prod.*, 228, 882–900, 2019.
21. Ferrari, A.G., Jugend, D., Armellini, F., Barbalho, S.C.M., de Carvalho, M.M., Crossing actors' boundaries towards circular ecosystems in the organic food sector: Facing the challenges in an emerging economy context. *J. Clean. Prod.*, 407, 137093, 2023.
22. Balsalobre-Lorente, D., Shah, S.A.R., Huseynova, R., Do circular economy, public-private Partnership and carbon policy manage the environmental stress? Developed countries' situation under the Prism of COP27. *Heliyon*, 10, 13, 2024.
23. Li, D., Zhang, B., Su, The impact of social Awareness and lifestyles on Household carbon emissions in China. *Ecol. Econ.*, 160, 145–155, 2019.
24. Liang, W. and Yang, M., Urbanization, economic growth and environmental pollution: evidence from China. *Sustain. Comput. Inform. Syst.*, 21, 1–9, 2019.
25. Freudenreich, B., Lüdeke-Freund, F., Schaltegger, S., A stakeholder theory perspective on business models: Value creation for sustainability. *J. Bus. Ethics*, 166, 3–18, 2020.
26. Geels, F.W., A socio-technical analysis of low-carbon transitions: Introducing the multi-level perspective into transport studies. *J. Transp. Geogr.*, 24, 471–482, 2012.
27. Tamba II, J.S., Abdulkarim, A., Shuaibu, A.N., Solar powered electric vehicle charging system: a comprehensive review. *Discov. Electron.*, 2, 1, 96, 2025.
28. Badjeena, B.P., Ali, E., Wonyra, K.O., Tamou, K., Green entrepreneurship: Opportunities and challenges for the transition to a circular economy in Togo, West Africa. *World Dev. Sustain.*, 5, 2024.
29. Ali, E., Climate change and agricultural development in West Africa: role of renewable energy and trade openness. *Environ. Econ.*, 12, 1, 14–31, 2021, 10.21511/ee.12(1).2021.02.
30. Andersen, M.M., Ogallo, E., Diniz Faria, L.G., Green economic change in Africa – green and circular innovation trends, conditions and dynamics in Kenyan companies. *Innov. Dev.*, 12, 2, 231–257, 2022, 10.1080/2157930X.2021.1876586.
31. Appiah, M.K., Sam, A., Twum, E., Godslove, E., Modelling the influencing of green entrepreneurship orientation on sustainable firm performance: A moderated mediation model. *Econ. Res.-Ekon. Istraživanja*, 36, 2, 2023.

32. Bayale, N., Ali, E., Tchagnao, A-F., Nakumuryango, A., Determinants of renewable energy production in WAEMU countries: New empirical insights and policy implications. *Int. J. Green Energy*, 18, 6, 602–614, 2021.
33. Berry, B., Haverkamp, J., Isenhour, C., Bilec, M.M., Lowden, S.S., Is convergence around the circular economy necessary? Exploring the productivity of divergence in US circular economy discourse and practice. *Circ. Econ. Sustain.*, 2022.
34. Centobelli, P., Cerchione, R., Esposito, E., Passaro, R., Shashi, Determinants of the transition towards circular economy in SMEs: A sustainable supply chain management perspective. *Int. J. Prod. Econ.*, 242, Article 108297, 2021.
35. De Jesus, A., Mendonça, S., Lost in transition? Drivers and barriers in the eco-innovation road to the circular economy. *Ecol. Econ.*, 145, 75–89, 2018.
36. Geisendorf, S., Pietrulla, F., The circular economy and circular economic concepts—a literature analysis and redefinition. *Thunderbird Int. Bus. Rev.*, 60, 5, 771–782, 2018.
37. Henrysson, M. and Nuur, C., The Role of Institutions in Creating Circular Economy Pathways for Regional Development. *J. Environ. Dev.*, 30, 2, 149–171, 2021.
38. Living, O., Nnamchi, S.N., Ukagwu, K.J., Abdulkarim, A., Jagun, Z.O., Minimization of Electric Power Losses on 132 kV and 220 kV Uganda Electricity Transmission Lines. *Energy Power Eng.*, 15, 02, 127–150, 2023.
39. Mamba, E., Natural resource rents, manufacturing trade, and manufacturing growth: Evidence from linear and nonlinear regressions for ECOWAS countries. *Omp. Econ. Stud.*, 2024.
40. Cui, M.-L., Feng, T.-T., Wang, H.-R., How can blockchain be integrated into renewable energy? --A bibliometric-based analysis. *Energy Strateg. Rev.*, 50, 2023.
41. Valdivia, A.D. and Balcell, M.P., Connecting the grids: a review of blockchain governance in distributed energy transitions. *Energy Res. Soc. Sci.*, 84, Article 102383, 2022.
42. Yahaya, A.S., Javaid, N., Alzahrani, F.A., *et al.*, Blockchain based sustainable local energy trading considering home energy management and demurrage mechanism. *Sustainability*, 12, 8, 3385, 2020.
43. Rasiah, R., Kari, F., Sadoi, Y., Mintz-Habib, N., Climate change and sustainable development issues: Arguments and policy initiatives. *J. Asia Pac. Econ.*, 23, 2, 187–194, 2018.
44. Mahmud, I., Ismail, I., Abdulkarim, A., Shehu, G.S., Olarinoye, G.A., Musa, U., Selection of an appropriate maintenance strategy using analytical hierarchy process of cement plant. *Life Cycle Reliab. Saf. Eng.*, 13, 2, 103–109, 2024.
45. Symons, E., Proops, J., Gay, P., Carbon taxes, consumer demand and carbon dioxide emissions: a Simulation analysis for the UK. *Fisc. Stud.*, 15, 2, 19–43, 1994.

46. Floros, N. and Vlachou, A., Energy demand and energy-related CO2 emissions in Greek manufacturing: assessing the impact of a carbon tax. *Energy Econ.*, 27, 3, 387–413, 2005.
47. Alper, A.E., Analysis of carbon tax on selected European countries: does carbon tax reduce emissions. *Appl. Econ. Finance*, 5, 1, 29–36, 2017.
48. Kirikkaleli, D. and Adebayo, T.S., Do public-private partnerships in energy and renewable energy consumption matter for consumption-based carbon dioxide emissions in India? *Environ. Sci. Pollut. Res. Int.*, 28, 23, 30139–30152, 2021.
49. Adebayo, T.S., *et al.*, Do public–private partnership investment in energy and technological innovation matter for environmental sustainability in the east Asia and pacific region? An application of a frequency domain causality test. *Sustainability*, 13, 2021.
50. García-Quevedo, J., Jové-Llopis, E., Martínez-Ros, E., Barriers to the circular economy in European small and medium-sized firms. *Bus. Strateg. Environ.*, 29, 6, 2450–2464, 2020.
51. Geissdoerfer, M., Pieroni, M.P., Pigosso, D.C., Soufani, K., Circular business models: A review. *J. Clean. Prod.*, 277, 123741, 2020.
52. Bakare, M.S., Abdulkarim, A., Shuaibu, A.N., Mundu, M.M., Predictive Energy Control for Grid-Connected Industrial Pv-Battery Systems Using GEP-ANFIS. *E-prime - Adv. Electr. Eng. Electron. Energy*, Elsevier, 9, 100647, September 2024, available https://www.sciencedirect.com/science/article/pii/S2772671124002274.
53. Geissdoerfer, M., Savaget, P., Bocken, N.M., Hultink, E.J., The circular economy—A new sustainability paradigm? *J. Clean. Prod.*, 143, 757–768, 2017.
54. Greco, M., Grimaldi, M., Cricelli, L., Open innovation actions and innovation performance: A literature review of European empirical evidence. *Eur. J. Innov. Manag.*, 18, 2, 150–171, 2015.
55. Hazen, B.T., Russo, I., Confente, I., Pellathy, D., Supply chain management for circular economy: Conceptual framework and research agenda. *Int. J. Logist. Manag.*, 32, 2, 510–537, 2021.
56. Abdollahi, S., Jafarzadeh Ghoushchi, S., Haseli, G., Evaluation of sustainable strategies for implementing blockchain technology in the solar energy supply chain under fuzzy ZE-numbers. *Appl. Soft Comput.*, 189, 2026.
57. Phung, M.D., De La Villefromoy, M., Ha, Q., Management of solar energy in microgrids using IoT-based dependable control. *2017 20th International Conference on Electrical Machines and Systems (ICEMS)*, Sydney, NSW, Australia, pp. 1–6, 2017. doi: 10.1109/ICEMS.2017.8056441.
58. Bakare, M.S., Abdulkarim, A., Shuaibu, A.N., Muhamad, M.M., Enhancing solar power efficiency with hybrid GEP ANFIS MPPT under dynamic weather conditions. *Sci. Rep.*, 15, 1, 5890, 2025, available https://www.nature.com/articles/s41598-025-90417-1,.

8

Metrics and Performance Measurement for Circular Economy

N. Prakash*, M. Dharshne, P. Karthikeyan, A. Kaviya Sree and S. Krishnashree

Department of Management Studies, Kongu Engineering College, Erode, Tamil Nadu, India

Abstract

As linear production systems transition to circular economy (CE) practices, the need for meaningful metrics and practices regarding performance measurement and improvement in manufacturing has never been more pressing. This chapter discusses how organizations can develop, implement, and assess indicators indicative of material efficiency, circularity, environmental performance, economic benefits, and social value. The motivation for using CE indicators comes from the limitations of traditional metrics associated with linear production systems, which often neglect to address issues such as resource depletion, externalized costs, and end-of-life situations and also compare traditional linear indicators to newly developed circular indicators that focuses on aspects of regenerative capacity, resilience, and the product-as-a-service offer. Several of the tools and frameworks available for measuring and assessing circularity are presented such as the Material Circularity Indicator, and the circular transition indicators, BS 8001 and ISO 14040/44, and their complementary functions in providing a means for manufacturers to benchmark, strengthen accountability, and improve decision-making. Life-cycle assessment and material flow assessment provide evidence-based methods for measuring the use of resources, evaluation trade-offs, and quantifying environmental impacts. Increasingly, there will be a more critical need to connect CE metrics to environmental, social, and governance frameworks while continuing to apply technology, such as Internet of Things, blockchain, and digital twins to strengthen transparency, comparison, and harmonization. By moving forward and focusing on developing reliable assessment systems, CE can change from an ambitious vision to a reliable, measurable practice.

**Corresponding author*: np.mba@kongu.edu

Jeyaprakash Natarajan, Milon Selvam Dennison, M. Bhuvanesh Kumar and Ganapathy Thirukkotti (eds.) Manufacturing and the Circular Economy, (253–288) © 2027 Scrivener Publishing LLC

Keywords: Circular economy, key performance indicators (KPIs), life-cycle assessment (LCA), material flow analysis (MFA), material circularity indicator (MCI), circular transition indicators (CTI), resource efficiency, sustainability reporting

8.1 Introduction

The manufacturing sector represents the central hub of the international economy, and it dictates the products, services, and livelihoods of billions globally. For the past century, the core operating model has been linear, i.e., "take, make, discard." In the linear system, raw materials are extracted and made into goods, be they products, services, or combinations of both, and disposed of as waste, with little consideration of long-term environmental or social outcomes [1]. Although the linear economy produced the industrial wealth and globalization, it also resulted in intolerable systems of extraction and waste considering devaluation of resources, greenhouse gas (GHG) emissions, loss of biodiversity, waste, etc. Increasing environmental restrictions, combined with shifts in societal expectation, regulations, etc., suggest that the linear growth model is not viable any longer. Business and industry across the planet are transitioning to a circular economy (CE), which is a system encouraging infinite use, reuse, and regeneration of resources.

Manufacturing sectors are starting to move from a traditional linear approach (take–make–dispose) to circular approaches where they attempt to continue products, materials, and resources in use through recycling, remanufacturing, and modularity in design [2]. This transition is necessary for industries to be sustainable and resource-efficient, to promote resilience, and return to profitable to allowing industries to mitigate their impacts on the environment, and for industries responding to social pressures affecting economic and regulatory frameworks. CE is more than recycling materials at the end of their life cycle. CE is a holistic reimagination of product and service design, manufacturing, consuming, and business models whereby materials, energy, and products are utilized productively to remain in use as long as possible [3]. CE is then extending the life of products through repair and remanufacturing and designing products for modularity and durability, and CE represents a critical transition in manufacturing firms to remain competitive, resilient, and legitimate as more boundaries are defined by the ecological limits of the earth.

Businesses and sectors expect to know whether they are improving, where the trade-offs are, and whether they are accountable. Metrics and performance measurements become invaluable for corporations. They become the "compass" for the organizations CE efforts and allow organizations to see if their strategies are resulting in real environmental, economic, and social value. They allow meaningful targets to be set, which are critical for managers to assess their own performance, investors to assess (them with respect to) risks and opportunities, and policymakers to assess their regulations or compliance, and to assess which sustainable products and sustainable business practices to purchase or use. Without metrics, circularity becomes an ambiguous goal; with metrics, circularity becomes a pragmatic and measurable approach [4].

In addition to standardized frameworks, digital tools such as Internet of Things (IoT), blockchain, and digital twins are becoming more integrated to improve accuracy, traceability, and decision-making in measurement of circular performance. Benchmarking and reporting mechanisms are just important as they provide organizations against which they can benchmark against their peers, report transparently to their relevant stakeholders, and approve reporting consistency against universal reporting frameworks such as the Global Reporting Initiative (GRI), integrated reporting (IR), and the EU's Corporate Sustainability Reporting Directive (CSRD). Transparent reporting with standardized metrics not only provides organization trust from their stakeholders but also drives action by providing organizations with common labeled parameters and language to assess progress on circularity [4]. Today, benchmarking and reporting provide insights, but the development of CE measurement points toward the evolution of next generation indicators that account for resilience, regenerative capacity, and integration with environmental, social, and governance (ESG) frameworks.

In the future, circular measures will be more dynamic, system-based, and integrated. New measures are beginning to capture ideas such as regenerative capacity, resilience, and product-service performance that represent an even more developed take on CE thinking. Most importantly, as circular measures are integrated with ESG measures, CE will be an enabler of sustainable business transformation into the future. Similarly, technologies such as digital twins, big data dashboards, and other real-time monitoring systems will increasingly play a role, improving the accuracy, prediction, and actionable assistance of a circular measure; however, this requires global harmonization to ensure that modifications to the measure can be regarded as comparable across either sector or region [5].

The point of metrics and performance assessments is to establish trust in organizational practices so that firms can assess the success of their circular initiatives and built momentum for value transition on their journey to circular practices. These are the infrastructure for the decisions and actions that will allow a manufacturer to be conscious about their intentions and opportunities for improvement, put transparency right through to beneficiaries about their value, and reinforce the adoption of best practices. This chapter is provided as a guide that lays out the basics of circularity measurement. This chapter provides KPIs for measuring circularity, followed by a review of frameworks that allow developers to assess multiple aspects of circularity. It then discusses quantitative methods such as life-cycle assessment (LCA) and material flow assessment (MFA) for enhancing performance evaluation, tracking resource use, and assessing impacts as part of decision-making processes. Building on this introduction, the following section explores why metrics are essential in a CE and how they guide performance assessment.

8.2 The Role of Metrics in CE

Conventional performance metrics in manufacturing—including costs, output, and efficiency—are troublesome to apply to CE because they are built around short-term productivity and profit and do not factor the wider implications across product life cycles or interrelated value chains. Traditional performance metrics do not account for resource recovery, environmental sustainability, extended producers' responsibility, or stakeholder well-being, all of which are key components to CE processes.

8.2.1 Drawbacks of Conventional Metrics

For decades now, manufacturers have measured success primarily based on financial and operational metrics, and have driven competitiveness based on cost per unit, return on investment (ROI), yield (production), and energy efficiency. Traditional metrics provide insights into firm operations, but when applied to the concepts of CE, these operational metrics create several issues [6]:

i. **Resource blindness**: Traditional metrics do not always recognize that manufacturers can account for the depletion of finite natural resources; a company can report great profits while relying only on scarce raw materials while exposing itself to risk in the long term.
ii. **Externalized impacts**: Multiple economic, social, and environmental costs—pollution, carbon emissions or labor across supply chains—are not included in financial accounts;

as a result, traditional metrics are limited in terms of representing the firm's performance.

iii. **Short-termism**: Conventional KPIs privilege immediate financial performance at the expense of sustainability. This is particularly evident in terms of production costs—e.g., cutting costs on production may incentivize the use of lower-quality materials, which reduce durability and increase waste.

iv. **End-of-life**: Metrics such as "units sold" or "uptime" do not capture what will happen when products reach the end of their life; waste disposal or potential for recycling or reuse is invisible.

v. **System fragmentation**: Linear metrics viewed traditional production as independent of supply chains, ecosystems, and communities—the CE perspective privileges that all systems are interdependent.

Shifting from a linear economy to a CE is more than a slightly changed business model or the use of new technology to develop new products; it requires a radical paradigm shift regarding success and how it is measured. Although unit cost, throughput, profit margin, and efficiency will still be relevant metrics in manufacturing, they are no longer sufficient. These metrics reflect performance within localized economic conditions and ignore the more encompassing social and environmental impacts convenience metrics capture. A true CE will not just account for utilization at the factory floor, but will also be comprehensively defined over full life cycles of resources, the health of people in communities, and resilience of ecosystems.

In contrast, CE metrics need to encompass a wider set of metrics that consider environmental, social, and systemic implications such as resource circularity, waste, renewable material flows, and responsible consumption. Social indicators such as those pertaining to job creation or community involvement must be equally valued in measuring holistic progress and equitable transitions. Although substantial progress with CE performance metrics is required, significant challenges with the implementation remain. These are largely related to the lack of standardization in definitions, appropriateness of metrics for sector-specific contexts, and continuing challenges with accessibility to data and data reliability [7]. Such challenges affect the transparency, comparability, and measurement system. It highlights the urgent need for continued development of actionable standardization and transparency metrics of circular manufacturing [8].

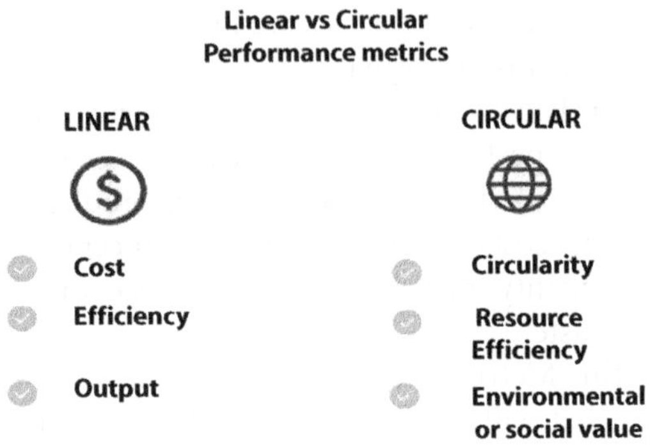

Figure 8.1 Linear versus circular performance metrics.

A linear economy basically goes down the path of take → make → dispose, using the basic model of extracting materials, making a product, using it, and throwing it away. This creates waste and depletes resources. A CE is focused on keeping products and materials in use for a longer duration of time. Companies do not sell their products to a consumer, but offer them as a service (leasing, sharing, repair) [9]. It emphasizes that value comes from durability, reuse, and efficiency as opposed to just overconsumption. This contrast between linear and circular economic systems is illustrated in Figure 8.1.

Although the contrast between linear and circular metrics provides the foundation, it is equally important to understand why metrics matter for organizations pursuing circular practices.

8.2.2 Importance of Metrics in CE

Metrics are vital to CE for three main reasons:

i. **Evaluation of performance**: An organization cannot assess whether its circular strategies are delivering improvements if it does not track quantitative indicators. For example, a transition from virgin plastics to bio-based alternatives may reduce reliance on fossil resources, but may simply shift pressures for land use elsewhere. In effect, metrics create a framework for evaluating trade-offs and ensuring circular interventions produce net positive outcomes.

ii. **Accountability to stakeholders**: Investors, regulators, customers, and employees are insisting on proof of progress toward sustainability. Transparent reporting, which can be backed by solid metrics, allows manufacturers to have credibility, fulfill requirements of policy frameworks, and open doors to green finance [10].

iii. **Catalyst for innovation**: Measuring circular performance can help pinpoint inefficiencies and catalyze new solutions. For example, tracking rates of material use may ultimately lead the firm to an industrial symbiosis opportunity, where the waste of one process is used as input for another. Metrics are thus an enabler of continual improvement.

With the role of metrics established, attention now shifts to specific key performance indicators (KPIs) that enable organizations to evaluate CE performance in practice.

8.3 KPIs for CE Success

KPIs for CE success are relevant to resource, circularity, environmental, economic, and social contexts, supporting implementation in sectors including manufacturing. Transitioning toward a CE necessitates changing how organizations define success and how they measure it. KPIs are central to this challenge. KPIs provide measurable, actionable information about where circular efforts are or are not delivering intended impacts from environmental, economic, and social perspectives [14]. In contrast to traditional measures of performance that are framed within linear objectives—doing more with less—circular KPIs focus less on efficiency and more on opportunities to regenerate value, eliminate waste, and extend the life of products and materials.

Assessment of CE best practices relies on measurable indicators, which capture the environmental, economic, and social dimensions of sustainability. Hence, although there are many ways to quantify CE practices, KPIs offer a structured and organized detail of how organizations can assess performance and where to improve and communicate results to interested stakeholders [11]. KPIs provide the components to measure circularity, but for those measures to provide credibility in comparing performance across sectors and organizations, there are various frameworks and standards to design into the implementation process. Table 8.1 shows some examples of general KPIs that are organized across five dimensions: resource efficiency, circularity, environmental, economic, and social. In addition, the table includes a measurement unit and how practitioners could ensure use in practice [12].

Table 8.1 Key performance indicators for circular economy in manufacturing.

Category	Example KPI	Unit of measurement	Application example
Resource efficiency	% of Renewable energy consumption	(Renewable energy/total energy) * 100	Organization's renewable energy usage can be identified
Circularity	% of circular inflow to outflow	(Circular inflow/ circular outflow) * 100	Measures share of renewable inputs and recovery performance
Environmental	E-factor (environmental factor)	(Mass of waste/ mass of product)	Highlights waste intensity in production processes across industries
Economic	Value-based resource	Value added/ weighted resource input value	Links economic output to resources use
Social	Warranty period	Duration (or) repairability score (%)	Brands offering lifetime warranty on recycled materials products

8.3.1 Functions of KPIs

i. **Strategic alignment**: They connect CE objectives to the business strategy so that leadership teams may track progress.
ii. **Decision-making**: KPIs provide the evidence for managers to make decisions on investments, to redesign processes, and to prioritize actions.
iii. **Transparency and accountability**: Reporting on KPIs gives credibility to all stakeholders, from investors to customers.
iv. **Benchmarking**: Comparable KPIs enable companies to measure themselves against their peers and industry benchmarks.

v. **Continuous improvement**: Reviewing progress against KPIs helps identify inefficiencies and promotes ongoing learning [13].

8.3.2 Resource Efficiency Indicators

- **Raw materials use intensity**: The mass (or weight) of raw materials consumed per unit of output, to identify opportunities for process improvements.
- **Energy/water use per unit produced**: The energy and water consumed per product, to support decision-making in lean and responsible manufacturing.
- **Waste minimization ratios**: The weight of waste produced compared to the output of a unit of operation, to inform the workforce about waste reduction and recycling activities.

8.3.3 Circularity Indicators

- **Percentage recycled/reused content**: The proportion of recycled materials in a product (e.g., electronics using recycled metals).
- **Remanufactured yield**: The number of parts/products that successfully underwent the remanufacturing process (e.g., number of automotive parts returned to service).
- **Product life years**: The extent by which products are kept in service before disposal, typically attributable to their repair or modular upgrade improvements.

8.3.4 Environmental Indicators

- **GHG emissions avoided**: The extent of GHGs avoided by implementing circular practices (e.g., remanufacturing a product instead of manufacturing a new product).
- **Reduced nonrenewable material consumption**: The quantity of reduction in the use of virgin (nonrenewable) resource consumption, which can be assessed in electronic products using incorporated reused rare earths.
- **Pollution reduction**: Reduction in air pollution, water pollution, and soil pollution as a result of improved activities in waste prevention, recycling/hazardous waste disposal, and eco-design.

8.3.5 Economic Indicators

- **Cost savings**: This can include financial benefits from avoiding resource use, recycling materials, and waste stream disposal (e.g., auto manufacturers have avoided material purchase costs by remanufacturing).
- **Extended asset value**: The value retained in products through circularity (e.g., keeping electronics in use through refurbishment).
- **ROI of circularity initiatives**: Is the financial return attributable to investments in circularity (e.g., manufacturers profiting more through closed-loop manufacturing systems).

8.3.6 Social Indicators

- **Green jobs produced**: This includes the number of jobs generated for recycling, remanufacturing, and renewable energy technologies.
- **Benefits to the local community**: This includes positive social outcomes (e.g., in community-based electronics recycling programs).
- **Employee upskilling**: Enabling training, accreditation, and reskilling to develop sustainable production practices.

To better understand how metrics and tools work in practice, case studies from automotive and electronics industries are outlined. For example, a European automotive manufacturer modified its operations to remanufacture engines and tracked KPIs related to the number of engines remanufactured, GHG emissions avoided, and cost savings achieved through reduced use of virgin materials. This manufacturer achieved a material reduction of 40% and a 20% reduction in energy per unit produced and created new green jobs in its remanufacturing facility [14].

Additionally, an electronics manufacturer moved to a closed-loop system established by KPIs: recycled content share, product life extension, and benefits to local communities. Over the course of 3 years, they achieved a 50% recycled metal footprint for each of their new devices, extended lifespan *via* modular designs, and addressed pollution mitigation including recycling waste [15]. KPIs serve as the building blocks of measurement; however, robust frameworks and tools are required to apply these indicators consistently across organizations and sectors.

8.4 Tools and Frameworks for Circular Performance Assessment

Although KPIs provide the building blocks for measuring progress toward a CE, organizations also need the structures and tools to help create consistency, comparability, and scalability [4]. Frameworks for managing CE specific KPIs not only help to guide firms in choosing relevant indicators and define boundaries and criteria, but they also help normalize results, whereas digital tools assist with detecting data collection and validation and increase transparency. Together, these represent the foundational components of circular performance assessment. This chapter will discuss the major tools and frameworks, including the Material Circularity Indicator (MCI), Circular Transition Indicator (CTI), BS 8001, and ISO 14040/14044, as well as the emerging role of digital tools such as the IoT, blockchain, and artificial intelligence (AI).

8.4.1 The Need for Frameworks in Circular Measurement

Transforming into a CE is a complicated and intricate system. The manufacturing system extends along global supply chains; there are many few stakeholders with multiple perspectives involved in the process, and the overall system-level impacts are apparent across economic, environmental, and social spectra. Therefore, using a series of *ad hoc* measurement approaches increases fragmentation and increases the pitfalls of inconsistency and reporting fatigue [16].

The frameworks provide a few advantages:

i. **Standardization**: Frameworks support standardization and can provide a common language to help create consistency in its application and methodologies that other organizations working in similar industries can use to compare.
ii. **Decision support**: It can offer a systematic way to support the linking of metrics to strategic action decision-making.
iii. **Credibility**: Their results are generally seen as more credible because it uses recognized frameworks and standards—stakeholders from outside the organization support this.

8.4.2 Material Circularity Indicator

MCI is a circularity indicator developed by the Ellen MacArthur Foundation that measures the circularity of a product or system. It examines the following:

- The amount of minimization of linear material flows (i.e., virgin raw materials, unrecoverable waste).
- The amount of maximization of restorative flows (i.e., recycled, reused, renewable input).
- How long people are using the product and usage intensity, compared with industry average [17].

MCI generates a score between 0 and 1, where 1 represents a fully circular product (only recycled or renewable materials fully recovered) and a 0 being fully linear (only virgin materials ending in landfill/incineration). It evaluates its key parameters, including material inputs, utility (on-product use period), and end-of-life recovery routes, to provide a circularity evaluation. This can be better understood with the example of a furniture company that trialed MCI using two chair designs, one a virgin plastic chair and the other a chair made from recycled polymers with a modular approach. MCI score for the modular, recycled design was 0.65, whereas the virgin plastic version had an MCI score of 0.28, which helped demonstrate the business case for scaling modular, recycled designs.

8.4.3 Circular Transition Indicators

CTI are corporate-level KPIs, meant to represent partnership progress to circularity. They represent multiple dimensions including resource management, business model innovation, and value chain partnerships. CTI are designed for companies to provide actionable insights, benchmarking capabilities for an organization's circular transition along with their stakeholders [18]. CTI, created by the World Business Council for Sustainable Development (WBCSD), provide a framework for assessment at a company level.

CTI supports organizations in evaluating and improving circularity in their operations by:

- Quantifying and mapping flow of materials.
- Establishing the proportion of secondary raw materials.
- Evaluating new product-utility and business models (e.g., service, rather than selling product).

- Understanding risks and opportunities connected to circular strategies.

The CTI have numerous strengths that had made it one of the important tools in circular flow assessment. Holding a broad scope and being suitable for all organizations, easy adaptation in multiple industries, integrating circularity with business risk, and assistance in strategic planning are some of its vital strengths. As shown in Table 8.2, the CTI (WBCSD) framework provides organizations with a common and quantitative means of undertaking corporate-level circularity globally because it is sector agnostic. MCI is at the tactical product level of HBR and uses metrics for whether recycled content is present, product lifespan, and waste. MCI has been adopted by several organizations as part of their

Table 8.2 Comparison of circular economy assessment frameworks.

Framework	Scope	Strengths	Limitations	Industry adoption
CTI (WBCSD)	Corporate-level circularity	Standardized, quantitative, cross-sector metrics	Requires detailed internal data	Applied and used by organizations across globe
MCI	Product-level circularity index	Integrates recycled content, lifespan, and waste	Data-intensive calculation	It is the emerging and popular framework in reporting companies
BS 8001:2017	Organization-level circular economy framework	First global standard offering principles and guidance for CE (systems thinking, stewardship, value optimization, etc.)	Guidance-oriented, not quantitative; flexibility can reduce comparability	Widely referenced as a guideline standard, especially in Europe and the UK
ISO 14040/14044	Life-cycle assessment (LCA) for products and services	Scientifically rigorous, internationally recognized method to assess environmental impacts	Complex, resource- and data-intensive; requires expertise	Broadly adopted across industries for environmental impact assessment and sustainability reporting

reporting, but requires leadership to work with exhaustive, intensive data and calculations. In contrast, BS 8001:2017 is a principles-based framework that encourages organizations to incorporate CE elements into their organizational strategy and operations. It is a relatively well-used standard to reference in organizational settings, because it is UK/European focused, but qualitative features make it difficult to compare with other organizations. Finally, ISO 14040/14044 is a set of standards for LCA, which outlines the internationally agreed way of determining a products overall environmental impacts through the life-cycle stages.

8.4.4 BS 8001:2017

BS 8001:2017 is the British Standard for which guidance is provided for organizations about applying CE principles. It offers flexible framework for developing, managing, and measuring CE and strategies by providing details to organizations [19].

BS 8001 is the first standard in the world aimed at helping organizations embed CE thinking into their governance, innovation, and operating functions [20]. Instead of specifying strictly defined requirements, it provides a new framework of principles, guidance, and steps to be adapted across various sectors and for organizations of all sizes. The standard focuses on key principles, systems thinking, innovation, stewardship, collaboration, value optimization, and transparency; all of these encourage organizations to step outside their current culture and governance systems to enact sustainable change.

BS 8001 is a significant strength in that it is adaptable and has credibility; to date, it has been endorsed by policymakers and industry as a solid reference point. One of the identified weaknesses is that although BS 8001 gives guidance about establishing CE thinking, it does not provide any numerical measurements; it is hoped that organizations will adapt the BS 8001 framework into their standard KPIs, or other tools, to record for progress accurately.

Leadership and culture for circularity:

- Product and service design for reuse and recyclability
- Resource flows and value retention
- Transparency and continuous improvement [21]

Organizations can align their CE practices with the framework of the standard to be able to integrate CE principles in their daily operations and reporting.

To understand its importance, a mid-sized manufacturer in the United Kingdom used BS 8001 as a roadmap for transitioning to a CE model. They formed a cross-functional steering group, embedded the principles of stewardship into their procurement activity, and used the framework to guide them in adopting a modular product design for their products.

8.4.5 Integration with ISO 14040/14044

ISO 14040 and 14044 provides a complementary environmental management standard, known as LCA, which organizations can use to assess the overall environmental impacts of a product or system [22]. When coupled with circularity measures such as measured by MCI, this holistic approach ensures organizations also measure circularity of the resource flows and the environmental impact in one overseen process. The tools and frameworks used for circular performance measurement are shown in Figure 8.2.

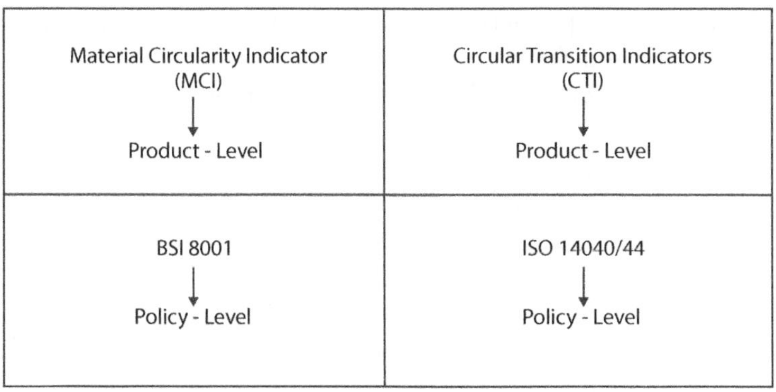

Figure 8.2 Tools and frameworks for circular performance assessment.

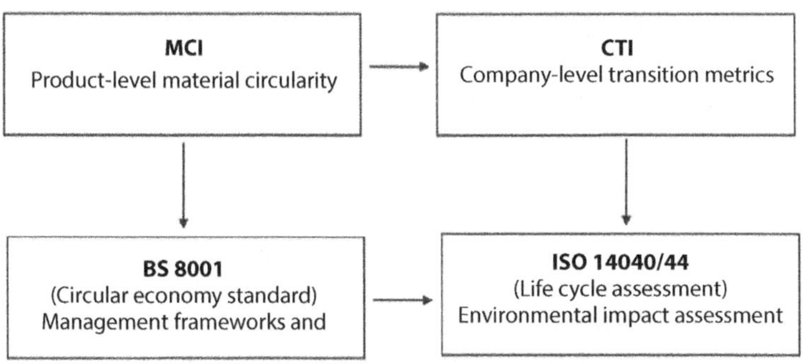

Figure 8.3 Complementary roles of MCI, CTI, BS 8001, and ISO 14040/44.

An automotive company sought to compare the environmental performance of aluminum components produced with virgin feedstock compared to those produced from recycled feedstock using LCA. They found that aluminum from a recycled feedstock reduced total energy use by 70% and made 60% less CO_2 emissions. This supported their business case for circulating materials. This case states the weightage of the ISO. The complementary roles of MCI, CTI, BS 8001, and ISO 14040/44 are presented in Figure 8.3.

8.4.6 The Role of Digital Tools

- The IoT can track items in products and supply chains to enhance transparency and leave less chance for making incorrect decisions around resource flows.
- Blockchain is used to keep records of recycled materials used and accurate traceability and keep trustworthy records of a product's life-cycle data, by providing unchangeable records.
- AI provides predictive analytics for maintenance, forecasting demand for renewable resources or surplus materials, and optimization of the design approach for circularity [23].

Digital tools and technologies not only improve the speed that organizations can implement a CE; these tools tackle and improve data quality, help organizations to collaborate with others, and aid decision-making to enhance circular performance [24].

The role of digital tools can be better understood with the example of blockchain in textiles. For instance, global apparel brand tracked the digital life of cotton fiber from farm, through processes and manufacturing to retail stores through blockchain. The ability to track the garment parts builds the brand's transparency and credibility on claims made on recycled content, while allowing the brand to accurately report on CE performance. Similarly, blockchain documents recycled plastic from the buyer all the way to bottling, verifies that bottles have recycled PET, and avoids double-counting or greenwashing. Some real-life examples are as follows:

- **Electronics (Dell)**: Blockchain is used to keep records of ownership and repairs; end of lease of laptop triggers return based on smart contracts for refurbish/reuse/recycle.
- **Fashion (H&M)**: Blockchain certifies that cotton is organic/fair-trade and tracked throughout supply chain, proof of ethical sourcing provided to consumers.

Frameworks and tools are essential enablers of circular performance measurement. From an organizational focus on frameworks such as CTI to the focused approach of MCI, to the organizational cultural reference of BS 8001, to the environmental standards provided by ISO 14040 and 44, they provide manufacturers with a reference in many different scenarios. Digital innovations through the ability to leverage IoT, blockchain, AI, and digital twins could provide additional resolution, traceability, and decision-making to the features of these frameworks. By bringing together different frameworks, organizations can start to move from disparate measures to a communal, integrated, system-level measure, enabling their CE aspirations to be validated and measured [25].

8.5 LCA and MFA

CE strategies are effective only when they provide organizations with approaches that reveal the true impacts and flows of resources throughout their systems. There are two popular and empirically robust approaches for organizations to make sense of their impacts and flows: LCA and MFA [26]. Both LCA and MFA can illustrate sustainability performance in organizations, but they tend to operate at different scales with different emphases: LCA measures environmental impacts across product life cycles, whereas MFA measures the quantities and direction of material flows within systems. This section describes both methods in detail and outlines their strengths and weaknesses while also explaining the ways in which they can work together to help organizations navigate their transition to CE.

8.5.1 Life-Cycle Assessment

LCA is a systematic orientation that evaluates the environmental impacts of a product, service, or system throughout its entire life cycle, from raw material extraction ("cradle") through production, distribution, consumption, and disposal or reuse/recycling ("grave"). LCA is particularly useful when there are linear and circular alternatives to evaluate, e.g., virgin inputs versus recycled input or single-use product versus reusable product [27]. LCA is an established methodology for evaluating environmental impacts over the entire life cycle of a product or system (also called, cradle-to-grave or cradle-to-cradle), from raw material extraction to disposal or recycling. LCA is an internationally recognized methodology for assessing the environmental impacts of a product or system over its entire life cycle, from the extraction of raw materials to disposal or recycling, also described as a "cradle-to-grave" assessment.

8.5.1.1 LCA Phases

i. **Goal and scope definition**: Identifies the purpose of the assessment, the system boundaries, and the functional unit of the assessment. This phase identifies what will be assessed, what life-cycle stages are included within its boundaries, and the environmental impacts the LCA will focus on.
ii. **Life Cycle Inventory (LCI)**: The data collection phase where the inputs (i.e., materials, energy) and outputs (i.e., emissions, waste) of the product system are collected and quantified.
iii. **Life-Cycle Impact Assessment**: The evaluation of potential environmental impacts resulting from the LCI data, based on categories such as global warming potential, human toxicity, acidification, and eutrophication.
iv. **Interpretation**: The results are analyzed and interpreted with conclusions and recommendations presented along with consideration for uncertainty, limitations, and opportunities for improvement [28].

8.5.1.2 Using LCA to Compare Linear and Circular Product Designs

LCA can help to draw comparisons between environmental footprints by presenting quantified impacts for conventional linear product life cycle compared to a circular design alternative (for instance, reuse, remanufacturing, or recycling) and identify trade-offs and hotspots along the product life cycle. Table 8.3 summarizes and displays the key strengths and weakness of LCA as applied in CE contexts.

For example, a beverage company used LCA to compare the impacts of single-use PET bottles, aluminum cans, and reusable glass bottles. They found that reusable glass was the better packaging option in regions with great collection systems, but worse in places where transportation distances were substantial due to the packaging being far heavier. The findings influenced the company to establish a regional approach in respect to packaging rather than simply a "one-size-fits-all" approach.

Table 8.3 Strengths and weakness of LCA.

Strengths	Weakness
Provide comprehensive view across product Life cycle	Time-consuming process
Helps to spot and identify hidden environmental impacts	Results can vary sometimes due to uncertainties
Helps in product-design decision-making, policy formulation and strategies planning	Costly process due to data collection and analysis
Promotes Eco-innovation and development	Larger datasets are needed

8.5.2 Material Flow Analysis

MFA is a systematic way of mapping and quantifying material flows and stocks over defined systems (e.g., in a manufacturing process or region) involving quantities and pathways of materials rather than inventorying environmental impacts. MFA identifies, maps, and quantifies material flows and stocks within systems. MFA focuses on quantities and flows, rather than connections to environmental impacts (e.g., impacts on resources are not emphasized) [29]. MFA is a technical procedure for determining the flows and stocks of materials in a defined system (such as a factory, industry, region, or nation). MFA is able to show where resources are extracted, how they are transformed as they move through processes, and where they ultimately end up. MFA surrounds the important easy-to-determine elements of resource efficiency, generation of wastes, and identifying opportunities to close materials loops.

For example, with the production of an automotive part, it is possible to describe total aluminum materials entering the production system, stocks of in-use vehicles, recapture rates of remanufactured parts, and waste outputs. In this way, MFA can glean systems-level material efficiency and circularity insights. MFA can be used to calculate the input and in-use stock of aluminum in vehicles, as well as recycling rates, and waste generated in the automotive manufacturing. These calculations can inform resource efficiency, the potential for circularity, and any system bottlenecks.

8.5.2.1 System-Level Information

MFA helps to understand how materials stock up and depopulate from a system, where materials accumulate in products and the efficiencies of the recycling loop, and to identify specific points of circular intervention [30]. For instance, an MFA of aluminum in the automotive sector showed all flows from mining aluminum to car production, use, and end-of-life. It found that whereas 95% of aluminum from scrapped cars was recycling-ready, only 70% was recovered due to failures in collection and sorting. This led to investment in new dismantling systems to recover more aluminum.

8.5.3 LCA and MFA as Complementary Assessments

LCA and MFA are essential tools for measuring performance in a CE. LCA provides a comprehensive picture of environmental impacts over the product life cycle, whereas MFA investigates material flows and losses at a system level. Each has shortcomings, but when used together, they provide an integrated understanding of environmental impacts and resource flows. The next generation of tools—driven by digital twins, big data, and hybrid models—has the potential to enhance the dynamism, accessibility, and usability of LCA and MFA. For the manufacturing sector, applying LCA and MFA is more than about meeting their current wants and needs; it lays the foundations for the evidence base to move forward with designing successful CE strategies, mitigate risks, and demonstrate effective sustainability performance.

LCA focuses on finding and quantifying the environmental impacts of material and energy related flows through a product's life cycle. MFA quantifies the mass balances and material flows through a system scale and does not explicitly relate it to environmental impacts. Together, MFA and LCA provide a comprehensive assessment [31]. MFA measures all material stocks and flows providing important information for determining resource management strategies; on the other hand, LCA reports on the environmental implications of these flows. This pairing contributes to improved decision-making related to CE strategies by combining environmental sustainability and efficient resource utilization. LCA helps to evaluate and quantify the production through its use and end-of-life phases. It helps in identifying trade-offs and potential unintended consequences of circular strategies. On the other hand, MFA offers quantitative approach for tracking the stocks and flows that helps in identifying losses and leakages, accumulated stocks. To compose in a nutshell, Table 8.4 states various differing aspects of LCA and MFA in context of its objectivities, scale, data requirements, outputs, and limitations in CE.

Table 8.4 LCA versus MFA in circular economy measurement.

Aspect	Life-cycle assessment	Material flow analysis
Objective	Evaluate environmental impacts across product life cycle	Track material flows through systems
Scale	Typically, product/ service-specific	Regional, national, or sector-wide
Data requirements	Detailed input/output, process data	Aggregate material flow data, less granular
Outputs	Environmental impact metrics (e.g., carbon footprint)	Flow diagrams such as Sankey, material quantities
Limitations	Data-intensive, complex modeling	Less detailed environmental insight, aggregate view

The comparative focus of LCA and MFA is highlighted in Figure 8.4, with LCA emphasizing environmental impacts across a product's life cycle, whereas MFA tracks material flows and stocks within systems. Although LCA and MFA allow detailed performance tracking, benchmarking and transparent reporting are essential for comparing results across organizations and communicating progress to stakeholders.

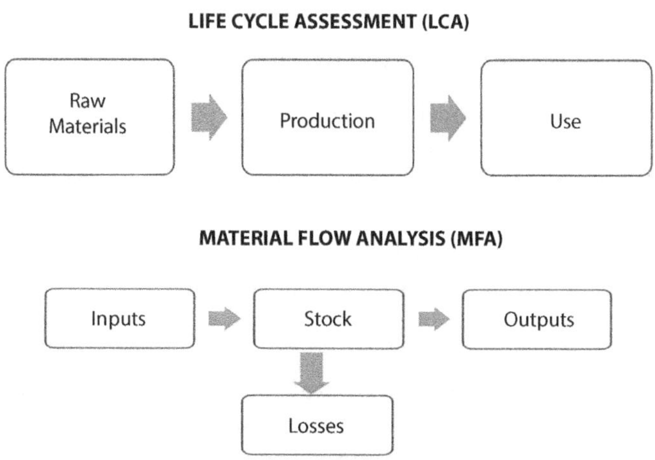

Figure 8.4 Life-cycle assessment (LCA) versus material flow analysis (MFA).

8.6 Benchmarking and Reporting Best Practices

Benchmarking and reporting are vital mechanisms for integrating CE principles into manufacturing. Although KPIs, frameworks, and tools provide options to measure performance, benchmarking allows organizations to compare their results against peers and industry levels, whereas reporting ensures that progress is communicated transparently to stakeholders [32]. Both practices facilitate accountability, trust, and improvement. This section examines the role of benchmarking in CE, reviews leading reporting standards, and outlines best practices for manufacturers.

8.6.1 The Role of Benchmarking in CE

Benchmarking is the practice of comparing an organization's performance against its internal targets or the performance of its peers, industry averages, or best practices. Within CE, benchmarking helps manufacturers to [33]:

i. **Identify gaps**: Identify areas where circular performance is behind their peers.
ii. **Drive continuous improvement**: Drive organizations to increase performance by competitive pressure.
iii. **Support strategic planning**: Align CE targets with sectoral or national priorities.
iv. **Increase credibility**: Show commitment to investors and regulators by placing results in a broader context.

8.6.2 Types of Benchmarking in CE

- **Internal benchmarking**: Comparing circular performance against other facilities, products, or business units.
- **Competitive benchmarking**: Comparing to direct competitors in the industry space.
- **Cross-industry benchmarking**: Learning from the best practices in unrelated sectors (e.g., automotive is learning from fashion).

Benchmarking is a formalized way to compare CE maturity and performance across firms or sectors. It also establishes leaders and followers, and gaps and opportunities, and can identify good practices and options for improvement. Furthermore, it will help organizations make decisions in regard to improvement, strategy, and investment. Benchmarking creates reference points that will allow organizations to measure and evaluate their own progress in circularity against their sector peers and will streamline the exchange of knowledge and the transition pathway.

8.6.3 Sector-Specific Benchmarks Examples

- **Steel sector**: The share of secondary raw material (the recycled content in steel) is a significant benchmark that will drive a reduction in imported primary iron ore.
- **Plastics sector**: The proportion of recycled plastics included in the production inputs targets circular-feedstock loops.
- **Electronics sector**: The percentage of overall product recyclability and recycled material content are benchmarks that can be utilized for electronics.
- **Automotive sector**: The yield of remanufacturing or proportion of recycled material in vehicle components.

The above benchmarks can be characterized as resource efficiency with respect to material input, resource efficiency with respect to product life cycle, and closed-loop design characteristics of the sector.

8.6.4 Linking to Global Reporting Standards

- **GRI**: The initiative's application tool provides waste and resource performance indicators for many levels of CE, and sustainability progress can be publicly reported to stakeholders in transparent way.
- **IR**: This kind of reporting tool enables organizations to identify the value creation cycle to demonstrate the effect of externalities in economic, environmental, social, and governance role. The reporting at a higher level of aggregating sustainability can provide the complete picture of CE aligned with IR, as it has an inclusive disclosure methodology.
- **EU CSRD and taxonomy**: These EU-incompatible regulations are to conform to sustainability reporting based on CE that enables reporting on sustainability financially and accountable.

8.6.5 Significance of Transparent Reporting and Stakeholder Trust

Transparent benchmarking and reporting are fundamental to developing confidence in CE claims and progress with stakeholders. A clear and credible disclosure process that aligns with international standards will help investors, regulators, customers, and communities assess their risks, impacts, and commitments. Transparency helps drive accountability and action compliance with regulatory and policy obligations and supports the development of trust, which is essential to continue to develop, implement, and scale CE initiatives within sectors across the economy. This systematic approach and integration of benchmarking with accepted frameworks and open communication are a foundation for ongoing CE improvement and shift to sustainable business models [34].

To understand the significance of benchmarking and reporting, the case of a European electronics manufacturer benchmarked their recycling rate against the EU WEEE target of 65% collection. At the outset, its performance was at 48%. After developing take-back programs and engaging with local recyclers, the electronics firm was able to raise its recycling rate to 67% in 3 years. It used GRI reporting standards to ensure transparency with regulators and consumers while having clearly benchmarked progress in increasing CE rates to further build confidence and trust with investors.

Establishing trust with stakeholders in CE claims and progress depends on transparent benchmarking and reporting. A transparent and credible disclosure and reporting process that conforms with international standards can allow investors, regulators, customers, and communities to understand better CE risks, impacts, and commitments. Transparency will help build accountability, action, regulatory and policy compliance, and trust and is important to continue to develop, implement, and scale CE initiatives at sectoral and economy-wide scales. Figure 8.5 pictorially maps out how different reporting initiatives, guidelines, and sector-specific tools are available in the benchmarking and reporting landscape.

Emerging KPIs that move beyond traditional efficiency metrics are shown in Figure 8.6.

As shown in Table 8.5, several international frameworks and standards have emerged to shape CE reporting metrics for organizations. The GRI is a common standard that reports on many indicators, including resource use, waste, energy, and circular inputs, across many industries.

IR is a standard that emphasizes value creation and resource stewardship, making it important for firms committed to sustainability through their corporate strategy. The EU CSRD requires public organizations in the

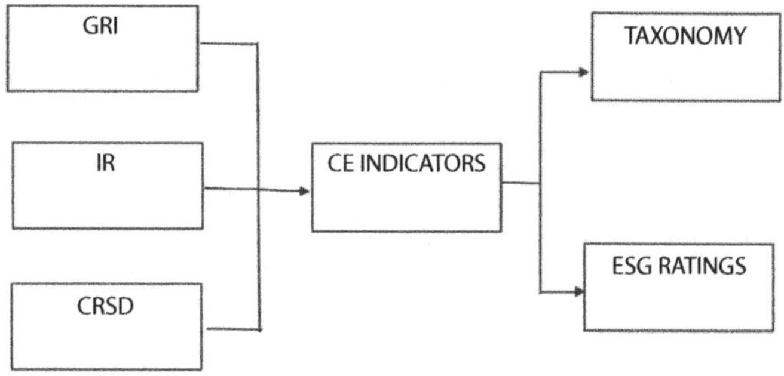

Figure 8.5 Benchmarking and reporting landscape.

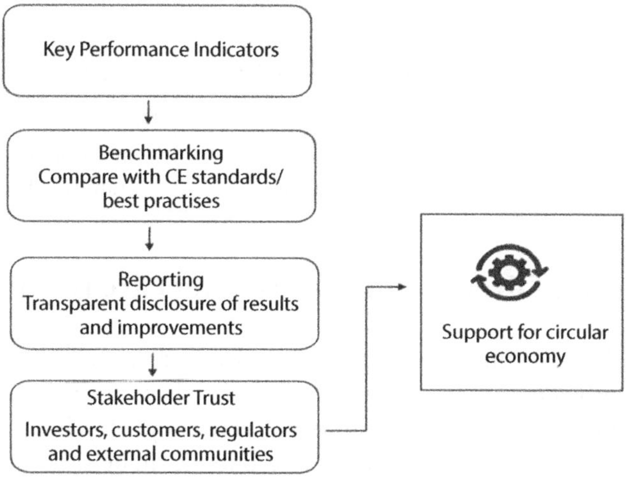

Figure 8.6 A flow of benchmarking and reporting.

European Union to make disclosures that include aspects of their CE targets and risk management. The EU Taxonomy helps identify circular and sustainable activities (mainly for the financial and regulated sectors) as well. The ESG Disclosure Guidelines blend environmental and social performance metrics, including CE efforts, and have been significant in shaping sustainability reporting frameworks across the globe. Together, these standards ensure that CE efforts can each be measured, disclosed, and compared to other industries and regions systematically. Although current benchmarking and reporting mechanisms provide a strong foundation, future developments will demand more dynamic, system-based, and integrated measures.

Table 8.5 Benchmarking and reporting practices in CE.

Framework/standard	CE metrics covered	Industry relevance
GRI (Global Reporting Initiative)	Resource use, waste, energy, circular inputs	It is being adapted in multiple industries
IR (integrated reporting)	Value creation, resource stewardship	Used by firms integrating sustainability into strategy
EU CSRD	Circular economy disclosures (targets, risks)	Mandatory for public organizations in EU
EU Taxonomy	Criteria for circular and sustainable activities	Used by financial and regulated sectors
ESG Disclosure Guidelines	Environmental and social metrics, including CE	Highly adapted in reporting frameworks

8.7 Future Directions in Measuring Circularity

The field of measuring CE is evolving rapidly. Current frameworks, KPIs, and tools provide a useful basis for assessing CE performance; however, they remain largely focused on resource efficiency, recycling, and waste reduction, reflecting the legacy of linear economic models. As CE thinking matures, new indicators will need to be developed that reflect deeper systemic characteristics (e.g., regeneration, resilience, elaboration of service performance, integration into ESG frameworks) [35]. Furthermore, the field is on the verge of being able to more reliably measure and report on circularity with new digital technologies and a greater level of global harmonization. This section examines the next-generation measurements of CE and focuses on new metrics, new digital technologies, and the impetus for harmonization. Future directions for measuring circularity will involve new metrics, ESG interaction, digital innovation, and global alignment.

8.7.1 Emerging Metrics

From a CE standpoint, the new metrics are meant to capture more expansive dimensions of circularity including the following:

- **Regenerative capacity**: Ability of a system to restore or renew its resources and ecosystems beyond recycling.
- **Resilience**: The ability of products, systems, or supply chains to absorb shocks while keeping circularity alive [36].
- **The performance of product-service systems**: Circular business models integrating products and services (e.g., leasing, sharing) that maximize life cycle and resource efficiency.

Table 8.6 indicates that emerging KPIs for CE activities go beyond traditional efficiency metrics that have often dominated measures of success. Regenerative capacity emphasizes an organization's ability to work within ecosystems or material value *via* the organization's operations—for example, possibly introducing composting, bio-based inputs, or land restoration into their manufacturing practices.

Table 8.6 Emerging circular metrics and trends.

New metric	Definition	Potential use in manufacturing
Regenerative capacity	Ability to restore ecosystem or material value through operations	Tracks practices such as composting, bio-based inputs, or land restoration tied to manufacturing processes
Resilience	Adaptability of operations amid supply chain/resource shocks	Measures how production adjusts to disruptions *via* repaired/refurbished components
Product-as-a-service (PaaS) performance	Success of service-based models extending product life cycle (leasing, PaaS)	Enables tracking of utilization rates and cost per service delivered
Secondary Market Value Index	Value retained in reused/recycled products	Encourages designing for remanufacture and resale value capture

Resilience considers the capacity of the manufacturing production system to absorb unpredicted disruption from external systems shocks such as supply chain challenges and could include the continuing use of made, repaired, or refurbished components in new products. Similarly, product-as-a-service performance provides an avenue to assess the outcomes/impact or effectiveness of service-based product business models, measuring product utilization and whether extending product life cycle through leasing or sharing is cost-effective and sustainable. The Secondary Market Value Index measures what value of reused or recycled products is retained, encouraging companies to work toward designing products capable for future remanufacturing and resale and to achieve carrying-long-term value. Collectively, these metrics indicate that there are potential avenues toward a more holistic, future-oriented means of measuring the success or contribution of CE practices related to manufacturing [15].

8.7.2 Integrating CE Metrics with ESG Frameworks

In a time where sustainability metrics are hard to disentangle, understanding that CE metrics are converging with ESG frameworks is helpful as they provide a holistic picture of sustainability [37]. This enables investors and stakeholders to measure and understand sustainability performance related to circularity as well as other sustainability measures such as climate action, social equity, governance factors, etc. And now, recommendations and support tools are updated including CTI link CE performance with the existing ESG framework to fulfill emerging CE/ESG reporting expectations with consistent, credible disclosures.

8.7.3 Digital Innovations

- **Digital Twins**: As digital counterparts of physical assets or systems, digital twins can support real-time monitoring of material flow and support simulation and visualizing interventions for circularity.
- **Big data and data analytics**: Big data technology allows ongoing assessments of large datasets across the supply chain to identify opportunities and risks relating to circularity (e.g., minimizing environmental impacts, ensuring resource availability, etc.).
- **AI-enabled dashboards**: Facilitate predictive analytics, scenarios modeling, and decision-making to optimize circular business models and transparency in reporting.

8.7.4 Need for Global Harmonization

Harmonization of CE metrics is critical for the following:

- Facilitating the comparison of circularity performance across industries and geographies
- Facilitating transparent and consistent reporting to regulators, investors, and consumers
- Facilitating policy coherence and tracking progress at a global level on CE goals

International collaborative efforts are underway to harmonize definitions, methodologies, and reporting frameworks for CE measurements or indicators to support harmonization and scalable circular transitions in different parts of the world [38].

These future directions collectively enable advancement of CE measurement beyond basic recycling rates to a comprehensive, integrated, data-driven, and globally harmonized approach that will ultimately support sustainable development.

8.7.5 System Metrics and Value-Chain Metrics

Measuring CE will move toward more system-based performance metrics rather than simply company or product level. Three examples include:

- **Sectoral circularity rates**: For example, % of secondary materials used' in certain sectors such as construction, textiles, electronics, etc.
- **Maps of value-chain circularity**: To identify material flow from suppliers, manufacturers, logistics, and retailers, which will identify bottlenecks/synergies.
- **Circularity indicators for regions**: For example, how the cities or regions look at material loop management can include indicators that support the need for municipal intervention.

To understand the system metrics, the city-level case of the Amsterdam developed a CE monitoring system at the city level to measure construction materials circularity, food waste minimization, and job development. Their whole system-focused approach allows them, for example, to measure their progress on construction materials independent of the company-as-unit-of-analysis, a concept that can be similarly applied to industrial ecosystems and clusters.

8.7.6 Future Metrics for Impact

Historically, metrics have extrapolated forward activities (e.g., recycling rates), rather than outcomes (e.g., less harm to the ecosystem). In the future, metrics are likely to emerge that measure impact by directly linking CE activities to global challenges such as climate change, biodiversity loss, and social inequity. The potential of measuring CE transition is in the shift from the current static and activity-based measurements to those that are dynamic, systemic, and ultimately impact-based. For instance, although emerging measures such as regenerative capacity, resilience, or product-service performance are still in inception stages, they indicate the advancements in CE mindset. Collaborative integration of CE with the ESG landscape will elevate circularity as an important part of financial and sustainability disclosure [17]. Digital technologies including IoT, AI, blockchain, and digital twins will create opportunities for continual and transparent measurement systems.

The world's efforts to harmonize measurement should be paramount to avoid fragmentation and promote consistent comparability across industries, regions, and contexts. At some point, measuring CE must evolve from simply tracking how the materials flow to how circular practices are regenerating ecosystems, strengthening communities, and drawing upon resilient economies. By considering a future direction for CE transition measurement, manufacturers and policymakers can begin to ensure that CE metrics are evolving with the impending challenges and opportunities presented by a fast-changing world.

Taken together, metrics, KPIs, frameworks, tools, and reporting mechanisms illustrate the progress made so far, but also highlight the continued need for harmonization, innovation, and stakeholder collaboration.

8.8 Conclusion

The shift toward a CE in the manufacturing sector is arguably one of the most significant industrial transformations of the 21st century. However, without a sound measurement approach in place, circularity may remain only an aspirational calling, rather than an actionable pathway. This chapter has established that measurement, metrics, KPIs, frameworks, and reporting practices are the core enablers that help us progress from vision to action and accountability from ambition.

The discussion began by establishing that traditional performance measures, concentrated on cost, output, and efficiency, are less capable (and suitable) for providing direction when transitioning to a CE. As such, it is essential to identify and develop metrics that represent a new generation of CE indicators. These should capture resource efficiency, material circularity, environmental performance, economic value, and social contribution—foundational elements that enable progress to be measured, opportunities to be identified, and innovation to be supported.

Organizations can rely on structured frameworks to ensure consistency and credibility, such as MCI to understand a product's aspects of circularity, CTI for various approaches for measuring circularity, BS 8001 to provide governance and principles for organizations, and ISO 14040/14044 for LCA-based assessment. These structured approaches, particularly when used as combined resources, provide a comprehensive landscape of assessment for product design, organizational operational performance, and system-level impacts.

Further, LCA and MFA provide holistic insight into both environmental impacts and resource pathways. Benchmarking and reporting practices subsequently extend the value of measurement, in that they provide a mechanism for companies to compare performance to peers, fit within regulatory frameworks, and develop stakeholder confidence through transparent reporting. Frameworks such as GRI, EU CSRD, and ESG ensure that circularity is a component of overall sustainability and financial reporting.

Going forward, CE measurement will likely show a trajectory toward more systemic, impact-based, and digitally enabled measurement practices. New metrics concerning regenerative capacity, resilience, and product-service performance illustrate that CE thinking is maturing. With ESG frameworks, circularity will begin to be institutionalized into the corporation's value-generating ecosystem, and digital innovations such as IoT, blockchain, AI, and digital twins will enable real-time, predictive insights into performance. Concurrently, attention to harmonizing global standards will also be fundamental to overcoming fragmentation and establishing any contextual comparability of performance across sectors and regions.

In conclusion, effective measurement is not simply a technical issue; it is a strategic imperative. It facilitates decision-making grounded in evidence, builds trust with stakeholders, and fosters shared learning across approaches. As such, it enables the shift from CE being an intent to being a stretchable metric, which puts into motion the transition from a take–make–dispose linear economy to a regenerative and resilient industrial future that is sustainable.

This will require industry, policymakers, academia, and communities to work collaboratively and continuously evolve toward building a measurement ecosystem that is intentionally designed to drive real change and secure a sustainable future within the limits of the planet.

AI disclosure statement: The author acknowledges the use of AI-based tools for minor language editing or grammatical correction. However, all intellectual contributions, analyses, and conclusions presented in this chapter are entirely the author's own.

References

1. Fobbe, L. and Hilletofth, P., Moving toward a circular economy in manufacturing organizations: the role of circular stakeholder engagement practices. *Int. J. Logist. Manag.*, 34, 3, 674–698, 2023.
2. Kulwant, M., Rai, N., Patel, D., Circular Economy and Waste Management: Advancing Sustainability Through Integration and Innovation, in: *A Vision for Environmental Sustainability: Overcoming Waste Management Challenges in Developing Countries*, pp. 309–334, Springer Nature Switzerland, Cham, 2025.
3. Mugoni, E., Shumbanhete, B., Nyagadza, B., The Nexus Between Circular Economy (CE) and Sustainable Supply Chain Management (SSCM): A Systematic Literature Review and Mapping of Future Research Agenda. *Circ. Econ. Sustainability*, 1–38, 2025.
4. Krasteva-Hristova, R., Papradanova, D., Vechev, V., Mapping the Landscape of Sustainability Reporting: A Bibliometric Analysis Across ESG, Circular Economy, and Integrated Reporting with Sectoral Perspectives. *J. Risk Financial Manag.*, 18, 8, 416, 2025.
5. Ali, Z.A., Zain, M., Hasan, R., Pathan, M.S., AlSalman, H., Almisned, F.A., Digital twins: cornerstone to circular economy and sustainability goals. *Environ. Dev. Sustain.*, 1–42, 2025.
6. Munonye, W.C., Towards Circular Economy Metrics: A Systematic Review. *Circ. Econ. Sustainability*, 1–43, 2025.
7. Shevchenko, T., Esfandabadi, Z.S., Ranjbari, M., Saidani, M., Mesa, J., Shevchenko, S., Cluzel, F., Metrics in the circular economy: An inclusive research landscape of the thematic trends and future research agenda. *Ecol. Indic.*, 165, 112182, 2024.
8. Remeikienė, R., Gasparėnienė, L., Bankauskienė, J., Assessment of the circular economy indicators in the EU Member States. *Discover Sustainability*, 6, 1, 1–19, 2025.
9. Nordström, E., Product life extension: A quantitative analysis of economic value retention in a circular economy business model, Unpublished master's thesis, Lund University, 2024.

10. Portillo-Tarragona, P., Kuba-Khoury, V., Aranda-Usón, A., Scarpellini, S., Environmental Management Accounting and Accountability for Circular Eco-Innovation Projects. *Sustainability*, 17, 6, 2392, 2025.
11. Gilsing, R., Wilbik, A., Grefen, P., Turetken, O., Ozkan, B., Adali, O.E., Berkers, F., Defining business model key performance indicators using intentional linguistic summaries. *Softw. Syst. Model.*, 20, 4, 965–996, 2021.
12. Baumer-Cardoso, M.I., Campos, L.M.D.S., Pigosso, D.C.A., Ashton, W., Measuring the adoption of circular economy at the company level: usefulness and applicability of the OCE index. *J. Ind. Prod. Eng.*, 40, 7, 572–588, 2023.
13. Abu-Bakar, H. and Charnley, F., Developing a strategic methodology for circular economy roadmapping: A theoretical framework. *Sustainability*, 16, 15, 6682, 2024.
14. Lahane, S., Kant, R., Shankar, R., Patil, S.K., Circular supply chain implementation performance measurement framework: A comparative case analysis. *Prod. Plann. Control*, 35, 11, 1332–1351, 2024.
15. Martín-Gómez, A.M., Pineda-Ganfornina, M., Ávila-Gutiérrez, M.J., Agote-Garrido, A., Lama-Ruiz, J.R., Balanced scorecard for circular economy: a methodology for sustainable organizational transformation. *Sustainability*, 16, 4, 1464, 2024.
16. Corona, B., Shen, L., Reike, D., Carreón, J.R., Worrell, E., Towards sustainable development through the circular economy—A review and critical assessment on current circularity metrics. *Resour. Conserv. Recycl.*, 151, 104498, 2019.
17. Kopnina, H., Fellinger, E., de Jong, J., Bowden, A., Bridging ESG and the Circular Economy. *EDITORS-IN-CHIEF*, 9, 2025.
18. Osei, A., Agyemang, A.O., Cobbinah, J., Strategic Sustainability Initiatives and the Circular Economy: Insights from Firm-Level Targets, Board Dynamics, Stakeholder Pressure, and Digital Transformation. *Bus. Ethics Environ. Responsib.*, 2025.
19. Senaratne, S., Gamage, I., Jayakodi, S., Perera, S., A taxonomy of circular economy terminologies: insights from the construction industry. *Built Environ. Proj. Asset Manag.*, 1–20, 2025.
20. Zils, M., Howard, M., Hopkinson, P., Circular economy implementation in operations & supply chain management: Building a pathway to business transformation. *Prod. Plann. Control*, 36, 4, 501–520, 2025.
21. Bertassini, A.C., Proposal of a roadmap for culture change towards a circular economy: application in a product-as-a-service business model, Doctoral dissertation, Universidade de São Paulo, 2023.
22. Ahmed, S., Liscio, M.C., Sospiro, P., Voukkali, I., Zorpas, A.A., Advancing Sustainable Development Through Environmental Performance Monitoring: The Organisational Life Cycle Assessment. *Bus. Strategy Environ.*, 34, 2, 2556–2570, 2025.

23. Turskis, Z. and Šniokienė, V., IoT-driven transformation of circular economy efficiency: an overview. *Math. Comput. Appl.*, 29, 4, 49, 2024.
24. Awan, U., Shamim, S., Khan, Z., Zia, N.U., Shariq, S.M., Khan, M.N., Big data analytics capability and decision-making: The role of data-driven insight on circular economy performance. *Technol. Forecasting Social Change*, 168, 120766, 2021.
25. Sakao, T., Bocken, N., Nasr, N., Umeda, Y., Implementing circular economy activities in manufacturing for environmental sustainability. *CIRP Ann.*, 73, 2, 457–481, 2024.
26. Iacovidou, E., Hahladakis, J.N., Purnell, P., A systems thinking approach to understanding the challenges of achieving the circular economy. *Environ. Sci. Pollut. Res.*, 28, 19, 24785–24806, 2021.
27. Gupta, R., Kushwaha, A., Dave, D., Mahanta, N.R., Waste management in fashion and textile industry: Recent advances and trends, life-cycle assessment, and circular economy, in: *Emerging Trends to Approaching Zero Waste: Environmental and Social Perspectives*, Hussain, C.M. and Singh, S. (Eds.), pp. 215–242, Elsevier, Amsterdam, Netherlands, 2022.
28. Ngan, S.P., Ngan, S.L., Lam, H.L., An overview of circular economy-life cycle assessment framework. *Chem. Eng. Trans.*, 88, 1123–1128, 2021.
29. Myers, R.J., Bide, T., Calzadilla Rivera, A., Hopkinson, P., Zils, M., Yayla, A., ... & Stegemann, J.A., Material flow analysis. NICER Programme Insight Report, 2025.
30. Cullen, J.M. and Cooper, D.R., Material flows and efficiency. *Annu. Rev. Mater. Res.*, 52, 525–559, 2022.
31. Saxegård, S.A., Wikström, F., Williams, H., Applying material flow assessment-based system expansion with multiple functions to solve for multifunctionality of recycling in life cycle assessment. *Int. J. Life Cycle Assess.*, 30, 2, 355–370, 2025.
32. Kochanski, M., Lotz, M.T., Korczak, K., Benchmarking circular economy measures in buildings along the 11R framework: A systematic review of quantified impacts on material use, energy consumption, GHG emissions, and costs. *J. Cleaner Prod.*, 144337, 2024.
33. Camp, R.C., *Benchmarking: The search for industry best practices that lead to superior performance*, CRC Press, Boca Raton, FL, USA, 2024.
34. Hassan, S.M., Circular economy and ESG: Building sustainable business models in the manufacturing sector. *J. Bus. Econom. Stud.*, 2, 1, 1–12, 2025.
35. Thimm, H., Digital Technologies for Enabling and Engineering the Circular Economy, in: *Applied Circular Economy Engineering: Technologies and Business Solutions to Implement Circularity*, Araujo, J.B., Hinderer, H., Viere, T. and Woidasky, J., (Eds.), pp. 171–196, Wiley-VCH, Weinheim, Germany, 2025.

36. John, C.K., Ajibade, F.O., Ajibade, T.F., Kumar, P., Adelodun, B., Adewumi, J.R., Navigating Circular Horizons: Introduction to the Concept of Circular Economy and Environmental Resilience, in: *Circular Economy and Environmental Resilience: Solutions for a Sustainable Tomorrow*, vol. 1, pp. 13–65, Springer Nature Switzerland, Cham, 2025.
37. Agyemang, A.O., Osei, A., Kongkuah, M., Exploring the ESG-circular economy nexus in emerging markets: A systems perspective on governance, innovation, and sustainable business models. *Bus. Strategy Environ.*, 2025.
38. Ritter, M., Schilling, H., Brüggemann, H., Fröhlich, T., Goldmann, D., Henze, R., ... & Kauffeld, S., Towards achieving the sustainable development goals: A collaborative action plan leveraging the circular economy potentials. *Gr. Interakt. Organ., Z. fur Angew. Organ. (GIO)*, 55, 2, 175–187, 2024.

9

Regulatory Compliance and Policy Considerations

Milad Heidari*, Jeyaprakash Natarajan, Sivasakthivel Thangavel, Pooyan Rahmanivahid and Lojin Jawad

Global College of Engineering and Technology (GCET), Muscat, Sultanate of Oman

Abstract

The decoupling of economic growth from resource depletion and environmental degradation is the principle behind the circular economy. It is a concept that has the ability to revolutionize the way we live, consume, and reuse our resources. This section is focused on discussing the changes that are taking place in terms of policies that are aimed at integrating CE into manufacturing, which is where concerns over resources and the environment are of major concern. This section provides an in-depth analysis of policies related to CE in various spheres of governance, including major issues that are of concern, such as policy fragmentation, cost of compliance, and regulating emerging technologies, among others, including a comparison of Europe, other parts of Asia, and developing countries. The chapter concludes by discussing future possibilities in the subject matter. Policy-makers, business leaders, and scholars who are keen on developing robust and sustainable circular manufacturing systems will find much value in this study.

Keywords: Circular economy, sustainable manufacturing, resource efficiency, environmental policy, policy fragmentation, circular manufacturing systems

9.1 Introduction

The revolutionary paradigm referred to as the "Circular Economy" (CE) seeks to achieve "decoupling" between economic growth and resource depletion and pollution. "Regenerating natural systems," "circulating

**Corresponding author*: milad@gcet.edu.om

Jeyaprakash Natarajan, Milon Selvam Dennison, M. Bhuvanesh Kumar and Ganapathy Thirukkotti (eds.) Manufacturing and the Circular Economy, (289–312) © 2027 Scrivener Publishing LLC

commodities and resources at the highest value," and "eliminating waste and pollution" are the three core principles of CE, which was first presented in Boulding's articles in 1966 and was later made popular by the "Ellen MacArthur Foundation." As global manufacturing is known to contribute to greenhouse gas emissions, and raw materials account for 9-39% of global emissions reductions in key industries, "Circular Economy" provides a strategic blueprint for aligning industry with Sustainable Development Goals [1–3].

Currently, there is an increase in pressure on the manufacturing industry, which has traditionally followed the linear "take, make, and dispose" approach, to integrate circularity into each and every aspect of their value chains. The history of the implementation of CE in the manufacturing industry has seen the development of component reuse, remanufacturing, and industrial symbiosis, which are all supported by laws and regulatory frameworks. Studies have shown that the development of the enabling policy framework has been found to be important for the successful implementation of CE in the manufacturing industry, despite the role of technology and enterprise flexibility [4, 5]. By the policy tools for the implementation of CE, which enable cooperation, reuse, and remanufacturing, the manufacturing industry can exchange materials, energy, and by-products in a mutually beneficial way, as shown in Figure 9.1.

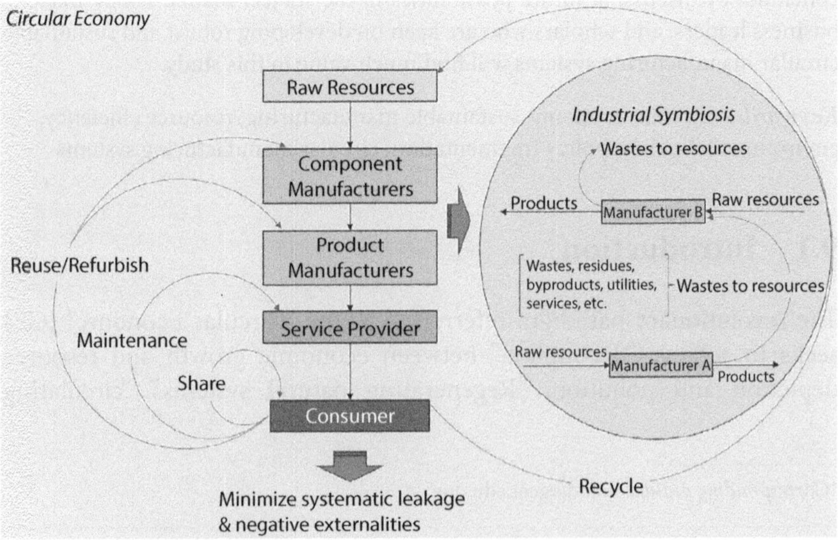

Figure 9.1 Conceptual diagram of industrial symbiosis and circular economy [6].

The transition of manufacturers to a circular economy is largely enabled by a policy and regulatory framework. This refers to regulations such as extended producer responsibility (EPR), eco-design regulations, and regulations related to resource efficiency and waste management. Notably, EPR schemes motivate producers to assume responsibility for products at the end of their life cycle, which is a critical aspect of a circular economy. Additionally, regulations such as mandatory eco-labeling and mandatory eco-design regulations, which affect manufacturing processes, are critical in embedding a circular economy into manufacturing processes. Figure 9.2 depicts EPR regulations that create a closed loop between recyclers, recyclers' financing, and product take-back.

This chapter aims to give a comprehensive analysis of the link between circular manufacturing and policy. For instance, we examine the global legal framework that includes new regulations in CE in developing countries, the EU's action plan, and China's promotion law. In addition, we look at how sector-specific regulatory modalities such as resource efficiency regulations and environmental licenses, as well as international organizations like UNEP, ISO, OECD, and WTO, impact cross-border CE governance.

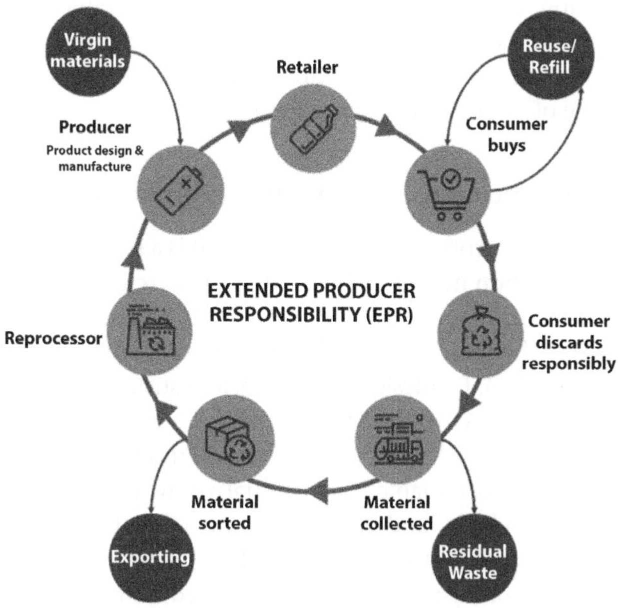

Figure 9.2 Circular flow representation of Extended Producer Responsibility (EPR) in packaging: producers fund and coordinate the collection, recycling, reuse, and eco-design efforts for packaging materials [7].

The three primary objectives of this chapter are to: (1) critically assess the exciting regulatory, economic, voluntary, and innovation-based CE policy tools; (2) recognize and identify the policy gaps and barriers to CE implementation in the manufacturing industry; and (3) offer practical recommendations based on case studies and best practices. By combining theoretical research with international policy initiatives, this chapter aims to help academics, industry practitioners, and policymakers develop reliable and efficient circular-based manufacturing systems.

9.2 Regulatory Landscape for Circular Economy

A regulatory framework of laws, intended to cut down on waste, foster resource efficiency, and encourage sustainable development, marks the CE regulatory framework. Most of these legislative actions, spearheaded by the European Union, include the formulation of laws such as the eco-design principles, the reduction of waste, and the incorporation of recycling procedures to accelerate the transition towards circular economies. Through trade and environmental diplomacy, transboundary actions such as the Global Alliance on CE and Resource Efficiency, spearheaded by the European Union, aim to enhance cooperation and establish global standards. When these actions are considered as a whole, they point to the growing realization of the need to transcend the borders of the CE principles in the face of global resource problems.

9.2.1 European Union (EU) Circular Economy Action Plan

A major part of the European Green Deal, which is a strategy planning document to reach carbon neutrality by 2050, is the Circular Economy Action Plan (CEAP), which was first introduced in 2015 and comprehensively revised in 2020. The sectoral plans for circular economy (e.g., electronics, batteries, and textiles), Ecodesign directives, and sustainable packaging are a few of the 35 measures outlined by CEAP for a circular economy along the entire product lifecycle. The preventive design of products is achieved by introducing the Sustainable Items Initiative, which requires products to be durable, recyclable, and repairable, and Digital Product Passports (DPPs) for supply chain transparency [8, 9].

CEAP is now more aspirational and enforced with the help of recent technological breakthroughs. The directive of 2009 has been replaced in July 2024 with Ecodesign for Sustainable Products Regulation (ESPR), which is more holistic and includes all physical products except cars and plants, along with binding regulations on carbon footprint, reparability, energy and resource efficiency, and recyclability. This is a major leap in regulations, which includes eco-modulated public procurement, outlawing the burning of unsold products, and setting DPP criteria under binding regulations. The Packaging and Packaging Waste Regulation (PPWR), which was implemented in early 2025 and includes recycled content limits (such as 65% in plastic bottles by 2040), outlaws single-use packaging materials and requires uniform labeling, is a key step towards reducing material leakage and recycling.

Some of the major impact sectors have been specifically addressed through the CEAP model. For example, the EU 2022 Strategy on Sustainable and Circular Textiles recommends the adoption of digital product passports by 2025, restrictions on microplastics, EPR schemes across all Member States, and eco-design standards. Initiatives such as the Circular Electronics Initiative and modifications to trash transport and construction regulations all improve the design of electronics and building products. These legally binding contracts represent a major shift by including circular economy principles not only in waste management but also in product design, purchasing, and trade.

9.2.2 United States and North American Regulatory Trends

Unlike the EU, the CE policy in the region is still in its infancy, yet gradually taking root in the North American region. Currently, the United States mainly uses voluntary state programs such as clean manufacturing tax incentives, zero-waste city initiatives, and EPR pilot programs. Canada has already put in place federal regulations on promoting circular building and sustainable procurement, which the provinces are already adopting. Notably, the two recent laws in the United States, which offer incentives for the production of clean-tech technologies, include the Inflation Reduction Act and the regional EPR laws on electronics and packaging materials. However, the lack of an overarching federal plan on the CE policy in the country indicates the fragmented nature and the need for state and provincial policy harmonization [10].

9.2.3 China's Circular Economy Promotion Law

The first legally binding foundation of CE globally was China's "2008 CE Promotion Law," which makes it legal for companies to practice recycling of packaging material and monitor their ecological footprint, besides using fewer resources, recycling more, and using cleaner production methods.

Other laws, such as the Cleaner Production Promotion Law (2002), along with ongoing tax advantages, funding options, and procurement policies, support the overall national policy on CE. Provinces also formulate policy targets in industrial areas with the help of recycling facilities and cleaner production facilities. These regulatory structures represent the top-down approach of the Chinese government in supporting industrial transformation in the country [11].

9.2.4 CE Policies in Developing Countries

In developing and emerging economies, the principles of CE have gradually begun to find their place in the national and regional policy structures. For example, in India, a comprehensive set of Plastic Waste Management Rules was enacted in 2016. These rules have since been amended in 2018, 2021, and 2024 to include provisions of a mandatory recycling rate of at least a certain percentage, Extended Producer Responsibility, limits on single-use plastics, and certification of biodegradable products. It appears to be a multi-layered policy framework that requires source segregation of waste, funding of waste collection by producers, and eco-design.

In South Asia and some parts of Southeast Asia, national-level initiatives as well as regional cooperation are fueling the pace of CE. In some countries like the Philippines, Vietnam, and Bangladesh, plastic bans as well as EPRs have been adopted to reduce pollution, as well as create new markets for product recovery. For instance, Bangladesh has improved its recycling infrastructure after adopting one of the earliest plastic bag bans in recorded history in 2002; however, enforcement remains inconsistent. Similarly, Vietnam's 2022 EPR law targets plastic packaging materials, which indicates a movement toward a globally accepted approach to CE (Figure 9.3). The major cases of regulatory developments in SSA include plastic bag bans and harmonization of regulations in various regional blocs in SSA, such as the EAC. In 2008, Rwanda led global efforts in plastic regulation through a ban on plastic bags. Kenya followed in 2017 with a similar ban. In 2020, the ban was extended to parks and beaches. The East African Community formulated a Regional Waste Management Strategy (2021) and a draft single-use plastics law as an example of harmonization of regulations in SSA aimed at reducing trade barriers in the region. However, implementation problems with plastic regulations in SSA underscore the need for institutional investment in SSA.

Figure 9.3 Infographic from the World Bank's 2021 Market Study for Vietnam: Plastics circularity opportunities and barriers [11].

9.2.5 Industry-Specific Regulations for Manufacturing

Table 9.1 shows the legislative advancements and differences in how these countries are utilizing these CE concepts in industry legislation. For waste management and EPR, the EU has led the way with its multi-layered approach to legislation. The US and Canada have adopted a decentralized approach to industry legislation. These legislative policies are working to ensure that producers are held responsible through advancements in supply chain management, waste recovery, and product design. Reverse logistics networks and infrastructure for recycling, along with financial incentives for recyclability, are quite effective.

The table also shows measures such as the Ecodesign Directive or France's repairability index, which involve integrating environmental criteria into product development processes, drive product manufacturers to focus on product durability and traceability; digital technologies such as Digital Product Passports promise to facilitate standardization in data collection across product lifecycles. On the other hand, data-driven oversight, circular economy business models, and shared responsibility are areas of focus under regulatory measures that are increasingly converging to support the objectives of the CE paradigm.

Table 9.1 Overview of industry-specific regulatory approaches in circular economy-oriented manufacturing.

Regulatory category	Region/ country	Instruments & examples	Objectives	Outcomes & impacts
Waste Management & EPR	EU	Waste Framework Directive (2008/98/EC); Packaging EPR regulations	Hierarchical waste treatment; producer accountability	Increased recycling rates, reduced landfill dependency
	Canada	CAP-EPR Framework; electronics, batteries, packaging sector schemes	Full life-cycle producer responsibility	Greater product take-back and material recovery
	USA (state-level)	California SB 54, Maine Packaging EPR Law	Incentivize recyclable packaging, reduce environmental burden	Fragmented implementation; improved design-for-recyclability in packaging
Resource Efficiency Standards	EU	Ecodesign Directive (2009/125/EC); ESPR (2024); End-of-Life Vehicle Directive (2000/53/EC)	Improve energy/material efficiency; mandate sustainable product attributes	341 TWh/year saved energy; mandated durability and disassembly design
	Global (electronics sector)	RoHS, WEEE, REACH	Restrict hazardous substances, enforce recycling/recovery	Eco-innovation in electronics, improved recyclability, and reduced toxic materials

(*Continued*)

Table 9.1 Overview of industry-specific regulatory approaches in circular economy-oriented manufacturing. (*Continued*)

Regulatory category	Region/ country	Instruments & examples	Objectives	Outcomes & impacts
Product Lifecycle Regulations	EU	Digital Product Passports (under ESPR); Right to Repair provisions; Repairability Index (France AGEC law)	Ensure traceability, reparability, and circular value retention	More durable products; consumer awareness; increased transparency across supply chains
	Global emerging frameworks	Lifecycle EPR; Repair labeling; Secondary materials quotas	Close material loops, reduce resource dependency	Circular procurement growth; emphasis on material passport standards

9.3 National and Regional Compliance Strategies

A methodical overview of the essential national and regional compliance strategies required in the application of the CE principles in the industrial sector is presented in Table 9.2. The four pillars of regulation—legal compliance, environmental permitting, integration of EIA, and compliance enforcement—are discussed in terms of their objectives, instruments, and processes.

To be legal in circular manufacturing, companies must follow the laws that make circularity a part of the production process. Such rules range from the basics of eco-design to Extended Producer Responsibility (EPR). For instance, within Europe and Canada, a firm must not only comply with resource use and emissions regulations, but it must also pay for the recycling of the product once it can no longer serve its purpose. The CAP-EPR system in Canada works like this: companies that produce electronics or packaging must monitor the number of their products that are recycled. This must be done on a regular basis. This way, companies are fully responsible for their products. This encourages them not to be wasteful in designing their products. Products must be eco-friendly to bear the CE mark for being compliant. This makes the transition to a circular economy

Table 9.2 Compliance strategies for circular manufacturing.

Compliance strategy	Description	Key instruments & examples	Objectives	Enforcement mechanisms
Legal Compliance in Circular Manufacturing	National/regional regulations ensuring adherence to CE laws	Mandatory EPR laws, eco-design mandates, emission/resource limits	Align manufacturing activities with CE principles	Legal reviews, mandatory reporting
Environmental Permits & Auditing	Permitting systems and periodic audits to ensure industrial pollution control & resource use efficiency	Environmental permits under RCRA/NEPA (US), UAE Circular Economy Strategy audits	Control emissions, validate CE measures	Inspections, ISO 14001 audits, permit renewal reviews
CE Integration into Environmental Impact Assessment (EIA)	Incorporation of CE principles (life-cycle, resource efficiency) into project-level EIAs	EU EIA Directive (2014/52/EU), Nigeria's NESREA EIA process	Evaluate CE impacts, ensure circular project planning	Mandatory EIA approval, public consultation
Compliance Monitoring & Enforcement	Mechanisms to ensure regulatory compliance through monitoring, data collection, and penalties	UAE Industrial Circular Economy Framework; China's provincial CE targets; US state-level EPR enforcement	Ensure adherence, deter violations	Inspections, audits, sanctions, public reporting

more feasible. Should a firm not comply with the regulations, they are likely to face sanctions, which may result in the use of green technology and sustainable design techniques. The regulations are nudging firms to incorporate circular economy principles into their overall environmental responsibilities as a business.

Environmental permitting is a fundamental requirement for industries, which ensures that pollution, resource usage, and waste management are in line with the circular economy vision set by the country. In the United States, licenses based on RCRA or NEPA regulations determine the usage of resources, pollution management, and dissemination of information on pollution to the general public. The same regulations apply in the countries that make up the Gulf Cooperation Council. For example, in the UAE, the Circular Economy Strategy, which is often backed by third-party audits like ISO 14001 audits, ensures that sustainability is integrated into the environmental permit by requiring evidence of resource reuse, implementation of eco-design, or reduction in waste. Both voluntary and compulsory environmental audits enhance the environmental permit by ensuring that regulations are adhered to and that any issues are addressed. Third-party audits like ISO 14001 audits provide credibility for the environmental permit. On the other hand, regulatory audits ensure that regulations are followed. The outcomes of audits often determine whether a permit is renewed or action is taken against a company. Audits ensure that manufacturers are held accountable for circular economy practices by linking them to compliance reports that are used for the advancement of the environment.

The EIAs are based on circular thinking since they assess upstream environmental damage, waste, reuse opportunities, and efficiency before any project is approved. The EU 2014/52/EU EIA directive requires an evaluation of alternatives, including those for design for the circular economy (CE). The Nigerian Environmental Study Action Group (NESREA) is the only agency of the Nigerian government that is authorized to certify EIAs. The agency uses circular economy metrics such as reduction targets for waste and reuse opportunities while carrying out project evaluation. By incorporating the circular economy into EIAs, the need for circular infrastructure is considered before any approvals are made. This also gives room for public participation since they can air their views regarding the circular economy. Therefore, EIAs are strategic tools for incorporating the circular economy into all stages of a project's life cycle. This means considering minimum recycled material requirements and take-backs. Monitoring is also done to ensure that the promises are kept.

Regulatory rules must be monitored and implemented for them to be effective. The UAE has an Industrial CE Policy Framework that outlines the goals for reducing waste in industry and reusing scraps. The rules require organizations to report to the Industrial Development Bureau. There is a centralized monitoring system for energy use and waste in China. The provinces have CE targets for the industrial zones. Organizations that fail to achieve the targets face penalties. However, for the rules to be effective, monitoring must be ongoing. The regulatory agencies use data analysis to identify any anomalies. Organizations publicly reporting their compliance with the rules is a powerful tool that encourages organizations to comply with the rules. The integration of technology with a systematic approach to monitoring has helped make CE rules more effective. The rules are not just measurable in terms of the circular impact on the production cycle. The rules are also more sustainable.

9.4 Policy Instruments Supporting the Circular Economy

9.4.1 Regulatory Instruments

Another important way of promoting circular economy principles *via* regulation is through a command-and-control approach, which is based on a set of design or performance rules that businesses must follow. An important example in this respect is the Ecodesign for Sustainable Products Regulation (ESPR), which will apply in the European Union as of 2024. This regulation makes eco-design recommendations binding, with a focus on resource efficiency, product durability, repairability, and recyclability. It requires that sustainable design be integrated into product design from the start, along with a call for supporting measures like digital product passports and repairability scores. The addition of a penalty mechanism underlines the regulatory power of a command-and-control approach in promoting circular economy principles in various industrial sectors.

CAC regulations can drive the achievement of environmental objectives through the enforcement of specific regulations. The EU's Single-Use Plastics Directive (2019/904) prohibits the use of a range of single-use plastics, including straws, cutlery, polystyrene food boxes, etc. The directive also sets a target for the use of at least 25% recycled content in drinks bottles by 2030. This not only reduces the use of difficult-to-recycle materials, which can now be eliminated from the market, but also increases the demand for secondary materials. The consistency of the rules across the EU, with no scope for regulatory arbitrage, aids the drive for circular manufacturing.

9.4.1.1 Command-and-Control Regulations

Currently, many countries are using bans and regulations on single-use items as one of the key measures to reduce plastics and encourage the use of greener products. In recent times, many countries have introduced similar regulations. In Ajman, UAE, for example, Ministerial Resolution No. 380/2022 was introduced to govern thin-walled single-use plastic bags. The regulation bans the bags unless they are of a minimum thickness. The regulations are set to take effect in January 2024. The regulations are meant to encourage people to adopt greener products. The neighboring countries to Ajman, including Saudi Arabia, Bahrain, and Oman, have all introduced similar regulations to ban single-use plastic bags based on their thickness. This promotes the use and availability of alternative products.

The Single Use Plastics Directive, which will ban various products starting in 2021, including cotton buds, plates, cutlery, and polystyrene containers, is another example of this strategy being implemented in Europe. Figure 9.4 demonstrates the EU's targeted regulatory strategy and the focus of the directive on material labeling and the identification of the specific single-use plastics that were banned. Additionally, any item that contains plastics must be labeled. These restrictions and bans encourage material

Figure 9.4 EU single-use plastics directive – Banned items (2021) [12].

circularity and recycling if combined with deposit return systems and recycling targets (such as the 90% recycling target for single-use plastic bottles by 2029). When combined, restrictions and bans force manufacturers to reassess their product lines, explore new resource availability, and develop circular economies.

9.4.2 Economic Instruments

Economic instruments are of critical importance in facilitating the transition to a CE by providing a means of ensuring that the financial benefits are aligned with environmentally friendly production and consumption practices. Among the most popular economic instruments for internalizing the environmental costs of manufacturing practices are fiscal subsidies and green taxation initiatives. For instance, green taxes are used to raise the cost of unsustainable production practices. However, incentives are provided to reduce the cost of eco-design, remanufacturing, and the development of green technology. The other effective financial mechanism that could encourage consumer engagement in a circular economy is the Deposit Refund System (DRS). The DRS is a system that encourages recycling, mainly of packages and beverage containers. The deposit that is charged for a product is refunded when the product is returned to a recycling center. The effectiveness of DRS is demonstrated by Germany and Norway, where more than 90% of beverage containers are collected from the market through DRS (European Commission, 2020). The DRS has a positive effect of closing the loop of materials that are used by producers to design products that are meant for reuse. The DRS has been adopted by different countries, such as various states in the U.S., like California and Oregon [13–15].

Extended Producer Responsibility (EPR) schemes, where producers are made responsible for the post-consumer stage of a product, are an important component of economic policy for circular manufacturing. EPR schemes shift waste management costs from public authorities to producers, thereby encouraging eco-design in product development. For example, the EU's Waste Framework Directive and Packaging and Packaging Waste Directive legally enforce EPR schemes on various product groups such as electronics, batteries, and automobiles. The Resource Circulation Act of South Korea and the Home Appliance Recycling Law of Japan are examples of how EPR has helped in the increased recycling rates and innovative product designs in these Asian countries. In developing countries like India, where the Plastic Waste Management Rules of 2024 have come into force, EPR schemes are gradually gaining popularity.

It is therefore essential to have a strong institutional basis that allows green taxes, subsidies, DRS, and EPR to be integrated into the broader policies for the circular economy. If these tools are not effectively harnessed, small and medium-sized enterprises might face challenges or suffer from negative effects. Governments are therefore increasingly using these tools in a hybrid form that effectively balances both economic and environmental viability. For example, tax reliefs for DRS infrastructure can attract private sector investments, while EPR and performance-based subsidies can reward firms that exceed set targets. As CE policies continue to develop, the use of these economic instruments is expected to become more sophisticated and possibly utilize technology such as blockchain.

9.4.3 Voluntary and Market-Based Instruments

Voluntary and market-based mechanisms support economic and regulatory strategies that encourage industry-driven and consumer-responsive strategies for the development of the CE. Instead of using regulatory restrictions, these strategies encourage sustainable practices through financial incentives, market recognition, and reputational rewards. Among the most popular strategies that fall under the category of voluntary mechanisms is the use of eco-labeling and green public procurement. These mechanisms can be quite useful in providing public and commercial actors with the flexibility of using circular practices due to the lack of regulatory support. With the growing popularity of the concept of sustainability, these technologies are quickly becoming popular.

The need to promote the concept of lifecycle thinking, circular economy business models, and product development from a sustainability perspective is facilitated by the concept of eco-labeling and environmental certification schemes. EU Ecolabel has been widely adopted by the Member States of the European Union, as depicted in Figure 9.5. Eco-labeling provides a platform for consumers to make environmentally conscious decisions through the provision of standardized information on the impact of a product on the environment. Such information may include the product's toxicity, energy consumption, material composition, and recyclability. Eco-labeling schemes encourage the development of environmentally friendly practices by producers. International trademarks such as the EU Ecolabel, the Blue Angel from Germany, the Eco Mark from Japan, and the Nordic Swan have encouraged producers to develop products that meet stringent regulations on environmental protection. According to the European Commission (2023), nearly 70,000 products and services bear

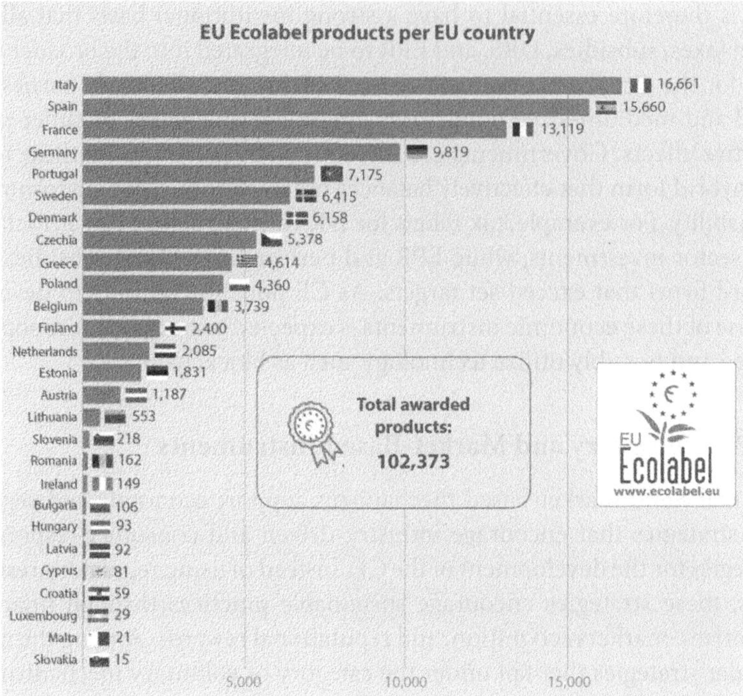

Figure 9.5 EU Ecolabel Certifications by Country. Total EU Ecolabel certified products and services by country (as of April 2025), illustrating leading adoption rates—the EU Ecolabel now covers over 102,000 certified items across 3,248 licenses, with Italy, Spain, France, and Germany leading in volume [16].

the EU Ecolabel. There is a relationship between the benefits to the environment and the trust that consumers have in the products.

Green or sustainable public procurement policies, which allow governments/public bodies to leverage their buying power to support CE principles, are another important strategy of voluntary markets. By establishing environmental and CE criteria for products and services that governments procure, such as product durability, reparability, or use of recycled materials, governments can help drive demand for more sustainable products. The European Union's Green Public Procurement Criteria and Japan's Green Purchasing Law are two examples of such policies that incorporate CE principles into procurement policies.

Voluntary and market instruments frequently function as a basis for more legally mandated regulations. For example, eco-labeling could one day become a basis for mandatory environmental statements. Moreover, these sites frequently facilitate collaboration between a wide range of stakeholders, such as corporations, NGOs, and certification bodies. However, there are challenges related to the coordination of standardization schemes, greenwashing, and engaging SMEs. Nevertheless, as demand is driven by consumers as well as institutional leadership, their power continues to grow. As digital technologies evolve, voluntary instruments are likely to become ever more vital for advancing CE transition in manufacturing and beyond.

9.5 Policy Challenges and Barriers

As shown in Table 9.3 below, some of the major barriers and challenges that are affecting the effective implementation of CE policies across various countries worldwide include: Fragmentation and lack of harmonization are some of the major challenges affecting CE policies. The fact that various countries have different and at times conflicting laws is a major challenge that is affecting businesses from implementing CE policies successfully. The lack of cohesive policies is affecting the efforts that are aimed at scaling up CE practices. The fact that there is a lack of clear policies is affecting CE practices from having a bigger systemic effect. The lack of clear policies is affecting investments in CE innovations due to the chance of sudden changes.

New technologies that could speed up circular economic transitions, like blockchain for traceability of products, and AI for predictive maintenance, are usually excluded from the existing restrictions. This creates a loophole in the law, which slows down the adoption of circular economic principles and creates a risk of legal challenges for businesses. Another significant challenge is the opposition of industries, which is a major threat, especially for SMEs, and is defined as the perceived cost of disruption of operations that is deemed too high. Finally, the absence of precise and detailed data on waste, resource use, and policy compliance limits the government's ability to monitor and enforce the law and adjust policy instruments.

9.6 Policy Recommendations and Future Directions

Table 9.4 presents a brief overview of the major strategic options available for lawmakers who aim to foster a robust transition towards a CE in a manner consistent with sustainability and economic resilience. First, circular solutions directly support the reduction targets for emissions by linking CE strategies with net-zero and climate strategies. This fosters systemic

Table 9.3 Policy challenges and barriers affecting circular economy implementation.

Challenge/barrier	Description	Impact on CE implementation
Fragmentation and Lack of Harmonization	Multiple overlapping policies across regions, countries, and sectors with inconsistent standards and definitions.	Leads to confusion, increased compliance complexity, and reduced cross-border circular trade.
Regulatory Uncertainty and Inconsistency	Frequent changes or lack of clarity in regulations create unpredictability for businesses and investors.	Discourages long-term investments in circular innovations; hinders strategic planning.
Policy Gaps for Emerging Technologies	Current regulations often lag behind rapidly evolving technologies like AI, blockchain, and advanced recycling methods.	Limits adoption of new CE enablers and innovation; legal grey areas increase risk exposure.
Industry Resistance and Compliance Costs	Resistance from industries due to perceived high costs, complexity, or disruption caused by new CE regulations.	Slows down CE adoption and creates lobbying pressures against stringent regulations.
Lack of Data for Monitoring and Decision-Making	Insufficient reliable data on material flows, environmental impacts, and compliance rates hampers evidence-based policymaking and enforcement.	Weakens policy effectiveness and accountability; impedes targeted CE interventions.

impact and agenda synergies for the environment. Entrepreneurs are encouraged to design low-carbon solutions by developing carbon metrics for businesses related to circularity, owing to the urgency for climate action on a global scale.

Secondly, the need to develop cross-sectoral and integrated regulatory frameworks meets the challenge of a fragmented legal environment, which might hinder the development of CE due to different regulations

Table 9.4 Policy recommendations and future directions for circular economy implementation.

Policy area	**Recommendations**	**Expected outcomes**	**Challenges addressed**
Aligning CE Policies with Climate and Net-Zero Goals	- Integrate CE targets with national climate and net-zero frameworks- Set measurable circularity-linked carbon reduction goals- Incentivize low-carbon circular innovations	- Synergized environmental policies- Reduced greenhouse gas emissions through circular strategies	Fragmented climate and CE policies
Building Integrated, Cross-Sectoral Regulatory Frameworks	- Harmonize regulations across manufacturing, waste, energy, and trade- Align EPR schemes and product standards- Facilitate cross-border cooperation on circular supply chains	- Streamlined compliance- Improved lifecycle management- Enabled circular supply chains	Regulatory fragmentation and lack of harmonization
Enhancing Stakeholder Engagement and Governance	- Foster multi-stakeholder collaboration and public participation- Build capacity for SMEs and local actors- Establish transparent monitoring and feedback mechanisms	- Increased policy legitimacy- Broader participation in CE transition- Better adaptation to local needs	Low stakeholder involvement; weak governance

(*Continued*)

Table 9.4 Policy recommendations and future directions for circular economy implementation. (*Continued*)

Policy area	Recommendations	Expected outcomes	Challenges addressed
Embracing Digitalization for Regulatory Compliance	- Deploy blockchain and IoT for product traceability and data integrity- Use AI for compliance monitoring and predictive analytics- Promote digital product passports	- Enhanced transparency and accountability- Improved regulatory enforcement- Real-time decision support	Data gaps; lack of transparency; compliance difficulties
Creating Adaptive Policies to Support Innovation and SMEs	- Design flexible regulatory sandboxes for CE innovations- Provide financial and technical support for SMEs- Regularly update policies based on technological advances	- Accelerated CE innovation- Inclusive economic growth- Policies resilient to emerging technologies	Regulatory rigidity; SME exclusion; innovation barriers

in different sectors and locations. Integrating trash regulations, extended producer responsibilities, and product regulations would ease compliance and the development of cross-border circular supply chains, which would offer opportunities for economies of scale.

Third, improving participation and governance in terms of stakeholders is very important in order to ensure effective and inclusive policy implementation. Multistakeholder participation is very important in improving the level of acceptance and enforcement. It provides an opportunity to bring together diverse viewpoints and areas of expertise in the decision-making process. Efforts to improve capacity, particularly in SMEs, can also help in democratizing the process and ensure that these players can make a significant contribution towards creating circular economies.

Fourth, digital technologies such as blockchain technology, Internet of Things (IoT), and artificial intelligence (AI) are seen to be potentially transformative in ensuring regulatory compliance through accurate traceability, data reliability, and predictability. These digital technologies are able to help companies and governments improve resource utilization through optimization by ensuring greater transparency in resource flow and product lifecycle. For example, digital product passports can offer detailed data on product sustainability to ensure circular product design and consumer confidence.

Finally, with SMEs playing a vital role in the advancement and development of the circular economy, regulations must be flexible in nature in order to support and foster such developments. A flexible regulatory sandbox, where there is less bureaucratic interference, allows for the testing and application of new technologies and innovations. This, with the help of financial and technological support, ensures the promotion of entrepreneurship and the adaptability and applicability of regulations with the advancement of technologies.

9.7 Conclusion

In this chapter, the role of regulatory compliance and policy in the promotion of CE in the manufacturing industry has been examined in detail. From the discussion of the foundational elements of CE in the manufacturing industry, it was evident that a paradigm shift from a traditional linear model of production and consumption to a circular model requires, besides technological and business innovations, enabling policy guidelines that regulate resource efficiency, waste management, and product lifecycle design, with policy playing a significant role as a facilitator and enforcer of CE principles.

The landscape is a lively and varied one, reflecting the goals and economic realities of the regions. One of the best examples of forward-thinking, wide-ranging regulation can be seen with the European Union's Circular Economy Action Plan, which outlines specific criteria for sustainability, eco-design, and product lifespan. On the other hand, the regulatory landscape in North America and the US reflects a highly fragmented and dynamic landscape, in which a greater focus is given to financial incentives and voluntary actions. A highly effective and comprehensive state-driven model is reflected in China's highly comprehensive and inclusive Circular Economy Promotion Law, in which national, provincial, and local initiatives are brought together to achieve circularity in industry. Developing countries are gradually incorporating CE principles in their regulatory landscape, with international cooperation, although infrastructure challenges persist.

Industry-specific regulations, including waste management regulations, Extended Producer Responsibility (EPR), resource efficiency regulations, and product lifecycle regulations, have proven essential in operationalizing the objectives of CE at the manufacturing stage. These regulations have helped reduce the impact on the environment and have helped in closing the loop through increased accountability and the promotion of innovation in green product design. However, as the chapter pointed out, policy issues in circularity have proven a challenge in the smooth implementation of circularity.

To address these challenges, national and regional compliance solutions have been developed, such as legal compliance procedures, environmental licenses, audits, and the application of CE principles in Environmental Impact Assessments. Monitoring and enforcement processes are significant in order to ensure that policy objectives are converted into results, and they need to be accompanied by open governance and stakeholder involvement. The analysis of policy initiatives identified a good mix of economic instruments like green taxes and subsidies, as well as command-and-control instruments, and voluntary market-based instruments like eco-labeling and green public procurement. These policy resources, when combined, create a good environment that encourages producers to adopt circular concepts through financial and regulatory means.

Ideas for the future of policy will also focus on the alignment of CE projects with broader climate and net-zero ambitions to deliver the most environmental benefits and economic resilience. A regulatory framework that is integrated and cross-sectoral will be essential to break down silos and deliver cross-border and cross-sectoral circular supply chains. More stakeholder engagement will be essential to deliver on inclusion and legitimacy. Finally, the use of digitization tools such as blockchain technology, AI, and IoT will be essential to deliver transparency and traceability. Finally, the development of flexible policy will be essential to support SMEs and innovation and maintain the speed of change of the circular economy.

To arrive at the resilient and circular manufacturing vision that the chapter has discussed so far, the chapter will conclude by illustrating the need for the policy strategy to be diverse, dynamic, cooperative, and technologically enabled. There is a need for the policy community, the corporate sector, and academics to come together and enhance the legislative environment that supports sustainability while also supporting innovation and inclusion. With the effective and visionary legislative efforts, the industrial sector will be able to overcome the challenges of circularity and assist the sustainable and resource-efficient global economy.

AI disclosure statement: The author acknowledges the use of AI-based tools for minor language editing or grammatical correction. However, all intellectual contributions, analyses, and conclusions presented in this chapter are entirely the author's own.

References

1. Kirchherr, J., Yang, N-H.N., Schulze-Spüntrup, F., Heerink, M.J., Hartley, K., Conceptualizing the Circular Economy: An Analysis of 221 Definitions. *Resour. Conserv. Recycl.*, 194, 107001, 2023, https://doi.org/10.1016/j.resconrec.2023.107001.
2. Dennison, M.S., Kumar, M.B., Jebabalan, S.K., Realization of circular economy principles in manufacturing: obstacles, advancements, and routes to achieve a sustainable industry transformation. *Discov. Sustain.*, 5, 438, 2024, https://doi.org/10.1007/s43621-024-00689-2.
3. Li, K., Salleh, H.B., Wang, R., Yang, Y., How do different policy instruments influence circular economy implementation in the construction sector? *Build. Res. Inf.*, 53, 3, 359–374, 2024, https://doi.org/10.1080/09613218.2024.2426466.
4. Sakao, T., Bocken, N., Nasr, N., Umeda, Y., Implementing circular economy activities in manufacturing for environmental sustainability. *CIRP Ann.*, 73, 2, 457–481, 2024. https://doi.org/10.1016/j.cirp.2024.06.002.
5. Leal, G.G., Vila, R.d.C., Dorado, A.B., Jäger, A., Circular Economy Adoption in Manufacturing Firms: Evidence From German Save Related Papers. *Bus. Strategy Environ.*, 2024, https://doi.org/10.1002/bse.4064.
6. Yu, Y., Yazan, D.M., Bhochhibhoya, S., Volker, L., Towards Circular Economy Through Industrial Symbiosis in the Dutch Construction Industry: A Case of Recycled Concrete Aggregates. *J. Clean. Prod.*, 293, 126083, 2021, 10.1016/j.jclepro.2021.126083.
7. The packaging industry, particularly the flexible packaging segment, has seen rapid growth due to its many advantages, https://epackagingsw.com/blog/extended-producer-responsibility-in-packaging?.
8. First Circular Economy Package including Regulation proposal on Sustainable Products and Sustainable Textiles Strategy, 2022. https://ec.europa.eu/newsroom/env/items/742027/en?.
9. Circular economy action plan, 2024. https://environment.ec.europa.eu/strategy/circular-economy-action-plan_en?.
10. Results and Indicators for Development circular economy, European Commission, Directorate-General for International Partnerships, Version 2021, https://capacity4dev.europa.eu/resources/results-indicators/circular-economy_en?utm_source=chatgpt.com.

11. World Bank Group, Market Study for Vietnam: Plastics Circularity Opportunities and Barriers. Marine Plastics Series;. © World Bank, 2021. http://hdl.handle.net/10986/36313 License: CC BY-NC 3.0 IGO.
12. Unpacking the New Single-Use Plastic Directive for the EU: What are the implications for packaging, retailers, and companies involved in foodservice? 2021. https://ecotensil.eu/blogs/blog/unpacking-the-new-single-use-plastics-directive-for-the-eu-what-are-the-implications-for-packaging-retailers-and-companies-involved-in-foodservice?.
13. Enriquez, S., Sánchez-Triana, E., Guerra López, M.G., *Economic Instruments and Financial Mechanisms for the Adoption of a Circular Economy* (pp. 455–482). Springer, Singapore, 2021. https://doi.org/10.1007/978-981-15-8510-4_23.
14. Huttmanová, E. and Mikča, R., Environmental Taxes as a Path to a Green Transition. *Eur. J. Sustain. Dev.*, 13, 3, 113, 2024, https://doi.org/10.14207/ejsd.2024.v13n3p113.
15. Davydenko, N., *et al.*, Fiscal regulation policy and financial incentives impact on the environmental management. *IOP Conf. Ser.: Earth Environ. Sci.*, 1269, 012010, 2023.
16. Directorate-General for Environment2 min read EU Ecolabel breaks record: setting the gold standard with more than 100.000 certifications, News blog, April 2025. https://environment.ec.europa.eu/news/new-eu-ecolabel-statistics-setting-gold-standard-more-100000-certifications-2025-04-15_en?.

10

Optimizing Material Handling in Manufacturing Production Shops

Milad Heidari*, Jeyaprakash Natarajan, Khalid Anwar, Amirhossein Ali Memari and Mohammad Ali Valikhani

Mechanical Engineering Department, Global College of Engineering and Technology (GCET), Muscat, Sultanate of Oman

Abstract

Material handling, defined as the movement, storage, control, and protection of materials, is a fundamental component of manufacturing systems. The efficiency of material handling has a direct impact on productivity, costs, worker safety, and quality of manufactured products." This chapter aims to present diverse strategies for optimizing material handling within the manufacturing production environment through the incorporation of lean manufacturing, sustainable manufacturing, and Industry 4.0 technologies. Initially, the chapter will address diverse material handling concepts, including the types of material handling equipment and the types of material handling systems. Subsequently, the chapter will address diverse material handling optimization approaches, including the design of the layout, workload balancing, material handling equipment, and the incorporation of diverse digital technologies for material handling optimization. Finally, the chapter will address diverse performance criteria for material handling, including diverse trends such as cybersecurity for smart manufacturing, human-robot collaboration, and predictive analytics, among many others. Throughout the chapter, material handling will be presented as an integral component for the development of sustainable manufacturing systems.

Keywords: Material handling, manufacturing optimization, lean manufacturing, automation

**Corresponding author*: milad@gcet.edu.om

Jeyaprakash Natarajan, Milon Selvam Dennison, M. Bhuvanesh Kumar and Ganapathy Thirukkotti (eds.) Manufacturing and the Circular Economy, (313–340) © 2027 Scrivener Publishing LLC

10.1 Introduction

Material handling refers to the movement, storage, control, and protection of materials, parts, and products during the entire process from the receipt of materials to the delivery of the final product. It is one of the fundamental aspects of the manufacturing process, which influences the scheduling of the manufacturing process, the layout of the manufacturing facility, the utilization of equipment, and the safety of the working environment. The modern material handling system combines manual operations with the use of automated equipment and advanced digital technology, such as robotic manipulators, conveyor systems, automatic guided vehicles, and Internet of Things technology for tracking and tracing materials. Thus, the evolution of the manufacturing process towards the creation of intelligent, lean, and responsive manufacturing systems has transformed the traditional material handling function from being a supporting aspect of the manufacturing process to a new and strategically important aspect of operational excellence (Figure 10.1) [1, 2].

The need to optimize the material handling function in the manufacturing process is significant, as the lack of an efficient material handling system could lead to increased worker fatigue, excessive work-in-progress (WIP), inventory, product damage, and higher costs of production. It has been observed that the material handling function could account for up to 70% of the total time spent during the manufacturing process and 20% to 50% of the total costs of operations in industrial settings. Thus, the need to optimize the material handling function has become significant, considering the need for customization of products, the reduction of product delivery time, and the need for flexible batch sizes in the manufacturing process. Optimization of the material handling function has also become significant to ensure the safety of the working environment, to address the ergonomic issues, and to minimize the environmental impact of the industrial process [4, 5]. Figure 10.2 presents the integration of cloud computing and IoT technology for the creation of efficient and intelligent material handling systems.

The design and operation of material handling systems undergo transformation through technological advancements, which mainly stem from Industry 4.0 developments. The combination of smart sensors, autonomous mobile robots, and real-time tracking systems, which include RFID, IoT, and predictive analytics technology, enables companies to achieve higher levels of operational accuracy, flexibility, and responsiveness. The technologies enable manufacturers to track materials throughout their

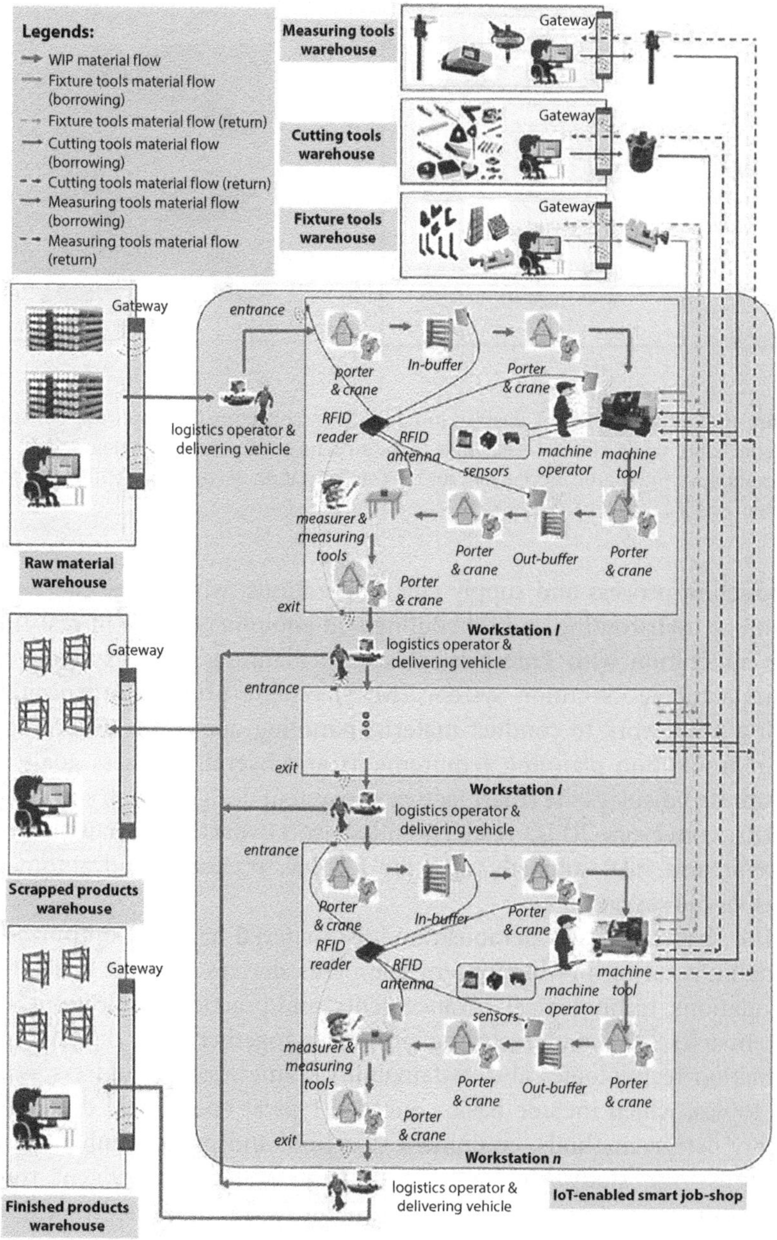

Figure 10.1 The material flow of manufacturing resources in IoT-enabled smart job shop [3].

Figure 10.2 Cloud-based IoT-enabled intralogistics architecture for supporting dynamic material handling decisions: (a) example of the structure of the racking system; (b) example of the shuttle mechanism for the transportation of containers within the same storage level [6].

production process and supply chain operations, which they can use to optimize their routing and scheduling and equipment usage in real-time. The integration with Enterprise Resource Planning (ERP) systems and Manufacturing Execution Systems (MES) systems provides organizations with a framework to conduct material handling operations according to their production planning requirements and overall business goals [7]. Figure 10.3 displays the smart factory ecosystem design, which shows how AMRs, conveyors, RFID readers, and sensors work together with cloud systems and ERP software to create flexible, traceable, and automated logistics operations.

The chapter aims to demonstrate how material handling optimization in manufacturing production environments derives from its theoretical foundations, technological advancements, and practical applications. The system uses lean manufacturing principles together with digital transformation technologies and sustainability frameworks to address essential topics, which include basic concepts, typical operational difficulties, facility design methods, equipment selection, and process enhancement methods. The study highlights automation systems, intelligent tracking solutions, and ergonomic design methods through case studies and upcoming technological advances. The material handling systems present engineers, researchers, and industrial specialists with a complete framework for designing and assessing systems that undergo ongoing updates in modern manufacturing settings.

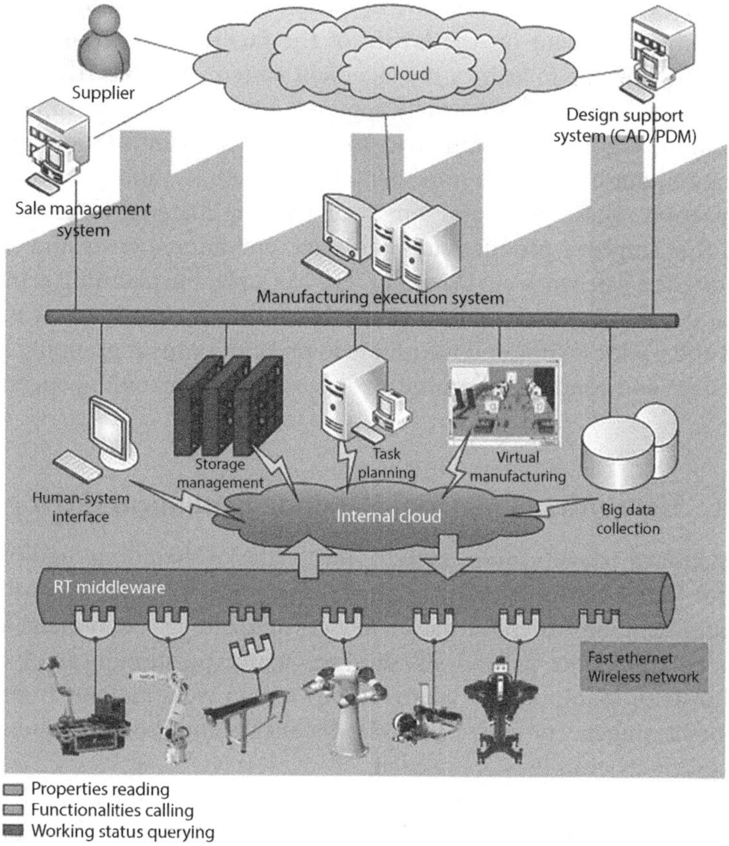

Figure 10.3 System architecture of a smart factory material handling ecosystem [8].

10.2 Fundamentals of Material Handling

"Material handling is the short-range movement, protection, storage, and control of materials and goods within a facility or between facilities, including that between a facility and vehicles." Material handling is different from manufacturing processes, which generate form utility, and material handling processes generate mostly time and place utility by ensuring that raw materials, work-in-progress, and finished goods are readily available at the required time and place within the production system. Material handling processes involve manual, semi-automated, and fully automated equipment, which are designed for material flow support throughout the production process.

Material handling is at the core of designing production systems, and it is highly dependent on the layout of the facilities, material handling equipment, and the inventory management system. For effective material handling, ten principles are widely accepted, and they are planning, standardization, ergonomics, unit load formation, space utilization, system integration, automation, environmental sustainability, and life cycle cost optimization. These principles aim at developing material handling processes that improve productivity, minimize operational costs and waste, and provide a safe work environment. For example, the planning principle aims at developing material flow paths that minimize unnecessary movements and backtracking, and the unit load principle aims at grouping items into pallets and containers to minimize the number of handling operations [9].

10.2.1 Categories of Material Handling Equipment (MHE)

The standard classification system for material handling equipment includes four main categories, which are transport equipment, positioning equipment, unit-load formation devices, and storage equipment. Unit-load formation (like pallets) standardizes loads; positioning equipment (like hoists or manipulators) aligns things within workstations; transport equipment transports materials over distances; and storage equipment holds products until they are needed.

Manual and semi-automated tools: The process of manual goods handling requires workers to perform various tasks, which include lifting, pushing, and carrying tasks that need expensive equipment to operate, but create serious challenges for worker health and result in decreased productivity. The handling equipment known as pallet jacks and lift tables, hoists, and manipulators represents a type of semi-automated tool which enables operators to control product movement through both manual and automated methods. The tools provide advantages through their affordable initial investment costs, which help improve production efficiency while decreasing physical strain and enhancing orientation precision.

Automated and intelligent systems: The category of automated and intelligent systems for MHEs includes robotic manipulators and AS/RS systems, AGVs, AMRs, and conveyors. AS/RS systems perform the task of handling goods in high-density storage areas; conveyors enable the movement of goods along established transport routes; AGVs handle goods transportation through their designated paths; intelligent adaptive machines provide manufacturing systems with flexible batch size capabilities through their real-time identification of various product characteristics.

10.2.2 Types of Material Flow in Manufacturing Shops

The flow of materials through production systems serves as a fundamental element that determines how efficiently systems operate and how much output they produce. Manufacturing environments display three main flow patterns, which include linear flow, loop flow, and cellular flow. Linear flow moves products through production stages in a sequential order, while loop flow enables products to go back to previous stations for rework or extra processing, and cellular flow creates workstations that operate in dedicated cells to process groups of similar parts. The choice of flow pattern depends on factors such as product complexity, production volume, and facility layout constraints.

Linear vs. Loop vs. Cellular Flow
Linear flow is most suitable for high-volume production environments that contain multiple products because this flow requires the least amount of backtrack movement.

Loop flow supports processes that involve repeated operations, such as inspection cycles or phased finishing procedures.

Cellular flow finds its application in lean manufacturing because it enables organizations to group various workstations which Process different materials into operational cells that need less time to transport between processing stations.

Production systems create two distinct material flow patterns that operate differently because of their unique characteristics. The production process in discrete manufacturing creates individual units or batches, which include electronic devices and automotive components, thus requiring manufacturers to use scheduled material flows that can be tracked. Continuous production systems, which operate in industries like chemicals and food processing, function without breaks while utilizing bulk material handling equipment. Discrete systems use flexible routing methods together with buffers, and they operate through intermittent material flows, while continuous systems depend on constant material flow processes, and they maintain operational uniformity.

10.3 Strategies for Optimization

The process of efficient material handling throughout manufacturing production facilities depends on the combined implementation of facility layout design, flow control systems, inventory movement systems, and

Table 10.1 Optimization strategies for material handling.

Optimization area	Strategies	Expected Benefits	Tools and technologies
Facility Layout Planning	- Adoption of cellular layouts for better efficiency in flow- Optimization of distances for material movement- Analysis of layout options through simulation	- Increased production throughput Reduced - material handling times - Reduced levels of work-in-progress inventory	AutoMod, FlexSim, Plant Simulation
Workstation and Aisle Design	- Application of ergonomic design for better workstation efficiency- Proper zoning of aisles- Analysis of bottlenecks	- Improved worker safety and ergonomics - Improved accessibility of materials - Reduced operational downtime	REBA, OWAS, Spaghetti Diagrams
Load Optimization and Scheduling	- Calculation of batch size according to takt-time - Optimization of loads for better efficiency in movement - Application of dynamic algorithms for scheduling	- Smoother production flows - Reduced internal transportation costs -Balanced production stages	ERP/MRP systems, AI-based scheduling, digital twins
Standardization	- Adoption of standardized pallets - Standardization of material handling - Application of modular containers	- Simplified training and operational processes - Improved system compatibility - Reduced variability in operational processes	5S, SOPs, ISO 6780 (Pallets), Lean 6σ
Cross-Docking and JIT	- Elimination of intermediate handling - Synchronization of material movement - Scheduling according to demand	- Reduced inventory holding costs - Reduced production lead times -Minimization of operational waste	Kanban, RFID tracking, EDI systems

workstation ergonomic design. The development of smart manufacturing, together with the adoption of lean production systems, has created new challenges for manufacturers because they must now eliminate all activities that do not contribute value to their work processes. Organizations have developed best practices together with optimization techniques that help improve material flow efficiency. The section brings together five main industrial sectors, which follow standard methods for facility layout planning and workstation and aisle design and load optimization, scheduling, process standardization, and lean logistics model execution, which includes Just-in-Time (JIT) and cross-docking. The strategies show intent to optimize material flow while reducing less effective operational activities and creating better production response times. Digital technologies now support these initiatives through their data analytics and automation and simulation tools, which help manufacturers synchronize their material handling processes with production schedules, customer demand patterns, and sustainability goals. The table presents all optimization strategies together with their real-world applications in Table 10.1 [10–12].

10.4 Role of Technology in Modern Material Handling

Automation and Robotics in Material Movement

Companies that operate current material handling systems depend on automated technologies and robotic systems to optimize their operational processes while decreasing their needs for human workers and creating safer work environments. Automated handling solutions include fixed conveyor systems, which use robotic manipulators and flexible mobile platforms that execute their work through automated processes that include palletizing, sorting, and part handling. The implementation of these technologies leads to greater production capacity while decreasing operational errors and enabling workers to avoid performing physical labor tasks. Research shows that automated robotic systems deliver their best results in dangerous production areas that have high operational volume because they maintain steady performance while working without breaks. Industries widely use robotic material handling systems, which include four-axis and six-axis robotic arms for processes that involve palletizing, part feeding, and assembly work. The robotic palletizing system, which operates with multiple conveyor lines, shows how robotic arms use vision systems to handle complicated material flows that occur in actual production environments.

Figure 10.4 Robots in manufacturing: (a) robotic palletizer for multiple conveyor belts that reduces human interaction in manufacturing; (b) robotic arms for raw lamb on the meat packing production line [14].

The robots use artificial intelligence and advanced machine vision technology to recognize, grasp, and position different components in unstructured environments. The implementation of simulation-based commissioning together with dynamic scheduling methods improves robotic integration because they match robot operations with production timelines to achieve maximum output while reducing downtime [13]. Figure 10.4 shows robotic palletizing systems integrated with multiple conveyors, robotic arms that handle raw meat within the packaging line.

Conveyors, AGVs, and AMRs

Conveyor systems serve as crucial elements that enable uninterrupted material transport between manufacturing units and across different production areas. The system operates efficiently in high-throughput environments because materials move through predetermined paths. The combination of conveyors with equipment such as vertical carousels and automated sorting systems permits efficient material handling, which enables large production operations (Figure 10.5). The fixed-path operation of conveyors restricts their ability to function in environments that require production to switch between different products and facilities that need to change their layouts frequently. The manufacturing industry now employs Automated Guided Vehicles (AGVs) and Autonomous Mobile Robots (AMRs) to overcome its existing operational challenges. AGVs navigate their routes through magnetic strips and markers and laser systems, which handle pre-established paths, while AMRs use LiDAR sensors and dynamic mapping algorithms to move independently and change their paths. AMRs present multiple benefits over conventional AGVs because they need less infrastructure work, allow for quick equipment restarts, and possess better abilities to identify obstacles in their path. The system requires organizations to decide between three

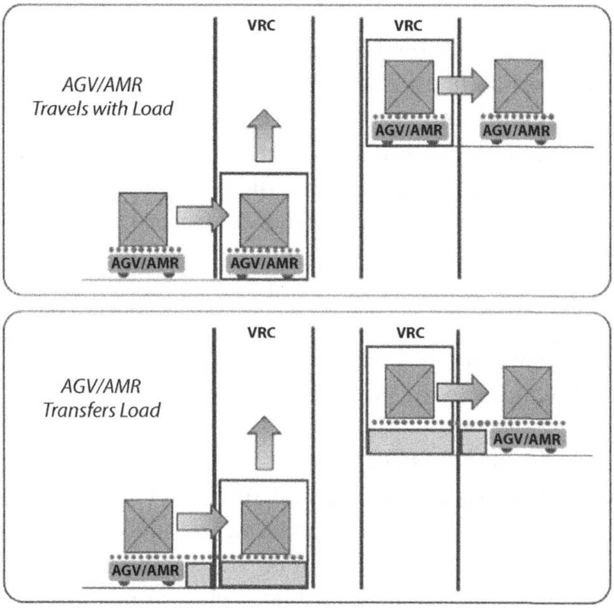

Figure 10.5 Vertical reciprocating conveyor (VRC) configurations for AGV/AMR load travel and load transfer between conveyor levels.

factors, which include expenses, facility needs, and the difficulty of running their operations. The solution requires facilities to implement hybrid material handling systems, which use conveyors and AGVs and AMRs to achieve operational flexibility and system dependability and cost-effective handling of materials [15, 16].

The vertical reciprocating conveyor shown in Figure 10.5 functions as an intermediate transfer layer between AGVs and AMRs in the facility through its connection to both fixed conveyor systems and mobile robotic platforms. The Internet of Things (IoT) and Radio Frequency Identification (RFID) technology enable organizations to track their assets throughout their entire lifecycle [17].

Use of IoT and RFID for Tracking and Traceability

The combination of Radio Frequency Identification (RFID) technology with the Industrial Internet of Things (IIoT) creates new capabilities that enable material handling systems to achieve complete real-time visibility and material traceability. The IoT sensors provide continuous updates about system locations and operational conditions and environmental factors, which the production monitoring systems and analytics platforms use to collect important information. The use of RFID tags for pallet, container, and product tracking enables organizations to achieve inventory accuracy through non-line-of-sight tracking, which functions across complex facilities and decreases their need for manual scanning. The combination of RFID technology and Internet of Things (IoT) sensors with digital twin platforms and simulation models enables organizations to make better operational decisions through their advanced digital twin platforms. Warehouse systems that utilize RFID-enabled digital twins for their storage retrieval operations show an optimization that results in reduced forklift idle time, according to studies. Scalable Internet of Things (IoT) frameworks enable manufacturing systems to connect all their components while providing control over automation, real-time system monitoring, and flexible material handling solutions in the production environment [13, 18].

Digital Twin and Simulation Tools for Layout Optimization

Digital twin technology enables manufacturers to create virtual representations of real-world production systems, which allow them to test design and operational choices before they build actual systems. The digital twin technology for material handling enables digital simulation of equipment layouts, traffic patterns, cycle times, and bottleneck conditions throughout the entire facility. Engineers use this capability to test different layout designs and robot arrangements and material movement pathways, which helps them achieve better results through data-based material flow optimization. Digital twin-based simulations demonstrate that material handling time decreases between 13 and 29 percent while production throughput increases by more than 15 percent, according to research from industrial and academic studies. Advanced simulation tools—such as Siemens Plant Simulation and reinforcement learning–enhanced modeling platforms—enable scenario-based optimization by training AI algorithms to recommend adaptive layouts and dispatching strategies. Digital twins support system design and help with commissioning and operational monitoring, and continuous performance optimization, which reduces implementation risks and enhances system efficiency over time [19].

Integration of Material Handling with MES and ERP Systems

The successful operation of manufacturing systems depends on properly connecting their physical material handling equipment with their digital control systems, which include Manufacturing Execution Systems and Enterprise Resource Planning systems. The manufacturing execution system operates from the shop floor to manage production operations and schedule work activities while dispatching material handling equipment based on production time constraints. Figure 10.6 shows a theoretical

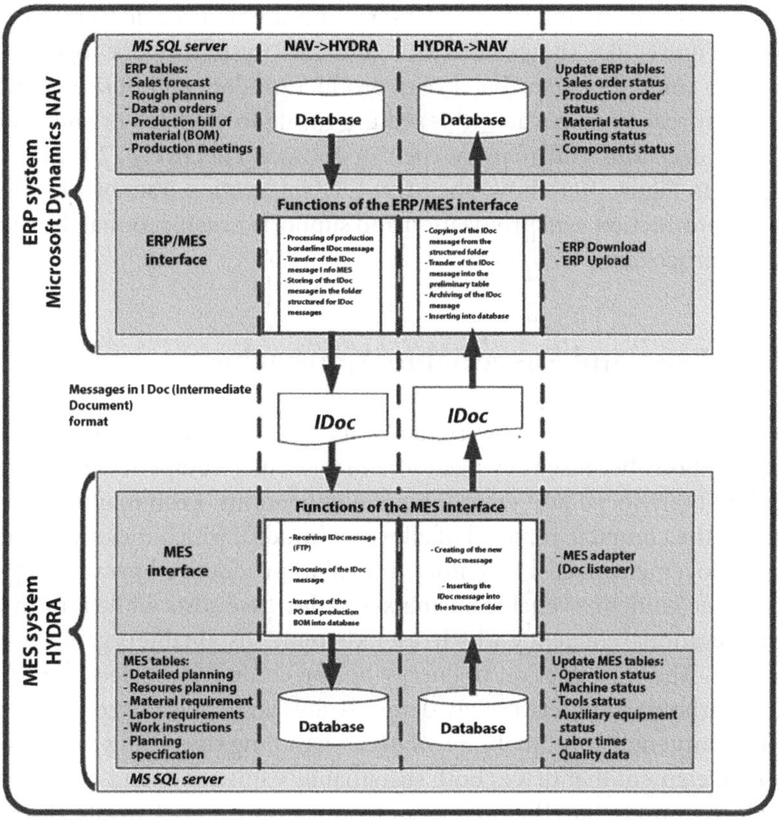

Figure 10.6 Conceptual model of MES–ERP integration [22].

two-way connection between MES and ERP systems, which demonstrates how operational information and enterprise-level data flow in two directions. The integration enables material handling equipment to transmit production information to MES systems in real-time, which includes cycle time data, machine operational data, and material flow information. The system establishes connections that allow immediate responses for production interruptions, changing order requirements, and ongoing schedule changes. The enterprise uses this data to align ERP systems with real-time shop floor operations, which synchronize demand forecasting and supplier management, and inventory control. Automated vehicles and handling systems use their arrival and departure signals to send data to ERP systems, which then use that information to make routing, inventory, and replenishment decisions. The digital synchronization enables lean operational methods to function because it decreases work-in-progress inventory and reduces costs for maintaining inventory, and it enhances delivery performance. Figure 10.6 shows how MES and ERP systems work together to provide a unified system that shares production data and business information in real-time, because this feature needs to exist for organizations to make decisions and manage their operations effectively [20, 21]. The diagram in Figure 10.6 shows the MES-ERP integration framework, which enables production synchronization and supports organizational decision-making processes.

10.5 Lean and Sustainable Approaches

Manufacturing facilities now require lean and sustainable material handling methods because they need to enhance their competitiveness while fulfilling their social and environmental obligations. Lean manufacturing requires the complete removal of all waste (muda), which includes unnecessary movement, excess inventory, and all unproductive operational processes. The guidelines enable businesses to decrease costs while improving their operational efficiency, which results in more sustainable organizational practices. The introduction of energy optimization, closed-loop logistics, and decarbonization technology demonstrates an increasing commitment to environmental accountability. Material handling operations serve as an essential element that drives both sustainability initiatives and operational excellence programs. The business organizations analyze waste through Value Stream Mapping (VSM) while they use energy-efficient and ergonomic handling tools to enhance employee productivity, and they follow circular economy principles by recycling and reusing pallets and containers to achieve their lean and green objectives. Organizations use cleaner energy sources together with improved logistical systems and transportation optimization methods to achieve their sustainability targets through lean and sustainable thinking. Table 10.2 presents essential lean and sustainability concepts used in material handling, which include their respective objectives and common strategies and measurable benefits [23–25].

10.6 Performance Metrics and Evaluation

The assessment process needs performance measurements that can detect operational problems and guide performance improvements while assessing return on investment for material handling systems. This section

Table 10.2 Lean and sustainable practices in material handling.

Focus area	Lean/sustainable principle	Key strategies/ tools	Benefits
Lean Manufacturing and Muda Elimination	Eliminate non-value-adding activities (transport, wait, excess motion)	5S, Kaizen, JIT, Kanban, Heijunka	Reduced WIP, shorter lead times, fewer handling steps
Value Stream Mapping (VSM)	Visualize and optimize material flow and information flow	VSM diagrams, takt-time alignment, flow balancing	Bottleneck reduction, improved flow efficiency
Ergonomic and Energy-Efficient Handling	Minimize human strain and reduce energy use during movement	Lift-assist devices, powered pallet jacks, LED lighting, regenerative braking	Lower injury rates, reduced power consumption
Circular Economy Practices	Maximize reuse and recovery of materials and containers	Reusable totes, reverse logistics, closed-loop packaging systems	Less material waste, lower packaging cost
Carbon Footprint Reduction	Reduce GHG emissions through optimized logistics and cleaner energy	Route optimization, load consolidation, electrified AGVs, renewable energy for warehouses	Lower emissions, better environmental compliance

provides optimization project cost-benefit analysis methods while presenting critical measurements, which include throughput, cycle time, inventory turnover, and equipment utilization. Manufacturers can achieve permanent development together with operational performance success, which meets business objectives by tracking these KPIs.

Throughput and Cycle Time

Throughput refers to the manufacturing process output, which measures the total finished products produced during an hour or a shift period. The Theory of Constraints defines throughput as the system's capacity to meet market demand, which can be measured through revenue minus actual variable costs. Production processes achieve efficient operations when they maintain high throughput levels, which demonstrate their capacity to produce goods without experiencing significant interruptions.

Contrarily, cycle time measures all processing activities plus the time spent waiting in queues to determine the duration needed to complete one unit from start to finish. The process of reducing cycle time enables businesses to enhance their ability to respond to customer needs while improving their order delivery times. The production process uses cycle time together with throughput as essential metrics that measure operational efficiency and production response capacity.

Inventory Turnover

Inventory turnover measures the rate at which inventory is used and replaced during a defined timeframe by calculating the cost of goods sold through the average inventory maintained by the business. The material handling process achieves optimal performance when higher turnover rates demonstrate that the organization successfully matches its requirements for materials and their storage with its production activities. The manufacturing industry can enhance its inventory turnover rates through the implementation of JIT systems, cross-docking operations, and real-time inventory tracking systems, which include RFID and ERP technology. The organization achieves efficient material movement because it eliminates buffer stock requirements while matching material supply with production requirements and decreasing stock obsolescence risks. The efficiency of working capital increases with every rise in turnover.

Equipment Utilization

The benchmark indicator known as Overall Equipment Effectiveness (OEE) combines three performance dimensions: quality, performance, and availability. The quality measurement records good parts production as a proportion of total output, whereas performance assesses production speed in relation to the ideal production rate, and availability assesses operational time in relation to planned operational time. OEE calculates the actual productive time through its two combined components, which achieve 100% when output reaches ideal production levels [26–28].

10.7 Case Studies and Best Practices

The process of material handling optimization within manufacturing production shops leads to three main advantages, which include better operational efficiency and lower operational expenses, plus higher product standards. Practical implementation of material handling solutions needs to be assessed through actual manufacturing processes, which demonstrate how companies have applied theoretical material handling concepts. The different case studies show how various approaches affect the efficiency of production operations. The analysis of current industrial methods from automotive, aerospace, and electronics to heavy manufacturing shows that organizations have improved their material handling operations through lean practices and automation, digital technologies, and ergonomic design improvements. The productivity and cost-saving achievements from these examples demonstrate measurable results, while the existing best practices will serve as a foundation for upcoming industrial and research initiatives.

Blockchain-Empowered Sustainable Manufacturing

Airbus used blockchain technology to create digital twin systems for managing materials during aircraft assembly operations [29]. The technology enables eco-friendly manufacturing processes and product lifecycle management through the implementation of an Industry 4.0 manufacturing system. The research analyzes how blockchain technology addresses challenges that hinder sustainable development from both manufacturing and product lifecycle management systems. The system demonstrates its capacity to process transactions through its decentralized network, which delivers clear transaction documentation and permits users to monitor their assets during smart contract operation. The implementation of blockchain technology in manufacturing operations provides complete visibility through its ability to trace products and eliminate the need for intermediary parties. The system enables users to make decisions through decentralized methods while organizations establish direct contact for optimization purposes using smart contract technology. The technology enables organizations to achieve better efficiency through its capacity reservation system, which reduces operational costs and eliminates the need for extra inventory and backup resources. The team conducted a simulation study to test logistics routes and parts movement before implementing the system. The system reached a 15% decrease in transport duration between manufacturing areas while experiencing reduced operational downtime. This study also points to a pressing need to address existing technical challenges and social barriers in order to improve the solution's accessibility to a larger population while realizing its full potential in terms of sustainability.

Equipment Optimization

In the production of steel and iron, the optimization of materials handling equipment has a significant impact on the reduction of the number of operating cycles. A case study is conducted to examine the impact of optimal materials handling equipment on the reduction of defects, along with the improvement of production efficiency. This case study highlights the importance of optimal materials handling equipment, which helps to improve product quality, thereby enhancing customer service. It is recommended that the management of manufacturing organizations should take the initiative to engage with optimal materials handling equipment.

Layout Design

A study carried out on GR Company's trouser workshop focused on investigating the impact of rearranging the workshop's layout in conformity with Systematic Layout Planning theory. The method of re-planning resulted in a reduction of material handling distances, thus promoting reduced costs and increased space utilization efficiency [31]. By preparing a comprehensive relationship map that includes logistics and non-logistics interdependencies in the production process and among operating units, it was possible to determine the interrelations in operations. There was a considerable contraction in the material handling distances among various operating units in the optimized layout. Such a contraction in handling distances is expected to bring about cost savings and increased efficiency in overall production processes and space utilization, thus promoting increased enterprise competitiveness and sustainable development.

Inventory Management

A case study of the automobile industry was carried out to introduce changes to the material handling management system, with positive outcomes for internal customer satisfaction within the organization [32]. The introduction of a unique vehicle system, i.e., an internally designated tug to pull wagons referred to as the 'train,' improved the accuracy of the delivery time of the materials within the enterprise. The system showed greater efficiency for the transportation of heavy loads for longer distances compared to the former system of forklifts. With the introduction of the novel system, cost savings were also realized, primarily due to the reduced high-maintenance costs of the forklifts and the high probability of breakdowns.

Table 10.3 Case studies for primary methods used, implemented practices, and practical outcomes.

Case study	Primary methods used	Implemented practices	Outcome
Aerospace digital twin pilot	Digital twin, BDA pipeline	IoT sensors, process DT, analytics	KPI visibility and closedloop control; quantified gains not reported [33]
CPS proactive shop-floor	CPS, digital twin, predictive TWMLR	Smart trolleys/ machines, proactive allocation	Large reductions in nonvalue energy and route optimization (no numeric in source) [34]
Raw material receiving	PDCA, 5S, rootcause	Layout reorg, labeling improvements	Receipt ≤7 days; labeling +253.4%; activities −45.9%; overtime eliminated [35]
Multirobot scheduling	MILP, genetic algorithm	Robot task allocation, buffer planning	PGA ARD 0.25% vs. BGA 0.38% (~34% better) on plant data [36]
ML logistics recommender	TFIDF, recommender ML	Recsys, integration with PFEP data	Improved material delivery punctuality and operational efficiency (no numeric in abstract) [37]

With the former system, high maintenance costs were a major constraint for budgetary control.

Although the above-mentioned case studies were useful for optimizing the material handling system, it is important to take into consideration the unique challenges posed by the manufacturing industry. These unique challenges need to be addressed while implementing the above-mentioned methods for optimal results. A tailored approach to the above-mentioned methods by incorporating the unique variables of the industry is crucial for the optimal results of the material handling optimization. Table 10.3 below represents a summary of the above-mentioned case studies, including the primary methods adopted for the implementation of the system.

In the recent study, several recommendations have been made for getting the best out of the materials being handled in ways that will add value to the overall production system of a manufacturer. Some examples of each recommendation are:

- **Integration of Industry 4.0 Tools:** By utilizing Industry 4.0 technological advancements such as IoT, AI, and digital twin technology, it is possible to monitor and control the material handling system in real-time. These tools provide the manufacturer with greater flexibility to market changes than traditional methods [38].
- **AGVs and Robotics for Smart Logistics:** The introduction of AGVs and/or robotics to the manufacturing industry's material-handling systems allows the manufacturer to achieve high levels of efficiency, as well as minimize labor costs and provide a constant flow of materials from their warehouse into the production floor. By utilizing AGVs and robotics in their manufacturing processes, a manufacturer will also be able to provide consistent production and meet the demands of their customers, thus strengthening their competitive advantage [39].
- **Lean–Digital Hybrid Models:** The implementation of the Lean-Digital Integrated Model in their material handling system allows for a balanced method in how they will handle materials. The Lean-Digital Integrated Model will help the manufacturer decrease waste in their operations while maintaining an appropriate level of production coordination [40].
- **Sustainability-Oriented Handling:** When manufacturers implement the Sustainability-Based Handling system in

their material handling systems, they have the opportunity to operate in a more sustainable manner while decreasing their operational costs. Increased focus on sustainability will help manufacturers benefit from this system being implemented in their production systems [41].

10.8 Future Trends and Research Directions

Material handling systems are witnessing a significant shift as the manufacturing industry moves towards higher intelligence, responsiveness, and sustainability. The future forms of material transportation, storage, and identification within industrial environments are increasingly being dictated by strategic innovations and emerging technologies. Some of the future trends and research areas that can be identified from Table 10.4 include the integration of Industry 4.0 philosophy, the implementation of artificial intelligence and predictive analytics techniques, human-robot collaboration, cybersecurity solutions, and the implementation of decentralized and adaptive material handling strategies. These technologies hold promise to change the paradigm of flexibility and safety within the entire value chain.

The development of Industry 4.0 leads to the increased use of material handling systems, which operate through cyber-physical systems that create the foundation for smart factory operations. The system operates through conveyors while robotic systems and sensor networks establish real-time communication through Internet of Things platforms and cloud-based services to create an integrated logistics network. The cellular transport system enables autonomous vehicles to operate their fleets through cooperative route planning and task distribution without requiring central leadership. The decentralized system design improves operational capacity while maintaining system stability and enabling adaptive system changes, which support manufacturing operations to adjust their processes according to production changes, operational disruptions, and market demand fluctuations.

Artificial intelligence (AI)–driven predictive analytics has become a force that enhances the efficiency of material handling operations. Machine learning algorithms use sensor data to estimate when equipment will break down, when production levels will change, and when operational delays will happen. The organization uses predictive capabilities to create maintenance schedules, create routing plans, and manage operations according to customer demand, thus achieving reduced equipment downtime

Table 10.4 Future trends and research directions in material handling.

Trend area	Key innovation	Expected benefits	Enabling technologies
Industry 4.0 and Smart Logistics	A comprehensive network of Intelligent manufacturing plants, creating a cyber-physical environment for material handling solutions.	Real-time optimization, adaptability, enhanced efficiency in controlling processes	IoT, CPS, cloud, digital twins
AI and Predictive Analytics	Anticipatory maintenance, routing capability that adjusts dynamically, forecasting product demand.	Reduced downtime, reduced energy consumption, and optimized production rate	Machine Learning Algorithms, Big Data Analysis Techniques, and Facilities for Data Analytic Processing
Human–Robot Collaboration (Cobots)	The use of collaborative robots, allocating jobs ergonomically, and adjusting in real-time.	Enhanced safety, enhanced flexibility, and reduced physical exertion of personnel	Collaborative Robots (Cobots) with sensing, vision, and developed artificial intelligence (AI)
Cybersecurity and Data Integrity	Converging the operational and information technology (OT/IT) securely with the use of encrypted communications and a blockchain technology protocol.	Higher levels of system reliability, enhanced trust in systems, and greater protection against cyber threats	Firewall Protection Systems, Intrusion Detection Systems (IDS)/Intrusion Prevention Systems (IPS), IEC 62443-1 Security Standards, and Blockchain Supported Technologies

(Continued)

Table 10.4 Future trends and research directions in material handling. (*Continued*)

Trend area	Key innovation	Expected benefits	Enabling technologies
Decentralized and Adaptive Systems	Self-organization of spatial layouts, decision-making based on edge technologies, and orchestrating fleets autonomously.	Greater responsiveness to disruptions, resilience from being disrupted, and scalability for reconfiguration	Edge Computer System Design Architecture, Digital Twins Technologies, and Multi-Agent System Design Architectures

and decreased power usage. The practical use of autonomous vehicles and robotic sorting systems demonstrates how AI algorithms enable systems to change their operational paths and duties, which leads to increased production capacity and decreased energy emissions. The development of predictive analytics will reach its full potential when data becomes more accessible and algorithms become more advanced.

The new operational model of Industry 5.0 establishes its foundation on human workers and robots working together inside industrial spaces. Collaborative robots (cobots) function as robotic arms with sensor capabilities, which enable them to work together with human operators in various applications, including assembly, palletizing, and packaging tasks. The research demonstrates that human operators who work with cobots experience less physical exhaustion and make fewer mistakes in their work, yet the complete safety measures required for their work need additional time to finish. Future studies need to investigate cognitive task assignment methods along with adaptive system control mechanisms and design methods that optimize human-robot interaction to maintain workplace safety and user-friendly design and social acceptance by employees.

The development of material handling systems that interconnect different systems has created two new security challenges because of the growing need to protect both information technology (IT) systems and operational technology (OT) systems. Industrial control systems show their susceptibility to cyber-attacks through dedicated malware attacks such as the Industroyer incident. The security threats require organizations to establish complete defense-in-depth security systems, which should include network division and safe user authentication methods, protected data transmission systems, and compliance with IEC 62443 cybersecurity standards. The protection of automated material handling systems from cyber-attacks depends on system resilience and data protection measures.

The upcoming material handling solutions, digitalization, and adaptive orchestration will receive implementation support from edge computing and multi-agent systems, and privacy-preserving federated artificial intelligence. The system enables autonomous robots, mobile platforms, and shuttle systems to execute their tasks through local coordination while they establish workload distribution and perform material rerouting during operational bottlenecks. The system decreases its need for centralized management systems but increases both its operational performance and system adaptability. Researchers face significant challenges because they must connect distributed decision-making systems while providing secure linkages between devices and enabling systems to work together with digital twin technologies. The developed technologies will create manufacturing ecosystems that exhibit high levels of resilience, flexibility, and capacity for reconfiguration.

10.9 Conclusion

Material handling has developed into a critical component of contemporary manufacturing operations because it improves productivity while reducing costs and protecting employee health and environmental resources. The chapter showed the basic material handling principles, which include equipment types and material movement patterns, while demonstrating the main optimization techniques, which include facility design, workstation ergonomics, workload management, and lean logistics implementation. The research proved that production environments benefit from advanced technologies, which include automation and robotics, automated guided vehicles, autonomous mobile robots, IoT tracking systems, and digital twin technology, because these systems provide improved operational visibility and flexibility and continuous operational response capabilities. The case studies from various industries demonstrated how companies used lean-digital integration and system optimization and sustainability-focused practices to achieve significant improvements in their operational efficiency and inventory management, production speed, and occupational safety. The research identified performance evaluation frameworks and operational metrics as vital resources that help organizations develop their operations while making better decisions. The combination of Industry 4.0 and Industry 5.0 systems will drive material handling system changes through the implementation of predictive analytics, human-robot collaboration, decentralized adaptive systems, and enhanced cybersecurity solutions. Future research and industrial practice need to develop future scientific and engineering advancements because they require creating links between innovative technologies and ergonomic, economic, and environmental elements.

AI disclosure statement: The author acknowledges the use of AI-based tools for minor language editing or grammatical correction. However, all intellectual contributions, analyses, and conclusions presented in this chapter are entirely the author's own.

Bibliography

1. Tompkins, J.A., White, J.A., Bozer, Y.A., Tanchoco, J.M.A., *Facilities Planning* (4th ed.). Wiley, Hoboken, NJ, 2010.
2. Destouet, C., Tlahig, H., Bettayeb, B., Mazari, B., Flexible job shop scheduling problem under Industry 5.0: A survey on human reintegration, environmental consideration and resilience improvement. *J. Manuf. Syst.*, 67, 155–173, 2023, https://doi.org/10.1016/j.jmsy.2023.01.004.
3. Wang, C., Jiang, P., Lu, T., Production events graphical deduction model enabled real-time production control system for smart job shop. *Proc. Inst. Mech. Eng. C. J. Mech. Eng. Sci.*, 232, 095440621772853, 2017, 10.1177/0954406217728531.
4. MHI, 2022 MHI Annual Industry Report: Evolution to Revolution. MHI, 2022. https://www.mhi.org/publications/report.
5. Womack, J.P. and Jones, D.T., *Lean Thinking: Banish Waste and Create Wealth in Your Corporation* (2nd ed.). Free Press, New York, NY, 2003.
6. Ponis, S.T. and Efthymiou, O.K., Cloud and IoT Applications in Material Handling Automation and Intralogistics. *Logistics*, 4, 3, 22, 2020, https://doi.org/10.3390/logistics4030022.
7. Zhong, R.Y., Xu, C., Chen, C., Huang, G.Q., Big Data Analytics for Physical Internet-based intelligent manufacturing shop floors. *Int. J. Prod. Res.*, 55, 9, 2610–2621, 2017, https://doi.org/10.1080/00207543.2015.1086037.
8. Wang, W., Zhu, X., Wang, L., Qiu, Q., Cao, Q., Ubiquitous Robotic Technology for Smart Manufacturing System. *Comput. Intell. Neurosci.*, 2016, 1–14, 2016, 10.1155/2016/6018686.
9. https://www.mbaknol.com/operations-management/principles-of-material-handling/?.
10. Heragu, S.S., *Facilities Design* (4th ed.). CRC Press, Boca Raton, FL, 2016. https://doi.org/10.1201/9781315382647.

11. Pawlak, S., Nowacki, K., Kania, H., Analysis of the impact of the 5S tool and Standardization on the duration of the production process - case study. *Prod. Eng. Arch.*, 29, 421–427, 2023, 10.30657/pea.2023.29.47.
12. Bhasin, S. and Laureani, A., A Lean longevity matrix steering an organization's journey towards higher levels of maturity. *SCIREA J. Econ.*, 9, 2, April 2024, https://doi.org/10.54647/economics790459.
13. Hakim, F., Khaled, T., Al-Kharaz, M., Gouabou, A.C.F., Amzil, K., Towards a Digital Twin Modeling Method for Container Terminal Port. *Procedia Comput. Sci.*, 246, 3113–3121, 2024, https://doi.org/10.1016/j.procs.2024.09.361.
14. Shen, Y., Guo, D., Long, F., Mateos, L., Ding, H., Xiu, Z., Hellman, R., King, A., Chen, S., Zhang, C., Tan, H., Robots under COVID-19 Pandemic: A Comprehensive Survey. *IEEE Access*, 1–1, 2020, 10.1109/ACCESS.2020.3045792.
15. https://locusrobotics.com/blog/amr-vs-agv?.
16. Melo, A.F. and Corneal, L.M., Case study: Evaluation of the automation of material handling with mobile robots. *Int. J. Qual. Innov.*, 6, 1, 1–14, 2020, ISSN 2363-7021, Springer, Heidelberg, https://doi.org/10.1186/s40887-020-00037-y.
17. Cobb and Hext, Vertical Reciprocating Conveyors Elevate AGVs and AMRs to New Levels of Efficiency, *PFlow Industries blog*, https://www.pflow.com/vrcs-elevate-agvs-and-amrs-to-new-levels-of-efficiency/.
18. Devarajulu, V.S., Real-Time Visibility and Tracking for Supply Chain Systems: Improving Inventory Management and Reducing Operational Costs Through Technology. *Int. J. Multidiscip. Res.*, 2, 1, 2020, https://doi.org/10.36948/ijfmr.2020.v02i01.3787.
19. Turgay, S. and Akar, N., Maximizing Efficiency and Cost Savings through Digital Twin Simulation: Optimizing Cellular Manufacturing. *Manuf. Serv. Oper. Manag.*, 4, 18–28, 2023, 10.23977/msom.2023.040403.
20. Brauckmann, O., *MES Manufacturing Execution System 4.0* (pp. 241–256). Springer Vieweg, Berlin, Heidelberg, 2019. https://doi.org/10.1007/978-3-662-58037-0_15.
21. Moon, Y.B. and Bahl, V., Assessing the impact of integrating a MES to an ERP system. *International Conference on Enterprise Information Systems*, 300–304, 2005. https://dblp.uni-trier.de/db/conf/iceis/iceis2005-1.html#MoonB05.
22. Oman, S., Leskovar, R., Rosi, B., Baggia, A., Integration of MES and ERP in supply chains: Effect assessment in the case of the automotive industry. *Teh. Vjesn.*, 24, 1889–1896, 2017, 10.17559/TV-20160426094449.
23. Indah, A.B.R., Nurwahidah, A., Mangngenre, S., Ikasari, N., Afifudin, M.T., A Review of the Combination of Lean and Green in manufacturing for Sustainable Development. *IOP Conf. Ser.: Earth Environ. Sci.*, 575, 012066, 2020, DOI 10.1088/1755-1315/575/1/012066.

24. Genç, R., *Lean Manufacturing Practices and Environmental Performance*. IntechOpen, London, UK, 2021. doi: 10.5772/intechopen.96973.
25. Resta, B., Dotti, S., Gaiardelli, P., Boffelli, A., *Lean Manufacturing and Sustainability: An Integrated View*. 659–666, 2016. 10.1007/978-3-319-51133-7_78.
26. https://www.asprova.eu/en/glossary/overall-equipment-effectiveness-oee/?.
27. https://new.abb.com/industrial-software/digital/oee-overall-equipment-effectiveness?.
28. https://www.tibco.com/glossary/what-is-overall-equipment-effectiveness?.
29. Leng, J., Ruan, G., Jiang, P., Xu, K., Liu, Q., Zhou, X., Liu, C., Blockchain-empowered sustainable manufacturing and product lifecycle management in industry 4.0: A survey. *Renew. Sustain. Energy Rev.*, 132, 110112, 2020.
30. Hama Kareem, J.A., Mohammed, B.I., Abdulwahab, S.A., Optimal materials handling equipment and defective product reduction skills in enhance overall production efficiency. *SAGE Open*, 12, 4, 21582440221128769, 2022.
31. Gong, W., Optimization Study of the Production Layout in the Trouser Workshop of GR Company. *J. Bus. Mark.*, 1, 3, 356–360, 2024.
32. Borges Vieira, G.B., Pasa, G.S., Borsa, M.B.N.D.O., Milan, G.S., Pandolfo, A., Materials handling management: A case study. *J. Oper. Supply Chain Manag.*, 4, 2, 19–30, 2011.
33. Dihan, M.S., Akash, A.I., Tasneem, Z., Das, P., Das, S.K., Islam, M.R., Islam, M.M., Badal, F.R., Ali, M.F., Ahamed, M.H., Abhi, S.H., Digital twin: Data exploration, architecture, implementation and future. *Heliyon*, 10, 5, 2024.
34. Wang, W., Zhang, Y., Zhong, R.Y., A proactive material handling method for CPS enabled shop-floor. *Robot. Comput.-Integr. Manuf.*, 61, 101849, 2020.
35. Realyvásquez Vargas, A., García Alcaraz, J.L., Satapathy, S., Díaz-Reza, J.R., Case Study 2. Raw Material Receipt Process Optimization. In *The PDCA Cycle for Industrial Improvement: Applied Case Studies* (47–77). Cham: Springer Nature Switzerland, 2023.
36. Shakeri, Z., Benfriha, K., Varmazyar, M., Talhi, E., Quenehen, A., Production scheduling with multi-robot task allocation in a real industry 4.0 setting. *Sci. Rep.*, 15, 1, 1795, 2025.
37. Chen, Y., Zhao, C., Cheng, M., Wu, Y., Zhu, J., Meng, Y., Liu, X., Optimizing production logistics through advanced machine learning techniques: A study on resource allocation for small-batch and multi-variety challenges. *Proc. Inst. Mech. Eng. Part. E: J. Process Mech. Eng.*, 09544089241234117, 2024.
38. Xu, L.D., Xu, E.L., Li, L., Industry 4.0: state of the art and future trends. *Int. J. Prod. Res.*, 56, 8, 2941–2962, 2018.
39. Vlachos, I., Pascazzi, R.M., Ntotis, M., Spanaki, K., Despoudi, S., Repoussis, P., Smart and flexible manufacturing systems using Autonomous Guided Vehicles (AGVs) and the Internet of Things (IoT). *Int. J. Prod. Res.*, 62, 15, 5574–5595, 2024.

40. Ferrazzi, M., Frecassetti, S., Bilancia, A., Portioli-Staudacher, A., Investigating the influence of lean manufacturing approach on environmental performance: A systematic literature review. *Int. J. Adv. Manuf. Technol.*, 136, 9, 4025–4044, 2025.
41. Vidakis, N., Petousis, M., Maniadi, A., Koudoumas, E., Vairis, A., Kechagias, J., Sustainable additive manufacturing: Mechanical response of acrylonitrile-butadiene-styrene over multiple recycling processes. *Sustainability*, 12, 9, 3568, 2020.

11

Future Trends and Opportunities in Circular Manufacturing

S. Arivazhagan[1], Thirukkotti Ganapathy[2], B. Arulmurugan[3] and N. Muthukumaran[3]*

[1]Center of Excellence in Drones and UAV, KPR Institute of Engineering and Technology, Coimbatore, Tamil Nadu, India
[2]Department of Mechanical Engineering, P. S. R. Engineering College, Sivakasi, Tamil Nadu, India
[3]Department of Mechanical Engineering, KPR Institute of Engineering and Technology, Coimbatore, Tamil Nadu, India

Abstract

Circular manufacturing (CM) integrates sustainable practices into industrial workflows to reduce environmental impact and boost economic growth. Growing use of Industry 4.0 technologies and anticipated benefits of Industry 5.0 are driving circularity. Many technological advances support this change. These innovations include digital twins, blockchain, robotics, artificial intelligence, and the Internet of Things. These instruments optimize material and energy use, enable condition-based maintenance, and improve process control. Product recalls, disassembly, and end-of-life recovery can use lifespan data from smart sensors in devices and products. Design for disassembly, modularity, and prefabrication demonstrate the importance of design in construction management. Material-efficient additive manufacturing accelerates the shift with modular, repairable, and recyclable products. Big data analytics and cloud computing allow companies to recreate product life cycles, assess environmental impacts, and improve circularity. These design ideas improve recovery and product life, supporting circularity. This chapter examines how circular supply chain management integrates recycling, remanufacturing, and reuse into production and logistics networks to promote closed-loop systems. With sector-specific uses, the construction, polymers, and textile sectors demonstrate CM implementation. Whereas the construction industry adopts modular building and sustainable materials, the plastics industry

**Corresponding author*: nmuthu1966@gmail.com

Jeyaprakash Natarajan, Milon Selvam Dennison, M. Bhuvanesh Kumar and Ganapathy Thirukkotti (eds.) Manufacturing and the Circular Economy, (341–368) © 2027 Scrivener Publishing LLC

is restructuring to prioritize recycling and reusability. However, modular building and sustainable materials are being used in construction. Entrepreneurial and innovative textile companies use environmentally friendly production methods and systematic design thinking to reduce waste and pollution. CM reduces emissions, preserves resources, and mitigates climate change. Creative thinking, job creation, and a competitive edge increase when raw materials are less scarce. The widespread adoption of this technology is hampered by a number of obstacles, including technological, legal, and cultural obstacles. To address these challenges, the chapter places an emphasis on legislative frameworks, worker competencies, and resilient digital infrastructure. The circular methodologies and scalable, long-term impact that these facilitators enable are both accomplished. The purpose of this chapter is to forecast the future of CM by analyzing the current trends, technological facilitators, sectoral applications, and strategic opportunities. For a circular economy, one of the most important pillars is CM, which is made possible by the technologies and agendas. In addition to putting an end to material cycles and reducing reliance on unspoiled resources, it encourages the establishment of a system that distinguishes economic activity from its effects on the environment. The information that is provided expands the data on how global supply chain management can direct businesses all over the world toward a more resilient and sustainable future.

Keywords: Circular economy, circular manufacturing, Industry 5.0, circular supply chain management, sustainability

11.1 Introduction

Circular economy (CE) is a big idea that was created to fix the problems that people make in nature that will not last. It tries to separate economic growth from getting resources and making trash by supporting systems that can be closed loop and grow back. CE is becoming more popular among policymakers, businesses, and academics because it can help the environment and create economic and social value. Because CE is at the center of both new technology and sustainability, it is a good choice for reaching these goals. Even though CE practices have a lot of potential, they are being used in different ways more and more, which is becoming a bigger problem. Some projects that have been pushed under the CE umbrella have been criticized for not really helping the environment. This is why we need to take a more critical and value-based look at circular transitions. The term "circular manufacturing" (CM) refers to a method that is both useful and smart. For a bigger picture, it builds on the ideas of CE. This model of "take, make, dispose" is not the same as conservation management. CM focuses on making the most of resources, making products last longer, remanufacturing, and recycling to keep materials valuable in the system. Companies can check their production plans to make sure they do not go over the limits set by the world. This helps the company stay strong over time, which is good for both the economy and the environment. With strategies based on basic ideas of sustainability [1–4], CM is an important part of creating a CE that will last. This is because it encourages responsible innovation and waste reduction.

Sustainability, personalization, and increased competition are accelerating change in the manufacturing industry. This transformation has been enabled by Industry 4.0 technologies such as Internet of Things (IoT), cloud computing, cyberphysical systems, artificial intelligence (AI), big data analytics, and the IoT. These technologies are required to implement CE principles because they enable more transparent operations, better resource utilization, and real-time monitoring in production systems. But the introduction of Industry 4.0 entails distinct problems. This technology is often underutilized due to several factors, such as insufficient comprehension of its functionality, reluctance to adopt new methods, the requirement for substantial investment, or the existence of obsolete infrastructure. In addition, integrating Industry 4.0 with CE introduces a variety of issues, including geographic dispersion, product traceability, and rigid linear production patterns. This technological shift is further aided by the rise of Industry 5.0, which takes a more human-centered approach to industrial transformation. Industry 4.0 focuses on automation and linking devices, whereas Industry 5.0 focuses on how smart systems and human intelligence may collaborate. It emphasizes the fundamental concepts of sustainable development with an emphasis on social inclusion, environmental resilience, and moral concerns. Industry 4.0 and 5.0 work together to establish a comprehensive set of guidelines for transitioning manufacturing to circularity. In addition to increasing operational efficiency and product customization, they provide the technological and ethical framework required to transition from linear to circular business models [5–8].

The global transition to circular models is being influenced by technological maturity, socioeconomic factors, and differences in material streams, and it is being implemented in a variety of industrial sectors. CE adoption is evident in the construction industry through the integration of alternative materials derived from industrial by-products and recycled waste, as well as practices such as modularization and life-cycle assessment (LCA). The sector is under significant pressure to decarbonize and reduce its reliance on raw materials, as it is responsible for nearly 39% of global carbon emissions and one-third of EU waste. Energy-efficient building design, waste management, and sustainable urban development are the primary focus of current research. Circular business models and building information modeling facilitate this transformation. The polymer and materials industry is being compelled to adopt CE principles by the development of biodegradable and bio-based polymers in response to the increasing concerns regarding plastic pollution and resource constraints. Enzymatic depolymerization, microbial and algal biomass, and renewable waste streams are among the cutting-edge alternatives to postconsumer waste management and sustainable manufacturing that are now under investigation. These projects are congruent with the EU Circular Economy Action Plan and the United Nations' Sustainable Development Goals (SDGs), which emphasize the importance of a carbon-neutral industrial future. In the same vein, the textile industry is currently undergoing a transformation, with a focus on circular design, material transparency, and product traceability. Closed-loop recycling systems, AI-enabled classification technologies, and digital product passports (DPPs) are being implemented by manufacturers to decrease landfill waste and extend the life cycle of products. These recent advancements illustrate the industry's convergence of sophisticated manufacturing, digital transformation, and sustainability. Among the most widely used concepts are design for disassembly, life-cycle thinking, and stakeholder engagement. Growing consumer awareness, changing legislative frameworks, and the advent of smart technologies are all contributing to the change, which is turning CE from an environmental strategy into a systemic industrial paradigm [9–11].

A robust policy environment is required to integrate CM initiatives across industries. Regulatory frameworks such as the European Green Deal and the Eco-Design for Sustainable Products Regulation provide a clear approach for incorporating circularity into product design, durability, and repairability [12]. Similarly, regulations such as the 2024 Repair Regulation mandate spare component availability and reparability indexes to encourage longer product life cycles [13]. These are supported globally by initiatives such as the United Nations' SDGs, namely, SDGs 9 and 12, which promote sustainable industrialization, innovation, and responsible resource use [14]. Recent regulations have prioritized eco-design guidelines, carbon-neutral production targets, and financial incentives for resource-efficient and low-carbon technology [15, 16]. These policies alter government. For economic planning and environmental protection, regulatory mechanisms, sustainability standards, and circularity regulations are essential. This chapter thoroughly reviews CM and its ability to address resource loss, waste creation, and environmental damage in main industry sectors. The evolution of CM and its implications for sustainable economic transformation are examined first. Next, we explore Industry 4.0 and 5.0 technologies. These technologies intelligently automate, digitize, and manage resources to implement circle tactics. The next section of the chapter discusses CM in polymer, textile, and construction industries. Innovative ideas such as biodegradable materials, modular design, and closed-loop production are stressed. In this study, the policy frameworks to evaluate the ways in which regulatory tools, environmental norms, and circularity criteria assist various businesses in integrating CE are investigated. The use of new methodologies and techniques is demonstrated through the use of case studies. At the end of the chapter, a discussion is held on the present obstacles that are being faced by circular processes, as well as proposed solutions that could bolster the industry's resilience and longevity.

11.2 Technological Enablers for CM

11.2.1 Industry 5.0 and Human-Centric Circularity

By reintroducing human-centric values into the manufacturing landscape, Industry 5.0 represents a progressive transition beyond the digital and automation-driven ethos of Industry 4.0. Industry 5.0 endeavors to strike a balance between technological advancement and human creativity, inclusivity, and sustainability, in contrast to Industry 4.0, which prioritized connectivity, cyberphysical systems, and machine learning. This paradigm is particularly relevant to CM, which strives for resource efficiency alongside social and environmental well-being [17]. Table 11.1 outlines the conceptual and functional differences between Industry 4.0 and Industry 5.0, emphasizing their respective implications for CM, especially in terms of human involvement, design priorities, and sustainability focus.

Industry 5.0 promotes collaborative intelligence, a framework wherein humans and robots work together to improve system adaptability and ethical accountability, unlike Industry 4.0, which often raised issues around worker marginalization due to automation. The deployment of collaborative robotics allows robots to perform repetitive or dangerous jobs, while permitting human workers to focus on circular innovation, repair methodologies, and design thinking [18]. This aligns neatly with the objectives of CM, which aim to promote repair and reuse, reduce waste, and prolong product life cycles through human-centered interventions. Moreover, Industry 5.0's customized manufacturing minimizes waste by obviating the necessity for mass production and surplus inventory. Products customized to individual customer requirements provide enhanced material

Table 11.1 Comparison between Industry 4.0 and Industry 5.0 in circular manufacturing.

Attribute	Industry 4.0 [17–19]	Industry 5.0 [20, 21]
Primary focus	Automation, smart systems	Human-centricity, personalization, sustainability
Technology role	Autonomous operation	Collaborative operation with humans (co-bots, AI)
Design objective	Functional efficiency	Ethical, modular, inclusive design
Worker involvement	System operators	Cocreators and decision-makers
Circularity orientation	Efficiency-oriented recycling and reuse	Human-driven regeneration and repair
Social impact	Limited focus on labor and equity	Worker empowerment, social sustainability

utilization, modularity incorporation, and repairability enhancement—all essential elements of CM [19]. Human-centric circularity also redefines the function of the workforce. In Industry 5.0, workers are perceived as value cocreators rather than simply operators of automated technologies. Their contributions to sustainability, ethical sourcing, and design for disassembly render them pivotal actors in facilitating CM. This cultural shift requires a new skills paradigm that integrates both digital competencies

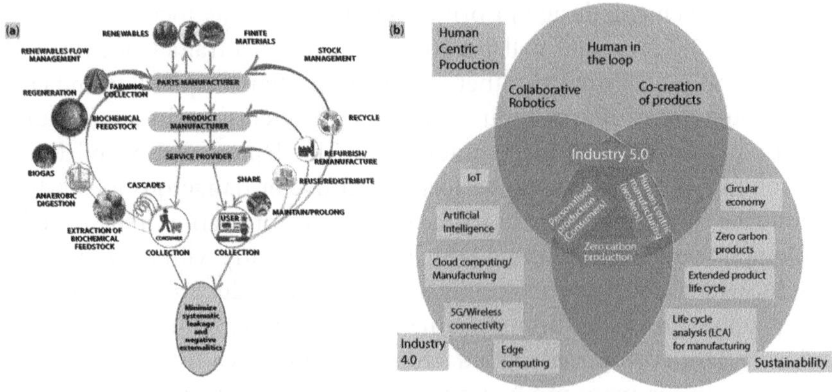

Figure 11.1 Integration of Industry 5.0 within circular economy principles [22].

and eco-literacy, ensuring inclusivity in circular transitions [20, 21]. Figure 11.1 illustrates the integration of CE mechanisms (a) and the technological–human–sustainability intersection driving Industry 5.0 (b). Figure 11.1(a), the Ellen MacArthur Foundation's butterfly diagram, visualizes the biological and technical cycles of a CE, including reuse, remanufacturing, and recycling flows. A Venn diagram (Figure 11.1(b)) highlights the convergence of Industry 4.0 technologies (e.g., IoT, AI, and cloud computing), human-centric production (e.g., cobots and personalized manufacturing), and sustainability outcomes (e.g., zero-carbon products and life-cycle analysis), which collectively define the scope of Industry 5.0.

11.2.2 Digital Twins and Circular Feedback Loops in CM

CM, an industrial implementation of CE, aims to reduce waste and enhance resource circularity throughout the manufacturing process. In this context, digital twins (DTs), virtual replicas of physical assets, are emerging as critical instruments for realizing CM by enabling real-time data-driven feedback loops across the design, operation, maintenance, and end-of-life (EoL) phases of goods and processes [23]. Figure 11.2 depicts how DTs interact with physical and social systems to optimize resource utilization, ensure supply chain continuity, and promote sustainability goals *via* real-time data exchange and predictive feedback loops. A DT in CM is more than just a simulation; it is a dynamic model that changes in real time with its physical counterpart. DTs integrate sensor data, AI, and machine learning to provide comprehensive visibility into the operating state, material utilization, energy consumption, and environmental performance of machines and components [25]. This real-time synchronization is crucial for achieving the circularity goals of increasing product longevity, decreasing resource inputs, and improving recyclability. For example, in remanufacturing environments, DTs can track component wear, detect anomalies, and initiate predictive maintenance or module replacement methods.

These interventions not only avoid failure, but also allow for modular product upgrades and design-for-disassembly (DfD), both of which are critical components of CM methods. Manufacturers can reduce the consumption of raw materials and facilitate reuse by anticipating when parts will approach the end of their service life [26]. DTs also offer closed-loop feedback systems that connect the production and post-use phases of a product. These loops influence eco-design, guide reverse logistics, and optimize EoL decision-making, such as reuse, refurbishment, or recycling. When combined with LCA and material flow analysis technologies, DTs help to evaluate environmental consequences and circularity metrics [27].

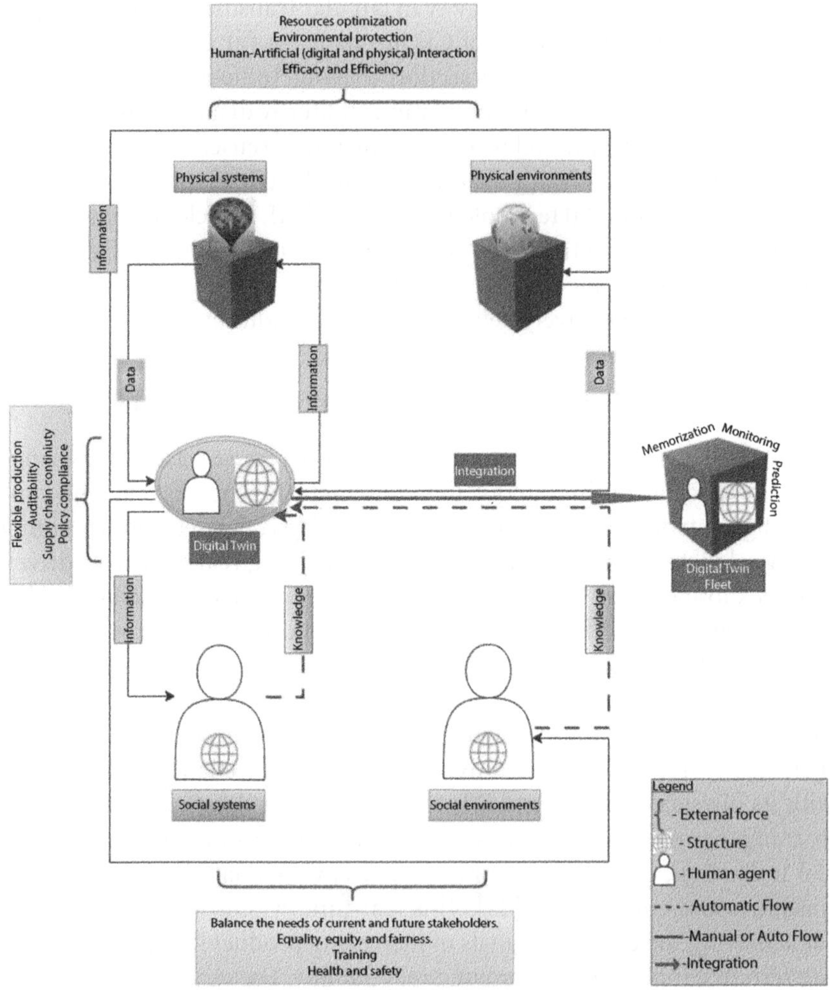

Figure 11.2 Integrated digital twin framework for circular manufacturing [24].

11.2.3 Blockchain and Digital Product Passports

In CM, blockchain provides a decentralized ledger that ensures transparency, traceability, and immutability of material flows across the product life cycle. Figure 11.3 shows that, when combined with DPPs, blockchain enables secure access to verified information on material composition, repair history, and recyclability essential for responsible sourcing, modular design, and EoL processing [28]. Table 11.2 outlines the key functionalities and advantages of integrating blockchain technology with DPPs in CM.

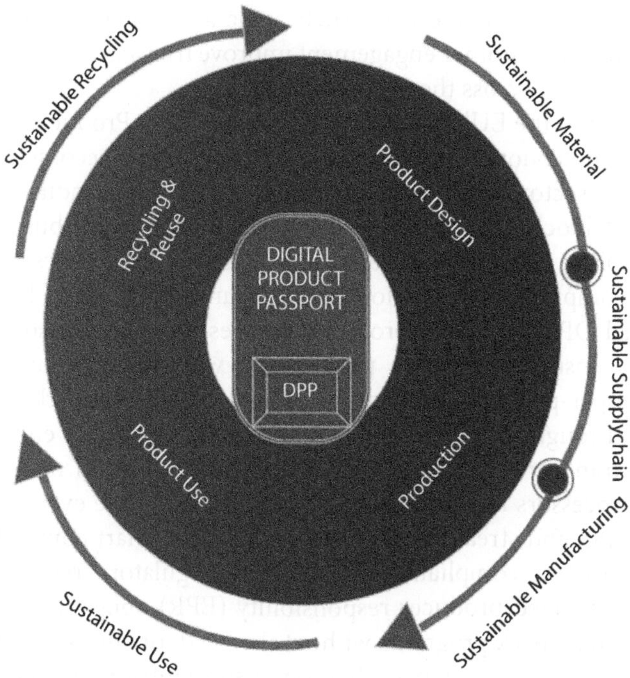

Figure 11.3 Circular product passport ecosystem [31].

Table 11.2 Role of blockchain in supporting DPPs for circular manufacturing [29].

Benefit	Description
Traceability	Immutable record of material origin and life-cycle events
Quality verification	Ensures authenticity of recycled and reused components
Smart contract automation	Triggers actions on EoL, recycling milestones, and compliance filings
Consumer engagement	Users access product history and sustainability credentials easily
Circular compliance	Supports extended producer responsibility (EPR) and sustainability laws

It highlights how characteristics such as data immutability, traceability, automation, and customer engagement improve transparency, compliance, and sustainability across the product life cycle.

According to the EU's Eco-Design for Sustainable Products Regulation and Circular Economy Action Plan, DPPs are set to become obligatory across many sectors, including electronics, textiles, and industrial batteries. Through blockchain integration, DPPs facilitate circular business models by enabling reuse, remanufacturing, and reverse logistics, while also ensuring compliance verification and consumer trust [30]. Blockchain-empowered DPPs offer numerous advantages that directly support CM. First, they ensure immutable provenance, which guarantees that data remain tamper-proof, thus safeguarding the integrity of recycled or reused materials throughout the product life cycle. Second, they enhance supply chain transparency by enabling all stakeholders from manufacturers to waste processors to reliably verify and trace life-cycle events, ensuring accountability and streamlined operations. Third, smart contracts can be used to automate compliance by executing regulatory reporting tasks, managing extended producer responsibility (EPR) obligations, and facilitating EoL take-back programs without the need for administrative intervention. Lastly, consumer participation is substantially enhanced by the implementation of technologies such as QR codes or NFC tags, which enable end-users to access critical information regarding product origin, material composition, sustainability credentials, and repair instructions. This promotes responsible consumption and product stewardship [32].

11.2.4 AI-Driven Sustainability Intelligence

AI plays a transformative role in enabling advanced decision-making, optimization, and automation for CM systems. Moving beyond conventional control systems, AI is now being deployed to offer predictive and prescriptive analytics across the manufacturing value chain. One of its key contributions is design optimization, namely, design for disassembly, modularity, and recyclability. By evaluating big datasets and simulating different configurations, AI can suggest product layouts that reduce material complexity while increasing EoL recovery potential [33]. Figure 11.4 shows how AI technologies interact with major CM stages design, logistics, manufacturing, and recycling to maximize resource efficiency, service life, and waste reduction across product life cycles. AI applications simulate closed-loop logistics in circular supply chains, anticipating material returns, optimizing reverse logistics routing, and lowering carbon emissions during product retrieval and remanufacturing. These tools also enable scenario modeling,

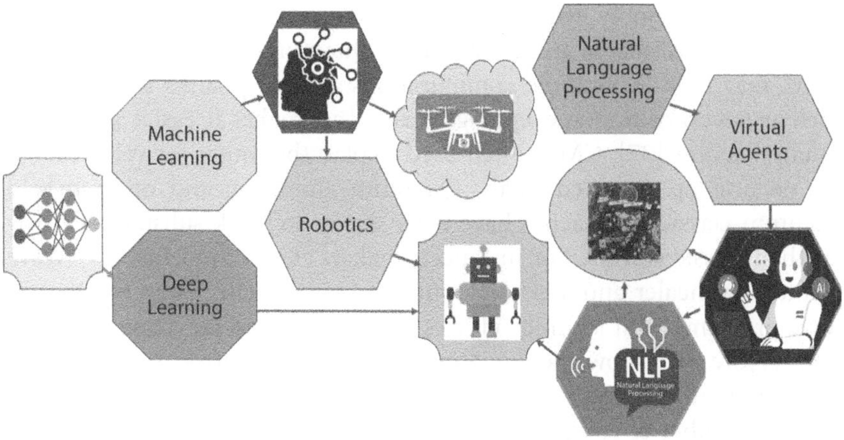

Figure 11.4 AI enabled circular manufacturing flowchart [35].

which accounts for disruptions in material flows and assists industry in transitioning to more resilient, resource-efficient operations [34].

Furthermore, in recycling and waste processing sectors, AI-driven robotic systems equipped with computer vision are automating the identification, sorting, and segregation of mixed waste streams with remarkable precision. This reduces contamination rates and increases the recovery of high-quality recyclers. AI-powered sustainability intelligence solutions are increasingly being utilized to monitor real-time environmental implications across the entire life cycle. These platforms use environmental, social, and economic variables to inform strategic decisions about material selection, process scheduling, and energy use. For example, AI models can recommend switching to lower-impact feedstocks or modifying production schedules to accommodate renewable energy availability. The system's ability to learn over time ensures that sustainability measures adapt to operational data and environmental changes [36]. As a result, AI is more than just a tool for making things go more smoothly; it is also a critical component in ensuring that CM ecosystems continue for a long time in terms of both the environment and the economics.

11.2.5 Quantum Computing and Optimization

By enabling the rapid and effortless identification of solutions to optimization problems that current technologies are unable to address, quantum computing has the potential to revolutionize CM. In high-dimensional, nonlinear situations, conventional approaches to vehicle routing in reverse logistics, disassembly sequencing, and energy flow coordination across complex supply chains are not effective. Quantum systems, on the other hand, may look at multiple configurations at once, thanks to properties such as superposition and entanglement. This makes it easier to explore solution spaces [37]. CM is often used to plan the routes for vehicles that are picking up returned items. Quantum annealing and other hybrid quantum-classic approaches have been shown to work substantially better than classic solvers. For instance, Neukart *et al.* found that a D Wave quantum annealer and a classic optimizer worked effectively together to solve problems with routing vehicles in decentralized recycling networks [38]. Figure 11.5 shows how quantum optimization moves traffic around in a way that keeps it from getting too crowded. The better map shows that the number of congested areas has gone down a lot. In the improved scenario, there are a lot fewer red zones that show heavy traffic. Table 11.3 compares classic and quantum computing methods for key optimization tasks in CM.

Classic approaches are occasionally limited by their complexity and computing time. In contrast, quantum techniques such as quantum annealing and QAOA allow for faster, parallel processing and greater adaptability. This makes them extremely vital for circular supply chains, which are constantly evolving and need significant resources. Tambunan *et al.* defined vehicle routing as a QUBO (quadratic unconstrained binary optimization)

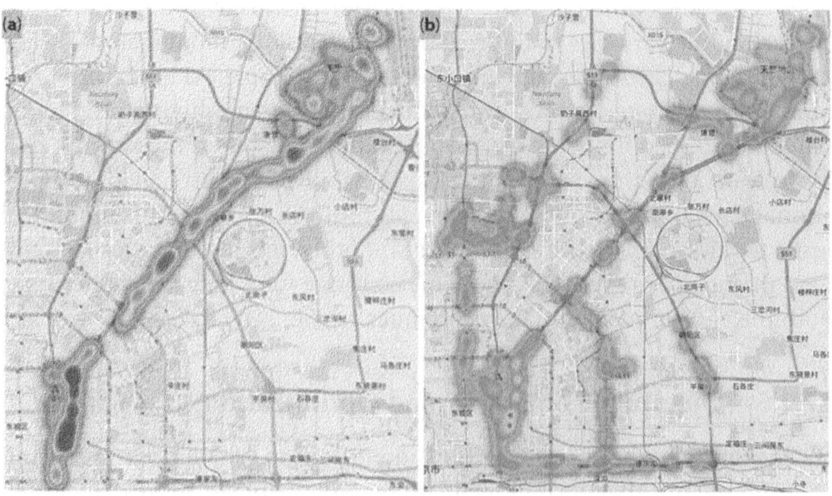

Figure 11.5 Traffic heatmaps before (a) and after (b) optimization using quantum-based qbsolv [38].

Table 11.3 Optimization performance: quantum versus classic approaches in circular manufacturing [39, 40].

Task	Classic method	Quantum-enhanced method
Reverse logistics routing	Heuristic algorithms; slow	Quantum annealing with fast convergence and better scaling
Job-shop scheduling	Iterative solvers; NP-hard	QAOA provides near-optimal solutions in reduced time
Disassembly flow planning	Sequential planning	Parallel state-space exploration *via* quantum techniques
Energy-flow coordination	Static analysis	Real-time, multivariable optimization with quantum inputs

problem, proving the use of quantum annealing to optimize route selection under real-world constraints, such as road weights [39]. Quantum approaches improve job-shop scheduling, which is critical for the disassembly and remanufacturing processes. Techniques such as QAOA (quantum approximate optimization algorithm) facilitate the parallel evaluation of scheduling permutations, frequently yielding solutions of comparable quality to classic heuristics while significantly reducing computation time [40]. The advancements highlight the significance of hybrid quantum-classic frameworks in CM, facilitating real-time adaptive optimization in sectors requiring efficient and responsive resource loop closure.

11.3 Sectoral Innovations and Future Applications

11.3.1 Textiles: BioBased Fibers and ClosedLoop Fashion

The textile industry is undergoing a cyclical transition as it embraces bio-based fibers and closed-loop fashion systems. Recent research in ChemSusChem highlights the importance of biocatalytic processes such as enzymatic depolymerization in recovering high-quality fibers from mixed and synthetic textile blends, paving the way for real fiber-to-fiber recycling. These techniques facilitate chemical and biological recycling, allowing materials to be reconstituted to near-virgin quality even from polyester–cotton blends [41]. Innovations include using agricultural residues (e.g., corncob, lignin) to create second-generation bio-based fibers, as well as microbial cellulosic fibers derived from CO_2 *via* novel biosynthesis. Trade items such as circular apparel and garment leasing are gaining traction, supported by textile-to-textile recycling pilots in Europe and enzymatic recycling technologies (e.g., by Carbios and ReO Eco), in step with expanded EPR frameworks [42].

11.3.2 Electronics: Urban Mining and EPR

The electronics industry is experiencing an increase in the popularity of urban mining, which involves the extraction of valuable metals and other basic materials from electronic waste. Urban mining is a viable alternative to virgin extraction due to its ability to rapidly extract precious commodities, including gold, cobalt, and rare earth elements, from accumulated e-waste. Figure 11.6 depicts CM developments from four main sectors.

It compares traditional and circular textile life cycles, displays clever packaging for traceability and waste reduction, depicts material flows in urban mining plans, and demonstrates design ideas for reusing lumber in construction. Each panel emphasizes circularity through smart design,

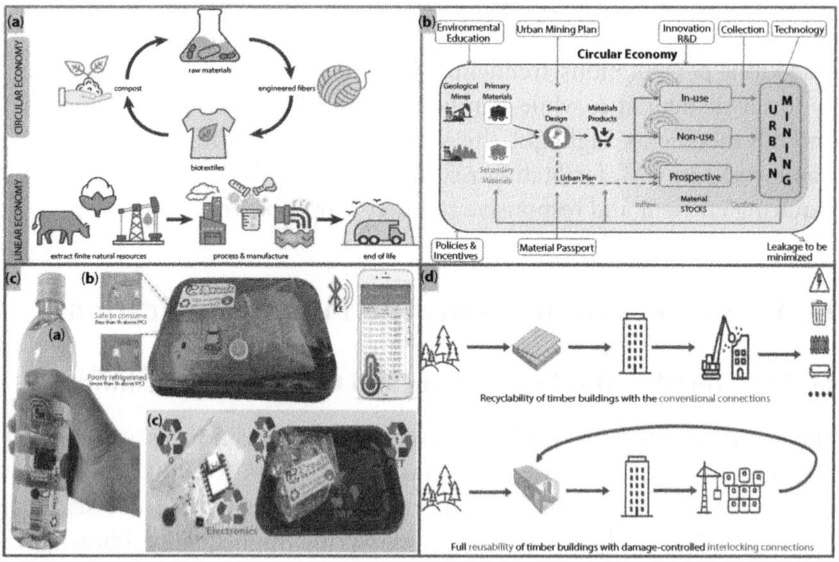

Figure 11.6 Sector-specific applications of circular economy in textiles, electronics, packaging, and construction: (a) linear and circular textile production systems, (b) urban mining framework with material recovery, (c) smart packaging innovations with recyclability features, and (d) conventional and interlocking timber building systems, reusability of modular construction under circular design [44–47].

material efficiency, and system-wide planning. This is comparable to EPR, which mandates that producers develop products that can be disassembled and establish mechanisms for their return. Tagging and digital product certificates that are integrated with the IoT facilitate the tracking of electrical components, enabling them to be disassembled and the materials to be returned. For urban mining to work, there needs to be better recycling technology, legislative support, and infrastructure that works together. Urban mining gets far higher concentrations of precious metals than traditional mining does. It also has less of an impact on the environment and less risk in the supply chain [43].

11.3.3 Polymers and Packaging: Smart Materials

The polymer and packaging sectors are undergoing substantial transformations to adhere to CM principles. This encompasses the utilization of recyclable, biodegradable, and advanced materials to enhance the sustainability and functionality of products. This enhancement enables CM to attain its objectives of extending product longevity, closing material loops, and promoting system-level intelligence. Sensors can now be integrated into bio-based smart packaging to monitor freshness, spoilage, humidity, and gas emissions. These sensors, which are frequently composed of cellulose or other biodegradable materials, not only monitor the safety and quality of food, but also ensure that the materials can be composted or recycled, as required by circular EoL regulations. These devices reduce food waste by revealing the state of food in real time, preventing people from tossing it away prematurely simply because it has an expiration date [48]. Digital circularity also includes smart materials. Technology such as printed RFID tags, flexible electronic circuits, and blockchain-based smart labeling enables resource accountability, reverse logistics, and traceability essential components of an intelligent circular supply chain. By monitoring used packaging and streamlining material retrieval with smart bins and return programs, these systems encourage EPR. CM also benefits from industrial symbiosis, which is when smart packaging materials are made more and more from waste from farms or food. Biopolymers made from algae, maize husk, starch, or lignocellulosic feedstocks are used to make smart films and sensors that are worth a lot of money. This shows how to use resources in a way that does not waste them. Finally, smart packaging enables service-oriented business models such as material leasing and packaging-as-a-service. The incorporation of intelligent elements enables real-time monitoring and control of the packaging lifespan, enabling circular logistics systems and lowering environmental footprints at different supply chain levels [49].

11.3.4 Construction Industry: Modular and Regenerative Design

The building business is shifting toward circularity, making adaptive and sustainable design increasingly crucial. Businesses can use prefabrication to create identical modules that are easy to disassemble. These components can be easily built and then recycled or reused. Regenerative design features such as dynamic facades and carbon-storing materials help to make the environment more resilient. Using DfD frameworks allows construction elements to be reused and recycled when no longer needed, hence closing material cycles. Digital siblings and material passports allow you to trace where parts originate from, how long they endure, and how likely they are to be reused. Also, these solutions encourage circularity and long-lasting buildings by making them adaptive and flexible so that they can fulfill the needs of users as they change. This not only cuts down on waste and resource use, but it also encourages circularity. This all-encompassing method encourages long-term growth in cities and has economic and social benefits for the whole life of the building [50].

11.4 Policy and Regulatory Frameworks

11.4.1 Global Harmonization of Circular Metrics

India is linking its CE efforts to global standards such as ISO/TC 323 and ISO 59010, which deal with circular business models. The Bureau of Indian Standards is working hard to create Indian standards that comply with ISO frameworks so that circularity may be measured and certified in India. Indian producers may compare their work to the finest practices throughout the world, acquire greater access to export markets, and follow global trade rules with the help of harmonized indicators such as product-level circularity datasheets and life-cycle evaluation tools. The India Circular Economy Forum and NITI Aayog are examples of public–private partnerships (PPPs) that want all jurisdictions to disclose circularity in the same way [51, 52]. Table 11.4 provides a detailed summary of India's emerging policy framework for promoting the transition to a CE. Beginning with the Municipal Solid Waste Management Rules of 2000, India has gradually aligned its waste management and resource efficiency initiatives with CE principles, particularly since the Swachh Bharat Mission's debut in 2014. The 2016 Waste Management Rules, based on the 5R principles (reduce, reuse, recycle, recover, and remanufacture), were a crucial step toward

Table 11.4 Promoting circular economy principles in India: policies and initiatives.

Category	Policy/initiative	Year and agency	Circular economy relevance
Waste management framework	Municipal solid waste management rules	2000, MoEFCC	Early step towards regulated waste handling; limited implementation
	Swachh Bharat Mission	2014, MoHUA	National cleanliness campaign; integrated waste management under CE principles
	Waste management rules (six sets)	2016, MoEFCC	Introduced the 5R principles: reduce, reuse, recycle, recover, remanufacture
	EPR guidelines	2022	Holds producers accountable for end-of-life product recovery
Updated CE-aligned regulations	Plastic waste management rules	2016 (Amended 2022)	Circularity in packaging and recycling targets
	E-waste management rules	2016 (Amended 2022)	Promotes recovery of rare earths/metals from discarded electronics
	Battery waste management rules	2022	Recovery and reuse of critical battery materials such as lithium, cobalt
	Construction and demolition waste rules	2016	Facilitates reuse of building material and debris
	Solid waste management rules	2016	Focus on source segregation, composting, and resource recovery

(Continued)

Table 11.4 Promoting circular economy principles in India: policies and initiatives. (*Continued*)

Category	Policy/initiative	Year and agency	Circular economy relevance
	Biomedical waste rules	2016	Ensures proper treatment and potential energy recovery
	Hazardous waste rules	2016 (Amended 2021)	Regulates transboundary movement and recycling of hazardous wastes
	National resource efficiency policy (draft)	2019, MoEFCC	Aims to mainstream CE and secondary raw material markets
Swachh Survekshan (SS)	National Cleanliness Assessment Survey	2016 onwards	Evaluates urban CE adoption: segregation, recycling, energy recovery
	SS 2023—8th edition	2023	Circularity-based metrics included in 9500-point scoring system
Industrial initiatives	Zero defect, zero effect (ZED) certification	2015, MoMSME	Encourages green manufacturing and CE adoption
	Metal recycling policy	Ongoing	Promotes end-of-life recovery and formal scrap management
Government coordination (focus areas)	11 Interministerial CE committees	2021	Action plans for CE in key sectors: batteries, tires, ELVs, etc.

mainstreaming CE. Subsequent initiatives, such the EPR guidelines and sector-specific laws on e-waste, plastic, batteries, and hazardous materials, demonstrate a regulatory commitment to resource recovery and pollution reduction. The table also highlights industry projects such as zero-emission discharge (ZED) certification and policy coordination through interministerial committees focused on CE in important areas such as EoL cars, used oil, and lithium-ion batteries. The Swachh Survekshan, which began in 2016, provides an evaluative mechanism for measuring urban CE uptake. These policies and programs demonstrate India's systematic approach to incorporating CE into national development plans [53].

11.4.2 Carbon Border Adjustments and Trade

Carbon border adjustment mechanisms (CBAMs) are developing as critical tools for global trade, reflecting the carbon content of imported commodities. India, a major exporter in carbon-intensive sectors such as steel, aluminum, and cement, will be heavily impacted by the EU's planned CBAM rollout from 2026. To retain trade competitiveness, Indian businesses are stepping up efforts in energy efficiency, green hydrogen, and green steel production. The government has previously added a green steel rating to its Production Linked Incentive (PLI) plan, establishing emissions requirements for five-star certification. Furthermore, India is looking into local carbon pricing and a voluntary carbon market to coincide with global carbon accounting. These measures, in line with the National Mission for Enhanced Energy Efficiency and the Perform Achieve Trade scheme, aim to reduce carbon intensity in industries exposed to CBAM. Indian exporters are likewise planning to comply with EU reporting rules that require transparency in Scopes 1 and 2 emission declarations [54, 55].

11.4.3 Circular Economy Legislation 2.0

India is transforming its regulatory landscape with next-generation CE legislation. The 2023 Eco Mark Certification Rules, developed by the Bureau of Indian Standards, now include life-cycle environmental standards and recycling thresholds. EPR standards for plastics, electronics, and batteries have been enhanced to include a minimum recycled content and mandatory take-back obligations. The upcoming Green Steel Policy, which will be unveiled in 2024, will feature procurement incentives for environmentally friendly products as well as prizes for circular behaviors. These legislative improvements encourage manufacturers to design for durability and remanufacturability, which is regulated by DPPs and modular design incentives that fit with national CM targets [56].

11.5 Strategic Opportunities

11.5.1 Business Model Innovation

Innovative circular business models are becoming increasingly prevalent in India's manufacturing sector, notably with the deployment of product-as-a-service (PaaS), sharing platforms, and reverse logistics networks. The PaaS model, which prioritizes access over ownership, encourages producers to retain responsibility for maintenance, updates, and recycling, a strategy that has gained support in India's PLI program, which incentivizes modular, repairable product designs. Simultaneously, organizations such as RentSher and Vyomo are promoting collaborative consumerism in India by offering services for the rental of equipment, appliances, and garments. This is consistent with the findings that Indian customers are increasingly adopting shared-use models due to perceived utility and cost benefits. Leena Ajit Kaushal's study, which discovered increased engagement in the Indian sharing economy, supports this tendency. Another detailed investigation emphasized the importance of sharing networks in production systems, highlighting their ability to improve resource efficiency and reduce waste. EPR standards and digital plastic credit systems are boosting reverse logistics frameworks by encouraging businesses to plan for recycling and resource recovery from the start [59]. These measures help the Indian sector migrate from linear to circular value retention tactics, which are bolstered by rising digital infrastructure and climate-tech investment [57–59].

11.5.2 Circular Procurement and Public–Private Partnerships

India's public procurement system accounting for roughly 20% to 30% of GDP represents a powerful driver for CE adoption. Green Public Procurement (GPP) reforms, such as the Eco Mark certification and mandatory procurement of energy-efficient goods, establish foundational policies amenable to scale-up into low-carbon materials such as green cement, steel, and appliances These reforms have been underpinned by recent studies, such as the RMI–TERI roadmap, which offer practical procurement thresholds for green building materials in public infrastructure projects (public housing, railways, highways). For example, the MITRA textile parks initiative has been instrumental in the advancement of circular concepts through PPPs. This initiative unites the government, manufacturers, and entrepreneurs to create closed-loop manufacturing methods and textile recycling. These collaborations are enabled by the development of digital infrastructure, such as India's Government e-Marketplace, which can proactively integrate circular criteria into bidding processes (e.g., material take-back provisions or recycled content). According to industrial ecology studies, well-designed GPPs serve not only as a demand-side instrument, but also as a stimulus for innovation, shifting supply networks toward circular results. Academic case studies reveal that initial pilots of circular tenders in the Netherlands reduced life-cycle emissions by an estimated 7% to 10%, implying a similar potential for use in Indian public projects [60–63].

11.5.3 Skill Development and Education

Building a truly circular industrial ecosystem requires a well-trained workforce. Education must go beyond typical technical skills to include design thinking, systems thinking, life-cycle evaluation, and digital literacy. A recent open-access study presents a comprehensive skills framework for CE in manufacturing. It focuses on four clusters of competencies: technical, digital, soft (for example, collaborative), and systemic, which are adapted to both higher education and vocational training, ensuring congruence with real-world CE needs [64]. Innovative education models are gaining popularity. For example, Maastricht University's "Circular Pathway" combines problem-based learning and industry case studies to foster critical thinking on product redesign and system looping. Although this European case study offers useful insights, efforts to bring such integrative education to India are already underway. Indian efforts such as SWAYAM provide MOOCs on sustainability, whereas numerous technical institutes incorporate CE modules into engineering courses, a trend supported by new research on India-centric curriculum. The Indian government's National Policy on Skill Development, introduced in 2009 and updated through initiatives such as PMKVY and DAY-NULM, is broadening its scope to incorporate sustainability-driven vocational programs. To increase CM adoption, curriculum should include systems thinking, life-cycle design tools, and problem-solving modules as part of broader workplace skill development activities for technicians, factory managers, and product designers [65].

11.5.4 Circular Startups and Investment

Startups are the innovative backbone of CM. A 2023 open-access study in the *Journal of Cleaner Production*, which surveyed 165 firms, found that younger entrepreneurs prefer inner-circle strategies such as recycling, repair, and remanufacturing, whereas older entrepreneurs prefer outer-circle approaches such as resource recovery and shared platforms.

Table 11.5 Essential competencies for circular manufacturing workforce [67].

Competency cluster	Key skills	Relevance to circular manufacturing
Technical	Product design, material science, life-cycle assessment (LCA) tools, remanufacturing	Enables eco-design and efficient use of materials across life-cycle stages
Digital	Data analytics, IoT, digital twins, CE software platforms	Supports tracking of resource flows and predictive maintenance
Systems thinking	Interdisciplinary integration, systems mapping, complexity navigation	Helps in designing closed-loop, cross-sectoral circular solutions
Soft skills	Collaboration, innovation, change management, problem-solving	Facilitates cultural shift in industry and enables CE leadership and teamwork

Such findings highlight that startups are responding dynamically to resource availability and market signals [66]. Table 11.5 infers about CM workforce skill set.

India's venture capital scene is increasingly funding circular startups, especially in materials innovation, digital design platforms, and reverse logistics. A recent conference paper supports promoting green entrepreneurship in India through public and incubator support, particularly for early-stage businesses, in line with the SDGs. RecyKal, a digital marketplace for EPR compliance, has grown to handle more than 200,000 MT yearly, demonstrating commercial viability and environmental benefit. To unleash additional potential, specialized governmental support is required, such as innovation grants, green credit guarantees, and SME-specific circularity criteria. These measures, combined with growing investor demand for climate-aligned portfolios, have the potential to catalyze India's leading circular startup ecosystem.

11.6 Conclusion

CM is a new approach of making things that prioritizes creating value that can be reused over simply making things faster. This chapter discussed the technological, sectoral, policy, and strategic problems that would shape the future of CM. AI, blockchain, quantum computing, and DTs are some of the most recent technologies that allow for intelligent resource management, predictive maintenance, and material monitoring throughout the product's life cycle. Advancements in construction, electronics, textiles, and packaging all demonstrate scalable closed-loop solutions based on material circularity, digital infrastructure, and innovative design.

The integration of CE ideas into national development goals has been aided by India's evolving policy framework, which includes EPR, Eco-Mark certification, and the establishment of interministerial CE committees. Strategic mechanisms such as GPP, business model innovation, talent development, and startup ecosystems help to speed the transfer of theory to practice.

To fully achieve the promise of CM, future initiatives must focus on standardizing circularity measures, establishing cross-sector cooperation, and equipping the workforce with interdisciplinary skills. As the industrial sector faces increasing climate and resource restrictions, CM provides a sustainable and economically feasible solution that balances environmental stewardship and industrial competitiveness. The convergence of enabling technology, supportive laws, and collaborative governance models establishes CM as a necessity for a long-term industrial future, rather than an option.

AI disclosure statement: The author acknowledges the use of AI-based tools for minor language editing or grammatical correction. However, all intellectual contributions, analyses, and conclusions presented in this chapter are entirely the author's own.

References

1. Kazakova, E. and Lee, J., Sustainable Manufacturing for a Circular Economy, 2022.
2. Pinzone, M. and Taisch, M., Key Competencies for Circular Manufacturing, 80, 120–125, 2023.
3. Patwa, N., Seetharaman, A., Arora, A., Agrawal, R., Mandalia, H., Circular economy: Bridging the gap in sustainable manufacturing, 55, 1, 2021.
4. Acerbi, F., *et al.*, Role of Artificial Intelligence in Circular Manufacturing: A Systematic Literature Review. *IFAC Pap.*, 54, 1, 367–372, 2021, doi: 10.1016/j.ifacol.2021.08.040.
5. Luiz, D., Nascimento, M., Garza-reyes, J.A., Rocha-lona, L., Exploring Industry 4.0 technologies to enable circular economy practices in a manufacturing context A business model proposal, 30, 3, 607–627, 2019, doi: 10.1108/JMTM-03-2018-0071.

6. Stecke, K.E. and Von Cieminski, G., Advances in Production, 2019, doi: 10.1007/978-3-030-29996-5.
7. Ciliberto, C. and Ioppolo, G., Enabling the Circular Economy transition: a sustainable lean manufacturing recipe for Industry 4.0, January, 3255–3272, 2021, doi: 10.1002/bse.2801.
8. Korhonen, J., Honkasalo, A., Seppälä, J., Circular Economy: The Concept and its Limitations. *Ecol. Econ.*, 143, 37–46, 2018, doi: 10.1016/j.ecolecon.2017.06.041.
9. RameshKumar, S., Shaiju, P., O'Connor, K.E., P, R.B., Bio-based and biodegradable polymers - State-of-the-art, challenges and emerging trends. *Curr. Opin. Green Sustain. Chem.*, 21, 75–81, 2020, doi: 10.1016/j.cogsc.2019.12.005.
10. Norouzi, M., Chàfer, M., Cabeza, L.F., Jiménez, L., Boer, D., Circular economy in the building and construction sector: A scientific evolution analysis. *J. Build. Eng.*, 44, May, 2021, doi: 10.1016/j.jobe.2021.102704.
11. Pieroni, M.P.P., McAloone, T.C., Pigosso, D.C.A., Circular economy business model innovation: Sectorial patterns within manufacturing companies. *J. Cleaner Prod.*, 286, 124921, 2021, doi: 10.1016/j.jclepro.2020.124921.
12. European Commission, Ecodesign for Sustainable Products Regulation and Repair Directive, https://ec.europa.eu/commission/presscorner/detail/en/IP_24_3043.
13. Ministère de la Transition Écologique, Loi Anti-Gaspillage pour une Économie Circulaire (AGEC), 2024, [Online]. Available: https://www.ecologie.gouv.fr/loi-anti-gaspillage.
14. United Nations, Transforming our World: The 2030 Agenda for Sustainable Development, 2015, [Online]. Available: https://sdgs.un.org/goals.
15. J., Ministry of the Environment, Green Growth Strategy Through Achieving Carbon Neutrality in 2050, 2021, [Online]. Available: https://www.env.go.jp/en/headline/2485.html.
16. Australian Government, Circular Economy Strategy and Circular Future Fund, 2024, [Online]. Available: https://www.dcceew.gov.au/environment/protection/circular economy.
17. European Commission, Industry 5.0: Towards a sustainable, human-centric and resilient European industry, Directorate-General for Research and Innovation, 2021, [Online]. Available: https://research-and-innovation.ec.europa.eu/system/files/2021-01/industry-5.0_report_0.pdf.
18. Nahavandi, S., Industry 5.0—A human-centric solution, *Sustainability*, [Online]. Available: https://doi.org/10.3390/su11164371.
19. Ojo, E.O., *et al.*, Industry 5.0 and circular economy: A review and research agenda. *Sustainable Oper. Comput.*, [Online]. Available: https://doi.org/10.1016/j.susoc.2021.03.001.
20. Xu, M., *et al.*, The fusion of digitalization and circular economy: Towards human-centric manufacturing. *J. Cleaner Prod.*, [Online]. Available: https://doi.org/10.1016/j.jclepro.2020.124962.

21. Longo, F., Padovano, A., Umbrello, S., Value-oriented and ethical technology design for Industry 5.0: A human-centric perspective. *Information*, [Online]. Available: https://doi.org/10.3390/info11030110.
22. Ellen MacArthur Foundation, Circular Economy System Diagram, 2019, https://ellenmacarthurfoundation.org.
23. Jones, D., Snider, C., Nassehi, A., Yon, J., Hicks, B., Characterising the Digital Twin: A systematic literature review. *CIRP J. Manuf. Sci. Technol.*, 29, 36–52, 2020.
24. Barata, J. and Kayser, I., How will the digital twin shape the future of industry 5.0?. *Technovation*, 134, 103025, 2024.
25. Liu, M., Fang, S., Dong, H., Xu, C., Review of digital twin about concepts, technologies, and industrial applications. *J. Manuf. Syst.*, 58, 346–361, 2021.
26. Tao, F., Zhang, H., Liu, A., Nee, A.Y., Digital twin in industry: State-of-the-art. *IEEE Trans. Ind. Inform.*, 15, 4, 2405–2415, 2018.
27. Kritzinger, W., Karner, M., Traar, G., Henjes, J., Sihn, W., Digital Twin in manufacturing: A categorical literature review and classification. *Ifac-Pap. Online*, 51, 11, 1016–1022, 2018.
28. Abid, I., Fuad, S.M., Chowdhury, M.J.M., Chowdhury, M.S., Ferdous, M.S., A Systematic Literature Review on the Use of Blockchain Technology in Transition to a Circular Economy, *arXiv preprint arXiv:2408.11664*, 2024.
29. Kühn, M., Baumann, M., Volz, F., Stojanovic, L., Digital Product Passport Design Supporting the Circular Economy Based on the Asset Administration Shell. *Sustainability*, 17, 3, 969, 2025.
30. Govindan, K., Tunneling the barriers of blockchain technology in remanufacturing for achieving sustainable development goals: A circular manufacturing perspective. *Bus. Strategy Environ.*, 31, 8, 3769–3785, 2022.
31. https://www.circularise.com/blogs/digital-product-passports-dpp-what-how-and-why.
32. Hulea, M., Miron, R., Muresan, Digital product passport implementation based on multi-blockchain approach with decentralized identifier provider. *Appl. Sci.*, 14, 11, 4874, 2024.
33. Wuest, T., Weimer, D., Irgens, C., Thoben, K.D., Machine learning in manufacturing: advantages, challenges, and applications. *Prod. Manuf. Res.*, 4, 1, 23–45, 2016.
34. Arocena, P., Orcos, R., Zouaghi, F., The impact of ISO 14001 on firm environmental and economic performance: The moderating role of size and environmental awareness. *Bus. Strategy Environ.*, 30, 2, 955–967, 2021.
35. Ali, Z.A., Zain, M., Hasan, R., Al Salman, H., Alkhamees, B.F., Almisned, F.A., Circular Economy Advances with Artificial Intelligence and Digital Twin: Multiple-Case Study of Chinese Industries in Agriculture. *J. Knowl. Econ.*, 1–37, 2024.
36. Chen, H., Zhang, Y., Research on the path of sustainable development of China's logistics industry driven by capital factors. *Sustainability*, 15, 1, 297, 2022.

37. Dubey, R., Gunasekaran, A., Childe, S.J., Blome, C., Papadopoulos, T., Big data and predictive analytics and manufacturing performance: integrating institutional theory, resource-based view and big data culture. *Br. J. Manag.*, 30, 2, 341–361, 2019.
38. Neukart, F., Compostella, G., Seidel, C., Von Dollen, D., Yarkoni, S., Parney, B., Traffic flow optimization using a quantum annealer. *Front. ICT*, 4, 29, 2017.
39. Tambunan, T.D., Suksmono, A.B., Edward, I.J.M., Mulyawan, R., Quantum annealing for vehicle routing problem with weighted segment. *AIP Conf. Proc.*, 2906, 1, AIP Publishing, 2023, November.
40. Jiang, H., Shen, Z.J.M., Liu, J., Quantum computing methods for supply chain management, in: *2022 IEEE/ACM 7th Symposium on Edge Computing (SEC)*, 2022, December, IEEE, pp. 400–405.
41. Ribul, M., Lanot, A., Mechanical, chemical, biological: Moving towards closed-loop bio-based recycling in a circular economy of sustainable textiles. *J. Cleaner Prod.*, 326, 129325, 2021, https://doi.org/10.1016/j.jclepro.2021.129325.
42. Jönsson, C., Wei, R., Biundo, A., Landberg, J., Schwarz Bour, L., Pezzotti, F., Syrén, P.O., Biocatalysis in the recycling landscape for synthetic polymers and plastics towards circular textiles. *Chemsuschem*, 14, 19, 4028–4040, 2021.
43. Ouro-Salim, O., Urban mining of e-waste management globally: Literature review. *Cleaner Waste Syst.*, 100162, 2024.
44. Schiros, T.N., Mosher, C.Z., Zhu, Y., Bina, T., Gomez, Lee, C.L., Obermeyer, A.C., Bioengineering textiles across scales for a sustainable circular economy. *Chem.*, 7, 11, 2913–2926, 2021.
45. Medkova, K., Trilogy on Circular Economy, 2016.
46. Li, S., Tang, W., Chen, S., Si, Y., Liu, R., Guo, X., Flexible organic polymer gas sensor and system integration for smart packaging. *Adv. Sens. Res.*, 2, 11, 2300030, 2023.
47. Li, Z., Tsavdaridis, K., Katenbayeva, A., Reusable timber modular buildings, material circularity and automation: The role of inter-locking connections. *J. Build. Eng.*, 2024.
48. Rodrigues, C., Souza, G.L., Coelhoso, I., Fernando, A.L., Bio-based sensors for smart food packaging—Current applications and future trends. *Sensors*, 21, 6, 2148, 2021.
49. Halonen, N., Pálvölgyi, P.S., Bassani, A., Fiorentini, C., Nair, R., Spigno, G., Kordas, K., Bio-based smart materials for food packaging and sensors–a review. *Front. Mater.*, 7, 82, 2020.
50. Jayawardana, J., Sandanayake, M., Kulatunga, A.K., Jayasinghe, J.A.S.C., Zhang, G., Osadith, S.U., Evaluating the circular economy potential of modular construction in developing economies—A life cycle assessment. *Sustainability*, 15, 23, 16336, 2023.
51. https://eepcindia.com/event/2024/circular-economy.

52. Yamaguchi, S., International trade and circular economy-Policy alignment, OECD Trade and Environment Working Papers, 2021, 2, 0_1-80, 2021.
53. Ghosh, S.K., Circular Economy and Sustainable Development Goals: Policy, Legislation and ISO Standards, 2023.
54. Erdogdu, E., The Carbon Border Adjustment Mechanism: Opportunities and Challenges for Non-EU Countries. *WIRES Energy Environ.*, 14, 1, e70000, 2025.
55. Makol, N., Gupta, P., Mital, M., Syal, M., Adapting to Global Carbon Policies: Economic Impact of Carbon Border Adjustment Mechanism on Indian Businesses. *OIDA Int. J. Sustain. Dev.*, 18, 06, 11–20, 2025.
56. https://www.teriin.org/sites/default/files/2024-08/GPP_SDG_Charter.
57. Jayakumar, J., K, J., KEK, Hasibuan, S., Modelling of sharing networks in the circular economy. *J. Mode. Manag.*, 15, 2, 407–440, 2020.
58. Kaushal, L.A. and Prashar, A., Determinants of service consumers' attitudes towards the sharing economy for sustainable consumption. *J. Glob. Inf. Technol. Manag.*, 25, 2, 137–158, 2022, doi:10.1080/1097198X.2022.2062993 tandfonline.com.
59. Ministry of Environment, Forest & Climate Change (MoEFCC), EPR Guidelines for Plastic Packaging, Government of India, 2022.
60. Zijp, M., Dekker, E., Hauck, M., De Koning, A., Bijleveld, M., Tokaya, J., Posthuma, L., Measuring the effect of circular public procurement on government's environmental impact. *Sustainability*, 14, 16, 10271, 2022.
61. Koul, S., Kashyap, P., Singh, A., Planning sustainability: The future of green public procurement in India, in: *Resilient Businesses for Sustainability*, vol. 34, pp. 31–46, Emerald Publishing Limited, 2024.
62. Singhal, R., Recourse to the Circular Economy: The Path Ahead, in: *Sustainable Development Insights from India: Selected Essays in Honour of RamprasadSengupta*, pp. 261–280, Springer Singapore, Singapore, 2021.
63. Karnavos, D., Mitoula, R., Tragaki, A., Apostolopoulos, C., Green Public Procurement as a tool for the transition from the linear model of economy to the circular economy. *Adv. Soc. Sci. Res. J.*, 9, 7, 566–579, 2022.
64. Trevisan, A.H., Boscarato, A., Acerbi, F., Terzi, S., Sassanelli, C., Enhancing Circular Economy education and training for the manufacturing sector: A holistic skills framework. *J. Environ. Manage.*, 380, 124982, 2025.
65. Garcia-Saravia Ortiz-de-Montellano, C., Ghannadzadeh, A., van der Meer, Y., The CIRCULAR pathway: a new educational methodology for exploratory circular value chain redesign. *Front. Sustain.*, 4, 1197659, 2023.
66. Van Opstal, W. and Borms, L., Startups and circular economy strategies: Profile differences, barriers and enablers. *J. Cleaner Prod.*, 396, 136510, 2023.
67. Ti, W., Ng, D.K., Andiappan, Optimal integration of hydrogen production process with carbon dioxide capture, utilisation and storage. *J. Cleaner Prod.*, 415, 137697, 2023.

12

Circular Manufacturing and Biomedical Engineering Applications

V. Sivaprakash[1]*, R. Narayanan[2], A. Revathi[3], S. Balakrishnan[4] and Thirukkotti Ganapathy[5]

[1]*Department of Mechanical Engineering, Sathyabama Institute of Science and Technology, Chennai, India*
[2]*School of Mechanical Engineering, VIT Chennai Campus, Chennai, India*
[3]*Department of Chemistry, Kongu Engineering College, Erode, India*
[4]*Department of Mechanical Engineering, Nandha Engineering College, Erode, India*
[5]*Department of Mechanical Engineering, P.S.R Engineering College, Sivakasi, India*

Abstract
Materials possess significant potential in the biomedical field due to their functional methods and properties. Implant materials require specific mechanical, chemical, physical, and biocompatibility properties for successful implantation. It is essential for implant biomaterials to be absorbed by the human body environment, adopt cellular structures, and accept biological growth. Attachment toward the bone and growth along with the tissues enable the material to remain biologically active. Researchers have focused on developing novel biomaterials and manufacturing techniques for medical devices. Choosing the right material is very important when making a medical device because it affects how well the device works and how successful it is. The article provides an overview of biomaterials, including metals, polymers, ceramics, and composites.

Keywords: Biomaterials, biocompatibility, metals, composites, tissue engineering

12.1 Introduction

Materials are essential for biomedical applications which adopt the environment of biological systems. Biomaterials function in the replacement or

**Corresponding author*: spkgopi@gmail.com

Jeyaprakash Natarajan, Milon Selvam Dennison, M. Bhuvanesh Kumar and Ganapathy Thirukkotti (eds.) Manufacturing and the Circular Economy, (369–406) © 2027 Scrivener Publishing LLC

reconstruction of bone, hips, and teeth [1]. Biomaterials are often used in everyday surgery, drug delivery, and heart valve applications [2]. The term "biomaterials" is difficult to formulate for specific applications, as there are various methods to fabricate them for the human body environment. Mostly, biomaterials are naturally occurring or manmade substances which can replace living structures wholly or partially, or biomaterials can be used to replace natural organs [3, 4]. Spongy biomaterials are among the most common types of materials as they easily adapt to the human environment. The use of orthopedic applications as bone graft substitutes, drug delivery systems, and scaffolds for bone tissues is remarkable in this current century [5].

Human body parts such as the hip, knee, shoulder, heart valves, dental structures, intravascular stents, and ears are major parts replaced by biomedical materials. Biomaterials science focuses on both treatments and diagnostics [6]. It includes fundamental sciences (biology, chemistry, physics), engineering, and medicine [7]. It further includes fundamental sciences (biology, chemistry, physics), engineering, and medicine [8, 9]. Materials are not only simple bioimplants but are also visually appealing. The implant materials, including their qualities, benefits, and downsides, are highly focusable [8, 10].

12.2 Biocompatibility Property

In the replacement or reconstruction of a human living system, the consideration of biocompatibility is essential. Biocompatibility is a crucial part of implanting materials into living tissue. Avoiding toxic release and harmful effects while operating inside human living tissues take high priority. Factors of material biocompatibility, surface properties, mechanical properties, surface characterization, corrosion resistance, and degradation behaviors play an important role in biocompatibility [11]. Titanium (Ti) and stainless steel (SS) are the generally used biological replacement materials due to their nature, corrosion resistance, and high strength-to-weight ratio. Modifying the surface of the material makes them even more effective as bioinert materials. The characterization of surface texture, wettability, and surface roughness (SR) of the material requires specific surface treatments [12, 13].

Attachment between the metal and tissue SR is essential. SR of biomaterials affects cell and tissue response by making the SR area near to the bone, leading to better bonding between the bones and cells [14, 15]. Cell adhesion and proliferation promotion in human tissue, as well as the importance of smooth and nanosurfaces, are reported by various researchers. Material surfaces can be tailor-made with proteins, which are highly used for tissue and bone regrowth. Initial interaction between the blood and materials takes place through serum proteins, which are highly recommended. The first approach between the cell and immune systems is decided by the initial layer [13, 16]. Proteins are another factor that creates a high biological surrounding for material interaction with cells and tissues. Bone scaffolds promote cell adhesion, and proteins increase regeneration toward the bone [17].

12.3 Biomaterials

Human anatomy is made of different types of bone with different types of structures. Human bodies are subjected to different kinds of loads, both internal and external. Owing to these loads, body parts may be damaged by internal or external, gradual or sudden loads [18]. For replacing bone or body parts, researchers use different types of materials according to the classification of metals, ceramics, polymers, and composite materials, depending on bone types and human requirements. Each material has unique properties.

The materials and their properties are discussed below. For the safe and effective use of biomaterials, the implant metals, ceramics, polymers, and composites need specific mechanical, chemical, physical, and environmental properties. The tensile strength of a material must withstand high loads and remain strong after implantation. The surface of the metal and bioimplant requires tailor-made surface nanomodifications [1, 19, 20]. In surface treatment, various powder materials play unique roles. The bonding between materials and the doping of compositions make the biomaterials even harder, and the results follow. Involving aluminum alloys can make the materials smooth with a fine shape on the surface. Involving silicon carbide (SiC) creates SR; chromium (Cr) [21] materials increase machining efficiency, and microcracks are observed; involving Ti composition increases corrosion resistance and surface hardness, while involving molybdenum (Mo) has a high impact on tensile strength [15, 22–24].

12.4 Metals Biomaterials

In the use of metals for orthopedic replacement, metals play an important role. As-fabricated (nontreated) metals may contain harmful chemicals such as arsenic, cadmium, lead, and mercury. Metallic bioimplants are given high priority in load-bearing applications due to their higher yield strength, lower degradation, and higher fracture toughness compared to ceramics, polymeric materials, and polymer/ceramic composite materials (Table 12.1).

Table 12.1 Biomaterials types and applications [25–28].

Biomaterials	Types	Applications
Metals	Stainless steel, titanium, magnesium, cobalt, etc.	Bone, hip, knee, dental
Ceramics	Cement, alumina, calcium phosphates, glass-ceramics, bioactive glasses, hydroxyapatite, carbon, aluminum oxides, etc.	Dental, drug delivery carrier, tooth fillings, load-bearing implant covers, medical sensors, dental and orthopedic implants, etc.
Polymers	Dextrans, poly-l-lysine, polyethylene glycol, Poly (octanediol-co-citrate), polycaprolactone, acrylic bone cements, cyclodextrin, poly(methylmethacrylate), etc.	Heart valves, blood vessels , contact lenses socket, artificial hearts, hip joint, etc.
Composites alloys	Ti, Ti– A l– B, Ti– Mo–Zr– Sn , Ti– A l– Nb, Ti–Al– N b – Ta, Ti–Al– V, Ti–Fe–Ta, Ti–Ta–Zr, Ti– Mo, Ti– Mo–Al, Ti–Mo–Ga, Ti– Nb–Ta–Sn, Ti– Nb–Ta–Zr, Ti–Ta, Ti– Zr, Ti–Mo–Ge, Ti–Mo–Nb, Ti–Mo–Nb–Si, Ti–Mo–Zr– Al, Ti–Mo–Zr– Fe, Ti– Nb–Hf, Ti–Nb–Sn, Ti– Nb–Ta–Mo, Ti– Nb–Zr, Ti– Sn–Nb–Ta and etc., **Alpha alloys**: Ti-6Al-2Sn-1.5Zr-1Mo-0.35Bi-0.15Si (Ti-11), Ti-5Al-6Sn-2Zr-1Mo-0.25Si, and i-2.25Al-11Sn-5Zr-1Mo-0.2Si **Alpha-beta type**: Ni- Ti, Ti-6Al-2Sn-2Zr-2Mo-2Cr/0.25 Si, Ti-6Al-2Sn-4Zr-6Mo, Ti-6Al-6V-2Sn, Ti-5Al-2Sn-2Zr-4Mo-4Cr (Ti-17), and Ti-3Al-2.5V. Ti-4.5Sn-6Zr-11.5Mo; Ti-8Mo-8V-2Fe-3Al; Ti-13V-11Cr-3Al; Ti-13Nb-13Zr; Ti-12Mo-5Zr-5Sn; Ti-15Mo; Ti-15Mo-2.8Nb-0.2Si. Ti-15Mo-5Zr-3Al, Ti-30Ta, Ti-45Nb, Ti-35Zr-10Nb, Ti-35Nb-7Zr-5Ta (TNZT), Ti-29Nb-13Ta-4.6Zr (TNTZ), Ti-35Nb-4Sn, Ti-50Ta, Ti-8Fe-8Ta, Ti-8Fe-8Ta-4Zr, Ti-35Nb-2Ta-3Zr, Ti-22.5Nb-0.7Zr-2Ta, Ti-23Nb-0.7Ta-2.0Zr-1.2O (Gum Metal), Ti-28Nb-13Zr-85n **Beta-rich**: Ti-13Nb-13Zr; Ti-24Nb-4Zr-8Sn. **Beta - Near**: Ti-33Zr-3Fe-2Cr, Ti-20Nb-10Zr-5Ta. Ti-4.5Al-3V-2Mo-2Fe, Ti-5Al-2Sn-2Zr-4Mo-4Cr, Ti-5Al-5Mo-1Cr-1Fe. Ti-10V-2Fe-3Al is metastable with Ti-29Nb-13Ta-4.6Zr, Ti-25Nb-8Zr-4Cr, Ti-26Nb-4Zr-3Mn, Ti-11Nb-3.5Fe, Ti-25Nb-3Sn-4Cr, Ti-11.5Mo-6Zr-4.5Sn, Ti-5V-3Cr-3Sn-3Al, and Ti-15Mo-2.6Nb-3Al-2Si. Ti-35Nb-2Ta-3Zr, Ti-15Mo, Ti-12Mo-6Zr-2Fe, Ti-4.5Fe-6.5Mo-1.5Al, Ti-7Fe-11Nb, Ti-8Fe-5Ta, Ti-6V-6Mo-5.7Fe-2.7Al, and Ti-27Nb-7Fe-2Cr	Joint replacements, bone cement, dental implants

The use of these modified chemical and physical treatment metal implants is a time-sensitive procedure that involves a vital connection between eventual implant failure and biological recovery. Although this is currently complex for researchers, incremental improvements may assist in minimizing bone and metal failures over time. *In situ*, this race is partially determined by bone quality. Various metallic implant materials now used include SS, cobalt-chrome alloys, and Ti alloys. Generally, biological metal implantations pose two primary issues. The first challenge is a mismatch between the mechanical properties of the metallic alloy and the surrounding blood environment and human bone tissue. SS (SS 316 Young's modulus 205–210 GPa, yield strength 170–750 GPa, ultimate tensile strength 465–950 MPa) and cobalt-Cr alloys have ten times the elastic modulus (Young's modulus 220–230 GPa, yield strength 275–1585 GPa, ultimate tensile strength 600–1785 MPa) of bone. Conversely, Ti alloys such as Ti-6Al-4V (Young's modulus 105–125 GPa, yield strength 840–1100 GPa, ultimate tensile strength 590–1024 MPa) have a five-fold increase [29].

Based on microstructure properties, SS is classified into four major categories. Austenitic steels, containing 8% nickel and low carbon, provide high corrosion resistance, weldability, and mechanical strength. These biomaterials possess cold-work ability and nonmagnetic properties that make them unique even within the SS category. Globally, they represent around 70% of usage. Metal ions in SS can sometimes be toxic, and the release of these ions may cause malignancies if corrosion resistance fails. For this unpredictable reason, SS sometimes fails to remain in the human body during long-term medical conditions. After the desired effect is achieved, the SS is withdrawn from human contact [30–32].

12.5 Ceramics Biomaterials

Ceramics are among the best materials utilized for bioimplants due to their high corrosion resistance, biocompatibility, electrical conductivity, and good compressive strength when incorporated into bone structures associated with hydroxyapatite (HAp) and tricalcium phosphate (TCP) [33]. Ceramic implants are divided into three categories: nonabsorbable (relatively inert), bioactive or surface-reactive (semi-inert), and biodegradable or resorbable (non-inert). Inert types such as Si nitrides, carbons, alumina, and zirconia are used under the ceramics category. Thick HAp bioreactives serve as semi-inert materials known as glass-ceramics, whereas calcium (Ca) or calcium phosphates are utilized as resorbable ceramics [34].

Initially used for bone repair and mostly as a bone filler material, ceramics were later used as bone replacement materials due to their unique properties. Because of hygienic porcelain manufacturing and the local usage of ceramics, there is a high demand for SiO_2-Al_2O_3-K_2O. The addition of crystal phases of feldspar ($KAlSi_3O_8$) and leucite ($KAlSi_2O_6$) ($K_2O \cdot Al_2O_3 \cdot 4SiO_2$) improved the biocompatibility of ceramics. Based on historical development, ceramics remain a frequent material used for dental implants. The feldspathic coating composition contains 52–62 wt% SiO_2, 11–16 wt% Al_2O_3, 9–11 wt% K_2O, and 5–7 wt% Na_2O, among additional components such as Li_2O or B_2O_3 [4, 35].

12.6 Polymers Biomaterials

Based on different structures and functional groups, polymers are available in various shapes and characteristics, allowing for precise control over desired architectures for different types of biomedical applications. Naturally occurring polymers and manufactured polymers are available in two categories for bioimplantation. Collagen, alginate, and chitosan are examples of naturally occurring polymers [36]. Synthetic types are categorized as either nonbiodegradable or biodegradable. Biodegradable polymers play a crucial role in biomaterials and tissue engineering (TE) by eliminating the need for subsequent surgery to remove implants or scaffolds.

Polyethylene, polypropylene, polyvinyl chloride, polyacrylate, elastomers, polycarbonate, fluoropolymers, polyurethane, polyester, polystyrene, polyethylene terephthalate, and Si are synthetic polymers highly utilized in medical devices [37]. For drug delivery systems, a variety of polymers, such as polyesters, polyacrylates, isopropylacrylamides, polyethylenimines, and poly(2-oxazoline)s, are commonly used, as are naturally occurring polymeric materials such as collagen and chitosan [38]. The natural process of biodegradation breaks down materials through hydrolytic or enzymatic mechanisms. In literature, biodegradation is also referred to by the terms "absorbable," "erodible," and "resorbable." In the current and past decade, biodegradable polymeric biomaterials have been widely used in surgery, blood-carrying packages, heart valves, and contact lenses.

Biodegradable materials offer significant benefits in implantation sites [39]. They do not persist longer than necessary after implantation; they are easily absorbed by the human body and do not remain at the implant site. Polyethylene, polypropylene, polyvinyl chloride, polyacrylate, elastomers, polycarbonate, fluoropolymers, polyurethane, polyester, polystyrene, polyethylene terephthalate, and Si are synthetic polymers highly utilized in medical devices [40]. For drug delivery systems, a variety of polymers, such as polyesters, polyacrylates, isopropylacrylamides, polyethylenimines, and poly(2-oxazoline)s, are commonly used, alongside naturally occurring polymeric materials such as collagen and chitosan. Hydrogel formulations also utilize poly(ethylene glycol)s [41].

12.7 Composites Biomaterials

Bone is a naturally occurring composite material made with proteins, collagen fibrils, and HAp nanocrystals distributed throughout the collagen fibers, forming a high hierarchical composite. With a high elastic modulus (approximately 100 GPa), cortical bone has a combined elastic modulus of 10 to 20 GPa, which is lower than that of metals commonly used for bone fixation, such as Ti and SS, which have elastic moduli of around 118 and 206, respectively [42]. For combinations of high strength and low elastic modulus, polymer-reinforced composites are recommended for biomedical applications. Natural polymer-based composites possess high corrosion and fatigue resistance. These materials have versatile qualities that can be tailored to specific needs. For femoral head applications, CoCr alloys, SS alloys, and alumina-zirconium alloys are recommended [30, 43].

The variation between the Young's modulus of native bone (10–30 GPa) and bulk biomaterials (110 GPa for Ti) may lead to bone loosening or resorption when Ti materials are implanted [44]. α-Phase Ti materials have a higher elastic modulus compared to β-phase titanium. For low elastic modulus and high biocompatibility, titanium alloys composed of 12% Mo, 6% zirconium, and 2% iron (Ti-12Mo-6Zr-2Fe ["TMZF"]) are β Ti alloys with a lower Young's modulus (~70 GPa) and a corrosion rate of 1.2 μm/year, which are also used in aerospace. Ti with 15% Mo, 5% zirconium, and 3% aluminum (Ti-15Mo-5Zr-3Al) with 700 MPa tensile properties, and Ti-13Nb-13Zr (β-type alloy), are highly used in dental applications [44, 45]. Ti with 6% aluminum and 4% vanadium (Ti-6Al-4V) offers high strength, good corrosion resistance (0.480 μm/year), and bioactivity. Due to unfavorable toxicity, inert materials such as vanadium, zirconium, aluminum, and niobium in Ti alloys may pose risks for human implantation.

With advancements in manufacturing technology, cobalt-Cr and cobalt-based alloys are widely used in dental applications. The mechanical characteristics of cobalt-Cr alloys, such as tensile strength, yield strength, compressive strength, and hardness, were enhanced by incorporating various component compositions [46]. For improving tensile, corrosion, wear resistance, and yield strength, cobalt-Cr with Mo (CoCrMo) is the best combination. Cobalt-based alloys typically have two allotropic crystalline phases. Cobalt-natured alloys are stable at ambient temperature with a hexagonal closed-packed (HCP) structure; when the temperature increases above 1243 K, based on the components or alloys, the stable phase reaches face-centered cubic (FCC). Certain implants must endure significant wear caused by prolonged usage and strain on high-stress joints. CoCrMo achieves high wear performance due to strain-induced FCC to HCP phase transformation occurring *in situ* under high shear stress by recrystallization [47].

12.8 Biomaterials for Tissue Engineering

TE is the study of how cells, scaffolds, biomaterials, and biologically active chemicals may be used to create functional tissue. The main objective of TE is to repair and enhance damaged or injured tissues [48]. Essentially, TE is divided into two categories: *ex vivo* and *in situ*. (i) *Ex vivo* TE takes stem cells from a donor and plants them on an external scaffold within an appropriate environment using bioreactors to promote cell proliferation and differentiation into the desired tissue. The tissue created following cell multiplication is the intended tissue; thus, it must be the same size and shape as the targeted problem site. The scaffold diminishes over time, allowing the substitution of freshly regenerated tissues [49]. Meanwhile, (ii) *in situ* TE differs from *ex vivo* in that the scaffold is made of biocompatible material with the same size and shape as the desired tissue and is implanted directly into the required site without prior cell seeding; the attached scaffold directly attracts surrounding cells and promotes host tissue regeneration [50]. This technology offers an immune-compatible alternative to *ex vivo* techniques, preventing the implanted scaffold from being rejected. Biomaterials interact directly with biological systems through their surface, materials, and structure. For the complete or partial replacement of tissues, naturally occurring or fabricated materials are utilized in TE. The implant material must be biodegradable (disappearing after performing its purpose), avoid inducing immunological reactions, be safe after absorption by host tissues, be bioactive and sterilizable, and respond to driving tissue growth [10].

12.9 Three-Dimensional Printing of Biomaterials

Three-dimensional (3D) printing, also known as additive manufacturing, is a cutting-edge process that prints components for the accurate assembly of parts, live cells, biomaterials, and biological factors to create tissue-engineered structures for therapeutic, pharmacological, and diagnostic applications [2]. Biological structures are fabricated with specific shapes and sizes to accomplish activities including tissue regeneration, medication release, and signal collection when implanted in patients. These constructions can act as bioscaffolds to guide cells and macromolecules to specific areas or as stiff sensors to detect pathophysiological changes in biological substances such as sweat, tears, and blood [51].

Bioprinting *via* additive manufacturing closely mimics human tissue format, microstructures, topology, geometry, and composition to respond to inputs and trigger desired transformations, properties, or functions. Recent advances in intelligent materials include stimuli-sensitive hydrogels, shape-memory polymers, liquid crystal polymers, and responsive additives such as graphene oxide, magnetic media, and electroconductive chemicals [52]. 3D-bioprinted constructions have tailored microstructures, topology, geometry, and composition to respond to inputs and trigger desired functions. Inkjet printing is a type of printing that uses binder jetting to transfer computer data or information onto a substrate [53, 54]. In the past decade, 3D printing has made material fabrication easier, and current technologies utilize these techniques for accurate biomaterial fabrication.

During the 3D bioprinting process, a liquid substrate is printed using an inkjet nozzle onto a powdered or receiver platform to create new objects or separate components in a single setting. 3D bioprinting involves computer-generated, commanded, and programmed designs. When an electrical pulse or pressure is applied to the nozzle, a vapor bubble is formed. The droplet ejects from the nozzle as the pressure increases. Droplets can combine with particles in powder beds or be deposited on the substrate to form layers. TE and regenerative medicine (RM) utilize modified cells and biomolecules to repair and regenerate damaged tissues and organs [55]. This includes enhancing the interactions between the constructs and the host body. 3D printing can manufacture complex 3D structures from biomaterials such as bioactive polymers, metals, ceramics, and glass, allowing for the development of implants and surgical equipment for personalized treatment.

Creating pH-sensitive biomaterial inks improves medicine release efficiency during tumor treatment. Polymers evaluated for pH responsiveness include polyacrylate, poly(N-isopropylacrylamide), n-vinylcaprolactam, sodium alginate, and carrageenan [56]. Bivalent copper can be used with alginate to generate biomaterial ink. This study found that the encapsulating system maintained structural integrity at pH 1.2. The sluggish release of substances in the digestive system was observed only at pH values greater than 5, indicating a delayed process. Many tissues and organs generate endogenous electrical impulses, which play an important role in processes such as mitosis, cell signaling, migration, wound healing, and angiogenesis [56]. The ability to respond to electrical signals enhances the functionality and homeostasis of natural tissues and organs. Exogenous electrical impulses can influence stem cell development and maturation in engineered tissues/organs. Conductive biomaterials are rapidly being used in brain interface research, drug or chemical release from engineered structures, and cell mechanical stimulation. Conductive polymers are commonly used in biomaterials to interact with cells [57].

12.10 Smart Biomaterials

In this past year, biomaterials have advanced significantly due to extraordinary transformations in materials for their applications. Smart materials are a groundbreaking invention that has the potential to transform biomedical engineering and healthcare. Smart materials respond to environmental stimuli, including temperature, pH, light, and magnetic fields, to affect their properties and behavior [58]. Their unique properties make them ideal for various applications, including medicine delivery, TE, biosensors, and medical devices. Smart biomaterials are indispensable for cell growth and regeneration, highly responsive to physiological stimuli, and quick to engage with tissue formation.

Smart biomaterials also respond to external sources such as light, magnetic forces (often through the incorporation of Fe_2O_3), and electric fields [59]. Biomagnetic nanoparticles (NPs) are used in drug delivery systems to transport drugs to targeted locations, minimizing side effects. These magnetic NPs respond to external magnetic fields by changing their volume, shape, or mechanical properties, which is used to release drugs at specific locations. Additionally, photoresponsive smart biomaterials react to light and change their properties [60]. These materials contain light-sensitive chromophores and undergo chemical or structural changes when exposed to specific light wavelengths. Light-induced alterations can be reversible, such as the isomerization of azobenzene, or irreversible, such as the photolysis of certain molecules [61].

The most popular electric field-sensitive smart biomaterials are conductive polymers, which modify their conductivity and mechanical characteristics in reaction to electric fields. Conductive polymers include polypyrrole and poly(3,4-ethylenedioxythiophene) (PEDOT); these combinations have been used for nerve-type regeneration and drug delivery [62]. Smart biomaterials are also involved in controlling or manipulating immune responses, making them applicable for treating various illnesses. Furthermore, smart biomaterials are resulting in novel therapeutics for cancer, autoimmune disorders, and infections [63]. In immune engineering, smart materials produce immunomodulatory cancer therapeutics that regulate the immune system to boost the patient's defenses and attack cancer cells. Biomaterials directly deliver immune-stimulating chemicals (β-glucans, lactoferrin, levamisole, and saponins) to tumor sites, activating immune cells and developing anti-tumor responses [64].

12.11 Antimicrobial Features of Biomaterials for Biomedical Applications

In the biomedical industry, biomaterials have revolutionized wound healing, drug delivery systems, grafts, stents, and vascular implant coatings. Biomaterials composed of metals, alloys, ceramics, and polymers are popular due to high demand. For long-term use, biocompatibility is essential. Antimicrobial biomaterials defend against biofilm development to prevent and treat illnesses caused by bacteria [65]. Antimicrobial elements are included in biomaterials through various means, such as polymers, marine extracts, NPs, and peptides. These materials must be biocompatible, nontoxic, cost-effective, stable over time, and possess broad-spectrum actions [66].

Biomaterials may be sealed with antimicrobial chemicals, such as superhydrophobic surfaces or zwitterionic polymers, to prevent germs. In medical implants, polymers provide antibacterial properties by releasing biocides or incorporating contact-killing moieties. Surface-functionalized polymers directly contact biofilms to eliminate bacteria. To reduce risk after implantation, contact-active techniques are effective, killing germs upon touch. Compared to leaching materials, the effectiveness of antimicrobial agents on contact-active materials is more stable [67]. NPs have a small size and a large surface-area-to-volume ratio, making a huge impact even at low concentrations. NPs exhibit antibacterial action by disrupting bacterial cell walls and generating reactive oxygen species. They attach to bacterial metabolic enzymes, limiting respiratory function. The compounds bind to DNA and inhibit metabolic activities, effectively eliminating resistance. Ag, Au, CuO, and ZnO NPs are effective for wound healing, tissue scaffolding, surgical equipment coating, and implants [68].

Smaller NPs exhibit better bacterial effects; for example, particles at 20 nm and 40 nm show enhanced activity compared to types ranging from 90 nm to 210 nm [69]. Smaller particles have a higher surface area for interacting with bacteria. Gold NPs for biomedical applications typically range from 1 to 100 nm. Particles of 2–20 nm are highly applicable for drug delivery, whereas 50–100 nm sizes are used for imaging and photothermal therapy [70, 71]. Copper oxide NPs show similar effectiveness and are available as spheres, rods, or nanowires. CuOs are involved in anticancer and antioxidant activities, deliver good antimicrobial results, and encourage cell prolongation [72].

12.12 Biomaterials Fabrication Process

TE combines clinical, genetic, biotechnological, biomedical, and mechanical engineering fields. It involves complications across several parameters, including surface characterization, material porosity, cell-cell interactions, mechanical properties, solubility, and biodegradation after implantation [73]. Accidents and illnesses such as osteomyelitis, arthritis, anemia, cancer, hereditary multiple exostoses, and hereditary bone marrow failure syndromes can all cause considerable bone, cartilage, and tissue damage. Biomaterials are fabricated based on basic properties determined by analyzing tissue attractions and complexity [74].

Several studies have reported advances in biomaterial manufacturing techniques and the construction of scaffolds that improved cell proliferation, survivability, and printability without causing stress. Plant-based biomaterials, including plant proteins, lignin, polysaccharides, and plant extracts, provide bioactive compounds used to restore and enhance scaffold creation. However, synthetic and animal-derived biomaterials have drawbacks, including high cost, high cell mortality, limited availability, and poor biocompatibility [75, 76].

12.12.1 Solvent Casting

Films protect against microorganisms, preserve gas permeability, and allow for *in-situ* medication delivery while being adaptable to individual morphology. Solvent casting aims to use film dressings as medicine carriers to manage infections and inflammation. Dressings promote wound repair by keeping the area wet, eliminating exudates, and promoting tissue regeneration. However, it is crucial to recognize product limits, such as challenges in treating surface and interior wounds simultaneously [77].

Solvent casting is a common method for producing biomaterial scaffolds due to its affordability, ease of use, and capacity to produce porous structures. It consists of dissolving a polymer in a solvent, potentially adding a porogen (such as salt particles), casting the solution into a mold, and then evaporating the solvent to leave behind a solid matrix [78, 79]. Several studies aim to improve the longevity of biomedical implants, which normally last ten to fifteen years. Metal implants pose issues due to low bioactivity and the emission of harmful ions. Poor bioactivity can lead to fixation issues, requiring revision surgery [80]. Hazardous elements can be released when metals biocorrode quickly. Surface treatment enhances mechanical, chemical, and biological properties when surfaces are exposed to living tissues.

316L SS enhances biological function through the formation of ultra-fine grains on its surface. Reducing grain size from 30 μm to 0.86 μm reduced wear and pitting corrosion resistance while improving local corrosion resistance and nearly doubling hardness (from 172 VHN to 300 VHN). Surface nanotopography can be created with multiple chemicals; for instance, researchers produced a nanotopographic layer of TiO_2 doped with Nb_2O_3 on CP-Ti, improving bonding strength, biocompatibility, and corrosion resistance [81, 82].

Creating composite materials with a metal-ceramic matrix, such as 316L fibers and 45S5 Bioglass, is another option. 316L fiber-reinforced bioceramic scaffolds are made to improve bending strength, fatigue strength, and fracture toughness. Coating approaches combine metal and bioactive characteristics. Bioactive coatings improve implant fixation, reduce mechanical failure (from 1% to 6.9% for fully HA-coated implants), prevent ion release, and prevent fibrous tissue formation. Various coating processes include physical vapor deposition (PVD), plasma spray, laser cladding, and

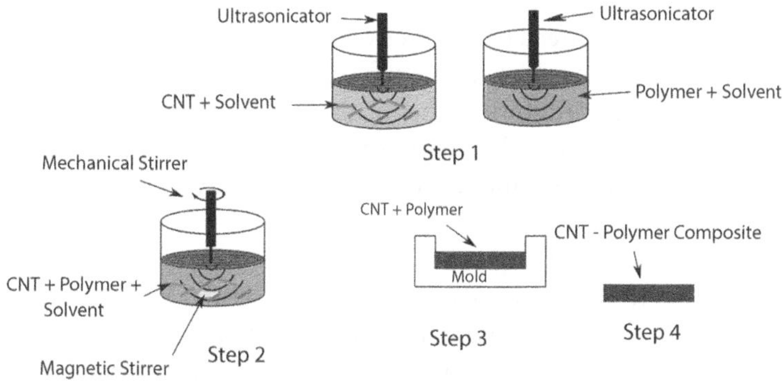

Figure 12.1 Schematic illustration of solvent casting diagram of the solvent casting procedure for creating carbon nanotube (CNT)–polymer composites utilizing a cosolvent approach.

solution-based techniques such as sol–gel and electrochemical deposition [83, 84]. Carbon nanotubes (CNTs, Figure 12.1) contribute to mechanical performance due to their stiffness and strength. Co-solvent methods are also useful for enhancing CNT dispersion, which lowers degradation and improves performance across various scales [85].

12.12.2 Physical Vapor Deposition

Coating technologies are applied, utilized, and marketed in a number of different fields, such as optoelectronics, semiconductors, aircraft, medical technologies, manufacturing, and solar energy. Coatings produced by PVD and chemical vapor deposition are aimed at increasing production quality and energy efficiency. PVD is defined by processing a material into a gas phase and then returning it to a film phase.

Three measures are taken into consideration during PVD: (1) Evaporation, separation, or sputtering are all considered forms of coating material vaporization; (2) migration of coatings occurs as a result of particle collisions; and (3) atoms or molecules are deposited as high-temperature vapor onto a low-temperature substrate [83]. PVD reduces SR and facilitates smooth film deposition. To attain successful thin-film fabrication or deposition on the surface of any material or alloy, it is critical to understand the process and reactions held inside the chamber during the process cycle. It is important to clean the material surface before the process begins, as the adhesion between the material and the coating is highly important; without prior cleaning, the adherent materials can easily peel off. Various researchers report that an ultrasonic bath cleaning process on the substrate is highly recommended. A vacuum sputtering chamber can be used to clean surfaces and subsequently deposit coatings [86].

PVD coatings can offer a barrier between the corrosive environment and the metal to protect the substrate's surface, and this protection is achieved by doping corrosion-inhibiting chemicals into the coating materials. To offer adequate protection, the coating must be pore-free, consistent, and self-healing, as well as promote the connection between bone tissue and the metallic implant [87].

The PVD vacuum coating provides improved corrosion resistance and wear characteristics. Vacuum PVD coating is essential for practical applications such as tools, ornamental items, optical enhancements, molds, dies, and blades. Maintenance of the machine is controllable, and there is an absence of unwanted chemical or physical reactions with the environment. Coatings fabricated using PVD technology offer distinct benefits

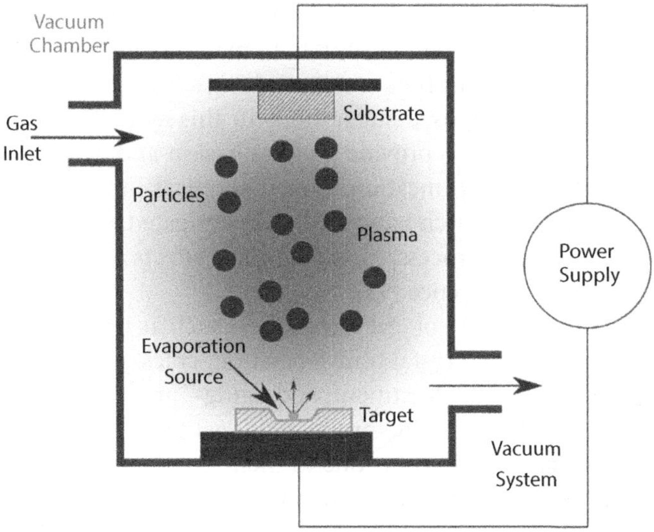

Figure 12.2 Schematic illustration of physical vapor deposition (PVD) process.

that enhance product durability and value. The PVD fabrication process allows for deposition in mono-layer, multilayer, and multigraduated coating systems [88].

In PVD, the material is vaporized from a solid or liquid source using the target's evaporation source, which serves as a cathode. Atomic-sized particles evaporate when heated by an electron beam. These particles are accelerated by collisions between the released particles and the gas molecules added to the chamber. This creates a plasma, which travels through the deposition chamber *via* a vacuum pump to the surface, where it condenses to create a thin coating. PVD is capable of creating both multilayered coatings and thin films. These films may range in thickness from a few nanometers to thousands of nanometers. Figure 12.2 shows a schematic of the PVD procedure [89].

12.12.3 Sol-Gel Technique

In recent years, numerous processes have been used to fabricate biomaterials, and Sol-Gel is one of the most popular and cost-effective ways to achieve biocompatible materials. Preparation involves the creation of a solution (Sol) where Ca and phosphorous (CaP) precursors are used, followed by the addition of two common solvents: distilled water and pure ethanol [90].

Ethanol is typically used to dissolve phosphorous precursors, such as phosphorus pentoxide or triethyl phosphite. A small quantity of water is then added to increase the hydrolysis of the resulting sol.

There are several proposed suggestions in this area. Although sol–gel techniques are expected to provide good adhesion and minimize delamination, the necessary clarifications and theoretical proofs remain complicated. Additional research is needed to investigate the impact of novel precursors on the base process, including their effects on corrosion resistance and substrate adherence [91].

The parameters for the sol–gel technique—such as temperature, molar ratio, curing, hydrolysis, crystal transformation, crack propagation during drying, pH, solvents, heat treatment, and aging—are often unpredictable under the control of the coating process. Sol–gel techniques are currently limited in industrial applications due to their lengthy preparation, aging, and curing times. Additionally, heat treatment can cause phase separation, especially in hybrid coatings [55]. Analyzing and optimizing the sol–gel approach remains challenging.

Sol–gel coating takes several forms, including dip coating, spraying, and spinning. During the sol–gel procedure, the objective is to achieve a uniform solution of precursors and alcohols. To prepare a homogeneous solution, the involvement of alcohol, water, or organic solvents improves solubility and allows the solution to gel easily. Particularly, a precise concentration of a combination of two solvents is used to dissolve the precursors. Metallic organic precursors may need to be dissolved in a water-soluble solvent before being mixed with water, whereas metal salts can easily dissolve in water without the need for an organic solvent [92].

Since HAp degrades at high temperatures, the sol–gel method is appropriate for processing and depositing it due to its low sintering temperature. Several researchers have used the sol–gel method to coat Ti substrates with a thin coating of HAp [93] or functional graded material (FGM) to improve biocompatibility. Because HAp degrades at high temperatures, the sol–gel method is ideal for processing and depositing it due to its low sintering temperature. Several studies have used the sol–gel method to coat Ti substrates with a thin layer of HAp or FGM to improve biocompatibility [94].

A schematic illustration of the sol–gel process in Figure 12.3 illustrates the many phases of the procedure, from the precursor to the aerogel. Salts of varying chemical compositions are combined to create binary or tertiary hybrid systems [95]. The pace of the reaction varies for each of the major salts, and variables such as pH, concentration, solvent type, and temperature all affect how quickly salts react. Voids are joined to form the

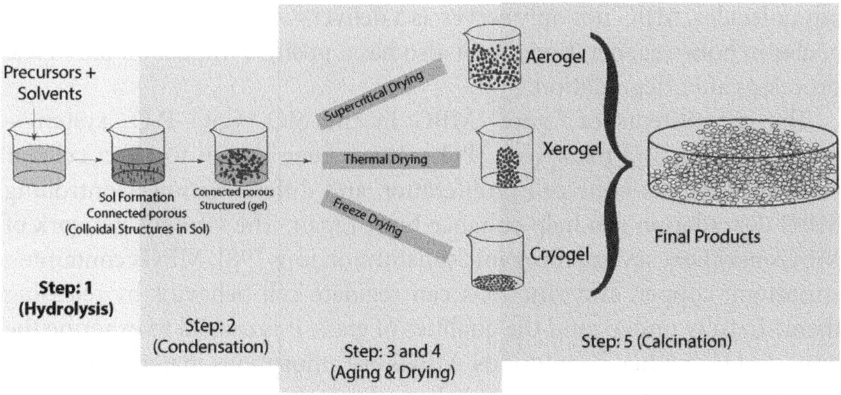

Figure 12.3 Schematic illustration of sol–gel process: from precursor to aerogel.

three-dimensional polymer gel created from the cell density. Volumetric shrinkage causes the gel to solidify and become hard after drying. It should be mentioned that nanosized porosity can be achieved by regulating the drying conditions of the gel. Compared to regular porosity, nanoporosity has the advantage of having a very large specific surface area. For instance, hydrogen can be captured and stored in the porosity of carbon materials by using nanoporous carbon materials [89].

12.12.4 Bioglass Coatings

Bioactive glasses are used on the surface of specific biological locations; these bioglasses (BGs) are applied as thin films using various methods to ensure they adopt or attach to the bone tissue and interact with the biological surroundings. By mimicking the composition of natural bone, these coatings are intended to strengthen the link between the implant and the surrounding tissue. They are widely utilized in metallic implants to combine the glass's bioactivity with the metal's mechanical durability [96].

Combining sol–gel technology with surfactants to create mesoporous bioactive glasses (MBGs) provides a solid foundation for developing multifunctional materials for many applications. MBGs have a highly organized system of channel-like pores ranging from 5–20 nm, a substantial pore volume, and a much higher specific surface area than conventional BGs [97]. Since their creation in the early 2000s, MBGs have been proposed for a number of medicinal uses, either alone or embedded in other biomaterials. They use their distinctive mesostructure to distribute medicines and biomolecules. MBG not only serves as a delivery vehicle for bioactive molecules in bone regeneration, but it also has a positive impact on biological processes after degradation.

The constituents of "pure" MBG in the SiO_2-CaO-P_2O_5 system—namely, Si, Ca, and phosphate (PO_4)—have been shown to affect cellular processes such as bone cell proliferation and differentiation. Controlling MBG degradation can help enhance bone repair. The vitreous network of MBGs may host several inorganic substitution ions [98]. MBGs containing strontium, copper, and zinc ions can regulate cell behavior by releasing them. To fully understand the qualities of glass, it is crucial to examine the impact of individual compounds. MBGs are amorphous materials made of silicate and PO_4 that are covalently bound together.

During stepwise alkoxysilane condensation, oxygen atoms bridge to produce the vitreous network [99]. If this network is disrupted, degradation increases and network stability decreases. By introducing nonbridging oxygen atoms, Ca acts as a network modulator, upsetting the glass network. Changes in Ca content have been linked to variations in MBG degradation, according to earlier research. There is a correlation between the Ca concentration and the surface reactivity of (M)BGs in aquatic environments. The production of carbonated HAp on the glass surface, a sign of bioactivity, is the consequence of a series of surface processes set off by the hydrolysis of Si-OCa bonds and the release of Ca ions. In the vitreous network of (M)BGs, PO_4 plays two roles: the glass network can be strengthened by PO_4 tetrahedral units, which provide connection and degradation resistance, yet PO_4 has also been connected to higher reactivity [100].

12.12.5 Plasma Spray Coating

In the early 1980s, plasma spraying became a popular approach for developing bioceramic coatings on metal components. It quickly became the industry's favored method for formulating HAp coatings for hip prostheses. A form of thermal spray called plasma spraying uses high energy to melt and propel tiny particles onto the surface of a component. Molten particles, known as "droplets," cool and solidify upon contact with the component surface, forming a robust coating with a lamellar structure through heat transfer [101].

Plasma spraying involves creating and using a high-temperature plasma stream within a spray torch. As shown in Figure 12.4, the plasma torch is made up of a cylindrical copper anode and a cone-shaped tungsten

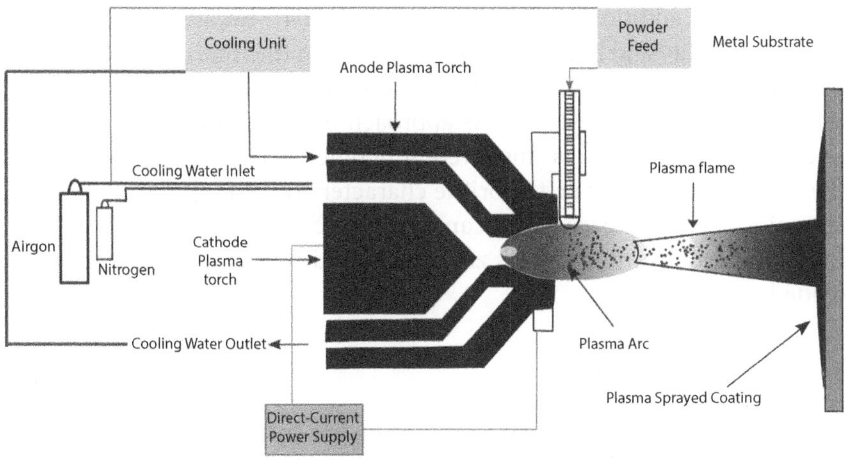

Figure 12.4 Schematic illustration set-up of plasma spray technique.

cathode. When gases are allowed to move between two electrodes and an arc with a high-frequency discharge is initiated, plasma is produced [102].

The gas stream between two electrodes stretches the arc, resulting in a plasma flame emerging from the torch nozzle. The most commonly used arc gases are nitrogen, helium, hydrogen, and argon. Temperatures of 10,000 to 15,000 °C are frequently reached by plasma flames. Almost any material, including metals, ceramics, refractory materials, and oxides, can be coated by plasma spraying. Feedstock materials, such as powder, wire, or rod, are melted in a high-temperature plasma flame during the spraying process [20]. Plasma flames often reach temperatures ranging from 10,000 to 15,000 °C. Plasma spraying can create coatings from practically any substance, including metals, ceramics, refractory materials, and oxides. A high-temperature plasma flame melts feedstock materials, such as powder, wire, or rod, during the spraying process. This approach creates a hard coating with a lamellar structure by using a plasma jet to force melted materials onto the substrate's surface [103].

Ceramic coatings sprayed by plasma not only meet mechanical requirements but also promote tissue and bone cell proliferation, thanks to recent breakthroughs in Ti coating technology. It has been demonstrated that ceramic coatings sprayed with plasma enhance mechanical properties, corrosion resistance, and wear resistance. Bioceramic coatings perform better due to their heat stability, dense microstructure, and chemical composition. Proper heat treatment can impact the mechanical characteristics of coatings in addition to their composition [104]. Because they enhance biocompatibility and bone regeneration between the implant and bone tissue, plasma-sprayed HAp coatings are widely used for surface modification in biomedical implants. This approach for developing HAp coatings offers advantages such as improved adherence between the coating and the component. However, the brittle characteristic of HAp results in weak ceramics. Composite coatings can be created by combining HAp with hard bioinert ceramics such as zirconium oxide, Ti oxide, and aluminum oxide [105].

12.12.6 HAp Coating

An alternative to conventional CaP coating has surfaced in HAp coatings. The bactericidal and osteoinductive properties of HAp are improved by ionic replacements. HAp coatings can improve biomechanical fixation and address pathological conditions including infection and osteoporosis. The discovery of therapeutic elements and ions during the past 50 years has fueled the fast growth of research on substituted HAp coatings. Furthermore, ion incorporation *via* interstitial and substitutive pathways is facilitated by the crystalline structure of HAp. Coatings can help alleviate diseases and speed up bone repair after implantation. The therapeutic applications of metallic implants are expanding beyond their conventional substitutive functions to encompass bone regeneration thanks to substituted HAp coatings and additively made metallic scaffolds. Combining substituted HAp with nanostructures has led to innovative coatings for orthopedic applications [106].

Thermal spraying is a key physical deposition technique for creating HAp coatings. These techniques include heating and spraying coating ingredients (or precursors) on the substrate. Thermal spraying might be atmospheric, vacuum, suspension, liquid phase, high velocity, oxy-fuel, or gas tunnel type, depending on the heating technique. Disparities between the feedstock and deposited layer are unavoidable because of the high temperatures needed for these procedures. Oxyhydroxyapatite (OA) and other CaP phases are produced when deposited and substituted HAp undergoes partial degradation and dehydroxylation. Amorphous calcium phosphate (ACP), α- or β-TCP, OA, HAp, and CaO are examples of multiphase coatings known as HAp coatings. The feedstock material has an impact on the coating composition, as do the cooling ratio and the heating and cooling methods used during the plasma's lifetime [107, 108].

The biocompatibility of a coating is determined by its multiphasic composition, which includes soluble phases such as ACP. In contrast to α-TCP, β-TCP, tetracalcium phosphate, and CaO content, which should not exceed 5% by mass, ISO standards require that the HAp content surpass 95% by mass. The coating crystallinity must be at least 45% of that of normal HAp after 15 hours of calcination at 1000 °C [109]. Charged colloidal HAp particles are deposited onto a conductive substrate with an opposite charge using a physical coating technique called physical deposition. The substrate serves as an electrode, whereas HAp particles are suspended in a liquid media and deposited using a DC electric field. The applied voltage can modify coating thickness and morphology, resulting in increased particle size and deposited HAp. The implant is usually heated to 850 °C to 950 °C under high vacuum after deposition. Electrophoretic deposition is effective for covering porous materials, although it might cause shrinkage and cracking during sintering [110].

Chemical deposition methods differ based on whether they use solutions or suspensions. During the coating process, the feedstock material experiences chemical reactions that, at the end of manufacture, produce a new compound. Temperature, pH, and solution supersaturation have the biggest effects on chemical deposition processes at moderate temperatures. However, the use of nucleators, inhibitors, and other additives can alter coating properties. This process requires pre-conditioning the substrate surface. For Ti implants, pre-treatment with acid or alkaline creates a rich Ti-OH layer, allowing for calcium phosphate nucleation and development [111].

Biomimetic synthesis can improve the biocompatibility of dental and orthopedic implants by producing artificial bone-like HAp using natural production procedures. The most common method is the low-temperature crystallization of nonstoichiometric carbonate-substituted HAp (C-HAp) from physiological fluid simulations. ACP or octacalcium phosphate (OCP) is nucleated during biomimetic HAp crystallization, producing substituted and Ca-deficient HAp (CDHAp). Si-OH, Ti-OH, Zr-OH, and Nb-OH substrates with OH-containing surfaces are necessary for biomimetic deposition, just like for other chemical deposition techniques. These substrates can be produced by acidic or alkaline treatments [112].

Regenerative TE is used in tissue transplantation to restore biological function to tissues or organs. The second most popular tissue transplant is a bone graft. To ensure a successful bone transplant, one must consider aspects such as cost, practicality, biological material, biomechanical and morphological qualities, viability, bone integration, and ethical considerations. Allografts and xenografts are easier to obtain but lack osteogenesis compared to autografts. Although autografts are regarded as the "gold standard" of bone transplantation, their usage in clinics is limited by their disadvantages, which include potential donor site morbidity and vascular injury [113].

Micro-arc oxidation (MAO) is a room-temperature electrochemical method that forms native ceramic layers on value metals such as Al, Mg, and Ti, improving wear and corrosion resistance. MAO electrolytes comprising Ca and P have been used to coat Ti surfaces with HAp. MAO treatment resulted in amorphous films with low Ca and P ion concentration, preventing the formation of crystalline HAp. The researchers hypothesized that the samples lacked sufficient hydroxyl groups, which can induce bone-like apatite, including HAp. Hydrothermal treatment following MAO was proposed to enhance film crystallinity. MAO creates a porous nanostructure on Ti surfaces, leading to improved osseointegration capabilities. MAO-produced nanostructured HAp is a synthetic scaffold that promotes osteoconductivity, osteoinductivity, and angiogenesis on Ti surfaces [114].

The porous scaffold's nano-HAp structure promotes osteoblast growth and endothelial cell angiogenesis. Small diameters on nano-HAp scaffolds can hinder cell proliferation, extracellular matrix (ECM) formation, and neovascularization, making controlled scaffolds crucial for successful bone transplantation. Steam-hydrothermal treatment can regulate the size of porous nanostructures on a Ti surface, affecting osseointegration [115, 116].

The Zn-HAp/Ca silicate coating increased the resistance of CP-Ti to corrosion; however, because of the presence of a secondary phase in the coating, the effect was not exclusively due to Zn in the HAp structure. Various authors have discussed the ideal quantity of Zn to achieve desired biological results. Webster *et al.* found that even small doses of Zn (1.3%) increased osteoblast responses [117]. Strong reactivity to low Zn^{2+} concentrations is beneficial since it limits the quantity of Zn^{2+} that can be incorporated, especially when high-temperature processes are used [118, 119].

Zn-HAp coatings have not been shown to have a favorable effect *in vivo*, and the consequences of Zn^{2+} cation release in bone marrow remain debatable. Through *ex-vivo* studies, Sogo *et al.* created Zn-substituted β-TCP/HAp composites and discovered that a suitable Zn concentration of 0.316% by weight encourages bone growth [120]. The researchers conducted *in vivo* investigations and found that adding Zn to β-TCP had both positive and negative outcomes. This substance undoubtedly showed better bone apposition to the implant surface. Extended studies have revealed heightened bone resorption in the area of the medullary cavity. Substituted HAp coatings are being studied to improve bonding strength with substrates. Bone strength, which is greatly impacted by the coating process, especially at the substrate-coating interface, is greatly impacted by the phase

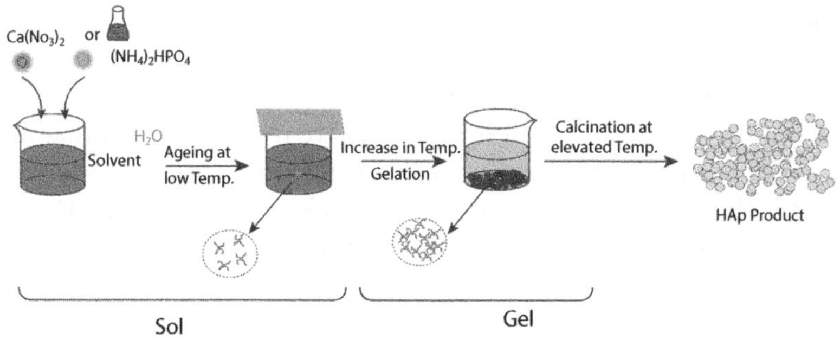

Figure 12.5 Schematic illustration preparation of nanoparticles of HAp.

composition and coating morphology. Ionic replacements may strengthen the interaction between coatings and substrates, according to research. The interfacial properties of Ti substrates and HAp coatings are changed by Zn substitution. This is because Zn^{2+} ions have an impact on the [002] and [211] orientations of HAp crystal formation [121].

Azzaoui *et al.* developed analytical grade reagents (Figure 12.5); Ca nitrate tetrahydrate and di-ammonium hydrogen phosphate served as the first ingredients in the manufacture of HAp. A modified wet chemical technique was used to manufacture HAp. First, 11.76 g of $Ca(NO_3)_2 \cdot 4H_2O$ was dissolved in 100 mL of water at 25 °C. After dissolving 4.06 g of $(NH_4)_2HPO_4$ in 100 mL of water, the solution was added to the $Ca(NO_3)_2 \cdot 4H_2O$ solution over the course of 30 minutes. A Ca/P molar ratio value of 1.67, or a stoichiometric HAp, was obtained by calculating the number of reagents in the solution. The mixture was then combined with polyethylene glycol. During the precipitation reaction, the slurry's pH was digitally monitored and ultimately reached 10.5 [122].

12.13 Tissue Engineering

As the largest organ in the body, the skin performs a number of tasks, including temperature regulation, excretion, protection, and sensory perception. The epidermis, dermis, and subcutaneous fat layer make up the soft, smooth, and elastic skin tissue. Whereas the epidermis has nerve endings but no blood vessels, the dermis and subcutaneous fat layer contain blood vessels, lymphatic vessels, nerves, sweat glands, and hair follicles. Significant skin damage can result from burns, abrasions, trauma, and surgical procedures. Hemostasis, inflammation, proliferation, and tissue remodeling are the four steps that wound healing usually goes through. Temperature, pH, sugar levels, and bacterial infection are examples of external factors that can impact this process.

The epidermis, dermis, and hypodermis are the three layers that make up the skin tissue. Every layer contributes differently to the tissue's functionality. The epidermis, located on the skin's outermost layer, is a thin (<1.5 mm) physiologically active area that is primarily acellular. This zone protects against external environmental pressures such as toxins, infections, UV radiation, and endotoxins. The epidermis not only serves as a barrier but also plays a role in hormone production [123, 124]. Enzymes, stem cell niches, blood vessels, nerves, adipose tissue, muscle fibers, glands, and hair follicles are all found in the dermis, a thick connective tissue that lies under the epidermis.

The hypodermis layer, located underneath the dermis, is made up of vascularized adipose tissue. It strengthens the tissue and regulates its temperature. The skin's three layers have distinct cellularity, functions, mechanical characteristics, biological compositions, and phenotypes. For instance, the outermost, thinner layer is called the epidermis [125]. About 95% of the tissue is composed of fully grown keratinocytes, followed by melanocytes, Langerhans cells, and Merkel cells. The skin's outermost layer is continuously impacted by outside factors. Keratinocytes flow into the epidermal layer, causing cell phenotypes to change frequently. Based on cellular activity and type, the epidermis layer is divided into four types: stratum corneum, stratum granulosum, stratum spinosum, and stratified basale. The dermal proximal layer makes it easier for nutrients to be transported to nearby cells for differentiation [126, 127].

Using 3D printing, bioprinting is a state-of-the-art method for producing intricate biological tissues and organs. 3D bioprinting allows for precise interactions between inorganic biomaterials and live cells. Bioprinting is a promising method for creating composite skin tissue-engineered scaffolds, notwithstanding its early stages [128]. Recent research conducted by our group revealed significant advantages of including bioactive silicates into bioinks for 3D bioprinting multicellular skin replacements. Silicate-based micro/NPs in bioactive inorganic/organic composite bioinks have the potential to both support cells and promote differentiation for tissue regeneration. In order to construct an engineered living system for skin regeneration, bioprinting enables the direct printing of cell-encapsulated bioink with inorganic particles or the layer-by-layer printing of inorganic/organic composite ink with living cells [129].

Raw biomaterials can be easily co-printed using a cutting-edge solvent-free extrusion-based 3D printing method. Composite scaffolds containing a PCL-based polymer matrix, HA, and bioactively enhanced SrHA phases at concentrations of 0%, 10%, and 20% weight percent, respectively, were made using a single-step, solvent-free 3D printing approach [130]. *In vitro* studies showed that SrHA-containing scaffolds had greater mineralization levels than bare PCL and PCL/HAp scaffolds. In rabbit adipose-derived stem cells (ADSCs), the material improved osteogenic differentiation, adhesion, proliferation, and cell infiltration. In rabbit femoral lesions, ADSC-containing Sr10-HA-g-PBLG microcarriers outperformed ADSC-free microcarriers in terms of bone mineralization and regeneration [131].

Scaffolds are used based on two essential factors: the biomaterial used and the construction process. Research has focused on altering and developing novel biomaterials. Any material that interacts with living processes is referred to as a biomaterial. Biomaterials are categorized according to their origin, biodegradability, physical and chemical makeup, and changes throughout time. The tissue being targeted dictates which biomaterial is used. A lot of work has been put into creating biodegradable biomaterials in recent years [132]. Based on their chemical composition, biomaterials can be divided into three categories: ceramics, polymers, and composites. Ca salts and/or inorganic metal complexes make up the majority of ceramic biomaterials. The majority of orthodontic treatments use these biomaterials. Because polymers imitate connective tissues, they are used in soft tissue engineering.

Composite biomaterials are made of polymers and ceramics. Orthopedic and dental TE can benefit from these materials. Both synthetic and natural polymers are frequently used in TE and RM. Natural biomaterials such as alginate, hyaluronic acid, collagen, and chitosan are frequently used due to their abundance, biodegradability, and biocompatibility. Degradation of biomaterials is a crucial characteristic of naturally occurring polymers [133]. Biomaterials in the ECM promote cell compatibility and proliferation. Collagen, a naturally occurring biomaterial, is frequently used in scaffolds for numerous purposes. These proteins are widespread and can be used across species without causing immunogenic responses. Among the commercially available collagen-based scaffold materials are Contigen, Zyplast, Zyderm, and Collagen Meniscal Implant. Another naturally occurring scaffolding material that is frequently used is chitosan. Chitosan's molecular structure is comparable to hyaluronic acid, another ECM component [134, 135].

The acetylation level affects the rate of disintegration of this biomaterial. Intact ECM is a new method for producing scaffolds from biomaterials that exist naturally. Decellularization is used to prepare organs and tissues from many animals. By removing the cellular components, this method maintains the entire ECM. Many people have been treated clinically with scaffolds of xenogenic origin [136]. Typically, bioprinting uses 3D printing techniques based on extrusion and inkjet processes. Two kinds of 3D printed structures are available for TE and RM: cell-laden scaffolds for tissue imitation and acellular scaffolds, which contain biological components. Mini-tissue building blocks, autonomous self-assembly, and biomimicry are the three main strategies used in 3D bioprinting. Whereas autonomous self-assembly uses early embryonic components to construct their own ECM, cell signaling, and architecture, biomimicry replicates biological components to mimic live tissue. Putting together the tiniest structural and functional components of a tissue to create a larger tissue or organ is known as mini-tissue manufacturing [137, 138]. Combining these three methods is required to produce intricate, multifunctional tissues.

Inkjet printing involves layering biological materials onto a build platform to create a desired structure. Thermal actuation or piezoelectric actuation are used to create droplets. Whereas thermal actuation uses a heating element to vaporize the biomaterial and deposit droplets, piezoelectric droplet generation uses voltage pulses to induce pressure changes [139, 140]. The speed, accuracy, and wide compatibility of inkjet printers with biomaterials are well known. Precise and detailed prints can be produced by printers that have good control over droplet size and deposition velocity. Biomaterials are extruded from the printer using mechanical or pneumatic pressure in extrusion-based bioprinting. With this method, adding cells and bioactive materials is simple and does not require heating [141, 142]. Extrusion-based 3D printing makes it easier to use and provides a wider variety of possibilities by enabling a continuous flow of biomaterials, such as polymers, decellularized matrices, and cell-laden hydrogels [143, 144], as well as spheroids and aggregates [145].

12.14 Conclusion

Biomaterials can influence an immunological response. The characteristics of the biomaterials—such as surface topography, particle size, porosity, pore size, and ion release—dictate the type of interaction. The biological behaviors of bone cells are significantly impacted by elements of degraded materials and chemical cues released by the interaction of the immune system with implants, which in turn affects the outcome of bone regeneration. This paper evaluates the most regularly utilized biomaterials. The article provides an overview of biomaterials, including metals, polymers, ceramics, and composites. Each type is discussed in detail, including their characteristics and applications in medical devices. TE may alter biomaterials, but it still relies on them. RM reduces the demand for synthetic materials in the body. Many applications will continue to require synthetics, and biomaterials are expected to be needed long beyond the century.

AI disclosure statement: The author confirms that no artificial intelligence (AI)-generated content or AI-assisted writing tools were used in the preparation of this chapter (including summaries and the abstract). All text, analysis, and conclusions are the result of the author's original work.

References

1. Huo, Y., Lyu, Y., Bosiakov, S., Han, F., A critical review of the design, manufacture, and evaluation of bone joint replacements for bone repair. *Materials*, 15, 153, 2021.
2. Zielińska, A., Karczewski, J., Eder, P., Kolanowski, T., Szalata, M., Wielgus, K., Szalata, M., Kim, D., Shin, S.R., Słomski, R., *et al.*, Scaffolds for drug delivery and tissue engineering: The role of genetics. *J. Controlled Release*, 359, 207–223, 2023.
3. Rodrigo-Navarro, A., Sankaran, S., Dalby, M.J., del Campo, A., Salmeron-Sanchez, M., Engineered living biomaterials. *Nat. Rev. Mater.*, 6, 1175–1190, 2021.
4. de Buffrénil, V., Quilhac, A., Bone tissue types: a brief account of currently used categories, in: *Vertebrate Skeletal Histology and Paleohistology*, pp. 147–190, Taylor & Francis, CRC Press, 2021.
5. Sun, Y., Bai, Y., Yang, W., Bu, K., Tanveer, S.K., Hai, J., Global trends in natural biopolymers in the 21st century: a scientometric review. *Front. Chem.*, 10, 915648, 2022.
6. Chu, S., Wang, A.L., Bhattacharya, A., Montclare, J.K., Protein based biomaterials for therapeutic and diagnostic applications. *Prog. Biomed. Eng.*, 4, 012003, 2021.
7. Rabiee, N., Dokmeci, M.R., Zarrabi, A., Makvandi, P., Saeb, M.R., Karimi-Maleh, H., Jafarzadeh, S., Karaman, C., Yamauchi, Y., Warkiani, M.E., *et al.*, *Green Biomaterials: fundamental principles*, vol. 1, pp. 1–4, Taylor & Francis, 2023.
8. Glauser, R. and Schupbach, P., Early bone formation around immediately placed two-piece tissue-level zirconia implants with a modified surface: an experimental study in the miniature pig mandible. *Int. J. Implant Dent.*, 8, 37, 2022.
9. Obiedat, Q., The modern main changes in dental implants surfaces. *Smile Dent. J.*, 14, 10–24, 2019.

10. Bružauskaitė, I., Bironaitė, D., Bagdonas, E., Bernotienė, E., Scaffolds and cells for tissue regeneration: different scaffold pore sizes—different cell effects. *Cytotechnology*, 68, 355–369, 2016.
11. Bauer, S., Schmuki, P., Von Der Mark, K., Park, J., Engineering biocompatible implant surfaces: Part I: Materials and surfaces. *Prog. Mater. Sci.*, 58, 261–326, 2013.
12. Gutiérrez Púa, L.D.C., Rincón Montenegro, J.C., Fonseca Reyes, A.M., Zambrano Rodrıǵuez, H., Paredes Méndez, V.N., Biomaterials for orthopedic applications and techniques to improve corrosion resistance and mechanical properties for magnesium alloy: a review. *J. Mater. Sci.*, 58, 3879–3908, 2023.
13. Brash, J.L., Horbett, T.A., Latour, R.A., Tengvall, P., The blood compatibility challenge. Part 2: Protein adsorption phenomena governing blood reactivity. *Acta Biomater.*, 94, 11–24, 2019.
14. Li, Y., Qi, Y., Gao, Q., Niu, Q., Shen, M., Fu, Q., Hu, K., Kong, L., Effects of a micro/nano rough strontium-loaded surface on osseointegration. *Int. J. Nanomedicine*, 4549–4563, 2015.
15. Gugulothu, B., Rao, G.K.M., Rao, D.H., Influence of drinking water and graphite powder concentration on electrical discharge machining of Ti-6Al-4V alloy. *Mater. Today Proc.*, 27, 294–300, 2020.
16. Popov, S., Paderin, N., Chistiakova, E., Sokolova, A., Konyshev, I.V., Belozerov, V.S., Byvalov, A.A., Swelling, protein adsorption, and biocompatibility of pectin–chitosan hydrogels. *Gels*, 10, 472, 2024.
17. Teimouri, R., Abnous, K., Taghdisi, S.M., Ramezani, M., Alibolandi, M., Protein-Based Hybrid Scaffolds: Application in Bone Tissue Engineering. *J. Polym. Environ.*, 32, 4102–4129, 2024.
18. Egbo, M.K., A fundamental review on composite materials and some of their applications in biomedical engineering. *J. King Saud Univ.-Eng. Sci.*, 33, 557–568, 2021.
19. Rahmati, M., Silva, E.A., Reseland, J.E., Heyward, C.A., Haugen, H.J., Biological responses to physicochemical properties of biomaterial surface. *Chem. Soc. Rev.*, 49, 5178–5224, 2020.
20. Thakur, A., Kumar, A., Kaya, S., Marzouki, R., Zhang, F., Guo, L., Recent advancements in surface modification, characterization and functionalization for enhancing the biocompatibility and corrosion resistance of biomedical implants. *Coatings*, 12, 1459, 2022.
21. Mahmoodi, M. and Ghazanfari, L., Fundamentals of biomedical applications of biomorphic SiC, in: *Properties and Applications of Silicon Carbide*, pp. 297–344, INTECH Open Access Publisher, 2011.
22. Omarov, S., Nauryz, N., Talamona, D., Perveen, A., Surface modification techniques for metallic biomedical alloys: A concise review. *Metals*, 13, 82, 2022.
23. Hourmand, M., Sarhan, A.A.D., Farahany, S., Sayuti, M., Microstructure characterization and maximization of the material removal rate in nano-powder mixed EDM of Al-Mg 2 Si metal matrix composite—ANFIS and RSM approaches. *Int. J. Adv. Manuf. Technol.*, 101, 2723–2737, 2019.

24. Kassapidou, M., Hjalmarsson, L., Johansson, C.B., Johansson, P.H., Morisbak, E., Wennerberg, A., Stenport, V.F., Cobalt–chromium alloys fabricated with four different techniques: Ion release, toxicity of released elements and surface roughness. *Dent. Mater.*, 36, e352–e363, 2020.
25. Niinomi, M., Titanium and its alloys, in: *Encyclopedia of Biomaterials and Biomedical Engineering*, Taylor & Francis, 2005.
26. Chen, L.-Y., Cui, Y.-W., Zhang, L.-C., Recent development in beta titanium alloys for biomedical applications. *Metals*, 10, 1139, 2020.
27. Niinomi, M. and Boehlert, C.J., Titanium alloys for biomedical applications, in: *Advances in Metallic Biomaterials: Tissues, Materials and Biological Reactions*, pp. 179–213, Springer Berlin Heidelberg, Berlin, Heidelberg, 2015.
28. Niinomi, M., Liu, Y., Nakai, M., Liu, H., Li, H., Biomedical titanium alloys with Young's moduli close to that of cortical bone. *Regener. Biomater.*, 3, 173–185, 2016.
29. Festas, A.J., Ramos, A., Davim, J.P., Medical devices biomaterials–A review. *Proc. Inst. Mech. Eng., Part L: J. Mater.: Des. Appl.*, 234, 218–228, 2020.
30. Alawadhi, A.A., The Effect of Reduced Sulphur Species on the Localised Corrosion of Stainless Steels, 1999.
31. Oladele, I.O., Onuh, L.N., Agbeboh, N.I., Alewi, D.D., Lephuthing, S.S., The relationship and functional links between human age, growth, and biomedical implants: A review on the application of bulk and nanomaterials. *Nano Select*, 4, 419–441, 2023.
32. Davis, R., Singh, A., Jackson, M.J., Coelho, R.T., Prakash, D., Charalambous, C.P., Ahmed, W., da Silva, L.R.R., Lawrence, A.A., A comprehensive review on metallic implant biomaterials and their subtractive manufacturing. *Int. J. Adv. Manuf. Technol.*, 120, 1473–1530, 2022.
33. Hayashi, K., Kishida, R., Tsuchiya, A., Ishikawa, K., Honeycomb blocks composed of carbonate apatite, β-tricalcium phosphate, and hydroxyapatite for bone regeneration: effects of composition on biological responses. *Mater. Today Bio.*, 4, 100031, 2019.
34. Islam, M.K., Phase equilibria study of the CaO-Al2O3-SiO2-(Na2O/B2O3) slag system to recover valuable metals from e-waste, 2023.
35. Fernandez de Grado, G., Keller, L., Idoux-Gillet, Y., Wagner, Q., Musset, A.-M., Benkirane-Jessel, N., Bornert, F., Offner, D., Bone substitutes: a review of their characteristics, clinical use, and perspectives for large bone defects management. *J. Tissue Eng.*, 9, 2041731418776819, 2018.
36. Chauhan, N.P.S., JABGID, N.K., Punjabi, P.B., *et al.*, Polyurethanes: silicone-polyurethane copolymers and, *Polyurethane*, 13, 6712–6723, 2015.
37. Sokolsky-Papkov, M., Agashi, K., Olaye, A., Shakesheff, K., Domb, A.J., Polymer carriers for drug delivery in tissue engineering. *Adv. Drug Deliv. Rev.*, 59, 187–206, 2007.
38. Kaczmarek, B., Sionkowska, A., Chitosan/collagen blends with inorganic and organic additive—A review. *Adv. Polym. Technol.*, 37, 2367–2376, 2018.

39. Kumar, R., Singh, N., Singh, R., An introduction of biodegradable polymers, modes of biodegradation and designing of biodegradable polymers. *Res. J. Pharm. Technol.*, 10, 625–640, 2017.
40. Lechner, M.D., Polymers, in: *Springer Handbook of Materials Data*, pp. 489–540, Springer International Publishing, Cham, 2018, 489–540.
41. Geanaliu-Nicolae, R.-E. and Andronescu, E., Blended natural support materials—collagen based hydrogels used in biomedicine. *Materials*, 13, 5641, 2020.
42. Rodriguez, A.J., Guzman, M.E., Lim, C.-S., Minaie, B., Mechanical properties of carbon nanofiber/fiber-reinforced hierarchical polymer composites manufactured with multiscale-reinforcement fabrics. *Carbon*, 49, 937–948, 2011.
43. Aherwar, A., Singh, A.K., Patnaik, A., Cobalt Based Alloy: A Better Choice Biomaterial for Hip Implants. *Trends Biomater. Artif. Organs*, 30, 2016.
44. Yang, X., Mechanical behaviour of Ti-12Mo-6Zr-2Fe (TMZF) β-titanium alloy in physiological environments, 2017.
45. Niinomi, M., Recent progress in research and development of metallic structural biomaterials with mainly focusing on mechanical biocompatibility. *Mater. Trans.*, 59, 1–13, 2018.
46. Barazanchi, A., Li, K.C., Al-Amleh, B., Lyons, K., Waddell, J.N., Mechanical properties of laser-sintered 3D-printed cobalt chromium and soft-milled cobalt chromium. *Prosthesis*, 2, 28, 2020.
47. de la Peña O′ Shea, V.A., de la Piscina, P.R., Homs, N., Aromi, G., Fierro, J.L.G., Development of hexagonal closed-packed cobalt nanoparticles stable at high temperature. *Chem. Mater.*, 21, 5637–5643, 2009.
48. Pilliar, R.M., Metallic biomaterials, in: *Biomedical Materials*, pp. 1–47, Springer International Publishing, Cham, 2021.
49. Alaribe, F.N., Manoto, S.L., Motaung, S.C.K.M., Scaffolds from biomaterials: advantages and limitations in bone and tissue engineering. *Biologia*, 71, 353–366, 2016.
50. Nikolova, M.P. and Chavali, M.S., Recent advances in biomaterials for 3D scaffolds: A review. *Bioact. Mater.*, 4, 271–292, 2019.
51. Villiger, M., Stoop, R., Vetsch, T., Hohenauer, E., Pini, M., Clarys, P., Pereira, F., Clijsen, R., Evaluation and review of body fluids saliva, sweat and tear compared to biochemical hydration assessment markers within blood and urine. *Eur. J. Clin. Nutr.*, 72, 69–76, 2018.
52. Ahmed, M.M.M. and Imae, T., Electrochemical properties of a thermally expanded magnetic graphene composite with a conductive polymer. *Phys. Chem. Chem. Phys.*, 18, 10400–10410, 2016.
53. Barui, S., 3D inkjet printing of biomaterials: Principles and applications. *Med. Devices Sens.*, 4, e10143, 2021.
54. Mishra, A. and Srivastava, V., Biomaterials and 3D printing techniques used in the medical field. *J. Med. Eng. Technol.*, 45, 290–302, 2021.

55. Xia, H., Li, X., Gao, W., Fu, X., Fang, R.H., Zhang, L., Zhang, K., Tissue repair and regeneration with endogenous stem cells. *Nat. Rev. Mater.*, 3, 174–193, 2018.
56. Levin, M., Pezzulo, G., Finkelstein, J.M., Endogenous bioelectric signaling networks: exploiting tage gradients for control of growth and form. *Annu. Rev. Biomed. Eng.*, 19, 353–387, 2017.
57. Muskovich, M. and Bettinger, C.J., Biomaterials-based electronics: polymers and interfaces for biology and medicine. *Adv. Healthc. Mater.*, 1, 248–266, 2012.
58. Dai, B., Guo, J., Gao, C., Yin, H., Xie, Y., Lin, Z., Recent advances in efficient photocatalysis *via* modulation of electric and magnetic fields and reactive phase control. *Adv. Mater.*, 35, 2210914, 2023.
59. Khan, I., Morishita, S., Higashinaka, R., Matsuda, T.D., Aoki, Y., Kuzmann, E., Homonnay, Z., Katalin, S., Pavić, L., Kubuki, S., Synthesis, characterization and magnetic properties of ε-Fe2O3 nanoparticles prepared by sol-gel method. *J. Magn. Magn. Mater.*, 538, 168264, 2021.
60. Wei, H., Cui, J., Lin, K., Xie, J., Wang, X., Recent advances in smart stimuli-responsive biomaterials for bone therapeutics and regeneration. *Bone Res.*, 10, 17, 2022.
61. Shamsipur, M., Ghavidast, A., Pashabadi, A., Phototriggered structures: Latest advances in biomedical applications. *Acta Pharm. Sin. B*, 13, 2844–2876, 2023.
62. Gaihre, B., Ashraf, S., Spinks, G.M., Innis, P.C., Wallace, G.G., Comparative displacement study of bilayer actuators comprising of conducting polymers, fabricated from polypyrrole, poly (3, 4-ethylenedioxythiophene) or poly (3, 4-propylenedioxythiophene). *Sens. Actuators A: Phys.*, 193, 48–53, 2013.
63. Tang, B., Xie, X., Lu, J., Huang, W., Yang, J., Tian, J., Lci, L., Designing biomaterials for the treatment of autoimmune diseases. *Appl. Mater. Today*, 39, 102278, 2024.
64. Koshy, S.T. and Mooney, D.J., Biomaterials for enhancing anti-cancer immunity. *Curr. Opin. Biotechnol.*, 40, 1–8, 2016.
65. Gottenbos, B., Busscher, H.J., Van Der Mei, H.C., Nieuwenhuis, P., Pathogenesis and prevention of biomaterial centered infections. *J. Mater. Sci. Mater. Med.*, 13, 717–722, 2002.
66. Asadi, N., Del Bakhshayesh, A.R., Davaran, S., Akbarzadeh, A., Common biocompatible polymeric materials for tissue engineering and regenerative medicine. *Mater. Chem. Phys.*, 242, 122528, 2020.
67. Bhattacharjee, B., Ghosh, S., Patra, D., Haldar, J., Advancements in release-active antimicrobial biomaterials: A journey from release to relief. *WIRES Nanomed. Nanobiotechnol.*, 14, e1745, 2022.
68. Chong, W.J., Shen, S., Li, Y., Trinchi, A., Simunec, D.P., Kyratzis, I.L., Sola, A., Wen, C., Biodegradable PLA-ZnO nanocomposite biomaterials with antibacterial properties, tissue engineering viability, and enhanced biocompatibility. *Smart Mater. Manuf.*, 1, 100004, 2023.

69. Nicolae-Maranciuc, A., Chicea, D., Chicea, L.M., Ag nanoparticles for biomedical applications—Synthesis and characterization—A review. *Int. J. Mol. Sci.*, 23, 5778, 2022.
70. Woźniak, A., Malankowska, A., Nowaczyk, G., Grześkowiak, B.F., Tuśnio, K., Słomski, R., Zaleska-Medynska, A., Jurga, S., Size and shape-dependent cytotoxicity profile of gold nanoparticles for biomedical applications. *J. Mater. Sci. Mater. Med.*, 28, 1–11, 2017.
71. Daraee, H., Eatemadi, A., Abbasi, E., Fekri Aval, S., Kouhi, M., Akbarzadeh, A., Application of gold nanoparticles in biomedical and drug delivery. *Artif. Cells Nanomed. Biotechnol.*, 44, 410–422, 2016.
72. Naz, S., Gul, A., Zia, M., Javed, R., Synthesis, biomedical applications, and toxicity of CuO nanoparticles. *Appl. Microbiol. Biotechnol.*, 107, 1039–1061, 2023.
73. Modaresifar, K., Ganjian, M., Angeloni, L., Minneboo, M., Ghatkesar, M.K., Hagedoorn, P.-L., Fratila-Apachitei, L.E., Zadpoor, A.A., On the Use of Black Ti as a Bone Substituting Biomaterial: Behind the Scenes of Dual-Functionality. *Small*, 17, 2100706, 2021.
74. Chen, F.-M. and Liu, X., Advancing biomaterials of human origin for tissue engineering. *Prog. Polym. Sci.*, 53, 86–168, 2016.
75. Gomes, A. and Sobral, P.J.d.A., Plant protein-based delivery systems: An emerging approach for increasing the efficacy of lipophilic bioactive compounds. *Molecules*, 27, 60, 2021.
76. Bahú, J.O., de Andrade, L.R.M., de Melo Barbosa, R., Crivellin, S., da Silva, A.P., Souza, S.D.A., Cárdenas Concha, V.O., Severino, P., Souto, E.B., Plant polysaccharides in engineered pharmaceutical gels. *Bioengineering*, 9, 376, 2022.
77. Ghosal, K., Chandra, A., Snigdha, S., Roy, S., Agatemor, C., Thomas, S., Provaznik, I., Electrospinning over solvent casting: tuning of mechanical properties of membranes. *Sci. Rep.*, 8, 5058, 2018.
78. Amani, H., Arzaghi, H., Bayandori, M., Dezfuli, A.S., Pazoki-Toroudi, H., Shafiee, A., Moradi, L., Controlling cell behavior through the design of biomaterial surfaces: a focus on surface modification techniques. *Adv. Mater. Interfaces*, 6, 1900572, 2019.
79. Lubineau, G. and Rahaman, A., A review of strategies for improving the degradation properties of laminated continuous-fiber/epoxy composites with carbon-based nanoreinforcements. *Carbon*, 50, 2377–2395, 2012.
80. Ibrahim, M.Z.A.A., Laser Cladding of FeCrMoCB Metallic Glass on Nickel-Free Stainless-steel to Develop Durable and Cost-effective Biomedical Implants, 2019.
81. Faisal, N.H., Prathuru, A., Ahmed, R., Rajendran, V., Hossain, M., Venkatachalapathy, V., Katiyar, N.K., Li, J., Liu, Y., Cai, Q., *et al.*, Application of thermal spray coatings in electrolysers for hydrogen production: advances, challenges, and opportunities. *ChemNanoMat*, 8, e202200384, 2022.

82. Sivaprakash, V. and Narayanan, R., Anodic synthesis of TiO2 nanotubes by step-up tages. *J. Compos. Mater.*, 55, 3775–3784, 2021.
83. Jones, A.C. and Hitchman, M.L., Overview of chemical vapour deposition, in: *Chemical Vapour Deposition: Precursors, Processes and Applications,* vol. 1, pp. 1–36, Royal Society of Chemistry, London, UK, 2009.
84. Sivaprakash, V. and Narayanan, R., Anodic synthesis of TiO2 nanotubes influence of water content and the analysis of the nano-mechanical application. *J. Bio Tribo-Corros.*, 6, 105, 2020.
85. Yaqoob, S., Ali, Z., Ali, S., D'Amore, A., Polystyrene–carbon nanotube composites: Interaction mechanisms, preparation methods, structure, and rheological properties—A review. *Physchem*, 5, 14, 2025.
86. Baptista, A., Silva, F.J.G., Porteiro, J., Mıǵuez, J.L., Pinto, G., Fernandes, L., On the physical vapour deposition (PVD): evolution of magnetron sputtering processes for industrial applications. *Procedia Manuf.*, 17, 746–757, 2018.
87. Pereira, H.F., Cengiz, I.F., Silva, F.S., Reis, R.L., Oliveira, J.M., Scaffolds and coatings for bone regeneration. *J. Mater. Sci. Mater. Med.*, 31, 1–16, 2020.
88. Ahanger, Z.A., Saleem, S.S., Dey, A., Physical vapour deposition technologies of functionally graded coatings. *Proc. Inst. Mech. Eng. Part L J. Mater. Des. Appl.*, 14644207251332077, 2025.
89. Mattox, D.M., *Handbook of physical vapor deposition (PVD) processing*, pp. 1–945, William Andrew, 2010.
90. Han, J.-H., Pack, S.P., Chung, S., Solvo-hydrothermal synthesis of calcium phosphate nanostructures from calcium inositol hexakisphosphate precursor in water-ethanol mixed solutions. *Korean J. Chem. Eng.*, 37, 891–897, 2020.
91. Wang, H., Zhu, Y., Hu, Z., Zhang, X., Wu, S., Wang, R., Zhu, Y., A novel electrodeposition route for fabrication of the superhydrophobic surface with unique self-cleaning, mechanical abrasion and corrosion resistance properties. *Chem. Eng. J.*, 303, 37–47, 2016.
92. Wilson, A.M., Bailey, P.J., Tasker, P.A., Turkington, J.R., Grant, R.A., Love, J.B., Solvent extraction: the coordination chemistry behind extractive metallurgy. *Chem. Soc. Rev.*, 43, 123–134, 2014.
93. Mohammad, N.F., Ahmad, R.N., Rosli, N.M., Manan, M.A., Marzuki, M., Wahi, A., Sol gel deposited hydroxyapatite-based coating technique on porous titanium niobium for biomedical applications: A mini review. *Mater. Today Proc.*, 41, 127–135, 2021.
94. Yılmaz, E., Kabataş, F., Gökçe, A., Fındık, F., Production and characterization of a bone-like porous Ti/Ti-hydroxyapatite functionally graded material. *J. Mater. Eng. Perform.*, 29, 6455–6467, 2020.
95. Bokov, D., Turki Jalil, A., Chupradit, S., Suksatan, W., Javed Ansari, M., Shewael, I.H., Valiev, G.H., Kianfar, E., Nanomaterial by sol-gel method: synthesis and application. *Adv. Mater. Sci. Eng.*, 2021, 5102014, 2021.
96. Joy-anne, N.O., Su, Y., Lu, X., Kuo, P.-H., Du, J., Zhu, D., Bioactive glass coatings on metallic implants for biomedical applications. *Bioact. Mater.*, 4, 261–270, 2019.

97. El-Fiqi, A., Buitrago, J.O., Yang, S.H., Kim, H.-W., Biomimetically grown apatite spheres from aggregated bioglass nanoparticles with ultrahigh porosity and surface area imply potential drug delivery and cell engineering applications. *Acta Biomater.*, 60, 38–49, 2017.
98. Migneco, C., Fiume, E., Verné, E., Baino, F., A guided walk through the world of mesoporous bioactive glasses (MBGs): fundamentals, processing, and applications. *Nanomaterials*, 10, 2571, 2020.
99. Schumacher, M., Habibovic, P., Van Rijt, S.J.B.M., Mesoporous bioactive glass composition effects on degradation and bioactivity. *Bioact. Mater.*, 6, 1921–1931, 2021.
100. Abodunrin, O.D., El Mabrouk, K., Bricha, M., A review on borate bioactive glasses (BBG): effect of doping elements, degradation, and applications. *J. Mater. Chem. B*, 11, 955–973, 2023.
101. Yi, H., Qi, L., Luo, J., Zhang, D., Li, H., Hou, X., Effect of the surface morphology of solidified droplet on remelting between neighboring aluminum droplets. *Int. J. Mach. Tools Manuf.*, 130, 1–11, 2018.
102. Prashar, G. and Vasudev, H., Thermal sprayed composite coatings for biomedical implants: a brief review. *J. Therm. Spray Eng.*, 2, 50–55, 2020.
103. Fanelli, F. and Fracassi, F., Atmospheric pressure non-equilibrium plasma jet technology: general features, specificities and applications in surface processing of materials. *Surf. Coat. Technol.*, 322, 174–201, 2017.
104. Huang, R., Sone, M., Ma, W., Fukanuma, H., The effects of heat treatment on the mechanical properties of cold-sprayed coatings. *Surf. Coat. Technol.*, 261, 278–288, 2015.
105. Tiwari, N., Preparation and Characterization of Hydroxyapatite-Alumina-Zirconia Composite, 2017.
106. Mondal, S.V., Dorozhkin, S., Pal, U., Recent progress on fabrication and drug delivery applications of nanostructured hydroxyapatite. *WIRES*, 10, e1504, 2018.
107. Sarraf, M., Rezvani Ghomi, E., Alipour, S., Ramakrishna, S., Sukiman, N.L., A state-of-the-art review of the fabrication and characteristics of titanium and its alloys for biomedical applications. *Bio-Des. Manuf.*, 1–25, 2021.
108. Navarrete-Segado, P., Tailoring calcium phosphate powder properties for additive manufacturing, 2021.
109. Yan, B., Zhang, Y., Chen, G., Shan, R., Ma, W., Liu, C., The utilization of hydroxyapatite-supported CaO-CeO2 catalyst for biodiesel production. *Energy Convers. Manage.*, 130, 156–164, 2016.
110. Dorozhkin, S.V., There are over 60 ways to produce biocompatible calcium orthophosphate (CaPO4) deposits on various substrates. *J. Compos. Sci.*, 7, 273, 2023.
111. Mahmod, D.S.B.A., Sintering of Zirconium Diboride-Silicon Carbide (ZrB2-SIC) and Titanium Dibor'ide-Silicon Carbide (TiB2-SIC) Ceramic Composites and Laser Surface Treatment: Application in Low Temperature Protonic Ceramic Fuel Cells (LTPCFCs), 2017.

112. Vatanatham, M., Surface nucleation of hydroxyapatite onto titanium substrates thermally treated with oxygen, 2000.
113. Arcos, D. and Vallet-Regí, M., Substituted hydroxyapatite coatings of bone implants. *J. Mater. Chem. B*, 8, 1781–1800, 2020.
114. Baldwin, P., Li, D.J., Auston, D.A., Mir, H.S., Yoon, R.S., Koval, K.J., Autograft, allograft, and bone graft substitutes: clinical evidence and indications for use in the setting of orthopaedic trauma surgery. *J. Orthop. Trauma*, 33, 203–213, 2019.
115. Wang, R., Ni, S., Ma, L., Li, M., Porous construction and surface modification of titanium-based materials for osteogenesis: A review. *Front. Bioeng. Biotechnol.*, 10, 973297, 2022.
116. Xie, H., Li, C., Wang, Q., A critical review on performance and phase separation of thermosetting epoxy asphalt binders and bond coats. *Constr. Build. Mater.*, 326, 126792, 2022.
117. Webster, T.J., Massa-Schlueter, E.A., Smith, J.L., Slamovich, E.B., Osteoblast response to hydroxyapatite doped with divalent and trivalent cations. *Biomaterials*, 25, 2111–2121, 2004.
118. Chillemi, G., D'Angelo, P., Pavel, N.V., Sanna, N., Barone, V., Development and validation of an integrated computational approach for the study of ionic species in solution by means of effective two-body potentials. The case of Zn2+, Ni2+, and Co2+ in aqueous solutions. *J. Am. Chem. Soc.*, 124, 1968–1976, 2002.
119. Vidilli, A.L., Afonso, C.R.M., Kiminami, C.S., Amigo, V.B., Amigo, A.M., Riva, R., *et al.*, Laser cladding of high energy ball milled powder of nanocrystalline Ti-Fe-Nb-Sn alloys, 2016.
120. Sogo, Y., Sakurai, T., Onuma, K., Ito, A., The most appropriate (Ca+ Zn)/P molar ratio to minimize the zinc content of ZnTCP/HAP ceramic used in the promotion of bone formation. *J. Biomed. Mater. Res.*, 62, 457–463, 2002.
121. Garbo, C., Locs, J., D'Este, M., Demazeau, G., Mocanu, A., Roman, C., Horovitz, O., Tomoaia-Cotisel, M., Advanced Mg, Zn, Sr, Si multi-substituted hydroxyapatites for bone regeneration. *Int. J. Nanomedicine*, 1037–1058, 2020.
122. Azzaoui, K., Lamhamdi, A., Mejdoubi, E., Berrabah, M., Elidrissi, A., Hammouti, B., Zaoui, S., Yahyaoui, R., Synthesis of nanostructured hydroxyapatite in presence of polyethylene glycol 1000. *J. Chem. Pharm. Res.*, 5, 1209–1216, 2013.
123. Prescott, S.L., Larcombe, D.-L., Logan, A.C., West, C., Burks, W., Caraballo, L., Levin, M., Etten, E.V., Horwitz, P., Kozyrskyj, A., *et al.*, The skin microbiome: impact of modern environments on skin ecology, barrier integrity, and systemic immune programming. *World Allergy Organ. J.*, 10, 1–16, 2017.
124. Thakur, L. and Vasudev, H., *Thermal Spray Coatings*, CRC Press, 2021.
125. Biggs, L.C., Kim, C.S., Miroshnikova, Y.A., Wickström, S.A., Mechanical forces in the skin: roles in tissue architecture, stability, and function. *J. Invest. Dermatol.*, 140, 284–290, 2020.

126. Brandner, J.M. and Schulzke, J.D., Hereditary barrier-related diseases involving the tight junction: lessons from skin and intestine. *Cell Tissue Res.*, 360, 723–748, 2015.
127. Rezaei, M., Davani, F., Alishahi, M., Masjedi, F., Updates in immunocompatibility of biomaterials: applications for regenerative medicine. *Expert Rev. Med. Devices*, 19, 353–367, 2022.
128. Chen, J., Fan, Y., Dong, G., Zhou, H., Du, R., Tang, X., Ying, Y., Li, J., Designing biomimetic scaffolds for skin tissue engineering. *Biomater. Sci.*, 11, 3051–3076, 2023.
129. Fang, H., Xu, J., Ma, H., Liu, J., Xing, E., Cheng, Y.Y., Wang, H., Nie, Y., Pan, B., Song, K., Functional materials of 3D bioprinting for wound dressings and skin tissue engineering applications: A review. *Int. J. Bioprint.*, 9, 757, 2023.
130. You, J., Zhang, Y., Zhou, Y., Strontium functionalized in biomaterials for bone tissue engineering: A prominent role in osteoimmunomodulation. *Front. Bioeng. Biotechnol.*, 10, 928799, 2022.
131. Borciani, G., Ciapetti, G., Vitale-Brovarone, C., Baldini, N., Strontium functionalization of biomaterials for bone tissue engineering purposes: a biological point of view. *Materials*, 15, 1724, 2022.
132. Song, R., Murphy, M., Li, C., Ting, K., Soo, C., Zheng, Z., Current development of biodegradable polymeric materials for biomedical applications. *Drug Des. Devel. Ther.*, 3117–3145, 2018.
133. Mndlovu, H., Kumar, P., du Toit, L.C., Choonara, Y.E., A review of bio material degradation assessment approaches employed in the biomedical field. *Npj Mater. Degrad.*, 8, 66, 2024.
134. Almalik, A., Donno, R., Cadman, C.J., Cellesi, F., Day, P.J., Tirelli, N., Hyaluronic acid-coated chitosan nanoparticles: Molecular weight-dependent effects on morphology and hyaluronic acid presentation. *J. Control. Release*, 172, 1142–1150, 2013.
135. Arokiasamy, P., Abdullah, M.M.A.B., Abd Rahim, S.Z., Luhar, S., Sandu, A.V., Jamil, N.H., Nabiałek, M., Synthesis methods of hydroxyapatite from natural sources: A review. *Ceram. Int.*, 48, 14959–14979, 2022.
136. Wong, M.L., Wong, J.L., Vapniarsky, N., Griffiths, L.G., *In vivo* xenogeneic scaffold fate is determined by residual antigenicity and extracellular matrix preservation. *Biomaterials*, 92, 1–12, 2016.
137. Kang, D., Hong, S., Kim, S.-J., Choi, H., Kim, K., Jang, J., Robotics-assisted modular assembly of bioactive soft materials for enhanced organ fabrication. *Virtual Phys. Prototyping*, 19, e2390484, 2024.
138. Azari, R., Rezaie, H.R., Khavandi, A., Effect of titanium dioxide intermediate layer on scratch and corrosion resistance of sol–gel-derived HA coating applied on Ti-6Al-4V substrate. *Prog. Biomater.*, 10, 259–269, 2021.
139. Li, L., Wu, E., Jia, K., Yang, K., Temperature field regulation of a droplet using an acoustothermal heater. *Lab Chip*, 21, 3184–3194, 2021.
140. Gil-Chávez, G.J., Villa, J.A., Ayala-Zavala, J.F., Heredia, J.B., Sepulveda, D., Yahia, E.M., González-Aguilar, G.A., Technologies for extraction and

production of bioactive compounds to be used as nutraceuticals and food ingredients: An overview. *Compr. Rev. Food Sci. Food Saf.*, 12, 5–23, 2013.
141. Ming, X., Wu, Y., Zhang, Z., Li, Y., Micro-arc oxidation in titanium and its alloys: Development and potential of implants. *Coatings*, 13, 2064, 2023.
142. Obagi, Z.A.I.D.A.L., Damiani, G., Grada, A., Falanga, V.I.N.C.E.N.T., *et al.*, Principles of wound dressings: a review. *Surg. Technol. Int.*, 35, 0–57, 2019.
143. Yang, C.-W. and Lui, T.-S., Hydrothermal Crystallization with Microstructural Self-Healing Effect on Mechanical and Failure Behaviors of Plasma-Sprayed Hydroxyapatite Coatings, in: *Biological and Biomedical Coatings Handbook: Processing and Characterization,* p. 237, CRC Press, 2011.
144. Rao, K.M., Rao, K.S.K., Ha, C.-S., Stimuli responsive poly (vinyl caprolactam) gels for biomedical applications. *Gels*, 2, 6, 2016.
145. Sharma, S.J., Gupta, R., Gupta, M., Advanced testing and biocompatibility strategies for sustainable biomaterials. *Biotechnol. Sustain. Mater.*, 1, 18, 2024.

13

Sustainable Supply Chain Management and Procurement Strategies

S. Deepika

Department of Civil Engineering, Sri Krishna College of Engineering and Technology, Coimbatore, Tamil Nadu, India

Abstract

The rising transition toward circular economy models has made sustainable supply chain management and procurement strategies central to achieving environmental, social, and economic resilience in manufacturing. This chapter provides a detailed explanation of how procurement, as a key function of the supply chain, can promote the circularity cycle through methods such as green sourcing, active supplier collaboration, life-cycle costing, and closed-loop resource use. Using recent frameworks and international case studies, the discussion also shows how ethical concerns—such as labor rights, fair trade, and transparency—shape procurement choices that influence global, multitier supply chains. At the same time, it acknowledges the most important challenges, including the need to balance cost efficiency with sustainability, manage risks in global sourcing, and overcome the absence of common sustainability benchmarks. By combining theory with practice, the chapter lays out a pathway for embedding sustainability into procurement—from supplier evaluation and contract design to monitoring performance. Ultimately, it argues that sustainable procurement is not just about compliance but a strategic necessity that strengthens competitiveness, lowers environmental impacts, and delivers long-term value for all stakeholders within circular manufacturing systems.

Keywords**:** Sustainable procurement, supply chain strategies, green sourcing, ethical sourcing, supplier engagement, life-cycle costing, circular manufacturing

Email: deepikongu13@gmail.com

Jeyaprakash Natarajan, Milon Selvam Dennison, M. Bhuvanesh Kumar and Ganapathy Thirukkotti (eds.) Manufacturing and the Circular Economy, (407–428) © 2027 Scrivener Publishing LLC

13.1 Introduction

Sustainable supply chain management (SSCM) is now widely recognized as a driving force in the global transition toward a circular economy [1]. Unlike traditional supply chains, which tend to prioritize short-term cost reduction, operational efficiency, and faster delivery, SSCM broadens the focus to include minimizing environmental damage, upholding social responsibility, and ensuring long-term economic resilience [2]. In this context, procurement functions as a cornerstone because the choices made at the sourcing stage strongly influence the flow of materials, supplier practices, and the overall sustainability profile of a manufacturing system [3].

Circular manufacturing requires procurement strategies that go beyond conventional cost-based decision-making. Increasingly, organizations are selecting renewable, recyclable, and reusable materials while also encouraging suppliers to implement eco-efficient processes and socially responsible policies [4]. These practices not only support closed-loop production systems but also strengthen long-term supplier relationships and improve transparency across supply chains [5]. Green procurement, supplier collaboration, and life cycle–oriented purchasing are thus emerging as practical tools for achieving circularity. Importantly, these tools are no longer seen as simple compliance measures; instead, they are viewed as strategic levers that enhance competitiveness in industries facing intense global pressure to meet sustainability targets [6].

International examples demonstrate this shift in action. Leading multinational corporations are adopting circular procurement policies to cut waste generation, extend the useful life of products, and adapt to evolving regulatory requirements [7]. For instance, the European Union's Circular Economy Action Plan has motivated companies across diverse industries to redesign sourcing and procurement policies in ways that align with both business goals and broader environmental standards [4]. At the same time, firms are increasingly aware that sustainability commitments influence customer trust, investor confidence, and long-term market positioning [8].

Despite these positive trends, integrating sustainability into procurement is not without challenges. Organizations must balance cost efficiency with environmental and social objectives, manage risks in global sourcing networks, and address the persistent lack of standardized sustainability indicators [9]. These hurdles highlight the need for frameworks that combine theoretical insights with practical tools to support decision-makers [10]. By embedding sustainability considerations directly into procurement—from evaluating suppliers and drafting contracts to monitoring performance—companies can ensure that circular economy principles are not just aspirational goals but operational realities [11].

Ultimately, SSCM demonstrates that sustainable procurement is far more than a regulatory or compliance requirement. It represents a strategic imperative that helps firms achieve resilience, reduce environmental footprints, and deliver long-term value to all stakeholders [12]. When applied thoughtfully, procurement becomes a transformative function that can accelerate the shift toward circular manufacturing ecosystems [13].

Ethical considerations are another critical dimension of SSCM [5]. Beyond environmental performance and cost efficiency, procurement must address social concerns such as labor rights, fair trade, and the responsible sourcing of materials from regions that often present complex social and political risks [8]. As stakeholder awareness grows and consumers increasingly demand transparency, organizations are being held accountable for ensuring that sustainability principles are embedded in their contracts, supplier selection criteria, and ongoing evaluations. Integrating measurable sustainability indicators into procurement practices not only helps to mitigate reputational risks but also builds trust and credibility across markets [14].

However, the path toward fully sustainable procurement remains challenging. High costs associated with eco-friendly materials, limited supplier readiness to adopt new practices, and the absence of universally accepted sustainability benchmarks create significant barriers [15]. Additionally, managing multitier global supply chains—where visibility often diminishes beyond the first tier—further complicates efforts to monitor compliance and ensure responsible practices [16]. The procurement roles in circular economy manufacturing is shown in Figure 13.1.

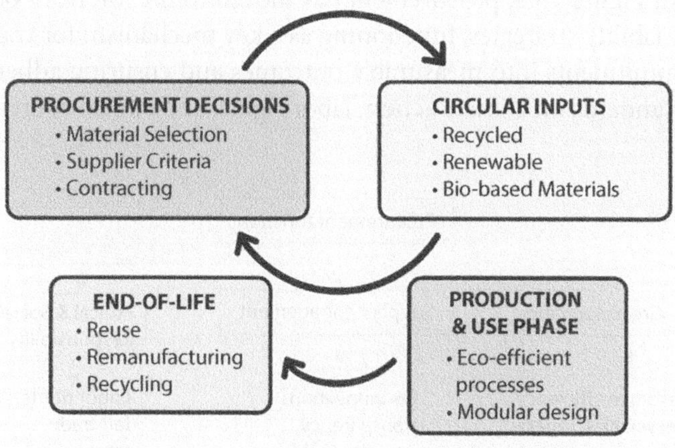

Figure 13.1 Procurement roles in circular economy manufacturing.

Overcoming these barriers requires a multifaceted approach. Innovative procurement strategies, such as performance-based contracting or incentivized supplier engagement, can help align economic and sustainability goals. Collaborative partnerships between firms, suppliers, and policymakers are essential to drive industry-wide progress [17]. The adoption of digital technologies, such as blockchain for traceability and big data analytics for supplier risk assessment, also provides promising avenues for enhancing transparency and accountability [18]. Coupled with strong policy support, these measures can create the structural conditions needed to embed ethics and sustainability into the heart of supply chain management [19].

This chapter examines the changing role of procurement in shaping circular and sustainable supply chains. It highlights green sourcing strategies, supplier engagement models, ethical frameworks, and proven practices that organizations can use to align their procurement activities with the principles of a circular economy [8]. By weaving together theoretical perspectives, real-world case studies, and practical applications, the discussion seeks to offer valuable insights for both scholars and practitioners committed to advancing sustainable and responsible manufacturing [4].

Over the past decade, procurement has undergone a significant transformation. Once regarded mainly as a transactional cost center focused on price negotiation and contract administration, it is now recognized as a strategic driver of sustainability, resilience, and innovation [20]. This shift has been accelerated by rising regulatory requirements, growing stakeholder expectations, and the widespread acknowledgment that supply chains represent the largest share of a company's environmental and social impact [20]. As a evidence from Figure 13.2, procurement has moved to the forefront of corporate sustainability strategies, functioning as a key mechanism for translating policy commitments into measurable outcomes and ensuring adherence to evolving standards on climate action, labor rights, and ethical sourcing [21].

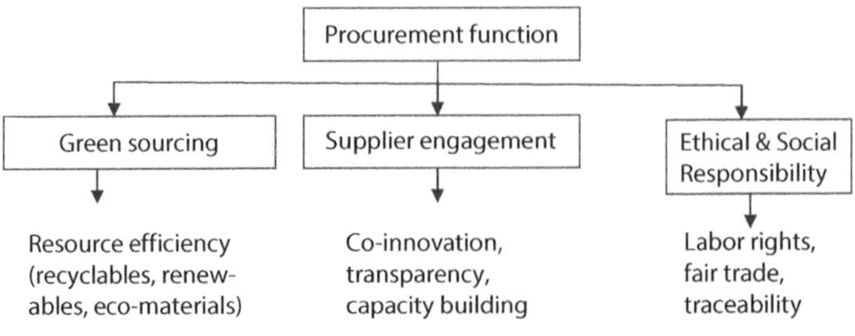

Figure 13.2 Procurement roles in circular economy manufacturing (flowchart).

A notable milestone in this transformation has been the incorporation of sustainability metrics into supplier performance evaluations [22]. Traditional measures such as price, lead time, and quality are now increasingly complemented by indicators that assess carbon intensity, waste reduction efforts, gender equity, and ethical governance practices [23]. This multidimensional framework enables organizations to move beyond short-term cost considerations and instead select suppliers based on their capacity to contribute to long-term resilience, innovation, and shared value creation [24].

Procurement's role in advancing the circular economy extends far beyond the choice of sustainable materials. It now encompasses the creation of collaborative ecosystems where buyers, suppliers, and regulators work together to codevelop products, processes, and systems that reduce resource dependency and support closed-loop supply chains [25]. Such collaboration has proven especially critical in resource-intensive sectors such as construction, electronics, and textiles, where procurement decisions directly affect both upstream resource extraction and downstream waste management [26].

At the same time, rapid advances in digital technologies are reshaping procurement's influence over sustainability governance [3]. Tools such as blockchain, Internet of Things (IoT) sensors, and advanced analytics provide real-time visibility across supply networks, enhance traceability of raw materials, and enable predictive decision-making that aligns with environmental and social priorities. As procurement becomes increasingly data-driven, its capacity to embed accountability and transparency throughout global value chains continues to expand [27].

Ultimately, the success of sustainable and circular procurement lies in balancing economic performance with social and environmental imperatives. Organizations that adopt this integrated approach not only mitigate risks and maintain regulatory compliance but also enhance competitiveness by appealing to consumers, investors, and stakeholders who value ethical and responsible business practices. This shift underscores the importance of procurement professionals cultivating new skills, fostering cross-sector partnerships, and championing innovative business models that connect day-to-day purchasing decisions with long-term sustainability goals [28].

13.2 Role of Sustainable Procurement

Sustainable procurement is increasingly recognized as the cornerstone of circular manufacturing because it connects resource efficiency with responsible sourcing practices. Unlike conventional procurement, which primarily focuses on minimizing costs and achieving short-term efficiency, sustainable procurement emphasizes the use of renewable, recyclable, and biodegradable inputs while embedding environmental and social considerations into supplier selection and contract management [28]. By adopting these principles, organizations can reduce dependence on virgin resources and promote closed-loop material flows, thereby aligning operational strategies with the broader objectives of a circular economy [29].

From a strategic perspective, procurement has shifted from being a purely transactional function to a value-creating mechanism that directly shapes corporate sustainability outcomes. Incorporating sustainability criteria—such as carbon footprint reduction, life-cycle costing, and supplier innovation capacity—into tendering processes strengthens compliance with regulatory frameworks while also improving resilience against market volatility and supply chain disruptions [30]. For example, procurement policies that prioritize bio-based plastics or recycled metals help stimulate secondary material markets, generating economic incentives for circular resource recovery [31].

At the operational level, sustainable procurement fosters long-term partnerships with suppliers that adopt eco-certifications, closed-loop logistics, and product stewardship practices. These approaches not only reduce environmental impacts but also enhance organizational reputation and strengthen competitive advantage [17]. Nonetheless, challenges remain—particularly the difficulty of harmonizing sustainability standards across diverse global supply networks and managing the cost premiums often associated with sustainable materials. Addressing these barriers requires collaborative industry approaches, the application of digital technologies

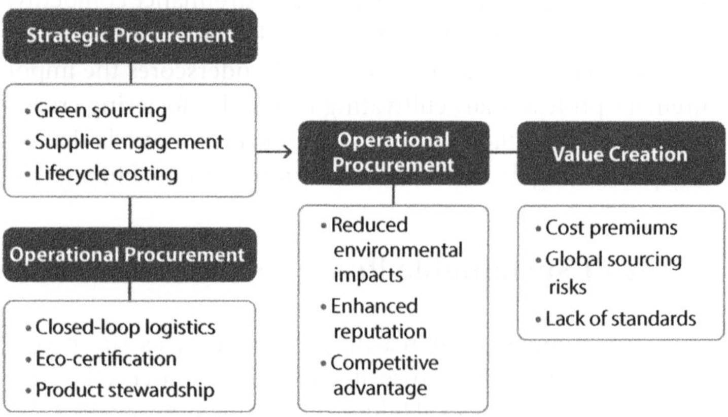

Figure 13.3 Framework of sustainable procurement in circular manufacturing.

for supply chain traceability, and a stronger alignment between corporate strategies and sustainability performance indicators.

In summary, as per the Figure 13.3 sustainable procurement operates both as a practical tool and a strategic lever for advancing circular manufacturing. By embedding environmental, social, and governance (ESG) considerations into procurement processes, organizations can drive systemic transformation, lower ecological footprints, and generate long-term value for stakeholders.

13.3 Green Procurement Strategies

Green procurement represents a forward-looking approach to sourcing, where organizations intentionally prioritize goods and services that meet environmental standards across the supply chain. Unlike conventional purchasing, which often centers on cost savings and lead times, green procurement evaluates suppliers against criteria such as energy efficiency, recyclability, reduced toxicity, and lower carbon emissions. By integrating these considerations, companies not only reduce the ecological footprint of their operations but also stimulate innovation in sustainable product design and material use.

Within circular manufacturing, green procurement plays an enabling role by supporting closed-loop systems in which resources are recovered, reused, and repurposed. Examples include firms adopting biodegradable packaging, renewable energy inputs, or modular construction materials that extend product life cycles and minimize waste. Such practices align closely with global initiatives such as the European Union's Circular Economy Action Plan, which advances eco-design standards and extended producer responsibility (EPR) policies.

At a strategic level, adopting green procurement calls for a shift in supplier engagement models. Instead of short-term, transactional arrangements, companies increasingly develop long-term partnerships based on coinnovation, shared knowledge, and certification compliance. Life-cycle costing has also become a core consideration, ensuring that environmental and social impacts are measured across the entire product use phase, rather than being overshadowed by upfront price comparisons.

Despite its promise, the implementation of green procurement is not without obstacles. Common barriers include the limited availability of eco-certified suppliers, higher procurement costs, and the absence of harmonized sustainability standards across industries and regions. Addressing these challenges requires capacity-building among supply chain actors, stronger regulatory support, and the integration of digital technologies—such as blockchain and artificial intelligence (AI)—to improve transparency, traceability, and accountability in sourcing practices.

In conclusion, green procurement provides a foundation for embedding circularity within manufacturing systems. By aligning purchasing decisions with broader ecological and social objectives, organizations can build more resilient supply chains that balance environmental responsibility

Table 13.1 Key differences between traditional procurement and sustainable procurement.

Dimension	Traditional procurement	Sustainable procurement
Primary focus	Cost minimization, efficiency, and lead time	Triple bottom line: economic, environmental, and social value
Supplier selection	Based on price and delivery performance	Includes sustainability criteria (eco-certification, ethics, labor standards)
Materials	Preference for cheapest available inputs	Preference for renewable, recyclable, or eco-friendly materials
Life-cycle perspective	Limited to purchase and immediate use	Full product life cycle considered (design, use, disposal, recovery)
Risk management	Financial and delivery risks	Broader risks including environmental, reputational, and regulatory
Contracting approach	Short-term, transactional contracts	Long-term, collaborative partnerships with suppliers
Performance measurement	Based on cost savings and on-time delivery	Includes carbon footprint reduction, social compliance, and circularity indicators
End-of-life management	Disposal without responsibility	Closed-loop strategies: reuse, remanufacturing, recycling

Source: Compiled by author from Kumar *et al.*, [57]; Ahi & Searcy, [58].

with long-term business competitiveness. Table 13.1 shows the key difference between traditional and sustainable procurement.

13.4 Supplier Engagement and Collaboration in Sustainable Procurement

Supplier engagement is central to sustainable procurement, as an organization's sustainability is strongly influenced by the practices of its upstream partners [32]. Effective engagement goes beyond transactional relationships by building trust, fostering collaboration, and aligning suppliers with ESG objectives [33, 34].

A key approach to achieving this is through sustainability-oriented evaluation systems, which incorporate eco-certifications, emissions reporting, labor standards, and compliance with EPR regulations. Many firms also rely on supplier scorecards and audits to monitor performance and encourage continuous improvement [34]. Beyond monitoring, collaborative programs with suppliers—such as codeveloping recyclable packaging, modular construction components, or low-carbon transport solutions—redefine procurement as a source of shared value and align it with circular economy principles.

Table 13.2 presents four key approaches to engaging suppliers in sustainable procurement. Evaluation and monitoring involve assessing supplier compliance with sustainability standards through tools such as scorecards and audits, ensuring accountability and mitigating risks. Collaborative innovation emphasizes joint development with suppliers to create solutions like recyclable packaging or modular components, transforming procurement into a driver of shared value and product innovation. Digital integration, using technologies such as blockchain and AI, enhances transparency, enables real-time monitoring of supplier performance, and supports predictive risk assessment across multitier supply chains [35]. Finally, supplier capacity building focuses on addressing knowledge and resource gaps among smaller suppliers through training and technical support, fostering more inclusive and resilient networks [36]. Despite these advances, challenges persist. Small- and medium-sized suppliers often lack the expertise or resources to meet strict sustainability standards, creating asymmetries in buyer–supplier relationships. Addressing these gaps requires investment in supplier training, knowledge transfer, and capacity-building initiatives, making sustainability a shared responsibility across the value chain.

In summary, Table 13.2 shows the evidence of supplier engagement goes well beyond compliance [36]. When approached strategically, it enables

Table 13.2 Approaches to supplier engagement in sustainable procurement.

Engagement strategy	Description	Expected benefits	Example tools/ practices
Evaluation and monitoring	Assess supplier compliance with sustainability criteria	Risk reduction, accountability	Scorecards, third-party audits
Collaborative innovation	Joint development of sustainable solutions	Shared value creation, product innovation	Codesign of recyclable packaging, modular systems
Digital integration	Use of digital platforms for transparency	Real-time traceability, predictive risk management	Blockchain, AI-based analytics
Supplier capacity building	Support SMEs with resources and training	Inclusive sustainability, stronger networks	Training programs, technical support

coinnovation of circular solutions, strengthens supply chain resilience, and ensures that sustainability commitments extend across the entire network.

13.5 Ethical Procurement Framework

Ethical and responsible procurement represents a key advancement in SSCM, combining environmental stewardship with social justice and good governance. Beyond simply choosing eco-friendly materials or implementing closed-loop systems, ethical procurement ensures that purchasing decisions uphold human rights, support fair labor practices, promote diversity, and prevent corruption throughout global supply chains [37].

In recent years, international initiatives such as the United Nations Global Compact, the OECD Guidelines for Multinational Enterprises, and ISO 20400 (the Sustainable Procurement Standard) have set clear expectations for organizations to integrate ethical principles into procurement policies. These frameworks encourage companies to extend accountability beyond first-tier suppliers, reaching deeper into the supply chain where risks of child labor, unsafe working conditions, and exploitative practices are often most significant [38].

At the heart of ethical procurement lies the principle of responsible sourcing, which focuses on acquiring materials and services in ways that minimize harm while maximizing positive impact. In industries such as construction and electronics, responsible sourcing involves avoiding conflict minerals, using fair-trade certified inputs, and ensuring the traceability of raw materials. Similarly, in food and textiles, ethical procurement promotes gender equity, living wages, and environmentally sustainable agricultural practices [39].

Technological innovations are increasingly transforming the practice of responsible procurement. Blockchain provides an unalterable record of material origins, enhancing transparency across supply chains, whereas AI allows real-time monitoring of supplier compliance with ethical and sustainability standards [40]. Together, these tools help organizations move beyond reactive audits toward proactive risk management, integrating social and environmental performance into procurement decisions.

Despite these technological advances, operationalizing ethical procurement remains challenging. The absence of harmonized global standards, the high costs of certification, and the limited capacity of small- and medium-sized enterprises (SMEs) to meet stringent requirements often slow widespread adoption. Addressing these obstacles requires investment in supplier development initiatives, collaborative auditing systems, and cross-industry partnerships that facilitate knowledge sharing and reduce compliance burdens [2].

In conclusion, ethical and responsible procurement extends sustainability principles by embedding fairness, transparency, and accountability throughout global value chains. When implemented effectively, these frameworks not only mitigate regulatory and reputational risks but also enhance stakeholder trust, strengthen supply chain resilience, and generate shared value for both society and the environment [41].

Figure 13.4 illustrates how ethical and responsible procurement is grounded in the three pillars of ESG, and how these dimensions collectively guide procurement strategies to achieve sustainable outcomes [42].

1. **Environmental Dimension**
   - Focuses on incorporating green sourcing practices, reducing carbon footprints, and utilizing circular inputs such as recyclable, renewable, and eco-friendly materials in procurement decisions.
   - Ensures that suppliers align with climate targets and principles of resource efficiency, supporting long-term environmental sustainability.

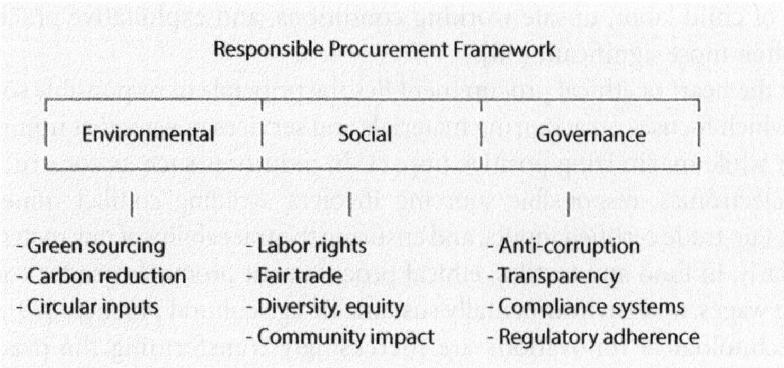

Figure 13.4 Ethical and responsible procurement framework.

2. **Social Dimension**
   - Prioritizes the protection of labor rights, promotion of fair trade, and advancement of diversity, equity, and inclusion, while contributing to the well-being of local communities.
   - Encourages procurement policies that prevent exploitative practices, including child labor, unsafe working conditions, and wage disparities.
3. **Governance Dimension**
   - Focuses on anticorruption measures, transparency in supplier relationships, and adherence to international regulations such as ISO 20400, OECD guidelines, and the UN Global Compact.
   - Establishes accountability frameworks that make procurement decisions traceable, auditable, and aligned with ethical standards.

An often-overlooked aspect of ethical procurement is the connection between local and global supply networks [34]. Whereas multinational corporations face pressure to adhere to international ethical standards, small local suppliers may lack the knowledge, resources, or infrastructure to meet these expectations. In such cases, organizations implementing ethical frameworks should go beyond mere enforcement and actively support capacity building by offering training, shared technology platforms, and financial assistance [32]. By doing so, compliance shifts from being a punitive requirement to a collaborative pathway toward sustainable practices.

Another important development is stakeholder-driven accountability. Consumers, investors, and civil society groups are increasingly demanding transparency in corporate procurement decisions. ESG-focused investment funds assess how procurement strategies align with long-term ethical objectives, whereas consumer advocacy promotes product labeling and certification schemes [43]. This growing scrutiny requires companies to integrate responsible procurement into corporate reporting and disclosure mechanisms, moving from internal compliance toward external legitimacy.

Strategically, ethical procurement is no longer just about minimizing risks; it also provides a source of competitive advantage [44]. Organizations that embed responsible sourcing practices often benefit from stronger supplier relationships, enhanced brand reputation, and improved resilience in responding to disruptions such as geopolitical conflicts or global pandemics. For example, companies with transparent, ethically managed supply chains were able to adapt sourcing strategies more effectively during COVID-19, highlighting the resilience benefits of ethical frameworks [45].

The integration of digital governance is also shaping ethical procurement. Modern procurement platforms with built-in compliance modules allow organizations to define supplier requirements, track progress, and generate audit-ready reports. When combined with blockchain-enabled traceability, these systems reduce information asymmetry and provide real-time visibility into supplier performance. This convergence of governance and technology demonstrates that ethical procurement is no longer a standalone CSR activity but an essential part of enterprise-wide risk management and strategic planning [46].

Looking ahead, the trajectory of ethical procurement is shifting from voluntary adoption to formal regulation. Governments across the EU, US, and Asia are introducing laws on supply chain due diligence, modern slavery, and carbon reporting, requiring companies to embed ethical procurement into their legal compliance frameworks [45]. As regulatory pressures increase, aligning procurement practices with ESG standards will become both a reputational necessity and a legal imperative.

13.6 Sustainable Procurement Metrics & Tools

Successfully implementing sustainable procurement requires effective tools and performance indicators that enable organizations to evaluate, monitor, and continuously improve their practices. Such measurement frameworks help procurement professionals balance economic efficiency with environmental and social objectives, ensuring that procurement strategies align with broader corporate sustainability goals and global regulatory standards [5].

Evaluating sustainable procurement calls for a comprehensive toolkit capable of capturing economic viability, environmental responsibility, and social accountability simultaneously. One of the most widely used instruments is lifecycle costing (LCC), which goes beyond traditional price-focused decision-making by assessing the total cost of ownership for goods and services over their entire lifecycle—from acquisition and operation to maintenance and eventual disposal [47].

By offering a long-term economic perspective, LCC enables decision-makers to weigh upfront expenditures against enduring benefits such as lower maintenance costs, improved energy efficiency, and reduced disposal expenses. In this way, procurement shifts from being a purely transactional function to a strategic lever for creating long-term value [48].

In addition to economic considerations, organizations are increasingly adopting Carbon and Environmental Footprint Assessments to measure the ecological impacts of their procurement activities, including greenhouse gas emissions, water usage, and resource depletion. Often aligned with internationally recognized standards such as ISO 14040/14044, these assessments help companies identify environmental externalities and uncover opportunities for decarbonization and improved resource efficiency across complex, multitier supply chains [49].

To ensure that sustainability goals are translated into actionable accountability, many organizations implement Supplier Sustainability Scorecards. These tools provide a structured framework for evaluating

Table 13.3 Indicators for measuring sustainable procurement.

Dimension	Indicators
Economic	Life-cycle cost savings, procurement efficiency, supplier innovation capacity
Environmental	Carbon footprint reduction, renewable/recyclable materials usage, waste diversion rate
Social	Labor rights compliance, fair-trade inputs, diversity in supplier base
Governance	Contract transparency, anticorruption compliance, regulatory adherence

supplier performance against ESG criteria, covering aspects such as labor rights compliance, emissions reduction, ethical sourcing, and adherence to circular economy principles [50].

From Table 13.3 by linking these evaluations to performance-based incentives or contractual obligations, companies encourage continuous improvement and embed sustainability expectations directly into supplier relationships. In doing so, procurement becomes a strategic lever for promoting responsible practices throughout the entire value chain [19].

Beyond individual firm assessments, standardized global frameworks such as the Global Reporting Initiative (GRI) and ESG metrics provide widely recognized benchmarks that enhance comparability and transparency in reporting sustainability outcomes related to procurement [51]. These frameworks transform broad sustainability commitments into concrete, measurable indicators, fostering stakeholder trust while ensuring alignment with investor expectations, regulatory requirements, and international sustainability standards.

The ongoing digital transformation of procurement further strengthens these measurement capabilities by providing unprecedented transparency, traceability, and predictive insight [23]. Blockchain technology offers immutable records of material origins, reducing risks of fraud, counterfeiting, and unethical sourcing, while building confidence among stakeholders across global networks. AI equips procurement professionals with predictive analytics to anticipate supplier risks, forecast sustainability performance, and identify optimization opportunities in real time [52]. Similarly, the IoT generates continuous data on supplier emissions, energy consumption, and resource use, closing the information gaps that have historically limited visibility in multitier supply chains [53]. The following Figure 13.5 shows the distribution of tools for measuring sustainable procurement.

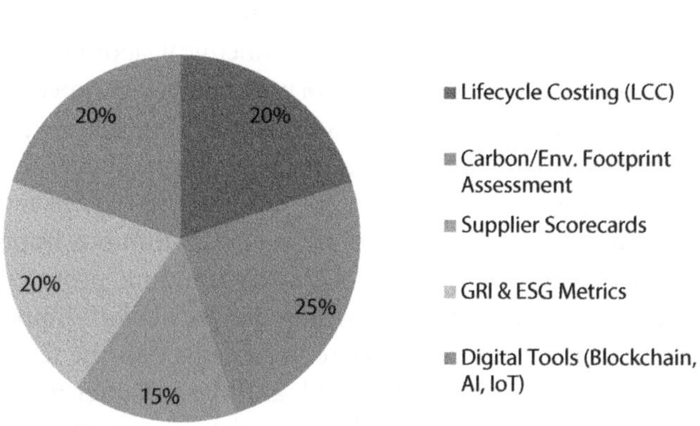

Figure 13.5 Distributions of tools for measuring sustainable procurement.

Together, these digital tools shift procurement from retrospective auditing toward proactive, data-driven governance, integrating sustainability objectives directly into strategic decision-making. By combining economic efficiency with environmental stewardship and social accountability, organizations can evaluate procurement not merely as a cost function but as a powerful enabler of sustainable value creation [54]. This integrated ecosystem provides a rigorous foundation for benchmarking, improving, and scaling procurement strategies in alignment with global circular economy goals.

13.7 Challenges and Future Directions

Although sustainable procurement has become a key driver of circular manufacturing, its widespread adoption still faces several significant challenges. One of the most prominent barriers is the higher upfront cost of sustainable materials and eco-certified products [43]. Even though LCC often demonstrates long-term financial and environmental benefits, many organizations—particularly those with limited resources—remain hesitant to invest in options that carry an initial price premium [55]. This challenge is further compounded by the limited availability and preparedness of suppliers, especially SMEs, which frequently lack the technical expertise and financial capacity to meet stringent sustainability standards [17].

Another persistent obstacle is the lack of harmonized standards and metrics for evaluating procurement sustainability. Despite frameworks such as ISO 20400, GRI, and ESG indicators, inconsistencies across industries and regions make it difficult to compare performance and ensure transparency [47]. These gaps complicate the integration of sustainability into tendering, supplier evaluation, and contract management processes. The complexity of global supply chains, often spanning multiple tiers and geographies, also reduces visibility into upstream practices, increasing the risk of unethical labor practices, greenwashing, and noncompliance with regulatory or stakeholder expectations [28].

Addressing these challenges requires a combination of strategic, technological, and policy-driven approaches. Strategically, organizations need to move beyond transactional procurement models and engage suppliers as long-term partners, fostering collaboration and continuous improvement in sustainability performance [28]. Capacity-building programs, training initiatives, and coinvestment strategies are particularly important for enabling SMEs to meet sustainability requirements. On the technological front, innovations such as blockchain, AI, and the IoT offer new opportunities for improving traceability, enhancing data accuracy, and enabling predictive risk management across complex supply networks [56].

Looking ahead, sustainable procurement is likely to evolve along three key trends. First, AI-driven decision-making will allow procurement professionals to incorporate sustainability metrics into predictive models, balancing cost, risk, and environmental performance in real time [53]. Second, blockchain-enabled traceability systems are expected to become standard practice, fostering trust and accountability throughout multitier supply chains. Third, global harmonization of standards may accelerate, as governments and industry consortia push for unified procurement frameworks that support carbon neutrality and circular economy goals [5].

In conclusion, sustainable procurement is at a pivotal stage of transformation. Although cost, complexity, and supplier readiness remain significant challenges, the combined potential of digital technologies, collaborative partnerships, and regulatory frameworks points toward a future in which procurement functions act as strategic levers for systemic sustainability. Successfully navigating current barriers while embracing emerging pathways will be essential for embedding procurement as a cornerstone of circular manufacturing systems.

AI disclosure statement: The author acknowledges the use of AI-based tools for minor language editing or grammatical correction. However, all intellectual contributions, analyses, and conclusions presented in this chapter are entirely the author's own.

References

1. Khulud, K., Masudin, I., Zulfikarijah, F., Restuputri, D.P., Haris, A., Sustainable Supplier Selection through Multi-Criteria Decision Making (MCDM) Approach: A Bibliometric Analysis. *Logistics*, 7, 4, Dec. 2023, doi: 10.3390/logistics7040096.
2. Li, Y., Omain, S., Tan, K., Supply Chain Resilience: A Review and Research Direction. *Int. J. Acad. Res. Bus. Soc. Sci.*, 11, Dec. 2021, doi: 10.6007/IJARBSS/v11-i12/11985.
3. Badi, S. and Murtagh, N., Green supply chain management in construction: A systematic literature review and future research agenda. *J. Cleaner Prod.*, 223, 312–322, Jun. 2019, doi: 10.1016/j.jclepro.2019.03.132.
4. Kim, S.-Y. and Nguyen, T., Supply chain management in construction: critical study of barriers to implementation. *Int. J. Construct. Manage.*, 22, 16, 3148–3157, Dec. 2022, doi: 10.1080/15623599.2020.1843768.
5. Sodhi, M.S. and Tang, C.S., Supply Chain Management for Extreme Conditions: Research Opportunities. *J. Supply Chain Manag.*, 57, 1, 7–16, 2021, doi: 10.1111/jscm.12255.

6. Al-Werikat, G., Supply Chain Management In Construction; Revealed. *Int. J. Sci. Technol. Res.*, 6, 106–110, Mar. 2017.
7. Seyedan, M. and Mafakheri, F., Predictive big data analytics for supply chain demand forecasting: methods, applications, and research opportunities. *J. Big Data*, 7, 1, 53, Jul. 2020, doi: 10.1186/s40537-020-00329-2.
8. Schinckus, C., Akbari, M., Clarke, S., Corporate Social Responsibility in Sustainable Supply Chain Management: An Econo-Bibliometric Perspective. *Theor. Econ. Lett.*, 9, 1, Jan. 2019, doi: 10.4236/tel.2019.91020.
9. Naeemah, A.J. and Wong, K.Y., Selection methods of lean management tools: a review. *Int. J. Prod. Perform. Manag.*, 72, 4, 1077–1110, Jan. 2021, doi: 10.1108/IJPPM-04-2021-0198.
10. Su, C., Horng, D.-J., Tseng, M.-L., Chiu, A., Wu, K.-J., Chen, H.-P., Improving sustainable supply chain management uses a novel hierarchical Grey-DEMATEL approach. *J. Cleaner Prod.*, 134, May 2015, doi: 10.1016/j.jclepro.2015.05.080.
11. Obianyo, J.I., Okey, O.E., Alaneme, G.U., Assessment of cost overrun factors in construction projects in Nigeria using fuzzy logic. *Innov. Infrastruct. Solut.*, 7, 5, 304, Aug. 2022, doi: 10.1007/s41062-022-00908-7.
12. Hendiani, S. and Bagherpour, M., Developing an integrated index to assess social sustainability in construction industry using fuzzy logic. *J. Cleaner Prod.*, 230, 647–662, Sep. 2019, doi: 10.1016/j.jclepro.2019.05.055.
13. Mentzer, J.T., *et al.*, Defining Supply Chain Management. *J. Bus. Logist.*, 22, 2, 1–25, 2001, doi: 10.1002/j.2158-1592.2001.tb00001.x.
14. Maghsoodi, A.I. and Khalilzadeh, M., Identification and Evaluation of Construction Projects' Critical Success Factors Employing Fuzzy-TOPSIS Approach. *KSCE J. Civ. Eng.*, 22, 5, 1593–1605, May 2018, doi: 10.1007/s12205-017-1970-2.
15. Deepika, S., Anandakumar, S., Bhuvanesh Kumar, M., Baskar, C., Performance appraisement of supplier selection in construction company with Fuzzy AHP, Fuzzy TOPSIS, and DEA: A case study based approach. *J. Intell. Fuzzy Syst.*, 45, 6, 10515–10528, Jan. 2023, doi: 10.3233/JIFS-231790.
16. Das, N., Supplier Selection Criteria and Methods in Supply Chain (A Statistical Approach), in: *Proceedings of the 3rd Asia Pacific Management Research Conference (APMRC 2019)*, Atlantis Press, Bali, Indonesia, 2020, doi: 10.2991/aebmr.k.200812.002.
17. Kosanoglu, F. and Kus, H.T., Sustainable supply chain management in construction industry: a Turkish case. *Clean Techn. Environ. Policy*, 23, 9, 2589–2613, Nov. 2021, doi: 10.1007/s10098-021-02175-z.
18. Singh, A., Kumar, Verma, P., Sustainable supplier selection in a construction company: a new MCDM method based on dominance-based rough set analysis. *Constr. Innov.*, Jan. 2023, doi: 10.1108/CI-12-2022-0324.
19. Cigolini, R., Gosling, J., Iyer, A., Senicheva, O., Supply chain management in construction and engineer-to-order industries. *Prod. Plann. Control*, 33, 9–10, 803–810, Jul. 2022, doi: 10.1080/09537287.2020.1837981.

20. Memari, A., Dargi, A., Akbari Jokar, M.R., Ahmad, R., Abdul Rahim, Abd.R., Sustainable supplier selection: A multi-criteria intuitionistic fuzzy TOPSIS method. *J. Manuf. Syst.*, 50, 9–24, Jan. 2019, doi: 10.1016/j.jmsy.2018.11.002.
21. Broft, R.D. and Koskela, L., Supply chain management in construction from a production theory perspective, in: *IGLC 2018 - Proceedings of the 26th Annual Conference of the International Group for Lean Construction*, Jul. 2018, vol. 1, pp. 271–281, doi: 10.24928/2018/0538.
22. Saeli, M., Micale, R., Seabra, M.P., Labrincha, J.A., La Scalia, G., Selection of Novel Geopolymeric Mortars for Sustainable Construction Applications Using Fuzzy Topsis Approach. *Sustainability*, 12, 15, Jan. 2020, doi: 10.3390/su12155987.
23. Viet, N.Q., Behdani, B., Bloemhof, J., The value of information in supply chain decisions: A review of the literature and research agenda. *Comput. Ind. Eng.*, 120, 68–82, Jun. 2018, doi: 10.1016/j.cie.2018.04.034.
24. Evans, O., Socio-economic impacts of novel coronavirus: The policy solutions. *BizEcons Q.*, 7, 3–12, 2020.
25. Yin, R. K., *Case Study Research and Applications Design and Methods*, 6th ed., Sage, Scientific Research Publishing, Thousand Oaks, CA, 2018, Accessed: Nov. 09, 2023. [Online]. Available: https://www.scirp.org/(S(lz5mqp453edsnp55rrgjct55.))/References/referencespapers.aspx?referenceid=2914980.
26. Qin, G., Zhang, M., Yan, Q., Xu, C., Kammen, D.M., Comprehensive evaluation of regional energy internet using a fuzzy analytic hierarchy process based on cloud model: A case in China. *Energy*, 228, 120569, Aug. 2021, doi: 10.1016/j.energy.2021.120569.
27. İki̇nci̇, M. and Ti̇pi̇, T., Food supplier selection in the catering industry using the analytic hierarchy process. *Food Sci. Technol.*, 42, e48420, Mar. 2021, doi: 10.1590/fst.48420.
28. Konys, A., Green Supplier Selection Criteria: From a Literature Review to a Comprehensive Knowledge Base. *Sustainability*, 11, 4208, Aug. 2019, doi: 10.3390/su11154208.
29. Rahman, M.M., Bari, A.B.M.M., Ali, S.M., Taghipour, A., Sustainable supplier selection in the textile dyeing industry: An integrated multi-criteria decision analytics approach. *Resour. Conserv. Recycl. Adv.*, 15, 200117, Nov. 2022, doi: 10.1016/j.rcradv.2022.200117.
30. Chopra, S., Meindl, P., Supply Chain Management Strategy, Planning, and Operations. Kemampuan Koneksi Matematis Tinjauan Terhadap Pendekatan Pembelajaran Savi, 53, 71–85, 2019, Scientific Research Publishing, Accessed: Nov. 09, 2023. [Online]. Available: https://www.scirp.org/(S(vtj3fa45qm1ean45vvffcz55))/References/referencespapers.aspx?referenceid=3528587.
31. Badi, S. and Murtagh, N., Green supply chain management in construction: A systematic literature review and future research agenda. *J. Cleaner Prod.*, 223, 312–322, Jun. 2019, doi: 10.1016/j.jclepro.2019.03.132.

32. (PDF) Sustainable Procurement in Multinational Corporations: A Conceptual Framework for Aligning Business and Environmental Goals, ResearchGate, Aug. 2025, doi: 10.54660/.IJMRGE.2023.4.1.774-787.
33. (PDF) Role of supplier engagement to reduce Scope 3 emissions in circular supply chains, ResearchGate, May 2025, doi: 10.1002/BSE.3994.
34. Li, K., Bashiri, M., Lim, M.K., Akpobi, T., How to improve supply chain sustainable performance by resilience practices through dynamic capability view: Evidence from Chinese construction. *Resour. Conserv. Recycl.*, 212, 107965, Jan. 2025, doi: 10.1016/j.resconrec.2024.107965.
35. (PDF) Collaborative Innovation for a Sustainable Future: How Tech Partnerships Drive Supply Chain Sustainability, ResearchGate, Aug. 2025, doi: 10.56025/IJARESM.2024.121024567.
36. Taddei, E., Sassanelli, C., Rosa, P., Terzi, S., Circular supply chains theoretical gaps and practical barriers: A model to support approaching firms in the era of industry 4.0. *Comput. Ind. Eng.*, 190, 110049, Apr. 2024, doi: 10.1016/j.cie.2024.110049.
37. Alland, D., Countermeasures of General Interest. *Eur. J. Int. Law*, 13, 5, 1221–1239, Dec. 2002, doi: 10.1093/ejil/13.5.1221.
38. Xia, Z., Wang, X., Zhang, L., Qin, Z., Sun, X., Ren, K., A Privacy-Preserving and Copy-Deterrence Content-Based Image Retrieval Scheme in Cloud Computing. *IEEE Trans. Inf. Forensics Secur.*, 11, 11, 2594–2608, Nov. 2016, doi: 10.1109/TIFS.2016.2590944.
39. Aljuneidi, T., Bhat, S.A., Boulaksil, Y., A comprehensive systematic review of the literature on the impact of the COVID-19 pandemic on supply chains. *Supply Chain Anal.*, 3, 100025, Sep. 2023, doi: 10.1016/j.sca.2023.100025.
40. Li, Y., Empirical Studies on Online Information Privacy Concerns: Literature Review and an Integrative Framework. *Commun. Assoc. Inf. Syst.*, 28, 453–496, Jan. 2011, doi: 10.17705/1CAIS.02828.
41. Sarker, I.H., Data Science and Analytics: An Overview from Data-Driven Smart Computing, Decision-Making and Applications Perspective. *SN Comput. Sci.*, 2, 5, 377, Jul. 2021, doi: 10.1007/s42979-021-00765-8.
42. (PDF) Supply chain integrating sustainability and ethics: Strategies for modern supply chain management, ResearchGate, Aug. 2025, doi: 10.30574/wjarr.2024.22.1.1259.
43. Ibn-Homaid, N.T., A comparative evaluation of construction and manufacturing materials management. *Int. J. Project Manage.*, 20, 4, 263–270, May 2002, doi: 10.1016/S0263-7863(01)00013-8.
44. Phong, N.T., Application of Supply Chain Management in Construction Industry. *Adv. Sci. Technol. Res. J.*, 12, 2, 11–19, 2018, doi: 10.12913/22998624/92112.
45. Ketchen, D. and Hult, G.T.M., Bridging Organization Theory and Supply Chain Management: The Case of Best Value Supply Chains. *J. Oper. Manage.*, 25, 573–580, Mar. 2007, doi: 10.1016/j.jom.2006.05.010.

46. Govindan, K. and Rajendran, S., Green supplier selection and order allocation in a low-carbon paper industry: integrated multi-criteria heterogeneous decision-making and multi-objective linear programming approaches. *Ann. Oper. Res.*, 238, Mar. 2016, doi: 10.1007/s10479-015-2004-4.
47. Joshi, G., Bhattarai, S., Bhandari, K., Journal of Management Research and Analysis A comparative study of supply chain management in building construction projects within Kathmandu valley. *J. Manage. Res. Anal.*, 10, 21–32, Apr. 2023, doi: 10.18231/j.jmra.2023.005.
48. Azadnia, A.H., Saman, M.Z.M., Wong, K.Y., Sustainable supplier selection and order lot-sizing: an integrated multi-objective decision-making process. *Int. J. Prod. Res.*, 53, 2, 383–408, Jan. 2015, doi: 10.1080/00207543.2014.935827.
49. Zhang, J., Li, D., Wang, Y., Toward intelligent construction: Prediction of mechanical properties of manufactured-sand concrete using tree-based models. *J. Cleaner Prod.*, 258, 120665, Jun. 2020, doi: 10.1016/j.jclepro.2020.120665.
50. Stević, Ž., Vasiljević, M., Vesković, S., Blagojević, A., Đorđević, Ž., Defining The Most Important Criteria For Suppliers Evaluation In Construction Companies, in: presented at the *The Sixth International Conference Transport and Logistics - til 2017*, May 2017, pp. 91–96.
51. Mojumder, A. and Singh, A., An exploratory study of the adaptation of green supply chain management in construction industry: The case of Indian Construction Companies. *J. Cleaner Prod.*, 295, 126400, May 2021, doi: 10.1016/j.jclepro.2021.126400.
52. Karamoozian, A., Wu, D., Luo, C., Green Supplier Selection in the Construction Industry Using a Novel Fuzzy Decision-Making Approach. *J. Constr. Eng. Manage.*, 149, 6, 04023033, Jun. 2023, doi: 10.1061/JCEMD4.COENG-13058.
53. Alayet, C., Lehoux, N., Lebel, L., Logistics approaches assessment to better coordinate a forest products supply chain. *J. For. Econ.*, 30, C, 13–24, 2018.
54. Zhu, J., Wan, L., Zhao, H., Yu, L., Xiao, S., Evaluation of the integration of industrialization and information-based entropy AHP–cross-efficiency DEA model. *Chin. Manag. Stud.*, Jan. 2023, doi: 10.1108/CMS-03-2022-0098.
55. Nursal, A., Omar, M., Mohd Nawi, M.N., Criteria Requirement for IBS Vendor Selection. *Int. J. Supply Chain Manag. (IJSCM)*, 5, 108–114, Jul. 2016.
56. Demand Forecasting in Supply Chain Explained, Relevant Software, Accessed: Nov. 09, 2023. [Online]. Available: https://relevant.software/blog/demand-forecasting-in-supply-chain.
57. Kumar, N., Patel, A., Financial benefits of IT integration in procurement processes. *J. Operational Efficiency*, 15, 1, 87–99, 2022.
58. Ahi, P., Searcy, C.A., Comparative literature analysis of definitions for green and sustainable supply chain management. *J. Cleaner Prod.*, 52, 329–341, 2013.

14

Integration of Digital Technologies (AI, IoT, and Blockchain) for Circular Manufacturing

Val Hyginus Udoka Eze[1*], George Uwadiegwu Alaneme[2], Vincent Chukwudi Chijindu[3], Awafung Emmanuel Adie[4] and N. Poyyamozhi[5]

[1]*Department of Electrical and Electronics Engineering, Mbarara University of Science and Technology, Mbarara, Kihumuro, Uganda*
[2]*Department of Civil Engineering, School of Engineering and Applied Sciences, Kampala International University, Western Campus, Bushenyi-Ishaka, Uganda*
[3]*Department of Electronic and Computer Engineering, University of Nigeria, Nsukka, Enugu State, Nigeria*
[4]*Department of Biomedical Engineering, School of Engineering and Applied Sciences, Kampala International University, Western Campus, Bushenyi-Ishaka, Uganda*
[5]*Department of Mechanical Engineering, Panimalar Engineering College, Chennai, Tamil Nadu, India*

Abstract
Manufacturing remains a cornerstone of industrial advancement and economic prosperity; however, the prevailing linear "take–make–dispose" paradigm has led to escalating environmental degradation, resource depletion, and industrial inefficiencies. In response, the circular economy (CE) has emerged as a transformative framework rooted in industrial ecology, systems thinking, and cradle-to-cradle design, promoting regenerative, restorative, and closed-loop industrial systems. This chapter presents a rigorous and comprehensive examination of how digital technologies—particularly artificial intelligence (AI), the Internet of Things

**Corresponding author*: udoka.eze@must.ac.ug; ORCID: https://orcid.org/0000-0002-6764-1721
Vincent Chukwudi Chijindu: ORCID: https://orcid.org/0000-0002-2700-4584
Awafung Emmanuel Adie: ORCID: https://orcid.org/0009-0007-3574-7234

Jeyaprakash Natarajan, Milon Selvam Dennison, M. Bhuvanesh Kumar and Ganapathy Thirukkotti (eds.) Manufacturing and the Circular Economy, (429–494) © 2027 Scrivener Publishing LLC

(IoT), blockchain, digital twins, and cyberphysical systems (CPSs)—are catalyzing the transition toward circular manufacturing. By integrating CE principles with Industry 4.0 innovations, digital circular manufacturing (DCM) fosters real-time monitoring, predictive analytics, intelligent decision-making, smart inventory management, and closed-loop supply chains that reduce waste, extend product life cycles, and regenerate material value. AI facilitates intelligent material recovery, fault prediction, and circular product design; IoT enables continuous tracking and performance optimization of assets and processes; and blockchain enhances transparency, traceability, and trust across reverse logistics and material provenance. The chapter articulates an interoperable digital framework that unifies these technologies to support system-wide automation, traceability, and resilience. As this chapter demonstrates, the way industries simulate, monitor, and optimize processes throughout a product's entire life cycle is being revolutionized by digital twins and CPSs. Better resource efficiency, reduced carbon emissions, increased operational uptime, and increased stakeholder participation in circular practices are just a few of the observable benefits demonstrated through real-world examples from the automotive, electronics, and textile industries. It also critically examines the barriers to broader adoption, including disparate digital infrastructure, cybersecurity issues, uneven regulations, and workforce skill shortages. The chapter concludes by outlining potential future directions, such as developing unified sustainability metrics, using explainable AI to assist in the design of sustainable products, and constructing massive, networked digital twins. Ultimately, it makes the case that DCM represents a fundamental rethinking of value creation that aims to achieve net-zero goals while respecting planetary boundaries.

Keywords: Artificial intelligence, Internet of Things, blockchain, circular manufacturing, predictive maintenance, smart manufacturing, resource optimization

14.1 Introduction

The inefficiencies and unsustainable trajectory of the linear economy, which predominates in global production and consumption systems, gave rise to the circular economy (CE) [1, 2]. The linear model, which has its roots in the Industrial Revolution and was heightened during the 20th-century boom in mass production and globalization, follows the "take–make–use–dispose" cycle [3]. Waste accumulation, resource depletion, and environmental degradation have all increased as a result of this model.

In response, the CE paradigm gained traction in the late 20th and early 21st centuries, drawing from foundational schools of thought such as Industrial Ecology, Cradle-to-Cradle Design, Biomimicry, and the Performance Economy. CE fundamentally reimagines economic activity by emphasizing resource efficiency, the regeneration of natural systems, and the elimination of waste through closed-loop cycles [4]. Unlike the linear model, CE decouples economic development from resource extraction by designing out waste and pollution, keeping materials in use, and regenerating ecosystems.

As global material consumption surpassed 100 billion tons annually, coupled with stagnating recycling rates (only about 8.6% of materials were cycled back into the economy as of 2020), the urgency for systemic transformation has intensified [5, 6]. CE responds by promoting restorative and regenerative systems that prioritize product longevity, reuse, refurbishment, remanufacturing, repurposing, and responsible material substitution. These strategies contribute to climate mitigation, biodiversity protection, and ecosystem health, while also offering economic opportunities through innovation and job creation. Moreover, CE embodies a shift from throughput-based industrial logic (focused on volume and velocity) to a performance-based logic, in which value is created by the service or function a product delivers over its life cycle [7]. Within this transformative framework, circular manufacturing arises as a key operational and technological domain that enables the practical implementation of CE principles in industrial production systems.

Traditionally, manufacturing has been a linear, resource-intensive process, but circular manufacturing reconfigures this paradigm by embedding sustainability, adaptability, and circularity into product and process design [8, 9]. Chronologically, this shift has been enabled by advancements in materials science, digital technologies, and industrial symbiosis. Circular manufacturing integrates principles such as eco-design, where products are engineered for modularity, reparability, and recyclability, thereby facilitating product life extension and component recovery.

Moreover, the use of bio-based, renewable, and recyclable inputs intended for repeated reuse promotes material circularity [10]. Reverse logistics and closed-loop supply chains enable the recovery and reuse of goods and materials, and product-service systems displace owner-based business models in favor of access-based models such as leasing, sharing, and performance-based contracts. These developments enhance supply chains, reduce the throughput of materials, and decrease dependence on volatile virgin resource markets [11]. The transition to circular manufacturing requires a structural and coordinated effort across the entire design, production, consumption, and postconsumption phases to be successful. This necessitates collaboration between industry, academia, policymakers, civil society, and stakeholders, supported by financial incentives, learning opportunities, and regulation.

By bringing economic systems into line with the planet's ecological limits, CE and circular manufacturing provide a route to an inclusive, low-carbon, and resource-resilient industrial future as they continue to develop [12]. The evolution of the convergence between digital transformation and CE principles marks a paradigm shift in how societies manage resources and the process of regeneration. Digital technologies have demonstrated that the incorporation of intelligence, traceability, and automation into the life cycles of products and materials can effectively overcome well-known impediments to circularity, such as data asymmetry, system fragmentation, and a lack of transparency [13, 14]. This is not merely additive but transformative, enabling circular business models to operate in data-rich environments in real time and scale properly. At the heart of this transition is the Internet of Things (IoT), which leverages embedded sensors, RFID tags, and actuators to bridge the gap between digital platforms and physical assets, goods, machinery, and infrastructure [15]. Life-cycle intelligence and real-time monitoring rely on highly detailed data regarding asset condition, usage, location, and environmental exposure as produced by the IoT. This type of visibility is necessary for predictive maintenance (PdM), longer product lifetimes, and inventory dematerialization, all of which are pillars of CE strategies such as reuse, repair, and refurbishment [16]. Artificial intelligence (AI) and machine learning (ML) enhance the cognitive functions that help make better decisions and optimize system behaviors by building on this layer of real-time information [17]. The use of AI allows for intelligent waste sorting, automated disassembly planning, and the detection of material compositions within the specific context of CE. ML can enhance demand forecasting and closed-loop material flow by identifying high-value recovery pathways through the analysis of historical and contextual data [18]. To enable higher throughput and purity, for example, AI vision systems on smart sorting robots in electronic waste (e-waste) recovery plants can recognize components and evaluate recyclable properties based on shape, color, and inferred material. Concurrently, the problem of establishing traceability and trust in intricate, decentralized supply networks is addressed by blockchain and distributed ledger technologies (DLTs) [19].

Digitized product passports and circular tokens, which track ownership, composition, repair history, and recycling eligibility, are made possible by the immutable and decentralized record-keeping system of blockchain technology. This is particularly relevant for regulatory compliance under frameworks such as the EU Green Deal, right to repair, and extended producer responsibility (EPR), where traceable product information empowers consumers and enforces producer accountability. Additive manufacturing (AM), or 3D printing, enhances circularity by shifting manufacturing from mass production to mass customization and decentralized production [20]. AM minimizes material waste through layer-by-layer fabrication, supports design for disassembly, and enables on-site component regeneration, thereby reducing transportation emissions and supporting localized repair economies. Furthermore, AM facilitates the use of recycled feedstocks and biodegradable polymers, contributing to the material circularity loop [21, 22].

Another transformative tool is the Digital Twin, which creates a virtual mirror of physical systems, capturing dynamic performance data over time [23, 24]. When applied to products, infrastructure, or even entire supply chains, digital twins allow for scenario analysis, stress testing, and life-cycle optimization. For instance, a digital twin of an industrial machine can forecast wear and schedule timely maintenance, thereby extending service life and minimizing downtime [25]. In construction, digital twins model building material flows and support adaptive reuse planning in circular urban development. Big Data Analytics integrates and interprets vast, heterogeneous datasets derived from IoT, enterprise resource planning (ERP) systems, environmental sensors, and consumer interfaces [26]. By deploying descriptive, predictive, and prescriptive analytics, stakeholders can monitor CE performance metrics such as the circular material use rate, material recovery efficiency, embodied carbon footprint, and end-of-life value retention [27]. This capacity enables data-driven circularity assessments and supports adaptive policy interventions.

These digital enablers, when synergistically integrated, form the digital nervous system of a modern CE, driving real-time responsiveness, system resilience, and regenerative design thinking [28]. They facilitate the emergence of circular value networks, replacing traditional linear flows with multinodal, interoperable ecosystems where materials, information, and value are continuously cycled. Moreover, the digitalization of circular systems aligns with global sustainability frameworks such as the UN SDGs, particularly SDG 9 (Industry, Innovation and Infrastructure), SDG 12 (Responsible Consumption and Production), and SDG 13 (Climate Action) [29]. To sum up, digital technologies are fundamental facilitators of the shift to a CE rather than supplementary improvements. To promote sustainable competitiveness and long-term environmental stewardship, they speed up the transition from linear, resource-intensive economies to adaptive, regenerative, and low-carbon systems by integrating intelligence, transparency, and flexibility into production and consumption systems [30].

The main goal of this chapter is to thoroughly examine how digital technologies are facilitating the transition from conventional linear manufacturing models to circular manufacturing paradigms. The chapter examines how data-driven tools and intelligent systems act as catalysts for integrating circularity throughout product life cycles and industrial value chains, operating at the nexus of sustainability science and industrial innovation.

To achieve this, the chapter first explains the theoretical underpinnings of the CE and circular manufacturing by referencing important conceptual frameworks like industrial ecology, systems thinking, and socio-technical transitions theory. These frameworks provide the analytical lens through which the complex interplay between technology, process innovation, and sustainability outcomes is assessed. The chapter further explores the enabling capabilities of digital technologies by analyzing both product-centric applications—such as smart product design, embedded sensors for condition monitoring, and digital twins for life-cycle optimization—and system-centric applications, including supply chain transparency, reverse logistics optimization, and decentralized resource recovery. Emphasis is placed on how technologies such as IoT, AI, blockchain, additive manufacturing, and big data analytics function not in isolation but as interconnected components of a cyberphysical infrastructure that supports circular operations at scale. This chapter further synthesizes empirical case studies from diverse manufacturing sectors, including electronics, automotive, textiles, and consumer goods. These case illustrations serve to highlight sector-specific best practices, measurable environmental benefits, economic value creation, and operational scalability. Rather than being merely celebratory, the review critically evaluates the main obstacles preventing the widespread use and efficacy of digital circular solutions. These difficulties include institutional inertia within established manufacturing systems, cybersecurity vulnerabilities, fragmented digital infrastructure, lack of data interoperability, and skills shortages. The chapter outlines the new frontiers of digital circular manufacturing (DCM) and highlights game-changing innovations such as digital product passports, AI-powered performance metrics for the CE, and legislative frameworks that encourage the adoption of new technologies and adherence to regulations. In addition to strategic insights from consulting reports (e.g., McKinsey & Company, Accenture), these developments are discussed in light of international initiatives and guidelines from organizations such as the European Commission, the United Nations Environment Programme, and the World Economic Forum (WEF). To guarantee both conceptual soundness and practical relevance, the chapter incorporates insights from engineering, sustainability studies, information systems, and industrial management using an interdisciplinary and multiscale approach. The chapter's ultimate goal is to provide a forward-looking, action-oriented framework for those involved in cocreating a resilient, low-carbon, and resource-efficient industrial future powered by digital innovation. These stakeholders include manufacturers, researchers, policymakers, and providers of digital solutions.

14.1.1 Overview of Circular Manufacturing

14.1.1.1 Definition and Principles of Circular Manufacturing

Circular manufacturing represents a transformative paradigm within production systems, firmly grounded in the foundational concepts of the CE [31, 32]. Diverging from the traditional linear "take–make–dispose" approach, it seeks to close material loops by extending the life cycle of products, components, and raw materials. This is achieved by embedding circularity principles throughout manufacturing processes and supply chains, with an emphasis on minimizing waste, reducing emissions, and improving energy efficiency. The ultimate objective is to create regenerative industrial systems that uphold economic value while mitigating environmental impacts [32]. Rooted in interdisciplinary frameworks such as systems thinking, industrial ecology, and sustainability science, circular manufacturing challenges prevailing resource extraction and consumption patterns by prioritizing resource preservation and value retention [2]. It requires a systemic redesign spanning product design, material selection, production, usage, and end-of-life management. This holistic approach supports the development of resilient and low-impact manufacturing ecosystems that respect planetary boundaries. The core principles underpinning circular manufacturing include designing for longevity and disassembly, which ensures products are durable, modular, and easily repairable or refurbishable, facilitating the recovery of valuable components and preventing premature disposal [33]. Resource efficiency and material circularity are prioritized by using recycled or bio-based materials and minimizing toxic inputs, thereby optimizing material use and reducing waste generation. Figure 14.1 shows evidence of closed-loop material flows, where outputs from one process are redirected as inputs into the same or other processes. This approach is essential because it reduces dependence on landfills and minimizes the use of virgin raw materials, thereby supporting a more circular and sustainable resource management strategy.

Through the 6Rs framework—reduce, reuse, repair, refurbish, remanufacture, and recycle—circular manufacturing operationalizes value retention. Each of these strategies helps maintain both functional and economic value throughout a product's life cycle [34]. Furthermore, the emphasis shifts from ownership to usage through servitization and product-as-a-service (PaaS) models, which encourage manufacturers to create durable, easily recoverable products while promoting sustainable consumption [35].

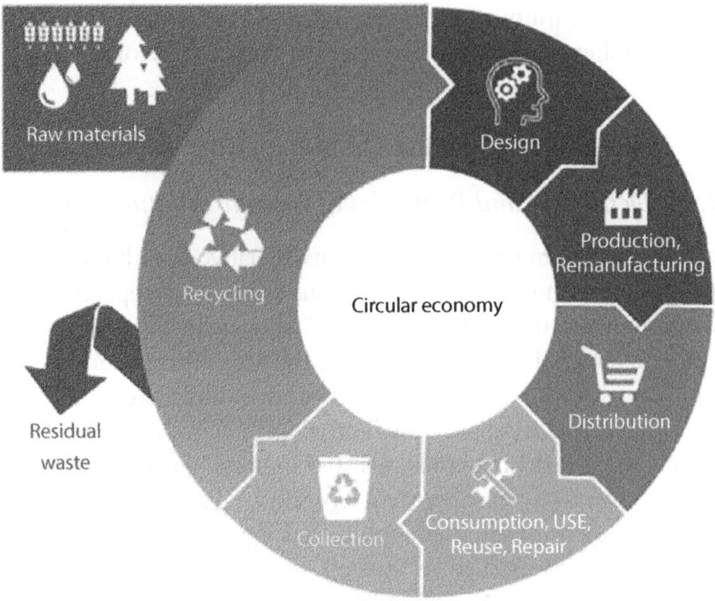

Figure 14.1 Principles of circular economy [23].

The use of instruments such as life-cycle assessment (LCA), material flow analysis, and circularity indicators to measure environmental effects and maximize resource efficiency across entire value chains is crucial for system-level integration. This data-driven approach enables well-informed decisions that optimize both economic and ecological benefits [36]. Collectively, these ideas establish circular manufacturing as a major force behind the transformation of production systems toward resilient, sustainable, and regenerative futures.

14.1.1.2 Linear versus Circular Manufacturing Models

Figure 14.2 shows the evidence of traditional linear manufacturing, which follows a sequential "cradle-to-grave" production and consumption path: raw material extraction → manufacturing/production → product use → end-of-life disposal. This model shows one-way material flow, with limited reuse, recycling, or recovery. The main objectives of this linear model are economic growth and throughput maximization. However, it inevitably results in widespread waste accumulation through landfill disposal or incineration, severe environmental degradation, and the excessive depletion of limited resources. Consequently, it contributes to unsustainable ecological footprints and elevated greenhouse gas emissions [37].

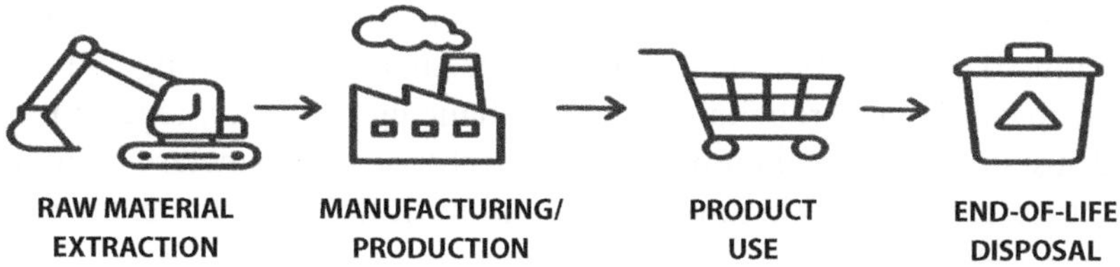

Figure 14.2 "Cradle-to-grave" production and consumption path in traditional manufacturing.

In contrast, circular manufacturing embraces a cradle-to-cradle philosophy aimed at maximizing resource retention and minimizing environmental impacts throughout the product life cycle [38]. Rooted in systems thinking and industrial ecology, this model emphasizes closed material loops, the regeneration of natural capital, and systemic resilience. Waste is reconceptualized as a valuable resource, and products are designed to enable the continuous recovery of materials and functionality. The fundamental distinctions between linear and circular manufacturing are summarized in Table 14.1.

Table 14.1 Summary of the differences between linear and circular manufacturing in CE.

Aspect	Linear manufacturing	Circular manufacturing
Resource flow	One-way, linear flow: input → output → waste	Closed-loop, cyclical flow: reuse, repair, refurbish, remanufacture, recycle
Design intent	Optimized for cost-efficiency and product functionality	Optimized for durability, modularity, maintainability, and material circularity
Waste treatment	Externalized disposal *via* landfill or incineration	Internalized as a resource input through recovery and regeneration
Business model	Product ownership and transactional sales	Product-as-a-service or performance-based models encourage longevity
Environmental impact	High carbon footprint, resource-intensive, polluting	Low-carbon footprint, resource-efficient, regenerative

This circular manufacturing paradigm represents a systemic innovation in industrial production. It redefines value creation by shifting emphasis from maximizing throughput toward enhancing resilience, regeneration, and sustainability. By aligning economic activity with planetary boundaries, it fosters sustainable resource use and mitigates environmental externalities [39].

14.1.1.3 Challenges in Traditional Manufacturing Systems

A complex web of deeply ingrained issues in traditional industrial systems continues to impede the shift from linear to circular manufacturing. The adoption of circular strategies and advancements in sustainability and resource efficiency are hampered by these barriers, which span technical, material, economic, organizational, and policy-related dimensions [40, 41].

1. **Product design rigidity**: Traditionally, product design frameworks have prioritized short-term functionality, low-cost mass production, and aesthetic appeal over long-term sustainability. It is common to overlook end-of-life factors such as material recovery, modularity, repairability, and ease of disassembly. The linear production-disposal paradigm is reinforced by this rigidity, which locks products into single-use trajectories and makes them incompatible with circular practices such as refurbishment, remanufacturing, and component reuse.
2. **Material complexity**: To improve product performance, modern manufacturing commonly uses hybrid material systems, laminated structures, and multimaterial composites. These intricate formulations are advantageous in terms of functionality, but they make recycling and post-use separation much more difficult. Due to a lack of environmentally sound, economically feasible, and scalable separation technologies, valuable resources are diverted to landfilling or incineration, resulting in significant material losses and widespread downcycling.
3. **Planned obsolescence and short product lifespans**: Planned obsolescence, whether intentional or unintentional, shortens product life cycles and speeds up turnover rates. Due to financial incentives or design constraints, consumers are frequently encouraged to replace rather than repair devices. This promotes greater extraction of virgin raw

materials, increases waste production, and directly opposes the concepts of circularity and life-cycle stewardship.

4. **Fragmented and opaque supply chains**: Conventional supply chains are typified by a lack of cooperation among actors, fragmentation, and restricted data interoperability. These conditions obstruct the development of critical circular mechanisms such as product take-back systems, component traceability, and reverse logistics infrastructures. The absence of real-time tracking and integrated life-cycle data further constrains the visibility required for efficient resource recovery and end-of-life decision-making.
5. **Economic lock-ins and infrastructural inertia**: Existing capital investments in linear manufacturing infrastructure—including production facilities, logistics networks, and workforce capabilities—create significant economic lock-ins. The perceived risk, financial cost, and complexity of transitioning to circular systems discourage experimentation and innovation. This infrastructural inertia sustains outdated production models, even as the long-term environmental and economic benefits of circularity become increasingly evident.
6. **Regulatory and standardization gaps**: One significant institutional obstacle is the absence of industry standards, incentive programs, and unified regulatory frameworks specifically designed for circular manufacturing. Regulatory frameworks often fall behind technological advancements and are unable to offer precise definitions, performance standards, or compliance metrics. Companies are less motivated to incorporate circularity into their operational and business strategies as a result of this governance gap, which also creates uncertainty.

Thus, a transformation strategy is required to effectively remove the barriers to circular manufacturing by addressing organizational, technological, policy, and sociocultural dimensions [42, 43]. Technological innovation—such as advances in modular construction, circular product design, and next-generation recycling technologies capable of handling complex material streams—must lead the way [43]. There is also a need to reorganize organizations to encourage cross-sector collaboration, digitalization, and the practice of servitization models that decouple economic value from material movement [44]. To impact these changes, policy shifts should introduce a favorable enabling environment through the adoption of performance-based standards, standardized regulation, and incentive schemes such as EPR. Finally, sociocultural evolution is a prerequisite to the adoption of circular principles in society by shaping sustainable consumption trends, encouraging a culture of repair and reuse, and increasing consumer awareness. When combined, these coupled levers can turn traditional manufacturing systems into resource-efficient, adaptable, and regenerative industrial ecosystems. This is completely in line with CE demands and the overall objectives of sustainable development [42–44].

14.1.1.4 Enablers of Circular Manufacturing

The shift toward circular manufacturing is underpinned by a multifaceted constellation of enablers that span digital technologies, design innovations, regulatory frameworks, novel business models, and collaborative ecosystems [45]. These enablers provide the structural, technological, and behavioral foundations necessary to embed circularity across product life cycles, from conception and production to use, recovery, and reintegration [46]. Central to this transformation is the deployment of digital technologies and Industry 4.0 tools, which unlock visibility, intelligence, and traceability across value chains. Technologies such as the IoT enable real-time monitoring of product performance and usage conditions, supporting PdM and circular service models [47]. AI and ML drive data-driven optimization of material flows and demand forecasting, whereas digital twins allow virtual simulations of life-cycle outcomes, facilitating eco-optimization. Blockchain technology ensures immutable traceability, enabling verification of material provenance and recycling claims. Additive manufacturing (AM) further supports on-demand, low-waste, and modular production systems, which are key prerequisites for circularity [48].

Complementing these technologies, eco-design and life-cycle thinking ensure that products are conceived with circularity in mind. Design-for-disassembly, design-for-repair, and design-for-recycling methodologies promote material recovery and reuse, whereas LCA and cradle-to-cradle certifications provide frameworks for evaluating environmental impacts and validating sustainable design principles [49]. The effectiveness of these designs is amplified through reverse logistics and circular supply chains, which facilitate the collection, inspection, reconditioning, and reintegration of used products. Digitally enabled traceability supports closed-loop flows and end-of-life take-back schemes, enhancing secondary material utilization [50].

Policy and regulatory instruments further institutionalize circular practices. Mechanisms such as EPR and Green Public Procurement place the onus on producers and public agencies to drive circularity through design innovation and market incentives [51]. Eco-labeling schemes and circularity standards provide regulatory clarity and consumer trust, whereas national CE roadmaps outline strategic directions and targets for systemic transformation. Simultaneously, business model innovation plays a pivotal role in decoupling value creation from material throughput. Models such as PaaS and servitization realign revenue structures with sustainability by incentivizing long-term use, maintenance, and material recovery [35]. Sharing economy platforms further reduce redundancy by promoting the collective utilization of underused assets.

Lastly, effective circular manufacturing is contingent upon stakeholder engagement and cross-industry collaboration. Value chain integration ensures alignment among suppliers, manufacturers, retailers, consumers, and recyclers, whereas customer cocreation fosters product attachment and participatory reuse [52]. Industrial symbiosis leverages byproducts and waste streams from one enterprise as inputs for another, mimicking regenerative natural systems and fostering closed-loop industrial networks. Collectively, these enablers constitute the technological, institutional, and sociocultural architecture necessary for transitioning from extractive, waste-intensive production models to regenerative, adaptive, and resource-efficient circular manufacturing systems. Their strategic coordination is essential to achieving resilience, resource sovereignty, and alignment with global sustainability imperatives such as the United Nations Sustainable Development Goals (SDGs) and the safe operating space defined by planetary boundaries [53].

14.2 Role of AI in Circular Manufacturing

AI is pivotal in enabling circular manufacturing by transforming traditional linear production models into intelligent, closed-loop systems that prioritize sustainability, efficiency, and resilience. AI facilitates real-time decision-making, intelligent automation, and adaptive control across the product life cycle through predictive analytics, ML, computer vision, and digital twin technologies. This not only improves material utilization and energy efficiency but also significantly reduces environmental impact by minimizing waste and maximizing resource circularity [54–56].

14.2.1 AI for Data-Driven Decision-Making

AI acts as a cornerstone for real-time, context-aware decision-making across the manufacturing value chain, particularly within circular economy frameworks [53, 57]. By integrating high-volume, high-velocity data streams from sensors, machines, enterprise systems, and supply chain actors, AI transforms raw data into actionable intelligence [51, 52]. This enables manufacturing firms to shift from static and linear decision processes to dynamic, adaptive, and circular strategies. In circular manufacturing systems, AI facilitates:

1. **Material flow monitoring**: Advanced AI models track the quantity, quality, location, and status of materials throughout their life cycle, from raw material acquisition to end-of-life. By analyzing data from RFID tags, IoT sensors, and production logs, AI helps identify material leakages, optimize stock levels of reusable components, and monitor material degradation. This enhances material circularity by ensuring that resources remain within the loop as long as possible.
2. **Design optimization for circularity**: AI supports sustainable product design by utilizing real-time usage analytics, LCAs, and historical performance data. ML algorithms, for instance, can suggest material replacements that improve durability, recyclability, or disassembly simplicity. Furthermore, product variations that optimize for maximum reuse potential and minimal environmental impact can be automatically created using AI-enabled generative design tools.
3. **Production planning and process efficiency**: AI-powered forecasting tools anticipate future resource requirements, plan preventive maintenance, and optimize energy use by utilizing sensor inputs, market demand trends, and historical production data. AI-powered life-cycle costing models can assess production routes according to their overall economic and environmental costs—including energy consumption, embedded carbon, and recyclability—enabling comprehensive circular production planning.

These capabilities collectively enable organizations to transition from reactive, end-of-pipe approaches to proactive, closed-loop strategies. AI not only improves operational efficiency but also provides high-resolution, real-time insights that support system-wide circularity goals. As a result, decision-making becomes anticipatory rather than corrective, aligning economic performance with environmental stewardship. AI-driven data analytics empowers manufacturers to embed intelligence at every node of the circular manufacturing value chain, creating a feedback-rich ecosystem where resources are continuously monitored, optimized, and revalorized [58].

14.2.2 Machine Learning for Material Recovery and Process Optimization

ML, a core subset of AI, provides advanced capabilities for autonomous pattern recognition, predictive analytics, and data-driven optimization by learning from large, complex, and heterogeneous datasets [59]. In the context of circular manufacturing, ML is increasingly vital for driving intelligent automation, enhancing material circularity, and optimizing end-of-life product handling and recovery systems.

1. **Material classification and recovery in CE**: Modern recycling facilities are using increasingly sophisticated supervised and unsupervised ML algorithms—such as K-means clustering, support vector machines (SVMs), and convolutional neural networks (CNNs)—to improve material classification and recovery procedures [60]. To precisely detect and classify heterogeneous waste streams in real time, these algorithms examine a variety of data modalities, such as spectral (e.g., hyperspectral imaging), visual (e.g., computer vision), and structural (e.g., X-ray imaging or acoustic signatures) data. Fiber-reinforced composites can be isolated during product deconstruction, specific metal alloys can be identified within complex e-waste, and PET, HDPE, and PVC polymers can be distinguished from one another. By greatly increasing throughput, improving material purity, reducing cross-contamination, and increasing recovery efficiency, intelligent sorting systems help advance closed-loop recycling and a sustainable CE [61].
2. **Process optimization in remanufacturing and waste treatment**: Within the domains of remanufacturing, refurbishing, and waste treatment, ML models—specifically supervised regression-based algorithms and reinforcement learning (RL)—are vital in optimizing process parameters [62]. To ensure that optimal process control procedures can be actively recognized and implemented, these models utilize constantly flowing operational data such as temperature, pressure, material throughput, and defect rates. Through knowledge gained both in real time and from past

information, ML models can optimize machine settings to minimize energy, water, and chemical usage, as well as defects and turnaround time [63]. For example, an RL-based system might autonomously adjust parameters on a cleaning or disassembly line based on real-time performance data, promoting adaptive control and continuous optimization. This intelligent optimization not only increases productivity but also ensures product quality and supports cost-effective, eco-friendly remanufacturing systems.

3. **Quality prediction and residual life estimation**: Advanced ML models such as recurrent neural networks, random forests, and gradient boosting are gaining momentum in predicting quality and estimating residual life [64]. By integrating sensor data, historical usage records, and known failure trends, these models can accurately predict the remaining functional life and integrity of recovered components. With such predictive analytics, it is feasible to identify repairable or reusable components, determine maintenance requirements after reconditioning, and conduct full component-level life-cycle analyses (LCAs) [65]. This philosophy ensures the reintegration of only those parts whose performance and safety are guaranteed, significantly enhancing customer satisfaction, operational safety, and product performance.

Figure 14.3 demonstrates evidence of machine learning integration in circular manufacturing by highlighting how machine learning enhances material recovery and process optimization workflows, thereby delivering transformative benefits to circular manufacturing systems [66]. By lowering material contamination and improving recovery accuracy, intelligent sorting and predictive analytics enhance resource circularity. PdM and real-time process control prolong equipment life and minimize downtime, whereas precise optimization methods cut down on material and energy waste. Aligned with sustainability objectives and the larger vision of Industry 4.0, these developments collectively hasten the transition from linear to circular production models [67].

14.2.3 Predictive Analytics for Waste Minimization

Proactive decision-making in circular manufacturing is made possible by predictive analytics, which uses both historical and real-time data to forecast system behaviors [68]. Manufacturers can predict product and

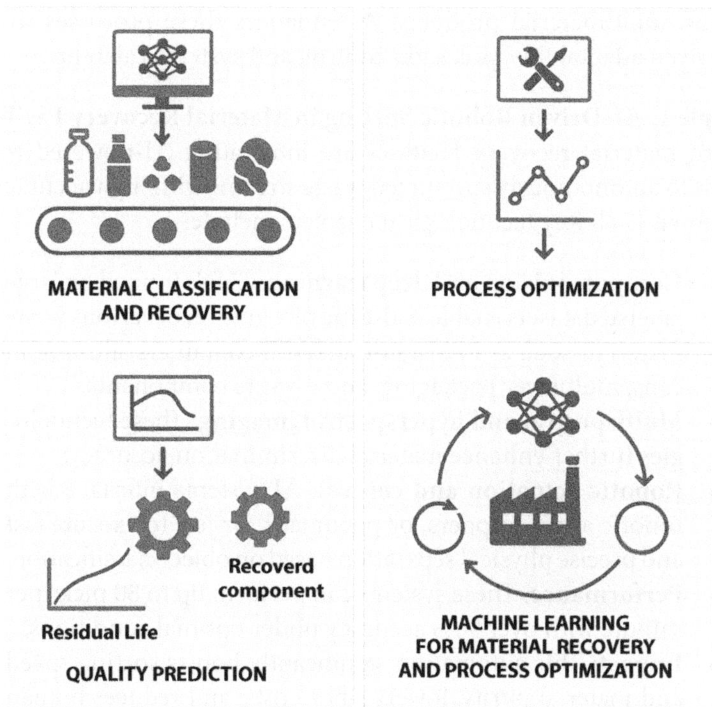

Figure 14.3 Machine learning for material recovery and process optimization.

component failures and replace or maintain them in a timely manner by utilizing sophisticated AI models. This is especially useful in PaaS models where uptime and longevity are crucial [69]. To anticipate and reduce waste generation, such as scrap, rework, and overproduction, predictive tools also find patterns in production variability. Predictive analytics-based life-cycle emission monitoring also makes it possible to estimate carbon footprints and other environmental impacts throughout the life stages of products, which helps to guide strategic interventions for impact reduction [70]. These predictive capabilities are essential to the development of CE principles and environmentally sustainable manufacturing because they are necessary to achieve zero-waste, closed-loop production systems.

14.2.4 Case Study: AI in Sorting and Automated Disassembly

A compelling and increasingly implemented application of AI in circular manufacturing is the deployment of intelligent systems for automated sorting and disassembly. These operations form the cornerstone of effective material recovery, enabling the high-quality reuse and recycling of complex, multimaterial products. AI enhances these processes through data-driven adaptability, precision control, and system scalability.

Example 1: AI-Driven Robotic Sorting in Material Recovery Facilities
Modern material recovery facilities are integrating AI-powered robotic systems to autonomously sort mixed waste streams with high accuracy and throughput [71]. Key technological enablers include:

- **Computer vision and deep learning**: CNNs trained on large labeled datasets enable real-time recognition of various waste materials such as PET bottles, HDPE containers, aluminum cans, multilayer packaging, and e-waste components.
- **Multispectral and hyperspectral imaging**: These technologies further enhance material discrimination accuracy.
- **Robotic actuation and control**: AI systems interface with robotic arms, grippers, or pneumatic air jets to execute fast and precise physical separation based on object classification.
- **Performance**: These systems can perform up to 80 picks per minute with over 90% accuracy under optimal conditions.
- **Impact**: This automation significantly boosts sorting speed and material purity, lowers labor costs, and reduces human exposure to potentially hazardous waste, thereby improving overall facility efficiency and safety.

Example 2: AI-Enabled Automated Disassembly of E-Waste
E-waste contains high-value materials (e.g., gold, palladium, rare earths), yet manual disassembly is labor-intensive, inconsistent, and hazardous [72]. AI facilitates efficient and intelligent disassembly through:

- **Component and fastener recognition**: Using 2D/3D imaging and ML algorithms, systems identify screws, clips, adhesives, PCBs, and other structural elements within electronic devices.
- **Robotic path planning and manipulation**: Vision-guided disassembly robots use AI to sequentially dismantle devices.
- **RL**: This enables the robot to adapt disassembly strategies in real time based on the detected condition, make, and model of the product.
- **Hazardous material handling**: AI-based hazard detection allows safe removal of toxic or dangerous components such as batteries, capacitors, or CRTs, thereby improving worker safety and reducing environmental risks.

- **Impact**: These systems enhance disassembly throughput, increase material recovery rates by up to 40%, and enable closed-loop recycling of rare and strategic materials with minimal contamination.

Strategic Contribution to Circular Manufacturing
AI-enabled sorting and disassembly systems contribute to circularity in the following strategic ways [73]:

- **Scalability**: Automating labor-intensive tasks allows for large-scale material processing with consistent quality.
- **Resource efficiency**: AI reduces process waste, enhances material yield, and improves energy efficiency across the value chain.
- **System intelligence**: Data generated from AI systems can inform product redesign for disassembly, recycling, or remanufacture, supporting design for circularity principles.

AI empowers circular manufacturing by embedding intelligence into postconsumer product recovery systems. These cognitive systems transform previously unstructured and inefficient waste processing into precise, adaptable, and high-value material recovery workflows. Ultimately, AI accelerates the shift toward a resilient, regenerative, and resource-efficient industrial ecosystem [71–73].

14.3 IoT Applications in Circular Manufacturing

The IoT serves as a pivotal enabler in the realization of circular manufacturing systems by embedding sensing, connectivity, and computational intelligence into products, machinery, and infrastructure. IoT provides improved visibility, traceability, and control throughout the whole product life cycle through ubiquitous data collection, edge computing, and bidirectional communication among dispersed systems. In the end, it aligns industrial processes with CE principles such as material retention, waste minimization, and asset longevity by supporting closed-loop material flows, facilitating data-driven decision-making, and optimizing resource utilization [74].

14.3.1 IoT Sensors for Real-Time Monitoring

The sensors of IoT play a crucial role in harnessing circular manufacturing due to their ability to provide 24/7 surveillance of the key physical parameters in production lines, warehouses, and distribution channels such as temperature, vibration, humidity, energy, and material wear out [74, 75]. This sensor-based visibility makes PdM possible but can also assist in early fault detection and increasing the lifetime of machines and parts. It also facilitates environmental conditions tracking to properly handle and store recyclable, remanufacturable, and perishable materials. On top of that, the IoT-based closed-loop process control will also reduce defects, waste of energy, and loss of material because it allows dynamically changing manufacturing control to a certain level [76]. Monitoring using IoT sensors provides the backbone of sustainable and effective circular manufacturing systems because it ensures the materials flow along the chains of circulation without compromising their quality and functionality.

14.3.2 Smart Inventory and Resource Management

Smart inventory systems powered by IoT technologies offer real-time visibility into the status, location, and condition of raw materials, in-process goods, and reusable components [77]. By enabling dynamic inventory tracking, these systems help prevent overproduction, minimize storage costs, and reduce the likelihood of material obsolescence. Through embedded sensors and RFID technologies, returned or surplus items can be automatically classified and sorted, streamlining reintegration into production or recycling streams. Furthermore, life-cycle tagging and monitoring provide detailed insights into the usage history, performance, and degradation patterns of individual components [78]. This granular intelligence empowers manufacturers to reallocate resources effectively, lower dependence on virgin materials, and route materials through the most efficient and sustainable circular pathways, ultimately enhancing the resilience and resource efficiency of the manufacturing system.

14.3.3 IoT-Enabled Closed-Loop Supply Chains

The IoT serves as a foundational catalyst for the implementation of closed-loop supply chains, which are integral to the realization of circular manufacturing systems [79]. By embedding interconnected sensors, actuators, and communication modules across the product life cycle, from raw material extraction and production to consumption, collection, and reintegration, IoT enables real-time visibility, PdM, and dynamic stakeholder coordination. This continuous digital connectivity supports data-driven interventions that facilitate the systematic recirculation of materials, thereby transforming linear supply chains into regenerative loops.

Unlike conventional linear models that culminate in waste disposal, closed-loop supply chains, empowered by IoT, prioritize the recovery, reuse, and valorization of products and materials [79].

Through sensor-enabled feedback systems and intelligent data flows, firms can monitor the physical condition of products in use, automate reverse logistics processes, and route items through optimal end-of-life pathways. For instance, IoT-enabled tracking using RFID, GPS, and NFC technologies allows the precise localization and condition assessment of postconsumer goods, thereby improving the efficiency of retrieval operations and minimizing environmental externalities [80]. Moreover, condition-based product routing becomes feasible as embedded diagnostics and AI-driven analytics assess returned items in real-time [81]. This enables strategic decisions regarding reuse, component harvesting, remanufacturing, or recycling, each aligned with preserving the maximum possible material value. In parallel, IoT fosters collaborative, data-centric ecosystems by integrating disparate actors, suppliers, OEMs, recyclers, and logistics providers within a unified digital infrastructure. Such synchronization enhances secondary material forecasting, supports decentralized remanufacturing, and ensures resilient supply chain adaptability in the face of market and environmental volatility [82]. Strategically, the deployment of IoT in closed-loop systems marks a paradigm shift in industrial resource management. It empowers manufacturers to eliminate waste, retain embedded value, and decouple economic growth from finite resource dependence. When synergized with complementary digital technologies, such as blockchain for traceability and AI for anticipatory logistics, IoT unlocks unprecedented levels of transparency, accountability, and operational agility. As industries advance toward circularity and climate neutrality, IoT-enabled closed-loop supply chains will be essential in constructing intelligent, regenerative, and future-proof manufacturing ecosystems.

14.3.4 Case Study: IoT in Remanufacturing and Product Life-Cycle Tracking

Caterpillar Inc.'s CAT® Reman Program provides a compelling demonstration of how the IoT can be strategically leveraged to enhance remanufacturing and product life-cycle tracking within circular manufacturing frameworks. Central to this initiative is the integration of embedded IoT devices, including RFID tags, onboard telematics, and connected sensors, within critical machinery components such as engines and drivetrains [83]. These devices continuously collect high-fidelity operational data encompassing cumulative usage hours, load cycles, thermal stresses, vibration signatures, fault diagnostics, environmental conditions, and detailed maintenance histories. The resulting comprehensive digital product passport facilitates sophisticated data analytics that inform each stage of the remanufacturing process [84]. By leveraging this granular life-cycle data, Caterpillar effectively assesses remanufacturability, determining both the technical integrity and residual economic value of returned components. Parts that exhibit wear or damage beyond predefined thresholds are excluded, thereby safeguarding product quality and minimizing resource waste. Additionally, knowledge of precise component histories enables optimized disassembly and reconditioning workflows, reducing unnecessary machining, lowering energy and water consumption, shortening turnaround times, and enhancing workplace safety and productivity [85]. Beyond operational efficiencies, the program's traceability protocols ensure full certification and documentation of remanufactured parts, reinforcing customer confidence, regulatory compliance (e.g., EU Ecodesign and US EPA mandates), and the company's sustainability brand [86]. Strategically, this IoT-driven approach enables Caterpillar to capture residual value from used products, diminish reliance on virgin materials, mitigate supply chain volatility, and significantly reduce life-cycle greenhouse gas emissions [87]. The program exemplifies how digitization and CE principles converge to deliver both environmental benefits and competitive advantage, positioning Caterpillar as an industrial sustainability leader. In summary, the CAT® Reman Program highlights the transformative potential of IoT-enabled life-cycle tracking and data analytics to operationalize efficient, transparent, and resilient remanufacturing ecosystems. As industries increasingly adopt such intelligent circular models, IoT will remain indispensable for closing material loops, extending product value, and advancing sustainable manufacturing [86, 87].

Table 14.2 is the IoT-enabled remanufacturing systems performance metrics.

14.4 Blockchain for Transparency and Traceability

Blockchain technology has emerged as a transformative enabler of transparency, traceability, and trust within circular manufacturing systems. By leveraging a decentralized and immutable digital ledger to record transactions and data exchanges, blockchain ensures the integrity and verifiability of information flows among multiple stakeholders. This decentralized infrastructure mitigates reliance on single authoritative intermediaries, thereby reducing risks associated with data tampering and single points of

Table 14.2 Performance metrics of IoT-enabled remanufacturing systems.

Metric	CAT® Reman Program (Caterpillar)	Industry benchmark/ reference case	Description
Reduction in virgin material usage	85%–90%	80%–95% (e.g., Cummins, Bosch Reman)	Achieved by recovering components such as housings, heads, blocks, and injectors
Energy savings in manufacturing	65%–80%	60%–85%	Remanufacturing consumes significantly less energy than producing new parts
Water savings per unit	70%	~68% (Based on US EPA data)	Optimized disassembly and cleaning protocols reduce water-intensive operations
Greenhouse gas (GHG) emissions reduction	50%–60%	45%–65%	Life-cycle emissions are reduced due to decreased extraction, machining, and logistics
Remanufacturing yield rate	>85% for core parts	80%–90%	Supported by condition-based sorting using IoT diagnostics
Turnaround time reduction	20%–30% improvement with life-cycle data integration	15%–25%	Real-time operational data streamlines inspection and reconditioning steps
Product return rate for Reman	Over 75% (participation in take-back programs)	70%–80%	Encouraged *via* service agreements and RFID-tracked logistics
Customer acceptance of Reman parts	80%–90% (in targeted markets)	70%–85%	Enhanced by certification, warranties, and IoT-based traceability
Regulatory compliance achieved	Meets US EPA Tier 4, EU Ecodesign, and ISO 14001 standards	Varies by region	IoT supports traceability and documentation for regulatory audits and life-cycle claims

failure [88]. In circular manufacturing contexts, blockchain's robust data provenance capabilities underpin collaborative supply chain governance, facilitating sustainable resource management and reinforcing accountability throughout product life cycles.

14.4.1 Fundamentals of Blockchain Technology

At its core, blockchain is a DLT distinguished by four fundamental characteristics [89]. First, decentralization ensures that the ledger is replicated and maintained across numerous independent nodes globally, eliminating centralized control and enhancing system resilience [90, 91]. Second, immutability guarantees that once transactions are validated and appended to the blockchain, they become permanent and tamper-proof, creating an auditable and verifiable historical record. Third, network users can collectively verify new entries using consensus mechanisms such as proof of work and proof of stake, which guarantees ledger consistency and guards against fraudulent changes. Fourth, cryptographic security protects against cyber threats by using secure hashing functions to link data blocks, maintaining data authenticity and confidentiality. These characteristics enable stakeholders in circular manufacturing to accurately and transparently document the provenance of materials, manufacturing process steps, and transaction histories [92]. By guaranteeing that all participants in intricate supply networks have access to reliable and consistent information, such thorough traceability not only improves operational visibility but also fortifies consumer trust, regulatory compliance, and CE performance.

14.4.2 Smart Contracts for Sustainable Supplier Management

Blockchain networks with smart contracts, which are autonomous, self-executing protocols, offer strong automation features that radically improve sustainable supplier management. Smart contracts allow agreements to be automatically enforced once predetermined conditions are met by directly encoding sustainability criteria and contractual terms into programmable logic [93]. This greatly lessens the need for time-consuming and prone-to-mistakes manual audits in the context of circular manufacturing supply chains by enabling the smooth verification of suppliers' adherence to environmental, social, and governance (ESG) standards. Furthermore, smart contracts facilitate dynamic incentive structures that allow for the instantaneous issuance of rewards or penalties contingent on suppliers' compliance with circular practices, including waste reduction goals and thresholds for the use of recycled materials. By giving all authorized stakeholders constant access to verified supplier performance data, this embedded automation removes information asymmetry and improves transparency and accountability [94]. Ultimately, smart contracts reduce administrative overhead, promote cooperation, and guarantee steady progress toward sustainability goals across intricate supply networks by incorporating trust, efficiency, and real-time governance into supplier relationships.

14.4.3 Blockchain in Material Provenance and Recycling Verification

Accurately verifying the provenance of raw materials and validating recycling claims remain pivotal challenges within circular manufacturing. Blockchain technology addresses these challenges by enabling comprehensive, end-to-end traceability of materials throughout their entire life cycle, from extraction and manufacturing through distribution, use, and eventual recovery at end-of-life [95]. The immutable nature of blockchain records ensures the certification of recycled, reclaimed, or remanufactured content, thereby facilitating adherence to stringent regulatory frameworks and green procurement policies. Furthermore, blockchain significantly mitigates the risk of greenwashing by providing consumers, regulators, and supply chain participants with transparent, verifiable, and tamper-proof evidence of sustainability claims. By linking physical assets to their digital representations, often referred to as "digital twins," on the blockchain, stakeholders acquire enhanced visibility and trust in product life-cycle data, which fundamentally supports and accelerates CE objectives [96].

14.4.4 Case Study: Blockchain-Enabled Reverse Logistics

The TradeLens platform, a pioneering collaboration between IBM and Maersk, exemplifies the practical application of blockchain technology to optimize reverse logistics, an essential process within circular supply chains. By creating a decentralized, transparent digital ecosystem, TradeLens integrates real-time shipment tracking, customs documentation, and product return management on a single blockchain-based platform [97]. This integration provides unparalleled visibility into the flow of returned goods and secondary materials, enabling stakeholders to streamline reverse logistics operations and enhance circular resource recovery. Additionally, TradeLens automates compliance workflows with complex customs and environmental regulations, reducing administrative burdens while ensuring regulatory adherence. The platform's shared, immutable ledger facilitates seamless collaboration among diverse actors, including manufacturers, logistics providers, recyclers, and regulatory bodies, by granting them access to trustworthy, verifiable data. Consequently, TradeLens reduces delays, minimizes fraud risks, and significantly improves the efficiency and resilience of reverse logistics processes [98]. This case vividly illustrates blockchain's capacity to underpin scalable, transparent, and trustworthy circular supply networks.

14.5 Integration of AI, IoT, and Blockchain

The combination of blockchain, IoT, and AI systems signifies a new point in DCM research and development. Individually, each technology addresses specific manufacturing issues; however, the combination of all of these results in unheard-of efficiency, transparency, resiliency, and sustainability [99]. Within this section, the role of cyberphysical systems (CPSs) in a manufacturing setting is contextualized, the interactive dynamics of such systems are analyzed, a holistic configuration of a digital framework is suggested, and digital twins are discussed as an important enabler.

14.5.1 Synergistic Interactions among the Technologies

Together, the IoT, blockchain, and AI form a revolutionary digital triad that propels the development of intelligent, transparent, and circular manufacturing ecosystems [100]. Although each of these technologies individually tackles unique industrial challenges, such as AI's ability to optimize and be autonomous based on data, IoT's role in real-time sensing and connectivity, and blockchain's decentralized trust architecture, their combination creates synergistic dynamics that significantly improve manufacturing efficiency, sustainability, and accountability. The system's cognitive core is AI, which uses ML, deep learning, and RL algorithms to analyze large datasets for closed-loop process design, equipment failure prediction, resource allocation optimization, and quality assurance automation [101]. Through intelligent decision-making and adaptive control, these capabilities help manufacturing operations decrease waste, increase yield, and conform to the principles of the CE.

Concurrently, IoT functions as the sensory and connective infrastructure of the manufacturing environment by deploying a dense mesh of sensors, actuators, and embedded devices throughout the production chain. These devices continuously collect high-frequency, granular data related to machinery status, process parameters, environmental conditions, energy consumption, and product tracking [100, 102]. This influx of data, characterized by both volume and velocity, not only fuels AI models for improved predictive performance but also enhances operational visibility and responsiveness. Furthermore, edge computing enables localized data processing, whereas cloud platforms provide centralized analytics and long-term data storage, creating a layered architecture for intelligent manufacturing. By embedding smart tags and sensors in materials, components, and finished goods, IoT also facilitates comprehensive traceability across the entire life cycle, from raw material acquisition and manufacturing to usage, return, and recycling, thereby supporting circularity and compliance monitoring [102].

Blockchain complements AI and IoT by introducing a cryptographically secure, distributed ledger system that guarantees the integrity, transparency, and immutability of both sensed data and algorithmic decisions [100]. This technological layer eliminates data tampering risks, facilitates trusted inter-organizational collaboration, and ensures regulatory compliance through verifiable audit trails. Smart contracts, deployed on blockchain networks, automate complex processes such as enforcing sustainability standards, managing recycling quotas, and triggering supplier payments based on sensor-validated conditions. By enabling multistakeholder trust without centralized control, blockchain empowers secure data exchange among manufacturers, suppliers, regulators, recyclers, and consumers, thereby ensuring that each actor in the value chain adheres to environmental and ethical standards. Moreover, blockchain's capability to record the provenance and life-cycle events of products reinforces the authenticity of circular manufacturing claims and enables transparent validation of material recovery flows [100, 103].

The synergistic integration of these three technologies results in a feedback-rich, cyberphysical ecosystem characterized by intelligent automation, traceable workflows, and resilient operations. AI benefits from the high-quality, real-time data streams generated by IoT, whereas blockchain ensures the credibility and auditability of that data, effectively closing the loop of trusted information exchange and decision-making. This triadic interaction enables the emergence of autonomous, policy-compliant manufacturing systems where AI-enforced smart contracts govern resource use, and IoT sensors monitor real-time adherence to sustainability metrics. In such environments, resource recirculation, energy efficiency, and life-cycle extension are not only technologically feasible but operationally optimized and transparently verifiable [99–103]. Ultimately, the coalescence of AI, IoT, and blockchain forms the digital foundation of Industry 4.0-enabled circular manufacturing, one that is predictive, adaptive, secure, and inherently aligned with long-term environmental and economic sustainability goals.

14.5.2 Integrated Framework for Digital Circular Manufacturing

The realization of a digitally-enabled circular manufacturing paradigm necessitates a structured and interoperable framework that unifies AI, IoT, and blockchain technologies into a cohesive architecture [104]. This integrated framework is designed to facilitate seamless data exchange, ensure operational transparency, and enable intelligent decision-making across all phases of the product life cycle, from raw material acquisition through production, usage, return, and reintegration. Organized into four interdependent layers, the framework provides a cyberphysical backbone that transforms conventional linear manufacturing into an intelligent, circular, and resilient system [100]. At the foundation lies the Perception Layer, comprising a distributed mesh of IoT-enabled devices, smart sensors, actuators, and embedded systems embedded within machines, infrastructure, and products. These devices capture high-resolution data in real time, monitoring critical operational and environmental parameters such as temperature, vibration, energy consumption, emissions, wear patterns, and positional data [105]. For example, RFID tags trace material flow across supply chains, accelerometers detect anomalies in rotating equipment, and GPS modules provide geolocation data for logistics optimization. The pervasive sensing capabilities of this layer enable detailed traceability, facilitate condition-based monitoring, and support data granularity essential for driving closed-loop systems and end-of-life strategies.

Building upon this sensory layer is the Data Processing and Analytics Layer, where AI techniques are used to convert raw IoT data into actionable insights [106]. ML algorithms analyze historical and real-time data to predict failures, detect quality deviations, and optimize production workflows. Deep learning enables pattern recognition in complex datasets such as image-based quality assessments, whereas RL supports continuous process improvement through adaptive feedback. Edge computing platforms enable low-latency analytics near data sources, facilitating immediate responses in time-sensitive operations, whereas cloud infrastructures offer scalability and centralized model training. This layer serves as the cognitive hub, transforming sensor-derived signals into dynamic, self-improving control mechanisms that minimize waste, extend asset lifespans, and enable predictive resource management in alignment with CE goals [107].

The blockchain layer introduces a decentralized ledger infrastructure that ensures the security, immutability, and provenance of all data transactions within the system. Every data record generated by IoT sensors or derived by AI algorithms can be cryptographically hashed, time-stamped, and stored in a distributed ledger, ensuring tamper-resistance and auditability. Smart contracts, which are programmable, rule-based agreements encoded on the blockchain, automate the execution of sustainability protocols, such as releasing payments upon successful recovery of recyclable materials or initiating product recalls based on sensor alerts [108]. Furthermore, the decentralized nature of blockchain facilitates secure data exchange among multiple stakeholders, including manufacturers, suppliers, recyclers, regulators, and consumers, without reliance on a central authority, thereby fostering trust, enhancing transparency, and reinforcing compliance with CE mandates.

At the apex of the architecture lies the Application and Interaction Layer, where digital interfaces and control systems translate data-driven insights into actionable operations. Key components include digital twins, which are real-time virtual models that replicate the behavior and status of physical systems using sensor and AI data, and CPS, which integrate computational intelligence with physical processes to enable autonomous control and adaptation [109]. These systems allow manufacturers to simulate performance, predict maintenance needs, and evaluate life-cycle impacts before physical interventions occur. User dashboards, augmented by AI-driven visualizations, enable operators and decision-makers to monitor performance metrics, conduct diagnostics, and assess sustainability indicators such as energy intensity, carbon footprint, and material recirculation rates. This layer ensures that human oversight, machine intelligence, and environmental accountability coalesce in an interactive and responsive

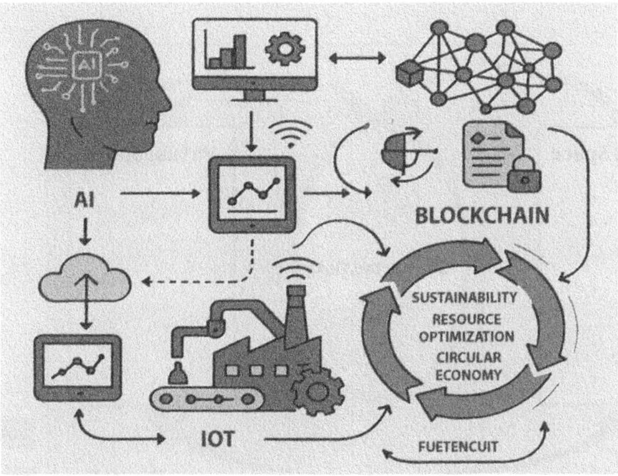

Figure 14.4 Architectural framework of systematic integration of blockchain, AI, and IoT for circular manufacturing [110].

environment [107, 109]. Together, these four layers form a robust, scalable, and interoperable framework that supports end-to-end life-cycle management of products and processes. The architecture framework enables continuous data exchange across physical and digital domains, ensuring that sustainability interventions are informed, traceable, and dynamically responsive. Closed-loop feedback mechanisms allow each layer to influence and be influenced by others, fostering system-wide adaptability in the face of shifting environmental, economic, and market conditions. Most importantly, this integrated framework, as illustrated in Figure 14.4, enables the simultaneous pursuit of environmental stewardship, resource efficiency, and industrial competitiveness, which are key pillars for achieving circular manufacturing at scale within the Industry 4.0 landscape and beyond [110].

14.5.3 Digital Twins: Architecture, Function, and Benefits

Digital twins constitute an advanced cyberphysical paradigm that enables the creation of real-time, data-driven digital replicas of physical assets, processes, or entire systems, as illustrated in Figure 14.5.

Within the realm of DCM, digital twins act as foundational enablers of continuous monitoring, adaptive control, and closed-loop optimization across all stages of the product life cycle, from initial design and fabrication to end-of-life recovery, remanufacturing, and recycling [111]. At their core, digital twins harness the synergistic capabilities of IoT sensors for data acquisition, AI for data-driven inference and decision-making, and

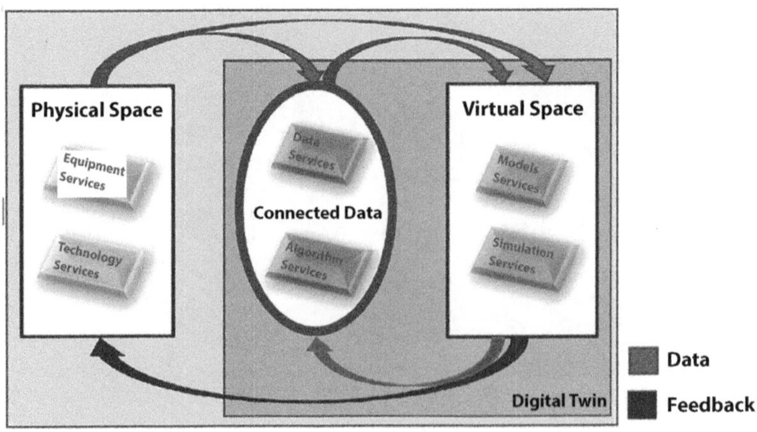

Figure 14.5 General digital twin architecture [115].

blockchain technologies for ensuring data immutability, auditability, and stakeholder trust. This convergence forms the cognitive and operational nucleus of next-generation cyberphysical production systems [112].

The architecture of digital twins in circular manufacturing is characterized by a multilayered construct. The physical layer comprises the tangible entity, be it a robotic assembly arm, smart product, or process line, subject to digital replication [113]. Overlaid on this is the IoT-based sensing layer, which integrates real-time telemetry through embedded sensors and actuators that capture key operational variables such as temperature, vibration, throughput, emissions, and material degradation. These data streams are funneled into the data integration and processing layer, where edge or cloud computing platforms clean, normalize, and contextualize raw inputs. Here, AI models perform diagnostic analytics, fault detection, and predictive forecasting. This is followed by the simulation and intelligence layer, which uses advanced digital physics engines, ML algorithms, and optimization routines to simulate "what-if" scenarios, evaluate material circularity, and guide resource-efficient interventions. Critically, a blockchain layer underpins the architecture, offering immutable records of life-cycle events, enabling multiparty trust, and facilitating decentralized governance of shared digital twin models across supply chain stakeholders. This cohesive architecture supports real-time synchronization and bidirectional data exchange between the digital twin and its physical counterpart, allowing the twin to evolve dynamically alongside the asset it represents [114].

In functional terms, digital twins in circular manufacturing provide a rich, interactive platform for asset supervision, simulation, and control [116]. They enable real-time monitoring of operational health, energy consumption, emissions compliance, and usage trends, thus allowing for timely interventions and system optimization. Through PdM, AI-driven models analyze historical and real-time data to forecast potential failures and schedule proactive maintenance, minimizing unplanned downtimes and extending asset longevity. In addition, digital twins facilitate process and design optimization by simulating production scenarios under varying constraints to identify configurations that reduce waste, material usage, and energy inputs while enhancing productivity. Their capability for life-cycle tracking, when coupled with blockchain, enables transparent traceability of materials and components from sourcing to postconsumer recovery, supporting circularity evaluations and informed decisions on refurbishing, remanufacturing, or recycling pathways. Furthermore, what-if analyses and stress testing under varying economic, environmental, or operational conditions empower manufacturers to design for resilience, sustainability, and agility in the face of uncertainty [117].

The benefits of integrating digital twins into DCM span strategic, operational, environmental, and economic domains [118]. From a strategic standpoint, the blockchain-enabled traceability of life-cycle data fosters transparency and trust, ensuring compliance with regulatory frameworks and ESG standards. Operationally, digital twins support data-driven decision-making that enhances process efficiency, resource optimization, and risk mitigation. Environmentally, the optimization of product designs and industrial processes yields measurable reductions in energy usage, material waste, and greenhouse gas emissions, outcomes that are directly aligned with CE objectives. Economically, benefits include cost savings through reduced downtimes, extended equipment lifespans, and more efficient use of secondary and recovered materials. Moreover, digital twins enable accelerated innovation through virtual prototyping and simulation, which shorten development cycles and promote the design of regenerative products. Finally, the adoption of standardized and interoperable digital twin frameworks, anchored by blockchain, facilitates collaborative governance, allowing distributed stakeholders to codesign, comonitor, and co-optimize circular supply chains across organizational boundaries [119].

In summary, digital twins transcend their role as passive digital reflections of physical systems; they operate as intelligent, autonomous agents capable of real-time orchestration, foresight, and systemic optimization within manufacturing ecosystems. When embedded within a DCM context, digital twins become the central nervous system of industrial intelligence, bridging physical operations with cyber insights to harmonize sustainability, efficiency, and economic viability. Their integration with AI, IoT, and blockchain catalyzes the evolution of manufacturing paradigms from static, linear value chains to resilient, regenerative, and transparent circular ecosystems, emblematic of Industry 4.0 and the future of sustainable industrialization [116–119].

14.5.4 Cyberphysical Systems in Manufacturing Environments

CPSs are foundational to the realization of intelligent, adaptive, and interconnected manufacturing ecosystems in the age of Industry 4.0 and emerging digital CE paradigms. These systems integrate computational intelligence, networked communication, and physical actuation into a cohesive, feedback-driven infrastructure capable of real-time monitoring, autonomous control, and dynamic optimization of manufacturing operations [120].

By tightly coupling the cyber and physical realms, CPS enable manufacturing environments to evolve from reactive and siloed operations into proactive, resilient, and self-optimizing ecosystems. In the context of DCM, CPS provides the operational infrastructure that synchronizes and orchestrates the synergistic functions of AI, IoT, and blockchain technologies. This synergy supports closed-loop resource flows, intelligent remanufacturing, traceable material usage, and sustainable value creation. A robust CPS framework comprises a multilayered architecture encompassing four interdependent strata: physical, communication, computation, and integration. At the base lies the physical layer, which encapsulates the tangible elements of the manufacturing system, including machines, smart materials, and embedded sensors and actuators. These components facilitate continuous, high-fidelity data capture on operational states, material degradation, energy consumption, and environmental parameters. In circular manufacturing settings, this layer is critical for enabling LCAs, predicting product end-of-life status, and initiating disassembly or remanufacturing workflows [121].

The communication layer functions as the digital circulatory system, ensuring reliable, secure, and low-latency data exchange across machines, devices, and platforms. Utilizing protocols such as OPC UA, MQTT, and emerging 5G/6G standards, this layer guarantees seamless machine-to-machine (M2M) and machine-to-cloud (M2C) interactions. Advanced cybersecurity frameworks within this layer, encompassing encryption, authentication, and fault-tolerant networking, safeguard sensitive manufacturing data and ensure system integrity across distributed value chains [122]. Above this is the computation layer, the cognitive engine of CPSs. It leverages edge computing to enable real-time data processing at or near the data source, reducing latency and bandwidth requirements. Simultaneously, cloud computing supports complex analytics, AI model training, and cross-site coordination. AI-driven models within this layer forecast machine failures, optimize resource usage, and evaluate product circularity based on real-time operational data and historical trends. This computational intelligence underpins key CE functions such as PdM, adaptive scheduling, and waste minimization [123].

Crowning the architecture is the integration layer, which facilitates interoperability between CPSs and higher-order enterprise systems such as blockchain networks, ERP platforms, and smart contracts [124]. Blockchain ensures data immutability, traceability of life-cycle events, and trusted collaboration across stakeholders, whereas smart contracts automate actions such as reverse logistics, incentive payments for recyclers, and enforcement of circular design standards. This layer establishes the governance mechanisms essential for implementing decentralized, transparent, and circular manufacturing ecosystems. The operational functionality of CPSs in circular manufacturing extends far beyond automation. CPS enables

Table 14.3 Comparative analysis of traditional versus CPS-enabled manufacturing.

Dimension	Traditional manufacturing	CPS-enabled circular manufacturing
System architecture	Isolated physical systems with minimal digital interaction	Integrated cyberphysical architecture with real-time data flow
Data acquisition	Periodic manual monitoring	Continuous sensor-driven data collection
Control systems	Static, preprogrammed logic (PLC-based)	Adaptive, AI-assisted control with feedback mechanisms
Decision-making	Human-centric, reactive	Autonomous or human-in-the-loop, predictive and proactive
Communication	Limited connectivity, often offline	Networked, secure M2M and M2C protocols with cloud access
Traceability	Paper-based, fragmented across life-cycle stages	Blockchain-backed, tamper-proof life-cycle traceability
Resource efficiency	Optimized for throughput, not sustainability	Optimization focused on circularity, reuse, and waste minimization
Maintenance strategy	Scheduled or reactive	Predictive and condition-based
Flexibility and adaptability	Low flexibility to changes in demand or disruptions	High adaptability *via* real-time reconfiguration
Collaboration across stakeholders	Limited integration; siloed data and operations	Shared digital twins and blockchain foster multistakeholder collaboration
Environmental monitoring	Often external and postprocess	Embedded and real-time with immediate corrective capabilities
Innovation cycle	Long product development times	Accelerated through simulation, virtual prototyping, and feedback loops

adaptive manufacturing by dynamically adjusting production parameters in response to supply chain disruptions, material inconsistencies, or shifting customer demands, thus optimizing material usage and production efficiency. Their capacity for resilient operations *via* self-diagnosing, self-healing algorithms and redundancy protocols ensures uninterrupted functionality even amid equipment malfunctions, grid instabilities, or cyber threats. Furthermore, CPS supports sustainable resource management by continually tracking energy flows, emissions, water use, and material inputs, thereby facilitating closed-loop material cycles and real-time environmental impact monitoring [125].

Strategically, the deployment of CPSs catalyzes the emergence of data-driven, sustainable, and human-centric factories that align with both Industry 4.0 and the broader vision of Industry 5.0. CPS-based systems are transparent; every operational state and decision point is traceable and auditable [126]. They are agile, able to reconfigure in real time to accommodate dynamic production or regulatory constraints. They are sustainable, underpinned by life-cycle thinking, resource optimization, and environmental consciousness. Finally, they are scalable and extensible, offering architectural flexibility for future integration with quantum computing, green hydrogen systems, or bio-based material loops [127]. In summary, CPSs constitute the digital nervous system of next-generation manufacturing. They transform the theoretical frameworks of DCM into operational realities by bridging the digital-physical divide. Their integration with AI, IoT, and blockchain not only enhances process efficiency and product traceability but also embeds sustainability, resilience, and collaboration into the very fabric of industrial production. As such, CPSs are not merely technological enablers but are strategic imperatives for navigating the complex interdependencies of modern manufacturing, CE imperatives, and socio-environmental accountability in the decades ahead [120–125].

Table 14.3 is the comparative summary of the traditional and CPS-enabled manufacturing analysis.

14.6 Predictive Maintenance and Smart Manufacturing

PdM is a core enabler of smart manufacturing and a critical component of CE strategies. By leveraging real-time sensor data, AI algorithms, and IoT infrastructure, PdM allows for data-driven diagnostics and failure forecasting, optimizing equipment performance while minimizing resource waste, unplanned downtime, and environmental impact [128].

14.6.1 Definition and Importance of Predictive Maintenance

PdM is a proactive, data-centric maintenance methodology that utilizes real-time operational parameters, historical performance data, and advanced computational analytics, most notably, ML and statistical inference techniques, to accurately forecast the impending failure or degradation of equipment, components, or systems [129]. Unlike traditional approaches such as reactive maintenance (performed postfailure) or preventive maintenance (scheduled at fixed intervals regardless of actual condition), PdM is condition-based and dynamically responsive. By detecting underlying patterns of degradation and only recommending maintenance interventions when scientifically justified, it reduces needless service actions and prevents major malfunctions.

This paradigm offers notable gains in operational efficiency, cost control, and asset longevity by improving the reliability, availability, and maintainability of industrial systems. More significantly, by providing real-time insight into the condition of machinery and components, it strongly supports the ideas of smart manufacturing and the CE. This helps make well-informed decisions throughout the life cycle of products and equipment. By minimizing unscheduled downtime, PdM enhances operational resilience and production continuity in smart manufacturing environments.

Maintenance activities can be strategically scheduled during noncritical periods, ensuring minimal disruption to workflows and enhancing throughput. Furthermore, by eliminating the inefficiencies of calendar- or usage-based servicing, PdM enables precision maintenance, which conserves parts, labor, lubricants, and other resources, thereby contributing to material and energy efficiency [130]. From a technical standpoint, PdM systems rely on an ecosystem of IoT-enabled sensors, edge and cloud computing, and AI algorithms that process vibration, thermal, acoustic, and electrical data to detect anomalies, assess wear and fatigue, and predict the remaining useful life (RUL) of components [131]. These insights drive timely, targeted interventions that extend equipment lifespans, particularly valuable for capital-intensive and mission-critical industrial assets. The reduction in catastrophic failure rates not only safeguards productivity but also results in lower total cost of ownership (TCO) and improved return on assets. Equally important are the environmental and circularity dimensions of PdM. By reducing unnecessary replacements and preventing early decommissioning of machinery, PdM decreases the demand for virgin material inputs and lowers embodied carbon emissions associated with equipment production and disposal. This contributes to climate mitigation goals and supports the shift toward regenerative industrial systems [132].

Table 14.4 Comparison of reactive, preventive, and predictive maintenance strategies.

Feature	Reactive maintenance	Preventive maintenance	Predictive maintenance
Definition	Maintenance performed after a failure occurs	Maintenance scheduled at regular intervals, regardless of condition	Maintenance based on real-time and historical data to predict failures
Trigger mechanism	Failure-driven	Time-based or usage-based	Condition-based, using sensor data and analytics
Goal	Restore functionality postfailure	Prevent failure through scheduled servicing	Forecast failure and intervene only when necessary
Data dependency	Low or none	Low (uses basic operational metrics or time schedules)	High (relies on sensors, IoT, AI, and machine learning)
Downtime risk	High—often unplanned and disruptive	Moderate, planned, but possibly unnecessary	Low failures are anticipated and avoided
Resource efficiency	Low—can cause overuse of labor and replacement parts	Moderate, risk of overservicing and wasted resources	High maintenance is targeted and efficient
Cost implication	Low short-term, high long-term due to breakdowns	Moderate, fixed costs from routine servicing	Higher upfront costs, lower long-term costs, and TCO

(Continued)

Table 14.4 Comparison of reactive, preventive, and predictive maintenance strategies. (*Continued*)

Feature	Reactive maintenance	Preventive maintenance	Predictive maintenance
Impact on asset life	Reduces lifespan due to unmanaged stress or damage	Can extend lifespan if properly scheduled	Maximizes lifespan through timely interventions
Technological requirements	Minimal	Basic tools and scheduling systems	Advanced: sensors, IoT devices, edge/cloud computing, AI
Suitability	Simple, noncritical systems	Moderate complexity systems	High-value, critical, and complex assets
Sustainability and circularity impact	Negative—frequent replacements, high material waste	Neutral—scheduled part replacements	Positive, supports reuse, reduces waste, and lowers emissions

In DCM systems, PdM plays a pivotal role in preserving embedded value and extending product and component life cycles [133]. Condition-based diagnostics enable the selective reuse, refurbishment, or remanufacturing of parts based on quantified health metrics rather than predetermined schedules. Furthermore, predictive insights can be fed into digital twin platforms and blockchain-enabled supply chains, enabling adaptive life-cycle management, smarter reverse logistics, and design-for-maintenance strategies. This encourages the preservation of sustainable value and strengthens closed-loop material flows. In conclusion, PdM is a strategic enabler of intelligent, sustainable, and circular manufacturing, and it goes far beyond merely improving traditional maintenance procedures. PdM helps companies move from reactive maintenance cultures to robust, resource-efficient, and future-ready production ecosystems by utilizing AI, IoT, and real-time analytics. Its integration into cyberphysical infrastructures underscores its transformative potential in achieving not only operational excellence but also broader sustainability and CE objectives [129–133]. The comparative summary of the reactive, preventive, and predictive maintenance strategies is illustrated in Table 14.4.

14.6.2 AI and IoT for Equipment Health Monitoring

The successful implementation of PdM in advanced manufacturing environments is underpinned by the synergistic integration of AI and the IoT, which together establish an intelligent, responsive, and data-driven infrastructure for real-time equipment health monitoring [134]. This convergence facilitates a closed-loop diagnostic ecosystem wherein data from physical assets is continuously acquired, analyzed, and acted upon to enable predictive diagnostics, failure forecasting, and condition-aware decision-making. The AI-IoT framework forms the operational core of smart and circular manufacturing systems, enabling self-aware, self-correcting maintenance regimes that extend asset life and optimize resource utilization. At the foundation of this architecture lie IoT-enabled sensors, which are embedded within critical machinery, tools, and infrastructure to monitor a wide range of operational parameters.

These sensors capture high-frequency data such as temperature, vibration, acoustic emissions, torque, humidity, pressure, and electrical signatures. This real-time telemetry is timestamped and transmitted *via* secure communication protocols to computational platforms for analysis [135]. The data acquisition layer is complemented by a hybrid connectivity architecture, wherein edge computing enables low-latency anomaly detection and initial response near the asset, whereas cloud computing facilitates scalable storage, historical trend analysis, and enterprise-level integration. This distributed intelligence ensures both immediate responsiveness and long-term learning.

Within this ecosystem, AI algorithms serve as the analytical engine that transforms sensor data into actionable insights. ML models, including supervised, unsupervised, and semisupervised methods, are used to classify equipment states, identify deviations from normal behavior, and forecast incipient faults.

More advanced deep learning architectures, such as CNNs and long short-term memory networks, are applied to high-dimensional, unstructured datasets, including acoustic signals, image streams, and sensor fusion outputs, allowing for nuanced failure mode identification and severity assessment. Complementing these are prognostics models that estimate the RUL of components through degradation modeling and survival analysis, providing a quantitative basis for maintenance scheduling and asset management [136].

Further enhancing the AI-IoT framework is the integration of digital twins, virtual replicas of physical assets continuously synchronized with live sensor data [137]. Digital twins offer a high-fidelity simulation environment in which predictive models can be validated, stress scenarios can be explored, and maintenance interventions can be optimized without disrupting physical operations. By visualizing system health in real time and enabling scenario-based forecasting, digital twins enhance transparency, control, and confidence in PdM strategies.

To ensure data integrity, provenance, and stakeholder trust, especially in multiactor manufacturing ecosystems, this framework can be fortified by blockchain technology [138]. Blockchain enables immutable logging of sensor data, alerts, maintenance actions, and compliance metrics, ensuring traceability and accountability throughout the asset life cycle. Additionally, smart contracts can automate the enforcement of service-level agreements, warranty conditions, and third-party payment triggers based on verified equipment health states [139]. This cryptographically secured infrastructure is essential for distributed, circular manufacturing systems where collaborative governance and transparent life-cycle documentation are prerequisites. Strategically, the integration of AI and IoT into health monitoring infrastructures supports CE principles by maximizing equipment productivity, reducing maintenance-related material waste, and enabling condition-based reuse and remanufacturing of components.

Furthermore, the continuous performance feedback generated by this system informs design-for-maintenance and design-for-disassembly strategies, closing the loop between operational insight and sustainable innovation [140]. When combined with blockchain and digital twin technologies, the AI-IoT ecosystem forms a resilient and autonomous foundation for intelligent circular production systems that are capable of self-optimization across technical, environmental, and economic dimensions.

14.6.3 Reducing Downtime and Extending Asset Lifespan

The integration of PdM into smart and circular manufacturing environments delivers a profound impact by minimizing unplanned downtime and extending the operational lifespan of critical industrial assets [141]. This paradigm shift replaces reactive and time-based maintenance strategies with condition-aware, data-driven interventions that anticipate failure trajectories and optimize service timing.

The approach supports not only operational resilience and cost reduction but also advances circularity by conserving material and energy embedded in high-value equipment. At the core of downtime reduction is the ability of PdM systems to continuously monitor sensor-derived data, such as temperature, vibration, torque, and acoustic emissions, against dynamically learned performance baselines.

When anomalies are detected or thresholds are breached, the system triggers real-time alerts, prompting targeted maintenance actions before significant deterioration or catastrophic failure occurs. These condition-based alerts ensure that servicing occurs only when required, thus preventing unnecessary inspections and minimizing production interruptions [142]. Maintenance schedules can be strategically aligned with noncritical periods, further enhancing equipment availability and throughput. Complementing this, early diagnostic capabilities powered by AI algorithms identify incipient failure patterns long before they manifest as operational disruptions [143]. Models trained on historical failure data can detect subtle precursors such as motor misalignment, bearing fatigue, seal degradation, or coolant inefficiencies. Timely identification of these signals prevents cascading mechanical failures, significantly reducing repair time and resource expenditure. This intelligence also enables failure containment, isolating issues before they compromise interconnected systems or escalate into multicomponent breakdowns. Intelligent spare part management is another essential component that facilitates uptime and life-cycle extension. Inventory strategies are informed by predictive analytics, which establishes a correlation between machine operating conditions and component wear rates [144]. This makes it easier to acquire replacement parts just when they are needed, preventing stock shortages and obsolescence. The right parts and procedures are proactively provided to maintenance teams, which streamlines servicing operations and reduces downtime.

Additionally, this data-aligned logistics model eliminates waste from unused or expired components and capital invested in idle inventory. The assistance that PdM offers to circularity-driven maintenance initiatives is equally significant. Predictive systems classify parts according to their remaining functional potential as they near the end of their useful lives, determining which are appropriate for material recycling, remanufacturing, or repair. This classification facilitates more efficient reverse logistics and end-of-life decision-making because it is based on condition monitoring rather than set schedules. Instead of being thrown away too soon, components are now directed into suitable circular flows that maintain their inherent value and lessen the environmental impact [145].

PdM can reduce total maintenance costs by 30–50%, reduce unexpected equipment failures by 70–75%, increase equipment uptime by 20–40%, and extend asset lifespans by 20–30%, according to reports from McKinsey & Company, Deloitte, and the WEF. These results translate into quantifiable gains in overall equipment effectiveness, reduced TCO, and improved return on capital employed [146, 147]. Strategically, these advantages reinforce manufacturing system resilience, lower capital replacement frequency, and support long-term asset productivity, which are core objectives in CE models.

By reducing material consumption, energy use, and emissions associated with overmaintenance and premature obsolescence, PdM contributes directly to sustainability metrics and corporate ESG compliance. In DCM ecosystems, PdM thus emerges not merely as a maintenance tactic but as a system-level enabler of regenerative industrial performance [147].

14.7 Case Studies of Digital Circular Manufacturing

DCM represents the fusion of Industry 4.0 technologies—AI, IoT, blockchain, and CPSs—with CE principles such as reuse, remanufacturing, recycling, and resource efficiency. This section presents empirical case studies highlighting the application of DCM across key industrial sectors, evaluating outcomes, and extracting strategic lessons [148–154].

14.7.1 Industry 4.0 Adoption in Circular Practices

The advent of Industry 4.0 technologies has fundamentally transformed the capabilities of manufacturers to embed CE principles within their operations. By leveraging IoT-enabled sensors, manufacturers can track material flows and product usage in real time, providing granular visibility into resource consumption and facilitating dynamic decision-making across the supply chain [148].

Concurrently, the integration of AI and digital twins enables precise prediction of product failures and supports life-cycle extension strategies by simulating operational conditions and maintenance scenarios. Furthermore, the deployment of blockchain-based smart contracts enhances transparency and trust in reverse logistics and recycling processes, ensuring the integrity of data exchanges among stakeholders and automating compliance with circularity standards [149].

Additionally, CPSs facilitate the simulation and optimization of circular production systems by tightly coupling physical processes with computational analytics and control mechanisms, enabling real-time adaptation to changing conditions. These digital interventions yield pronounced benefits in industries characterized by complex supply chains, high resource intensity, or stringent regulatory sustainability requirements, thus accelerating the transition toward regenerative and resilient manufacturing ecosystems [150].

Case 1: Digital Twin-Driven Remanufacturing at Choisy-le-Roi Plant (Renault Group France)

Renault's Choisy-le-Roi plant exemplifies a cutting-edge implementation of digital twin technology to revolutionize remanufacturing processes within the automotive sector. This facility integrates a sophisticated network of IoT sensors that continuously monitor the condition of returned engines and gearboxes throughout their life cycle [151]. Advanced analytics are based on the vital real-time operational data that these sensors record, including vibration signatures, temperature variations, and wear metrics. Renault uses AI-driven diagnostic algorithms to accurately classify parts for reuse, reconditioning, or material recycling by utilizing this data. By replacing traditional blanket refurbishment strategies with this condition-based decision-making framework, resources can be optimized and each part can be treated differently. Thus, an intelligent, flexible remanufacturing process that optimizes component recovery rates while reducing waste is fostered by the combination of sensor data and AI [152]. This innovation's foundation is the implementation of a high-fidelity digital twin. Renault is able to model, examine, and improve refurbishment processes in a dynamic digital setting by building a virtual version of the complete remanufacturing process. This allows for continuous process improvements through scenario testing, PdM scheduling, and real-time operational adjustments, resulting in enhanced efficiency, reduced turnaround times, and superior quality control. Empirical outcomes underscore the success of this digital transformation: approximately 75% of returned parts achieve remanufactured performance levels comparable to new components, underscoring the reliability and durability of the process.

Additionally, energy consumption is reduced by an estimated 43% relative to traditional manufacturing, contributing substantially to the facility's sustainability goals. Raw material usage is curtailed by up to 80%, significantly lowering dependency on virgin resources and mitigating environmental impacts associated with mining and material extraction.

Collectively, Renault's integration of IoT, AI, and digital twin technologies at the Choisy-le-Roi plant serves as a benchmark for sustainable circular manufacturing in the automotive industry. It demonstrates how digital innovation can drive systemic improvements in resource efficiency, operational agility, and environmental stewardship while maintaining product quality and customer satisfaction [151, 152].

Case 2: 3D Printing and Closed-Loop Cartridge Recycling (HP Inc.)

HP Inc. has established a pioneering CE framework in the electronics sector by integrating advanced digital technologies to enhance sustainability and operational efficiency across its global printing ecosystem [153]. Central to this initiative is the deployment of IoT-enabled printers equipped with sophisticated sensors that continuously monitor critical life-cycle parameters of printer cartridges. These sensors give precise insight into the condition and functionality of consumables by gathering data in real-time on cartridge usage, wear levels, and end-of-life status. HP has added blockchain technology to this IoT infrastructure to create a safe, unchangeable ledger that carefully monitors the origin, ownership, and flow of returned plastic materials across the supply chain for recycling and remanufacturing.

In addition to reducing the risks associated with illegal diversion and counterfeit materials, this blockchain-enabled traceability framework promotes stakeholder trust throughout the circular supply network by guaranteeing transparency, authenticity, and accountability [154]. HP is leading the way in large-scale electronics circularity by effectively processing over a million recycled cartridges every day by utilizing these digital innovations [155]. By reusing the recovered plastics in production streams, both for new printer cartridges and 3D-printed replacement parts, the environmental impact of conventional manufacturing processes is reduced and dependency on virgin plastic resins is greatly reduced. Moreover, HP uses supply chain analytics powered by AI to streamline reverse logistics processes. Cartridge returns, sorting, and reprocessing operations can be dynamically scheduled with the help of these analytics, which successfully lowers transportation costs, minimizes delays, and distributes the workload evenly among several recycling facilities [156]. This intelligent orchestration enhances operational agility and scalability, underpinning the economic sustainability of HP's closed-loop manufacturing model. Through the synergistic integration of IoT, blockchain, and AI technologies, HP exemplifies a robust digital enabler paradigm that advances the electronics industry's transition towards a circular, resource-efficient, and resilient manufacturing ecosystem [157].

Case 3: AI and IoT in Circular Fashion Operations (H&M Group Sweden)

H&M Group has embraced digital innovation to advance circularity within the fashion industry by integrating smart tagging technologies and AI into its reverse logistics and garment processing workflows. Central to this approach is the deployment of RFID-enabled smart tags embedded in garments, which provide real-time identification and material composition data throughout the product life cycle. Combined with the use of high-tech AI algorithms, the technology enables automatic sorting of returned garments based on the type of material they are made of, fabric blends, and quality.

To facilitate the proper routing of the clothing to destination end-of-life solutions, such as recycling, resale, or repairing, such a granular analysis based on the data entry is highly beneficial in terms of downstream processing choices [158, 159]. On top of the technological infrastructure, H&M uses digital platforms to generate recommendations based on data that can be used to optimize circular pathways of each piece of clothing. This integrated system enhances an efficient and sustainable supply chain with the potential to optimize material recovery rates, minimize manual sorting errors, and streamline operations. H&M's circular initiatives have yielded quantifiable operational and environmental gains. Approximately 60 percent of clothing returns are diverted out of landfills [159] to the appropriate textile recycling operations or resale markets.

Because of these results, the amount of virgin textile fibers consumed has significantly decreased, which has reduced the production's environmental impact. Moreover, provided programs have led to a massive decrease in life-cycle CO_2 emitted regarding the production and disposal of garments [160]. H&M's blockchain-powered customer engagement platform, which guarantees end-to-end transparency and traceability, is another tool that promotes circularity. This platform can also help in increasing consumer awareness and consumer trust by recording valuable data such as where the garment was produced or where the garment materials (e.g., label information) have come from in their life cycle and how to care for them within this platform. Moreover, it incentivizes customer participation in circular programs through rewards and return incentives, reinforcing sustainable consumption behaviors and closing the loop between producer and consumer. Through the synergistic application of IoT, AI, and blockchain technologies, H&M Group exemplifies how digital transformation can underpin scalable, transparent, and effective circular fashion operations that address both environmental imperatives and evolving consumer expectations.

14.7.2 Comparative Analysis of Implementation Outcomes

A comparative evaluation of DCM practices across the automotive, electronics, and textile sectors reveals sector-specific deployment of Industry 4.0 technologies that yield measurable environmental and economic benefits. The analysis underscores that strategic customization of digital tools, such as IoT, AI, blockchain, and digital twins, drives differentiated impacts aligned with the structural and material complexities of each industry [161].

In the automotive sector, the integration of IoT, AI, and digital twin technologies enables real-time component assessment and optimized remanufacturing workflows [162]. This has led to a 75% remanufacturing success rate and an 80% reduction in raw material usage, contributing to lower material procurement costs and prolonged asset life cycles. The electronics sector benefits from IoT and blockchain for cartridge life-cycle monitoring and secure material traceability, resulting in the recycling of over one million cartridges per day and significant plastic reuse. These outcomes translate into reduced production costs and enhanced supply chain transparency. Meanwhile, the textile sector uses AI-powered sorting algorithms, IoT-based material tracking, and blockchain-backed customer platforms to achieve a 60% circular diversion rate, with substantial revenue generated from resale markets and consumer engagement in sustainable return programs [163]. This cross-sector analysis highlights how digitalization enables CE outcomes tailored to sectoral dynamics, emphasizing remanufacturing efficiency in automotive, reverse logistics in electronics, and consumer-driven loops in textiles. The convergence of digital and circular strategies is thus not one-size-fits-all but is most effective when aligned with industry-specific value chains, regulatory pressures, and material flows. The digital circular practice implementation outcomes are summarized in Table 14.5.

Table 14.5 Comparative implementation outcomes of digital circular practices.

Sector	Digital tools used	Circular impact metrics	Economic impact
Automotive	IoT, AI, digital twin	75% remanufacturing rate; 80% reduction in raw material usage	Reduced material costs; increased equipment asset value
Electronics	IoT, blockchain, AI	Over 1 million cartridges recycled daily; significant plastic reuse	Lower production costs; enhanced supply chain traceability
Textile	AI, IoT, blockchain, smart tags	60% of returns diverted from landfill; circular processing enabled	New revenue from resale/ secondhand markets; consumer loyalty

14.7.3 Lessons Learned and Key Performance Indicators of Digital Circular Manufacturing

The implementation of DCM across diverse industrial sectors has yielded a set of actionable lessons and performance metrics that inform future scaling, replication, and procedure development. These insights emphasize the need for technological, organizational, and systemic alignment to realize the full value of Industry 4.0 tools in advancing CE outcomes [164, 165].

Lessons Learned

- **Digital infrastructure readiness is foundational**: The effectiveness of circular strategies is highly dependent on the maturity, interoperability, and scalability of digital infrastructure. Successful use of IoT, AI, digital twins, and blockchain requires robust sensor networks, data acquisition systems, edge/cloud computing platforms, and cybersecurity safeguards. Without these, predictive analytics, real-time traceability, and intelligent automation cannot be effectively operationalized.
- **Cross-sector collaboration is essential for circularity**: Achieving closed-loop systems necessitates the integration of diverse actors, including manufacturers, recyclers, logistics providers, and regulators, through shared data ecosystems and interoperable platforms. Seamless information exchange enables synchronized material flows, reverse logistics coordination, and life-cycle accountability.
- **Product design must align with digital circular tools**: The benefits of digital traceability and decision automation are significantly enhanced when embedded within design-for-disassembly, modularization, and material tagging frameworks. Digital systems must be codeveloped with circular product design strategies to ensure that repair, reuse, remanufacturing, and recycling are viable at scale.
- **Policy and consumer incentives catalyze adoption**: The uptake of digital circular technologies is accelerated by regulatory mechanisms, such as carbon pricing, EPR, and ESG disclosure mandates, and consumer-facing incentives, such as eco-labels, take-back schemes, and loyalty programs. These mechanisms create both top-down and bottom-up pressures for industrial transformation.

To quantitatively assess the effectiveness of DCM strategies, key performance indicators (KPIs) (Table 14.6) are recommended. The convergence of digital and circular manufacturing reveals that technological sophistication alone is insufficient; success hinges on an ecosystemic approach involving collaborative governance, user-centric design, and performance-driven

Table 14.6 Key performance indicators (KPIs) of digital circular manufacturing [164–166].

Category	Key performance indicator	Description
Circular efficiency	Remanufacturing/ recycling rate (%)	Percentage of components or materials successfully recovered and reintegrated into production
Resource optimization	Reduction in raw material consumption (%)	Comparative decrease in use of virgin resources enabled by digital monitoring and reuse loops
Operational uptime	Equipment downtime reduction (%)	Improvement in asset availability and performance *via* predictive maintenance
Carbon reduction	CO_2 emissions avoided (kg CO_2e/unit)	Life-cycle emissions reduction achieved through circular redesign and process optimization
Traceability coverage	Traceable material volume (%)	Share of products/components with end-to-end digital tracking (*via* RFID, blockchain, etc.)
Customer engagement	Return/resale participation Rate (%)	Proportion of consumers engaging in circular programs (returns, repairs, resale, or recycling)
Economic impact	Cost savings from circular operations (US $/ unit)	Net financial benefit achieved by implementing digital circular strategies
Innovation index	Percentage of SKUs redesigned for circularity (%)	Share of product portfolio incorporating circular design and digital feedback systems

measurement. Establishing and tracking clear KPIs ensures that digital circular strategies are not only visionary but verifiably effective across environmental, economic, and social dimensions [165, 166]. The deployment of DCM practices across the automotive, electronics, and textile sectors reveals measurable improvements in resource efficiency, operational resilience, and environmental performance. By leveraging Industry 4.0 technologies strategically, manufacturers can accelerate the transition from linear to circular systems, enhancing both competitiveness and sustainability in the evolving global economy.

14.8 Challenges and Future Directions

The adoption of Industry 4.0 technologies within circular manufacturing ecosystems offers transformative potential for achieving resource efficiency, waste minimization, and value retention across industrial sectors [99]. However, this transition is fraught with complex, multidimensional challenges encompassing technological integration, organizational inertia, regulatory fragmentation, cybersecurity vulnerabilities, and human capital readiness. Addressing these barriers is pivotal to the scalability, security, and inclusivity of digital circular transitions. Concurrently, emergent research trajectories and policy frameworks are reshaping the contours of digitally enabled circularity, demanding a forward-looking, systems-level approach to innovation and governance [101].

1. Technological, Organizational, and Regulatory Barriers
Despite considerable progress in digital manufacturing, structural constraints continue to impede widespread adoption of circular innovations. Chief among these is interoperability; the lack of standardization and seamless integration across heterogeneous digital platforms, legacy systems, and proprietary protocols stifles end-to-end visibility and data fluidity within supply chains [167]. Moreover, high capital expenditure requirements and uncertain return on investment pose significant entry barriers for small- and medium-sized enterprises (SMEs), particularly in the Global South. Regulatory uncertainty further compounds these challenges. Fragmented frameworks surrounding EPR, data sovereignty, and digital waste classification hinder cross-border collaboration and legal harmonization. Additionally, the absence of standardized metrics and taxonomies for assessing digital circularity obstructs benchmarking, certification, and investor alignment. To mitigate these constraints, there is a critical need for coherent transnational regulatory architectures, blended

financing models that de-risk private investments, and open-source digital infrastructures that democratize access to circular technologies and lower systemic entry thresholds [168].

2. Cybersecurity and Data Privacy Concerns

The proliferation of interconnected devices, platforms, and assets in circular manufacturing increases the system's vulnerability to cyber threats. Industrial IoT environments, often lacking robust endpoint security, are susceptible to malware infiltration, ransomware attacks, and data breaches that can severely disrupt closed-loop operations or compromise proprietary product data [169]. Compounding these risks are emerging data privacy regulations, notably the EU General Data Protection Regulation and forthcoming Artificial Intelligence Acts, which impose complex compliance obligations, especially for blockchain-enabled traceability systems that record immutable personal or material data. The prevailing deficit in cyber risk governance within manufacturing enterprises exacerbates exposure and limits organizational resilience. A secure digital circular infrastructure must be underpinned by end-to-end cybersecurity architectures, including zero-trust security models, blockchain-based identity management, and privacy-preserving AI analytics. These technologies should be complemented by real-time threat detection systems and sector-specific cyber hygiene standards [170].

3. Skills Gap and Workforce Adaptation

DCM necessitates a paradigm shift in workforce capabilities, emphasizing hybrid proficiencies in engineering, data analytics, and sustainability. However, many industrial workers lack exposure to AI/ML model interpretation, cybersecurity protocols, digital twin management, and IoT system operations [171]. The accelerating pace of technological change has outstripped the ability of most education and training systems to respond effectively, particularly in vocational and technical education domains. This skills mismatch not only threatens the competitiveness of firms but may also exacerbate technological unemployment and regional disparities, especially in economies with labor-intensive, low-digitization industrial bases. To address these risks, policy and industry actors must invest in lifelong learning ecosystems, modernize technical and vocational education and training programs, and embed green-digital hybrid curricula that prepare workers for AI-augmented, sustainability-oriented production environments. Equity-focused training initiatives should prioritize vulnerable populations, including women and youth in underrepresented regions [171].

4. Future Research Trends and Policy Implications
Advancing DCM requires a forward-looking research and policy agenda centered on systemic innovation, cross-sectoral integration, and ethical stewardship.

Key emerging trends include:

1. **AI for circular design**: The development of generative design algorithms, materials informatics, and life cycle–optimized digital tools that embed circularity at the design stage, enabling smarter material selection and modular product architecture.
2. **Ethical and explainable AI**: Building transparent, auditable, and accountable AI systems that govern circular decision-making processes, such as automated waste sorting, secondary resource allocation, and value chain optimization.
3. **Cross-scale digital twins**: Extending beyond single-machine or factory models toward ecosystem-level digital twins, capable of simulating interdependent industrial flows across eco-industrial parks, urban symbiosis networks, and regional circular clusters.
4. **Integrated policy alignment**: Synchronizing digital and CE agendas through alignment with frameworks such as the EU Circular Economy Action Plan, UN SDGs, and OECD Digital Transformation strategies.
5. **Next-generation impact metrics**: Moving beyond economic indicators to incorporate multidimensional performance metrics that capture environmental equity, digital inclusivity, and socio-economic resilience across value chains.

14.9 Concluding Remarks

DCM represents a paradigm shift at the intersection of the CE and Industry 4.0, offering a transformative pathway toward sustainable, resource-efficient, and resilient industrial systems. This chapter has demonstrated that the integration of advanced digital technologies—AI, IoT, blockchain, digital twins, and CPSs—fundamentally enhances the visibility, traceability, and adaptability of manufacturing processes. These tools collectively enable closed-loop material cycles, intelligent product life-cycle management, and data-driven decision-making, thereby accelerating the transition from linear to circular value creation. Theoretical frameworks such as industrial ecology, systems thinking, and LCA have provided a robust foundation for understanding how digital enablers operationalize CE principles in real-world manufacturing contexts.

Through empirical case studies across the automotive, electronics, and textile sectors, this chapter has highlighted the tangible economic, environmental, and operational benefits of DCM, including reductions in raw material consumption, CO_2 emissions, unplanned downtime, and waste generation, while also generating new value through remanufacturing, servitization, and consumer engagement. However, realizing the full potential of DCM necessitates overcoming several multidimensional challenges. These include the fragmentation of digital infrastructure, cybersecurity vulnerabilities, a widening skills gap, and regulatory misalignments. Interoperability remains a critical issue, underscoring the need for standardized architectures and protocols that seamlessly integrate AI, IoT, and blockchain technologies. Furthermore, aligning policy incentives, market mechanisms, and education systems with circular and digital transitions is essential for inclusive and equitable deployment, particularly among SMEs and developing regions.

Looking ahead, future research and innovation must focus on developing ecosystem-scale digital twins, explainable AI models tailored for circularity, and integrative metrics that holistically assess circular and sustainability performance. Interdisciplinary collaboration among technologists, policymakers, business leaders, and academics will be vital to shaping governance frameworks, ethical guidelines, and institutional support for DCM.

In sum, DCM is not merely a technological advancement; it is a systems-level reimagination of industrial production, consumption, and regeneration. By uniting the intelligence of digital systems with the regenerative goals of the CE, it offers a viable pathway toward achieving net-zero emissions, economic resilience, and global sustainability. This convergence marks a decisive step toward the Fourth Industrial Revolution's alignment with planetary boundaries and human well-being.

14.10 Exercise Questions

1. Define the CE and explain how it differs fundamentally from the traditional linear "take–make–use–dispose" model.
   - Hint: Use concepts such as closed-loop systems, resource efficiency, and product-service systems in your explanation.
2. List and briefly explain the six components of the 6Rs framework in circular manufacturing. How do they support sustainable industrial systems?
3. Discuss the role of AI in enabling circular manufacturing. Focus on at least two specific applications, such as predictive analytics and material recovery.

4. How does the integration of IoT sensors contribute to real-time monitoring and life-cycle tracking in circular supply chains? Provide an example from the case studies.
5. Explain how blockchain technology enhances traceability and trust in circular manufacturing. What are smart contracts, and how do they promote sustainable supplier management?
6. Using the case of Renault Group or HP Inc., describe how digital tools have been used to achieve measurable outcomes in circular manufacturing. Include KPIs.
7. Critically analyze the key challenges that hinder the implementation of DCM, such as data interoperability and infrastructure fragmentation. Suggest at least two strategies to overcome them.

AI disclosure statement: The author acknowledges the use of AI-based tools for minor language editing or grammatical correction. However, all intellectual contributions, analyses, and conclusions presented in this chapter are entirely the author's own.

References

1. Chizaryfard, A., Trucco, P., Nuur, C., The transformation to a circular economy: Framing an evolutionary view. *J. Evol. Econ.*, 31, 475–504, 2021.
2. Ghisellini, P., Cialani, C., Ulgiati, S., A review on circular economy: the expected transition to a balanced interplay of environmental and economic systems. *J. Cleaner Prod.*, 114, 11–32, 2016.
3. Sasu-Boakye, Y. and Olsson, V., The impact of consumer-to-consumer online platforms on the competitive strategies of traditional second-hand retail stores in Southern Sweden, 2024.
4. Kara, S., Hauschild, M., Sutherland, J., McAloone, T., Closed-loop systems to circular economy: A pathway to environmental sustainability?. *CIRP Ann.*, 71, 2, 505–528, 2022.
5. Bashmakov, I.A., Nilsson, L.J., Acquaye, A., Bataille, C., Cullen, J.M., Fischedick, M., Geng, Y., Tanaka, K., Climate Change 2022: Mitigation of Climate Change, in: *Contribution of Working Group III to the Sixth Assessment Report of the Intergovernmental Panel on Climate Change, Chapter 11*, 2022.
6. Lima, A.T., Kirkelund, G.M., Lu, Z., Mao, R., Kunther, W., Rode, C., Slabik, S., Hafner, A., Sameer, H., Dürr, H.H., Flörke, M., Mapping circular economy practices for steel, cement, glass, brick, insulation, and wood–A review for climate mitigation modeling. *Renew. Sustain. Energy Rev.*, 202, 114697, 2024.

7. Milios, L., Policies for Resource Efficient and Effective Solutions: A review of concepts, current policy landscape and future policy considerations for the transition to a Circular Economy, 2016.
8. Elf, P., Werner, A., Black, S., Advancing the circular economy through dynamic capabilities and extended customer engagement: Insights from small sustainable fashion enterprises in the UK. *Bus. Strategy Environ.*, 31, 6, 2682–2699, 2022.
9. Koilo, V., Driving the Circular Economy Through Digital Servitization: Sustainable Business Models in the Maritime Sector. *Businesses*, 5, 1, 12, 2025.
10. Dahiya, S., Katakojwala, R., Ramakrishna, S., Mohan, S.V., Biobased products and life cycle assessment in the context of circular economy and sustainability. *Mater. Circ. Econ.*, 2, 1–28, 2020.
11. Wautelet, T., of thesis: Exploring the role of independent retailers in the circular economy: a. *Prod. Eng.*, 33, 5, 308–320.
12. Naicker, P., Climate Change Projections and Public Behaviour Towards Adopting Integrated Mitigation and Adaptation Approaches at a Household Level in Urban Areas, the EThekwini Municipality, KwaZulu-Natal, Doctoral dissertation, University of KwaZulu-Natal, Westville, 2018.
13. Han, Y., Shevchenko, T., Yannou, B., Ranjbari, M., Shams Esfandabadi, Z., Saidani, M., Bouillass, G., Bliumska-Danko, K., Li, G., Exploring how digital technologies enable a circular economy of products. *Sustainability*, 15, 3, 2067, 2023.
14. Greer, C., Burns, M., Wollman, D., Griffor, E., Cyber-physical systems and internet of things, 2019.
15. Gbadamosi, A.Q.O., An internet of things enabled system for real-time monitoring and predictive maintenance of railway infrastructure, Doctoral dissertation, Dissertation, University of the West of England, Bristol, 2023.
16. Soori, M., Arezoo, B., Dastres, R., Artificial intelligence, machine learning and deep learning in advanced robotics, a review. *Cognit. Rob.*, 3, 54–70, 2023.
17. Delbari, S.A. and Hof, L.A., Glass waste circular economy-Advancing to high-value glass sheets recovery using industry 4.0 and 5.0 technologies. *J. Cleaner Prod.*, 142629, 2024.
18. Farahani, B., Firouzi, F., Luecking, M., The convergence of IoT and distributed ledger technologies (DLT): Opportunities, challenges, and solutions. *J. Network Comput. Appl.*, 177, 102936, 2021.
19. Roeck, D., Sternberg, H., Hofmann, E., Distributed ledger technology in supply chains: a transaction cost perspective. *Int. J. Prod. Res.*, 58, 7, 2124–2141, 2020.
20. Ben-Ner, A. and Siemsen, E., Decentralization and localization of production: The organizational and economic consequences of additive manufacturing (3D printing). *Calif. Manage. Rev.*, 59, 2, 5–23, 2017.
21. Nyamekye, P., Lakshmanan, R., Tepponen, V., Westman, S., Sustainability aspects of additive manufacturing: Leveraging resource efficiency *via* product design optimization and laser powder bed fusion. *Heliyon*, 10, 1, 2024.

22. Turner, C. and Oyekan, J., Personalised production in the age of circular additive manufacturing. *Appl. Sci.*, 13, 8, 4912, 2023.
23. Ragaert, K., Delva, L., Van Geem, K., Mechanical and chemical recycling of solid plastic waste. *Waste Manag.*, 69, 24–58, 2017.
24. Fuller, A., Fan, Z., Day, C., Barlow, C., Digital twin: enabling technologies, challenges and open research. *IEEE Access*, 8, 108952–108971, 2020.
25. Soori, M., Arezoo, B., Dastres, R., Digital twin for smart manufacturing, A review. *Sustainable Manuf. Serv. Econ.*, 2, 100017, 2023.
26. Dai, H.N., Wang, H., Xu, G., Wan, J., Imran, M., Big data analytics for manufacturing internet of things: opportunities, challenges and enabling technologies. *Enterp. Inf. Syst.*, 14, 9–10, 1279–1303, 2020.
27. Onyeje, C.C., Oshilalu, A.Z., Fadojutimi, B., Data-driven analytics and modelling of circular supply chains for net zero manufacturing. *World J. Adv. Res. Rev.*, 23, 3, 1097–1121, 2024.
28. D'Amico, G., Arbolino, R., Shi, L., Yigitcanlar, T., Ioppolo, G., Digital technologies for urban metabolism efficiency: Lessons from urban agenda partnership on circular economy. *Sustainability*, 13, 11, 6043, 2021.
29. Mondejar, M.E., Avtar, R., Diaz, H.L.B., Dubey, R.K., Esteban, J., Gómez-Morales, A., Hallam, B., Mbungu, N.T., Okolo, C.C., Prasad, K.A., She, Q., Digitalization to achieve sustainable development goals: Steps towards a Smart Green Planet. *Sci. Total Environ.*, 794, 148539, 2021.
30. Sharma, H.B., Vanapalli, K.R., Samal, B., Cheela, V.S., Dubey, B.K., Bhattacharya, J., Circular economy approach in solid waste management system to achieve UN-SDGs: Solutions for post-COVID recovery. *Sci. Total Environ.*, 800, 149605, 2021.
31. Korhonen, J., Nuur, C., Feldmann, A., Birkie, S.E., Circular economy as an essentially contested concept. *J. Cleaner Prod.*, 175, 544–552, 2018.
32. Korhonen, J., Honkasalo, A., Seppälä, J., Circular economy: the concept and its limitations. *Ecological Economics*, 143, 37–46, 2018.
33. Den Hollander, M.C., Bakker, C.A., Hultink, E.J., Product design in a circular economy: Development of a typology of key concepts and terms. *J. Ind. Ecol.*, 21, 3, 517–525, 2017.
34. Reike, D., Vermeulen, W.J., Witjes, S., The circular economy: new or refurbished as CE 3.0?—exploring controversies in the conceptualization of the circular economy through a focus on history and resource value retention options. *Resour. Conserv. Recycl.*, 135, 246–264, 2018.
35. Langley, D.J., Digital product-service systems: The role of data in the transition to servitization business models. *Sustainability*, 14, 3, 1303, 2022.
36. Ioppolo, G., Cucurachi, S., Salomone, R., Shi, L., Yigitcanlar, T., Integrating strategic environmental assessment and material flow accounting: a novel approach for moving towards sustainable urban futures. *Int. J. Life Cycle Assess.*, 24, 1269–1284, 2019.
37. Garcia-Muiña, F.E., González-Sánchez, R., Ferrari, A.M., Settembre-Blundo, D., The paradigms of Industry 4.0 and circular economy as enabling drivers

for the competitiveness of businesses and territories: The case of an Italian ceramic tiles manufacturing company. *Soc. Sci.*, 7, 12, 255, 2018.
38. De los Rios, I.C. and Charnley, F.J., Skills and capabilities for a sustainable and circular economy: The changing role of design. *J. Cleaner Prod.*, 160, 109–122, 2017.
39. Brenner, B., Transformative sustainable business models in the light of the digital imperative—A global business economics perspective. *Sustainability*, 10, 12, 4428, 2018.
40. Pereira, T., Kennedy, J.V., Potgieter, J., A comparison of traditional manufacturing vs additive manufacturing, the best method for the job. *Procedia Manuf.*, 30, 11–18, 2019.
41. Khan, A. and Turowski, K., A survey of current challenges in manufacturing industry and preparation for industry 4.0, in: *Proceedings of the First International Scientific Conference "Intelligent Information Technologies for Industry" (IITI'16)*, vol. 1, Springer International Publishing, pp. 15–26, 2016.
42. Bertola, P. and Colombi, C., Can fashion be sustainable? Trajectories of change in organizational, products and processes, and socio-cultural contexts. *Sustainability: Sci. Pract. Policy*, 20, 1, 2312682, 2024.
43. Limon, G.Q., Lean Manufacturing and ERP Integration: A Systematic Review of Process Efficiency Tools in the Apparel Sector, 2023, Available at SSRN 5268414.
44. Dzhengiz, T., Miller, E.M., Ovaska, J.P., Patala, S., Unpacking the circular economy: A problematizing review. *Int. J. Manage. Rev.*, 25, 2, 270–296, 2023.
45. Mishra, J.L., Chiwenga, K.D., Ali, K., Collaboration as an enabler for circular economy: A case study of a developing country. *Manage. Decis.*, 59, 8, 1784–1800, 2021.
46. Bressanelli, G., Pigosso, D.C., Saccani, N., Perona, M., Enablers, levers and benefits of Circular Economy in the Electrical and Electronic Equipment supply chain: A literature review. *J. Cleaner Prod.*, 298, 126819, 2021.
47. Bressanelli, G., Adrodegari, F., Perona, M., Saccani, N., Exploring how usage-focused business models enable circular economy through digital technologies. *Sustainability*, 10, 3, 639, 2018.
48. Geng, X., Wang, F., Wu, H.H., Wang, S., Wu, G., Gao, J., Zhao, H., Zhang, C., Mao, X., Data-driven and artificial intelligence accelerated steel material research and intelligent manufacturing technology. *Mater. Genome Eng. Adv.*, 1, 1, e10, 2023.
49. Garg, D., Mustaqueem, O.A., Kumar, R., Sustainable circular manufacturing in the digital era: analysis of enablers, in: *Advances in Industrial and Production Engineering: Select Proceedings of FLAME 2020*, Springer Singapore, pp. 541–554, 2021.
50. Ghadimi, P., O'Neill, S., Wang, C., Sutherland, J.W., Analysis of enablers on the successful implementation of green manufacturing for Irish SMEs. *J. Manuf. Technol. Manage.*, 32, 1, 85–109, 2021.

51. Domenech, T., Doranova, A., Roman, L., Smith, M., Artola, I., Cooperation fostering industrial symbiosis: market potential, good practice and policy actions, A Report for the European Commission, DG Internal Market, Industry, Entrepreneurship and SMEs, 2018.
52. Watson, R., Wilson, H.N., Smart, P., Macdonald, E.K., Harnessing difference: a capability-based framework for stakeholder engagement in environmental innovation. *J. Prod. Innov. Manage.*, 35, 2, 254–279, 2018.
53. Ranängen, H., Cöster, M., Isaksson, R., Garvare, R., From global goals and planetary boundaries to public governance—a framework for prioritizing organizational sustainability activities. *Sustainability*, 10, 8, 2741, 2018.
54. Wilson, M., Paschen, J., Pitt, L., The circular economy meets artificial intelligence (AI): Understanding the opportunities of AI for reverse logistics. *Manag. Environ. Qual.: Int. J.*, 33, 1, 9–25, 2022.
55. Ghoreishi, M. and Happonen, A., Key enablers for deploying artificial intelligence for circular economy embracing sustainable product design: Three case studies. *AIP Conf. Proc.*, AIP Publishing, 2233, 1, 2020, May.
56. Ronaghi, M.H., The influence of artificial intelligence adoption on circular economy practices in manufacturing industries. *Environ. Dev. Sustainability*, 25, 12, 14355–14380, 2023.
57. Chen, S.C., Chen, H.M., Chen, H.K., Li, C.L., Multi-Objective Optimization in Industry 5.0: Human-Centric AI Integration for Sustainable and Intelligent Manufacturing. *Processes*, 12, 12, 2723, 2024.
58. Aldoseri, A., Al-Khalifa, K.N., Hamouda, A.M., AI-powered innovation in digital transformation: Key pillars and industry impact. *Sustainability*, 16, 5, 1790, 2024.
59. Rathore, M.M., Shah, S.A., Shukla, D., Bentafat, E., Bakiras, S., The role of ai, machine learning, and big data in digital twinning: A systematic literature review, challenges, and opportunities. *IEEE Access*, 9, 32030–32052, 2021.
60. Moraga, G., Huysveld, S., Mathieux, F., Blengini, G.A., Alaerts, L., Van Acker, K., De Meester, S., Dewulf, J., Circular economy indicators: What do they measure?. *Resour. Conserv. Recycl.*, 146, 452–461, 2019.
61. Bernat, K., Post-consumer plastic waste management: From collection and sortation to mechanical recycling. *Energies*, 16, 8, 3504, 2023.
62. Peng, H., Jiang, Z., Wang, H., Research on ecological efficiency for the remanufacturing process considering optimization and evaluation. *Processes*, 7, 9, 567, 2019.
63. Peng, H., Wang, H., Chen, D., Optimization of remanufacturing process routes oriented toward eco-efficiency. *Front. Mech. Eng.*, 14, 422–433, 2019.
64. Sharma, P. and Bora, B.J., A review of modern machine learning techniques in the prediction of remaining useful life of lithium-ion batteries. *Batteries*, 9, 1, 13, 2022.
65. Ferreira, C. and Gonçalves, G., Remaining Useful Life prediction and challenges: A literature review on the use of Machine Learning Methods. *J. Manuf. Syst.*, 63, May, 550–562, 2022.

66. Lin, K.Y. and Wei, S.H., Advancing the industrial circular economy: the integrative role of machine learning in resource optimization. *J. Green Econ. Low-Carbon Dev.*, 2, 3, 122–136, 2023.
67. Lopes de Sousa Jabbour, A.B., Jabbour, C.J.C., Godinho Filho, M., Roubaud, D., Industry 4.0 and the circular economy: a proposed research agenda and original roadmap for sustainable operations. *Ann. Oper. Res.*, 270, 273–286, 2018.
68. Mishra, S., Jena, L., Tripathy, H.K., Gaber, T., Prioritized and predictive intelligence of things enabled waste management model in smart and sustainable environment. *Plos One*, 17, 8, e0272383, 2022.
69. Söderlund, S. and Lilja, T., What KPIs are fundamental for the business model "Equipment-as-a-Service" at one of Sweden's largest automotive manufacturers?. 2023.
70. Enyejo, J.O., Fajana, O.P., Jok, I.S., Ihejirika, C.J., Awotiwon, B.O., Olola, T.M., Digital Twin Technology, Predictive Analytics, and Sustainable Project Management in Global Supply Chains for Risk Mitigation, Optimization, and Carbon Footprint Reduction through Green Initiatives. *Int. J. Innov. Sci. Res. Technol.*, 9, 11, 2024.
71. Lakhouit, A., Revolutionizing Urban Solid Waste Management with AI and IoT: A review of smart solutions for waste collection, sorting, and recycling. *Results Eng.*, 104018, 2025.
72. Bhardwaj, K. and Soryan, R., Advancing Circular Economy Through AI-Driven E-Waste Management: A Comprehensive Review of Current Research, Challenges, and Future Directions, 2025.
73. Hettiarachchi, B.D., Brandenburg, M., Seuring, S., Connecting additive manufacturing to circular economy implementation strategies: Links, contingencies and causal loops. *Int. J. Prod. Econ.*, 246, 108414, 2022.
74. Cavalieri, A., Reis, J., Amorim, M., Circular economy and internet of things: Mapping science of case studies in manufacturing industry. *Sustainability*, 13, 6, 3299, 2021.
75. Syafrudin, M., Alfian, G., Fitriyani, N.L., Rhee, J., Performance analysis of IoT-based sensor, big data processing, and machine learning model for real-time monitoring system in automotive manufacturing. *Sensors*, 18, 9, 2946, 2018.
76. Barton, K., Maturana, F., Tilbury, D., Closing the loop in IoT-enabled manufacturing systems: Challenges and opportunities, in *2018 Annual American Control Conference (ACC)*, IEEE, pp. 5503–5509, 2018, June.
77. Soori, M., Arezoo, B., Dastres, R., Internet of things for smart factories in industry 4.0, a review. *Internet Things Cyber-Phys. Syst.*, 3, 192–204, 2023.
78. da Costa, T.P., da Costa, D.M.B., Murphy, F., A systematic review of real-time data monitoring and its potential application to support dynamic life cycle inventories. *Environ. Impact Assess. Rev.*, 105, 107416, 2024.
79. Jum'a, L., Ikram, M., Jabbour, C.J.C., Towards circular economy: A IoT enabled framework for circular supply chain integration. *Comput. Ind. Eng.*, 192, 110194, 2024.

80. Alam, S.S., Latif, M.M., Kokash, H.A., Ahsan, M.N., Relationship among Industrial IoT, Circular Supply Chain Management Practices and Sustainable Performance of Manufacturing Companies: an Empirical Study. *Circ. Econ. Sustainability*, 1–28, 2025.
81. Ochella, S.M., Advanced data-driven methods for prognostics and life extension of assets using condition monitoring and sensor data, 2021.
82. Ferreira, B., Artificial Intelligence Applied to Supply Chain Management and Logistics: Systematic Literature Review, 2023.
83. Kerin, M. and Pham, D.T., Smart remanufacturing: a review and research framework. *J. Manuf. Technol. Manag.*, 31, 6, 1205–1235, 2020.
84. Garrido-Hidalgo, C., Roda-Sanchez, L., Javier Ramírez, F., Olivares, T., IoT-driven digital twin for improved product disassembly in remanufacturing, in: *International Workshop on Autonomous Remanufacturing*, pp. 281–291, Springer Nature Switzerland, Cham, 2023, October.
85. Fofou, R.F., Jiang, Z., Wang, Y., A review on the lifecycle strategies enhancing remanufacturing. *Appl. Sci.*, 11, 13, 5937, 2021.
86. Ambiado, V., Enhancing Circular Practices in the Automotive Manufacturing Industry-Exploring Opportunities and Challenges of Remanufacturing Electronic Control Units (ECUs), 2023.
87. Kandasamy, J., KEK, V., Ethirajan, M., Murali, N., Role of Industry 4.0 in the Future Circular Supply Chain Management, in: *Circular Supply Chain Management: A Sustainability Approach*, pp. 143–178, Springer Nature Switzerland, Cham, 2025.
88. Sunny, J., Undralla, N., Pillai, V.M., Supply chain transparency through blockchain-based traceability: An overview with demonstration. *Comput. Ind. Eng.*, 150, 106895, 2020.
89. Jeppsson, A. and Olsson, O., Blockchains as a solution for traceability and transparency, 2017.
90. Komalavalli, C., Saxena, D., Laroiya, C., Overview of Blockchain Technology Concepts, in: *Handbook of Research on Blockchain Technology*, pp. 349–371, Academic Press, Cambridge, MA, 2020.
91. Selvaprabhu, P., An examination of distributed and decentralized systems for trustworthy control of supply chains. *IEEE Access*, 11, 137025–137052, 2023.
92. Politou, E., Casino, F., Alepis, E., Patsakis, C., Blockchain mutability: Challenges and proposed solutions. *IEEE Trans. Emerging Top. Comput.*, 9, 4, 1972–1986, 2019.
93. Groschopf, W., Dobrovnik, M., Herneth, C., Smart contracts for sustainable supply chain management: Conceptual frameworks for supply chain maturity evaluation and smart contract sustainability assessment. *Front. Blockchain*, 4, 506436, 2021.
94. Dal Mas, F., Dicuonzo, G., Massaro, M., Dell'Atti, V., Smart contracts to enable sustainable business models. A case study. *Manage. Decis.*, 58, 8, 1601–1619, 2020.

95. Wilson, S., Adu-Duodu, K., Li, Y., Sham, R., Almubarak, M., Wang, Y., Solaiman, E., Perera, C., Ranjan, R., Rana, O., Blockchain-enabled provenance tracking for sustainable material reuse in construction supply chains. *Future Internet*, 16, 4, 135, 2024.
96. Xu, J., Lou, J., Lu, W., Wu, L., Chen, C., Ensuring construction material provenance using Internet of Things and blockchain: Learning from the food industry. *J. Ind. Inf. Integr.*, 33, 100455, 2023.
97. Hrouga, M., Sbihi, A., Chavallard, M., The potentials of combining Blockchain technology and Internet of Things for digital reverse supply chain: A case study. *J. Cleaner Prod.*, 337, 130609, 2022.
98. Zhang, X., Feng, X., Jiang, Z., Gong, Q., Wang, Y., A blockchain-enabled framework for reverse supply chain management of power batteries. *J. Cleaner Prod.*, 415, 137823, 2023.
99. Mamudu, U.U., Obasi, C.D., Awuye, S.K., Danso, H., Ayodele, P., Akinyemi, P., Circular economy in the manufacturing sector: Digital transformation and sustainable practices. *Int. J. Sci. Res. Arch.*, 12, 02, 129–141, 2024.
100. Bhumichai, D., Smiliotopoulos, C., Benton, R., Kambourakis, G., Damopoulos, D., The convergence of artificial intelligence and blockchain: The state of play and the road ahead. *Information*, 15, 5, 268, 2024.
101. Chadha, U., Abraham, A., Anilkumar, K., Kuriyakkattil, V., Singh, H., Bane, S., Chadha, A., Armstrong, S., Patterson, A., Synergizing Lean Six Sigma Framework Using Artificial Intelligence, Internet of Things, and Blockchain for Sustainable Manufacturing Excellence, Authorea Preprints, 2024.
102. Gallicchio, C., Micheli, A., Dragone, M., Saffiotti, A., and Simoens, P., Internet of Robotic Things: Converging Sensing/Actuating, Hyperconnectivity, Artificial Intelligence and IoT Platforms. *Cognitive Hyperconnected Digital Transformation*, pp. 97–155, River Publishers, Gistrup, Denmark, 2022.
103. Rane, N., Choudhary, S., Rane, J., Blockchain and Artificial Intelligence (AI) integration for revolutionizing security and transparency in finance, 2023, Available at SSRN 4644253.
104. Dolci, V., Bigliardi, B., Petroni, A., Pini, B., Filippelli, S., Tagliente, L., Integrating Industry 4.0 and circular economy: a conceptual framework for sustainable manufacturing. *Procedia Comput. Sci.*, 232, 1711–1720, 2024.
105. Alaba, F.A., IoT Architecture Layers, in: *Internet of Things: A Case Study in Africa*, pp. 65–85, Springer Nature Switzerland, Cham, 2024.
106. Ilmudeen, A., Artificial intelligence, big data analytics and big data processing for IoT-based sensing data, in: *Transforming management with AI, big-data, and IoT*, pp. 247–259, Springer International Publishing, Cham, 2022.
107. Paramesha, M., Rane, N.L., Rane, J., Big data analytics, artificial intelligence, machine learning, internet of things, and blockchain for enhanced business intelligence. *Partners Univ. Multidiscip. Res. J.*, 1, 2, 110–133, 2024.
108. Ahmed, S., Enhancing Data Security and Transparency: The Role of Blockchain in Decentralized Systems. *Int. J. Adv. Eng., Manag. Sci.*, 11, 1, 593258, 2025.

109. Groshev, M., Guimaraes, C., Martín-Pérez, J., de la Oliva, A., Toward intelligent cyber-physical systems: Digital twin meets artificial intelligence. *IEEE Commun. Mag.*, 59, 8, 14–20, 2021.
110. Trakadas, P., Simoens, P., Gkonis, P., Sarakis, L., Angelopoulos, A., Ramallo-González, A.P., Skarmeta, A., Trochoutsos, C., Calvo, D., Pariente, T., Chintamani, K., An artificial intelligence-based collaboration approach in industrial iot manufacturing: Key concepts, architectural extensions and potential applications. *Sensors*, 20, 19, 5480, 2020.
111. Qian, C., Liu, X., Ripley, C., Qian, M., Liang, F., Yu, W., Digital twin—Cyber replica of physical things: Architecture, applications and future research directions. *Future Internet*, 14, 2, 64, 2022.
112. Roopa, M.S. and Venugopal, K.R., Digital Twins for Cyber-Physical Healthcare Systems: Architecture, Requirements, Systematic Analysis and Future Prospects. *IEEE Access*, 2025.
113. Redelinghuys, A.J.H., Basson, A.H., Kruger, K., A six-layer architecture for the digital twin: a manufacturing case study implementation. *J. Intell. Manuf.*, 31, 6, 1383–1402, 2020.
114. Atalay, M., Murat, U., Oksuz, B., Parlaktuna, A.M., Pisirir, E., Testik, M.C., Digital twins in manufacturing: Systematic literature review for physical–digital layer categorization and future research directions. *Int. J. Computer Integr. Manuf.*, 35, 7, 679–705, 2022.
115. Steindl, G., Stagl, M., Kasper, L., Kastner, W., Hofmann, R., Generic digital twin architecture for industrial energy systems. *Appl. Sci.*, 10, 24, 8903, 2020.
116. Javaid, M., Haleem, A., Suman, R., Digital twin applications toward industry 4.0: A review. *Cognit. Rob.*, 3, 71–92, 2023.
117. Preut, A., Kopka, J.P., Clausen, U., Digital twins for the circular economy. *Sustainability*, 13, 18, 10467, 2021.
118. Pehlken, A., Dawel, L., Meyer, O., Digital twins: enhancing circular economy through digital tools. *Procedia CIRP*, 122, 563–568, 2024.
119. Van Dyck, M., Lüttgens, D., Piller, F.T., Brenk, S., Interconnected digital twins and the future of digital manufacturing: Insights from a Delphi study. *J. Prod. Innovation Manage.*, 40, 4, 475–505, 2023.
120. Ferrer, B.R., Mohammed, W.M., Lastra, J.L.M., Villalonga, A., Beruvides, G., Castaño, F., Haber, R.E., Towards the adoption of cyber-physical systems of systems paradigm in smart manufacturing environments, in: *2018 IEEE 16th International Conference on Industrial Informatics (INDIN)*, pp. 792–799, IEEE, 2018, July.
121. Pesce, D., Franzè, C., Paolucci, E., Meeting the closed-loop challenge: The "Who-What-How" strategic choices for a successful remanufacturing approach. *Bus. Strategy Environ.*, 33, 6, 5661–5680, 2024.
122. Ma, Z., Xiao, M., Xiao, Y., Pang, Z., Poor, H.V., Vucetic, B., High-reliability and low-latency wireless communication for internet of things: Challenges,

fundamentals, and enabling technologies. *IEEE Internet Things J.*, 6, 5, 7946–7970, 2019.

123. Mahmood, H.S., Abdulqader, D.M., Abdullah, R.M., Rasheed, H., Ismael, Z.N.R., Sami, T.M.G., Conducting In-Depth Analysis of AI, IoT, Web Technology, Cloud Computing, and Enterprise Systems Integration for Enhancing Data Security and Governance to Promote Sustainable Business Practices. *J. Inf. Technol. Inform.*, 3, 2, 2024.
124. Eom, S.J., The emerging digital twin bureaucracy in the 21st century. *Perspect. Public Manag. Gov.*, 5, 2, 174–186, 2022.
125. Fatorachian, H. and Smith, C., Impact of CPS on Enhancing Supply Chain Resilience, with a Focus on Solutions to Pandemic Challenges. *Cyber-Physical Systems*, pp. 109–125, CRC Press, Boca Raton, FL, 2022.
126. Bongomin, O., Positioning Industrial Engineering in the Era of Industry 4.0, 5.0, and Beyond: Pathways to Innovation and Sustainability, 2025.
127. Lou, S., Hu, Z., Zhang, Y., Feng, Y., Zhou, M., Lv, C., Human-cyber-physical system for Industry 5.0: A review from a human-centric perspective. *IEEE Trans. Autom. Sci. Eng.*, 22, 494–511, 2024.
128. Çınar, Z.M., Abdussalam Nuhu, A., Zeeshan, Q., Korhan, O., Asmael, M., Safaei, B., Machine learning in predictive maintenance towards sustainable smart manufacturing in industry 4.0. *Sustainability*, 12, 19, 8211, 2020.
129. Sivakumar, M., Maranco, M., and Krishnaraj, N., Data Analytics and Artificial Intelligence for Predictive Maintenance in Manufacturing. *Data Analytics and Artificial Intelligence for Predictive Maintenance in Smart Manufacturing*, pp. 29–55, CRC Press, Boca Raton, FL, 2024.
130. Singh, A.K. and Tewari, P.C., An overview of reliability, availability, maintainability, and safety strategies for complex systems in various process industries. *Int. J. Perform. Eng.*, 19, 12, 788, 2023.
131. Okokpujie, I.P., Tartibu, L.K., Omietimi, B.H., Improving the Maintainability and Reliability in Nigerian Industry 4.0: Its Challenges and the Way Forward from the Manufacturing Sector. *Int. J. Sustain. Dev. Plan.*, 18, 8, 2023.
132. Roda, I., and Garetti, M., Application of a Performance-Driven Total Cost of Ownership (TCO) Evaluation Model for Physical Asset Management. *Value Based and Intelligent Asset Management: Mastering the Asset Management Transformation in Industrial Plants and Infrastructures*, pp. 65–78, Springer International Publishing, Cham, Switzerland, 2020.
133. Lee, J., Ni, J., Singh, J., Jiang, B., Azamfar, M., Feng, J., Intelligent maintenance systems and predictive manufacturing. *J. Manuf. Sci. Eng.*, 142, 11, 110805, 2020.
134. Gupta, N., Khosravy, M., Patel, N., Dey, N., Gupta, S., Darbari, H., Crespo, R.G., Economic data analytic AI technique on IoT edge devices for health monitoring of agriculture machines. *Appl. Intell.*, 50, 11, 3990–4016, 2020.
135. Silva, A. and Souza, G.F., Prognosis Smart System AI-based Applied to Equipment Health Monitoring in 4.0 Industry Scenario, in: *2021 Annual*

Reliability and Maintainability Symposium (RAMS), pp. 1–6, IEEE, 2021, May.

136. Chen, Z., Shao, H., Han, T., Gryllias, K., AI-enabled industrial equipment monitoring, diagnosis and health management. *Meas. Sci. Technol.*, 35, 5, 050102, 2024.
137. Mon, B.F., Hayajneh, M., Ali, N.A., Ullah, F., Ullah, H., Alkobaisi, S., Digital Twins in the IIoT: Current Practices and Future Directions Toward Industry 5.0. *Comput., Mater. Contin.*, 83, 3, 2025.
138. Alghamdi, W.Y., Alshamrani, R.M., Aloufi, R.K., Ba Lhamar, S.O., Altwirqi, R.A., Alotaibi, F.S., Althobaiti, S.M., Altalhi, H.M., Alshamrani, S.A., Alazwari, A.S., Exploring the Synergy Between Digital Twin Technology and Artificial Intelligence: A Comprehensive Survey. *Int. J. Adv. Comput. Sci. Appl.*, 16, 3, 2025.
139. Staifi, N. and Belguidoum, M., Adapted smart home services based on smart contracts and service level agreements. *Concurrency Comput. Pract. Exp.*, 33, 23, e6208, 2021.
140. Boorsma, N., Polat, E., Bakker, C., Peck, D., Balkenende, R., Development of the circular product readiness method in circular design. *Sustainability*, 14, 15, 9288, 2022.
141. Rashad, H., Managing of aging assets and ways for its remnant life extension, in: *Abu Dhabi International Petroleum Exhibition and Conference*, p. D021S043R005, SPE, 2017, November.
142. Adegboye, A.O., Reliability Culture—The Key to a Reliable and Sustainable Asset Uptime, in: *2024 Annual Reliability and Maintainability Symposium (RAMS)*, IEEE, pp. 1–5, 2024, January.
143. Vanaparthi, R. and Rao, S.V.A., Revolutionizing Health Care: Ai-Enabled Disease Diagnosis, Outcome Prediction & Operational Efficiency. *Turk. J. Comput. Math. Educ.*, 14, 3, 993–1001, 2023.
144. Al Bashar, M., Taher, A., Johura, F.T., Utilizing Predictive Analytics for Enhanced Production Planning and Inventory Control in the US Manufacturing Sector. *Int. Res. J. Modern. Eng. Technol. Sci.*, 6, 8332–8339, 2024.
145. Singh, S., Batheri, R., Dias, J., Predictive analytics: How to improve availability of manufacturing equipment in automotive firms. *IEEE Eng. Manag. Rev.*, 51, 4, 157–168, 2023.
146. Gupta, K. and Kaur, P., Application of Predictive Maintenance in Manufacturing with the utilization of AI and IoT Tools, Authorea Preprints, 2024.
147. Gupta, K. and Juneja, P.K., Predictive Maintenance Using AI and IoT in Manufacturing, Authorea Preprints, 2025.
148. Sharma, M., Luthra, S., Joshi, S., Kumar, A., Jain, A., Green logistics driven circular practices adoption in industry 4.0 Era: A moderating effect of institution pressure and supply chain flexibility. *J. Cleaner Prod.*, 383, 135284, 2023.

149. Yu, Z., Khan, S.A.R., Umar, M., Circular economy practices and industry 4.0 technologies: A strategic move of automobile industry. *Bus. Strat. Environ.*, 31, 3, 796–809, 2022.
150. de Sousa Jabbour, A.B.L., Jabbour, C.J.C., Choi, T.M., Latan, H., 'Better together': evidence on the joint adoption of circular economy and industry 4.0 technologies. *Int. J. Prod. Econ.*, 252, 108581, 2022.
151. Lei, Z., Cai, S., Cui, L., Wu, L., Liu, Y., How do different Industry 4.0 technologies support certain Circular Economy practices?. *Ind. Manag. Data Syst.*, 123, 4, 1220–1251, 2023.
152. Blanchet, M., The Dimension of Markets for the Digital Twin, in: *The Digital Twin*, p.65–96, Springer International Publishing, Cham, 2023.
153. Shi, J., Zhou, J., Zhu, Q., Barriers of a closed-loop cartridge remanufacturing supply chain for urban waste recovery governance in China. *J. Cleaner Prod.*, 212, 1544–1553, 2019.
154. Pavlo, S., Fabio, C., Hakim, B., Mauricio, C., 3D-printing based distributed plastic recycling: a conceptual model for closed-loop supply chain design, in: *2018 ieee international conference on engineering, technology and innovation (ice/itmc)*, IEEE, pp. 1–8, June, 2018.
155. Rajabi-Kafshgar, A., Seyedi, I., Tirkolaee, E.B., Circular closed-loop supply chain network design considering 3D printing and PET bottle waste. *Environ. Dev. Sustain.*, 1–37, 2024.
156. Schumacher, K., Green, M.L., Circular economy in the high-tech world workshop report, NIST Special Publication, 10, 1500–204, 2021.
157. McIntyre, K., and Ortiz, J. A., Multinational Corporations and the Circular Economy: How Hewlett Packard Scales Innovation and Technology in Its Global Supply Chain. *Taking Stock of Industrial Ecology*, pp. 317–330, Springer Cham, Cham, Switzerland, 2016.
158. Alatalo, A., Ekelund, E., Industry 4.0 as an Enabler of Circular Business Models: Within the clothing industry, 2021.
159. Bångsbo, J., The effect of circularity and automation on the textile system in Sweden, 2025.
160. Edirisinghe, L.G.L.M., de Alwis, A.A.P., Prakash, S., Wijayasundara, M., Optimizing material circularity pathways in industrial waste streams: A decision-making model. *Methodsx*, 13, 102813, 2024.
161. Hill, L.G., Cooper, B.R., Parker, L.A., Qualitative comparative analysis: a mixed-method tool for complex implementation questions. *J. Prim. Prev.*, 40, 69–87, 2019.
162. Liu, H., Zhang, B., Wu, V., Yang, X., Wang, L., Review of Digital Twin in the Automotive Industry on Products, Processes and Systems. *Int. J. Automot. Manuf. Mater.*, 6–6, 2025.
163. Rahmani, R., Jesus, C., Lopes, S.I., Implementations of Digital Transformation and Digital Twins: Exploring the Factory of the Future. *Processes*, 12, 4, 787, 2024.

164. Aljamal, D., Salem, A., Khanna, N., Hegab, H., Towards sustainable manufacturing: A comprehensive analysis of circular economy key performance indicators in the manufacturing industry. *Sustainable Mater. Technol.*, 40, e00953, 2024.
165. Aljamal, D., Hegab, H., Ajaj, R., Sustainability in Manufacturing: A Guide to Circular Economy Practices and Key Performance Indicators, in: *IISE Annual Conference. Proceedings*, Institute of Industrial and Systems Engineers (IISE), pp. 1–6, 2024.
166. Kanellou, E., Alexakis, K., Kapsalis, P., Kokkinakos, P., Askounis, D., The DigiPrime KPIs' framework for a circular economy transition in the automotive industry. *Procedia Manuf.*, 54, 302–307, 2021.
167. Engberg, R., Altmann, P., Regulation and technology innovation: a comparison of stated and formal regulatory barriers throughout the technology innovation process. *J. Technol. Manag. Innov.*, 10, 3, 85–91, 2015.
168. Psara, K., Papadimitriou, C., Efstratiadi, M., Tsakanikas, S., Papadopoulos, P., Tobin, P., European energy regulatory, socioeconomic, and organizational aspects: An analysis of barriers related to data-driven services across electricity sectors. *Energies*, 15, 6, 2197, 2022.
169. Wylde, V., Rawindaran, N., Lawrence, J., Balasubramanian, R., Prakash, E., Jayal, A., Khan, I., Hewage, C., Platts, J., Cybersecurity, data privacy and blockchain: A review. *SN Comput. Sci.*, 3, 2, 127, 2022.
170. Black, K.D., Alam, C.B., Bucher, S.M., Giannetti, A.J., Godfrey, L.D., Wear, J.D., Recent developments in cybersecurity and data privacy. *Tort Trial Ins. Prac. Law J.*, 54, 2, 403–434, 2019.
171. Jandrić, M., Ranđelović, S., Adaptability of the workforce in Europe–changing skills in the digital era. *Zbornik Radova Ekonomskog Fakulteta U Rijeci: Časopis Za Ekonomsku Teoriju I Praksu*, 36, 2, 757–776, 2018.

15

Energy Efficiency and Renewable Energy Utilization in Circular Manufacturing

Mutiu Shola Bakare[1], Abubakar Abdulkarim[1,2*], Ismail Muhamud[2], Sulaiman Haruna Sulaiman[2], Ibrahim Sani Madugu[1,3] and Val Hyginus Udoka Eze[1]

[1]*Department of Electrical Engineering, Kampala International University, Ishaka, Western Region, Uganda*
[2]*Department of Electrical Engineering, Ahmadu Bello University, Zaria, Kaduna State, Nigeria*
[3]*Department of Electrical Engineering, Aliko Dangote University of Science and Technology, Wudil, Kano State, Nigeria*

Abstract

Globally, the circular economy is focused on eliminating waste and using resources efficiently. In view of these goals, the emphasis of the circular economy is on the generation of electricity from renewable energy resources, recycling, and the design-out of waste. Furthermore, efficient, available, and reliable power supply, increasingly enhanced by Artificial intelligence (AI) for predictive optimization, is becoming the heart of the circular economy in modern society. However, distant loads and communities far from the electricity grid still face acute shortages of economical, reliable, and efficient power supply. This is due to several reasons, such as technical, economic, and environmental challenges. These challenges are causing the circular economy to face many setbacks, especially in developing countries. In view of these issues, this chapter carries out a comprehensive review of the global status of renewable energy necessary for the circular economy to thrive. The most recent AI-driven modeling techniques for renewable energy resources have been proposed, and advances in site analysis for realistic renewable energy resources have been investigated. In addition, suitable energy management strategies for a realistic circular economy, powered by machine learning algorithms,

**Corresponding author*: aabdulkarim@kiu.ac.ug

Jeyaprakash Natarajan, Milon Selvam Dennison, M. Bhuvanesh Kumar and Ganapathy Thirukkotti (eds.) Manufacturing and the Circular Economy, (495–534) © 2027 Scrivener Publishing LLC

have been developed. In the same vein, various reliability techniques suitable for a realistic circular economy have been analyzed, and different battery storage options are investigated for more efficient usage of renewable energy resources. Finally, AI-enhanced maintenance strategies for renewable energy power systems are examined for better reliability and efficiency. This chapter is expected to be a reference resource for policymakers, researchers, and experts in the circular economy with an emphasis on renewable energy system utilizations across the globe.

***Keywords*:** Energy management, circular economy, power systems, renewable energy systems, artificial intelligence

15.1 General Introduction

Circular manufacturing (CM) is an innovative approach to manufacturing and consumption aimed at creating sustainable, closed-loop systems that save resources, minimize waste, and mitigate environmental effects [1]. Moving away from the common linear "make-use-dispose" model, CM focuses on strategies of reuse, remanufacturing, and recycling throughout the life cycle of the product [2]. The implementation of circular economy principles in manufacturing processes not only encourages environmental stewardship but is also a source of competitive advantage and market potential for those companies that are ready to innovate [3].

Easy realization of CM, nevertheless, relies significantly on the sharing and alignment of data across heterogeneous stages—from production and design to end-of-life—but continues to be held back by challenges such as data silos, incompatibility frameworks, and system interoperability [4]. Artificial intelligence (AI) has emerged as a vital tool to bridge these gaps by synthesizing complex datasets for better transparency. Master data management has been recognized as a critical, yet understudied, facilitator for enhancing strategic decision-making throughout change management [5].

The change in public expectation of industrial production practices has also driven the industry further toward circular models aimed at resource maximization through high-level reuse, remanufacturing, and recycling practices [3, 4]. Technological innovations associated with Industry 4.0, including AI-integrated cyber-physical systems, blockchain technology, augmented and virtual reality, digital twins, big data analytics, and autonomous robots, are major drivers in this development by enabling real-time monitoring, predictive maintenance, and better resource management [5]. However, in spite of these innovations, CM adoption is confronted with challenges such as technological constraints, low consumer awareness, and budget limitations [6]. Stakeholder collaboration throughout the supply chain is crucial, but research demonstrates a knowledge gap concerning the relational and cooperative aspects required for a totally integrated CM strategy [4].

At the heart of the CM transformative potential model is the need to enhance energy efficiency and harness renewable energy (RE) potentials throughout the manufacturing system, as shown in Figure 15.1. The combination of these practices, often optimized by AI-driven smart grids, can effectively decouple economic growth from environmental degradation and thus promote long-lasting sustainability and resilience [7, 8]. The durable, repairable, and recyclable product design is supported by innovative recycling technologies that extract high-quality materials from advanced products such as electronics and automotive parts [3]. As the production sector embarks on system change, the synergistic combination of RE technologies, circular economy concepts, and advanced AI data management becomes the primary approach to speed up the transformation toward a low-carbon, resource-efficient world [1, 9].

The circular economy transformation in RE systems is a key approach to sustainable development, which calls for efficient resource utilization, waste minimization, and material life extension through creative design, production, and recycling strategies [10]. Main tenets, including the removal of

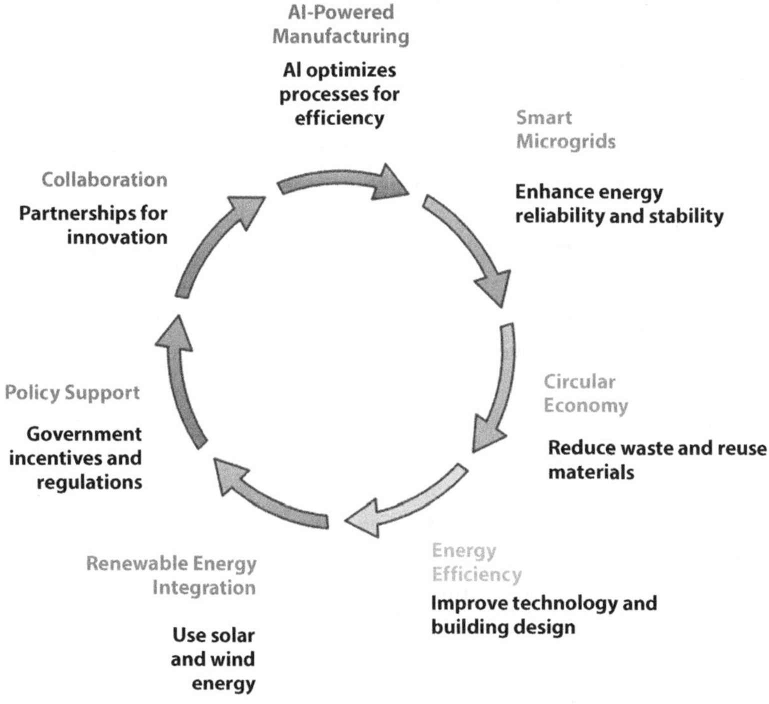

Figure 15.1 Cycle of sustainable manufacturing.

pollution and waste, regeneration of natural ecosystems, and optimization of resource efficiency, are the pillars of this model that allows for significant minimization of landfill rubbish, limiting environmental pollution, and initiating new economic potential *via* material recycling and recovery industries [11]. Integrating energy efficiency and RE utilization into circular frameworks—supported by AI-enabled demand-response systems—not only helps achieve sustainable resource management but also enhances corporate sustainability profiles and supply chain risk resilience, allowing industries to attract investment and stimulate economic growth [12].

Circularity is critical to delivering global climate goals and targets of sustainable development *via* RE and energy efficiency. RE technologies already reduce greenhouse gas emissions in the world by up to 55%, and integrating the principles of the circular economy multiplies these benefits by promoting efficient use of materials and life-cycle minimization of waste [13]. AI further enhances these benefits by optimizing material sorting and predicting the remaining useful life of energy assets through machine learning-based degradation models. Energy efficiency measures are essential in lowering the consumption of resources and the production of waste, in line with circular economy systems that emphasize eco-innovation and sustainable resource utilization [14].

Recycling material in industries such as the construction sector can achieve up to 65% environmental impact reduction, thereby illustrating the synergy potential that exists within circular systems and RE technologies [15, 16]. Interestingly, Germany's leadership efforts, as embodied by the German Circular Economy Act and the PV Cycle partnerships illustrated in Figure 15.2, showcase the success of national policy frameworks and public-private partnerships in successfully integrating circularity into RE systems, specifically solar energy [10].

Furthermore, process integration, RE technology innovations, and design improvements have been shown to improve economic and environmental performances, thus offering strategic avenues for circularity achievement [17]. Improved material circularity and energy efficiency, often optimized through AI-driven predictive analytics, minimize dependence on carbon-intensive activities and costly mitigation processes, for example, Carbon Capture and Storage [18]. The integration of circular economy strategies with ambitious climate policy enables industries to realize deep emissions cuts simultaneously with underpinning objectives found in the Paris Agreement [19]. In this way, the symbiosis of energy efficiency and RE use is an inherent part of a circular economy, a comprehensive strategy that espouses environmental protection, stimulates economic innovation, and facilitates robust sustainable development.

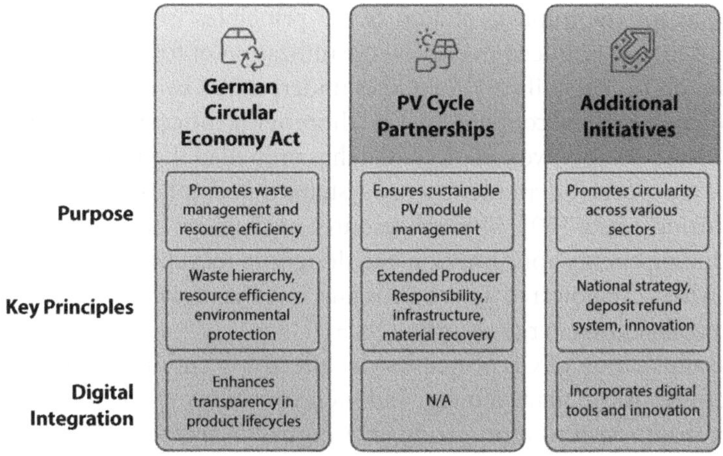

Figure 15.2 Circular economy initiatives in Germany.

The immediate need for a transition to RE in industry stems from the intersecting needs of climate goals, energy security, and regulatory drivers. With the pace of global warming, the rapid decarbonization of energy systems has become imperative to reduce greenhouse gas emissions, which are largely linked with fossil fuel consumption [20, 21]. The sector, as a heavy energy user, is responsible for increasing emissions, pointing to the sector's key position in assisting the achievement of global climate targets, e.g., limiting warming to 1.5°C as promoted by the IPCC [22, 23]. Meanwhile, dependence on non-RE sources exposes economies to geopolitical risk and volatility in the market, introducing the strategic imperative of RE deployment to underpin long-term energy security [24, 25]. Investment in clean energy technology, particularly when managed by AI-enabled smart grids, not only reduces climate change threats to energy but also builds resilience, especially for nations with strong governance structures [26].

However, integrating RE into industry has disadvantages such as high up-front capital costs, technological challenges, as well as the sensitivity of commodity markets to volatility, e.g., the fluctuation of green metal prices that can affect renewable investments [27, 28]. Recognizing the mutual dependence of energy security and climate policy, regulatory environments increasingly demand the incorporation of sustainability considerations into industrial energy planning [21], which demands a concerted effort through enabling policies, technology development, and multistakeholder collaboration to unlock the complete value of RE transformation in industry [27].

Global issues such as climate change and natural resource depletion represent major challenges to sustainable energy development but also create prospects for the implementation of CE principles in the energy sector. Climate change, induced mainly by the utilization of fossil energy sources, requires an urgent shift to RE sources underpinned by novel technologies and enhanced global cooperation [29]. Improving the cost-competitiveness of wind and solar power, in particular, has propelled their uptake, improving the prospects for circular energy systems that emphasize efficiency and minimizing waste [30]. Limited resource availability also focuses efforts on reducing energy consumption and designing recycling into energy systems, where AI-powered smart grids and intelligent controls can improve sustainability and energy security [30, 31].

The application of CE principles can effectively cut down carbon emissions, foster waste management, and increase energy efficiency, and it is a practical approach to minimizing environmental impacts to support sustainable development agendas [32, 33]. Despite such prospects, challenges still exist, including the high cost of carbon removal technologies and little corporate commitment to climate goals, necessitating an urgent transition by private and public entities from linear to circular economic frameworks to ensure long-term environmental and economic sustainability [33, 34].

In spite of increasing momentum for RE deployment and energy efficiency, the intersection of these measures with the principles of CE is still inadequately addressed within the framework of manufacturing transformation. This chapter has identified a key gap in literature and practice: the ongoing disconnection between energy transition viewpoints and CM approaches. Although climate imperatives and sustainability aspirations are motivating huge investments in decarbonization, the absence of synthesis frameworks linking RE adoption, circular material flows, and systemic innovation—such as AI-driven life-cycle assessment (LCA)—still slows down the actualization of integrated and sustainable industrial ecosystems. Most studies to date fail to consider how energy-efficient systems, waste-to-energy facilities, and RE systems can be designed in manners complementary to circular approaches such as remanufacturing, eco-design, and material recovery.

As a reply, this chapter discusses the critical contribution of energy efficiency to the development of sustainable manufacturing, explores the inclusion of RE sources in circular economy transitions, presents strategic practices in minimizing energy use throughout production systems, and provides model case studies of energy-efficient factories to demonstrate realistic application and effect.

The chapter is structured to give a detailed presentation of how energy efficiency and RE integration facilitate CM. It starts with placing energy efficiency at the center of facilitating sustainable production as presented in Section 15.1, followed by a description of how RE resources facilitate circular economy transformations in Section 15.2. The chapter subsequently proceeds to present practical means of minimizing energy use within production activities such as technological and operational interventions, including AI-driven process optimization, as discussed in Section 15.3. For the sake of applying these theories to practice, it presents a set of case studies demonstrating the effective application of energy conservation interventions within a range of industries as evident in Section 15.4. The Sections collectively present an overall approach to coordinating energy optimization and circular economy thinking in industry.

15.1.1 Importance of Energy Efficiency in Sustainable Manufacturing

As global energy demands surge, the manufacturing sector—responsible for approximately 24% of global energy consumption and over 20% of greenhouse gas emissions—faces escalating pressure to optimize energy use while minimizing its carbon footprint [35]. Energy efficiency has thus emerged as a critical driver of sustainability, cost reduction, and operational excellence, earning its place as the "fifth fuel" after coal, gas, nuclear, and renewables [36]. Implementing advanced energy-efficient technologies, such as AI-based industrial Internet of Things (IoT), can reduce industrial energy use by 20–30%, yielding significant operational cost savings; this importance is detailed in Table 15.1, particularly for energy-intensive industries such as steel, semiconductors, ceramics, and paper [37].

Energy efficiency is at the nexus of economic sustainability and AI-driven environmental stewardship, and it represents a primary point of entry for manufacturers to mitigate emissions, save costs, and transition toward a circular and sustainable future [40]. Proper measurement of energy efficiency in the manufacturing industry, often enhanced by machine learning, is essential for realizing economic enhancement as well as environmental sustainability, especially against the background of increasing energy prices and the pressing need for CO_2 emissions reduction. The main indicators are energy performance indicators (EnPIs), specific energy consumption (SEC), load factor analysis, energy cost per unit, carbon footprint metrics, energy utilization index (EUI), and Energy Intensity. All of these give measurable data about the consumption of energy in terms of productivity, as seen in Figure 15.3 [41, 42].

Some of the most critical energy performance management tools are EnPIs, which allow for benchmarking, setting targets, and AI-enhanced performance monitoring in manufacturing systems [43]. These indicators may either be energy intensity ratio-based or sophisticated statistical

Table 15.1 Importance of energy efficiency in sustainable manufacturing [38, 39].

Pillar	Key benefit	Supporting actions	Example/impact
Cost savings	Lower operational costs	1. Upgrade to efficient lighting, HVAC, motors 2. Use variable frequency drives (VFDs)	1. Reduces energy bills and equipment wear 2. Cuts maintenance and replacement costs
	Equipment longevity	Efficient equipment uses less energy and wears slower	Extends machinery life, reduces unplanned downtime
	Reinvestment potential	Redirect savings into R&D, training, or scaling up	Drives innovation and growth
Environmental impact	Lower emissions	Use less energy, especially from fossil fuels	Decreases carbon footprint, helps meet climate goals
	Resource conservation	Use renewables; reduce fossil fuel consumption	Conserves finite resources such as coal, oil, and gas
	Waste minimization	Streamline processes to reduce energy and material waste	Supports cleaner production and sustainable use of materials
Competitiveness	Cost efficiency	Cut production costs *via* energy reduction	Allows for competitive pricing or higher profit margins
	Stronger brand reputation	Publicize green initiatives and efficiency efforts	Attracts eco-conscious customers and partners
	Innovation stimulation	Adopt new technologies to improve energy use	Spurs broader operational and product innovation

(*Continued*)

Table 15.1 Importance of energy efficiency in sustainable manufacturing [38, 39]. (*Continued*)

Pillar	Key benefit	Supporting actions	Example/impact
Regulatory compliance	Legal alignment	Comply with energy efficiency standards and audits	Avoids fines and legal repercussions
	Incentive access	Qualify for tax breaks, subsidies, grants	Reduces implementation costs for energy-saving solutions
	Future-proofing	Stay ahead of policy changes and mandates	Ensures smoother transition into stricter regulatory environments

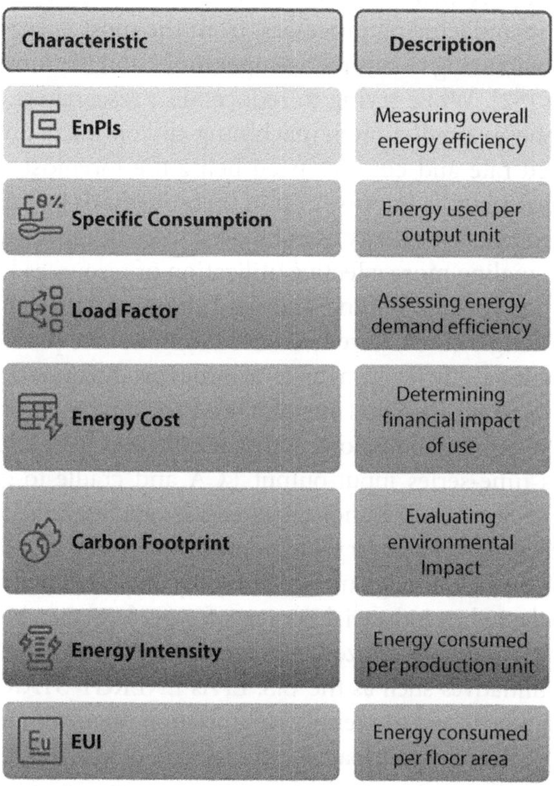

Figure 15.3 Key energy efficiency metrics.

models, such as linear regression and neural networks, and the selection is typically based on data quality, reliability, and analytical strength [44]. Recent developments have applied EnPIs to industry-specific use, such as using AI to assess energy performance in rubber and cement production from mandatory energy audit data to inform targeted interventions [45, 46].

Yet, the limitations of current indicator systems have necessitated the creation of more advanced measures that utilize real-time sensor data and machine learning to identify inefficiencies at both the machine and production line level, thereby introducing concepts such as downtime energy bottlenecks and power bottlenecks [47]. Energy intensity, conventionally expressed as the energy used per unit of output or sales, continues to be a fundamental indicator for cross-sectoral comparisons [48, 49]. This metric is influenced by a range of determinants including firm size, ownership, technology utilization, and R&D investment, leading to wide variations in energy efficiency within and across national contexts [49–51].

No less significant is the analysis of SEC, which quantifies energy usage per unit of processed material. Empirical results show a broad spectrum of variability in manufacturing processes, from the most energy-consuming additive manufacturing to subtractive operations and the most economical bulk-forming [52]. While trying to reduce SEC, researchers have utilized AI to model energy prediction in machining and optimize process parameters, with feed rate and cutting speed being the foremost variables [53, 54]. Load factor analysis improves upon these methods by quantifying the consumption of electric energy as compared to peak capacity, with higher load factors signaling more effective utilization of resources [55, 56].

Tools such as process mining and load duration curve analysis, often powered by AI algorithms, have been used to minimize peak demand and enhance operational efficiency in make-to-order production settings [57, 58]. Concurrently, carbon footprint metrics are providing environmental data through the tracking of emissions across production life cycles. AI-driven tools, such as time-series input-output LCA and cradle-to-gate analyses, have mapped sectoral contributions to emissions and identified high-impact processes such as nickel recovery and petroleum refining [59–61].

In addition, the EUI, though more commonly utilized in buildings, is being increasingly adapted in industrial contexts for performance benchmarking. Benchmarking using standardized indicators and AI-supported data sets, as promoted by initiatives such as the U.S. EPA's ENERGY STAR, additionally empowers manufacturers to identify optimization opportunities and incorporate energy practices into broader sustainability objectives [43, 62].

The combination of these indicators, as shown in Table 15.2, enables manufacturers to realize a decrease in energy costs, backed by

Table 15.2 Related work on energy efficiency in sustainable manufacturing.

Ref.	Work done	Country	Area of application	Energy efficiency metrics	Lessons learned
[66]	Decomposition analysis of energy intensity in Indian manufacturing	India	Cement, chemicals, steel	Energy intensity	Structural changes (e.g., fuel substitution) drive energy intensity reduction more than efficiency improvements
[50]	Firm-level analysis of energy intensity in Indian manufacturing using PROWESS data	India	Steel, textiles	Energy intensity	U-shaped relationship between energy intensity and firm size; foreign-owned firms are less energy-intensive. Technology imports reduce intensity
[67]	Kaya identity analysis of energy intensity and carbon goals in Latvian manufacturing	Latvia	Large manufacturing industries	Energy intensity, carbon intensity	Manufacturing growth threatens EU carbon goals; energy-saving strategies needed for industrial practices
[68]	Sectoral energy intensity analysis of five Indian manufacturing industries (2005–2014)	India	Aluminum, cement, iron and steel, textile, fertilizer	Energy intensity	Energy intensity varies widely across sectors; sector-specific policies are critical for improvement

(*Continued*)

Table 15.2 Related work on energy efficiency in sustainable manufacturing. (*Continued*)

Ref.	Work done	Country	Area of application	Energy efficiency metrics	Lessons learned
[69]	Carbon footprint analysis of latex foam production	Not specified	Rubber	Carbon footprint	Fertilizer use in cultivation doubles emissions; 47% of emissions come from cultivation, 45% from production
[54]	Optimization of cutting parameters to minimize SEC in machining	Not specified	Machine tools	EnPIs, load factor analysis	Feed rate is the dominant factor affecting SEC. Optimal parameters: feed = 0.12 mm/rev, speed = 46.2 m/min
[63]	Production scheduling to minimize energy costs in plastic bottle manufacturing	Belgium	Plastic manufacturing	Energy cost per unit	Proposed scheduling method reduces electricity costs by 21% compared to conventional methods
[48]	Inter-industry comparison of energy intensity in seven Indian manufacturing sectors	India	Paper, aluminum, iron, and steel	Energy intensity	Energy intensity varies significantly by industry and over time; industries are more energy-intensive than the aggregate manufacturing sector

(*Continued*)

Table 15.2 Related work on energy efficiency in sustainable manufacturing. (*Continued*)

Ref.	Work done	Country	Area of application	Energy efficiency metrics	Lessons learned
[45]	Energy audits and EnPI analysis in the Italian rubber industry	Italy	Rubber and tire manufacturing	EnPIs	Energy audits identify cost-effective efficiency measures (e.g., CHP, renewables). Payback <4 years for many interventions
[46]	Methodology for EnPI calculation in Italian nonmetallic mineral products	Italy	Cement manufacturing	EnPIs , SEC	SEC-based EnPIs enable benchmarking; methodology applicable across sectors
[70]	Taxonomy for energy end-use in the Swedish engineering industry	Sweden	Engineering industry	EnPIs	Classification of energy use aids in identifying efficiency measures. Production processes dominate energy use
[71]	Taxonomy for energy end-use in the Swedish food industry	Sweden	Food industry	EnPIs, carbon footprint metrics	Two-thirds of energy used in production processes; heat processing and space heating are most energy- and carbon-intensive

(*Continued*)

Table 15.2 Related work on energy efficiency in sustainable manufacturing. (*Continued*)

Ref.	Work done	Country	Area of application	Energy efficiency metrics	Lessons learned
[72]	Analysis of EnPIs in Italian pharmaceutical plants using energy audits	Italy	Pharmaceuticals	EnPIs	70% of energy used in auxiliary services (unrelated to production). EnPIs should be calculated per plant surface area
[73]	Energy and carbon performance assessment of offshore oil platforms	Brazil	Oil production	EnPIs, carbon footprint metrics	Multilevel EnPIs detect deviations; optimizing gas turbine operations reduces carbon emissions
[74]	Evaluation of EnPIs (SEC, CUSUM) in an Egyptian refinery	Egypt	Oil refining	SEC, cumulative summation (CUSUM)	Combining multiple EnPIs provides accurate tracking of energy performance
[75]	Machine learning-based prediction of SEC in cutoff grinding	Not specified	Manufacturing (machining)	SEC	Gaussian process regression outperforms ANN and regression trees in SEC prediction

simulation-based studies and AI predictive modeling showing possible savings of up to 21%. In addition, the method supports movement toward overall sustainability goals by combining energy optimization with strategic resource planning [63–65].

15.2 Role of Renewable Energy Sources in Circular Economy Transitions

The circular economy is the core of global sustainability, aiming for resource productivity, waste reduction, and the continuous use of materials in a closed loop, as presented in Figure 15.4. In this regard, AI-optimized RE resources are instrumental in decoupling economic growth from environmental pollution [76].

A circular energy economy entails creating and structuring systems wherein energy inputs, primarily from renewables managed by smart grids and AI forecasting, facilitate sustainable production, reuse, and recycling activities without exhausting finite natural resources. Contrary to the traditional linear "take-make-dispose" paradigm, circularity redesigns energy flows by integrating green technologies and AI-driven efficiency that restore, rather than destroy, ecosystems [77]. This paradigm is especially crucial as nations strive to limit climate change and shift toward more resilient, autonomous energy systems.

Renewable power that comes from inexhaustible resources, such as solar, wind, and biomass, fosters circularity because it generates clean, stable, and renewable power. Solar and wind energies, in particular, do not harness finite inputs during electricity generation, whereas biomass, although being

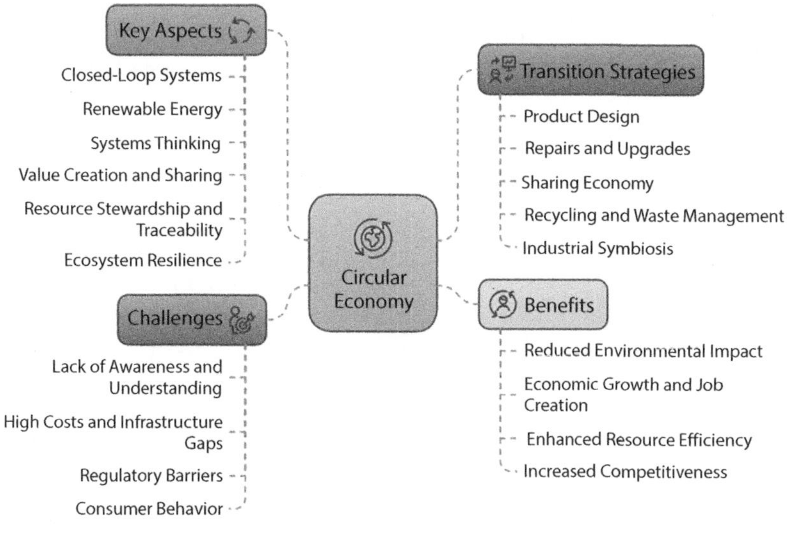

Figure 15.4 The transition to a circular economy.

consumable, can be restored by sustainable farming [77, 78]. The transition to energy is characterized by the International Renewable Energy Agency (IRENA) as transitioning away from fossil-based systems to zero-carbon ones by 2050—a trajectory that is required if global warming is to be limited to less than 1.5°C above pre-industrial levels [79]. The change is not merely environmental but also socioeconomic, with opportunities for generating jobs, improving public health through mitigated pollution, and anchoring energy prices by decoupling from volatile fossil fuel markets. IRENA reiterates that AI-managed, renewable-powered electrification can considerably decarbonize all sectors; thus, RE is the foundation of climate mitigation efforts [80].

Besides, the integration of RE into circular economy ideas, as presented in Figure 15.5, enhances technological sustainability by encouraging the reuse, recycling, and refurbishment of materials utilized in energy infrastructure. Some of these processes, which can be optimized *via* AI-driven sorting and material tracking, include recycling lithium-ion batteries to recover essential minerals, silicon reuse from photovoltaic cells, and the disassembly of wind turbines for the recovery of valuable metals such as copper and rare earth elements [81]. These processes minimize the

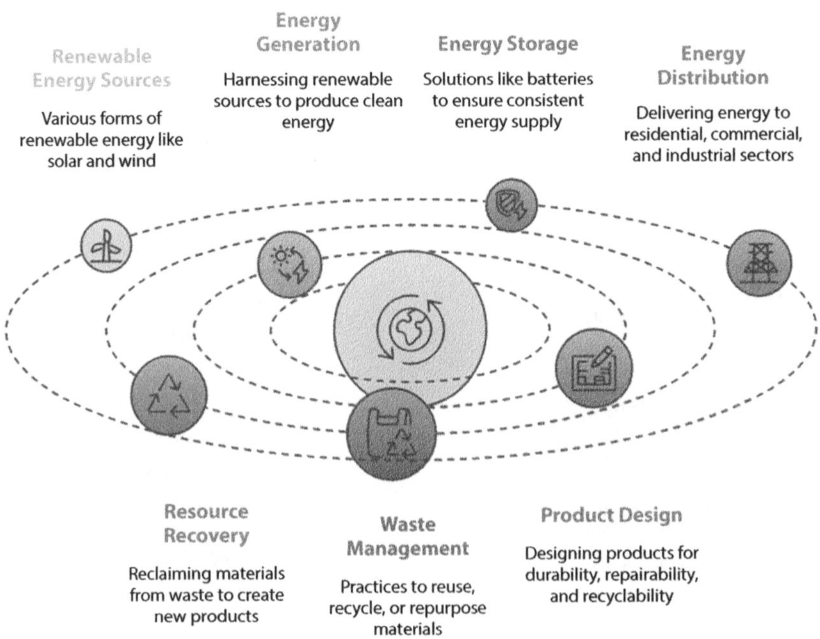

Figure 15.5 Integrating renewable energy into a circular economy.

Table 15.3 Examples of industries using renewable energy to support circular practices [88–90].

Industry	Country	Company	Circular strategies	Circular materials	Circular process	Innovation	Renewable energy used	Impact
Chemicals and materials	The Netherlands	ReSolved Technologies	Green chemistry, bio-based materials, chemical leasing, industrial symbiosis	Bioplastics, solvents	Solvent-based recycling of engineering plastics	Closed-loop plastic recycling with additive removal	Waste heat recovery from industrial processes	Enhances recyclability, reduces virgin material demand
Food and beverage	Italy	Circular food	Upcycling food waste, predictive inventory, plant-based transition	Upcycled flour, biogas	Converts fermentation waste into flour	Upcycled flour from distillation by-products	Biogas (from anaerobic digestion of food waste)	Reduces waste, creates added value from food waste
Packaging	United Kingdom	Treetop Biopak	Biopolymers, eco-design, compostables	Corn starch-based packaging	Makes durable compostable packaging	Compostable alternatives to plastic	Solar PV used in sustainable packaging facilities	Reduces landfill impact, biodegradable material use
Manufacturing	The Netherlands	Batch.Works	Product-as-a-service, remanufacturing, digital manufacturing	3D-printed recycled goods	Digital, on-demand, circular material production	Smart and local circular production	Green electricity (solar + wind mix)	Minimizes waste, shortens supply chains

(Continued)

Table 15.3 Examples of industries using renewable energy to support circular practices [88–90]. *(Continued)*

Industry	Country	Company	Circular strategies	Circular materials	Circular process	Innovation	Renewable energy used	Impact
Fashion and textiles	United States	Circular Fashion LA	Zero-waste fashion, textile recycling, take-back models	Recycled and redesigned garments	Subscription-based wardrobe renewal and recycling	Repair, refit, redye services with recycling	Solar PV and green textile processing	Reduces fast fashion waste, promotes garment longevity
Automotive and transport	Germany	Circunomics	Battery reuse, on-demand mobility, remanufacturing	Reused EV batteries	Battery analytics and second-life simulation	Circular battery platform for OEMs	Energy from EV battery repurposing	Extends EV battery life cycle, supports recycling
Renewable energy	Canada	Varme Energy	Service models, battery repurposing, smart grids	Waste-to-energy systems	CCS-enabled waste heat conversion	Waste-to-energy with carbon capture	Waste heat → electricity + CCS	Reduces emissions, diverts nonrecyclables from landfills

(Continued)

Table 15.3 Examples of industries using renewable energy to support circular practices [88–90]. (*Continued*)

Industry	Country	Company	Circular strategies	Circular materials	Circular process	Innovation	Renewable energy used	Impact
Agriculture	France	SWING Biomethane	Regenerative farming, waste composting, biofertilizer	Biomethane, digestate	Converts organic residues to biogas and fertilizer	Biomethane from agricultural residues	Biomethane/ Bio-LNG from agri-waste	Reduces synthetic fertilizer use, supports farm sustainability
Construction	France	revitalyze.io	Design for disassembly, modular builds, reused materials	Building material reuse	Digital inventory and component matching	Component reuse *via* digital marketplace	On-site solar and green grid power	Reduces construction waste, cuts emissions from new materials
Electronics	Italy	Circular Technologies	Modular design, e-waste recovery, energy efficiency	Refurbished IT devices	IT asset life-cycle management and certification	Circular IT procurement and sustainability certification	Renewable-powered data centers	Reduces e-waste, promotes IT reuse and carbon accounting

environmental impact of production and raw material extraction and encourage innovation in the life-cycle management of renewable technology. Practices such as OMV's used cooking oil sustainable aviation fuel demonstrate the potential of bio-based fuels for achieving waste minimization as well as energy generation [82]. With these technologies, RE is not merely a clean source of energy but also an encouragement of circularity across all industries [83].

At a global scale, the circular economy's complementarity with RE is being achieved across industries and geographies, as presented in Table 15.3. In construction, low-energy designs are followed by renewables; for clothing and furniture, companies such as Patagonia and IKEA use recycled products and circular energy strategies; whereas in Africa, distributed solar power and recycled batteries power development targets. European countries, particularly Sweden and Luxembourg, have high circular economy performance through the integration of renewables, while varying still [16]. Pioneering solar business models, Portuguese offshore energy clusters, and cooperative renewable initiatives in Brazil and India also signal the development of global resilient, circular energy systems [84, 85]. Thus, RE is not merely supportive but essential to achieving a regenerative, low-carbon future that reconciles economic growth with the well-being of the planet [86, 87].

15.3 Strategies for Reducing Energy Consumption in Production Processes

Industrial energy efficiency has become a mainstay of international sustainability agendas. The manufacturing industry alone consumes about 45% of the world's industrial energy, based on International Energy Agency figures, which is the highest among industrial sectors [91]. This is because the industry depends greatly on high-temperature processes, large machinery, and the round-the-clock running of motors, compressors, and pumps. Consequently, industrial firms are ever more compelled to conserve energy—not only to comply with climate policy but also to improve production efficiency, reduce costs, and establish long-term competitiveness [92]. Energy conservation in manufacturing processes is no longer a peripheral endeavor but a strategic imperative in accordance with AI-enhanced decarbonization trajectories and resource efficiency [93].

To achieve deep and long-lasting reductions in energy consumption, manufacturers are pursuing multidimensional strategies that include AI diagnostics, technology retrofitting, process optimization, and behavior modification [94]. Detailed energy audits often initiate the process, examining current consumption patterns and revealing inefficiencies. Audits inform the retrofitting of energy monitoring and control systems, enabling AI-driven data decision-making and real-time optimization [95, 96]. They are followed by technological improvements, such as the replacement of aging equipment with energy-efficient equipment, preferably certified by programs such as Energy Star. Advanced smart manufacturing technologies, including IoT sensors, automation, and machine learning algorithms, provide fine-grained control over energy-consuming processes, which improves accuracy and minimizes wastage [97, 98].

In parallel with technological innovation, the process optimization of production is fundamental. Workflow reorganization, more efficient heating and cooling systems, and heat recovery from residues are the principal levers for consumption reduction [99]. Passive design principles, such as natural light exploitation, insulation, and ventilation, reduce the need for energy-hungry HVAC systems [100, 101]. In addition, the use of RE resources such as solar photovoltaics, wind, or geothermal systems enables firms to replace fossil fuels with cleaner, cost-stable resources. AI-integrated grid-connected installations bring resilience and reduce peak-load demand. Collectively, these actions constitute a comprehensive energy management approach that supports environmental performance along with profitability [102, 103]. To launch this strategy successfully, the strategic fragmentation in Table 15.4 recognizes main areas of implementation.

Recent literature attests to the viability of such approaches. Nota *et al.* emphasize the integration of Industry 4.0 technologies and AI management principles for the sake of quantifying and reducing energy losses in batch operations [104]. Similarly, Hamrol *et al.* present the 2E-DAmIcS approach, which recognizes inefficiency and facilitates intervention [105]. Scheduling power-down for idling machinery and energy-aware scheduling through reinforcement learning also yield substantial savings, as demonstrated by [106]. In the design phase, the inclusion of AI-based energy consumption modeling offers a competitive edge in terms of system performance optimization right from the beginning [107]. Production planning can be made as much as 40.9% more energy efficient using mathematical modeling and heuristic algorithms [108].

Further research applies the argument to industrial practice. Diaz *et al.*, for instance, propose kinetic energy recovery and the optimization of process parameters in machine tool design [109]. Müller *et al.* propose an integrated approach to pharmaceutical manufacture, where energy conservation is balanced against risk, GMP compliance, and safety [110].

Table 15.4 Energy efficiency strategies in manufacturing [116–118].

Technology/ strategy	Description	Benefits	Tools/examples	Recommended application
Energy management planning	Develop a site-specific plan to monitor, control, and reduce energy use	Tracks usage, optimizes processes, reduces waste	HVAC systems, sensors, energy dashboards	All manufacturing environments
High-efficiency equipment	Replace outdated machines with energy-efficient models	Reduces consumption and heat loss, improves performance	High-efficiency motors, compressors, boilers	Heavy equipment and processing industries
Automated lighting and sensors	Use LED and sensor-based lighting to reduce usage when not needed.	Saves electricity, reduces heat output, extends lamp life	LED lights, occupancy sensors, smart switches	24/7 operations, warehouses
Use of natural light	Utilize daylight through design to reduce artificial lighting needs	Lowers lighting costs, improves material performance	Skylights, reflective panels, daylight controls	New construction, energy-smart layouts
Onsite renewable energy	Install systems such as solar panels or wind turbines to generate electricity	Cuts grid reliance, reduces emissions, lowers long-term cost	Solar PV, microwind, hydro units	Remote or mini-grid factories
Passive cooling techniques	Design for natural airflow and thermal regulation to reduce AC load	Enhances comfort, reduces energy usage	Ventilation design, shading, thermal mass materials	Hot and arid climate zones
Thermal insulation	Install effective insulation to regulate internal temperature	Reduces heating/ cooling load, boosts energy retention	Foam boards, fiberglass, sealing wraps	Large surface-area buildings

(Continued)

Table 15.4 Energy efficiency strategies in manufacturing [116–118]. (*Continued*)

Technology/ strategy	Description	Benefits	Tools/examples	Recommended application
Smart building automation	Use IoT and automation to optimize heating, cooling, and lighting systems	Real-time efficiency, automated shutdowns, analytics	Smart thermostats, BMS, programmable controllers	Digital or Industry 4.0–ready facilities
Employee engagement	Train staff in energy-saving practices and eco-conscious behavior	Cultural buy-in, behavior-based energy reductions	Workshops, incentives, visual dashboards	All staff-involved operations
Reuse and recycling	Repurpose waste materials to avoid energy-intensive new production	Conserves resources, reduces waste emissions	Recycled steel, wood, glass, shredded tires	Construction-heavy or material-diverse facilities

Wolff *et al.* show that utilizing AI-triggered power-off for nonessential components during idle periods delivers additional energy savings [111]. Jędrzejewski and Kwaśny stress the importance of designing machine tools on the basis of adequate energy modeling and introducing intelligent control systems, particularly for drives of axes and machining operations [112].

Despite the apparent benefits, implementation barriers cannot be underplayed. Firms are typically faced with a hefty capital investment, particularly small- and medium-sized enterprises (SMEs) which may not be in a financial position to support investments in upgrades. Staggered implementation schedules, government incentives, and energy performance contracting through ESCOs can fill this barrier [113]. In addition, behavioral resistance, operation disruption, and a lack of technical AI expertise can be obstacles. Solutions comprise energy consultants, off-peak retrofits, and comprehensive employee training programs. Regulatory nuances and compatibility with existing infrastructure are also a concern, which may be met by continuous policy monitoring, infrastructure audits, and modular and extendable technology deployment [114].

Lastly, reducing energy consumption in production activity requires more than technological change; it requires changing industrial culture, operations, and design. By combining AI diagnostics, innovation, and far-sighted management, industries can not only be cost-effective and reduce their environmental impact but also achieve long-term competitiveness and resilience in a decarbonizing world economy [115].

15.4 Case Studies of Energy-Efficient Manufacturing Facilities

With increasing environmental and economic pressures in the modern world, the manufacturing sector is being faced with increasing imperatives for energy efficiency and carbon savings. Factory buildings are some of the biggest energy consumers globally and account for huge shares of industrial energy consumption. In this context, AI-enhanced energy efficiency does not just seem like an environmental necessity but is also a good business proposition. Recent case studies set out the disruptive impact of strategic energy efficiency measures across different manufacturing settings, where companies have realized considerable cost savings as well as sustainability benefits through technology change and systematic AI-driven intervention [119]. These findings substantiate that energy management is not a marginal factor but a core business imperative.

Specifically, industry-based empirical research highlighted the need to adopt holistic and tailored energy efficiency programs, as presented in Table 15.5. Thiede provides an approach focusing analytical activity away from single machines to entire process chains and demonstrates large efficiency gains in processes such as aluminum die casting and printed circuit board assembly through AI process modeling [120]. Ketenci and Wolf subsequently apply this perspective to SMEs, suggesting industry-specific reductions of 1.3 million kWh and 22% cost savings in the automotive and environmental industries using predictive analytics [121]. Such measures are subsequently drawn upon by Silva *et al.*, who present an estimate for the potential of HVAC system upgrading in U.S. manufacturing, estimating annual savings of $744 million with associated carbon emissions reductions [122]. Along with this trend, the replacement of old air compressors with AI-controlled variable speed drives and the redesign of air distribution at 3M Cumberland saved 40% energy and achieved a payback on investment within 2.9 years, demonstrating the potential for the strategic replacement of systems to create quick paybacks [123].

Such corporate initiatives as Toyota's Environmental Challenge 2050 and Siemens' Siemens Energy Management System initiative have also shown the promise of integrated AI energy management systems to curb carbon emissions by up to 35% and achieve multimillion-dollar savings [124].

Table 15.5 Some selected case studies of energy-efficient manufacturing facilities.

Ref.	Company name	Goods produced	Country	Energy strategy	Technology/ approach	Energy savings (%)	Cost savings/ ROI
[123]	3M Cumberland	Floor pads, abrasives	USA	Compressed air upgrade	Variable speed compressors	40%	$3500/month, ROI: 2.9 years
[124]	Toyota	Automobiles	Japan/USA	Environmental Challenge 2050	Renewables, process improvement	35%	$279 million
[124]	Siemens	Electronics, industrial systems	Germany	Siemens Energy Management System	Smart sensors, energy analytics	20%	$108 million
[124]	Philips Lighting	Lighting equipment	Belgium	LED retrofit	LEDs, motion sensors	50%	$150,000/year
[124]	Toyota (Kentucky)	Automobiles	USA	Paint booth optimization	Infrared and airflow drying	45%	$1.2 million/ year
[124]	Dow Chemical	Chemicals	USA	HVAC optimization	High-efficiency chiller, VAV system	30%	$600,000/year
[124]	Procter & Gamble	Consumer goods	USA	Motor system upgrade	VFDs, high-efficiency motors	25%	$750,000/year

(*Continued*)

Table 15.5 Some selected case studies of energy-efficient manufacturing facilities. (*Continued*)

Ref.	Company name	Goods produced	Country	Energy strategy	Technology/ approach	Energy savings (%)	Cost savings/ ROI
[125]	Tex Plastics	Plastic molding	UK	Energy monitoring	Eniscope + VEM	26.7%	£237,000/year
[126]	Unnamed Industrial Client	Industrial	USA	Energy monitoring	Eniscope	36%	$84,000/year, quick ROI
[132]	ArcelorMittal	Steel	Global	Energy recovery	ERS—heat to electricity	20%	Significant
[133]	Nucor	Steel	USA	Electric Arc Furnace (EAF) upgrades	Advanced EAF, real-time management	15%	Significant
[133]	POSCO	Steel	South Korea	Holistic upgrades	Furnace control, EMS, lighting	18%	Substantial
[133]	JSPL	Steel	India	Waste heat recovery	WHRPP with steam/gas turbines	30%	Substantial
[133]	ThyssenKrupp	Steel	Germany	Rolling mill upgrades	Motors, insulation, process control	10%	Improved quality, lower costs

(*Continued*)

Table 15.5 Some selected case studies of energy-efficient manufacturing facilities. (*Continued*)

Ref.	Company name	Goods produced	Country	Energy strategy	Technology/ approach	Energy savings (%)	Cost savings/ ROI
[134]	De Bortoli Wines	Wine	Australia	Refrigeration optimization	Smart refrigeration controls	17%	960 MWh/ year, >800 tons CO_2 saved
[135]	Wacker Chemie AG	Chemicals	Germany	CHP and steam recovery	Heat networks, gas/steam turbines	High	465,000 MWh saved
[135]	SATECMA	Chemicals	Spain	Lighting, PV, HVAC upgrades	LED, natural light, solar PV	20%	Significant
[136]	AMB Alloys	Ferroalloys	Georgia	New energy-efficient plant	Techno-economic analysis	Unknown	€220,000/year, ROI: ~4 years
[137]	Aerospace Component Mfr.	Aerospace parts	Not specified	Job-shop scheduling	MO optimization algorithm	Not specified	Reduced energy, time, cost
[138]	Unnamed Beverage Factory	Beverages	Not specified	IoT-enabled EPE monitoring	Real-time energy sensing	Significant	163,000 kWh saved in 2017

(*Continued*)

Table 15.5 Some selected case studies of energy-efficient manufacturing facilities. (*Continued*)

Ref.	Company name	Goods produced	Country	Energy strategy	Technology/ approach	Energy savings (%)	Cost savings/ ROI
[139]	J. R. Simplot	Frozen French Fries	USA	Better Plants Challenge	Blending tank, process optimization	24%	$161,000/year
[140–142]	General Motors	Automobiles	USA/ Canada	ENERGY STAR® Treasure Hunts, ECO toolbox	Data-driven audits, supplier engagement	6.5% (2022–2023), >25% cumulative	$2M site + $0.5M supplier savings
[143–145]	General Mills	Cereal, flour, yogurt	USA	DOE Better Plants Challenge	Projects + behavior-based programs	11% intensity, 20% efficiency	$5M past + $13.5M annual target

Organization-level activities, such as retrofitting with LED lighting at Philips Lighting, high-efficiency HVAC retrofits at Dow Chemical, and high-efficiency motor drives at Procter & Gamble, have obtained 25% to 50% savings on energy, highlighting the reproducibility of these measures [124]. Furthermore, real-time AI monitoring systems, such as Eniscope and Tex Plastics, have established up to 36% visibility-based savings [125, 126]. Together, these examples reveal that energy efficiency initiatives, when harmonized with operating conditions and technological AI abilities, yield high investment returns and sustainability in the long term.

The effectiveness of such initiatives is complemented by developments in diagnostic technologies and system integration practices. Energy audits and AI simulation packages are now the norm for finding inefficiencies in equipment, processes, and infrastructures [127, 128]. Nevertheless, accuracy limits of models still constitute a hindrance to direct application [129]. Moreover, the supremacy of standby energy, contributing up to 63% of overall consumption, indicates the importance of AI monitoring and control technologies [127]. The work of Sean Kapp *et al.* identifies untapped thermal system savings, including heat recovery and chiller optimization, and related economic returns that are in excess of implementation costs [130]. Berglund *et al.* are of the view that process energy, production systems, and facility operations need to be integrated *via* AI to achieve sustainable

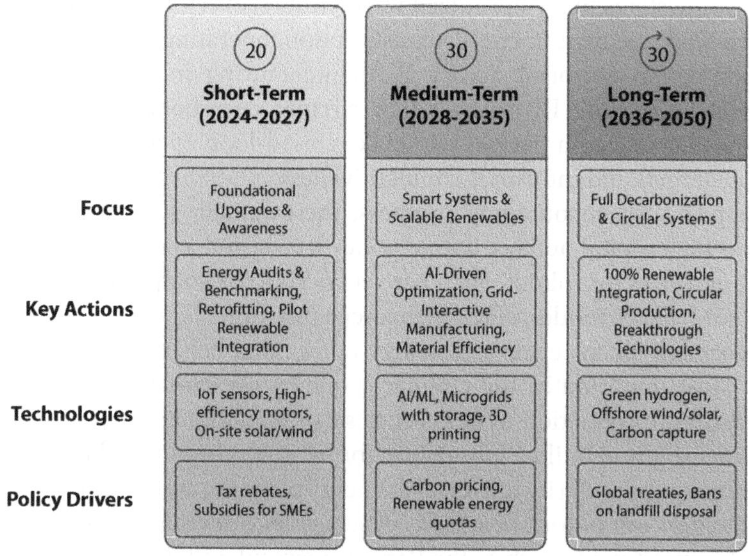

Figure 15.6 Energy efficiency and renewable integration roadmap.

manufacturing outcomes [131]. These converging lines of evidence confirm the role of formal, data-driven, and sector-specific AI interventions in driving energy efficiency across the manufacturing industry.

With decarbonization accelerating worldwide, manufacturing industries must adopt a formal long-term strategy to improve energy efficiency and integrate renewable forms of energy. Figure 15.6 offers this roadmap in the form of a phased strategy integrating phases, priority measures, AI technologies, and policy drivers for inducing sustainable industrial transformation.

15.5 Conclusion

The shift to CM requires a balanced strategy that combines energy efficiency and RE utilization with systemic change, policy consistency, and AI-driven digitalization. This chapter has illustrated that circularity in manufacturing is more than local actions; it needs the convergence of next-generation energy management technology, intelligent AI control systems, and life-cycle thinking. With the integration of best global practices, case studies, and AI analysis approaches, this program focuses on the fact that energy efficiency is not only a sustainability requirement but also an enabler of strategic resilience, competitiveness, and decarbonization.

The application of the latest technology, ranging from smart energy metering systems to AI-optimized waste heat recovery, has provided measurable improvement in energy consumption, operating expenditure, and environmental footprint across all manufacturing industry categories. Further, integrating RE sources into circular decarbonization improves energy efficiency as a necessity to make closed-loop operations viable for climate targets and industrial competitiveness.

Despite such encouraging progress, there remain structural barriers, such as high capital outlays, flaccid policy levers, and a lack of coordinated AI frameworks for rollout. Such barriers need to be conquered by cooperative governance modes, efficient financial instruments, and human capital development for fostering technology uptake and behavioral transformation. Most importantly, the circular economy presents the possibility of reimagining production systems that seize natural capital, reduce fossil fuel intensity, and build a foundation for socio-environmental justice.

By making circularity universal in energy planning and industrial policy, stakeholders can unlock new fields of sustainable development and call on global commitments such as the Paris Agreement and the UN Sustainable Development Goals. By conducting this analysis, the review thus offers a strategic reference to policymakers, practitioners, and researchers who wish to leverage the interlinkage of RE and CM, and thus drive the world toward the development of a regenerative, low-carbon industrial economy.

AI disclosure statement: The author acknowledges the use of AI-based tools for minor language editing or grammatical correction. However, all intellectual contributions, analyses, and conclusions presented in this chapter are entirely the author's own.

References

1. Jamal, A., The Role of Circular Economy Principles in Revolutionising Sustainable Manufacturing Practices. *Int. J. Multidiscip. Res. (IJFMR)*, 2024.
2. Garg, D., Mustaqueem, O.A., Kumar, R., Sustainable circular manufacturing in the digital era: analysis of enablers, in: *Advances in Industrial and Production Engineering: Select Proceedings of FLAME 2020*, Springer, 2021.
3. Moorthy, K.S., *et al.*, Embracing Circular Economy Principles for Sustainable Green Supply Chain Management in Manufacturing Industries, in: *Convergence of Human Resources Technologies and Industry 5.0*, pp. 85–110, IGI Global, 2024.
4. Abdel-Aty, T.A., *et al.*, Unlocking the potential of data in circular manufacturing: opportunities for data sharing and stakeholders' collaboration, in: *Low-Cost Digital Solutions for Industrial Automation (LoDiSA 2023)*, IET, 2023.
5. Andersen, T., *et al.*, Information systems and circular manufacturing strategies: the role of master data, in: *IFIP International Conference on Advances in Production Management Systems*, Springer, 2022.
6. Fohl, F., *et al.*, Circular Manufacturing, in: *International Conference "Coordinating Engineering for Sustainability and Resilience"*, Springer Nature Switzerland, Cham, 2024.
7. Vangeri, A.K., *et al.*, Green Supply Chain Management in Eco-Friendly Sustainable Manufacturing Industries, in: *Environmental Applications of Carbon-Based Materials*, pp. 253–287, IGI Global, 2024.
8. Balaji, S., *et al.*, Circular Economy Strategies for Resource Efficiency and Sustainable Development in Manufacturing Industries. *J. Neonatal Surg.*, 14, 13s, 2025.
9. Nair, K., *et al.*, Integrating policy, technology, and knowledge: a roadmap to circular manufacturing adoption. *Int. J. Sustainable Eng.*, 18, 1, 1–11, 2025.
10. EMRC, Circular Economy in Renewable Energy, Energy Market and Rates Consultants Limited, EMRC Nigeria, 2025.
11. Velenturf, A.P. and Purnell, P., Principles for a sustainable circular economy. *Sustain. Prod. Consum.*, 27, 1437–1457, 2021.

12. Abdirahman, A.A., Asif, M., Mohsen, O., Circular Economy in the Renewable Energy Sector: A Review of Growth Trends, Gaps and Future Directions. *Energy Nexus*, 100395, 2025.
13. Eyo-Udo, N.L., *et al.*, Advances in circular economy models for sustainable energy supply chains. *Gulf J. Adv. Bus. Res.*, 2, 6, 300–337, 2024.
14. Rosen, M.A., The circular economy and energy, in: *Towards a Circular Economy: Transdisciplinary Approach for Business*, pp. 133–149, Springer, 2022.
15. Papadaki, D., Nikolaou, D.A., Assimakopoulos, M.N., Circular environmental impact of recycled building materials and residential renewable energy. *Sustainability*, 14, 7, 4039, 2022.
16. Jakubelskas, U. and Skvarciany, V., Circular economy practices as a tool for sustainable development in the context of renewable energy: What are the opportunities for the EU?, 2023.
17. Klemeš, J.J., *et al.*, Towards efficient and clean process integration: utilisation of renewable resources and energy-saving technologies. *Energies*, 12, 21, 4092, 2019.
18. Mallick, S., Link between innovation in the circular economy design and efficiency improvement in the renewable energy technologies, 2021, Available at SSRN 3900035.
19. Fragkos, P., Analysing the systemic implications of energy efficiency and circular economy strategies in the decarbonisation context. *AIMS Energy*, 10, 2, 2022.
20. Christoff, P., Energy Security and Climate Change—Tensions and Synergies, in: *Energy Security in the Era of Climate Change: The Asia-Pacific Experience*, pp. 217–239, Springer, 2012.
21. Nyman, J., Rethinking energy, climate and security: a critical analysis of energy security in the US. *J. Int. Relat. Dev.*, 21, 118–145, 2018.
22. Scott, M., Planning for a Just Energy Transition: If Not Now, When?, pp. 321–326, Taylor & Francis, 2022.
23. Renna, P. and Materi, S., A literature review of energy efficiency and sustainability in manufacturing systems. *Appl. Sci.*, 11, 16, 7366, 2021.
24. Setiyono, J. and Nabela, N., Renewable Energy Regulatory Urgency in Global Energy Security, in: *IOP Conference Series: Earth and Environmental Science*, IOP Publishing, 2023.
25. Mayer, M. and Peters, S., Energy technology, climate change, and security in Anthropocene, in: *Handbook on Climate Change and International Security*, pp. 238–256, Edward Elgar Publishing, 2023.
26. Iyke, B.N., Climate change, energy security risk, and clean energy investment. *Energy Econ.*, 129, 107225, 2024.
27. Usman, E.C.A., Ebirim, W., Montero, D.J.P., Olu-lawal, K.A., Ninduwezuor-Ehiobu, N., Integrating Renewable Energy Solutions in the Manufacturing Industry: Challenges and Opportunities: A Review. *Eng. Sci. Technol. J.*, 2024.

28. Igeland, P., *et al.*, The energy transition: The behavior of renewable energy stock during the times of energy security uncertainty. *Renew. Energy*, 221, 119746, 2024.
29. Tamang, B., Global Climate Change: Challenges, Opportunities, and Multilateral Strategies for Sustainable Development. *NPRC J. Multidiscip. Res.*, 1, 4, 65–76, 2024.
30. Lund, P. and Byrne, J., Energy strategies to confront climate change. *WIRES Energy Environ.*, 1, 1, 1–2, 2012.
31. Marcucci, A. and Turton, H., Swiss energy strategies under global climate change and nuclear policy uncertainty. *Swiss J. Econ. Stat.*, 148, 2, 317–345, 2012.
32. Yang, M., *et al.*, Circular economy strategies for combating climate change and other environmental issues. *Environ. Chem. Lett.*, 21, 1, 55–80, 2023.
33. Ghazanfari, A., An analysis of circular economy literature at the macro level, with a particular focus on energy markets. *Energies*, 16, 4, 1779, 2023.
34. De Abreu, V.H.S., *et al.*, The role of the circular economy in road transport to mitigate climate change and reduce resource depletion. *Sustainability*, 14, 14, 8951, 2022.
35. Pawanr, S. and Gupta, K., A Review on Recent Advances in the Energy Efficiency of Machining Processes for Sustainability. *Energies*, 17, 15, 3659, 2024.
36. Shao, S., Huang, T., Yang, L., Using latent variable approach to estimate China's economy-wide energy rebound effect over 1954–2010. *Energy Policy*, 72, 235–248, 2014.
37. Worrell, E., *et al.*, Industrial energy efficiency and climate change mitigation, in: *Renewable energy*, vol. 1, pp. 548–568, Routledge, 2018.
38. Elfaham, G., Energy Efficiency Training 101: Metrics & Measurement: Part (2/9), linkedlin, 2023.
39. SYMESTIC, Energy Monitoring in Manufacturing, Linkedlin, 2025.
40. Micieta, B., Markovic, J., Binasova, V., Advances in Sustainable Energy Efficient Manufacturing System. *MM Sci. J.*, 2016.
41. Andersson, E., *et al.*, Decarbonization of industry: Implementation of energy performance indicators for successful energy management practices in kraft pulp mills. *Energy Rep.*, 7, 1808–1817, 2021.
42. Carreno Perez, A.X., Innovative KPIs for sustainability and energy management: Creation, value generation, visualization, 2024.
43. Dutrow, E. and Boyd, G.A., Motivating industrial energy efficiency through performance-based indicators, in: *ACEEE Summer Study on Energy Efficiency in Industry: Cutting the High Cost of Energy*, 2005.
44. Shim, H.S. and Lee, S.J., A study of determination of energy performance indicator for applying energy management system in industrial sector, in: *2018 Portland International Conference on Management of Engineering and Technology (PICMET)*, IEEE, 2018.

45. Piccioni, M., *et al.*, Evaluation of Energy Performance Indicators and Energy Saving Opportunities for the Italian Rubber Manufacturing Industry. *Energies*, 17, 7, 1584, 2024.
46. Bruni, G., *et al.*, From energy audit to energy performance indicators (EnPI): A methodology to characterize productive sectors. the Italian cement industry case study. *Energies*, 14, 24, 8436, 2021.
47. Brundage, M.P., *et al.*, Sustainable manufacturing performance indicators for a serial production line. *IEEE Trans. Autom. Sci. Eng.*, 13, 2, 676–687, 2014.
48. Ray, S., Measuring energy intensity in selected manufacturing industries in India. *J. Energy Technol. Policy*, 1, 1, 31–44, 2011.
49. Sahu, S. and Narayanan, K., Determinants of Energy Intensity: A preliminary investigation of Indian manufacturing, 2009.
50. Sahu, S. and Narayanan, K., Determinants of energy intensity in Indian manufacturing industries: a firm level analysis, 2010.
51. Dudzevičiūtė, G., Energy intensity in the Lithuanian manufacturing sector. 2013.
52. Yoon, H.-S., *et al.*, A comparison of energy consumption in bulk forming, subtractive, and additive processes: Review and case study. *Int. J. Precis. Eng. Manuf.-Green Technol.*, 1, 261–279, 2014.
53. Li, W. and Kara, S., An empirical model for predicting energy consumption of manufacturing processes: a case of turning process. *Proc. Inst. Mech. Eng., Part B: J. Eng. Manuf.*, 225, 9, 1636–1646, 2011.
54. Pawanr, S. and Garg, G.K., Selection of optimum cutting parameters for minimization of specific energy consumption during machining of Al 6061. *J. Phys.: Conf. Ser.*, 2019, IOP Publishing.
55. N, T.V. and G, D.E., Analysis of Energy Consumption by Load Factor. *J. Emerg. Technol. Innov. Res. (JETIR)*, 2019.
56. Gradelski, P., *et al.*, Performance analysis of a manufacturing shop: A case study, in: *[1991] Proceedings of the 30th IEEE Conference on Decision and Control*, IEEE, 1991.
57. Park, M., *et al.*, Workload and delay analysis in manufacturing process using process mining, in: *Asia Pacific Business Process Management: Third Asia Pacific Conference, AP-BPM 2015, Busan, South Korea, June 24–26, 2015, Proceedings 3*, Springer, 2015.
58. Surai, J. and Surapatana, V., Load factor improvement in industrial sector using load duration curves, in: *2014 International Electrical Engineering Congress (iEECON)*, IEEE, 2014.
59. Yang, Q. and Song, B., Improving the carbon footprint of secondary nickel recovered from industrial wastes, in: *2010 5th IEEE Conference on Industrial Electronics and Applications*, IEEE, 2010.
60. Egilmez, G., *et al.*, Carbon footprint stock analysis of US manufacturing: A time series input-output LCA. *Ind. Manag. Data Syst.*, 117, 5, 853–872, 2017.
61. Alsaffar, A.J., *et al.*, A process-based approach for cradle-to-gate energy and carbon footprint reduction in product design, in: *International*

Manufacturing Science and Engineering Conference, American Society of Mechanical Engineers, 2012.

62. Kreitlein, S., Rackow, T., Franke, J., Energy KPI's, challenges for sustainable manufacturing strategies, analysis of existing rules and indicators in an industrial environment in relation to the establishment of energy benchmark. *Adv. Mater. Res.*, 1018, 501–508, 2014.
63. Gong, X., *et al.*, A power data driven energy-cost-aware production scheduling method for sustainable manufacturing at the unit process level, in: *2016 IEEE 21st International Conference on Emerging Technologies and Factory Automation (ETFA)*, IEEE, 2016.
64. Gutowski, T.G., The carbon and energy intensity of manufacturing, in: *40th Seminar of CIRP, Keynote Address, Liverpool University*, Liverpool, UK, 2007.
65. Yuksek, Y.A., *et al.*, A unit product energy mapping framework for operation management in manufacturing industries. *Procedia CIRP*, 122, 873–878, 2024.
66. Reddy, B.S. and Ray, B.K., Decomposition of energy consumption and energy intensity in Indian manufacturing industries. *Energy Sustain. Dev.*, 14, 1, 35–47, 2010.
67. Rozentale, L. and Blumberga, D., Energy Intensive Manufacturers in State Economy: Case study of Latvia, in: *2019 IEEE 60th International Scientific Conference on Power and Electrical Engineering of Riga Technical University (RTUCON)*, IEEE, 2019.
68. Soni, A., Mittal, A., Kapshe, M., Energy Intensity analysis of Indian manufacturing industries. *Resour.-Efficient Technol.*, 3, 3, 353–357, 2017.
69. Gunathilaka, L. and Gunawardana, K., Carbon footprint calculation from cradle to grave: A case study of rubber manufacturing process in Sri Lanka. *Int. J. Bus. Soc. Sci.*, 6, 10, 82–94, 2015.
70. Kanchiralla, F.M., *et al.*, Energy end-use categorization and performance indicators for energy management in the engineering industry. *Energies*, 13, 2, 369, 2020.
71. Kanchiralla, F.M., *et al.*, Energy use categorization with performance indicators for the food industry and a conceptual energy planning framework. *Appl. Energy*, 304, 117788, 2021.
72. Bruni, G., *et al.*, On the energy performance and energy saving potential of the pharmaceutical industry: a study based on the Italian energy audits. *Processes*, 11, 4, 1114, 2023.
73. Barbosa, P.H.d.A., *et al.*, A practical Approach for Measuring Energy and Carbon Performance of Turbomachinery in Offshore Applications, 2021.
74. El-Shennawy, T., Practical Implementation of EnergyPerformance Indicators in Industry. *Int. J. Energy Manag.*, 4, 2022.
75. Awan, M.R., *et al.*, Machine learning-based prediction of specific energy consumption for cut-off grinding. *Sensors*, 22, 19, 7152, 2022.
76. Islam, N.F., *et al.*, Encouraging circular economy and sustainable environmental practices by addressing waste management and biomass energy production. *Reg. Sustainability*, 5, 4, 100174, 2024.

77. Röcken, R. and Moloney, P., Resource management and circular economy, Ramboll, 2023.
78. Kristia, K. and Rabbi, M.F., Exploring the synergy of renewable energy in the circular economy framework: a bibliometric study. *Sustainability*, 15, 17, 13165, 2023.
79. Marzouk, O.A., Expectations for the role of hydrogen and its derivatives in different sectors through analysis of the four energy scenarios: IEA-STEPS, IEA-NZE, IRENA-PES, and IRENA-1.5 C. *Energies*, 17, 3, 646, 2024.
80. Uzondu, N. and Lele, D., Socioeconomic challenges and opportunities in renewable energy transition. *Int. J. Appl. Res. Soc. Sci.*, 6, 1503–1519, 2024.
81. Kumar, S., Darshna, A., Ranjan, D., A review of literature on the integration of green energy and circular economy. *Heliyon*, 9, 11, 2023.
82. Alola, A.A., *et al.*, The role of renewable energy, immigration and real income in environmental sustainability target. Evidence from Europe largest states. *Sci. Total Environ.*, 674, 307–315, 2019.
83. Adeleke, O., *et al.*, Sustainable utilization of energy from waste: A review of potentials and challenges of Waste-to-energy in South Africa. *Int. J. Green Energy*, 18, 14, 1550–1564, 2021.
84. Strupeit, L., Bocken, N., Van Opstal, W., Towards a circular solar power sector: Experience with a support framework for business model innovation. *Circ. Econ. Sustainability*, 4, 3, 2093–2118, 2024.
85. Brown, H., Towards A Circular Energy Economy. *Consilience*, 20, 20, 23–42, 2018.
86. Lacy, P., *et al.*, Circular Economy: A Tale of 10 Industries, in: *The Circular Economy Handbook: Realizing the Circular Advantage*, pp. 75–85, 2020.
87. Bari, M.S., *et al.*, Circular Economy Models in Renewable Energy: Technological Innovations and Business Viability, 2024.
88. Blog, Explore the 10 Leading Circular Economy Examples in 2024, StartUs Insights Discovery Platform, 2024.
89. Green, S.O., 10 Examples of Circular Economy Solutions. 2017.
90. VR, A., The Circular Economy in Solar: Advancing Sustainable Practices for Solar Installers, Blogs, 2025.
91. Agency, I.I.E., Industry - Energy System, 2022.
92. Jiang, J., *et al.*, A review and perspective on industry high-temperature heat pumps. *Renew. Sustain. Energy Rev.*, 161, 112106, 2022.
93. Bakare, M.S., *et al.*, A comprehensive overview on demand side energy management towards smart grids: challenges, solutions, and future direction. *Energy Inf.*, 6, 1, 4, 2023.
94. Singh, M., *et al.*, Advancing Towards a Sustainable Future: The Synergy of Green Technology and Industry 4.0, in: *Advanced Manufacturing Processes*, pp. 300–324, CRC Press, 2025.
95. Company, A., A Comprehensive Guide to Energy Audit Measurements in the Industrial Sector, 2023.

96. Mbaye, A., Review on energy audit: Benefits, barriers, and opportunities. *Am. J. Energy Nat. Resour.*, 1, 1, 45–58, 2022.
97. Brown, R., Webber, C., Koomey, J.G., Status and future directions of the Energy Star program. *Energy*, 27, 5, 505–520, 2002.
98. Rehan, H., Energy efficiency in smart factories: leveraging IoT, AI, and cloud computing for sustainable manufacturing. *J. Comput. Intell. Robot.*, 1, 1, 18, 2021.
99. Beck, A., *et al.*, An integrated optimization model for industrial energy system retrofit with process scheduling, heat recovery, and energy supply system synthesis. *Processes*, 10, 3, 572, 2022.
100. Mashruwala, P., Impact of Passive Design Techniques on a Building Performance in Improving Thermal Comfort in a Hot and Dry Climate, Institute of Architecture & Planning, Nirma University, 2021.
101. Mashruwala, P. and Jadav, P., Impact of Passive Design Techniques on Building Performance in Improving Thermal Comfort in a Hot and Dry Climatic Zone, in: *Future is Urban: Livability, Resilience & Resource Conservation*, pp. 320–330, Routledge, 2023.
102. Bakare, M.S., *et al.*, A hybrid long-term industrial electrical load forecasting model using optimized ANFIS with gene expression programming. *Energy Rep.*, 11, 5831–5844, 2024.
103. Bakare, M.S., *et al.*, Energy management controllers: strategies, coordination, and applications. *Energy Inf.*, 7, 1, 57, 2024.
104. Nota, G., *et al.*, Energy efficiency in Industry 4.0: The case of batch production processes. *Sustainability*, 12, 16, 6631, 2020.
105. Hamrol, A., *et al.*, A Diagnostic Approach to Improving the Energy Efficiency of Production Processes—2E-DAmIcS Methodology. *Energies*, 17, 23, 5942, 2024.
106. Benedikt, O., *et al.*, Energy-aware production scheduling with power-saving modes, in: *Integration of Constraint Programming, Artificial Intelligence, and Operations Research: 15th International Conference, CPAIOR 2018, Delft, The Netherlands, June 26–29, 2018, Proceedings 15*, Springer, 2018.
107. Bähre, D., *et al.*, Energy consumption: one criterion for the sustainable design of process chains, in: *Sustainable Manufacturing: Shaping Global Value Creation*, pp. 163–168, 2012.
108. Jin, L. and Zhang, C., Process planning optimization with energy consumption reduction from a novel perspective: Mathematical modeling and a dynamic programming-like heuristic algorithm. *IEEE Access*, 7, 7381–7396, 2019.
109. Diaz, N., *et al.*, Machine tool design and operation strategies for green manufacturing, 2010.
110. Müller, G., *et al.*, Reducing energy consumption in pharmaceutical production processes: framework and case study. *J. Pharm. Innov.*, 9, 212–226, 2014.

111. Wolff, D., Kulus, D., Nagel, J., Simulationsgestützte Bewertung von Energiesparstrategien: Berichte aus der inpro-Innovationsakademie. *Zeitschrift Für Wirtschaftlichen Fabrikbetrieb*, 108, 3, 103–108, 2013.
112. Jędrzejewski, J. and Kwaśny, W., Study on reducing energy consumption in manufacturing systems. *J. Mach. Eng.*, 11, 3, 7–20, 2011.
113. Trianni, A., Leak, J., Hasan, A.M., Switching on ESCOs: Barriers, challenges and opportunities for the development of Australia's ESCO market. *Energy Policy*, 199, 114546, 2025.
114. Yazdi, M., Maintenance strategies and optimization techniques, in: *Advances in Computational Mathematics for Industrial System Reliability and Maintainability*, pp. 3–58, Springer, 2024,
115. Singh, B., Manjusha, A., Lal, B., 10 Chapter Decarbonizing Global Industry, in: *Gas Hydrate in Carbon Capture, Transportation and Storage: Technological, Economic, and Environmental Aspects*, p. 197, 2024.
116. Papilloud, L., 10 Ways to Reduce Energy Consumption on Construction Sites, Energy spacewell, 2023.
117. BECIS, 9 Efficient Energy Tips for Manufacturing Facilities, 2023.
118. Ocampo-Martinez, C., Energy efficiency in discrete-manufacturing systems: Insights, trends, and control strategies. *J. Manuf. Syst.*, 52, 131–145, 2019.
119. Boyd, G.A., Comparing the statistical distributions of energy efficiency in manufacturing: meta-analysis of 24 Case studies to develop industry-specific energy performance indicators (EPI). *Energy Effic.*, 10, 217–238, 2017.
120. Thiede, S., *Energy efficiency in manufacturing systems*, Springer Science & Business Media, 2012.
121. Ketenci, A. and Wolf, M., Advancing energy efficiency in SMEs: A case study-based framework for non-energy-intensive manufacturing companies. *Cleaner Environ. Syst.*, 14, 100218, 2024.
122. Peruchi Pacheco da Silva, R., *et al.*, Strategic Evaluation of Sustainable Practices for HVAC Systems in Small-and Medium-Sized US Manufacturers. *J. Eng. Sustainable Build. Cities*, 5, 3, 031002, 2024.
123. Seelig, K. and Schleppegrell, S., 3M Cumberland - Air Compressors, Green tier, 2025.
124. Singh, M.P., *et al.*, Energy-efficient manufacturing: Opportunities and challenges, in: *E3S Web of Conferences*, EDP Sciences, 2024.
125. Rumble, I.A. and Davies, J., UK Plastics Manufacturer, Tex Plastics, Saves 26.7% on Energy Bills, Best.Energy, 2025.
126. Chang, I., Eniscope Drives Huge Industrial Energy Savings, Best.Energy, 2020.
127. Le, C.V., Pang, C.K., Gan, O.P., Energy saving and monitoring technologies in manufacturing systems with industrial case studies, in: *2012 7th IEEE Conference on Industrial Electronics and Applications (ICIEA)*, IEEE, 2012.
128. Bakare, M.S., *et al.*, Predictive Energy Control for Grid-Connected Industrial Pv-Battery Systems Using Gep-Anfis. *E-Prime Adv. Electr. Eng., Electron. Energy*, 100647, 2024.

129. Moynihan, G.P. and Triantafillu, D., Energy savings for a manufacturing facility using building simulation modeling: A case study. *Eng. Manage. J.*, 24, 4, 73–84, 2012.
130. Kapp, S., Choi, J.-K., Kissock, K., Toward energy-efficient industrial thermal systems for regional manufacturing facilities. *Energy Rep.*, 8, 1377–1387, 2022.
131. Berglund, J., *et al.*, Energy efficiency analysis for a casting production system, in: *Proceedings of the 2011 Winter Simulation Conference (WSC)*, IEEE, 2011.
132. Winiarek-Erdoğan, S. and Rogozik, M., ArcelorMittal Poland and E. ON announce the launch of a modern heat recovery system, ArcelorMittal Poland communications, 2025.
133. Rajat, Case Studies Successful Energy Efficiency Projects in Metal Manufacturing, EXOS News, 2025.
134. Heiland, T., De Bortoli Wines: striving for better energy efficiency, De Bortoli Wines, 2024.
135. Gennitsaris, S., *et al.*, Energy efficiency management in small and medium-sized enterprises: current situation, case studies and best practices. *Sustainability*, 15, 4, 3727, 2023.
136. Europe, U.N.E.C.f., Guidelines and best practices for micro-, small and medium enterprises in delivering energy-efficient products and in providing renewable energy equipment.
137. Jiang, X., *et al.*, Energy-efficient scheduling of flexible job shops with complex processes: A case study for the aerospace industry complex components in China. *J. Ind. Inf. Integr.*, 27, 100293, 2022.
138. Jagtap, S., Rahimifard, S., Duong, L.N., Real-time data collection to improve energy efficiency: A case study of food manufacturer. *J. Food Process. Preserv.*, 46, 8, e14338, 2022.
139. Simplot, J.R., J.R., Simplot Company, Better building U.S department of energy, 2019.
140. Motors, G., DOE Recognizes General Motors for Energy Efficiency Leadership, Better buildings, 2024.
141. Motors, G., General Motors: Energy and Carbon Optimization Toolbox, Better building U.S department of energy, 2021.
142. Motors, G., Partner of the Year - Sustained Excellence - Energy Management, Energy star, 2023.
143. Mills, G., better energy management approach, better building U.S department of energy, 2018.
144. Mills, G., General Mills Implements Plant-Based Energy Management Plan to Achieve Significant Savings. better building U.S department of energy, 2015.
145. Thorsteinson, G., General Mills' energy management success story, in: *Energy Management and Efficiency for the Process Industries*, pp. 48–55, John Wiley & Sons, Ltd., Hoboken, New Jersey, USA, 2015.

16

Human Capital, Workforce Training, and Circular Economy Skills Development

Val Hyginus Udoka Eze[1*], Addah Kyarisiima[1], Zaina Kalyankolo[1], Josephine Najjobyo[2] and Eze Chidinma Esther[3]

[1]*Department of Electrical and Electronics Engineering, Mbarara University of Science and Technology, Kihumuro, Uganda*
[2]*Department of Civil Engineering, Mbarara University of Science and Technology, Kihumuro, Uganda*
[3]*Department of Educational Foundations, University of Calabar, Calabar, Nigeria*

Abstract

This chapter investigates the pivotal role of human capital, enhanced by artificial intelligence (AI)–driven workforce training, in accelerating the transition toward a circular economy (CE). Using a mixed-methods analytical framework that integrates competency mapping, AI-enabled skills taxonomy analysis, and key performance indicators, the study evaluates the statistical relationships among skills development, firm innovation capacity, and circular business model adoption across manufacturing sectors. Descriptive data synthesized from more than 60 international CE initiatives indicate that firms with structured, AI-supported reskilling programs record an average 28%–35% increase in resource recovery efficiency, a 22% reduction in production waste, and up to a 19% rise in remanufacturing productivity. Comparative meta-analysis of educational models reveals that AI-personalized modular credentialing systems, such as microdegrees and stackable certificates, improve learner employability by 26% and accelerate industry–academia collaboration outcomes by 31% relative to conventional programs. Furthermore, policy-level datasets from EU and OECD circular skills frameworks demonstrate that regions implementing AI-integrated skill-indicator dashboards experience a 0.67 correlation ($p < 0.01$) between CE skills investment and regional eco-innovation index performance. The chapter proposes a multitier competency architecture encompassing firm, institutional, and ecosystem levels, supported

**Corresponding author*: udoka.eze@must.ac.ug; ORCID: https://orcid.org/ 0000-0002-6764-1721

Jeyaprakash Natarajan, Milon Selvam Dennison, M. Bhuvanesh Kumar and Ganapathy Thirukkotti (eds.) Manufacturing and the Circular Economy, (535–568) © 2027 Scrivener Publishing LLC

by a visual framework linking human capital formation, AI-driven innovation adoption, and sustainability outcomes. Empirical insights underscore that strategic skills governance, data-driven training architectures, and the integration of AI-facilitated lifelong learning can yield a statistically significant and enduring impact on the circular manufacturing transition.

***Keywords*:** Circular economy, human capital, competency architecture, sustainable manufacturing, policy frameworks, artificial intelligence

16.1 Introduction

The transition to the circular economy (CE), and in particular, its manufacturing sector, will not merely demand technological innovation but will necessitate an overhaul of the capabilities of human capital and manpower through artificial intelligence (AI)–enhanced workforce development. The knowledge and coordination-intensive processes include circular manufacturing processes, such as remanufacture, repairing, refurbishing, reusing, high-quality recycling, and repair. Companies must learn how to apply AI-driven product redesign for multiple product life cycles, reverse logistics, product traceability, AI-powered materials analytics, and quality management on secondary feedstocks, as well as new business models such as the product-as-a-service (PaaS) model and take-back models. This compound problem marks the highest significance of people and skills, where AI-integrated workforce development becomes the core of the prosperity of the CE [1–3].

This immediate change to skilled manpower is being supported by international policy systems, market forces, and AI-based analytical tools. Green transition goals, changing indicators of the CE, and the evolving needs of the employer are adding to the increased attention on new competencies in accordance with sustainability goals. Circularity as one of the forms of workforce change mentioned by the most prominent organizations, including the International Labor Organization (ILO) and the United Nations Environment Program (UNEP), also needs the development of skills and appropriate metrics, rather than the simple adoption of technology. Besides these perceptions, surveys done by the World Economic Forum (WEF) have shown that the demand for green and systems thinking skills—increasingly augmented by AI literacy—will rise significantly by 2030, which creates strategic significance for intended workforce development and human capital investing in the successful realization of a prosperous CE.

16.1.1 Circular Manufacturing Competency Architecture

Circular manufacturing demands a flexible and extremely skilled workforce, grounded on an all-inclusive competency architecture optimized by AI. In academic literature and industry best practices, the most important set of skills is organized into seven distinct yet overlapping domains, each of which must involve AI-enabled insights to make the processes of circular manufacturing productive.

- Circular design and engineering specializes in designing products for more than one life cycle and is characterized by the following concepts: design for repair (DfR), design for disassembly (DfD), and design for manufacturing adjusted to remanufacturing. This also involves AI-driven material selection optimization for use in multiple loops, modularity, and enhanced contentment to enhance product durability and value recovery [3].
- Industrial operations for loops encompass the looping operational competencies necessary to sustain product value, such as AI-assisted condition assessment, cleaning, disassembly, remachining, and requalification. The competency of adhering to stringent requirements for remanufacturing parts—often monitored *via* AI quality-control systems—is essential to guarantee the same performance and safety as original devices [4, 5].
- Data and digital skills are fundamental, as circular manufacturing involves extensive asset tracking and life-cycle management tools. Competencies include optimizing product life-cycle management (PLM) and bill of materials (BoM) versioning across multiple life cycles, using AI and the Internet of Things (IoT) to track usage and health, using life-cycle assessment (LCA) tools, and using AI-driven learning analytics to constantly up-skill the workforce [5].
- Materials science and metrology expertise is needed for the characterization of secondary and recycled materials, contamination control, and performance recertification. The ability to use AI for feedstock quality management in the secondary phase directly affects material circularity and product reliability [6].
- Business model innovation skills help firms adopt and control new service models such as PaaS, AI-modeled residual

value pricing, take-back contracts, and risk management frameworks for CE strategies [5, 6].

- Policy, standards, and measurement competencies, such as understanding and applying CE metrics, ensuring conformity with emerging indicator frameworks, and integrating AI-monitored just transition principles for balancing economic and social sustainability [4].
- Change and transversal skills are vital in promoting systems thinking, cross-functional coordination, stakeholder engagement, and AI-supported continual improvement processes. These skills enable organizations to deal with the complexity and interdependencies, which are part of circular systems [2].

Collectively, these competency domains orient on developing job families in manufacturing from operators and technicians to designers, data analysts, and service managers. This shifting skills architecture, illustrated in Figure 16.1, fundamentally alters the nature of hiring criteria, training curricula, and career pathways within manufacturing ecosystems.

Evidence from the WEF and LinkedIn suggests that the demand for these types of multidisciplinary CE skills—increasingly powered by AI-driven talent analytics—is significantly outstripping supply in the job market. This discrepancy drives home the point of the sheer urgency to

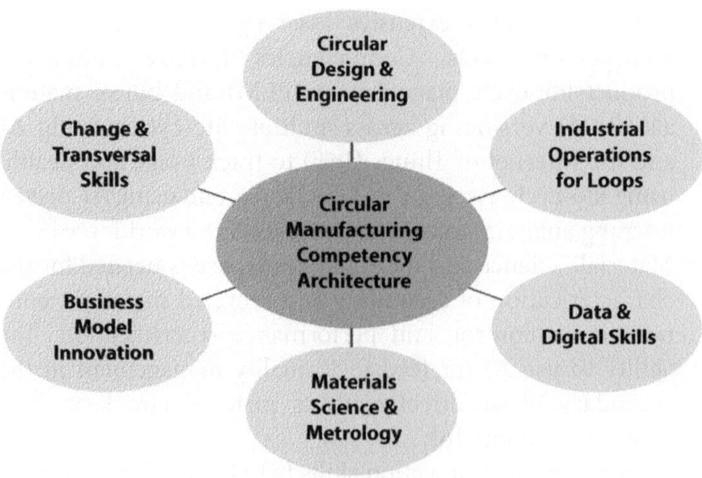

Figure 16.1 Competency architecture for circular manufacturing [7].

reskill and develop the workforce using AI-enhanced training platforms to realize the full potential of circular manufacturing [6, 7].

Table 16.1 outlines the multidimensional skill architecture behind circular manufacturing integrated with AI-driven capabilities. It categorizes competencies in seven interconnected domains: technical, digital, managerial, and policy-oriented, and these are explained in terms of specific AI tools, digital systems, and occupational roles. The framework focuses on systems thinking and cross-sectoral coordination, which is a reality in the integrated nature of circular value creation. It supports AI-enhanced curriculum and workforce design through the linkage of domain expertise with measurable operational outcomes [9].

Table 16.1 Competency domains for circular manufacturing [8].

Domain	Core focus	Typical tools/ examples	Primary roles
Circular design and engineering	DfD, DfR, multilife architectures	Modular BoMs, teardown laboratories	Product/ design engineers
Industrial operations for loops	Condition assesses, clean, disassemble, re-qualify	Reman standards, test stands	Technicians, operators
Data and digital	PLM across life cycles, IoT, LCA, learning analytics	PLM, xAPI/LRS, dashboards	Data/PLM analysts
Materials science and metrology	Secondary feedstock characterization	Contamination control, re-cert	Materials/QA engineers
Business model innovation	PaaS, take-back, residual value pricing	Contracting, pricing	Service/ product managers
Policy, standards, and metrics	CE indicators, conformity	UNECE/OECD frameworks	Compliance/ ESG leads
Change and transversal skills	Systems thinking, cross-functional ops	CI, stakeholder engagement	Supervisors, change leads

16.2 Program Design Principles

Developing human capital for a sustainable CE requires the development of modular, stackable, and competency-based curricula, optimized by AI for personalized learning, which will encourage lifelong learning and workforce adaptability. The best programs combine AI-curated microcredentials, which are short, targeted units of learning, into progressive qualification pathways that may lead to diplomas, postgraduate certificates, and master's degrees. This structure encourages inclusivity within a variety of learner groups and flexible, AI-guided entry and exit points for technicians, engineers, and managers [9, 10].

Curricular Focus and Assessment

CE curricula need to be a combination of conceptual and practical, experiential learning. Hands-on projects, such as product teardown laboratories, reverse engineering, and AI-powered LCA simulations, help learners internalize CE design principles and decision-making [10, 11]. Assessment systems should be explicitly linked with circular performance indicators, often monitored through AI-based analytics, which ensures that the educational outcomes reflect the sustainability goals of the industry. Some key performance metrics for CE include the following:

1. Percentage of parts requalified or reused
2. Average disassembly and reassembly time
3. Material recovery rate
4. Change in LCA results (ΔLCA) compared to baseline products

Such outcome-based evaluations promote alignment between learning deliverables and organizational key performance indicators (KPIs), bridging academia and industry through shared AI data environments [6].

Dual-Track and Dual-System Integration

To achieve both technical depth and operational breadth, CE programs should adopt a dual-track structure, one track focusing on technician-level practical competencies and the other on engineering and managerial problem-solving skills, both augmented by AI literacy. This should be complemented by a dual-system framework integrating academic coursework with industry-based learning experiences, including apprenticeships, cooperative placements, and rotational industry internships [12]. These immersive engagements should cover the core functional domains of circular practice, such as repair and refurbishment, remanufacturing, reverse

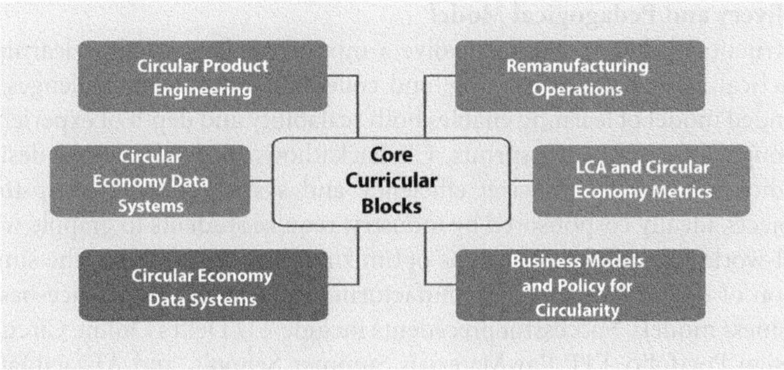

Figure 16.2 Core curricular blocks [15, 17].

logistics, materials tracking, and AI-driven service analytics. International initiatives such as the European Institute of Innovation and Technology (EIT) RawMaterials Academy and the EU Pact for Skills have increasingly endorsed and funded such collaborative education-industry models [13] (Figure 16.2).

Core Curricular Blocks

- **Circular product engineering**: DfD, modular product architectures, fixings and fasteners, AI-generated BoM and hotspot mapping, teardown laboratories, and component recovery simulation [13].
- **Remanufacturing operations**: AI-assisted diagnostics, remanufacturing standards (e.g., International Organization for Standardization [ISO] 8887, BS 8887 series), performance testing and validation, warranty integration, and AI-monitored quality assurance across product life cycles [14].
- **CE data systems**: Product serialization and digital traceability, PLM for multi-life cycles, AI- and blockchain-supported reverse logistics, and return-flow analytics [15].
- **LCA and CE metrics**: UNECE- and OECD-aligned CE indicators, AI-modeled carbon and material intensity, LCA practical sessions, and automated KPI dashboard visualization for sustainability reporting [16].
- **Business models and policy for circularity**: PaaS models, AI-optimized deposit-return and take-back schemes, extended warranty design, CE-compliant procurement strategies, and AI-tracked regulatory frameworks for ecodesign [17].

Delivery and Pedagogical Model

Instructional design should involve a mix of AI-driven online learning, practical factory-based training, and collective innovation challenges. A blended model of learning enables both scalability and depth of experience through on-site factory sprints, CE hackathons, and AI-assisted design studios focused on material efficiency and system redesign. Capstone projects, ideally cosponsored by industry, require students to grapple with real-world CE problems, such as optimizing disassembly lines, the simulation of digital twins for remanufacturing, or redesigning service-based business models. Successful precedents include TU Delft's Online Circular Design Portfolio, EIT RawMaterials Summer Schools, and AI-facilitated hackathons for sustainable product systems [18–20].

16.2.1 Upskilling and Reskilling Pathways in Firms

The transition toward circular manufacturing involves sustainable upskilling and reskilling frameworks that help firms build adaptive, AI-literate, sustainability-focused workforces [21]. Leading industrial organizations are increasingly setting up internal learning academies and AI-powered, data-driven training environments that blend technical training with digital learning analytics. These systems are used to support continuous professional development and to match employee capabilities with changing CE business models using AI-based talent mapping [22, 23].

A prominent example is Caterpillar Inc., which has created an experience API (xAPI)–based learning record ecosystem. This system combines several training platforms, consolidates learning histories, and uses AI analytics to directly correlate employee skill development with operational performance measures [24]. Such a model can be easily adapted to circular operations, allowing for the certification of specialist CE competencies in global dealer and service networks, such as AI-enhanced remanufacturing diagnostics, reverse logistics analytics, or component recovery optimization.

Workforce Transformation and Strategic Alignment

Upskilling initiatives should be strategically aligned with future manufacturing competitiveness. Recent corporate and policy efforts in Europe, North America, and Asia have focused on workforce investment as a key building block of industrial resilience and CE readiness [25, 26]. Firms are also increasingly incorporating AI-driven sustainability assessments into performance reviews and competency frameworks to ensure that CE principles—such as reuse, remanufacture, and material recovery—are embedded into day-to-day production processes.

Competency-Based On-the-Job Credentials

On-the-job credentialing creates a framework for accountability in both skills and performance. CE-aligned credentials should be mapped to clear role profiles and observable competencies, backed by AI-monitored production KPIs and operational outcomes [27, 28]. Typical job profiles for the CE include:

1. **Circular disassembly technician**: Proficient in AI-optimized teardown sequencing, component sorting, and safe material recovery procedures.
2. **Remanufacturing machining specialist**: Skilled in precision repair, tolerance restoration, and part qualification to remanufacturing standards, often utilizing AI-guided machining tools.
3. **CE quality engineer**: Responsible for process validation, AI-powered failure-mode analysis, and ensuring conformance with remanufacturing and CE quality frameworks.

Competency validation may use digital badges or microcertifications using interoperable credentialing technologies such as xAPI or the Open Badges standard. These mechanisms—increasingly managed *via* AI-driven credentialing platforms—provide transparent, portable, and verifiable records of circular skills achievement across firms and supply chains [30]. Ultimately, integrating AI-powered learning analytics, microcredential frameworks, and role-specific upskilling fosters a data-informed, agile workforce capable of operationalizing circularity in production, maintenance, and service functions.

Such internal CE learning ecosystems not only enhance individual career mobility but also drive measurable gains in resource efficiency, product longevity, and corporate sustainability performance. Table 16.2 organizes firm-level pathways to build circular-economy capabilities.

It links learning layers, roles, AI-integrated technologies, and portable credentials to concrete KPIs, showing how internal academies and AI-driven data analytics translate training into operational, commercial, workforce, and sustainability gains, scalable across plants and supply chains as shown in Figure 16.3.

Table 16.2 Upskilling and reskilling framework for circular manufacturing.

Layer/element	Purpose (what)	Key activities (how)	Data and tech enablers	Credentialing mechanism	Roles targeted	Performance link (KPIs)	Illustrative reference
Internal learning academy	Build a repeatable, CE-oriented training system	Modular courses (DfD, reman, reverse logistics); blended delivery; coach-the-coach	LMS + LRS; content libraries; virtual teardown laboratories	Microcredentials stacked to certificates	All shop-floor and engineering tracks	Training completion → DTT↓, RFPY↑, SR↓	[55]
Data-driven learning analytics	Tie learning to operations for ROI	Capture event-level learning; map to MES/QMS/ERP; cohort A/B or DiD evaluation	**xAPI/LRS**; ETL to KPI mart; dashboards	Digital skill passports	Training and ops leaders, analysts	Skill use on-the-job → COPQ↓, WCR↓, DT↑	[56]
Strategic alignment and governance	Align skills with CE strategy and competitiveness	Annual skills foresight; job–family maps; budget tied to CE KPIs	Workforce planning tools; HRIS integration	Role-based competency frameworks	Execs, HR, plant managers	CRS↑, TBR↑, SMIR↑; audit trail	[55]
Circular disassembly technician	Safe, efficient teardown and sorting	Sequencing; fixture/fastener methods; core triage	Work-instruction apps; torque/vision aids	**Open Badges** for DfD/teardown	Operators, maintenance	DTT (min/unit), tool count, nondestructive access ratio	[57]

(*Continued*)

Table 16.2 Upskilling and reskilling framework for circular manufacturing. (*Continued*)

Layer/element	Purpose (what)	Key activities (how)	Data and tech enablers	Credentialing mechanism	Roles targeted	Performance link (KPIs)	Illustrative reference
Remanufacturing machining specialist	Restore tolerances; qualify parts	Cleaning/ inspection; remachining; test-stand validation	CNC data capture; SPC; QMS links	Badge: Reman machining L2–L3	Machinists, QA techs	RFPY (%), Rework hours/1k, COPQ/€m	[58]
Circular economy quality engineer	Validate processes; ensure conformance	FMEA; capability studies; warranty feedback loops	QMS (ISO 9001); warranty DB; analytics	Badge: CE quality engineer	QA/process engineers	**WCR (‰)**, Hazard ratio (reman:new), audit pass rate	[58]
Reverse logistics and data ops	Make returns traceable and timely	Serialization; DPP fields; core tracking; lead-time reduction	PLM; UID/QR/ RFID; ledger/ traceability; SQL/Python	Badge: Traceability and PLM	Supply chain IT, analysts	Traceability %, core return lead time, TBR (%)	[56]
Microcredential framework	Portable, verifiable skill proof	Issue/bundle badges; expiry and recert rules; proctoring	xAPI, Open Badges; LRS registry	Stacked badges → diplomas	All CE roles	Credential-to-role alignment; redeployment rate	[57]
Change and just transition	Redeploy at-risk workers fairly	Pathways from linear → circular roles; mentoring; wage ladders	HRIS; equity dashboards	Recognition of prior learning (RPL)	Operators in legacy lines	RR (%), WP (%), RIR/DART safety	[55]

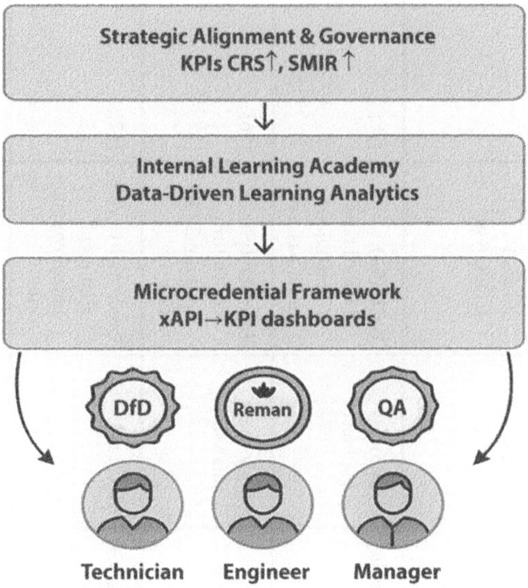

Figure 16.3 Upskilling and skilling framework for circular manufacturing [29].

16.3 The Role of Universities and Research Institutions

Curriculum design is a basic element of building an impactful educational response to the complex needs of the CE [10]. It includes a systematic process incorporating pedagogical principles, industry requirements, and sustainability objectives in a coherent manner. As understood from the field of academic curriculum studies, this process involves deliberate procedural development, strategic organization, and refinement to ensure that training programs generate pertinent competencies for the activities fulfilled by present industry and society. At its heart, curriculum design for CE focuses on integrating interdisciplinary content that creates systems thinking and circular practices [31].

This consists of a strategy of careful selection and sequence of subject matter, pedagogies of instruction, and strategies for assessing student progress and learning that collectively lead to desired learning outcomes. For instance, a well-designed curriculum would include modules related to circular design principles, remanufacturing processes, LCA activities, AI-powered digital tools for traceability, and policy compliance, all in an experiential learning context. Such curricula are not static; they must remain flexible to accommodate technological developments, regulations, and evolving industry standards, necessitating iteration in the development and revision of the curricula [32, 33].

In addition to this, designing curricula for CE has to consider contextual factors, including the sociocultural environment, resource availability, and regional industry practices [34]. The design process should therefore be participatory, involving industry stakeholders, educators, policymakers, and students to ensure relevance and practical applicability. This stakeholder engagement—increasingly facilitated by AI-driven collaboration platforms—increases the ability of the curriculum to bridge the gap between theory and practice, preparing learners to meet real-world challenges in circular manufacturing ecosystems [35].

A modern approach to curriculum design in CE also calls for the use of agile and flexible pedagogical models. In this context, curricula are designed to support project-based learning, problem-solving, and collaborative activities that reflect industry workflows. Such models encourage critical thinking, innovation, and entrepreneurial skills, which are fundamental for the further development of circular business models and technical solutions [35]. Flexibility in design means that institutions can introduce new topics, such as digital product passports, circular supply chain management, and new material standards, without the need to revamp their entire curriculum.

Effective curriculum design must also incorporate clear, measurable competencies, guided by official documents on curriculum design for higher education. This involves setting out precise learning goals, performance standards, and AI-enhanced assessment instruments that measure the mastery of skills and content in a CE—from the characterization of materials to the analysis of circular life cycles. Incorporation of industry-standard benchmarks, such as the ISO and the European Union Sustainable Products Regulation, ensures that learners acquire globally relevant skills that support regulatory and market requirements [36].

In conclusion, curriculum design for the CE must be an integrative, adaptive, and stakeholder-driven process focusing on interdisciplinary knowledge, practical skills, and continuous improvement. By taking such a holistic approach, educational institutions can promote the growth of a workforce capable of innovating, implementing, and sustaining circular manufacturing practices, contributing significantly to the transition toward a sustainable, resilient economy.

Figure 16.4 is a sample of an iterative, multilevel process in which universities incorporate AI-driven pedagogical foundational components, interdisciplinary content, pedagogy, content, contextual factors, and

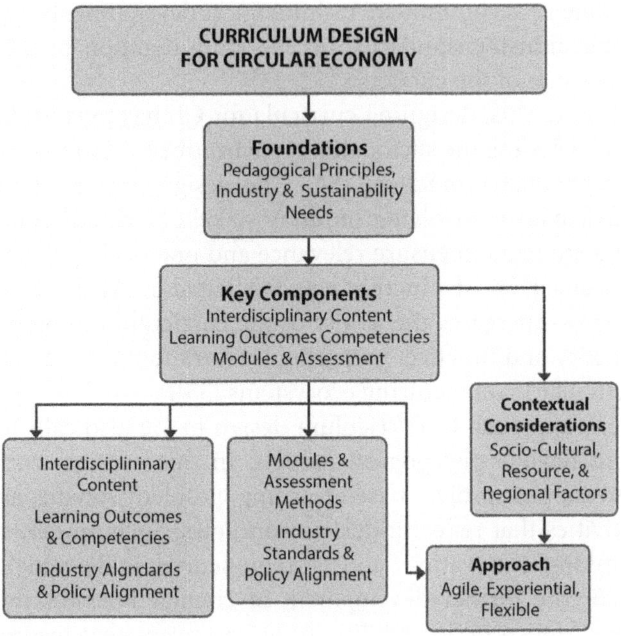

Figure 16.4 Curriculum design framework for circular economy in education [35, 36].

industry-aligned assessment into agile, experiential curricula. It focuses on the issues of flexibility, stakeholder involvement, and competency alignment to produce graduates ready for AI-integrated circular manufacturing and sustainability transitions [36].

A corporate learning ecosystem combining AI-powered digital academies, predictive analytics, and automated governance mechanisms is shown in Table 16.3. It matches the AI-enhanced training of employees to operational KPIs such as disassembly time, yield rates, and circularity scores. AI-enabled credentialing systems and data-driven dashboards have operational continuous improvement processes and link knowledge acquisition to plant-level productivity, quality, and sustainability metrics.

Universities and research institutions are the key enablers in AI-driven CE skills and innovation. They play important roles in the design of curriculum, applied research, and the creation of an AI-ready talent pipeline which together contribute to a system-level shift to circular manufacturing and sustainability [37]. University-led curriculum design is infusing the CE within higher education by equipping students with a level of interdisciplinary skills, AI literacy, and systems thinking that they require for CE challenges [38]. Flagship programs, including TU Delft's circular design

Table 16.3 Firm upskilling architecture for circular operations [35–38].

Layer	Enablers	Credentialing	Linked KPIs
Internal academy	LMS/LRS, virtual teardown	Stacked microcredentials	DTT↓, RFPY↑, SR↓
Learning analytics	xAPI → KPI mart	Digital skill passports	COPQ↓, WCR↓, DT↑
Governance and alignment	HRIS, job–family maps	Role frameworks	CRS↑, TBR↑, SMIR↑
Role exemplars	Work-instruction apps, QMS/SPC	Badges (DfD, machining, QA)	Traceability↑, rework↓

courses and Wageningen's circular bioeconomy degree program, prioritize AI-enhanced life-cycle engineering models, sustainable materials, and regulatory compliance practices so that graduates are prepared to creatively innovate within the confines of circular programs.

Curricula focus on agile and project-based learning, incorporating new emerging concepts such as AI-integrated Digital Product Passports and EU Sustainable Product Regulations in order to remain relevant in the face of constantly changing policies and technologies [37]. Applied research centers within universities bridge theory and industry practice by providing AI-enabled pilot lines for manufacturing, metrology laboratories, and innovation centers for prototyping circular processes. For example, Cranfield University's Sustainable Manufacturing Systems Centre is a facilitating organization for experimentation in AI-driven remanufacturing and circular supply chains working with industrial partners. This collaboration facilitates the real-world testing of disassembly techniques, AI validation of secondary material, and circular business models, which will accelerate the adoption of technology [37].

Furthermore, pan-European programs such as EIT Raw Materials recruit academic consortia for delivering advanced education, professional certification, and AI-centric entrepreneurial training across CE value chains [39, 40]. These efforts boost cross-border knowledge sharing and undergraduate standardization of essential abilities needed to scale CE jobs. Organizations, such as the Ellen MacArthur Foundation, have continuously updated AI-augmented resources and trainings to service the upskilling of a workforce to suit CE innovations, including a curated platform of lifelong learning resources [9, 41]. Collectively, these activities

Table 16.4 Ecosystem levers for policy and academic integration.

Actor	Main levers	Outputs
Policymakers	Skills funds, subsidized apprentices, CE centers	Inclusive green jobs, reporting dashboards
Universities	Living laboratories, industry capstones, agile curricula	Job-ready talent, applied CE research
Clusters/SMEs	Codesign programs, open laboratories	Local capability and absorption
Public buyers	CE-aligned tenders	Demand pull for CE skills

highlight that universities and research institutions must play a catalytic role in the development of the skilled and adaptive workforce needed to support transitions toward an AI-supported CE, and on this basis, sustainable industrial transformations are possible.

Table 16.4 identifies macrolevel AI enablers, which enhance the diffusion of skills among institutions. It focuses on collaboration among policymakers, universities, AI clusters, and public buyers for the institutionalization of circular competences. By creating maps of AI-driven levers and outputs, it highlights the potential of coordinating policy instruments and educational efforts to catalyze regional capacity building, innovation, and the sharing of inclusivity in green employment within the AI-enhanced CE transition [41].

16.4 Case Studies: Industry–Academic Collaboration for AI Skills

Case 1: Renault's Remanufacturing Lineage and the Re-Factory (France)
Renault's circular manufacturing legacy is well and truly in place thanks to its pioneering AI-supported remanufacturing operations at Choisy-le-Roi, which started in 1949 and specializes in important vehicle parts, such as engines, gearboxes, and pumps. This longstanding expertise helped lay the foundation for the creation of the Re-Factory in Flins, France, the first CE factory dedicated to the AI-integrated CE of sustainable mobility in Europe. The Re-Factory is a systemic integration of circular principles, which combines AI-driven vehicle life extension, robotic parts remanufacturing, and automated materials looping in one industrial ecosystem, which puts Renault at the forefront of automotive circularity [42–44].

The Re-Factory's structure is divided into four synergistic AI-powered business units:

- **Re-trofit**: Specializing in vehicle refurbishment, AI-guided retrofitting, and life extension strategies, having refurbished some 1,500 vehicles to date.
- **Re-energy**: Specializing in AI-optimized second-life battery applications and emerging energy solutions, with about 2,000 battery repairs done, partnering for continuous development on energy storage with partners such as Mobilize and HYVIA.
- **Re-cycle**: Combining AI-sorted parts and materials recycling with the remanufacturing of key parts, including the exchange of specialized teams from Choisy-le-Roi for maximum reuse of mechanical and electronic parts.
- **Re-start**: An AI-driven innovation and training center, driving innovation in CE, Industry 4.0 applications, and new commercial vehicle prototypes.

Human capital development is one of the strategic pillars. The Mobility Circular Industry Campus at Flins provides a structured and rigorous training in AI-assisted disassembly, diagnostics, repair, and reassembly skills to develop the adaptability of the workforce through links with outside training bodies and regional actors. This is AI-integrated skill development institutionalized on campus to facilitate job evolution in response to circular operations expansion [44].

Key human capital findings from Renault's Re-Factory initiative highlight the strategic role of AI-driven workforce development in industrial circularity [45]: First, the company's decades-long accumulation of technical expertise has built up deep organizational know-how in AI-enhanced remanufacturing and component recovery processes. Second, Renault has shown the power of upscaling workforce competencies by using dedicated AI training infrastructure to have employees across production tiers acquire and retain specialized CE skills. Most importantly, the firm matches the outcomes of training with plant-level AI-monitored KPIs such as parts throughput, first-time-right quality rates, and remanufacturing yield, in order to maintain an ongoing investment in workforce capability building [44]. By incorporating AI–CE competencies directly into its operational model, Renault's Re-Factory represents a best-practice model that integrates operational excellence with human capital development, positioning the company as a global leader in AI-driven sustainable mobility and industrial transformation. This integrated operational-human capital model provides a scalable blueprint for circular manufacturing that is aligned with global targets for AI-led sustainability and green industry.

Case 2: Caterpillar Analytics-Enabled Learning for AI Circular Operations

Caterpillar's strategy of modernizing circular operations workforce training is a best example of AI-driven, data-driven human capital transformation in the manufacturing industry. The company uses an advanced AI-powered xAPI-based learning ecosystem to unify and analyze training data across its global dealer network, remanufacturing centers, and production facilities [8]. This platform brings together different streams of learning such as compliance, safety, technical, and product-specific modules into a cohesive AI-rich learning platform that can track individual progress and associate learning outcomes with operational performance indicators. By merging xAPI learning records with AI-enhanced enterprise resource planning (ERP) and performance management systems, Caterpillar is able to correlate training achievements with plant-level measures, such as parts throughput, rework rates, and first-time-right quality scores [46, 47].

The AI-driven nature of the system allows for the identification of skills gaps and targeted AI-informed upskilling and reskilling interventions to be applied in specific areas of circular manufacturing (e.g., AI-assisted component teardown, inspection, precision remachining, and materials recovery) [48]. Embedded AI analytics enable managers to dynamically allocate training resources where they have the greatest operational value and thus keep human capital development closely linked to business performance. A unique feature of Caterpillar's model is AI-verified credential portability, the recognition of verified certifications between dealer networks and between factory sites around the world. This provides greater workforce mobility, flexibility, and cross-site transfer of knowledge, ensuring that AI best practices are efficiently propagated across geographically dispersed operations [49].

By having the ability to tie AI certifications and learning outcomes to measurable KPIs in real-time, Caterpillar is able to ensure that training investments make measurable improvements in production efficiency, quality consistency, and sustainability performance. The networked design of the AI learning ecosystem also supports best-practice dissemination across multiple facilities, building a common organizational learning culture of AI-driven circularity and continuous improvement. This approach allows not only the standardization of AI remanufacturing procedures but also the institutionalization of AI–CE competencies as fundamental aspects of the company's industrial identity [48, 49].

Recent workforce investment commitments reflect Caterpillar's continued commitment to grow this AI-based ecosystem, featuring advanced learning analytics, adaptive AI content delivery, and predictive capability mapping to personalize training paths in real time. The company's roadmap incorporates taking advantage of AI-powered recommendation services and performance dashboards to predict new AI skill requirements as circular processes evolve and technologies mature [50]. Key human capital learning from Caterpillar's model identifies three important points for the future of AI–CE workforce development:

1. Data-rich AI learning environments clearly accelerate the learning of skills and provide the ability to proactively clear competency gaps through constant AI analytics feedback.
2. Multisite AI digital learning networks enhance the spread of expertise, operational excellence, and common AI standards throughout global manufacturing ecosystems.
3. AI credential portability improves workforce agility, the ability to redeploy dynamically, and support for the future-ready organization.

Overall, Caterpillar's pioneering work with AI learning analytics and xAPI-driven credential systems is a world-class example of best practices in aligning employee AI capabilities with circular production demands. This integrated and scalable model is proof-of-concept that industrial companies can use AI digital learning ecosystems to enable both operational efficiency and sustainability in the context of the green industrial transition [50].

Case 3: University Networks Powering AI–CE Talent (EU)

University-industry cooperation has become a part of Europe's strategy to develop a well-trained AI workforce for the CE. One of the best is TU Delft's AI–Circular Economy Design portfolio that offers online and blended AI master classes codeveloped with industries. These programs use a combination of AI-facilitated teardown-based experiential learning and systems thinking to allow students and professionals to apply AI–CE principles directly to product redesign, reverse logistics, and materials optimization [9]. Similarly, the EIT Raw Materials Academy is an initiative of the EIT, which works as a pan-European education and innovation network to accredit top-quality AI-integrated master's and PhD courses, professional upskilling courses, and industry-sponsored AI hackathons and summer schools. These activities promote multidisciplinary AI problem-solving and expedite the delivery of research results into market-ready AI circular solutions [51, 52].

Complementing these institutional initiatives, the EU Pact for Skills is an AI-supported coordination platform of collective workforce commitments across strategic industrial ecosystems, including mobility as well as manufacturing and energy-intensive industries. Through this mechanism, universities, companies, and policy actors coordinate their efforts toward large-scale AI reskilling and green transition goals. Circle Economy, a Netherlands-based social enterprise, plays a facilitative role in this by delivering AI-driven labor-market intelligence and tools to align training programs with emerging AI–CE employment opportunities as well as AI competency frameworks [53–55]. Key human capital insights stemming from this networked AI approach are:

1. AI labeling and co-funding schemes, where EIT Raw Materials is used as an example for such schemes, add credibility to the programs and guarantee their conformity to AI industrial quality standards.
2. AI hackathons, challenge-based learning, and industrial master classes are effective ways of bridging the gap between academia and industry, creating immediately deployable AI–CE skills.
3. Collaborative AI governance structures across universities, industries, and EU institutions reduce coordination failures to be a more adaptive and AI innovation–ready talent pipeline.

Collectively, these university–industry–policy linkages depict how the AI–CE education ecosystem in Europe is evolving to become a multilevel human capital machine, which could produce the technical, managerial, and entrepreneurial AI capabilities needed to make industrial circularity and sustainable growth a reality.

16.5 AI Implementation Toolkit for Firms, Clusters, and Policymakers

16.5.1 Firms for OEMs and Suppliers

Transitioning toward AI-driven circular manufacturing requires not only technological innovation but also a systematic AI–human capital transformation. Firms, particularly OEMs (Original Equipment Manufacturers) and their supply networks, must institutionalize structured AI frameworks for skill identification, competency building, and continuous learning to support new AI production paradigms such as remanufacturing, repair, reuse, and recycling. The following toolkit provides a practical framework to help firms operationalize AI–CE skill development within their organizational strategies [59, 60].

1. AI Workforce Foresight and Skill Gap Mapping

The first step is strategic AI workforce foresight, in which firms identify their product portfolios against certain AI-loop strategies (e.g., AI remanufacturing, refurbishment, recycling, or PaaS models). Each loop strategy requires a set of unique technical and AI digital competencies [61]. Firms should use AI to quantify skill gaps within job families, engineering design, production operators, maintenance technicians, and service professionals, while analyzing the external AI labor market. Alignment with WEF AI skills outlooks and local labor market data allows organizations to anticipate emerging occupational shifts born from AI automation, sustainability regulations, and material circularity trends [61–64]. This AI foresight–driven approach ensures that upskilling investments will be both future-oriented and regionally adaptive and address local AI workforce readiness issues and global competitiveness at the same time.

2. AI Skills Standards and Microbadging Frameworks

In order to promote transparency and mobility of AI competencies on sites and between partners, firms should develop AI circular skills standards that are specific to job functions and linked with quantifiable AI measures of performance. For example, it could be demonstrated AI competence in teardown efficiency of components, AI-monitored defect reduction rate, and material recovery percentage [65] for a "Level 2 AI-Circular Disassembly Technician" badge. These AI microbadges can be stackable, creating a part of a larger system of AI professional credentials that are recognized at the level of the value chain. By creating mutual AI certification taxonomies, companies facilitate the portability of AI credentials from one company to another, increasing AI labor mobility and helping to enforce consistent quality standards across global AI remanufacturing and value recovery networks [66].

3. Integrated AI Learning Stack and Delivery Architecture

Build a one-stop AI learning ecosystem, enabling circularity in daily operations by combining [67]:

- (i) Lean AI online modules in CE design thinking, LCA, and material flow optimization

- (ii) On-site AI laboratories with actual components for teardown, diagnostics, and AI remanufacturing exercises
- (iii) Structured AI rotations through value recovery lines (repair, refurbishment, remanufacturing) to ground AI theory in context
- (iv) AI-enabled analytics credentialing—xAPI/LRS tracking linking individual progress to plant AI–KPIs

This is a blended, portfolio-style AI model that maintains adaptive and measurable training while closely coupling the acquisition of AI skills with production performance [68–70].

4. AI Change Management and Just Transition Strategies

Implementing AI circular models often involves substantial changes in the workforce and the content of the job, especially for employees from fossil-oriented or linear production operations. Firms thus need to implement structured AI change management and just transition frameworks with a focus on AI reskilling and redeployment, instead of redundancy [71]. Guided by the principles of social dialogue set out by the ILO, firms should engage employees and trade unions in AI transition planning in order to ensure trust, fairness, and inclusivity. Proactive engagement in ensuring that vulnerable groups such as older workers and low-skilled employees are part of the AI circular transition through accessible AI retraining pathways is essential. Furthermore, the incorporation of AI–CE skill development into corporate sustainability and ESG reporting frameworks demonstrates commitment to social responsibility and AI workforce resiliency, reinforcing investor and regulatory confidence [72]

Table 16.5 Program design and assessment for education/providers [71, 72].

Design element	What to implement	Evidence of mastery
Modular, stackable pathways	Microcredentials → diplomas/masters	Credential ladders, RPL
Experiential learning	Teardowns, reverse-engineering, LCA sims	Laboratory check-offs, project rubrics
Dual track/system	Technician and engineering tracks + co-ops	Placement rates, employer evaluations
KPI-linked assessment	Map learning to CE metrics	% Requalified, DTT, MRR, ΔLCA

Table 16.5 outlines a modular and evidence-driven model for AI-integrated CE education. It proposes stackable AI microcredentials, experiential learning formats, and dual academic–technical tracks aligned with industry needs. By incorporating AI-driven, KPI-linked assessments, the framework connects pedagogical delivery to quantifiable CE performance indicators, ensuring that educational outcomes translate into usable, future-proof competencies [73].

5. Strategic Impact

By incorporating AI-powered workforce foresight, standardized skill-based credentials, and integrated learning ecosystems into the corporate strategy, companies can bring the human capital development process in line with operational excellence and sustainability goals. This is institutionalizing the CE adoption so that it is no longer a technical exercise, but a strategic AI-driven workforce transformation, assuring that industrial competitiveness and environmental care move forward in parallel [72–74].

16.5.2 Universities and Training Providers

Universities and vocational training providers have a key role to play in supporting AI-enhanced CE transitions by equipping the workforce with skills and competences in line with industry needs, technological developments, and AI-driven sustainability principles [75]. Integration of curriculum architecture, AI assessment frameworks, and regional industrial ecosystems is necessary in designing and implementing well-functioning programs [76]. This section presents some of the key strategies to help universities and training providers operationalize AI–CE-oriented education and skills development.

16.5.2.1 Program Architecture

- **Stackable and AI modular credentials** [73]
  - Designing curricula that are organized around stackable AI credentials, so that learners may attend microcertifications sequentially toward diplomas and full degree programs.
  - Map each credential to the seven domains of AI–CE skills found in Section 16.1.1 (e.g., AI-driven resource recovery, product life extension, generative sustainable design, and digital tracking).

- Provide flexible learning pathways combining AI online modules, hands-on workshops, and laboratory work experiences that allow for the upscaling of both professionals and students.
- **AI industry–sponsored capstones** [72]
  - Incorporate capstone projects under the sponsorship and guidance of industry partners, such as AI-driven car manufacturers, smart battery recyclers, or electronic device manufacturers.
  - Focus projects on real-world challenges including AI-optimized remanufacturing and reverse logistics as well as the AI-based assessment of product circularity.
  - Facilitate mentorship by AI industry experts to increase the relevance of technical and business solutions.
- **AI living-laboratory facilities** [77]
  - Develop in-house hands-on facilities such as AI-monitored remanufacturing facilities, simulators of AI-driven reverse logistics, and material recovery laboratories so students can gain experience.
  - Use these laboratories for AI prototyping and to test circular design approaches while assessing the economic and environmental performance of AI–CE processes.
  - Facilitate students, SMEs, and corporate partners to address real-world challenges in the laboratories to scale AI solutions.

16.5.2.2 Assessment and AI Research Integration

- **Alignment with AI–CE indicators** [78]
  - Design assessment models that trace learning outcomes to AI-informed UNECE/OECD CE measures, including automated material recovery measures, product remanufacturing lifespan, and remanufacturing efficiency.
  - Encompass AI-driven quantitative (e.g., LCA delta, resource savings) as well as qualitative (e.g., stakeholder engagement, innovation capacity) measures to offer a comprehensive performance review of the student and program.
- **AI research–embedded learning** [79]
  - Publication of AI learning outcomes and project findings in the form of case studies or applied research reports

should be encouraged to expand the AI–CE knowledge base.
    - Encourage universities and SMEs to collaborate in developing AI experimental protocols, pilot projects, and process improvements that meet local industrial needs.
- **Open AI laboratories for SMEs** [80]
    - Create open-access AI laboratories to offer low-cost services to SMEs for demonstrating AI–CE technology, prototyping, and testing equipment.
    - Transfer AI knowledge, lower the barriers of entry to circular business models, and establish the possibilities of collaborative AI-driven innovation.

16.5.2.3 Regional Alignment and Cluster Integration

- **Codesign with AI industrial clusters** [81]
    - Collaborate with local geographical clusters (e.g., automotive, electronics, AI-driven battery manufacturing) to design the curriculum in co-need to meet the current and future AI skill requirements.
    - Discover major AI competencies required in cluster-based CE programs and include them within course units, internship programs, and research.
- **Engagement with AI public procurement agencies**
    - Work collaboratively with government and procurement agencies to see that graduates are in a position to fulfill AI sustainability and circularity conditions in tenders and projects.
    - Use public contracts as testbeds for student-led AI–CE projects, which improve the AI absorptive capacity of local industries.
- **Capacity building for AI regional ecosystems**
    - Synchronize education systems with local industrial strategies in developing an AI-ready talent pipeline capable of fostering the uptake of the CE in various industries.
    - Encourage collaboration between universities, SMEs, corporate actors, and local government to increase AI innovations in remanufacturing, recycling, and sustainable design.

16.5.2.4 Implementation Recommendations

- Do AI skills-gap analysis between industry partners so that programs can be localized to regional AI workforce requirements.
- Develop joint AI degree or certification programs with international institutions to incorporate global best practices in AI–CE education.
- Implement AI-driven monitoring and evaluation systems to track graduate employability, innovation outcomes, and industry uptake of student projects.
- Encourage interdisciplinary collaboration, linking AI engineering, business, and environmental science programs to foster holistic AI–CE competencies.

This is how universities and training providers can be catalysts of innovation in the circular economy, with the graduates and research outputs directly linked to the industry, regional development and global sustainability agendas.

16.5.3 For Policymakers and AI Ecosystem Orchestrators

Ecosystem orchestrators and policymakers have a key role to play by facilitating the development of an AI workforce in the CE through financial systems, AI monitoring, and inclusive job pipelines. AI platforms, measurement schemes, and regional inclusion should be part of the strategic interventions used to maximize environmental and socioeconomic influence [82–85].

16.5.3.1 AI Platforms and Finance

- **Partnerships in AI risk sharing**: Enter into agreements on AI skills-type partnerships between government, industry, and training providers to share risks and co-fund AI–CE workforce initiatives.
- **Subsidized AI apprenticeships:** Financial incentives, including wage subsidies or tax credits, are given for employer-led AI–CE apprenticeships to reduce barriers to entry for SMEs.
- **Consolidation**: Develop AI centers of excellence: Fund AI–CE research and training facilities associated with universities as living laboratories for AI-driven remanufacturing, repair, and material recovery practices.

16.5.3.2 *AI Measurement and Monitoring*

- **AI skills reporting dashboards:** Require the reporting of AI–CE-relevant indicators, such as AI training hours, attainment of AI credentials, redeployment rates, and productivity indicators.
- **AI benchmarking:** Use AI-aligned UNEP/UNECE principles to ensure international standards, benchmarking, comparability, and transparency of policies.
- **AI policy loops:** Basing decisions on data gathered through AI dashboards allows the adaptation of workforce programs in real-time in response to AI skill shortages.

16.5.3.3 *Inclusion and AI Regional Jobs*

- Localization of AI–CE programs to align workforce initiatives with regional priorities, including AI-driven repair economies and automated e-waste formalization.
- Build AI-ready pipelines for skilled employment in CE sectors, emphasizing inclusive access for all communities to the AI green economy.
- Leverage AI–CE training as a tool for broader social inclusion, employment generation, and sustainable regional development.

16.5.3.4 *Policy Recommendations*

i. Set up AI–CE skills funds at the national level controlled by multistakeholder boards.
ii. Require industry AI–CE skills reporting tied to measurable indicators.
iii. Encourage SME participation in AI–CE apprenticeships through subsidies.
iv. Establish regional AI centers of excellence as training and demonstration centers.
v. Encourage local sustainable job creation through AI inclusiveness.
vi. Periodically revise AI–CE workforce policies based on international AI standards.

16.6 Concluding Remarks

The shift to a CE is not only a technological revolution, but an AI–human capital revolution. The design, operation, and governance of circular systems across manufacturing ecosystems rely on an AI-trained, flexible, and innovation-driven workforce. This chapter has demonstrated that the success of circular manufacturing depends on the adoption of technical, digital, managerial, and AI policy competencies in an integrated format.

Circularity at the firm level involves the intentional insertion of AI reskilling and upskilling processes in operational strategies. Continuous learning systems made AI data-driven, such as the xAPI-based Caterpillar ecosystem, can directly improve productivity and sustainability. The inclusivity of this transformation is guaranteed by AI workforce foresight and standardized AI skills taxonomies.

For universities, the concept of an AI–CE requires dynamic curricula that link AI theory to industrial application through stackable AI credentials and living laboratories. Finally, the policy viewpoint shows how scaled AI workforce preparedness is made possible through enabling structures such as the EU Pact for Skills. When combined, these factors make the AI-driven CE a reality driven by knowledge, ability, and common interest.

AI disclosure statement: The author acknowledges the use of AI-based tools for minor language editing or grammatical correction. However, all intellectual contributions, analyses, and conclusions presented in this chapter are entirely the author's own.

References

1. Madu, C.N., Nnadi, V.E., Ezeudu, O., Madu, I.E., Ezeasor, I.C., Udokporo, E.L., Okolo, O.J., Systems design and innovations in circular economy: The industry and business perspective, in: *Handbook of Environmentally Conscious Manufacturing*, 2nd ed., C.N. Madu (Ed.), pp. 27–38, Springer International Publishing, Cham, Switzerland, 2022, doi: 10.1007/978-3-030-75834-9_3.
2. Zhao, B., Yu, Z., Wang, H., Shuai, C., Qu, S., Xu, M., Data science applications in circular economy: Trends, status, and future. *Environ. Sci. Technol.*, 58, 15, 6457–6474, 2024, doi: 10.1021/acs.est.3c08331.
3. Jorge, N.R., Dopper, S., van Valkenburg, W., Defining a pedagogical model: The TU Delft online learning experience, in: *EDEN Annual Conference –*

Expanding Learning Scenarios, Barcelona, Spain, June 9–12, 2015, European Distance and E-Learning Network, 2015.

4. Schandl, H., Boxall, N., MacMillan, C., Lau, D., Porter, N., CSIRO submission to consultation on Opportunities in the circular economy, CSIRO, Submission 24/089, Nov. 2024.
5. Björkdahl, J., Strategies for digitalization in manufacturing firms. *Calif. Manage. Rev.*, 62, 4, 17–36, Aug. 2020, doi: 10.1177/0008125620920349.
6. Thake, A.M., Transitioning to a Green Economy: The Impact on the Labor Market and Workforce Skills. *Greening Our Economy for a Sustainable Future*, pp. 163–175, Elsevier, Amsterdam, Netherlands, 2025.
7. Liao, M.H. and Wang, C.T., Using enterprise architecture to integrate lean manufacturing, digitalization, and sustainability: A lean enterprise case study in the chemical industry. *Sustainability*, 13, 9, 4851, 2021.
8. Sumter, D., de Koning, J., Bakker, C., Balkenende, R., Circular economy competencies for design. *Sustainability*, 12, 4, 1561, 2020.
9. Sikander, A., Innovative approaches to workforce training for a circular economy. *Green Environ. Technol.*, 1, 1, 47–57, 2024.
10. Del Vecchio, P., Secundo, G., Mele, G., Passiante, G., Sustainable entrepreneurship education for circular economy: Emerging perspectives in Europe. *Int. J. Entrep. Behav. Res.*, 27, 8, 2096–2124, 2021, doi: 10.1108/IJEBR-03-2021-0210.
11. Kirchherr, J. and Piscicelli, L., Towards an education for the circular economy (ECE): Five teaching principles and a case study. *Resour. Conserv. Recycl.*, 150, 104406, 2019, doi: 10.1016/j.resconrec.2019.104406.
12. Aizenman, J., Jinjarak, Y., Ngo, N., Noy, I., Vocational education, manufacturing, and income distribution: International evidence and case studies. *Open Econ. Rev.*, 29, 3, 641–664, 2018.
13. Mah, A., Future-proofing capitalism: The paradox of the circular economy for plastics. *Glob. Environ. Polit.*, 21, 2, 121–142, 2021, doi: 10.1162/glep_a_00594.
14. Odake, N. Circular Economy and Regional Systems. *Sustainable and Smart Cities, Routledge*, p. 55, London, United Kingdom, 2025.
15. Das, S., Barve, A., Sahu, N.C., Muduli, K., Enabling artificial intelligence for sustainable food grain supply chains: An agri 5.0 and circular economy perspective. *Oper. Manage. Res.*, 16, 4, 2104–2124, 2023, doi: 10.1007/s12063-023-00390-z.
16. Amicarelli, V. and Bux, C., Users' perception of the circular economy monitoring indicators as proposed by the UNI/TS 11820:2022: Evidence from an exploratory survey. *Environments*, 10, 4, 65, 2023, doi: 10.3390/environments10040065.
17. Grossi, T., and Rayner, L. The Socio-Ecological Dimension of the Green Deal Industrial Plan. *Social Policy in the European Union: State of Play 2023, European Trade Union Institute (ETUI) and European Social Observatory (OSE)*, p. 13, Brussels, Belgium, 2024.
18. Eekhout, M., and van Swieten, P. *The Delft Prototype Laboratory*, vol. 8, IOS Press, Amsterdam, Netherlands, 2016.

19. Torreggiani, A., *et al.*, RM@Schools: Fostering students' interest in raw materials and a sustainable society, in: *Conference Proceedings: The Future of Education 2020*, June 2020.
20. Happonen, A., Nolte, A., Bystriakova, N., Santti, U., Kärhä, K., Study on hackathons for new innovation seed and business model development needs in digitalization-driven sustainability, circularity and environmentally friendly solutions demanding digitalizing societies. *New Innov. Econ. Bus. Manag.*, 1–29, 2022.
21. Li, L., Reskilling and upskilling the future-ready workforce for Industry 4.0 and beyond. *Inf. Syst. Front.*, 26, 5, 1697–1712, 2024, doi: 10.1007/s10796-023-10373-9.
22. Leon, R.D., Employees' reskilling and upskilling for Industry 5.0: Selecting the best professional development programmes. *Technol. Soc.*, 75, 102393, 2023, doi: 10.1016/j.techsoc.2023.102393.
23. Hasan, M., Haque, M.A., Nishat, S.S., Hossain, M.M., Upskilling and reskilling in a rapidly changing job market: Strategies for organizations to maintain workforce agility and adaptability. *Eur. J. Bus. Manag. Res.*, 9, 6, 118–126, 2024, doi: 10.24018/ejbmr.2024.9.6.2285.
24. Muchiri, D.G., Skilling, reskilling, and upskilling a workforce: A perspective from Kenyan enterprises. *Strateg. J. Bus. Change Manag.*, 9, 4, 190–203, 2022.
25. Becker, B.E., Huselid, M.A., Beatty, R.W., The Differentiated Workforce: Transforming Talent into Strategic Impact, Harvard Business Press, 2009.
26. Grajek, S. and Reinitz, B., Getting ready for digital transformation: Change your culture, workforce, and technology, *EDUCAUSE Rev. Online*, 2019.
27. Klein-Collins, R., Competency-Based Degree Programs in the U.S.: Postsecondary Credentials for Measurable Student Learning and Performance, Council for Adult and Experiential Learning, 2012.
28. Boahin, P., Eggink, J., Hofman, A., Competency-based training in international perspective: Comparing the implementation processes towards the achievement of employability, *J. Curric. Stud.*, 46, 6, 839–858, 2014, doi: 10.1080/00220272.2014.923485.
29. Panagiotopoulou, V.C., Bikas, H., Paraskevopoulou, A., Stamatopoulos, F., Stavropoulos, P., A roadmap for reskilling and upskilling of the workforce towards aligning with twin transition in the manufacturing sector, in: *Conference on Learning Factories*, Mar. 2025, Springer Nature Switzerland, Cham, pp. 177–185.
30. Stamatopoulos, F. and Stavropoulos, P., A roadmap for reskilling and upskilling of the workforce towards aligning with twin transition in the manufacturing sector, in: *Advancing Learning Factories: Enabling Future-Ready Skills: Proceedings of the 15th Conference on Learning Factories 2025*, vol. 1, Springer Nature, 2025, p. 177.
31. Türkeli, S. and Schophuizen, M., Decomposing the complexity of value: Integration of digital transformation of education with circular economy transition, *Soc. Sci.*, 8, 8, 243, 2019, doi: 10.3390/socsci8080243.

32. Iacovidou, E., Hahladakis, J.N., Purnell, P., A systems thinking approach to understanding the challenges of achieving the circular economy, *Environ. Sci. Pollut. Res.*, 28, 19, 24785–24806, 2021, doi: 10.1007/s11356-021-13154-3.
33. Wandl, A., *et al.*, The circular economy concept in design education: Enhancing understanding and innovation by means of situated learning, *Urban Plan.*, 4, 3, 63–75, 2019, doi: 10.17645/up.v4i3.2238.
34. Ababio, B.K. and Lu, W., Barriers and enablers of circular economy in construction: A multi-system perspective towards the development of a practical framework, *Construct. Manage. Econ.*, 41, 1, 3–21, 2023, doi: 10.1080/01446193.2022.2109444.
35. Druzhinina, M., Belkova, N., Donchenko, E., Liu, F., Morozova, O., Curriculum design in professional education: Theory and practice, in: *SHS Web of Conferences*, vol. 50, p. 01046, 2018, doi: 10.1051/shsconf/20185001046.
36. Delmas, M. and Montiel, I., The diffusion of untary international management standards: Responsible Care, ISO 9000, and ISO 14001 in the chemical industry, *Policy Stud. J.*, 36, 1, 65–93, 2008, doi: 10.1111/j.1541-0072.2007.00255.x.
37. Renfors, S.M., Education for the circular economy in higher education: An overview of the current state, *Int. J. Sustain. High. Educ.*, 25, 9, 111–127, 2024, doi: 10.1108/IJSHE-07-2023-0270.
38. Nunes, B.T., *et al.*, University contributions to the circular economy: Professing the hidden curriculum, *Sustainability*, 10, 8, 2719, 2018, doi: 10.3390/su10082719.
39. Trippl, M., *et al.*, Addressing the regional dimension of open strategic autonomy and European green industrial policy, 2024.
40. Dede, C. and Richards, J. (Eds.), *The 60-Year Curriculum: New Models for Lifelong Learning in the Digital Economy*, Routledge, New York, NY, USA, 2020.
41. Van Looy, B., Debackere, K., Andries, P., Policies to stimulate regional innovation capabilities *via* university–industry collaboration: An analysis and an assessment, *R&D Manag.*, 33, 2, 209–229, 2003, doi: 10.1111/1467-9310.00294.
42. L'Allemand, J. and Ramström, S., Generic Design Requirement to Facilitate Remanufacturing of Electric Vehicle Components, 2024.
43. Schlie, T.W. and Goldhar, J.D., Advanced manufacturing and new directions for competitive strategy, *J. Bus. Res.*, 33, 2, 103–114, 1995, doi: 10.1016/0148-2963(94)00063-Q.
44. Schmidt, W.P., Sustainable product development, in: *Solutions for Sustainability Challenges: Technical Sustainability Management and Life Cycle Thinking*, pp. 115–147, Springer Nature Switzerland, Cham, 2024, doi: 10.1007/978-3-031-56201-8_7.
45. Hajoary, P.K., Ramani, Nuur, C., New for some, old for others: Circular economy practices in ancient time. *Circ. Econ. Sustainability*, 4, 2, 815–825, 2024, doi: 10.1007/s43615-023-00353-6.

46. Mohanty, S., Jagadeesh, M., Srivatsa, H., *Big Data Imperatives: Enterprise Big Data Warehouse, BI Implementations and Analytics*, Apress, Berkeley, CA, USA, 2013, doi: 10.1007/978-1-4302-6291-4.
47. Parwez, M.S., Rawat, D.B., Garuba, M., Big data analytics for user-activity analysis and user-anomaly detection in mobile wireless network, *IEEE Trans. Ind. Inform.*, 13, 4, 2058–2065, 2017, doi: 10.1109/TII.2017.2679745.
48. Kim, Y.H., Ye, W., Kumar, R., Bail, F., Dvorak, J., Tan, Y., May, M.C., Chang, Q., Athinarayanan, R., Lanza, G., Sutherland, J.W., Li, X., Nath, C., Unlocking the potential of remanufacturing through machine learning and data-driven models — a survey. *Algorithms*, 17, 12, 562, 2024, doi: 10.3390/A17120562.
49. Tsai, W., Knowledge transfer in intraorganizational networks: Effects of network position and absorptive capacity on business unit innovation and performance. *Acad. Manage. J.*, 44, 5, 996–1004, 2001, doi: 10.5465/3069443.
50. Aho, A.M., Product data analytics service model for manufacturing company, in: *Proc. Int. Conf. Knowledge Manage. Organizations*, Springer, Cham, Switzerland, pp. 282–296, 2015, doi: 10.1007/978-3-319-21009-4_24.
51. Morehouse, C. and Busse, M., *How to Keep a Competitive Edge in the Talent Game: Lessons for the EU from China and the US*, Rowman & Littlefield, Lanham, MD, USA, 2014.
52. Lopez, C., *et al.*, Academic Offer and Demand for Advanced Profiles in the EU, European Commission Joint Research Centre.
53. Müller, T., Platzer, H.W., Rüb, S., Transnational company policy and coordination of collective bargaining—new challenges and roles for European industry federations. *Transfer: Eur. Rev. Labour Res.*, 16, 4, 509–524, 2010, doi: 10.1177/1024258910383992.
54. Di Salvo, M., Talent Partnerships and Future Skills Needs, IEMed – European Institute of the Mediterranean, Barcelona, Spain, 2022.
55. European Commission, EU Pact for Skills: Building Skills Partnerships for the Green and Digital Transition, Brussels, 2022.
56. Torrance, M., Data & Analytics for Instructional Designers, Association for Talent Development, Alexandria, VA, USA, 2023.
57. Coenen, J., Makkink, H. and Zijderveld, M., Disassembly Strategies for Remanufacturing: Experiences from a Learning Factory, in: International Workshop on Autonomous Remanufacturing, pp. 501–512, Springer Nature Switzerland, Cham, 2023.
58. Parker, D., Riley, K., Robinson, S., Symington, H., Tewson, J., Jansson, K., Ramkumar, S. and Peck, D., Remanufacturing Market Study, European Remanufacturing Network, Brussels, Belgum, 2015.
59. Suchek, N., Fernandes, C.I., Kraus, S., Filser, M., Sjögren, H., Innovation and the circular economy: A systematic literature review. *Bus. Strategy Environ.*, 30, 8, 3686–3702, 2021, doi: 10.1002/bse.2834.
60. Kuik, S., Kumar, A., Diong, L., Ban, J., A systematic literature review on the transition to circular business models for small and medium-sized enterprises (SMEs). *Sustainability*, 15, 12, 9352, 2023, doi: 10.3390/su15129352.

61. Gayatri, G., Jaya, I.G.N.M., Rumata, M., The Indonesian digital workforce gaps in 2021–2025. *Sustainability*, 15, 1, 754, 2023, doi: 10.3390/su15010754.
62. Siikaniemi, L., Information pathways for the competence foresight mechanism in talent management framework. *Eur. J. Training Develop.*, 36, 1, 46–65, 2012, doi: 10.1108/03090591211192689.
63. Ngo, Q.D., Nguyen, Q.H., Vu, C., Envisioning future workforce adaptability: A multi-layered analysis of skills ecosystems in Vietnam's emerging economy. *Futures Foresight Sci.*, 7, 1, e70000, 2025, doi: 10.1002/ffo2.70000.
64. Chigbu, B.I., Advancing sustainable development through circular economy and skill development in EV lithium-ion battery recycling: A comprehensive review. *Front. Sustainability*, 5, 1409498, 2024, doi: 10.3389/frsus.2024.1409498.
65. Johnson, K.W., An exploration of employer participation in internships and other work-based learning experiences. *J. Career Tech. Educ.*, 37, 1, 1–20, 2022, doi: 10.21061/jcte.v37i1.1978.
66. Daugherty, M., Carter, Sumner, A., Standards for technological and engineering literacy and STEM education. *Technol. Eng. Teacher*, 80, 5, 1–20, 2021.
67. Genc, H., *et al.*, Gemmini: Enabling systematic deep-learning architecture evaluation *via* full-stack integration, in: *Proc. 58th ACM/IEEE Design Autom. Conf. (DAC)*, pp. 769–774, 2021, doi: 10.1109/DAC18074.2021.9586238.
68. Gbenle, P., *et al.*, A national education access platform model using MEAN stack technologies: Reducing barriers through cloud-based smart application systems, 2022.
69. Sarma, S. and Bagiati, A., Current innovation in STEM education and equity needs for the future, in: *Symposium on Imagining the Future of Undergraduate STEM Education*, National Academies of Sciences, Engineering, and Medicine, 2021, Available: https://www.nationalacademies.org.
70. Plaza, E., Aamodt, A., Ram, A., Van de Velde, W., Van Someren, M., Integrated learning architectures, in: *European Conf. Machine Learning*, Springer, Berlin, Germany, pp. 427–441, 1993, doi: 10.1007/3-540-56602-3_148.
71. Goddard, G. and Farrelly, M.A., Just transition management: Balancing just outcomes with just processes in Australian renewable energy transitions. *Appl. Energy*, 225, 110–123, 2018, doi: 10.1016/j.apenergy.2018.05.025.
72. Krawchenko, T.A. and Gordon, M., How do we manage a just transition? A comparative review of national and regional just transition initiatives. *Sustainability*, 13, 11, 6070, May 2021, doi: 10.3390/su13116070.
73. International Labour Organization, Guidelines for a Just Transition Towards Environmentally Sustainable Economies and Societies for All, ILO, Geneva, Switzerland, 2022.
74. TU Delft Online Learning, Circular Product Design and Lifecycle Thinking, Delft University of Technology, 2023.
75. Carnevale, A.P., *Training Partnerships: Linking Employers & Providers, Alexandria*, American Society for Training & Development, VA 1990.

76. Qu, D., Shevchenko, T., Saidani, M., Xia, Y., Ladyka, Y., Transition towards a circular economy: The role of university assets in the implementation of a new model. *Detritus*, 17, 3–14, 2021, doi: 10.31025/2611-4135/2021.15141.
77. Rane, J.R., Chaudhari, R.A., Rane, N.L., Resilience and Sustainability in Supply Chains through Circular Economy: Environmental Impact, Climate Change Mitigation, and Waste Management, in: *Enhancing Sustainable Supply Chain Resilience Through Artificial Intelligence and Machine Learning: Industry 4.0 and Industry 5.0 in Manufacturing*, pp. 111–120, 2025.
78. Alivojvodic, V. and Kokalj, F., Drivers and barriers for the adoption of circular economy principles towards efficient resource utilisation. *Sustainability*, 16, 3, 1317, 2024, doi: 10.3390/su16031317.
79. Greenhalgh, T. and Fahy, N., Research impact in the community-based health sciences: an analysis of 162 case studies from the 2014 UK Research Excellence Framework. *BMC Med.*, 13, 232, 2015, doi: 10.1186/s12916-015-0467-4.
80. Casciani, D. and D'Itria, E., Fostering Directions for Digital Technology Adoption in Sustainable and Circular Fashion: Toward the Circular Fashion-Tech Lab. *Systems*, 12, 6, 190, 2024, doi: 10.3390/systems12060190.
81. Uyarra, E. and Ramlogan, R., The effects of cluster policy on innovation, master dissertation.
82. Arthur-Mensah, N., Bridging the industry–education skills gap for human resource development. *Ind. Commer. Train.*, 52, 2, 93–103, 2020.
83. Nogueira, A., Ashton, W., Teixeira, C., Lyon, E., Pereira, J., Infrastructuring the circular economy. *Energies*, 13, 7, 1805, 2020, doi: 10.3390/en13071805.
84. Munonye, W.C., Towards Circular Economy Metrics: a Systematic Review. *Circ. Econ. Sustainability*, 1–43, 2025.
85. Fonseca, L. and Michie, R., Circular Economy Policies in Europe: Assessing Regional Policy Integration, European Policies Research Centre, Glasgow, 2024.

17

Investment, Business Models, and Financial Strategies for Circular Manufacturing

N. Prakash*, P. Karthikeyan, M. Dharshne, S. Brinda and M. Logitha

Department of Management Studies, Kongu Engineering College, Erode, Tamil Nadu, India

Abstract

In industrial contexts, circular production is becoming a key tactic to attain long-term sustainability, improve resource efficiency, and cut waste. Circular manufacturing, as opposed to the conventional linear "take–make–dispose" paradigm, emphasizes prolonging product life cycles, maximizing resource utilization, and restoring ecological systems. The financial drivers of this change are examined in this chapter, with special attention paid to the function of investment structures, new business models, and performance indicators. Government incentives, ESG rules, and investor demand for sustainable practices are driving an increase in global financial support for circular economy activities. There is a surge in venture capital, green bond issuance, and blended finance in industries such as electronics, textiles, automotive, and construction. Public–private partnerships and development banks are particularly important because they provide risk-sharing arrangements, tax breaks, and subsidies. Innovations in business models are essential to circular manufacturing. Recurring revenue and life-cycle control are made possible by tactics such as product-as-a-service, remanufacturing, and take-back initiatives. Xerox and Caterpillar's remanufacturing systems and Philips' "lighting-as-a-service" are noteworthy examples. These models increase economic and environmental value while decreasing reliance on material resources. By facilitating improved traceability, predictive maintenance, and performance tracking through tools such as digital twins and material passports, digital technologies such as blockchain, IoT, and AI are speeding up the adoption of the circular economy. Despite this, lengthy repayment periods continue to be a barrier to funding

**Corresponding author*: np.mba@kongu.edu

Jeyaprakash Natarajan, Milon Selvam Dennison, M. Bhuvanesh Kumar and Ganapathy Thirukkotti (eds.) Manufacturing and the Circular Economy, (569–604) © 2027 Scrivener Publishing LLC

for early-stage circular businesses. This is addressed by the introduction of the Circular Investment Readiness model, which provides a framework for evaluating financial sustainability, stakeholder alignment, and scalability. In the meantime, more recent KPIs are being used to assess both financial and environmental benefits, such as life cost savings (LCS), material circularity indicator, and return on circular investment. Successful circular transitions are illustrated by case studies from H&M and Renault, highlighting the significance of institutional cooperation, customer awareness, and supportive regulation in mainstream structures for the circular economy.

Keywords: Circular manufacturing, circular economy, material circularity indicator (MCI), linear cost savings (LCS), return on circular investment (RoCI), ESG, remanufacturing, green finance

17.1 Introduction

A sustainable alternative to the "take–make–dispose" linear model of production, the circular economy (CE) seeks to mitigate resource shortages and climate change by generating income from the use of finite resources. The main goals of a CE are waste reduction, material reuse, and product recycling, in contrast to a linear economy that uses resources and produces waste. Because of its significant resource consumption and waste production, the manufacturing sector is at the forefront of this change, highlighting the necessity of circularity in industrial operations [46, 47].

17.1.1 The Definitions and Application of CE in Manufacturing

An economic system that keeps resources and things in circulation for as long as feasible is known as the "circular economy." Key tactics include transitions from product ownership to service-oriented business models and closed-loop projects such as the "3 R's" (reduce, reuse, recycle) [24, 25]. In manufacturing, this translates into designing products for multiple life cycles (e.g., modular designs for easier repair), using recycled inputs, and developing reverse logistics to reclaim end-of-life materials. However, CE implementation in manufacturing remains nascent, with firms facing significant challenges in overhauling linear production systems.

An important focus of this research is how CE adoption affects corporate risk and incentives. Linear business models entail inherent "linear risks" (e.g., volatile input prices or regulatory liabilities), but circular strategies can mitigate these exposures. Empirical studies find that firms

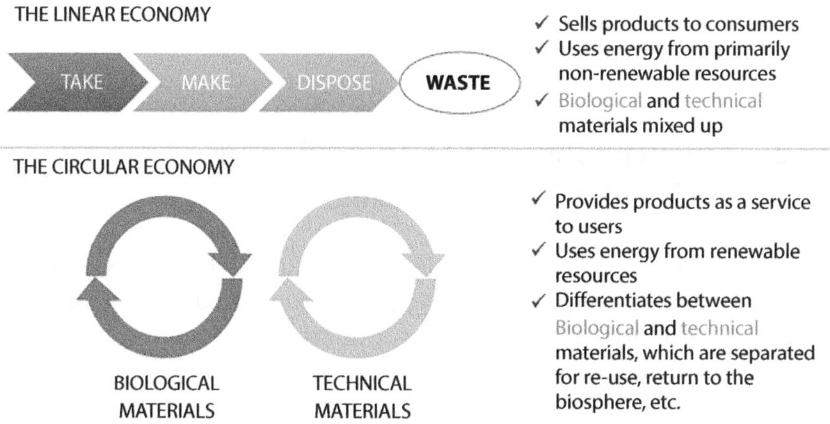

Sources: World Economic Forum with Ellen MacArthur Foundation and McKinsey & Company. Towards the Circular Economy: Accelerating the scale-up across global supply chains. Cologny/Geneva, Switzerland: January 2014; http://mbdc.com/ (accessed 13 April 2016)

Figure 17.1 Linear flow versus circular flow.

with greater circularity have significantly lower risk profiles and can even achieve superior risk-adjusted returns. Thus, a circular model can serve as a risk management strategy. The framework developed in this study bridges risk management with CE strategy, aiming to show how firms can realign risk assessment and investment decisions to support circular initiatives.

Figure 17.1 contrasts Linear Flow and Circular Flow models. In the linear flow, resources move in one direction from the initial phase to production, distribution, consumption, and finally disposal—leading to waste. In contrast, the circular flow emphasizes continuous reuse, where products are recycled after consumption and reenter the production cycle, minimizing waste and resource depletion.

17.1.2 Methodological Approach and Contribution

This study develops a framework integrating risk management with CE strategies. It analyzes sustainability data (circularity indicators and ESG disclosures) alongside risk measures to evaluate how circular practices affect firm performance. This integrated approach links circular initiatives with risk outcomes to identify key obstacles and the forces in the shift from a linear to a circular framework. By filling a gap at the intersection of CE and risk management, the research provides a novel perspective on CE adoption. In practical terms, it offers guidance for industry—showing manufacturers how circular strategies can improve risk-adjusted performance—and informs policymakers in designing effective incentives to facilitate the circular transition.

17.2 Financial Benefits of Transitioning to Circular Manufacturing

Implementing the transition to circular manufacturing has both environmental and strong financial rewards. This methodology is demonstrated by the EU-funded circular project, which aims to reduce production resources while converting end-of-life commodities into high-value goods [1]. Essentially, circular manufacturing helps organizations reduce expenses and open new revenue sources by segregating the value from the consumption of raw materials. Cost reduction, revenue growth, and asset productivity are the three financial benefits of circular manufacturing that are examined in this study. Key performance indicators (KPIs) such as the material circularity indicator (MCI), linear cost savings, and return on circular investment (RoCI) are reviewed to assess these benefits.

Figure 17.2 [45] shows that the same contextual levers can either burden or boost a circular project's bottom line. Taxes and fragmented laws may raise operating costs and depress asset value, yet compulsory take-back rules can also cut disposal expenses. Industry standards lower system-setup costs while reassuring customers, and access to green or public finance offsets high upfront spending—whereas scarce capital inflates costs and limits value capture.

	Financial performance	
Context	Cost	Value
Legislation	**Increased** due to taxation of labour and weight, and the disparity between national legislations. **Decreased** due to creating infrastructure for take-back.	**Decreased** due to regulatory obsolescence.
Standards	**Decreased** due to affecting system enablers.	**Increased** through standards for remanufacturing products removing customer uncertainty.
Financing	**Increased** from limited financing options for investment in cost reduction. **Decreased** from potential public financing in take-back	**Decreased** due to limited financing options for improved value capturing.

Figure 17.2 The impact of product return value and cost context.

17.2.1 Gains on the Cost Side

The elimination of unproductive linear processes in circular manufacturing leads to significant cost-side gains. Businesses can save money by using fewer raw materials, using less energy, disposing of garbage less frequently, and complying with regulations with greater ease.

The cost of acquiring resources is directly reduced when recycled or regenerated inputs are used instead of virgin materials. An organization can save more money if it uses fewer costly virgin resources. According to one analysis, by 2030, circular solutions might reduce material costs by up to $700 million annually [2]. These savings result from the fact that secondary (recycled) feedstocks are frequently less expensive than new ones; in fact, the more affordable and convertible the recycled inputs are, the more money can be recovered by accomplishing the materials loop [3]. Transforming end-of-life products into useful inputs lowers waste and raw material costs in the framework of the circular project [1].

Costs are further minimized by the energy efficiency of circular production processes. Remanufacturing a product, for instance, generally consumes a lot less energy than creating a new one from the ground up. Because the producer is responsible for the operational costs, servitization—the provision of goods as services—can encourage manufacturers to create long-lasting, energy-efficient devices. One example is Xerox's recent transition to an "everything-as-a-service" business model, which dramatically reduced the company's manufacturing energy usage and related expenses by maintaining and reusing items rather than mass-producing new ones [2]. In general, circular innovators such as SpaceX have shown incredible cost reductions; for example, reusing a rocket booster reduced launch expenses by almost 30% in one instance [4]—showcasing how designing for reuse yields energy and cost efficiencies.

Reducing trash production directly lowers waste management and compliance expenses. Businesses pay twice in a linear system: first for excess materials that end up as scrap and again for the disposal of that scrap. By using a circular strategy, this loop is closed. Businesses can save significant landfill fees, hazardous waste processing expenses, and environmental levies by designing items for reuse/recycling and putting take-back programs in place. Ninety-five percent of material value is currently lost after a single use in Europe's traditional take–make–dispose economy [5], which translates to wasted capital and additional disposal costs. Money is saved for each ton of waste that is avoided or recycled. A possible solution can be found in industrial symbiosis, which minimizes net waste by utilizing the byproducts of one process as the feedstock for another. For manufacturers, this translates into lower waste hauling costs and a chance to profit from residuals. For example, Hyundai implemented reverse logistics to recover spent auto parts, which reduced the requirement for trash disposal and, by recovering parts, reduced the cost of production overall [2].

Developing circular processes proactively can help lower the expenses associated with meeting environmental standards. Linear operations risk increased compliance costs and significant penalties when governments implement more stringent regulations on waste, emissions, and resource use (such as Europe's Circular Economy Action Plan and Green Deal [48]). Contrarily, circular manufacturers are ahead of rules because they naturally generate less waste and pollution. They escape the penalties linked to environmental noncompliance and pay less for emissions or waste disposal permits. To summarize it briefly, circularity serves as a kind of insurance against upcoming regulatory expenses. Businesses may minimize the cost of adapting processes to meet new regulations later by planning out waste and toxics today [2]. Furthermore, many businesses discover that a circular reputation enhances their interactions with communities and regulators, further smoothing operations.

Profitability is increased when these cost-side benefits—materials, energy, waste, and compliance—are combined. Manufacturers can boost operating margins by utilizing circular models to create more with less. Research has shown that implementing sustainability practices in production can have quantifiable financial benefits; for instance, manufacturers that emphasize sustainability have seen an average 18% increase in return on investment (ROI) compared to their counterparts [2]. Circularity's cost savings are a major factor in these enhanced returns.

17.2.2 Gains on the Revenue Side

An instance of industrial symbiosis occurs whenever a chemical manufacturer sells process by-products to adjacent industries as inputs. Waste steam, gases, or slurry from one factory can be sold to nearby facilities as inputs, as demonstrated by the traditional Kalundborg symbiosis in Denmark [3]. As a result, circular supply chains generate markets for remelted metals, recycled materials, reconditioned parts, and other byproducts. These sales generate additional revenue in addition to thereby compensating for disposal expenses.

This source of revenue rationale is precisely indicated in the circular project's focus on converting end-of-life items into high-value products [1]. Another example is Hyundai's remanufacturing program, which collects and refurbishes used car subassemblies from consumers for exchange or resale [2]. Through this circular system, an asset pool (old cars) that would otherwise be written off is converted into service revenue and parts sales. By retaining previous customers through trade-in programs, it also promotes recipient retention.

Remanufacturing prolongs a product's profitable life. A manufacturer can harvest components for reuse or remanufacture and subsequently sell a product several times instead of selling it all at once. Each cycle develops more revenue due to significantly lower production costs than the first cycle. According to research, remanufactured products often have higher profit margins than new ones because they are far less expensive to produce and can be sold for 75%–90% of the price of new ones [2]. Companies such as Caterpillar and John Deere that have successful remanufacturing departments accept used engines or equipment, fix them to like-new condition, and then sell them with warranties. This not only captures value that would be lost in a one-and-done purchase, but it also draws in budget-conscious customers. As a result, trade-in credits and less costly reconditioned options are valued by buyers, which encourages client loyalty. Companies that use circular strategies typically report improved brand perception and client retention [6], which boosts sales. Many Dutch manufacturers interviewed stated that adopting circular business models enhanced their customer loyalty and market uniqueness [6]—intangible assets that eventually generate income.

A defining characteristic of cyclical innovation in business is servitization, which is the practice of marketing a product's usefulness rather than its actual features. Manufacturers maintain ownership of the product and generate ongoing income under product-as-a-service (PaaS) agreements (lease, subscription, pay-per-use), whereas consumers pay for results or access. Because the manufacturer is responsible for upkeep, this model encourages businesses to create durable, upgradeable products and permits ongoing client connections.

The result is often a stable, annuity-like revenue stream in place of volatile one-off sales. For example, Philips Lighting now offers lighting-as-a-service where building owners pay for "lumens" delivered instead of buying lightbulbs [4]. Therefore, Philips accumulates a consistent flow of service revenue and can replace and return lighting equipment, which minimizes waste. Similarly, to increase its service income and retrieve discarded printers for remanufacturing, Xerox changed from selling printers to leasing them and charged by the page [4]. Other trailblazers include Patagonia, which makes money from clothing repair services and second-hand sales, and H&M, which gathers used clothing from consumers and recycles the fibers into new clothing, establishing a closed-loop product line and enhancing brand engagement [4]. These instances demonstrate how circular models create additional revenue streams, such as recycling credits, maintenance services, subscription fees, and take-back resale schemes.

An organization may retain customers in their ecosystem longer and increase the lifetime value of each product by designing it for longevity, reusability, and upgradeability. Offering upgrades or modular add-ons, for example, rather than requiring a complete product replacement, enables more sales over time. An actual example is Apple's iPhone trade-in and refurbishment program, which prolongs the device's life cycle and makes money from the sale of refurbished phones. Furthermore, a brand can be elevated by having strong CE credentials, drawing in premium-paying, sustainability-conscious customers. Price power and increased sales are frequently the results of a sustainable brand image. Consumers are increasingly choosing products with recycled content or take-back guarantees, in accordance with surveys [6]. Therefore, through improved brand equity and access to new client groups (such as green public procurement [GPP] markets), circular manufacturing can indirectly increase top-line growth in addition to opening direct income streams.

Manufacturers can increase income while utilizing fewer resources by switching from selling volume to selling value in usage. The circular paradigm increases the number of opportunities to generate revenue per unit of material by transforming what was previously considered waste or a one-time transaction into a continuous value cycle. Studies that predict trillions of dollars in economic opportunities demonstrate that this more regenerative paradigm is a route to sustained growth. For instance, if CE ideas are implemented widely, a McKinsey/Ellen MacArthur analysis estimated that Europe will profit economically by €1.8 trillion by 2030 [5], primarily from new companies and potential markets.

17.2.3 Asset Productivity and Resilience

Improved asset productivity and increased business resilience are two benefits of circular manufacturing models. Circular enterprises increase utilization rates, supply stability, and risk management by reconsidering how assets are used and how supply chains are organized. Many assets are drastically underutilized in traditional linear operations, which is a financial inefficiency. For example, the average office structure is only used 35 to 50 percent of working hours, and the average car is parked approximately 92 percent of the time [5]. Because of this low utilization, capital investment is locked up in underutilized assets. By using tactics that make assets sweat more, such as leasing, pooling, and sharing platforms, circular approaches seek to address this. A single vehicle can serve numerous users thanks to car-sharing programs (such as Zipcar or OEMs providing mobility services), significantly increasing its mileage and revenue per day. Similarly, operating products as a service or renting equipment to several clients guarantees that goods are being utilized rather than lying idle at a client location. Increased asset utilization increases return on assets (ROA) and postpones the need for additional capital expenditures. Customers just pay for what they require, which is a win–win situation. As mentioned, pay-per-use and leasing are examples of circular business models that retain product ownership and are successful in boosting utilization and value extraction from each product [3].

Businesses can increase overall capital efficiency by converting idle capacity into productive usage, which allows them to make more money from the same asset base. According to one industry analysis, circular models such as sharing and product-service systems not only decrease waste but also save businesses money on materials and the acquisition of new assets [4]. Better utilization effectively results in fewer total assets needed for a given level of service output, which lowers depreciation costs and frees up capital. Because circular manufacturing lessens reliance on global commodities and limited virgin inputs, supply networks become more robust. A circular model protects a company from unstable raw material markets by sourcing a greater proportion of input from locally recovered or recycled materials.

This is especially effective during periods of lack of resources or geopolitical unrest. A maker of electronics that extracts precious metals from outdated devices, for instance, has an internal supply of metals and is less vulnerable to changes in mining productivity or price surges in the international market. The European Commission has emphasized the significance of promoting circularity to guarantee businesses' long-term competitiveness and to disentangle economic growth from resource use [5]. Practically speaking, using secondary materials protects against supply shocks; a business that can use recycled inputs will be far less impacted if the price of virgin materials spikes or if tariffs are put in place. Furthermore, circular supply chains frequently reduce geographic distances (by means of nearby recycling and remanufacturing plants, etc.), which lowers logistical risks and delays.

Circular systems are also adaptive by design; for example, modular components can be switched to get around parts shortages, and goods made for disassembly can be fixed more readily during supply disruptions. A steadier production process with fewer expensive interruptions is the result of all these considerations. Manufacturers with strong take-back and refurbishment programs, for example, were able to repurpose returned inventory to satisfy demand during the COVID-19 pandemic, providing them with a resilience edge when new production was interrupted. Closing the loop essentially eliminates supply vulnerabilities, making businesses more independent and less susceptible to the boom and bust of commodities markets.

There is growing evidence that leaders in the CE perform better when risk is adjusted. Businesses lower environmental liability and the risk of future stranded assets by planning out waste and pollution [7]. Because it "hedges" against the hazards associated with the linear take–make–waste model, adopting circular processes can be viewed as a risk mitigation approach [7]. This de-risking effect is supported by quantitative research. Two hundred twenty-two European companies were studied, and it was discovered that those with higher circularity ratings had better risk-adjusted returns and lower risk than their fewer circular counterparts [7]. Implementing circular methods, such as decreasing and reusing resources, dramatically lowers both idiosyncratic risk and default risk, according to another survey of 1,150 EU enterprises [8].

Consider it in another perspective: circular businesses are less likely to experience financial difficulties. This resilience stems from several factors, including more reliable input sources, cost flexibility, and frequently a robust compliance stance. Furthermore, longer-term planning is more common in circular firms, which is consistent with improved risk management. Investors are beginning to pay attention, viewing a focus on the CE as a stand-in for robust, forward-thinking management. As a result of their lower risk profiles, we can anticipate that businesses with strong circularity will eventually benefit from better lending terms and insurance conditions. In conclusion, a company's financial resilience is strengthened by switching to circular manufacturing, which makes it more resilient to environmental and economic shocks than the linear model would permit.

Circular manufacturing increases capital efficiency by increasing utilization and decreasing risk, producing more output (or income) for every dollar of invested capital. A higher return on invested capital results from fewer write-offs and idle assets. For example, if a business can create products that are valuable at the end of their useful lives (by implementing take-back programs), the money spent on them will pay for itself several times over (original sale, after-market services, second-hand sale, etc.).

Figure 17.3 [43] illustrates two distinct approaches adopted by asset managers in relation to investing in the CE. In the upper section (A), labeled as "Trackers," asset managers exhibit limited engagement with CE by categorizing it under broader, dominant categories. Their actions are marked

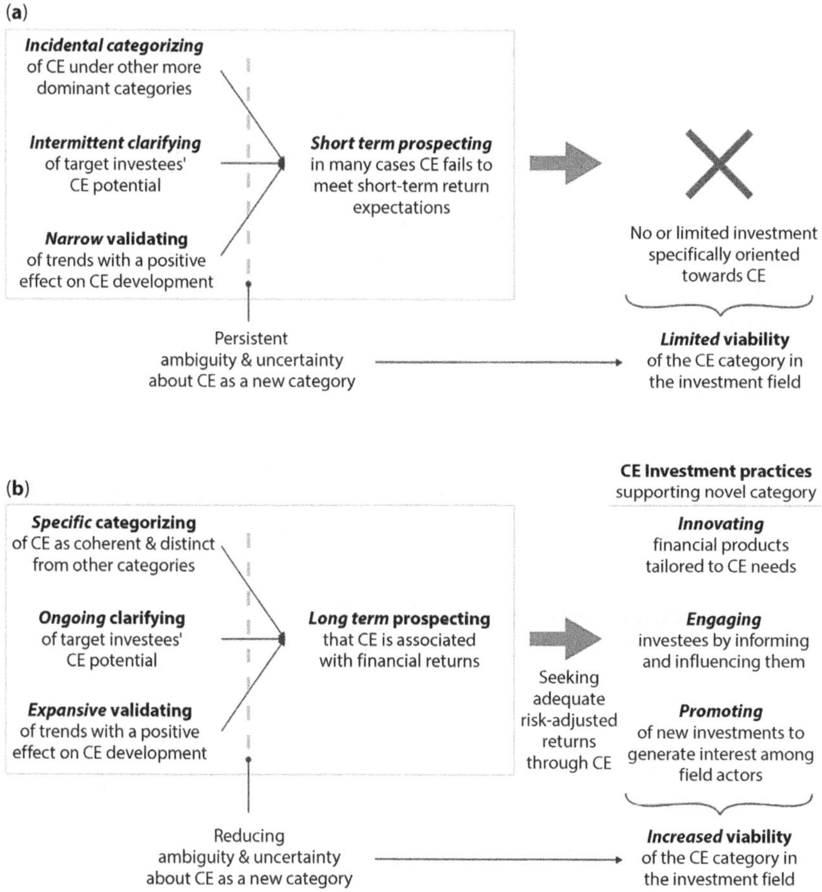

Figure 17.3 Patterns of asset managers' sensemaking.

by intermittent clarification and narrow validation, often driven by short-term return expectations. This results in persistent ambiguity around CE, leading to limited or no CE-specific investments and, consequently, low viability of CE as an investment category. In contrast, the lower section (B), titled "Trailblazers," represents a more active and constructive approach. These asset managers view CE as a distinct and coherent category, continuously clarify its potential, and validate trends that support CE development. Their focus on long-term financial returns fosters the creation of CE-specific financial products, active investor engagement, and promotion of CE opportunities. As a result, this approach significantly enhances the viability and legitimacy of the CE within the investment field. A linear sale, on the other hand, loses value after just one transaction. Stronger financial

KPIs such as ROI and ROA might result from increased capital productivity. As previously stated, leaders in sustainable manufacturing report higher returns on investment, suggesting that investing in circular capabilities makes sense financially [2]. By gradually reducing their expenditures on waste management and raw materials, businesses can also free up funds for expansion or innovation. These elements all work together to create a more competitive and lean cost structure, which can be a tactical advantage. These efficiency gains will be increasingly more important to sustaining margins as carbon pricing schemes grow and resource prices rise.

Circular manufacturing combines resilience and efficiency. It guarantees that resources, such as tangible machinery or inventory, are used and their worth is fully realized rather than being wasted or left idle. In this way, productivity is maximized. Additionally, it strengthens the company's financial performance by protecting it from outside shocks. These factors provide businesses with compelling financial incentives to adopt circularity, beyond the well-publicized environmental motivations.

17.2.4 Circular Performance Financial KPIs

Organizations and researchers are using KPIs to monitor and convey the financial advantages of circular manufacturing. The MCI, linear cost savings (LCS), and RoCI are three helpful indicators. These KPIs bridge the gap between technical and financial outcomes by helping to quantify circular performance in a combination of monetary and nonmonetary terms.

To measure how "circular" a system or product is, the Ellen MacArthur Foundation and Granta Design created the MCI, a comprehensive statistic. It reduces different circularity components to a single score that ranges from 0 (completely linear) to 1 (completely circular) [4]. A product's longevity and intensity of use (e.g., through reuse, repair, or shared use models), its end-of-life situation (i.e., how much of the product is collected for recycling or remanufacturing), and the effectiveness of recycling processes (i.e., ease of disassembly, fraction of material recovered) are all evaluated by the MCI. In practical terms, a higher MCI means the product uses more secondary inputs, stays in use longer (or more frequently), and yields materials that are largely recovered and cycled back. For instance, consider two smartphones: Phone A uses 20% recycled metals, is designed for easy battery replacement, and 90% of it is recyclable, whereas Phone B uses only virgin materials and is hard to recycle. Phone A would score much higher on the MCI.

A company can use the MCI at the product or even company level to track improvements in circular design and operations. Why is this financially relevant? Because a higher MCI often correlates with lower material costs and potential new revenue (from recaptured materials), it serves as a proxy for resource efficiency gains. Investors and stakeholders are increasingly interested in such metrics to evaluate how well a firm is future-proofing its resource dependence [4]. In sum, the MCI translates technical circularity into a measurable indicator that can be tied to financial performance (e.g., cost savings from higher recycled content). It is a valuable KPI for managers to identify where the biggest circular improvements (and hence cost reductions or risk reductions) can be made.

LCS refers to the cost reduction achieved by moving away from the linear "take–make–dispose" model toward circular processes. It is essentially a financial metric that captures how much expense has been avoided or eliminated thanks to circular initiatives. LCS can be computed by comparing the baseline costs under a linear scenario to the realized costs under a circular scenario. Key components of LCS include savings on raw material purchasing (by using recycled inputs or less material overall), savings on energy (via efficiency or renewable use), and savings on waste management and regulatory fees (due to waste reduction). For instance, if a manufacturer spent $100 per unit on virgin materials but now spends $80 by incorporating recycled feedstock, that $20 per unit difference is a linear cost saving [3]. Summed across all circular improvements, LCS provides a tangible dollar value of the benefit of circularity. This metric can be expressed as an absolute annual saving or normalized per product/unit. It can also be broken down by category (material cost savings, energy cost savings, etc.). Although LCS is not yet a standardized indicator such as the MCI, it is increasingly used internally in companies to justify circular projects [30]. It speaks the language of CFOs by directly linking CE actions to bottom-line impact. One could also frame LCS in percentage terms (e.g., a 15% reduction in input costs due to circular sourcing).

The concept is backed by economic logic; as noted earlier, the more a firm can substitute cheaper secondary materials for expensive primary ones, the greater the cost savings. Companies such as Renault and Unilever have reported multimillion-euro savings by redesigning products for circularity (e.g., material lightweighting and increased recyclability leading to procurement savings) [38, 39]. By tracking LCS, firms ensure that cost-side gains of circular manufacturing are quantified and recognized [24]. This KPI helps in building the business case for further circular investments—it answers the question, "How much money did we save this year by implementing circular initiatives?" in concrete terms.

RoCI is a proposed metric analogous to the traditional ROI, tailored for CE projects. It measures the financial return generated by an investment in circular practices or infrastructure. In formula terms, RoCI can be thought of as (net financial benefits of circular investment)/(cost of investment), often expressed as a percentage or ratio. For example, if a company invests $1 million in a new remanufacturing facility and reaps $1.5 million in increased profit (through cost savings and new sales) over a certain period, the RoCI would be 0.5 or 50%. The idea behind RoCI is to isolate the returns attributable to circularity—which might include cost savings (LCS, as above), additional revenue from circular offerings, and even risk mitigation value—and compare them to the upfront costs (such as new equipment, R&D, or training for circular processes). Using RoCI, managers and investors can evaluate and rank circular projects just as they would any capital project. This is important because, historically, many sustainability or circularity initiatives were justified on qualitative or environmental grounds, making finance departments cautious. RoCI puts these initiatives into a familiar financial framework. There is a growing effort to collect data and prove that circular business models provide strong ROI in the long run [4].

In fact, clear evidence of high returns would likely accelerate the adoption of a CE, as companies on the fence often need to "see the numbers" to be convinced [4]. Early signs are encouraging; research finds that companies with advanced CE integration tend to outperform financially, as noted with higher ROI and lower risk metrics [2, 7]. RoCI as a formal metric is still emerging, but some organizations have started using frameworks such as "return on sustainability investment," which are closely related, quantifying benefits from things such as improved resource efficiency, innovation, and brand value. In practice, to apply RoCI, one must account for all cash flows from a circular project—e.g., savings from using less material, earnings from selling recycled outputs, and the avoidance of future costs due to compliance or carbon taxes—and then calculate the rate of return. A positive RoCI (above 0 or above the company's hurdle rate) demonstrates that the circular investment is adding value to the firm. Using RoCI alongside traditional ROI helps ensure that long-term circular benefits are measured and not overlooked in favor of short-term gains. It essentially translates the ethos of the CE into the finance-centric metric of investment efficiency.

A manufacturing firm might use the MCI to benchmark the circularity of its product lines and set targets (e.g., "increase average MCI from 0.3 to 0.6 in five years"). As the MCI improves, the firm would expect to see proportional improvements in LCS; for example, higher recycled content should manifest as reduced material spending. LCS can be tracked annually, showing the growing cost advantage of circularity. Meanwhile, when proposing a new circular initiative (say, an in-house recycling plant), the firm can calculate the RoCI to ensure the project makes financial sense. These metrics are interconnected: a high-RoCI circular project will typically deliver notable LCS and boost the MCI. Together, they provide a balanced scorecard of circular performance: technical circularity (MCI), cost savings (LCS), and investment returns (RoCI).

By monitoring such KPIs, companies in the circular project and beyond can quantitatively demonstrate the financial merits of their sustainability efforts. This not only helps in internal decision-making but also in communicating value to external stakeholders such as investors, who increasingly seek evidence that sustainability initiatives contribute to financial success. As one report noted, integrating circular metrics into business cases helps "prove the business advantages" of circularity and gives executives the confidence that these models yield real financial returns [4].

Figure 17.4 [44] complements the KPI discussion by mapping a closed-loop, five-step workflow for managing CE metrics. It starts with definition, where firms derive or design KPIs (such as MCI, LCS, or RoCI) from

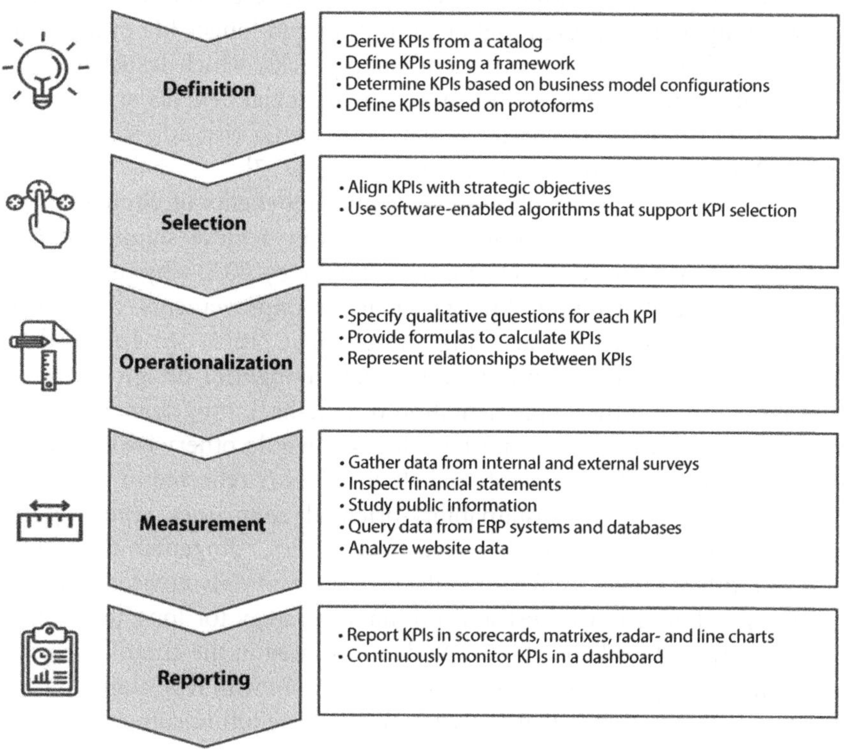

Figure 17.4 Business model KPI life cycle and identified approaches for each phase.

catalogs, frameworks, or prototypical business-model patterns. Selection follows, ensuring that only those indicators that truly support strategic objectives make it onto the scorecard—often aided by analytics engines that rank candidate KPIs. During operationalization, each KPI is translated into clear questions, formulas, and causal links so that engineers and finance teams know exactly how to calculate and influence the number. Measurement and reporting close the loop by detailing data sources (ERP pulls, surveys, web analytics) and visual formats (scorecards, radar charts, live dashboards) that keep circular performance—and its financial impact—visible to decision-makers.

The transition to circular manufacturing, as pursued by the circular project and many industry leaders, is more than an environmental imperative—it makes profound financial sense. Companies can achieve cost-side gains through lower raw material and energy bills, reduced waste, and lower compliance costs, thereby boosting their profit margins. Simultaneously, they unlock revenue-side gains by accessing new markets for recycled materials, offering remanufactured products, and delivering services that build ongoing revenue and customer loyalty. The result is often improved asset productivity (through higher utilization and longer life cycles) and greater resilience against market and supply risks, which translates to a more stable and competitive business. The financial benefits are increasingly being validated; empirical studies show better risk-adjusted returns and ROI for firms embracing circular practices [2, 7].

Table 17.1 above highlights the quantifiable benefits of circular manufacturing, demonstrating how companies can achieve significant raw material savings—up to $700 million annually by 2030—by using recycled or regenerated inputs. Energy efficiency improvements, as seen in practices such as remanufacturing and product reuse, can cut production energy costs by around 30%. Through thoughtful design for reuse and recycling, and the implementation of take-back programs, firms can avoid losing up to 95% of material value that would otherwise be wasted in a linear model. These operational efficiencies are reflected in improved financial returns, with sustainability-oriented companies reporting up to 18% higher ROI than their conventional peers. Altogether, these data points reinforce that circular manufacturing is not only environmentally responsible but also a robust and profitable strategy for long-term business growth and resilience [5, 7]. As demonstrated in the circular project, adopting such approaches allows firms to do more with less, aligning economic gains with sustainability goals and ensuring future competitiveness in a resource-constrained world.

Table 17.1 Financial benefits of circular manufacturing.

Benefit type	Mechanism/example	Numeric evidence
Raw material savings	Using recycled or regenerated inputs in production	Saves up to $700 million/ year in material costs by 2030 [5, 7]
Energy efficiency	Remanufacturing and product reuse (e.g., SpaceX rocket reuse, Xerox servitization)	Reduces production energy costs by roughly 30% [5, 7]
Waste reduction	Designing for reuse/ recycling and take-back programs	Avoids losing 95% of material value (linear model loss) [5, 7]
Improved financial returns	Sustainability and circular production initiatives	Sustainability-oriented firms achieve 18% higher ROI [5, 7]

17.3 Investment Opportunities in Circular Business Models

Investment in CE business models (CEBMs) has seen significant growth in recent years, indicating an increasing acknowledgment of the economic potential and sustainability advantages of the CE. In 2020, the global CE market was estimated to be worth approximately €148 billion, with projections suggesting it will reach €263 billion by 2030, marking a 78% increase [9]. As illustrated in Table 17.2, this market growth is mirrored by rising financial activity: the number of dedicated public equity funds focused on circular themes reached 13 by mid-2021, collectively managing $8 billion, whereas green and sustainability bonds for circular projects have exceeded 35 issuances since 2019. Even amidst challenging economic circumstances, investments in the CE have demonstrated resilience [13]. For instance, in the UK, the number of CE businesses receiving external funding increased from 42 in 2018 to 184 in 2023, with investment in these firms rising by 30% year-on-year in 2023, despite a general decline in deal-making activity [11]. This indicates a fundamental increase in investor interest.

Several factors contribute to this growth. Environmental and resource pressures serve as primary motivators; institutional investors are increasingly recognizing CE strategies as a means to alleviate climate and supply chain risks while seizing new value opportunities. Table 17.2 also highlights sector-specific trends, such as major funding rounds in the electronics and mobility sectors and the gap between current and required investment in plastics recycling. For example, $57 billion worth of recoverable materials is generated annually from e-waste, and circular electronics startups such as Back Market and battery recyclers such as Redwood Materials have attracted substantial investment. However, compared to the need, current investment levels are still small. Although increasing, venture capital

Table 17.2 Investment trends in circular economy business models.

Trend/metric	Details/example	Numeric evidence
Global market growth	Global circular economy market (2020 vs. 2030 projection)	€148 billion (2020) increases to €263 billion (2030) (78% increase) [9]
Dedicated investment funds	Public equity funds focused on circular themes	13 funds (by mid-2021) managing $8 billion [11]
Green bonds issuance	Bonds with proceeds for circular projects	More than 35 green/ sustainability bonds issued since 2019 [11]
Circular business growth (UK)	UK circular businesses receiving investment	Grew from 42 (2018) to 184 (2023); investment up 30% YoY (2023) [11]
VC investment share	Share of venture capital funding going to circular startups	Only 1.5% of global VC funding (2023) [14]
Plastics recycling funding	Private capital for plastics circular solutions	$32 billion per year (2018–2023) vs. $1 trillion needed by 2040 [15]
Electronics sector	E-waste recovery and refurbished electronics	$57 billion worth of recoverable materials/ year; Back Market raised $335 million (2021) [14]
Mobility sector	Battery recycling and automotive remanufacturing	Redwood Materials raised $700 million for battery recycling (2021) [14]

(VC) funding for circular businesses only made up about 1.5% of all VC investment worldwide in 2023 [14]. From 2018 to 2023, an average of $32 billion in private capital was allocated to circular solutions in the plastics recycling space, far less than the $1 trillion required by 2040 [15]. As the CE transitions from specialty to mainstream, this disparity suggests significant unrealized investment potential. Overall, the data in Table 17.2 underscores that although progress has been made, there is considerable room for future capital inflow as momentum builds and investors expand their commitments to circular sectors.

17.3.1 Sectoral Hotspots for Circular Investments

CE opportunities span many industries, but certain sectoral hotspots have emerged where investment activity and potential impact are especially high. Leading development finance institutions (DFIs) have identified areas such as the built environment, electronics, mobility, and textiles as high-potential sectors for circular business models [16]. These sectors are characterized by intensive resource use and waste generation, meaning circular innovations there can deliver outsized economic and environmental gains.

The built environment is one of the largest waste generators globally, accounting for approximately 25%–30% of total solid waste and about one-third of natural resource use [1]. This makes it a prime target for circular transformation. Investment is increasing in businesses that recover and reuse building and demolition materials (such as recycled concrete and steel), design structures for disassembly, and offer product-service arrangements such as "lighting-as-a-service." Specific circular design models can decrease costs and supply risks for architects while diverting colossal waste volumes from landfills. Governments are also upholding this change (e.g., through circular public procurement in construction projects), which further spurs private lending. In essence, we see new ventures acquiring capital to produce low-carbon cement from industrial byproducts, to operate marketplaces for recovered construction components, and to provide standardized "construction-as-a-service" offerings. Each of these innovations addresses the building industry's need to decouple growth from virgin material use—creating a compelling business case for financiers and builders alike.

The field of electronics has emerged as a significant area of concern due to the escalating issue of electronic waste. About 20% of the 50 million tons of e-waste produced annually worldwide is recycled through official routes [18]. This waste stream is estimated to contain recoverable materials worth around $57 billion annually, including precious metals and rare earth elements [18], highlighting a substantial economic opportunity for circular business models. Investors have recognized this potential, supporting companies that promote extended life cycles for electronics and facilitate materials recovery. Notable examples include recommerce platforms and refurbishment services for smartphones and laptops, as well as advanced recycling companies capable of extracting metals from circuit boards and batteries. There is indeed a significant surge of activity in the circular electronics sector, encompassing industry consortiums and substantial funding initiatives [18]. A prominent example is Back Market, a French online marketplace specializing in refurbished electronics, which secured $335 million in a growth round in 2021, valuing the company at $3.2 billion to enhance its service offerings [18]. Another noteworthy instance is ERI, a U.S.-based electronics recycling firm that attracted considerable strategic investment from Closed Loop Partners and other investors to expand its e-waste processing capabilities [18]. The rapid innovation cycles and valuable components within the electronics industry render it particularly appealing for circular investment, spanning from startups that provide device-as-a-service models to large manufacturers that implement recycling and take-back initiatives to ensure a steady supply of materials.

In the mobility sector, the shift toward electric vehicles (EVs) and the emphasis on sustainable transportation have created new opportunities for circular business models. EV batteries have emerged as a key focus—they house essential minerals such as lithium, nickel, and cobalt that can be recycled and repurposed, presenting a "recycling as the new mining" opportunity [9]. Significant investments are being directed toward battery recycling and reuse initiatives. For example, Redwood Materials, a U.S. battery recycling startup established by Tesla's former CTO, has secured over $700 million from a group of prominent investors to develop facilities that recover battery metals and reintegrate them into the supply chain [19]. By closing the loop on battery materials, these companies aim to lower production costs and lessen reliance on raw mineral extraction [19]. Automotive manufacturers are also supporting circular initiatives; numerous automakers now run or invest in remanufacturing plants for vehicle components, tire recycling programs, and car-sharing or leasing models that extend the lifespan of vehicles. In addition to electrification, mobility startups are investigating product-service system strategies (such as subscription-based access to cars or bikes instead of ownership) which can enhance asset utilization. Overall, the mobility sector's transition toward a CE is propelled by both economic incentives (e.g., reducing material supply risks and leveraging the secondary car market) and regulatory pressures (more stringent end-of-life vehicle regulations), rendering it a vibrant landscape for new investments and collaborations.

The textiles industry presents another critical hotspot for circular investment, as the current linear model of fast fashion generates tremendous waste and lost value. It is estimated that less than 1% of material used to produce clothing is recycled into new garments, representing over $100 billion in lost economic value each year [20]. This inefficiency, along with the industry's environmental impacts (e.g., 1.2 billion tons of CO_2 emissions annually from textile production) [20], has spurred numerous CE solutions in fashion. Investors are increasingly funding innovators in fiber recycling, sustainable materials, and new business models such as apparel resale and rental platforms. For example, textile recycling specialist Circ raised over $30 million in a Series B round headed by the recognizable apparel brand Inditex (Zara's parent company) and Breakthrough Energy Ventures to scale technology that chemically recycles blended textiles back into yarn [21]. Major fashion brands such as H&M have also launched corporate venture funds and accelerators to invest in circular startups (e.g., textile-to-textile recyclers, circular design software) as they commit to using more recycled content in their products [20]. On the consumer side, online resale marketplaces and subscription clothing rental services have attracted VC as they rapidly gain users. These circular fashion models cater to shifting consumer preferences while recapturing value from used clothing. Given the scale of the opportunity—hundreds of billions in potential savings from recirculating textiles [20]—the textiles sector is set to remain a vibrant field for CE investment and innovation.

17.3.2 Financing Instruments Supporting Circular Business Models

A variety of funding tools are being deployed to fund CE initiatives, ranging from traditional asset classes to creative blended structures. Green bonds have emerged as a powerful way to raise capital for CE projects. These fixed-income instruments place proceeds specifically toward green or circular endeavors (such as waste management facilities, recycling plants, or circular product design). Over the past few years, dozens of corporate and sovereign green bonds have been issued specifically to finance CE transitions [10]. For example, in 2023, Banco de Bogotá in Colombia issued a sustainability bond to fund loans for circular projects (alongside other social and green initiatives), with development banks such as IDB Invest and the IFC subscribing to the offering [16]. This demonstrates how public financiers can use bond markets to channel significant private capital into circular development. The EU's taxonomy for sustainable finance and corresponding frameworks are also beginning to define CE criteria, which is expected to further boost green bond issuance for circular assets.

CE projects—especially in emerging markets or those involving novel technologies—often face high perceived risks that can deter traditional financial investors. Blended finance addresses this by combining concessional funds (from governments, philanthropic organizations, or development agencies) with private capital to de-risk circular ventures. A notable model is the Circulate Capital Ocean Fund, which uses a blended structure where development agencies such as the IFC and Proparco provide anchor capital (including concessional equity) to mobilize additional private investment into plastic recycling and waste management startups [21]. This approach helped Circulate Capital raise over $165 million across its funds to invest in circular solutions in South and Southeast Asia [21]. Blended finance has also been used through public–private partnerships, guarantee facilities, and impact finance instruments to support circular SMEs and infrastructure. These instruments are vital for early-stage or infrastructure-intensive circular projects, as they absorb initial risks and unlock one or two orders of magnitude more capital from profit-seeking financiers [21].

VC is performing an increasingly central role in scaling circular business models by providing growth capital and strategic counseling to startups. Climate-tech and impact financiers have recognized the CE transition as central to their portfolios. Although still a small portion of overall VC (about 1%–2% globally [14]), capital for circular startups is increasing, and deal sizes are growing as the sector matures [22]. VC firms—including specialized funds such as Closed Loop Partners and mainstream firms such as Sequoia or Andreessen Horowitz—have supported companies in areas such as advanced recycling technology, circular supply chain tracking, PaaS platforms, and material innovation. For example, Closed Loop's venture arm has invested in the AI-driven recycling startup AMP Robotics and the fashion recommerce platform ThredUp, among others [18]. At the same time, private equity (PE) investors are looking at more established circular firms (for instance, remanufacturing firms or recycling plant operators) as acquisition targets, drawn by their stable cash flows and alignment with ESG investment criteria. In the UK, midmarket PE capital accounted for about 21% of CE deal volume in 2023, up from 17% the previous year [11], signifying climbing PE interest. Both VC and PE activity in this scope benefit from the clear impact narrative and the prospect of penetrating new markets created by circular consumption patterns.

DFIs and multilateral development banks have prioritized the CE within their climate and sustainability strategies. These entities utilize a combination of loans, equity investments, credit lines, and guarantees to facilitate CE initiatives, frequently collaborating with local banks and governmental bodies. For instance, the European Investment Bank (EIB) and its counterparts have established a joint working group focused on CE finance and are developing specific financial instruments to address the investment requirements of the CE throughout product life cycles [16]. They offer concessionary loans and technical support to municipalities for circular city projects, provide credit lines to commercial banks designated for circular business financing, and make direct investments in circular enterprises or funds. A notable example is the EBRD's backing of recycling firms in Eastern Europe through blended loans, as well as the World Bank and IFC's funding of waste management enhancements in Asia and Africa [15]. DFIs also play a vital role in establishing standards—the IFC-led Harmonized Circular Economy Finance Guidelines (2024) provide financial institutions with a unified framework for defining and monitoring CE investments [23]. By alleviating early-stage risks and focusing on inclusive, climate-resilient outcomes, public development finance has been instrumental in fostering a market for circular projects that may otherwise find it challenging to secure commercial financing.

17.3.3 Investor Typologies and Motives

The CE investment space is attracting a wide spectrum of investors—from mission-driven family offices to large institutional asset managers—each with distinct motives and strategies [12]. Table 17.3 summarizes the major investor typologies backing circular ventures and their primary motivations.

In the financing ecosystem for the CE, each of these investment groups has a beneficial function to play. Institutional investors bring scale and mainstream acceptance, channeling trillions of assets into circular opportunities because they are convinced of the risk-adjusted returns [10]. Corporates bring industry know-how and integration opportunities, commercializing circular startups and providing offtake markets for recovered materials. VCs invest in innovation, bringing risk capital and entrepreneurial mentoring to build next-generation circular technologies and business models. DFIs act as market enablers, using concessional finance and guarantees to seed projects and build a track record to "crowd-in" commercial actors. Finally, family offices and foundations frequently act as "patient capital" and thought leaders, providing funds for experimental modes (such as radical material science innovations or community-scale circular projects) that align with their missions. A significant point is that these categories are collaborating more frequently. A single round of finance or

Table 17.3 Key investor types in circular economy and their motivations.

Investor type	Key motivations and focus
Institutional investors	Focus on long-term returns and ESG integration. Invest in circular economy to reduce supply chain risk and align with sustainability trends. Example: BlackRock's $2B circular fund [10]
Corporate investors	Aim for strategic alignment and resource security. Invest to support sustainability goals, ensure supply of inputs, and gain market edge. Use VC arms or acquisitions
Venture capital (VC)	Driven by high-growth potential and innovation. Target scalable circular startups, especially in climate tech and waste reduction. Looking for disruptive opportunities
Development finance institutions (DFIs)	Prioritize development impact and market creation. Provide capital where risks are high, especially in emerging markets. Use loans, equity, and guarantees
Family offices and foundations	Motivated by mission impact and legacy value. Willing to accept lower short-term returns. Offer patient, flexible capital to support early-stage circular ventures

a blended fund might use corporates, DFIs, VCs, and family offices coinvesting—as seen in the Circulate Capital case and in large-scale deals such as Redwood Materials, where institutional investors banded together with corporate and impact-oriented funds [19]. The variety of backers mirrors a rising consensus: investment in circular business models can deliver environmental and social dividends while generating strong commercial financial returns, making it a compelling proposition for the entire range of investors.

17.3.4 Illustrative Deal-Flow Examples

Current funding activity in the CE scope provides concrete examples of how capital is being redistributed into circular business models. The following "snapshots" highlight deals and actions across various sectors and financier types.

Redwood Materials, a Nevada-based EV battery recycling startup, raised over $700 million in a 2021 Series D capital round to expand its operations [19]. The round was supported by an association of institutional financiers (including T. Rowe Price, Baillie Gifford, and Fidelity) in addition to strategic corporate financiers such as Amazon and climate-focused funds such as Breakthrough Energy Ventures [19]. This large deal, which valued Redwood at almost $3.7 billion, exemplifies the confidence in circular solutions for mobility. Redwood is utilizing the capital to scale up technologies that recover lithium, cobalt, nickel, and other materials from used batteries, aiming to feed these back into new battery production and severely cut the need for mining [19]. The deal underscores how collaborations between traditional financiers and impact investors can propel circular technology that addresses both supply security and environmental goals.

Back Market, a Paris-based online marketplace for refurbished electronics, provides another prominent instance of CE VC. In May 2021, Back Market secured a $335 million Series D funding round, increasing its valuation to $3.2 billion [18]. The round was led by General Atlantic and included other venture growth funds, indicating powerful investor appetite for the recommerce model. Back Market's platform extends the lifespan of smartphones, laptops, and appliances by connecting users with professional refurbishers, thereby keeping devices in use and lowering e-waste. The success of this deal—making Back Market a rare "unicorn" in the CE—demonstrates the scalability and value of circular marketplaces. It also indicates how shifting consumer preferences (with more customers opting for secondhand electronics) convert into solid market opportunities that VC is eager to fund.

In 2022, textile recycling innovator Circ secured over $30 million in Series B funding to accelerate its technology that isolates and recycles poly-cotton synthetic blends [21]. Notably, this round was co-led by fashion giant Inditex (parent company of Zara) alongside the multi-industry Breakthrough Energy Ventures fund founded by Bill Gates [21]. Additional participation came from global brands such as Patagonia and investors such as Circulate Capital. This diverse investor group highlights a trend of strategic venture partnerships in circular fashion startups; large clothing companies are stepping in to support innovations that help them meet sustainability goals (such as using recycled textiles) and mitigate sourcing risks. The Circ deal is a case where strategic corporate capital and impact-oriented VC capital converged on a promising circular solution. It provides a model for how established rivals in a value chain (including retailers) can become partners in financing a circular approach that benefits the entire industry's sustainability.

In early 2023, Banco de Bogotá issued a milestone sustainability bond that raised nearly $230 million, with a portion of the proceeds specifically assigned to CE initiatives [16]. This bond—subscribed by development finance organizations including IDB Invest and the IFC—represents one of the first instances in Latin America of using capital markets for CE funding. The capital is on-lent to projects such as upgrading recycling infrastructure, scaling recyclable packaging systems, and financing small and medium enterprises with circular business models. The deal represents the role of banks in not only providing direct funding but also enabling private debt financing for CE transitions. By anchoring a meaningful share of the bond issuance, these DFIs helped ensure its success and signaled to the market that CE projects are credible and bankable. This model shows an alternative to equity capital, utilizing fixed-income tools to redistribute capital at scale into CE assets, aligning investor returns with tangible impact goals.

Each of these case snapshots reinforces the vitality and momentum of circular business models across sectors. They further demonstrate the broad range of financial actors involved—from VC and corporates in early-stage equity deals to institutional fund managers and development banks in later-stage and structured finance deals. The Redwood Materials and Back Market cases prove that circular startups can achieve unicorn-level valuations and attract top-tier investors by targeting significant inefficiencies in current linear systems (battery metals and electronics waste, respectively). The Circ instance emphasizes the significance of partnerships between incumbents and innovators, with corporates not just adopting but also financing circular solutions relevant to their industry. At the same time, the Banco de Bogotá bond demonstrates innovation in financing mechanisms, merging CE goals into mainstream financial products (bonds) that attract yield-seeking and impact investors alike.

Going forward, the pipeline of such deals is expected to grow as the CE shifts from a concept to a concrete investment opportunity. Initiatives such as the Plastics Circularity Investment Tracker have documented over 5,500 circularity transactions in recent years [15], and large financial institutions are creating dedicated teams to source CE investments [10]. This deal flow, spanning multimillion-dollar startup fundings to hundred-million-plus project financings, illustrates that capital is beginning to be actively deployed to reinvent value chains on circular principles. For investors, these opportunities offer a chance to achieve positive environmental impact and capitalize on the economic upside of a more circular system—truly aligning profit with purpose in the next wave of sustainable development [10, 21].

17.4 Risk Management and Financial Incentives for Circular Manufacturing

Figure 17.5 [42] shows that CEBMs are squeezed between two mirrored sets of forces: internal/external barriers (e.g., strategy gaps, funding and technology limits, hesitant consumers, and legislative frictions) and internal/external drivers (e.g., resource-efficient leadership, product innovation, supportive policy, and supply chain collaboration). It illustrates how many factors—regulation, stakeholder pressure, or design choices—can serve as either a brake or an accelerator depending on the management response. Recognizing this symmetry helps firms link each risk in Section 17.4.1 to a matching mitigation lever or incentive in later sections.

17.4.1 A Risk Taxonomy

Market risk is severe, with revenues from secondary raw materials and remanufactured items swinging with the fortunes of commodity-price cycles rather than sales of their virgin counterparts. A panel of 1,150 listed

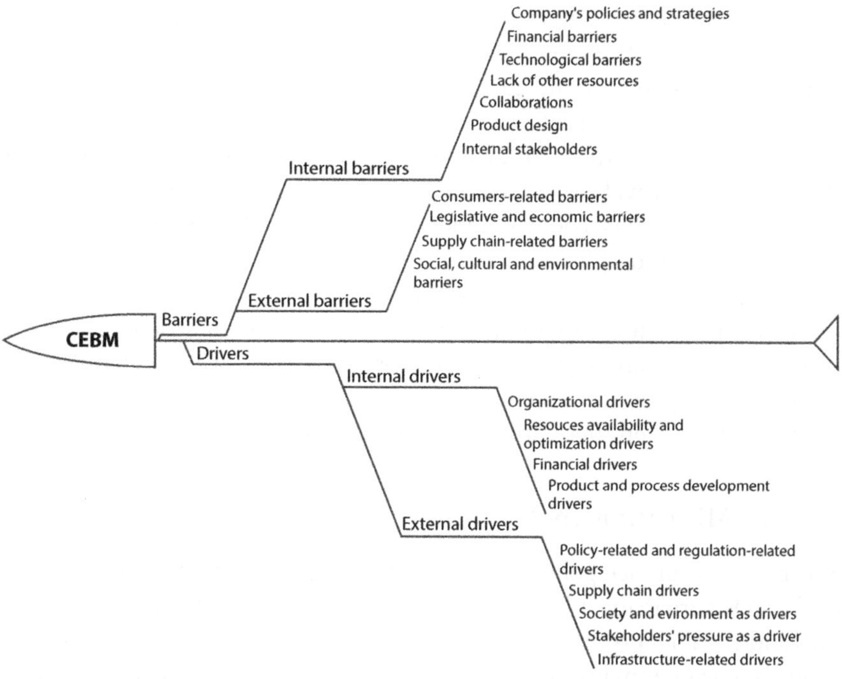

Figure 17.5 Barriers to circular economy business models' implementation.

firms in the EU (2010–2022) suggests that the adoption of "three R" practices—all together—has the effect of reducing both idiosyncratic volatility and Altman-style default probability; conversely, firms depending on recycling alone have found little downside protection [26]. A further study on European public equities supports a general "de-risking effect" and found that higher circularity scores tend to associate with lower beta and better Sharpe ratios for the period between 2013 and 2018 [27].

Reverse-logistics failures, contamination of returned flows, and inconsistent quality grades create bottlenecks in operational risk that are unknown in linear chains. Early European take-back-program studies show that firms lacking robust sorting and inspection protocols suffer cost overruns and service-level penalties [7, 28]. Regarding technology risk, circular-type innovations—biochemical recycling, product-passport tracking, and smart disassembly—are fast-evolving. If the board is not adequately funded, assets face the risk of becoming technologically obsolete and being written down [29]. Regarding regulatory risk, EU legislation, particularly the Circular Economy Action Plan of 2020 and the Sustainable Finance Regulation of 2020, tightens the rules on ecodesign, stipulates digital passports, and increases landfill charges [30]. If found noncompliant, firms can face sanctions or the restriction of market access.

The financial risk environment shows increased capital requirements for companies that operate PaaS models along with reverse-logistics systems; these systems extend cash-conversion cycle durations. Banks modify their collateral haircuts and covenant structures as a result of these changes. According to sector evidence, lenders incorporate CE scores into their credit approval procedures, whereas they charge interest rates that are between 7–10 basis points higher for businesses that practice reduction and reuse methods [26, 31]. The company encounters model risk when recycling revenues show unstable behavior [31]. The risks related to the CE exist as dependent components. The implementation of stricter extended producer responsibility fees as regulatory measures drives technological upgrades that produce amplified market-share losses and financial liquidity difficulties when these upgrades face implementation delays.

17.4.2 Mitigation Tools

Specialized insurance policies that activate based on pollution levels in recycled goods surpassing a limit shift risky but rare losses to insurance companies and even out profits. Credit boosts and assurances from national growth funds (such as Germany's KfW and the EIB) provide round-credit assurances that reduce interest rates on CE infrastructure loans and enable longer loan periods [32, 33]. Electronic and clothing companies acknowledge financial set-asides for disposal duties through take-back reserves, similar to mining's reclamation funds. Such devices—backed by proof of benefit in structured return programs [27]—shield reported earnings and satisfy auditors. Supply chain pooling, through shared storage centers and partnerships, distributes risk across many participants and reduces the cost of sorting each item. Scandinavian furniture makers, for example, set up breakdown centers close to city recyclers to ensure efficient processing. Financial hedging *via* exchanges tied to recycled-plastic measures is limited but enables sellers of recycled-plastic flakes to secure profits for 6–12 months—a method first introduced in the Dutch plastics sector. Combined risk management is now more frequent, with boards incorporating CE KPIs—such as the rate of material reuse and residual value ratios—into company-wide risk assessment tools and ensuring they correspond with COSO ERM frameworks. Bank directives now urge board risk groups to create methods for identifying circular-related risks [31]. Combining a process check (such as quality gates) with a financial exchange (such as insurance) creates the strongest risk posture.

17.4.3 Government Incentives That Tilt the Risk–Return Balance

Tax credits and accelerated depreciation in several OECD areas permit 40%–50% "super-deductions" for equipment that fulfills CE standards. Front-loaded tax benefits boost project value and reduce market volatility. Financial aid and business support from the European Union's Innovation Fund and Japan's "Circular Economy Vision 2027" jointly fund major projects that turn fixed expenses into partly public expenses, focusing on turning plastics into chemicals. The EIB's commitment to CE projects is a testament to its dedication to sustainable development and climate action.

Producer accountability charges, such as those in the EU Packaging Law, now adjust fees to give a bonus to recyclable designs; although fees increase the cost of compliance, they also establish steady cash-flow patterns that can be insured or protected. Eco-friendly government purchasing, motivated by the 2020 CE Action Plan, encourages public purchasers to demand reuse or rebuilding terms in IT and furniture bids, ensuring guaranteed sales and reducing demand uncertainty [30]. Diverse landfill and burning taxes in nations such as the Netherlands and Finland increase landfill fees yearly, decreasing the cost difference between recycled and new materials and lessening financial uncertainty for recyclers. Companies that work with tax-credit approvers and GPP overseers find better and more reliable ways to sell their products and reduce their borrowing expenses.

17.4.4 ESG & Disclosure Frameworks

Under the EU CSRD & ESRS E5 (mandatory for FY 2025), companies must reveal how many resources they use, how circular their products are, and how many products they take back to lessen information asymmetry. Research on equity connects more detailed CE information to reduced beta and narrower credit gaps [27]. The ISSB IFRS S1/S2 (global baseline 2024) demands the efficient use of materials and transition planning, aligning non-European and European regulations to simplify international investment movements. GRI 306: Waste 2020 links waste production to recycling plans, offering reviewers comparable measurements. The SASB Materiality Map provides industry-specific CE measures—such as fabric recycling rates and car component refurbishing—to aid investors in comparing top performers and underperformers. The EU Taxonomy Regulation and these frameworks are interconnected and mutually reinforcing. Financial products that fund activities "substantially contributing" to resource circularity qualify as sustainable investments. Starting in 2024, banks in Europe must reveal a ratio that measures their environmentally friendly investments, including those that align with CE standards [34]. Early alignment with ESRS E5, ISSB, and the EU Taxonomy widens the investor pool and can shave 15–30 basis points off debt spreads.

17.4.5 Managerial Implications

Managers should chart the complete risk landscape—market, operational, technological, regulatory, and financial—and acknowledge their interconnected effects. Pair every significant danger with a management strategy and a monetary safeguard or insurance method. Use public benefits—tax breaks, GPP agreements, and innovation funds—not only to increase internal rate of return but also to stabilize cash flows. Align disclosure with ESRS E5, ISSB, and GRI 306 to reduce information risk and access the rapidly expanding field of "circular finance."

17.5 CE Case Studies

17.5.1 Philips: Lighting-as-a-Service

Philips (now Signify) was an early pioneer in the service-based approach to lighting [35]. In this setup, Philips installs and maintains LED lights for clients and bills them based on brightness instead of selling the lights as complete products. This "light-as-a-service" (LaaS) model eliminates the customer's initial cost hurdle; the customer pays a yearly charge while Philips retains the equipment and manages upgrades or recycling when it is no longer needed. As a Philips leader stated, clients "only pay us for the light, and we handle the technology risk and the investment." This results in significant energy reductions and prolonged product durability. Philips has stated that by switching to LEDs, energy use typically drops by 50%–70%. They also mention that LED lights have a lifespan about five times that of conventional bulbs. These savings can also cover the service by cutting down on power expenses. In real-world applications, LaaS agreements (such as those with municipalities and airports) have resulted in reduced expenses for clients, with Philips responsible for reclaiming used lamps. Signify's commitment to sustainability is evident in its efforts to reduce carbon emissions and promote CE principles.

17.5.2 H&M: In-Store Garment Loop

H&M has piloted in-store fabric recycling with its "Looop" device, tested in 2020. This small box-like setup takes in clothes provided by customers and turns them into fresh clothes in one go. For instance, a shopper may place worn garments into Looop, where ozone purification and cutting machines transform them into new thread; this thread is subsequently woven into a fresh sweater, scarf, or infant blanket within approximately five hours. The method does not require water or chemicals, and H&M charges about €10–15 for each reused piece of clothing (balanced by a coupon) to cover the operational costs. The model enhances H&M's ongoing clothing return program (where people can drop off any brand's clothes for recycling) by providing a direct second use for returned textiles. Although still in the trial phase, the Looop project shows H&M's commitment to circular business models; it required updating a flagship store in Stockholm with the recycling system and training staff and customers how to use it. Although results are currently limited, experts point out that "quality remains intact and valuable natural resources are saved" when fabrics are reprocessed rather than thrown away. H&M considers Looop as a component of its broader aim to utilize entirely recycled or eco-friendly materials by 2030 [37, 38]. H&M considers Looop as a component of its broader aim to utilize entirely recycled or eco-friendly materials by 2030 [36, 37].

17.5.3 Caterpillar and Xerox: Remanufacturing Programs

Heavy equipment and electronics firms provide instructive examples of circular remanufacturing. Cat Reman® rebuilds off-highway engines and machine components (such as transmissions) to original, like-new condition. These refurbished parts perform "same-as-new" and are a cost-effective replacement option for components that eventually wear out. According to Caterpillar, remanufacturing "reduces waste, lowers greenhouse gas production, and reduces the need for raw materials" while providing customers with extended equipment life. In practice, dealers collect old "cores" and highly trained technicians replace thousands of parts so the rebuilt machine meets new standards [40].

Xerox introduced similar concepts in its office equipment as early as 1975, reclaiming copiers and toner cartridges. Today, its Green World Alliance program reclaims used toner cartridges in 183 countries. For instance, in 2017, customers returned more than 4.8 million cartridges (approximately 4,600 metric tons) to be reused. Approximately 90% of the returned parts are reused in remanufactured products to factory specifications. Xerox also leases copiers and demands 100% take-back at the end of life for the reuse of high-value parts. Both firms recognize that remanufacturing not only offers environmental benefits but also maintains or improves profit margins by cutting material costs. Because of these remanufacturing models, they have successfully generated new revenue from returned products and achieved a remarkable inventory reduction [41, 42].

Conclusion

For contemporary businesses, circular manufacturing is becoming a financially astute and sustainable approach. Businesses can save money, create new revenue streams, and increase asset productivity by abandoning the conventional linear "take–make–dispose" strategy. Remanufacturing, recycling, and PaaS models are strategies that businesses use to lower material and energy costs while increasing consumer value. Businesses can assess the financial advantages of circular operations by using key financial KPIs such as MCI, LCS, and RoCI. By bridging the gap between environmental performance and business value, these indicators facilitate the justification and expansion of circular projects.

Strong economic potential and increased ESG demands are driving investment interest in the CE. Funding sources, including VC and green bonds, are increasingly promoting circular models in high-impact industries including fashion, electronics, mobility, and construction. Businesses must use tools such as insurance, credit guarantees, and public incentives to handle risks associated with circular operations, such as supply unpredictability or regulatory change, if they want to thrive. All things considered, circular manufacturing provides a strong and lucrative way forward, assisting businesses in becoming more competitive over the long run and fostering a more sustainable future.

AI disclosure statement: The author acknowledges the use of AI-based tools for minor language editing or grammatical correction. However, all intellectual contributions, analyses, and conclusions presented in this chapter are entirely the author's own.

References

1. Denu, M., David, P., Landry, A., Mangione, F., Emerging digital technologies to support circular manufacturing systems implementation: a literature review, in: *Premier congrès de la SAGIP*, Jun 2023, SAGIP, Marseille, France.
2. Kazakova, E. and Lee, J., Sustainable Manufacturing for a Circular Economy. *Sustainability*, 14, 17010, 2022, https://doi.org/10.3390/ su142417010.
3. Chennak, A., Giannakas, K., Awada, T., On the Economics of the Transition to a Circular Economy. *Circ.Econ. Sust.*, 4, 3007–3023, 2024, https://doi.org/10.1007/s43615-023-00297-8.
4. Grady, B. and Grady, B., Measuring the ROI for circularity soon may be easier, Trellis, 2017, April 6, https://trellis.net/article/measuring-roi-circularity-soon-may-be-easier/.
5. Europe's circular-economy opportunity, McKinsey & Company, 2015, September 1, https://www.mckinsey.com/capabilities/sustainability/our-insights/europes-circular-economy-opportunity.
6. Ho, H.W.L., Haaker, T., Yishake, M., Barriers and Opportunities when Transitioning from Linear to Circular Business Models: Evidence from the Construction and Manufacturing Sectors in The Netherlands. *Circ. Econ. Sust.*, 2025, https://doi.org/10.1007/s43615-025-00524-4.
7. Zara, C., Iannuzzi, M., Ramkumar, S., The Impact of Circular Economy on Public Equity in Europe. Understanding De-Risking Effect and Risk-Adjusted Performance, October 8, 2021.
8. Allodi, E. and Soana, M.G., Circular Economy and Firm-Specific Risks: A Risk Management Perspective, 2024, SSRN: https://ssrn.com/abstract=5024911 or http://dx.doi.org/10.2139/ssrn.5024911.
9. On track for a circular economy?, https://www.db.com/what-next/responsible-growth/Circular-Economy--Kreislaufwirtschaft/Facts-Fakten/index.
10. The world's largest investor and the circular economy: BlackRock, 2021, September 23, https://www.ellenmacarthurfoundation.org/circular-examples/the-worlds-largest-investor-embraces-the-circular-economy-blackrock.

11. BDO and Mills, T., Investment into the UK Circular Economy, In Circular Economy Series [Report], 2024, https://www.bdo.co.uk/getmedia/4ebba463-246c-46ac-a8e9-1fe4339134be/BDO-Circular-Economy-Series-2024.pdf.
12. AlJishi, M., Investcorp's Second Global Mega Trends Survey Finds Digitization, Aging Population and Climate Change are Top of Mind for Institutional Investors and Family Offices, Investcorp, 2021, July 8, https://www.investcorp.com/investcorps-second-global-mega-trends-survey-finds-digitization-aging-population-and-climate-change-are-top-of-mind-for-institutional-investors-and-family-offices/.
13. Averina, E., Frishammar, J., Parida, V., Assessing sustainability opportunities for circular business models. *Bus. Strat. Environ.*, 31, 4, 1464–1487, 2022, https://doi.org/10.1002/bse.2964.
14. Circular Economy Start-up Landscape 2024, https://thankful-insect.files.svdcdn.com/production/uploads/circular-republic/Whitepapers/Circular_Startup_Economy_Whitepaper_v06.pdf.
15. Ocean Plastic, The Circulate Initiative, The Circulate Initiative issues call to action to financial community as investment gap widens to meet targets to tackle plastic pollution - Ocean Plastic | The Circulate Initiative, 2024, August 28, https://www.thecirculateinitiative.org/media-coverage/the-circulate-initiative-issues-call-to-action-to-financial-community-as-investment-gap-widens-to-meet-targets-to-tackle-plastic-pollution/.
16. European Investment Bank, How Multilateral Development Banks Are Advancing the Transition the Circular Economy in Motion 2024, 2024, https://www.eib.org/attachments/lucalli/20240173_the_circular_economy_in_motion_en.pdf.
17. Martin, H., Chebrolu, D., Chadee, A., Brooks, T., Too good to waste: Examining circular economy opportunities, barriers, and indicators for sustainable construction and demolition waste management. *Sustainable Prod. Consumption*, 48, 460–480, 2024, https://doi.org/10.1016/j.spc.2024.05.026.
18. Clancy, H. and Clancy, H., Circular economics and the $57B e-waste opportunity, Trellis, 2024, July 24, https://trellis.net/article/circular-economics-and-57b-e-waste-opportunity/.
19. Lienert, P., Battery recycling firm Redwood raises $700 mln from big fund managers, Reuters, 2021, July 28, https://www.reuters.com/business/finance/battery-recycling-firm-redwood-raises-700-mln-big-fund-managers-2021-07-28/.
20. Refashioning clothing's environmental impact, McKinsey & Company, 2019, July 25, https://www.mckinsey.com/capabilities/sustainability/our-insights/sustainability-blog/refashioning-clothings-environmental-impact.
21. Dunne, E., Circulate Capital achieves third close for Circulate Capital Ocean Fund I-B, led by the International Finance Corporation (IFC) and Proparco, Circulate Capital, 2023, April 20, https://www.circulatecapital.com/circulate-capital-achieves-third-close-for-circulate-capital-ocean-fund-i-b-led-by-the-international-finance-corporation-ifc-and-proparco/.

22. Net Zero Insights, European Circular Economy funding trends in 2024, 2025, February 18, https://netzeroinsights.com/resources/circular-funding-in-europe-2024/.
23. Harmonized Circular Economy Finance Guidelines, https://www.ifc.org/content/dam/ifc/doc/2025/harmonized-circular-economy-finance-guidelines-en.pdf.
24. Chabowski, B.R., Gabrielsson, P., Hult, G.T.M., Morgeson, F.V., Sustainable international business model innovations for a globalizing circular economy: a review and synthesis, integrative framework, and opportunities for future research. *J. Int. Bus. Stud.*, 2023, https://doi.org/10.1057/s41267-023-00652-9.
25. Ndoka, E., Alimehmeti, G., Shulla, K., Voigt, B.F., Transitioning to circular business models in developing countries: a systematic literature review of barriers, enablers, and future directions. *Discov. Sustain.*, 6, 1, 605, 2025.
26. Zara, C., Iannuzzi, M., Ramkumar, S., Equity de-risking and risk-adjusted performance in circular business models. *Int. Rev. Econ. Finance*, 2023.
27. Heese, H.S., Cattani, K., Ferrer, G., Gilland, W., Roth, A.V., Competitive advantage through take-back of used products. *Eur. J. Oper. Res.*, 164, 143–157, 2005.
28. Gennari, F. and Cassano, R., Circular economy and strategic risk. *Symphonya. Emerg. Issues Manag.*, 1, 136–148, 2020.
29. European Commission, A new Circular Economy Action Plan for a cleaner and more competitive Europe, 2020.
30. Ozili, P.K. and Opene, F., The role of banks in the circular economy. *World J. Sci. Technol. Sustain. Dev.*, 18, 2, 180–197, 2021.
31. European Investment Bank, The EIB in the circular economy, 2018.
32. European Investment Bank, Circular economy overview 2020, 2020.
33. European Banking Authority, Report on the role of environmental and social risks in the prudential framework, 2023.
34. Afolabi, J.A., Islam, M.R., Driving the circular economy in the European Union: Public environmental expenditure, private sector investment, and their synergy. *J. Environ. Manag.*, 394, 127529, 2025.
35. Kramer, M.R., Geradts, T., Nadella, B., Philips Lighting: Light-as-a-Service, Harvard Business School Case 419–023, 2019.
36. H&M Group, Let's close the loop – H&M's garment collecting program, 2020.
37. Azzarello, N., H&M's "Looop" recycling system transforms unwanted garments into new fashion favorites, 2020, October 16, designboom.
38. Renault Group, Refactory: The Flins site enters the circle of the circular economy, 2020, November 25, Renault Group.
39. Ellen MacArthur Foundation, Europe's first circular economy factory for vehicles: Renault, 2021, August 16, https://www.ellenmacarthurfoundation.org/circular-examples/groupe-renault.
40. Caterpillar Inc., Caterpillar's circular economy, Retrieved May 1, 2025, from https://www.caterpillar.com/en/company/sustainability/remanufacturing.html.

41. Xerox Corporation, Striving for a circular economy – 2018 CSR Report, 2018, https://www.xerox.com/corporate-social-responsibility/2018/environment/circular-economy.
42. Hina, M., Chauhan, C., Kaur, P., Kraus, S., Dhir, A., Drivers and barriers of circular economy business models: Where we are now, and where we are heading. *J. Cleaner Prod.*, 333, 130049, 2021, https://doi.org/10.1016/j.jclepro.2021.130049.
43. Gross, J.A., Blomsma, F., Djabbarov, I., Busch, T., The Micro-Processes of Transitioning to a Circular Economy Through Capital Allocation: A Case of the Investment Field. *Organ. Environ.*, 38, 2, 309–341, 2025, Original work published 2025, https://doi.org/10.1177/10860266251342567.
44. van de Ven, M.R., Lara Machado, P., Athanasopoulou, A., Aysolmaz, B., Türetken, O., Key Performance Indicators for Business Models: A Review of Literature, in: *European Conference on Information Systems (ECIS 2022): New Horizons in Digitally United Societies*, Article 126, AIS Electronic Library, 2022, https://aisel.aisnet.org/ecis2022_rp/126.
45. Uhrenholt, J.N., Kristensen, J.H., Rincón, M.C., Jensen, S.F., Waehrens, B.V., Circular economy: Factors affecting the financial performance of product take-back systems. *J. Cleaner Prod.*, 335, 130319, 2022, https://doi.org/10.1016/j.jclepro.2021.130319.
46. Kandasamy, J., K E K, V., Ethirajan, M., Murali, N., Circular Supply Chain Management: A Sustainability Approach, 2025, https://doi.org/10.1007/978-3-031-81750-2.
47. Kirchherr, J., Yang, N.N., Schulze-Spüntrup, F., Heerink, M.J., Hartley, K., Conceptualizing the Circular Economy (Revisited): An analysis of 221 definitions. *Resour. Conserv. Recycl.*, 194, 107001, 2023, https://doi.org/10.1016/j.resconrec.2023.107001.
48. The Green Deal: the future of Europe's economy? | Frans Timmermans | Summit 2020, 2020, September 9, https://www.ellenmacarthurfoundation.org/videos/the-green-deal-the-future-of-europes-economy.

Index

Also of Interest

Check out these other titles from Scrivener Publishing

Vibration Control Systems, by Kundan Meshram and Prashant Lahre, ISBN: 9781394358250. This comprehensive guide bridges the gap between theory and real-world application, giving you real-world access to cutting-edge damping technologies needed to safeguard today's most ambitious, high-risk architectural marvels.

Dictionary of Industrial Terminology 2nd Edition, by Michael D. Holloway and Emma Holloway, ISBN: 9781119363446. Greatly expanded and revised, this second edition is the most comprehensive and in-depth dictionary of industrial terms available, a must-have for any engineer, scientist, technician, or operator working in industry. *NOW AVAILABLE!*

Process Machinery Handbook: For Field Personnel, Decision Makers, and Students, Edited by Robert X. Perez, ISBN: 9781394214457. *Process Machinery Handbook: For Field Personnel, Decision Makers, and Students* equips newcomers and seasoned professionals with essential insights into the diverse world of process machinery, empowering them to understand unique performance characteristics, common failure modes, and effective strategies for enhancing reliability in their operations.

Basic Electrical and Instrumentation Engineering, by P. Sivaraman, C. Sharmeela, A. Thaiyal Nayagi, and R. Mahendran, ISBN: 9781119764465. Offering the most up-to-date coverage on the subject available, this new volume provides detailed concepts of AC circuits and power systems, transformers, DC machines, AC machines, measurement and instrumentation, and many other practical concepts for the engineer or engineering student. *NOW AVAILABLE!*

Electrical and Electronic Devices, Circuits, and Materials: Technological Challenges and Solutions, Edited by Suman Lata Tripathi, Parvej Ahmad Alvi, and Umashankar Subramaniam, ISBN: 9781119750369. Covering every aspect of the design and improvement needed for solid-state electronic devices and circuit and their reliability issues, this new volume also includes overall system design for all kinds of analog and digital applications and developments in power systems. *NOW AVAILABLE!*

Books in the series, "Rotating Machinery Fundamentals and Advances"

Condition Monitoring, Troubleshooting, and Reliability in Rotating Machinery, Edited by Robert X. Perez, ISBN: 9781119631545. This third volume in a broad collection of current rotating machinery topics, written by industry experts, is a must-have for rotating equipment engineers, maintenance personnel, students, and anyone else wanting to stay abreast with current rotating machinery concepts and technology.

DESIGN, MODELING AND RELIABILITY IN ROTATING MACHINERY, Edited by Robert X. Perez, ISBN: 9781119631682. This broad collection of current rotating machinery topics, written by industry experts, is a must-have for rotating equipment engineers, maintenance personnel, students, and anyone else wanting to stay abreast with current rotating machinery concepts and technology.

MAINTENANCE, RELIABILITY AND TROUBLESHOOTING IN ROTATING AND PROCESS MACHINERY, Edited by Robert X. Perez, ISBN: 9781119631644. For Rotating equipment professionals, maintenance personnel, project engineers, process engineers, mechanical engineering students, and anyone working around critical rotating equipment.

Troubleshooting Rotating Machinery: Including Centrifugal Pumps and Compressors, Reciprocating Pumps and Compressors, Fans, Steam Turbines, Electric Motors, and More, by Robert X. Perez and Andrew P. Conkey, ISBN: 9781119294139. A must-read for anyone whose job depends on operating or maintaining safe, reliable, and efficient machinery in a process facility, this volume shows the newcomer and veteran alike how you can start troubleshooting rotating equipment problems immediately by implementing this book's common-sense methodology. *NOW AVAILABLE!*

Operator's Guide to Process Compressors, by Robert X. Perez, ISBN: 9781119580614. The perfect primer for anyone responsible for operating or maintaining process gas compressors. *NOW AVAILABLE!*

Operator's Guide to General Purpose Steam Turbines: An Overview of Operating Principles, Construction, Best Practices, and Troubleshooting, by Robert X. Perez and David W. Lawhon, ISBN: 9781119294214. A must-read book for anyone operating or maintaining general purpose steam turbines in a process setting, this is a practical reference that includes a collection of field-tested procedures aimed at ensuring safe general purpose steam turbines start-ups, shutdowns, and over-speed tests. *NOW AVAILABLE!*

Printed and bound by CPI Group (UK) Ltd, Croydon, CR0 4YY

29/09/2026

14971772-0004